929.4 Ref   17453.

HARRAP'S
BOOK OF
NICKNAMES
AND THEIR
ORIGINS

A Comprehensive Guide to Personal Nicknames in the English-speaking World

BASIL FREESTONE

Nothing except scandal spreads so fast as
an apt nickname
– Hervey Allen

London

First published in Great Britain 1990
by HARRAP BOOKS LIMITED
Chelsea House, 26 Market Square,
Bromley, Kent BR1 1NA

ISBN 0 245-60019-1

Printed and bound in Great Britain
by The Bath Press, Avon

CONTENTS

PREFACE

Nicknames came before surnames – if indeed, they are not the same. Certainly, many of them may be equated with names from earlier times to which they have been added, as they were to a man I knew in the Army called Blanco White. For nicknames are 'added names', often described by dictionaries as 'substitutes for proper names'.

But are they?

Take a look at one or two first names, starting with Hebrew. Esau means 'hairy', Rachel, 'a ewe'; Simeon (and so Simon), 'a hyena', Enoch, 'a teacher', and David, 'beloved'. Then some British: Nigel means 'black', Gavin 'a hawk', Arthur (the Celtic Art), probably 'a bear', Alfred, 'elf counsel'; and Christopher, 'Christ-bearer', originally a nickname for a Christian who bore Christ in his heart.

And a few surnames. Nodder was someone who was sleepy, says Bardsley,[1] although not everyone agrees with him. Spilman is 'a jester,' (OE *spileman*, related to the German *spielen*, 'to play,' the origin of which, says Walshe,[2] is obscure). Dr. P. H. Reaney[3] comments on Spilman that it 'was one of those nicknames used as a personal name which were not uncommon in the 12th century'. Others are Puddifoot, originally Pudifat (twelfth century), a nickname for someone with a large stomach; Wyndswyft (1301) for someone who could run fast; Brown 'a man with brown hair' (Brunus, 1066); and, of course, Smith, 'a blacksmith'[4].

Nicknames, however, were not taken lightly, and are not even today. My insurance agent told me that a man had the name Digger Smith written on his policy, and when he died in about 1975, the company had great difficulty in determining that the man in the policy was the same person as the man named on the death certificate.

There is, nevertheless, an air of frivolity about them which sits ill with serious-minded scholars. Philologists and lexicographers, on the whole, have little affection for 'nickname', which first appeared in the English language in the fifteenth century from an Old English word '*ekename*', comparable with the Old Norse *aukanafn*.

'Nickname' got its present shape from the not uncommon mistake of running the 'an' into the word itself, as happened with 'newt', originally 'an ewt'. An ekename became a 'nekename', which showed itself in a fifteenth-century Anglo-Latin lexicon called for short *Promptorium parvulorum*.

In spite of its sound English parenthood, philologists seem to feel the word has not the academic ring of the French *sobriquet*, a mere youngster from the fifteenth century.

One actively hated it. G. L'Estrange Ewen did everything he could to avoid tracing a surname from a nickname. He called them 'characteristic descriptions' or 'manufactured appellations'.

1) *English Surnames* by C. W. Bardsley (Chatto and Windus, 2nd edition, 1875).
2) A *Concise German Etymological Dictionary* by M. O'C, Walshe (Routledge and Kegan Paul, 1951).
3) A *Dictionary of British Surnames*, by Dr. P. H. Reaney (Routledge and Kegan Paul, 1959).
4) Ibid.

Dr Reaney sadly regrets that the 'English language lacks terms corresponding to the French *sobriquet* and *nom de famille*'.[5] My French dictionary, however, translates sobriquet as 'nickname', and 'family name' seems a perfectly satisfying equivalent to *nom de famille*. But he does say in another book 'Strictly speaking, all names are nicknames'.

A single modern name may belong to more than one class of surname, Dr Reaney points out in his monumental dictionary of British surnames[6]: '*Low* may be a French nickname for the wolf, a Scandinavian nickname for a small man, a pet name from *Laurence*, or a local surname from *hlaw*, hill.'

'That many modern surnames were originally nicknames is proved conclusively by the material' in his book, he states. 'Names of animals may be nicknames descriptive of appearance or disposition. *Lamb* may denote meekness, *Bull* strength or a headstrong nature'. Bird names, names from dress and equipment, names of occupations, were all very often nicknames.[7]

When I was in West Africa the Ashantis (who are very good at that sort of thing) called a great drunken slob of a white man, rude, aggressive, greedy and unmannered, *kotoko*, 'bush pig'. However much this seemed to describe him, it was, I always felt, a wicked slander on the Red River Hog or porcupine.

One famous name of this character is the one added to the name of an English king, Harold I, who was called 'Harefoot', from the Old Norse *harfótr*, a nickname for a swift runner which survives in the surname Harfoot.

Bardsley was very apologetic about using the word 'nickname', even putting it into inverted commas in his chapter heading, but he quotes some telling examples. A Peter Blackbeard was 'brought up for not paying Easter reckonings, 1676' and John Orphanstrange is found in a Cambridge register for 1544.[8] Doubtless, says Bardlsey, he was a foundling. Anna Hellicate (hell-cat) was called before the Archdeacon of Durham 'for not coming to the Church, 27th July, 1673'.[9]

He suggests that the nickname Shakespeare was given to 'some over-demonstrative sergeant or clearer of the way'.

The Oxford Dictionary has no misgivings about the derivations of 'nickname' and 'sobriquet'. It plainly describes a sobriquet as 'an epithet, a nickname'. The French etymologist Albert Dauzat[10] thought it derived from *sous* with some obscure element. Professor Ernest Weekley's etymological dictionary[11] says it is Old French for 'a chuck under the chin', which is synonymous with the Italian *sottobecco*, 'under the beak'. The Italians, on the other hand, call a nickname not an 'under' but an 'over', *soprannome*.

The OED quotes, among other references, one from the antiquarian William Stukeley (1687–1765): 'Most of the names then [i.e. 15th c.] were what we call sobriquets, travelling names...what we call nick-names.'

The situation gets even more complicated when you examine the word 'surname,' particularly if you remember that 'nickname' means basically something which is added; for 'surname' originally meant exactly the same. In the words of the OED, it is 'a name, title or epithet added to a person's name or

5) Ibid.
6) Ibid.
7) Ibid.
8) Bardsley (1).
9) Dean Granville's letters, W. Surtees publications (quoted in (1)).
10) *Dictionnaire etymologique de la langue française* by Albert Dauzat (Larousse, 1938).
11) *A Concise Etymological Dictionary of Modern English* by E. W. Weekley (John Murray, 1924).

names, especially one derived from his birthplace or from some unique quality or achievement'.

It comes from the Anglo-French *surnoun*, equivalent to the Italian *soprannome*, and the OED quotes a sentence from John Hardyng's *Chronicle* (1457): '...kyng Edward with longshanks by surnoun;' and the first example of a surname sounds suspiciously like a nickname: 'His sirname was: hardi of hert' (*Arthur and Merlin*, c. 1330). Another from 1589 is: 'My surname is Peace-Maker, one that is but poorly regarded in England,' (Richard Harvey: *Plaine Perceuall the peace-maker of England*). In another English chronicle (c 1325), quoted by Joseph Ritson in *Ancient English Metrical Romances* (1802) is the phrase: 'Richard, queor de Lyoun. That was his surnoun.'

In his dictionary of nicknames and surnames (1904), Edward Latham[12] used 'surname' for what we would today call a nickname. e.g. 'The Exterminator, a surname for Montbars, a French buccaneer (b.c.1645), from his ferocity....'

So I think we are reduced to looking further back.

'Name' is the Old English *nama*, linked with the Old Norse *nafn* and related to the Latin *nomen*, the Greek *onoma* and the Sanskrit *naman*. It is possible, some philologists think, that the Indo-European root was **gna*, a form of *gan*. 'to know' (which survives in our words 'can' and 'ken') and that its meaning to early man was to distinguish one thing from another. And 'to know' in the earliest philosophy was to possess the secrets of magic – but that is another story.

These distinguishing marks – although I do not agree with John Stuart Mill's shallow observation that they were 'meaningless marks' – were in most cases nicknames since they described a person: in fact Professor Weekley asserts that 'in a sense all personal names are nicknames'.[13]

If you examine the names of Celts and Teutons you feel there is not a great deal of difference between them and the names given in more primitive societies. In Australia, for instance, the Aborigines around the Adelaide district give all children the same name in strict numerical order, as do the Malays. 'This custom is so confusing that nicknames have to be given to make any sense of the custom.'[14]

You are perhaps reminded of the Welsh, of Dylan Thomas's 'Mrs Dai Bread One; and 'Mrs Dai Bread Two'; as well maybe of the custom of calling the multifarious Joneses by their occupations, 'Jones the Post,' or 'Jones the Garage'. Nicknames proliferate in Wales where so many people have the same names. A Welsh friend told me that in Portmadoc, where there were a number of sea captains, people were often known by the names of the ships with which they had been connected. 'On my father's side, for example,' he said, 'I belonged to the Anna Brunswick family. My father was always referred to as Bob Jones Anna Brunswick, the name of the ship commanded by my grandfather.' The Joneses obviously acquired many nicknames, he added. Richard Jones, a greengrocer's son, was called 'Richie Bananas' and Richard Jones, the butcher's son, 'Dick Faggots'. There was Thomas-Never-no-more, who when his wife survived the ordeal of a difficult birth exclaimed whenever he was congratulated 'Thank you, thank you, but never no more, chum bach.' Griffith Roberts had a very pronounced stammer, and the family was, most uncharitably, spoken of as 'Teulu Quack-Quack.' *Teulu* is Welsh for 'family'.

This way of thought goes deeper than you may at first think.

12) *A Dictionary of Names, Nicknames and Surnames* by Edward Latham (Routledge, 1904).
13) *The Romance of Words*, by E. W. Weekley (John Murray, 1912).
14) *Primitive Culture*, by E. W. Tylor, Torchbook ed. U.S., 1958.

Among certain Red Indian tribes, a warrior earns a new name by his deeds or his appearance, and these are nothing short of nicknames. Many Indians do – or did – not use their real names, for they believe that an enemy by possession of them can destroy the owners' souls.

Kiowa children are not given names immediately after birth but a little later in life, and even then they are not called by their formal names every day, but by nicknames.[15] A Cherokee child is sometimes given a ridiculous name as a joke since his parents know that as he grows up 'new names will be acquired by this child...often descriptive of his physical features or misfortunes'.[16]

Often these names were mutilated by ill-educated white men who spoke less of the Indian language than they professed e.g. 'His Face is Like a Storm' became in English Chief 'Rain-in-the-Face'.

Compare that type of name with the Celtic Campbell, 'crooked mouth', Canmore, 'large head', Cruikshank, 'crooked leg', Howel Dda, 'the good', or with the Teutonic Sitric Silken Beard who was Viking ruler in Dublin in the eleventh century (sometimes Sigtrygg Silk-Beard) or Sigtrygg One-Eye, king in York.

Or, to take it a step further, put the Old Norse name *skeifr*, which became the English name Scafe, 'awkward, crooked'[17] side by side with the eighteenth-century nickname for Lord Temple (who was First Lord of the Admiralty in 1756), 'The Gawky Squire.'

Wherever you look, you will find a great many nicknames better known than the names of the man who bore them. Even the 'name' of St Francis of Assisi was a nickname. His real name was Giovanni, but Francesco ('the Frenchman') was given to him because of his schoolboy proficiency in French.[18] He was canonized under that nickname, not his given name.

The name of one of the earliest British resistance heroes may indeed have been a nickname: Caratacus, chief of the Catuvellauni, whose proud defiance of Rome brought life to him and his family after they were taken as prisoners before the emperor Claudius. Caratacus is a Latinization of the Welsh 'Caradoc' (from *cariad* = love) and that may well have been an expression of the affection his courage and leadership won him among the Silures, the southern Welshmen who fought beside his Catuvellauni and the Ordovices in a campaign which ended in defeat at a place known today as Caer Caradoc. Tacitus said 'He was joined by everyone who feared a Roman peace' and later 'The reputation of Caratacus spread beyond the islands and through the neighbouring provinces to Italy itself'.[19]

Pocahontas, the Indian 'princess', is known to us by a nickname; so is her father Powhatan. Attila the Hun ('Little Father') was named Etzel; Botticelli ('Little Barrel') was Alessandro di Mariano dei Filipepi; El Cid (the Arabic *sidi*, 'lord') was Rodrigo Diaz de Bivar. Then there are Brutus ('stupid'), Crassus ('fat') and, of course Robin Hood (and no one is quite sure what his real name was; if you disagree, read Professor Holt's book on him[20]).

Nicknames in very recent times have been taken as surnames. You will find two of them in this dictionary: Lely and Readymoney.

If we go deeper still, we find that a great deal of the thinking behind names,

15) *Social Anthropology of North American Tribes*, ed. by F. Eggan (University of Chicago, 1937).
16) Ibid.
17) Reaney (3)
18) *The Oxford Dictionary of English Christian Names* by E. G. Withycombe, (OUP, 1945).
19) *The Annals of Imperial Rome by Tacitus*; trans. Michael Grant (Penguin Classics, 1956).
20) *Robin Hood* by J. C. Holt, (Thames and Hudson, 1982).

and so nicknames, was originally magical, or, if you prefer, religious.

Many people thought – and think – like the Red Indians that if an enemy got hold of their real names, they could be destroyed. Many did and do in Africa and Australia. Some Africans have a true name which is never mentioned, because of the fear of what an evil sorcerer might do with it.

In a number of societies, to avoid the attention of a malevolent being – and this is often a deity – parents gave their children names like 'filth,' so that the magician or deity would think the child not worth his notice.

The most notable, perhaps, of the people who never revealed their names were the Kroo, in what is now the republic of Liberia, the men who served aboard British ships, including men-of-war, in tropical waters in the eighteenth and nineteenth centuries. Since they were consequently nameless, British sailors, traders and explorers gave them all nicknames like 'Pipe of Tobacco,' 'Snowball,' 'Flying Fish,' 'Bottle of Beer,' 'Mashed Potatoes', 'Bubble and Squeak', 'Straw Hat', 'Dry Toast', 'Corkscrew' and 'Jack the Ropeyarn'.

The Kroo faith is very much akin to the Semitic belief in the true properties of a name. For them both a name is not just a mark to differentiate one thing from another. It contains in some mysterious way the true nature of the thing it describes. A man's name, therefore, embraces his most personal characteristics; and that meant, of course, his relations with his god. Most names for the Jews, the Babylonians and the Assyrians were suggested by some aspect of the person's birth, and the name defined a course of life. When King Sargon II (who reigned 721–705 BC) laid down the dimensions of the city which was to bear his name as Dûr-Sharrukîn, he declared that the measurements should express the numerical value of his name.

That emphatically expressed the man's relationship with his god, for 'Sharru' was the name or title of his god Shamesh, and the king's Assyrian name, Sharru-ukîn, means 'the king has established' – the king in that case being Shamash.[21]

The Sumerian name Apil-Ê-Sharra means 'Son of Ê-Sharra;, where Ê-Sharra is the name of the temple, 'the house of the universe'. The Biblical Tiglathpilesar was in reality Tukultî-apil-E-Sharra, *tukultî* being 'my help'.[22]

But just as magic could produce good effect, it could equally well produce evil, and so real names of gods were masked by nicknames. The name of the god of Israel is not known. It was written YHWH, and the name Jehovah is a sobriquet created by putting the letters of *Adonai*, 'lord,' between the letters.

Adonai was spoken whenever YHWH was written and the letters of *Adonai* were put above YHWH. Scholars read the vowels of the word as the 'missing' characters of YHWH.

Very frequently the real name of the deity, says Professor Louis Gray[23] 'was kept secret and was made known to the initiate alone, with the result that the divinity was called only by some descriptive epithet'.

In medieval mysticism a *ba'al sem*, or Baal Shem, was the Master of the Name, one who knew the real name of YHWH (or so he claimed) and could exercise unlimited supernatural power with it. The most famous of them was one who came later, Israel ben Eliezer (*c* 1700–60), who was spoken of as Baal Shem Tov,

21) *The Religious Significance of Semitic Proper Names*, by the Rev. C. H. W. Johns (John Bohlen lectures for 1910: Dixon, Cambridge, 1912).
22) Ibid.
23) *Foundations of Language*, by Louis H. Gray (Macmillan, New York, 1939).

the Good Master of the Name, but even he was given a nickname: Besht formed by the initials of his title.

That belief stretches back even deeper into human history. The great Egyptian god Ra, bitten by a snake, could only be cured by Isis if he told her his secret names. He did, and thereafter Isis had power over him. And the worship of Ra was established before the unification of the two kingdoms of Upper and Lower Egypt, which has been put at 3100 BC. The goddesses of the two lands, the vulture and the cobra, had a nickname, 'The Two Ladies'. The king, at his assumption of power, preceded his name with a title, a *nesu-bit* meaning 'He who belongs to the sedge and the bee,' symbolizing the two kingdoms.[24]

A change of name, then often meant a change of personality – and still does. A Pope, for example, takes a new name to show he is no longer the man he was. Sick people in some societies are given a new name to 'make them well'. The sick one 'dies' with the old name.

It was in the eleventh and twelfth centuries that names in Europe began to assume the beginnings of their present shape, and many scholars think that happened under the influence of Arabs or Arabic-speaking Jews, or perhaps of returning crusaders. The Arabs had long been in the habit of adding family names to given names, e.g. Hamza ibn Abdul Muttalib, Mohammed's uncle. In fact, Abdul Muttalib was a nickname. Abdul was given the name of Shaiba, but he was taken to Mecca by his uncle Al Muttalib riding pillion on a camel. The people of Mecca imagined that Al Muttalib had bought a new slave and called the boy Abdul Muttalib, 'the slave of Al Muttalib' – and he never lost the label.

In Britain many nicknames became hereditary names, and here one might well ask: what real difference is there between a nickname, a sobriquet and a surname? I think very little, if any. Usage alone turned a nickname into a surname.

So if custom makes a nickname hereditary and calls it a 'surname', does that make it no longer a nickname? If a small boy uses a cash-book as a stamp album, does that volume thereby cease to be a cash-book and become what the small boy maintains it to be? It is a cash-book used as a stamp album, just as a nickname does not change its essential quality but remains a nickname used as a surname.

And nicknames came first, I am convinced, because, however hard I try, I find I cannot imagine that the men who discovered language in a hunters' society would have pushed their minds to the enormous task of conjuring up an abstract idea for the name of a companion when there were ready at hand spontaneous nicknames like 'Clumsy', 'Grim', 'Windswift', 'Fatty', 'Bull', 'Gawky', or 'Three fingers'.

24) *Archaic Egypt*, by W. B. Emery (Pelican Books, 1961).

KEY TO WORKS MENTIONED IN THE TEXT

Aubrey	*Brief Lives* by John Aubrey, ed. Richard Baker (Book Club Associates, 1983).
BLJ	Boswell's *Life of Johnson* (Odhams Press Ltd n/d)
Bowen	Frank Bowen's *Sea Slang* (Sampson Low, Marston & Co, n/d)
Brewer	Cobham Brewer's *Dictionary of Phrase and Fable* (1870–1978)
Cotgrave	Randle Cotgrave's *Dictionnaire de la langue française* (1611)
Dawson	Lawrence Dawson's *Nicknames and Pseudonyms* (Routledge, 1880)
AS Chron	*Anglo-Saxon Chronicle*
D'Israeli	Isaac D'Israeli's *Curiosities of Literature* (1839)
Enc Brit	*Encyclopaedia Britannica*, ed. W. Yust (Enc. Brit. Inc, 1949).
Farmer & Henley	John S. Farmer and W. E. Henley's *Dictionary of Slang and Colloquial English* (Routledge, 1905)
Fitzgerald	Percy Fitzgerald's *A New History of the English Stage* (2 vols., 1882).
Forster	John Forster's *The Life of Charles Dickens* (Chapman and Hall, 1872–4)
Fuller	Thomas Fuller's *The Worthies of England*, pub. 1662
Gronow	Captain Rees Howell Gronow's *Memoirs* (Selwyn and Blount, 1934; Bodley Head, 1964)
Grose	Captain Francis Grose's *A Classical Dictionary of the Vulgar Tongue* (ed. Routledge & Kegan Paul, 1963)
Harman	Thomas Harman's *A Caveat or Warning for Common Cursetors*
Hone	William Hone (1780–1842), political satirist
Lockhart	J. G. Lockhart's *Life of Sir Walter Scott* (Dent, Everyman, 1922)
NA	*Noctes Ambrosianae*, a series of imaginary conversations written by several people for *Blackwood's Magazine*, between 1822 and 1835. The idea is said to have come from William Maginn (*the Adjutant*), and bestowed a number of lasting nicknames.
OED	Oxford English Dictionary (13 Vols: Clarendon Press, Oxford, 1933).
Reaney	Dr P. H. Reaney's *Dictionary of British Surnames* (Routledge, 1958) and *The Origin of British Surnames* (Routledge, 1967)
Timbs	John Timbs's *A Century of Anecdote* (Warne, n/d)
Ware	J. Redding Ware's *Passing English of the Victorian Era* (Routledge, n/d)

ACKNOWLEDGEMENTS

My thanks to everyone who has helped, especially my wife and my two daughters, Susan in America and Lucinda in Australia, evidence of whose loving interest I can find in so many of these pages and to Roy Minton of Harrap, who on several occasions has pulled me to safety when my foot slipped.

A

A.B.C. Admiral of the Fleet Viscount Cunningham of Hyndhope (1883–1963); from his initials as Admiral Sir Andrew Browne Cunningham, C-in-C. Mediterranean Fleet (World War II). Also *Old-Close-the-Range*.

ABDAEL George Monk or Monck, 1st Duke of Albemarle (1608–69). Monk, a professional soldier, first served Charles I (the *Ahab of the Nation*) and then the Commonwealth. He turned down a generous offer by Charles II (the *Blackbird*), and remained loyal. After the Restoration – which he played some part in engineering – he was reconciled to the monarchy; so called by Dryden (*Asaph*). Also *Honest George* and *Old George*.

- Abdael or Abdiel (Hebrew: 'Servant of God') is mentioned in a cabbalistic work as the loyal seraph who refused Satan's inducement to revolt. He also features in Milton's *Paradise Lost*, but is not mentioned in the Bible.

ABE THE NEWSBOY Abraham Hollandersky, American boxer who fought 1,309 bouts between 1905 and 1918.

ABOMINABLE NO-MAN, THE Sherman Adams (1899–), former Governor of New Hampshire and chief White House aide to President *Ike* Eisenhower in a staff system comparable to that of the military; so called because he wrote 'no' on documents with such frequency and with as much force as the comments of the President. Also the *Iceberg*.

ABSALOM James Scott, Duke of Monmouth (1649–85), illegitimate son of Charles II (the *Blackbird*) by Lucy Walter (1630–58). He led a rebellion against James II (the *King Over the Water*), was defeated at Sedgemoor (1685) and executed; so called by Dryden (*Asaph*) in *Absalom and Achitophel* (1681). Also *King Monmouth*, the *Little Duke*, *Prince Perkin* and the *Protestant Duke*.

- Absalom, son of David, rebelled against his father (2 Sam. xiv–xviii).

Shaftesbury (*Achitophel*) tried to prevent James from becoming King, and to have Monmouth named as successor to Charles II.

ABSOLUTE WISDOM, THE Sir Matthew Wood (1768–1843). He was Lord Mayor of London (1816–17), a radical MP, a municipal and political reformer and friend and counsellor to Queen Caroline (1768–1821). George IV (*Adonis of Fifty*) called him 'that beast Wood'.

ABU SAUD Lieutenant-Colonel Harold Richard Patrick Dickson (1881–1959), local representative of the Kuwait Oil Co. Ltd.; so called by the Kuwaiti Bedouins. His son's name is Saud. Abu = Arabic for 'father'.

ABYSSINIAN BRUCE James Bruce (1730–94), Scottish traveller who explored Abyssinia to discover the source of the Blue Nile (1770–1). Also *Ethiopian Bruce*.

ABYSSINIAN PRINCE, THE George Augustus Polgreen Bridgewater (1780–1845), a mulatto violinist who first appeared at Drury Lane Theatre, London (1790) to play a solo between parts of Handel's *Messiah*. He gave many concerts in London at the beginning of the 19th century.

ACE OF ACES, THE Captain Edward (Eddie) Vernon Rickenbacker (1890–1973), commander of the 'Hat-in-the-Ring' squadron of the USAF, who shot down 26 German planes (World War I) and was awarded the Congressional Medal of Honor.

ACHILLES OF ENGLAND, THE
i) Arthur Wellesley, 1st Duke of Wellington (1769–1852), British general in the Napoleonic wars. The statue to the Duke in Hyde Park, London gives him the figure of Achilles. Also *Atty Conkey*, the *Captain of the Age*, *Conkey*, *Europe's Liberator*, the *Great Duke*, the

Hero of a Hundred Fights, the *Hero of the Peninsula*, the *Iron Duke*, *Nosey*, *Old Conkey*, *Old Douro*, *Old Nosey*, the *Peer*, the *Saviour of the Nations*, the *Sepoy General* and the *Waterloo Hero*.

ii) John Talbot, 1st Earl of Shrewsbury (c. 1373–1453), England's foremost fighter in the closing stages of the Hundred Years War against France. He was at the siege of Orleans, defeated the Burgundians before Crotoy and re-captured Harfleur. A dashing figure, he was killed at Castillon. Also the *English Achilles*, *Talbot Our Good Dog* and the *Terror of France.*

• Achilles, hero of *The Iliad*, was a formidable Greek warrior in the Trojan War, handsome and brave.

ACHILLES OF THE NORTH, THE Beowulf (? fl. 6th century), hero of Scandinavian legend and of the OE poem (10th century).

ACHITOPHEL Anthony Ashley Cooper, 1st Earl of Shaftesbury (1621–83); so called by Dryden (*Asaph*) in *Absalom and Achitophel* (1681) because he helped Monmouth (*Absalom*) in his rebellion. John Evelyn the diarist (1620–1705) described him as 'crafty and ambitious'. Also the *Little Machiavel*, *Old Tony*, *Shiftesbury* and *Tapsky.*

• Ahitophel, a counsellor to David, persuaded Absalom to join a conspiracy against the King (2 Sam. xv, xvi (21–23) and xvii).

ACID DROP, THE Horace Edward, 1st Baron Avory (1851–1935), English judge; because of his manner in court. Also the *Hanging Judge.*

• 'Acid' is slang for sarcasm, e.g. 'Don't come the acid.'

ACID RAINE Raine, Countess Spencer (1929–), the wife of Earl Spencer (1924–), the father of the Princess of Wales (1961–), from 'acid rain'.

ACTION MAN Michael Ray Dibdin Heseltine (1933–), Minister of Environment (1979–83) and Minister of Defence (1983–5). He resigned over the Westland helicopter affair; nickname mentioned by Julian Critchley, MP (1930–). Also *Goldilocks*, *Tarzan*, *Veronica Lake* and *Von Heseltine.*

ACTOR, THE William (Willie) Francis Sutton (1901–80), American bank robber; from his skill in disguise.

ACTORS' MP, THE Alfred Denville (1876–1955), pioneer of repertory companies and an MP (1931–45).

ADDIE Adrian Joss, American baseball pitcher in the Hall of Fame (1902–10). America honours prowess in various fields by election to a Hall of Fame, e.g. in aviation, baseball, basketball, bowling, football, theatre and athletics. Each sphere has its own building to perpetuate the awards, e.g. the National Aviation Hall of Fame at Daytona, Ohio. Ex-President Reagan (*Dutch*) was elected (1989) to the Cowboy Hall of Fame in Oklahoma City.

ADDISON OF AMERICA, THE Joseph Dennie (1768–1812), essayist overshadowed by Washington Irving (the *American Addison*).

• For Joseph Addison, see the *English Atticus*.

ADDISON OF THE NORTH, THE Henry Mackenzie (1745–1831), Scottish essayist and novelist who wrote after the style of Addison. Also the *Man of Feeling.*

ADJUTANT, THE William Maginn (1793–1842), English doctor of law and journalist; so called in *Noctes Ambrosianae*, which he may have originated. Also the *Doctor*, the *Ensign*, the *Modern Rabelais,* the *Prince of Pedagogues* and the *Standard Bearer.*

ADMIRABLE CRICHTON, THE James Crichton (1560–85), Scottish scholar who won an MA at fourteen; classical scholar, poet, musician, sculptor, artist, actor, brilliant conversationalist in twelve languages and an excellent swordsman; so called in John Johnston's *Heroes Scoti* (1603) and repeated by Sir Thomas Urquhart (1611–60) in his account of Crichton (1652).

ADMIRABLE CRICHTON OF HIS DAY, THE Sir William Jones (1746–94), English orientalist, jurist and linguist; a pioneer in the science of comparative philology through his mastery of Sanskrit; so called by George Lillie Craik (1789–1886) in his *History of English Literature* (1844). Boswell knew him as **Persian Jones**. Also **Linguist Jones**.

ADMIRABLE CRICHTON OF OXFORD, THE Charlton George Lane (1836–92), cricketer (captain of Oxford University for five years), oarsman in university eight, racquets player and footballer in the university XI. He played in the MCC centenary match at Lord's (1887). He became a clergyman. Also **White Lane**.

ADMIRABLE DOCTOR, THE Roger Bacon (c. 1214–94), English scholar, philosopher and scientist, who wrote treatises on grammar, logic, mathematics and physics, as well as philosophy. His scientific skills were so great that the superstitious thought him a necromancer. He was known to his successors as **Doctor Mirabilis** (the **Wonderful Doctor**), which was turned into 'The Admirable Doctor'. Also the **Father of Philosophy**.

ADMIRAL, THE Sir John Harvey-Jones (1924–   ), former chairman of ICI. He served in the Royal Navy, having been educated at the RN College, Dartmouth.

ADMIRAL BOOTH James Mallord William Turner (1775–1851), English artist who was so secretive that towards the end of his life he lodged in a small house in Chelsea kept by Mrs Booth, who had been his landlady in Kent. He was known to the children of the neighbourhood by this nickname. Also **Blackbirdy** and **Pugsy Booth**.

ADMIRAL OF THE LAKE, THE Professor John Wilson (1785–1854), English scholar and journalist ('Christopher North') who lived beside Lake Windermere. He was on the editorial staff of *Blackwood's Magazine*.

ADMIRAL (or CAPTAIN) STERNPOST Admiral Henry Paulet, 6th and last Duke of Bolton and 11th Marquis of Winchester (1719–94). In action with Admiral Hawke's fleet, Paulet's carpenter reported the ship's sternpost to be loose and dangerous. Paulet returned to Spithead. At his court-martial he was acquitted but was never employed actively again. The carpenter was found to have exaggerated and was dismissed. Latterly, Paulet was eccentric and lived near Lambeth church, London, where he was known as 'King of Vine Street and Governor of Lambeth Marsh'.

ADONIS OF FIFTY, THE George IV (1762–1830) when Prince Regent. In March 1812 the *Morning Post*, eulogizing the Prince, wrote 'You are an Adonis in loveliness.' Leigh Hunt (**Bacchus**), then editor of *The Examiner*, replied with 'this Adonis in loveliness is a corpulent man of fifty'. Hunt was imprisoned for two years. Also **Beau of Princes**, the **Fat Adonis**, the **First Gentleman in Europe**, **Florizel**, **Fum the Fourth**, **George the Greater**, the **Mere Dandini**, the **Nob** or **Nobs**, the **Prince of Princes**, the **Prince of Whales** and **Prinny**.

ADVERSITY HUME Joseph Hume (1777–1855), English MP, because of his prediction of a national disaster (*circa* 1825). He pressed for the introduction of a 4d. piece which was called a 'joey' after him; so called by **Boney Cobbett**. Also the **Revenue Cutter**.

AEDH OF THE AGUE Aedh Ui Neill, High King of Ireland (604–12)

- Aedh was one of the nicknames of the great Celtic god Dagda: Aedh Alainn ('the Lovely Aed'). Also spelt *Aed* and *Aodh*, all of which mean 'fire'. Dagda is not a name but a title, 'the Good God'.
- Ui or Ua is the old style of indicating relationship among the Irish, the predecessor of 'O'. It means a descendant, a member of the same clan or tribe.

AEOLUS

i) William Pitt, 1st Earl of Chatham (1708–78), British Prime Minister (1756–63 and 1766–8); so called by Chesterfield (the **English Rochefoucauld**). Also **Atlas**, the **British Cicero**, the **Distressed Statesman**, the **Elder**, the **Great Commoner**, the **Loggerhead of London**, the **Napoleon of Oratory**, the **Old Lion**, the **People's William**, the **Terrible Cornet of Horse** and the **Young Marshal**.

ii) George Canning (1770–1827), British Prime Minister (1827); so called by

Boney Cobbett. Also the *Cicero of the British Senate*, the *Jocular Samson* and the *Zany of Debates*.

- Aeolus, son of Poseidon, was ruler of the winds, which he could excite or smooth as he wished, as Pitt and Canning did with MPs by their oratory. See a *Diner-Out of the First Water*.

AESCULAPIUS OF THAT AGE, THE Dr William Butler (1535–1618), physician to James I (the *British Solomon*); so called by Fuller. Aubrey says that he was the greatest physician of his time.

- Aesculapius (Gk. Asklepios) was the god of medicine.

AESOP OF ENGLAND, THE John Gay (1685–1732), English poet and dramatist; from his authorship of *Fables* (1727) which were very popular. Also the *Orpheus of Highwaymen*.

- Aesop (fl. 570 BC) was a Greek writer of fables.

AESOP OF INDIA, THE Pilpay (fl. 3rd century BC) to whom a collection of fables is attributed. They are believed to have been a version of the *Panchatantra*. 'Pilpay' is thought to come from Bidyapat Vidapati, 'Master of Wisdom', a wise Brahman who may have played a part in the creation of the fables.

AETHELING, THE

i) Edward (1016–57), son of Edmund *Ironside*. He was taken into exile in Hungary when Canute the *Great* acceded to the throne (1016) but after forty years returned to England as heir. He died in London soon after landing. His son (below) was too young to succeed and Canute's son Harold I (*Harefoot*) became king. Also the *Outlaw*.

ii) Edgar or Eadgar (c. 1050–c. 1130), Edward's son, who led an uprising to try to make himself king, but was a nonentity like his father. Although he was the only male descendant of the old royal house, he never gained the throne. His sister Margaret married Malcolm *Canmore*.

iii) Aethelwold, son of King Alfred the *Great's* elder brother, Aethelred. He tried to ferment revolt.

iv) Aelfred (died 1036), son of Emma and Canute the *Great*.

- 'Aetheling' is an OE word which means 'heir apparent', 'son' or 'nobleman', but can also mean 'hero'. It was applied almost exclusively to members of the royal house of Wessex.

AFFIE Admiral of the Fleet Prince Alfred, Duke of Edinburgh (1844–1900), second son of Queen Victoria (*Drina*). He became Duke of Saxe-Coburg-Gotha (1893).

AFRICAN ASTRONOMER, THE Benjamin Banneker (1731–1806), self-taught American scientist who became the foremost astronomer of his day. For several years he computed and published almanacs which required complex mathematical and scientific study.

AFRICAN CHIEF, THE Andrew Hutton (1800–63), an eccentric miser who lived in Fife, Scotland.

AFRICAN LION, THE Michael (Mike) Chiliambe (1962–   ), Zambian middleweight boxer who lost to Nigel Benn (the *Dark Destroyer*) for the Commonwealth title (1989) in 67 seconds; so called after thirteen first-round knock-outs.

AFRICAN ROSCIUS, THE Ira Frederick Aldridge (1804–67), the first great negro actor, who became a naturalized Englishman (1863). He is believed to have become interested in the theatre by having been valet (1826) to Edmund Kean (1789–1833) on an American tour. One of Aldridge's notable parts in London was Othello.

- Quintus Roscius (died 62 BC) was a famous Roman actor and his name is a synonymous term for a consummate performer.

AHAB OF THE NATION, THE Charles I (1600–49); so called by the Levellers. Also the *Blood Man, Britain's Josiah,* the *Last Man*, the *Late Man*, the *Man of Blood*, the *Martyr King*, the *Royal Martyr, St Coloquintida* and the *White King*.

- Ahab, King of Israel (reigned *circa* 875–852 BC) married Jezebel and started the deterioration of the nation by his wickedness (1 Kings xvi 31–33).

- The Levellers were extreme republicans preaching total religious and social equality. They were even too much for Cromwell, who suppressed them (1649).

AIREDALE POET, THE John Nicholson (1790–1843) who wrote *Airedale*.
- Airedale, in west Yorkshire, was where Nicholson went to school.

ALABAMA ANTELOPE, THE Donald M. Hutson (1913–   ), American footballer granted a place in the Hall of Fame for his prowess with the Green Bay Packers (1935–45); with reference to his speed.

ALBERT THE GREAT
i) Albert Chevalier (1861–1923), British music-hall singer and comedian who specialized in cockney sketches. His most famous song was *My Old Dutch*. His real name was Albert Onesime Louis. Also the *Coster Laureate.*
- 'Dutch' = duch, rhyming slang for wife (Duchess of Fife).

ii) Albert Thurgood (c. 1875–1935), Australian Rules footballer, said to have been the greatest player of all time.

ALCAEUS James Montgomery (1771–1854), Scottish poet and journalist; so called by Byron (*Baby*). Also the *Bard of Sheffield* and *Classic Sheffield.*
- Alcaeus (fl. c. 600 BC) was the earliest of Aeolian lyric poets.

ALCIBIADES George Villiers, 2nd Duke of Buckingham (1628–87). Also *Zimri.*
- Alcibiades (c. 450–404 BC) was a handsome man of great ability and wealth, but something of a rake. Buckingham was a libertine as well as a chemist, a musician and statesman.

ALDERMAN MEDIUM William Abell (fl. 1620s–1640s), an alderman of the City of London and Master of the Vintners' Company (1637), unpopular because he supported a tax on wine. He was a notoriously venal champion of government and a place-hunter; so called in broadsheets. Also *Cain's Brother.*
- An obsolete meaning of 'medium' is money, from 'medium of exchange'.

ALEX Field-Marshal Harold Rupert Leofric George, 1st Viscount Alexander of Tunis (1891–1969), Deputy C-in-C, Allied Forces in North Africa and C-in-C, Allied Forces in Italy (World War II); Governor-General of Canada (1946–51) and Minister of Defence (1952–4).

ALEXANDER THE CORRECTOR Alexander Cruden (1701–70), a London bookseller who compiled a *Concordance of the Holy Scriptures* (1737). He had been a corrector of the press, and petitioned Parliament to make him 'Corrector of the People'. He was slightly insane, and went about with a sponge to wipe out graffiti. A self-chosen nickname; he published *The Adventures of Alexander the Corrector* (1755).

ALFALFA Carl Switzer (1926–59), American boy film actor in the 1930s, e.g. in *Our Gang.*

ALFALFA BILL William H. Murray (1869–1956), Governor of Oklahoma (1929–31) with a tendency to use the military to enforce his ideas.
- Oklahoma is one of the alfalfa-producing states of the USA.

ALFRED THE GREAT Alfred Mynn (1807–61), fast bowler and hard-hitting batsman. He was a member of the great Kent cricket team of the 1830s and 1840s; so called because of his size and power; he was more than 6 ft tall, and weighed about 18 stone (252 lb). Also the *Lion of Kent.*

ALICE IN WONDERLAND Princess Alice Mary Victoria Augusta Paulina, Countess of Athlone (1883–1981); nickname in royal circles. She was an avid reader of the children's books by Lewis Carroll (1832–98).

ALICKY Princess Alix of Hesse (1872–1918), granddaughter of Queen Victoria (*Drina*); became Tsarina of Russia and was murdered following the Russian Revolution. Also *Sunny.*

ALIST, THE Francis Foster Barham (1808–71), originator of Alism, who sought to reconcile all that he saw as divine truth.

ALLENO Sir Allen Young (1827–1915), son of a rich London merchant and friend of the Prince of Wales (the *Peacemaker*). He was an Arctic explorer and a member of the Royal Yacht Squadron.

ALMIGHTY NOSE, THE Oliver Cromwell (1599–1658), Lord Protector of England under the Commonwealth (1653–58); so called by Needham (the *Cobbett of His Day)* because of his large nose, in *Mercurius Pragmaticus* (c. 1649). Also the *Blasphemer,* the *Brewer, Copperface, Coppernose Saint, Crum-Hell,* the *English Attila,* the *Glorious Villain,* the *Great Independent,* the *Great Leviathan of Men, His Noseship,* the *Immortal Rebel,* the *Impious, Ironside, King Oliver,* the *Man of Sin, Nod-Noll, Nose Almighty, Nosey, Old Noll, Ruby Nose,* the *Sagest of Usurpers,* the *Saviour of the Nation* and the *Town Bully of Ely.*

ALNASCHAR OF MODERN LITERATURE, THE Samuel Taylor Coleridge (1772–1834), English poet who said he wrote *Kubla Khan* (1816) after a dream. Also the *Cumberland Poet* and *Old Man Eloquent.*

- Alnaschar in *The Arabian Nights,* selling glassware in the market, thought of being rich, but his fortune was wrecked when he kicked his wares over while day-dreaming of spurning the Vizier's daughter.

ALPHABET BAYLEY Frederick William Bayley (1808–53), first editor of *The National Standard* (January 1833) and first editor of *The Illustrated London News* (1842). He had a considerable facility for writing verse.

ALPHABET SMITH Thomas Berry Cusack Smith (1795–1866), Attorney-General for Ireland. He prosecuted O'Connell (the *Big Beggarman*) for unlawful assembly in the Queen's Bench, Dublin (1844). So called by O'Connell, who was convicted. Smith became Master of the Rolls, Ireland. Also the *Vinegar Cruet.*

AMBITIOUS THANE, THE James Boswell (1740–95), biographer of Johnson (*Blinking Sam*); so called by Wolcot (*Peter Pindar*) in a letter to Boswell. Also the *Bear-Leader, Bosy, Corsica Boswell,* the *Curious Scrap-Merchant, Dapper Jemmy, Johnson's Zany* and *Will o' the Wisp.*

- A thane in OE was originally a military attendant to a king; later one who held lands in the king's name and

so a lord. Although Boswell's father was Lord Auchinleck, he was a law lord; it was a title which carried no honours for wife or children. Boswell was in dispute with his father over the entail of his estates, the heirs to which Boswell wanted to be male only.

AMBLING ALP, THE Primo Carnera (1906–67), Italian-born American heavyweight, champion of the world (1933). He was 6 ft 53/4 in tall and weighed 18 st 8 lb (260 lb). He held the title for only 350 days. Also *Da Preem* and the *Vast Venetian.*

AMERICAN ADDISON, THE Washington Irving (1783–1859), was an essayist and novelist.

- Cf the *Addison of America* and see the *English Atticus.*

AMERICAN BEAUTY, THE Lilian Russell (1861–1922), actress and singer in light operas. Her real name was Helen Louise Lennard.

AMERICAN BEWICK, THE Alexander Anderson (1775–1870), the *Father of American Wood Engraving.*

- Thomas Bewick (1753–1828), an Englishman, was the first man to popularize wood engraving, by means of his illustrations to *British Quadrupeds* (1790) and *British Birds* (1797).

AMERICAN BLACKSTONE, THE James Kent (1763–1847), jurist and legal commentator who was professor of law at Columbia University. He wrote *Commentaries on American Law* (4 vols. 1826–30).

- Sir William Blackstone (1723–80) was a notable English jurist. His *Commentaries on the Laws of England* (1765–80) have had a powerful influence on legal thinking. His fame in the USA is even greater than in England.

AMERICAN CATO, THE Samuel Adams (1722–1803), who was an active agitator from 1764 onward and a leader of the movement which culminated in the Revolution and the Declaration of Independence. He helped to organize the Sons of Liberty and the Boston Tea Party (1773);

so called by the newspapers (c. 1781). Also the *Father of America,* the *Last of the Puritans*, the *Man of the Revolution*, *Man of the Town Meeting* and the *Would-Be Cromwell*.

- Marcus Porcius Cato (234–149 BC), called 'Cato the Censor', was a violent opponent of the Roman nobility, and also had a strong conviction that Rome would never be safe until Carthage was destroyed.

AMERICAN CINCINNATUS, THE or THE CINCINNATUS OF THE AMERICANS George Washington (1732–99) who was called from life as a planter in Virginia to head the colonial forces in the American War of Independence. Also the *American Fabius*, the *Atlas of America,* the *Deliverer of America,* the *Father of His Country,* the *Father of America* and *Lovely Georgius.*

- Lucius Quinctius Cincinnatus (*circa* 519–438 BC) was brought from work on his farm beyond the river Tiber to become dictator of Rome when it was besieged by the Aequi. He saved Rome (485 BC) and went back to his farm.

AMERICAN CHARLES LAMB, THE George William Curtis (1824–92), journalist, orator and author. His books include *Lotus Eating* (1852) and *The Potiphar Papers* (1853); was so called by Charles Francis Richardson (1851–1913) in *American Literature* (1887–8).

- For Charles Lamb, see the *Mitre Courtier*.

AMERICAN CRUIKSHANK, THE David Claypole Johnston (1799–1865), etcher; so called by William Hickling Prescott (1796–1859) in *Biographical and Critical Miscellanies* (1845).

- For Cruikshank, see the *Prince of Caricaturists.*

AMERICAN DUMAS, THE Kenneth Roberts (1885–1957), author of *Rabble in Arms* (1933) and of *North-West Passage* (1937).

- Alexandre Dumas the elder (1802–70), author of historical novels which included *The Three Musketeers* (1844).

AMERICAN EAGLE, THE Army general Mark Wayne Clark (1896–1984) who commanded Allied forces in Italy (World War II) and UN troops in Korea (1952–3); so called by Churchill (*Bricky*).

AMERICAN FABIUS, THE George Washington, the *American Cincinnatus*; so called by newspapers (1775–85) because in fighting the British he adopted the tactics of . . .

- Quintus Fabius Maximus (275–203 BC) who instead of meeting Hannibal in a set battle harassed him in every way, and so slowed him down. He was given the nickname of 'Cunctator', the Delayer.

AMERICAN GIANT, THE Charles Freeman (died 1845), pugilist who was 6 ft 10 in tall. He fought in England.

AMERICAN GOLDSMITH, THE Samuel Woodworth (1785–1842), journalist, author of *The Oaken Bucket* and poet.

- For Oliver Goldsmith, see the *Child of Nature*.

AMERICAN MILTON, THE William Wilberforce Lord (1819–1907), clergyman whose poems appeared in 1845.

- For John Milton, see *Black-Mouthed Zoilus*.

AMERICAN MONTAIGNE, THE Ralph Waldo Emerson (1803–82), philosopher, essayist and poet. Also the *Buddha of the West* and the *Sage of Concord*.

- Michel Montaigne (1533–92), famous for his *Essais* (1580), was an influence on Emerson's thinking.

AMERICAN RICHARD SAVAGE, THE Edgar Allan Poe (1807–49), poet, essayist and short-story writer. Also the *Father of the Detective Story*.

- Richard Savage (died 1743), poet and dramatist, was condemned to death for having killed a man in a tavern, but was pardoned.

AMERICAN SOCRATES, THE Benjamin Franklin (1706–90), philosopher, scientist and diplomat. His thinking was humanitarian and pragmatic; so called by Sir James Mackintosh (the *Apostate*). Franklin was also the *Liberator of the New World* and the *Wisest American*.

- Cf the *English Socrates*.

AMERICAN STUART, THE Gilbert Charles Stuart (1756–1828), artist; so called in the UK to distinguish him from James *Athenian Stuart*.

AMERICAN TUPPER, THE Josiah Gilbert Holland (1819–81), editor and author combining sentiment with a real desire to teach.

- Martin Tupper (1810–89), English writer, famous for *Proverbial Philosophy* (1838–42).

AMERICAN WORDSWORTH, THE William Cullen Bryant (1794–1878), poet, notable for *Poems* (1832), and editor for almost fifty years of the *New York Evening Post*. He was a poet of nature, like Wordsworth, whose work greatly influenced him. Also the *Father of American Poetry*.

- For Wordsworth, see the *Bard of Rydal Mount*.

AMERICA'S BOY FRIEND Charles *Buddy* Rogers (1904–   ), American film-star so called in the 1920s, but whose chief claim to fame now is that he married (1937) Mary Pickford (*America's Sweetheart*). Also the *Love Rouser.*

AMERICA'S FIRST LADY OF SONG Ella Fitzgerald (1918–   ), American jazz singer.

AMERICA'S SWEETHEART Mary Pickford (1893–1979), Hollywood's first great film-star, whose real name was Gladys Smith, born in Canada. Also the *Little Girl with the Golden Curls* and the *Sweetheart of a Nation*.

AMIABLE GERONIMO, THE William (Bill) Beaumont (1952–), captain of the English rugby team twenty-one times (1970s–1980s). Also *Bo-Bo.*

- Geronimo (1829–1909) was the fiercest of Apache leaders.

AMIABLE MATHEMATICIAN, THE Lady Anne Isabella (Annabella) Milbanke (1792–1860) who became Lady Byron. She had a flair for mathematics; so called by Byron (*Baby*) who also called her *Pippin* and the *Princess of Parallelograms*.

ANACREON MOORE Thomas Moore (1779–1852), an Irish poet who translated the odes of the Greek lyrical poet Anacreon (*circa* 563–478 BC); so called by Byron (*Baby*). Captain R.H. Gronow recalls that in Paris Moore was known as 'Monsieur Anacreon'. Also the *Bard of Erin,* the *Landsdowne Laureate*, the *Pander of Venus*, *Trumpet Moore* and the *Young Catullus of His Day.*

- 'Anacreon' became a favourite word in the mid-19th century with a sense of 'amatory' or 'convivial'. Anacreonic societies were popular around the 1850s.

ANACREON OF ANCIENT SCOTTISH POETRY, THE or THE SCOTTISH ANACREON Alexander Scott or Scot (c. 1530–70) of Edinburgh; so called by John Pinkerton (1758–1826), antiquary and critic.

- See the *Word Catcher.*

ANACREON OF THE TWELFTH CENTURY, THE Walter Map or Mapes (c. 1150–1208), Welshman who became Archdeacon of Oxford, an author linked with early Arthurian legends. Some of the poems attributed to him deal with the vices of monks. Also the *Jovial Toper.*

ANAK OF PUBLISHERS or STATIONERS, THE John Murray (1778–1843), second in the hierarchy of the great publishing firm. He started *The Quarterly Review* (1809) and extended the business, publishing Jane Austen, George Borrow and Byron (who gave him the nickname). Also *Barabbas*, the *Emperor of the West* and *Glorious John.*

- The children of Anak were giants (Numbers xiii.33). Cf the *Coxcomb Bookseller.*

ANASTASIUS

i) Thomas Hope (c. 1770–1831), English collector of works of art who travelled widely. He published *Anastatius, or the Memoirs of* a *Modern Greek* (1819), of which Byron said that he wept when he read it because he was not the author.

ii) Henry Drummond (1851–97), British theological writer, e.g. *Natural Law in the Spiritual World* (1883).

- Anastasius was the name of four Popes and two East Roman emperors, of whom Anastasius I was humane and philanthropic.

ANATOMICAL JOHN John Hilton (1804–78), greatest anatomist of his day and surgeon to Queen Victoria (*Drina*).

AN CRAOIBHIN AOIBHINN Dr Douglas Hyde (1860–1949), 1st President of Eire (1938), historian, Gaelic scholar and poet. The name means 'The delightful little branch'.

ANDREW AMBO Dr Andrew Perne (1596–1654), Master of Peterhouse, Cambridge University and Dean of Ely; a man who adjusted his theology to the monarch's beliefs. Also the *Doctor of Hypocrisie, Judas, Old Andrew Turncoat,* and *Old Father Palinode.*

- 'Ambodexter' is an obsolete form of 'ambidexter' and in the 16th and 17th centuries was slang for double-dealing, from the Latin *ambo*, 'both'. His name has given the verb 'to pern', to be a turncoat.

ANDREW PREVIEW André Previn (1929–), German-born musician who began as a jazz pianist and is notable as a conductor of symphony orchestras; mentioned by Gloria Hunniford (*Glorious Honeybun*) on TV.

ANGEL FACE Walter Probyn (1931–), Britain's most wanted criminal at one time, and master of prison breaks. He spent 30 of his first 44 years in prison and escaped 15 times. Also *Britain's Public Enemy No 1*, the *Houdini of the Underworld* and the *Terror of Hoxton*.

ANGEL OF THE BATTLEFIELDS, THE Clara Barton (1821–1912), volunteer nurse in the American Civil War and founder of the American Red Cross; so called by Union soldiers.

ANGLO-SAXON MILTON, THE Caedmon (died 680), a Northumbrian herdsman – almost certainly of Celtic stock – who said he received the power of writing poetry in a vision after he had become a monk at Whitby, Yorkshire. The Venerable Bede (the *Father of English History*) said Caedmon could quickly turn any passage of Scripture into moving verse. Also the *Dreamer of Whitby* and the *Father of English Song.*

- For John Milton, see *Black-Mouthed Zoilus.*

ANIMAL, THE Anthony Parnes (1946–), London stockbroker; so called in the City, not because of any savagery in his nature but because he paces his office floor growling instructions into a portable telephone.

ANN Adrienne Shirley Haydon (1938–), Mrs P.F. Jones, British tennis player and Wimbledon champion (1969).

ANNE OF SWANSEA Frances Anne (Fanny) Kemble (1809–93), actress and popular figure in London society.

ANNE'S GREAT CAPTAIN John Churchill, 1st Duke of Marlborough (1650–1722), who commanded British armies under Queen Anne (*Brandy Nan*) and won many great victories. Also *Le Bel Anglais*, the *British Pallas, Corporal John*, the *Handsome Englishman, Handsome Jack, King John, Queen Anne's Great Captain* and *the Silly Duke.*

ANN THE WORD Ann Lee (1736–84), head of the Shakers, a religious body which she led to America (1774) and founded the American sect. Also *Mother Ann.*

ANOTHER ROSCIUS Richard Burbage (?1567–1619), actor and theatre manager who performed in plays by Shakespeare, Ben Jonson and Beaumont and Fletcher. He created the parts of Hamlet and Macbeth. Nickname recorded by Camden (the *British Pausanias*). Also the *English Roscius.*

- See the *African Roscius.*

ANTHROPOSOPHUS Thomas Vaughan (1622–66), alchemist and twin brother of Henry (the *Silurist*); so called after he wrote *Anthroposophus teomagica* (1650), an allegory of life after death. For a time he held a living in Brecknockshire.

ANTINOUS Granville Leveson-Gower, 1st Earl Granville (1773–1846); so called by Lady Bessborough (*Lady Blarney*). Also *Le Wellington des Joueurs.*

- Antinous was a beautiful youth, favourite of the Emperor Hadrian (76–138). After the boy was drowned in the Nile (130), he was deified by the Emperor and had a city named after him.

10

ANTIPODEAN, THE Robert (Bob) James Prometheus Fitzsimmons (1862–1917), British boxer who won the world titles at middleweight (1891), heavyweight (1897) and light heavyweight (1903). Born in Cornwall, he emigrated to New Zealand where he began professional boxing. Also the *Cornishman, Fighting Bob,* the *Freckled Freak, Ruby Robert* and the *Village Blacksmith.*

ANTIQUARIAN POET, THE John Leland or Leyland (1506–52), earliest of modern antiquaries, famous for his *Itinerary* (not published until 1710).

ANTIQUARY OF POETRY, THE Joseph Ritson (1752–1803), British antiquarian who among other works published a catalogue of English poets from the 12th to the 16th centuries. Also the *Learned Cabbage-Eater* and the *Word Catcher.*

APACHE KID, THE Has-kay-bay-nay-ntay (1867–?94), American Indian scout turned outlaw and murderer.

APECLOGGE, THE William de la Pole, 1st Duke of Suffolk (1396–1450) who was unpopular and banished as a traitor, but was murdered in the Channel; so called because of his badge, a clog and a chain like that attached to a monkey. Also *Jack Napes.*

APE GABRIEL Gabriel Harvey (?1545–1630), poet who claimed to be the *Father of the English Hexameter.* He condemned *The Faerie Queene* by Spenser (the *Child of the Ausonian Muse*); so called by Nash (the *English Aretine*) in 1593. Also the *Aristarchus of His Day, Fame's Duckling,* the *Monarch of Crosbiters* and the *Ropemaker.*

- To ape = to imitate in an inferior way (since 1230).

APELLES OF HIS AGE, THE Samuel Cooper (1609–72), English miniaturist; inscribed on his epitaph. Walpole (the *Autocrat of Strawberry Hill*) called him *Van Dyck in Little.*

- Apelles (4th century BC), celebrated Greek painter, was contemporary with – and painted a portrait of – Alexander the Great (356–323 BC).

APE OF ENVY, THE John Lyly (?1554–1606), English dramatist and author who created the style of Euphuism by his two works *Euphues, the Anatomy of Wit* (1578) and *Euphues and his England* (1580); so called by *Ape Gabriel* Harvey.

- Euphuism became fashionable in the late 16th and early 17th centuries, and loosely means 'affected writing'.

APE OF EUPHUES, THE Robert Greene (1560–92), English dramatist; so called by *Ape Gabriel* Harvey in *Foure Letters* (1592). Also the *Dying Titan*, the *Homer of Women* and the *King of the Paper Stage.*

- See above. 'Ape' in this sense = to imitate.

APOLLO'S MESSENGER Philip Massinger (1583–1640), English dramatist, best known for *A New Way to Pay Old Debts* (1633); a pun on 'Massinger' by Sir Aston Cokain (1608–84) in his preface to Massinger's *Emperor of the East* (1632).

APOLOGIST FOR THE QUAKERS, THE Robert Barclay (1648–90), Scottish Quaker who wrote *An Apology for the True Christian Divinity held by the Quakers* (1678).

- 'Apology' for Barclay meant a plea or an explanation.

APOSTATE, THE Sir James Mackintosh (1765–1832); so called by Parr (the *Birmingham Doctor*). After Mackintosh's defence of the French Revolution, he recanted and accepted an Indian judgeship from Pitt (the *Bottomless Pit*), the enemy of the revolution. Also *Subscription Jaimie.*

APOSTLE OF CALEDONIA, THE St Columba (c. 521–97). A Celt reputed to have been descended from *Niall of the Nine Hostages*, Columba made missionary journeys from Iona among the Picts of northern Scotland. He is said to have driven away 'a water monster' from Loch Ness. His real name was Irish Colum, and so was *Columkille* or *Colum of the Church.* Also the *Apostle of the Highlanders.*

- Niall of the Nine Hostages was an O'Neill, and they were hereditary abbots of Iona.

APOSTLE OF CHEERFULNESS, THE John Kenyon (1784–1856), poet and philanthropist, a lover of good food.

APOSTLE OF COLONISATION, THE Abbé François-Xavier-Antoine Labelle (1833–91), explorer of northern Canada above Montreal. He became Deputy Minister for Colonisation (post-1887). Also *Le Roi du Nord*.

APOSTLE OF CULTURE, THE Matthew Arnold (1822–88), English poet and critic whose works include *Culture and Anarchy* (1869); so called first, it is believed, by Sir Francis Burnand (1836–1917) in *Punch* (1880). Also the *Sainte-Beuve of Criticism*.

APOSTLE OF ENGLAND, THE Hugh Latimer (*circa* 1490–1555), Bishop of Worcester, burnt at the stake in the reign of *Bloody Mary*. He was one of the chief promoters of the Reformation in England.

APOSTLE OF FREE TRADE, THE
i) Richard Cobden (1804–65), British political economist noted for his advocacy of free trade, and leader of the Anti-Corn Law League (1839–46).
ii) John Bright (1811–89), Liberal MP who was a vigorous opponent of the Corn Laws after having been incited by Cobden (above). Also the *Quaker Solon of Rochdale* and the *Tribune of the People*.
• See also the *Corn-Law Rhymer*.

APOSTLE OF GERMANY, THE St Boniface (*circa* 675–754), Englishman born in Devon, whose real name was Wynfrith. After having been a monk in England he went as a missionary to the heathen tribes of Germany.

APOSTLE OF IRELAND, THE St Patrick (*circa* 385–*circa* 461), a Romano-British evangelist who was the first missionary Bishop to pagan Ireland. Also *St Paddy*.

APOSTLE OF LIBERTY, THE
i) Henry Clay (1777–1852), American Secretary of State (1825–29). He supported the Latin American states in their revolts against Spain. Also *Gallant Harry of the West*, the *Grand Old Man*, the *Great Commoner*, the *Great Compromiser*, the *Great Pacificator*, *Harry of the West*, the *Judas of the West*, the *Mill Boy of the Slashes*, *Old*

Chief, the *Saviour of His Country* and the *Second Washington*.
ii) Thomas Jefferson (1743–1826), 3rd President of the USA. He was one of the original rebels against British colonial rule, and was the moving spirit behind the Declaration of Independence. Also *Long Tom* and the *Sage of Monticello*.

APOSTLE OF MARYLAND, THE Andrew White (1579–1656), English Jesuit missionary to the whites and Indians of Maryland for ten years.

APOSTLE OF TEMPERANCE, THE Father Theobald Mathew (1790–1856), an Irish Capuchin friar who became the greatest of all temperance missionaries. He travelled all over Ireland (1838–42), and later extensively in England and the USA. Also the *Sinners' Friend*.

APOSTLE OF THE ALLEGHANIES, THE Demetrius Augustine Gallitzin (1770–1840), a Russian-born Roman Catholic immigrant into the USA. He bought an estate in Cambria, Pennsylvania, and gave away or sold parts of it at low prices to Catholic immigrants. He died deeply in debt.
• The Alleghany or Allegheny Mountains range through Pennsylvania, Maryland and Virginia.

APOSTLE OF THE ANGLO-SAXONS, THE St Augustine or Austin (died 604), a Benedictine monk sent (597) by Pope Gregory I as a missionary to Kent. He established the See of Canterbury, and was England's first Archbishop. Also the *Apostle of the English*.

APOSTLE OF THE ENGLISH, THE St Augustine (above).

APOSTLE OF THE FRIESIANS, THE St Willibrord (658–739), English missionary to Friesland (690), and later Archbishop of the Friesians.

APOSTLE OF THE HIGHLANDERS, THE St Columba, the *Apostle of Caledonia*.

APOSTLE OF (or TO) THE INDIANS, THE John Eliot (1604–90), English missionary who preached to the Indians near Boston, Massachusetts, in their own language. He established fourteen villages and translated the Bible and a number of religious works into the Massachusetts dialect of the Algonkin language. Also the *Protector of the Indians*.

APOSTLE OF THE ISLE OF ELY, THE William Sedgwick (?1610–69), Puritan divine and mystic. Also *Doomsday Sedgwick*.

- The Isle of Ely in Cambridgeshire was once the stronghold of Hereward the *Wake*.

APOSTLE OF THE NORTH, THE or THE NORTHERN APOSTLE

i) Bernard Gilpin (1517–83), vicar of Houghton-le-Spring (Durham), who helped the poor, maintaining a number of children at his own expense. He endowed a grammar school and assisted some of the pupils to enter university. Also the *Father of the Poor*.

ii) John Macdonald (1779–1849), Scottish Presbyterian clergyman.

APOSTLE OF THE PEAK, THE William Bagshaw (1628–1702), a nonconformist missionary to the Peak district of Derbyshire.

APOSTLE OF THE PICTS, THE St Ninian (died 432), a British bishop reputed to have preached among the southern Picts (c. 400), although like much hagiography, traditions about his life are untrustworthy.

APOSTLE OF THE SCOTS, THE John Knox (c. 1505–72), preacher and reformer. He advocated a wide system of education, from a school in every parish in Scotland to three universities. Also the *Apostle of the Scottish Reformation*, the *Firebrand of His Country* and the *Religious Machiavel*.

APOSTLE OF THE SCOTTISH REFORMATION, THE John Knox (above) who established the Reformed Church in Scotland.

APOSTLE OF UNITARIANISM, THE William Ellery Channing (1780–1842), American Congregational minister who began to preach unitarianism in 1819.

APOSTLE OF VIRGINIA, THE Samuel Harris (1724–95), a fanatical American Baptist preacher.

APOSTLE OF WALES, THE St David (480–

544). He is reputed to have been born the son of a Cardiganshire chieftain and named Dewi. He founded twelve monasteries and became Primate of Wales. Also the *Waterman*.

APOSTLE OF YORKSHIRE, THE St Paulinus (597–644), Bishop of York and Rochester. He was a missionary to the North and baptized King Edwin of Northumbria and his court.

APPIUS John Dennis (1657–1734), English dramatist and critic who wrote *Appius and Virginia* (1709), savaged by Pope (the *Bard of Twickenham*) for its bombast. Dennis in reply called Pope 'a short squab gentleman'. Also the *Best-Abused Man in England*, *Python* and *Young Zoilus*.

- The decemvir Appius Claudius (c. 451 BC) was a lustful tyrant.

ARABIAN TAILOR, THE Henry Wild (1684–1734), a Norwich tailor who while working at his trade learned Latin, Greek, Hebrew, Syriac, Arabic and Persian. Also the *Learned Tailor*.

ARCH-DRUID, THE William Stukeley (1687–1765), English antiquary who wrote on Stonehenge and other remains which he labelled Druidical.

ARCHIE Field-Marshal Archibald, 1st Earl Wavell (1883–1950), C-in-C, Middle East Forces (World War II). He was later Viceroy of India (1943–47). Although this was his own name, it was so widely used among troops under his command as to become a nickname. Also the *Chief*.

ARCHIMAGUS George Dyer (1755–1841), English essayist and poet; so called by his close friend Lamb (the *Mitre Courtier*). Also *Copernicus*.

- An archimagus is a chief magician or enchanter; from the Persian *magus*.

ARCHIMEDES John Rennie (1761–1821), British engineer and inventor who drained and reclaimed vast areas of marshland; so called by Dibdin (the *Beau Brummell of Living Authors*).

- The great scientist and inventor Archimedes of Syracuse (287–212 BC) introduced the Archimedian Screw for irrigation among so much else.

ARCHITECT EARL, THE Henry Herbert, 9th Earl of Pembroke (c. 1689–1750), largely responsible for the erection of Westminster Bridge, London.

ARCH-KILLER OF CHICAGO, THE Charles Dion O'Bannion (1892–1924), American gang leader (1920s); so called by the Chicago police. Also *Deanie*.

ARCH-PIRATE, THE Captain John Avery (c. 1665– ?), English pirate (principally in the Red Sea and the Indian Ocean) who once captured a ship rich in treasures of the Grand Mogul, but, it is said, died in poverty somewhere in Devon, his birthplace. Also the *King of Madagascar* and *Long Ben*.

ARGONAUT Captain Basil Hall, RN (1788–1844), traveller and author, e.g. *Fragments of Voyages and Travels*; so called in *Noctes Ambrosianae*. Also *A Literary Sinbad*.

- The Argonauts were the sailors of the *Argo* which sailed to Colchis for the golden fleece.

ARIEL Percy Bysshe Shelley (1792–1822), British lyric poet. He had a small schooner in Italy called the *Ariel*. Also the *Atheist*, *Mad Shelley*, the *Poet of Poets* and the *Snake*.

- Ariel is the spirit in *The Tempest*.

ARIOSTO OF THE NORTH, THE Sir Walter Scott (1771–1832), poet and novelist; so called by Byron (*Baby*). Also the *Bard of Martial Lay*, the *Black Hussar of Literature*, the *Border Minstrel*, the *Caledonian Comet*, the *Charmer of the World, Colonel Grogg*, the *Duke of Darnick, Duns Scotus*, the *Father of the English Novel*, the *Great Magician of the North*, the *Great Minstrel*, the *Great Unknown*, the *Mighty Minstrel*, *Old Peveril*, *Peveril*, and the *Wizard of the North*.

- Ludovico Ariosto (1474–1553), Italian poet and author of *Orlando Furioso* (1510–32); later called 'The Southern Scott'.

ARISTARCH OF BRITISH CRITICISM, THE John Gibson Lockhart (1794–1854), British critic whose severity earned him the nickname of the *Scorpion*; so called by W.H. Prescott (1796–1859) in his *Bio-graphical and Critical Miscellanies* (1845).

- Aristarchus of Samothrace (fl. 156 BC) was a grammarian and critic, who founded a school in Alexandria.

ARISTARCHUS OF CAMBRIDGE, THE Richard Bentley (1662–1742), scholar and critic. He proved the *Epistles of Phalaris* (1695), edited by Lord Orrery, to be spurious.

- See *Phalaris Junior*.

ARISTARCHUS OF HIS DAY, THE *Ape Gabriel* Harvey.

ARISTARCHUS OF THE EDINBURGH REVIEW, THE Francis, Lord Jeffrey (1773–1850), critic, lawyer and politician. With Sydney Smith (*Diner-Out of the First Water*), he founded *The Edinburgh Review* (1802) and was a notable opponent of the Lake Poets (i.e. S.T. Coleridge, the *Alnaschar of Modern Literature*; R. Southey, the *Ballad Monger*; and W. Wordsworth, the *Bard of Rydal Mount*).

- The term 'Lake School' was first used in *The Edinburgh Review* (1817). All the poets lived in the English Lake District.

ARIZONA JOHN Major John M. Burke (1846–1917), *Buffalo Bill's* friend and partner; his nickname as an actor, though he never went to Arizona. He persuaded Sitting Bull (1831–90) to join the Wild West Show (1884). He wrote a life of Cody and died a few weeks after him.

ARKLE Derek Randall (1951–), Nottinghamshire and England cricketer; because of his 'dancing' at the wicket. He scored 209 and 146 in the same match against Middlesex. (1979).

- Arkle was a popular steeplechasing horse (1962–6).

'ARRY BOY Harry Cripps (1941–), British full back for Millwall F.C., with a habit of scoring goals; so called by Millwall fans.

ARSENIC SAL Sarah Chesham, executed 1851 for having poisoned her husband Richard (died 1850). She had previously been acquitted of poisoning three children.

ARTFUL JOE Joseph Chamberlain (1836–1914), British statesman; from his political adroitness. He was very ambitious – another of his nicknames was *Pushful Joe* – and as Liberal-Unionist Colonial Secretary pushed the Boers too far and so is accused of starting the Boer War (1899). Also *Brummagem Joe*, the *Grand Young Man*, the *Master, Moatlhodi*, the *People's Joe*, *Radical Joe* and *Tiger*.

ARTIFICER, THE Saer Gobban (fl. 7th century), builder of churches and fortresses in north and east Ireland.

ASAPH John Dryden (1631–1700), poet and dramatist; so called by Nahum Tate (1652–1715) in a second part of *Absolom and Achitophel* (1682) which Dryden revised. Also *Glorious John*, *Old Squab* and *Poet Squab*.

- Asaph was a musician who 'made a sound with cymbals' (Chronicles I, xvi, 5).

ASIAN MYSTERY, THE Benjamin Disraeli, 1st Earl Beaconsfield (1804–81), British Prime Minister (1868 and 1874–80), because he was of Jewish origin; so called by Beresford Hope (1867) during a Parliamentary debate on the Reform Bill. Also the *Chief*, *Dizzy*, the *Gay Lothario of Politics*, *Jingo*, the *Old Jew*, the *Primrose Sphinx* and the *Red Indian of Debates*.

ASPERS John Aspinall (1926–   ), London gambler and Kent zoo-owner.

ASSYRIAN, THE Charles Frederick Moberly Bell (1847–1911); staff nickname at *The Times*, of which he was managing editor (1890–1911). He was born in Egypt where he founded *The Egyptian Gazette* and was *Times* correspondent for twenty years.

ASTROLOGICAL RICHARD Richard Harvey (died 1623), astrologer and almanac-maker; brother of *Ape Gabriel* Harvey. Also *Donzel Dick* and *Lipsian Dick*.

ATCH Surgeon-Captain Edward Leicester Atkinson (1882–1929) who as a lieutenant was parasitologist on the Antarctic Expedition (1910–13) and found the Scott party dead.

ATHEIST, THE

i) P.B. Shelley, *Ariel*; his nickname at Eton. At Oxford University he wrote a pamphlet *The Necessity of Atheism*.

ii) Thomas Hobbes (1588–1679), philosopher who wrote *The Leviathan* (1651); so called by David Masson (1822–1907) in his *Life of Milton* (1859–80), accepting a contemporary view, although Aubrey (the *Little Boswell of His Day*) wrote 'For his being branded with atheism, his writings and virtuous life testify against it.' Hobbes was more concerned with nature and man than with spiritual matters. Also the *Bear*, *Crowe*, the *Mighty Leviathan*, the *Philosopher of Malmesbury* (and the *Malmesbury Philosopher*).

ATHEIST TAMBURLAN, THE Christopher Marlowe (1564–93) a dramatist who wrote *Tamburlaine* (c. 1587); so called by Greene (the *Ape of Euphues*). Also the *Father of English Dramatic Poetry* and the *Second Shakespeare*.

ATHENIAN ABERDEEN George Hamilton Gordon, 4th Earl of Aberdeen (1784–1860), British Prime Minister (1852–5). He visited Greece, founded the Athenian Society and wrote *An Inquiry into the Principles of Beauty in Grecian Architecture* (1822); so called by Byron (*Baby*) as 'The travelled Thane, Athenian Aberdeen'.

- See *Tear 'Em*.

ATHENIAN STUART James Stuart (1713–88), Scottish artist. As a result of a visit to Greece, he published *The Antiquities of Athens* (1751) which led to the introduction of Greek-style architecture in London.

- Cf the *American Stuart*.

ATHLING, THE see Aetheling.

ATLAS

i) William Pitt, Earl of Chatham, *Aeolus*; so called by Byron (*Baby*).

ii) David Garrick (1717–79), said to have been one of the greatest actors of all time; buried in Westminster Abbey. When discussing Garrick's proposed retirement with Johnson (*Blinking Sam*), Boswell (the *Ambitious Thane)*, observed that Garrick 'would be Atlas with the burden off his back'. Also the *British Roscius*, the *Great Roscius*, *Little Davy*, the *Proteus of the Stage*, *Roscius*

Britannicus and the *Whitefield of the Stage*.

- Atlas, Greek mythological giant, was condemned to bear heaven and earth on his head and shoulders.

ATLAS OF AMERICA, THE George Washington, the *American Cincinnatus*.

ATLAS OF ANTIQUARIANS, THE or THE ATLAS OF SCOTS ANTIQUARIANS George Chalmers (1742–1825), lawyer and political writer. He was an attorney in America for about ten years, and wrote the political annals of America to 1688 and a history of Northern Britain; so called by Dibdin (the *Beau Brummell of Living Authors*). Also *Aurelius*.

ATLAS OF POETRY, THE George Peele (1552–98), dramatist, actor and poet. He wrote a great deal: plays, pageants, lyrics, congratulatory poems and miscellaneous verse; so called by Nash (the *English Aretine*).

ATLAS OF THE SWORD, THE James Figg (died 1740), English pugilist, swordsman and cudgeller who kept a booth at Southwark Fair, London, and offered to meet anyone at each of his skills. He also had a 'theatre' in the Tyburn Road. Also the *Father of Boxing*.

ATTERBURY'S PAD Thomas, 1st Baron Coningsby (?1656–1729: later Earl: 1719). He criticized Bishop Francis Atterbury (1662–1732) of Rochester in the House of Lords (1718) for having likened himself to a prophet, and commented that he found a prophet very like him in Balaam who rode his ass so furiously that the ass reproved him. The bishop replied that Coningsby being the only person who had reproved him 'must needs take that character upon himself'. The nickname dates from that day.

- A pad (used here sardonically since Coningsby was sharp-tempered) was slang for an easy-paced horse (from German *pfad*).

ATTILA Mark Hateley (1961–   ), striker for Coventry, Portsmouth F.C. and England; so called in Italy where he played for Milan.

- See below.

ATTILA THE HEN Margaret Hilda Thatcher (1925–   ), British PM (1979–   ), from her uncompromising attitudes. She was the first Prime Minister for 150 years to be elected (1987) for a third term; so called by *Private Eye*. Also *Ayesha*, *Blessed Margaret*, *Boadicea*, the *Cold War Witch*, *'Er Indoors*, *Gladys Hacksaw*, *Gloriana*, *H.M.*, the *Iron Lady*, the *Mekon*, the *Milk Snatcher*, *Miss Floggie*, the *Plutonium Blonde*, *Rhoda the Rhino*, *She Who Must be Obeyed*, *Snobby Roberts*, *TBW*, *Tina* and the *Westminster Ripper*.

- Attila (c. 406–43), King of the Huns, noted for his ruthlessness, overran a great part of the Byzantine and west Roman empires. Attila (= Little Father) was a nickname for Etzel.

ATTORNEY FOR THE DAMNED, THE Clarence Darrow (1857–1938). American lawyer famous for his defences in 'impossible' cases, e.g. Leopold (*Babe*) and Loeb, the Chicago thrill killers (1924) and the Scopes 'monkey trial' (1925).

ATTY

i) Henry Seymour Pearsse (1869–1960), British racehorse owner and trainer.

ii) The Hon. Thomas Anthony Corbett (1921–   ), British amateur jockey.

ATTY CONKEY The Duke of Wellington, the *Achilles of England*; so called by his soldiers. It means 'Arthur the Long-Nosed'. He had been *Conkey* since 1805.

AUGUSTUS George II (1683–1760), the last British monarch to lead troops into action (Dettingen, 1743); so called by Pope (the *Bard of Twickenham*). Also *Dapper George*, the *Great Patron of Mankind* and *Old Squaretoes*.

- The Roman emperor Augustus (63 BC–AD 14) had personal command of the Roman army. He was also the patron of the Augustan Age, the finest days of Roman literature, so Pope's tribute was not entirely disinterested. 'Augustus' was George's second name.

AUGUSTUS DRURIOLANUS Sir Augustus Henry Glossop Harris (1852–96), theatre manager, controller of Drury Lane Theatre, London (1880s). Also *Druriolanus* and the *Emperor Augustus*.

- See above; a word-play on 'Coriolanus'.

AuH2O Senator Barry Goldwater (1980–), American Presidential candidate (1964); mock chemical formula as a pun on his name. He used it as an election slogan. Also *Beelzebub M. Goldwater.*

AUK, THE Field-Marshal Sir Claude John Eyre Auchinleck (1884–1981), C-in-C, Middle East (1941–2); his army nickname since before World War II.

AULD MICHAEL Michael Scot or Scott (?1175–c. 1232), Scottish mathematician and astrologer who won a reputation as a wizard. He appears in Dante's *Inferno* as one of the magicians and soothsayers. He wrote books on astronomy, astrology and the occult; so called in Northumberland. Also the *Devil's Piper.*

- *The Inferno* is part of *The Divine Comedy* (c. 1300), written by Dante Alighieri (1265–1321). See Aubrey's comment at the *Coryphaeus of Mathematicians*.

AURELIUS George Chalmers, the *Atlas of Antiquarians*; so called by Dibdin (*The Beau Brummell of Living Authors*).

- Marcus Aurelius (121–180), Roman emperor and Stoic philosopher.

AURORA Jane Elizabeth Digby (1807–81), daughter of Admiral Digby (the *Silver Captain*). She married and divorced Lord Ellenborough (the *Elephant*), and after many adventures across Europe became the wife of a Bedouin sheikh, Medjuel el Mesrab; so called by an admirer from Byron's Aurora Raby, a beautiful and innocent heiress in *Don Juan* (1819–24); nickname mentioned by Thomas Creevy (1768–1838). Jane was the original of Balzac's Lady Arabella Dudley. Also *Ianthe.*

AUSSIE JOE Joseph (Joe) Bugner (1949–), Hungarian-born heavyweight boxer who settled in Australia after a brief career in England. He once defeated Henry Cooper (*'Enery*) on points.

AUSTRALIAN BOB Robert Trimbole (1931– 87), born Bruno Trimboli of Italian parents in Australia, head of a drugs ring and Australia's most wanted man; partner of Terry Sinclair (*Mr Big*). Trimbole fled from Australia to Europe and was arrested in Ireland. He was extradited, but died mysteriously in Spain on the journey. His body was only identified by the fingerprints.

AUSTRALIAN MARIE LLOYD, THE Florrie Forde (1876–1940), music-hall star in London (post-1897). Her real name was Florence Flanagan (born Melbourne). She was the first to sing *Pack Up Your Troubles* and *It's a Long Way to Tipperary*.

- For Marie Lloyd, see *Our Marie*.

AUSTRALIAN PATRIOT, THE William Charles Wentworth (1793–1872), was a champion of Australian self-government. President of the Legislative Assembly (post-1861) which he fought to create.

AUSTRALIA'S QUARTZ REEF KING J.B. Watson (1824–89), English-born Australian millionaire who made a fortune in the *Bendigo* gold-mine.

AUSTRALIA'S QUEEN OF SONG Dame Nellie Melba (1861–1931), soprano whose real name was Nellie Porter Mitchell (Melba, from Melbourne).

AUTIE Major-General George Armstrong Custer (1839–76), cavalry leader in the American Civil War; died at the battle of Little Big Horn. Also the *Boy General*, *Iron Butt*, *Long Hair*, *Ringlets* and *the Squaw Killer*.

AUTOCRAT OF STRAWBERRY HILL, THE Horace Walpole, 4th Earl of Orford (1717–97), author and antiquarian. He turned a villa at Strawberry Hill, Twickenham into what was virtually a baronial mansion; so called by Mrs S.C. Hall (1800–81) in *Pilgrimages to English Shrines*. Also the *Last of the Romans*, the *Lying Old Fox*, the *Parasite of Genius* and *Ultimus Romanorum.*

- See the *Toy Woman à la Mode*.

AWESOME WELLES Orson Welles (1915– 85), American actor and producer; so called by Tony Curtis (1925–); because of his size (281/2 stone: 399 lb in 1983).

AYESHA Margaret Thatcher, *Attila the Hen*; mentioned by Patrick Jenkin (1926–) when Environment Secretary; from Rider Haggard's *She* (1887): '*She Who Must be Obeyed*'.

AYRSHIRE POET, THE Robert Burns (1759–96), Scottish poet from Ayrshire. Also the *Bard of Ayrshire*, the *Glory and*

Reproach of Scotland, the *Heaven-Taught Ploughman* and the *Peasant Bard*.

AXIS SALLY

i) Rita Zucca (1912–   ), announcer of Rome radio (World War II); so called by Allied soldiers in the Anzio bridgehead (1944) whom she invited to desert.

ii) Mildred Elizabeth Sisk (1900–   ).

- Germany, Italy and Japan were known in World War II as 'The Axis'.

B

BAB Baptist May (1629–98), Keeper of the Privy Purse to Charles II (the *Blackbird*); brother to Hugh May, architect who worked on Windsor Castle.

BABA Dorothy Pim (1901–   ), Mrs John B. Beck, Irish Ladies golf champion (1938).

BABBLETONGUE Thomas Babbington, 1st Baron Macaulay (1800–59), British historian and poet; from 'Babbington' and his fluency in speaking. He was said to have been inexhaustible as a conversationalist at Cambridge University. Also a *Book in Breeches*, the *Burke of Our Age*, and the *Son of the Saint*.

BABE
i) George Herman Ruth (1894–1948), American baseball player who during his career with the New York Yankees (1914–35) hit more than 700 home runs; so called because of his size. It has become a slang term for any fat baseball player, but George Ruth made it a 'title' of honour; elected to the Hall of Fame. Also the *Bambino*, the *Behemoth of Bust*, the *Colossus of Clout*, the *Home Run King*, *Slambino* and the *Sultan of Swat*.
● See *Home Run* and *Hammerin' Hank*.
ii) Mildred Didrikson (1914–56), later Mrs Zaharias, all-round American athlete who at the age of eighteen won Olympic gold medals for the 80 metres hurdles and the javelin (1932). Also a champion professional golfer.
iii) Patrick Macdonald (1878–1954), American athlete, the oldest to win an Olympic title (56 lb throw, Antwerp, 1920).
iv) Nathan F. Leopold, jnr., (1906–71), one of the Chicago 'thrill killers' (1924); imprisoned for life and paroled (1958).
v) Woolf Barnato (1855–1948), British motor-racing driver; son of the *Kaffir King*.
vi) Floyd Herman (1903–87), American, an outstanding batter for the Brooklyn Dodgers baseball team from 1925 until 1931. In 1930 he scored 393 runs. He set several Dodgers' records.
vi) Oliver Hardy, see the *Fiddle and the Bow*. He was fat like (i).

BABY
i) George Gordon Noel, 6th Baron Byron of Rochdale (1788–1824), poet; so called by his mistress, Lady Caroline Lamb (*Caro*). Also the *Bard of Corsair*, the *Comus of Poetry* and the *Old English Baron*.
ii) Princess Beatrice (1857–1944), youngest child of Queen Victoria (*Drina*). She married Prince Henry of Battenberg (1858–96).
iii) Lillie Langtry (1877–1965), British music-hall singer. Also the *Electric Spark*. She was no relation to the *Jersey Lily*.
iv) Warren Dodds (1898–1959), American jazz drummer.

BABY CORNWALL Bryan Procter (1787–1874), English poet. He wrote under the pseudonym of 'Barry Cornwall', e.g. *Mirandola* (1821). Also the *Moral Byron*.

BABYFACE George Nelson (1908–34), American bank-robber and murderer; shot by the FBI. His nickname behind his back in the underworld. Also *Public Enemy No 1*.

BABYFACED COMEDIAN, THE Harry Langdon (1884–1944), early American film comic; mentioned by Harold Lloyd (1893–1971).

BABY FLO Flora Mae King (1930–65), later Mrs Jackson, the heaviest woman in the world. An American negress, she weighed 60 stone (840 lb) just before her death. She used the nickname in show business.

BABY MONROE Melanie Griffith (1958–   ), American film actress, star of *Working Girl* (1989). Also the *New Kim Novak*.
● Marilyn Monroe (1926–62), American film actress and sex symbol. Her real name was Norma Jean Dougherty.

BABY PEGGY Peggy Montgomery (1917–), American child film actress.

BABY SANDRA Sandra Henville (1938–), American child film actress.

BACCHUS

i) James Henry Leigh Hunt (1784–1859), British journalist, poet and essayist who translated Radi's *Bacco in Toscana* (1825). Also *King Leigh* and the *Jove of Modern Critical Olympus.*

ii) Ensign, later Colonel, Lascelles (fl. early 19th century) of the Guards. Captain R.H. Gronow (then an ensign) said in 1813 that 'good living at St Jean de Luz agreed so well with my friend that he waxed fat and from that period to his death was known to the world by the jovial appellation of Bacchus'.

• Bacchus was the Roman god of wine.

BACHELOR PAINTER, THE Sir Joshua Reynolds (1723–92), fashionable painter and leader of the English School. He never married; so called by John Timbs in *Anecdotal Biographies.* Also the *Raphael of England*.

BACKSTAIRS DRAGON, THE Robert Harley, 1st Earl of Oxford (1661–1724), British Chief Minister (1710), who was a secret intriguer and undermined the confidence of Queen Anne (*Brandy Nan*) in her ministers. Also the *Dragon*, *Harlequin*, *Hermodactyl*, the *King of Book Collectors* and *Robin the Trickster*.

• One historian wrote of him that 'he functioned most efficiently behind the scenes, "backstairs".'

BACON FLY, THE Macveigh Napier (1776–1847), British journalist who published a book on Bacon (the *Father of Inductive Philosophy*). He was editor of *The Edinburgh Review*. Also *Macveinus Napier* and *Supplement Napier*.

BACON OF THEOLOGY, THE Joseph Butler (1692–1752), Bishop of Durham who wrote *The Analogy of Religion* (1736), a defence of Christian philosophy against Deists, advocates of 'natural religion', who put reason before revelation.

• Bacon, see above and see the *Father of English Deism*.

BACON'S ALTER EGO Sir Tobie Matthew (1577–1655), English courtier, diplomat and writer; so called because Bacon (above) submitted his later work to him for criticism.

BAD, THE Hywel ab Ieuaf, Welsh king (reigned 979–85), killed by the Saxons.

BADONICUS See the *Wise*.

BAD NEWS George Cafego (1915–), American footballer. His skill made him 'bad news' for his opponents.

BAD OLD MAN, THE General Jubal Anderson Early (1816–94) of the Confederate army; so called by his soldiers in the American Civil War because he opposed the principle of secession for which they felt they were fighting. Also *Old Jube*.

BAGATELLE Richard Seymour-Conway, 4th Marquis of Hertford (1793–1874) who lived a great deal in Paris.

BAHAWDER JAW Sir John Malcolm (1769–1833), was an Anglo-Indian soldier and administrator, and first chairman of the Oriental Club, London; so called by Canning (*Aeolus*). Sir John talked long and volubly.

BALAAM Theophilus Hastings, 7th Earl of Huntingdon (1650–1701), follower of Monmouth (*Absalom*) and imprisoned for treason (1692); so called by Dryden (*Asaph*).

• Balaam was a prophet who told the Midianites how to bring disaster on the Israelites by 'causing them to commit trespass against the Lord' (Numb. xxxi).

BALD EAGLE James (Jim) Smith (1940–), player for Sheffield United and manager for Queen's Park Rangers Football Club, who took them to the final of the Milk Cup (1986). He left Queen's Park Rangers Football Club for Newcastle United in 1988. He is bald.

BALD EAGLE OF FOGGY BOTTOM, THE President Truman's Secretary of Defense, Robert Lovett, was bald. He had worked in the State Department at one time, and since that was nicknamed (appropriately enough, some maintained) Foggy Bottom, the two elements combined into this splendid nickname. The bald eagle is of course the symbol of the United States.

BALLAD MONGER, THE Robert Southey (1774–1843), British poet and biographer; so called by Byron (*Baby*) in an attack on him in *English Bards and Scotch Reviewers* (1809). Also the *Bard of the Bay*, the *Blackbird*, the *Cumberland Poet*, the *Epic Renegade*, the *First Man of Letters in Europe*, *Mouthy* and the *Poet of Greta Hill*.

BALLCRUSHER, THE Leonard (Len) Ganley (1943–   ), top British snooker referee; after a beer TV advertisement had shown him crushing a snooker ball to dust.

BALLOON TYTLER James Tytler (1747–1804), first Englishman to go up in a fire-balloon (1784). He contributed much to the first two editions of the *Encyclopaedia Britannica* (1778–83).

BAMBI Lance D. Alworth (1940–   ), American footballer for San Diego Chargers; in the Hall of Fame for his performances (1962–70); from the Walt Disney cartoon deer.

BAMBINO *Babe* Ruth.
• *Bambino* is Italian for 'Babe'.

BAN Byron Bancroft Johnson (1864–1931), founder of the American League of Baseball Clubs, its first president and one of the game's great influences.

BANANA NOSE Edward (Eddie) Arcaro (1916–   ), leading American jockey (fl. 1945–50). Also the *King of the Stakes Riders*.

BANDIT QUEEN, THE Belle Starr (1848–89), whose real name was Myra Belle Shirley, horse-thief and receiver of stolen goods; shot by an unknown gunman. She married an Oklahoma Indian named Sam Starr. She is said to have ridden with Jesse James (*Dingus*). Also the *Petticoat of the Plains*.

BANGTAIL David Armstrong, border reiver (late 16th century); a poor horseman?

BANJO Andrew Barton Paterson (1864–1941), Australian journalist and ballad-writer, credited with having been the author of *Waltzing Matilda* (*circa* 1898).

BANJO EYES Eddie Cantor (1892–1964), American vaudeville comedian and film star with large eyes. His real name was Edward Iskavitz.

BANKER POET, THE
i) Samuel Rogers (1763–1855), son of a banker, and a rich man. Also the *Bard of Memory*, the *Dug-Up Dandy*, the *Last English Maecenas* and the *Nestor of English Authors*.
ii) Edmund Clarence Stedman (1833–1908), American poet and successful Wall St broker. He wrote *Pan in Wall Street* (1869).

BANK NUN, THE Sarah Whitehead (fl. early 19th century), a 17-year-old girl whose brother was executed for embezzlement from the Bank of England. She did not know of his death, and, half-mad, haunted Threadneedle St for 25 years, asking for him. She lived on charity from bank employees and is thought to have been fifty-five or sixty when she died.

BANZU MOHR AR CHAT Elizabeth, Countess of Sutherland (1765–1839) who succeeded to the earldom in her own right (1766). The Gaelic nickname means the *Great Lady of the Cat*; so called by Scott (the *Ariosto of the North*).
• The badge of the Sutherland earldom is a wild cat.

BAPU Rameshchandra Gangara Nadkarni (1932–   ), Indian cricketer who bowled 21 six-ball maiden overs during a match between India and England (Madras, 1964).
• *Bap* is Hindi for 'father'.

BARABBAS
i) Thomas Longman (1770–1842), nephew of the founder of that publishing firm and controller of the business from 1755; so called by Campbell (the *Bard of Hope*).
ii) John Murray, the *Anak of Publishers*; so called by Byron (*Baby*).
• Most publishers in those days bought the copyright of a book for a small sum. The stricture is, of course, no longer applicable. Barabbas was the thief and murderer released by Pontius Pilate in place of Jesus. 'Barabbas' is now the telegraphic address of the London publisher Robert Hale. Cf the *Dey of Algiers*.

BARBER'S DEMON, THE Joe Walcott

(1872–1935) who won the world welter-weight boxing championship (1901).

• Cf *Jersey Joe*.

BARD NANTGLYN Robert Davies (?1769–1835), Welsh poet from Nantglyn, a town south-west of Denbigh.

BARD OF ALL TIME, THE William Shakespeare (1654–1616), England's greatest dramatic poet. Also the *Bard of Avon*, the *Divine*, *Fancy's Child*, the *Glory of the English Stage*, the *Glory of the Human Intellect*, the *Homer of Dramatic Poets*, the *Immortal Bard*, the *Incomparable*, the *Matchless*, *Nature's Darling*, the *Swan of Avon* and the *Sweet Swan of Avon*.

• Ben Jonson (the *Bricklayer*) wrote in his eulogy after Shakespeare had died: 'He was not of an age, but for all time.'

BARD OF ARTHURIAN ROMANCE, THE Alfred, 1st Baron Tennyson (1809–92), poet-laureate who wrote *Morte d'Arthur* (1842), *Idylls of the King* (1859) and *The Holy Grail* (1869). Also the *English Virgil*, the *Poet of Haslemere* and *Schoolmiss Alfred*.

BARD OF AVON, THE William Shakespeare, the *Bard of All Time*; usually clipped to 'The Bard' in theatrical circles.

BARD OF AYRSHIRE, THE Robert Burns, the *Ayrshire Poet*.

BARD OF DEMOCRACY, THE Walt(er) Whitman (1819–92), American poet who wrote *The Democratic Review'* (1841–5) and published *Democratic Vistas* (1871). Also the *Good Gray Poet*.

BARD OF EMPIRE, THE Rudyard Kipling (1865–1936), British poet and novelist who won a Nobel Prize for Literature (1907); because of his imperialistic verses. Also the *Singer of Empire*.

• See the *Widow of Windsor*.

BARD OF ERIN, THE Thomas *Anacreon Moore* who was born in Dublin and wrote *Irish Melodies* (1807–35). He became national lyricist of Ireland.

BARD OF HOPE, THE Thomas Campbell (1777–1844), Scottish poet who wrote *The Pleasures of Hope* (1799). Also the *Dromedary*.

BARD OF HYDE, THE John Critchley Prince (1808–66), British poet and bohemian who lived at Hyde, Cheshire.

BARD OF MARTIAL LAY, THE Scott, *the Ariosto of the North*; so called by Sir James Mackintosh (the *Apostate*).

BARD OF MEMORY, THE Samuel Rogers, the *Banker Poet*, author of *The Pleasure of Memory* (1792); so called by Scott (the *Ariosto of the North*).

BARD OF OLNEY, THE William Cowper (1731–1800), poet who lived at Olney, Bucks. Also the *Domestic Poet* and the *Stricken Deer*.

BARD OF PENBRYN, THE Sir Lewis Morris (1833–1907), poet of *Songs of Two Worlds* (1871) and the *Epic of Hades* (1876–7); born and lived at Penbryn, north-east of Cardigan.

BARD OF RYDAL MOUNT, THE William Wordsworth (1770–1850), English poet who lived at Rydal Mount, near Grassmere, Cumbria. Also the *Cumberland Poet*, the *Great God Pan*, the *Great Laker*, *Old Ponder*, the *Poet of Nature* and *Poet Wordy*.

BARD OF SHEFFIELD, THE James Montgomery, *Alcaeus*, who became proprietor of *The Sheffield Register* (1795) after having been on the staff for three years.

BARD OF THE BAY, THE Robert Southey, the *Ballad Monger*; from *Botany Bay Eclogues* (1794).

BARD OF THE BRITISH NAVY, THE Charles Dibdin (1745–1814), dramatist and writer of sea songs, e.g. *Tom Bowling*, written on the death of his brother, Captain Thomas Dibdin. Also the *True Laureate of England*.

BARD OF THE CORSAIR, THE Lord Byron, *Baby*; so called by Maginn (the *Adjutant*) from *The Corsair* (1814).

BARD OF IMAGINATION, THE Mark Akenside (1721–70), physician and poet of *The Pleasures of Imagination* (1744–57).

BARD OF THE NORTH, THE Dr James Beattie (1735–1803), Scottish poet; professor of Moral Philosophy at Marischal College, Aberdeen; so called by Hayley (the *King of Poets*).

BARD OF THE SILVERY TAY, THE William Topaz McGonagall (1825–1902), poetaster of Perth. Also the *People's Poet*.

BARD OF TWICKENHAM, THE Alexander Pope (1699–1744), English poet who lived at Twickenham, Middlesex for the last twenty years of his life. Also the *English Horace, Gunpowder Percy*, the *Little Man of Twickenham*, *Little Nightingale*, the *Nightingale of Twickenham*, the *Paper-Saving Pope*, *Poet Pug*, the *True Deacon of his Craft*, the *Wasp of Twickenham* and the *Wicked Wasp of Twickenham*.

BARNACLE, THE Trevor Edward Bailey (1923–   ), cricketer for Cambridge University, Essex and England (61 Tests) and cricket commentator for the BBC (post-1965); so called because he sticks to something when he has started it. Also the *Boil*.

BARNARDO

i) Bernard Darwin (1876–1961), English international golfer and grandson of Charles Darwin (*Gas*). He played golf for England for twenty years and was golfing correspondent of *The Times* for the greater part of his life.

ii) Joseph Haselwood (1769–1811), bibliographer; so called by Dibdin (the *Beau Brummell of Living Authors*).

BARNUM OF RELIGION, THE Aimée Semple McPherson (1890–1944), Canadian-born US evangelist (fl. 1920s); so called from her flamboyant circus-orientated style of religious service. Also the *Hot Gospeller*.

• For Barnum, see the *Prince of Humbugs*.

BARON, THE

i) The 7th Baron Hawke (1860–1938), captain of Yorkshire cricket team (1883–1920). He was Major Martin Blades Hawke until he succeeded to the title (1887). The nickname was given to him in the late 1880s.

ii) A Mr Courtney, chairman of the South London music-hall in the 1870s–80s.

BARON BAN Francis Farquharson of Monaltrie who fought at Culloden (1746).

BARON GEORGE George Parkes (1827–95), lessee (1880s) of the Alhambra and Elephant and Castle theatres, London. He was fat and the nickname soon became applied to any fat, prosperous man; sometimes 'Baron Parkes'.

BARON OF SUNSET STRIP, THE Milton B. Scott (1922–   ), 'M.B.', an American millionaire, because of the amount of property he owns in Hollywood.

BARROW BOY, THE Sir Gerald Nabarro (1913–73), MP for Kidderminster (1950–64) and a colourful figure in the House of Commons; so called from the rhyme with 'Nabarro'. Also the *Kidder from Kidderminster* and *Nab*.

BARRYMORE OF THE WHITE HOUSE, THE Franklin Delano Roosevelt (1882–1945), 32nd President of the USA. He was the only President to have a third term of office (it is now unconstitutional); so called from his many newsreel appearances. Also the *Philatelic President* and the *Poor Man's Friend*.

• See the *Great Profile*.

BART Henry Guy Bartholomew (1884–1962), chairman of the *Daily Mirror* and *Sunday Pictorial* (1944–51).

BASHER Prince William (1982–   ), son of the Prince of Wales (*Fishface*) and Heir Apparent after his father; so called at school because he is arrogant, bossy and aggressive.

BASKERVILLE OF AMERICA, THE Isaiah Thomas (1749–1831), printer, editor and publisher. He issued specimens of type (1785) and wrote a *History of Printing in America* (1810); so called by Franklin (the American Socrates), himself a printer in his early days. Also the *Diderot of America*.

• Baskerville, the *Jenson of His Day*, invented his own typefaces and printed many fine editions.

BASKET-MAKER POET, THE Thomas Miller (1807–74) of Gainsborough, Lincs., rural poet.

BASTARD, THE William I (*circa* 1027–87), first Norman king of England who was the bastard son of Robert (the *Devil*), Duke of Normandy. His mother was

Arletta, daughter of a tanner of Falaise. Also the *Conqueror*.

- 'Bastard' was not then derogatory if a child was sired by a noble.

BASTARD OF FAUCONBERG, THE Thomas Neville (died 1471), son of William Neville, Baron Fauconberg and Earl of Kent (*circa* 1405–63). Thomas was a follower of the *Kingmaker*.

BAT William Barclay Masterson (1855–1921), lawman in Dodge City, Kan. and Deadwood, S. Dakota. He used a cane to stun lawbreakers. Dodge City presented him with a golden cane. Another version gives him the christian name 'Bartholomew' which he disliked and changed, keeping 'Bat', a shortened form.

BAT LUGS King George VI (1895–1952); so called by cadets at the RN College, Dartmouth. His family nickname was 'Bertie', from his first name Albert. Also *Mr Johnson*.

- See comment at *Cut-Lugged Willie.*

BATCHY Air-Marshal Sir Richard Llewellyn Roger Atcherley (1904–70), C-in-C, Flying Training Command.

BATH ROSCIUS, THE John Henderson (1747–85), actor who first appeared at Bath as Hamlet (1772) and stayed there for several years. He was also a success on the London stage.

- See the *African Roscius*.

BATHING TOWEL General Robert Stephenson Smyth, 1st Baron Baden-Powell (1857–1941), hero of the siege of Mafeking (1899–1900) and founder of the Boy Scout movement (1908). The nickname dates from his schooldays at Charterhouse. Also *Bups*, the *Butterfly Spy* and 'BP'.

BATHSHEBA Louise Renée de Penancoet de Kéroualle, Duchess of Portsmouth (1649–1734), mistress of Charles II (the *Blackbird*). She was his love in his old age as Bathsheba was for David; so called by Dryden (*Asaph*). Also *Fubbs*, *Madam Carewell* and the *Weeping Willow*.

- See 2 Sam. xi. 3 and 4.

BATTERED CHERUB, THE Joseph (Joe), 1st Baron Gormley (1917–   ), president of the British National Union of Mineworkers (1971–82).

BATTLING BILLY William (Billy) Wells (1889–1967), British heavyweight boxing champion (1911–19). He defended his title thirteen times during that period and was so famous that a big gun in the 1914–18 war was nicknamed after him. In his early days he was nicknamed *Beautiful Billy* and later *Bombardier Billy*. Towards the end of his life, he was the renowned gong-beater of Rank films.

BATTLING JACK Sir John Allsebrook, 1st Viscount Simon (1873–1954), British Foreign Secretary (1931–35); so called sardonically in the Foreign Office where the nickname was picked up by newspapermen. He was Lord Chancellor (1940–5).

BATTLING NELSON Oscar Matthew Nelson (1882–1954), American world lightweight boxing champion (1908–10). He took part in the longest title fight, losing to Joe Gans (1874–1910) in the 42nd round. Also the *Durable Dane.*

BAULD WILLIE or WULLIE Lord William Howard (1563–1640), 3rd son of the 4th Duke of Norfolk. He lived in Cumbria on the Scottish border and captured three reivers (1606) after an all-night chase. Also *Belted Will*. His wife was *Bessie with the Braid Apron*.

- 'Bauld' is the north country pronunciation of 'bold'. See *Slowlugs*.

BAX Sir Beverley (Bev) Baxter (1891–1964), MP and former editor of the *Daily Express*.

BAY

i) Captain George Middleton (1846–92), 12th Lancers, friend and guide to the Empress Elizabeth of Austria; a daredevil rider and dandy killed in a steeplechase in Warwickshire.

ii) Henry Baynton (died 1950) who directed a Shakespearian company which encouraged many young actors and actresses. He was an outstanding Hamlet.

BAYARD OF THE CONFEDERACY, THE General Robert Edward Lee (1807–70), commander of the Confederate army in the American Civil War, noted for his moral courage and noble nature. Also *Uncle Robert*.

- Pierre Terrail, Seigneur de Bayard (1473–1524), was called *Le chevalier sans peur et sans reproche*.

BAYARD OF INDIA, THE or THE BAYARD OF THE EAST General Sir James Outram Bart. (1803–63). The first nickname was given to him by Napier (*Old Fagin*) after Outram had shown himself a hero in the defence of Hyderabad (1842). Also the *Little General*.

BAYARD OF THE REVOLUTION, THE John Laurens (1754–82), present with Washington (the *American Cincinnatus*) at all battles of the War of Independence from Brandywine to Yorktown. His courage earned him the nickname. Washington said of him: 'He had not a fault that I could discover, unless it were intrepidity bordering upon rashness.'

BAZOOKA Robert (Bob) Burns (1892–1956), famous American radio comedian.

B.B. Riley King (1926–   ), American blues singer known as the Beale Street Blues Boy after the success of his song *Beale Street Blues*.

B.B.C. SPY, THE Johannes Dronkers (1896–1942), Dutch Nazi hanged as a spy after he had tried to infiltrate the BBC as an announcer.

BEACONSFIELD OF THE CONFEDERACY, THE Senator Judah Philip Benjamin (1811–84), Confederate Attorney-General who believed in an aristocratic form of government. Also the *Brains of the Confederacy*.

- Beaconsfield, see the *Asian Mystery*.

BEANS Coleman Hawkins (1904–69), American pioneer jazz musician.

BEANSIE Herman Rosenthal (murdered 1912), New York gambler. He was shot by police lieutenant Charles Becker after he had said he would name a corrupt policeman.

BEAR
i) Rupert Deen (1939–   ), Lloyds underwriter and London socialite; from the children's cartoon series *Rupert Bear*.
ii) James (Jim) Brady (1941–   ), press

secretary to President Reagan (*Dutch*) wounded in an assassination attempt on the President (1981) and crippled for life; childhood nickname of 'Pooh Bear'.
iii) Paul Bryant (1913–83), American football Coach of the Year (1957). In 1981 he scored his 315th coaching victory in college football.

BEAR, THE
i) Thomas Hobbes, the *Atheist*, so called by Charles II (the *Blackbird*) who had been his pupil for mathematics (1646–8), because of his bad temper and habit of swearing. When Hobbes was a man of seventy the King used to comment 'Here comes the bear to be baited.' He enjoyed Hobbes's wit in disputes. Aubrey quotes this nickname, and adds of 'bear': 'too low wit to be published'.
ii) Edward Ellice (1781–1863), British Cabinet Minister and first chairman of the Reform Club (est. 1830); from his association with the Hudson Bay fur trade. Also the *Nestor of the House of Commons*.

- Cf the *Young Bear*.

iii) Robert Hite (1943–81), American blues-rock musician (fl. 1960s).

- See the *Big Bear*.

BEAR COAT Major-General Nelson Appleton Miles (1839–1925); so called by Indians. He wore a rough bear-skin coat in winter campaigns.

BEAR LEADER, THE
i) James Boswell, the *Ambitious Thane*, biographer and friend of Johnson, one of whose nicknames was *Ursa Major*. Boswell's wife once commented: 'I have seen many a bear led by a man, but never before saw a man led by a bear.'
ii) William Gifford (1756–1826), critic with a bearish manner who had been tutor to Lord Belgrave (1731–1802), son of the 1st Earl of Grosvenor. Gifford had a hatred of radicals and attacked *Endymion* (1818) by Keats (*Pestleman Jack*); so called by Wolcot (*Peter Pindar*). Also the *Cobbling Wonder of Ashburton*, the *Censor of the Age*, the *Coryphaeus of Modern Literature*, the *Demon of Darkness* and *Grosvenor's Cobbler*.

- A bear-leader was a sardonic name for

a travelling tutor who took a young nobleman on a tour of Europe.

BEAR RIVER TOM Thomas Smith (1838–70) who put down a revolt at Bear River, Wyoming, and later became a lawman in Abilene, Kansas.

BEARD, THE Monty Woolley (1888–1963), born Edgar Montillion Woolley, former university professor and American film actor, e.g. *The Man Who Came to Dinner* (Broadway, 1939).

BEAST, THE

i) Denis Winston Healey (1917–), Deputy Leader of the Labour Party (1980s); because of his bushy eyebrows.

ii) John Mugabi (1951–), Uganda-born middleweight boxer.

BEAST 666 Aleister Crowley (1875–1947), British mountaineer, poet, eccentric and believer in black magic. His real first names were Edward Alexander. He adopted a string of fantastic names like Lord Boleskine and Master Therion, and published *The Diary of a Dope Fiend*. Also the **Great Beast** ('Therion' means 'beast'), the **King of Depravity** and the **Wickedest Man in the World.**

• For the Beast Crowley thought himself to be, see Rev. xiii, 18.

BEAST OF BOLSOVER, THE Dennis Skinner (1932–), Labour MP for Bolsover (1970–) from his fiery nature. He has been expelled from the House of Commons a few times; so called by Conservatives.

BEAST OF GEORGIA, THE Wayne Williams (1958–), negro photographer given two life sentences (1982) for the murders of two out of twenty-eight young people (1980–1) in Georgia.

BEAU

i) George Bryan Brummell (1778–1840), dandy and high priest of fashion, said to have made the Prince Regent (**Adonis of Fifty**) weep by disapproving the cut of his coat. Ironically, at the end of his life he was careless and dirty, and died poor and insane in Caen. Early in life he was called **Buck**. Also the **Dandy Killer**, **George the Lesser**, the **Prince of Beaux** and the **Prince of Dandies**.

ii) Richard Nash (1674–1762), gambler who became Master of Ceremonies at Bath. Also the **Count**, **Great** or **Grand Nash** and the **King of Bath**.

iii) Robert Feilding (?1651–1712), Restoration rake who 'married' Barbara, Duchess of Castlemaine (1641–1709), mistress of Charles II (the **Blackbird**). Feilding had a wife still living, and his union with the Duchess was void. He died in Scotland Yard, after having been convicted of bigamy. Also **Handsome Feilding** and **Orlando the Fair**.

• Scotland Yard was then a ruined palace.

iv) John Law (1671–1729), Scottish economist, infamous for his ruinous financial ideas. Also the **Paper King** and the **Projector**.

v) General D'Orsay, father of Count D'Orsay (**Le Jeune Cupido**). The general distinguished himself in Spain, especially at Salamanca (1812).

vi) Edward Wilson of Leicestershire, a London man-about-town, killed in a duel (1694) with **Beau** Law. He was a man of mystery.

vii) Nicholas James Hannon (1881–1972), English actor.

viii) Topham Beauclerk (1739–80), a fashionable young man; so called by Dr Johnson (**Blinking Sam**).

BEAU BRUMMELL OF LIVING AUTHORS, THE Thomas Frognall Dibdin (1776–1847), bibliographer. Also **Black-Letter Tom** and the **Prince of Bibliomaniacal Writers**.

• For **Beau** Brummell, see above.

BEAU BRUMMELL OF THE DAY, THE Colonel (later Major-General) John Palmer Brabazon (1843–1922), who commanded the 4th Hussars from 1893 and the 2nd Cavalry Brigade in South Africa; so called by *Vanity Fair*. He was handsome and always elegantly dressed. Also **Beautiful Bwab** and **Old Bwab**.

BEAUCLERC or BEAUCLERK Henry I (1068–1135). He could read and write in Latin and English and knew something of law (OF *beau clerc* = good scholar). Also the **Lion of Justice**.

- There was a Walter Mauclerc ('bad scholar') who was Bishop of Carlisle (1275).

BEAU JAMES James Walker (1881–1946), likeable but corrupt Mayor of New York in the Prohibition era (1920s). He dressed fashionably and frequented nightclubs, which earned him the nickname of the *Playboy Mayor*.

BEAU NASTY Samuel Foote (1720–77), actor and dramatist who wrote brilliant satires of contemporary life; so called by Peake in *Memoirs of the Colman Family*. Also the *English* or *Modern Aristophanes* and *Proteus*.

BEAU OF LEADENHALL STREET, THE Nathaniel Bentley (died 1809), a dandy who became *Dirty Dick*.

BEAU OF PRINCES, THE The Prince Regent, the *Adonis of Fifty*.

BEAUTIFUL BILLY William Wells, *Battling Billy*; so called when he was young and good-looking.

BEAUTIFUL BWAB Colonel J.P. Brabazon, the *Beau Brummell of the Day*.

BEAUTY OF BUTTERMERE, THE Mary Robinson, who was deceived into marriage (1802) with John Hatfield (the *Keswick Imposter*). Mary, daughter of an old couple who kept a public-house beside Lake Buttermere, Cumbria, was given the nickname in *A Fortnight's Ramble to the Lakes in Westmoreland, Lancashire and Cumberland* (late 18th century). She was also called the *Maid of Buttermere*.

BEAVER, THE William Maxwell Aitken, 1st Baron Beaverbrook (1879–1964), Canadian-born proprietor of a chain of newspapers including the *Daily Express*. He was Minister of Aircraft Production (1940–1) and, according to Churchill (*Bricky*), 'worked magic'; so called because of his title and energy. Also the *Pedlar of Dreams*; and see the *Wicked Uncles of Fleet Street*.

BEBE Virginia Daniels (1901–71), American film star who made her first film at the age of seven years.

BECKY Mary Wells (fl. 1780–1810), British actress, after her success in that part in *The Agreeable Surprise* by O'Keefe (the *English Molière*).

BEER-BOTTLE VC, THE Sgt. William (Bill) Speakman (1927–   ). He led charge after charge at Hill 217 in the Korean War (1950–3). He ran out of grenades but threw empty beer-bottles at the enemy.

BEETLES BABINGTON Charles Cardale Babington (1808–95), naturalist, founder of the British Entomological Society (1833); professor of botany, Cambridge University (post-1861).

BEELZEBUB M. GOLDWATER Barry Goldwater, *AuH$_2$O*; people were frightened of his politics.

- Beelzebub is a name for the devil.

BEGGING BISHOP, THE John Hacket (1593–1670), Bishop of Lichfield and Coventry (post-1661) because of his importunity in raising money to rebuild Lichfield Cathedral, almost in ruins after the English Civil War. He collected large sums.

BEHEMOTH OF BUST, THE *Babe* Ruth.

- A behemoth is a huge animal mentioned in Job (40:15); from the Hebrew word for a beast. It is thought to derive from the Egyptian *pehemau* (= water ox), and so to have been a hippopotamus.

BEL, LE Geoffrey *Plantagenet*, Count of Anjou (1129–51), father of Henry II (*Curtmantle*). Also *Greycloak* and the *Handsome*.

BEL ANGLAIS, LE The Duke of Marlborough, *Anne's Great Captain*; so called by French troops under Marshal Turenne (1611–75). As a captain, Marlborough was sent with 6,000 soldiers to help Louis XIV to subdue the Dutch.

BELLE HAMILTON, LA Elizabeth Hamilton, Comtesse Grammont (1641–1708), wife of Comte Philibert de Grammont (1621–1707), subject of the famous memoirs. She was one of the great beauties of the Court of Charles II (the *Blackbird*).

BELLE IRLANDAISE, LA Mary Ann Boyd (fl. 1760s–1770s), actress with whom James Boswell (the *Ambitious Thane*) fell in love.

BELLE JENNINGS, LA Francis Jennings, Duchess of Tyrconnel (1649–1730), wife of the Jacobite duke (*Lying Dick Talbot*) and sister to the Duchess of Marlborough (*Mrs Freeman*). Also the *White Milliner*.

BELLE SAUVAGE, LA or **THE BELL SAVAGE** Matoaka or Matsoaks'ats, *Pocahontas* (1595–1617), daughter of *Powhatan*. Her name is given on her monument at St George's church, Gravesend, Kent, as Matoaka. She married John Rolfe (1585–1622) and stayed at the Bell Savage inn, London (1616–17), where a painting of her was used as a sign. The inn was originally the Bell, kept (1579) by a Mr Savage. Also *Virginia's Tutelary Saint*.

• An inn sign at Boston, Lincs. (Rolfe's home) calls her 'The Indian Queen'.

BELLE STUART, LA Frances Teresa Stuart or Stewart, Duchess of Richmond and Lennox (1647–1702), with whom Charles II (the *Blackbird*) was infatuated before she married Charles, 3rd Duke of Richmond and 6th Duke of Lennox. She posed for the figure of Britannia on British coins.

BELL-THE-CAT Archibald Douglas, 5th Earl of Angus (circa 1449–1514); so called after a meeting to discuss getting rid of Robert Cochrane, Earl of Mar, favourite of James III of Scotland (1451–88). When the meeting was asked 'Who will bell the cat?' Angus replied instantly that he would, and captured Mar, it is said, in the presence of the King. Also the *Great Earl of Angus* and *Grey Steel*.

• The allusion is to an ancient fable in which an old mouse suggests belling the cat to save them from danger, but a wise young mouse asks 'Who will put the bell on the cat?' Belling the cat is mentioned in *Piers Plowman* (?1360), where the first speaker is a rat.

BELOVED MERCHANT, THE Sir William atte Pole (died 1366), 1st Mayor of Hull and MP in five Parliaments. He was a famous trader, being accounted 'second to no merchant in England.' He became a baron of the Exchequer. The nickname was given to him by Edward III (the *Father of English Commerce*). Sir William's son Michael (1330–89) became 1st Earl of Suffolk and Lord Chancellor.

• See *Green Park*.

BELTING EARL, THE John Colum, Earl of Dumfries (1958–), heir to the Marquis of Bute. The earl is a racing driver with ambitions to become a champion.

• To belt = to move at a very fast pace, to rush along: a pun on 'belted earl'.

BELTED WILL Lord William Howard, *Bauld Willie*. He wore a broad studded belt; so called by Scott (the *Ariosto of the North*).

BEN or **WEE BEN** Barnard Sayers (1857–1924), British Open golf champion (1880–1923) and professional at North Berwick. He was a small man.

BENJAMIN THE GOOD Sir Benjamin D'Urban (1777–1849), British general and Governor of the Cape Colony (1834–38), after whom Durban in South Africa is named. During his governorship, slavery was abolished and legislative and municipal councils were established. He was relieved of office (1837) after the Great Trek and Xosa war, but remained until January 1838.

BENDIGO William Thompson (1811–89), Nottinghamshire prize-fighter who won the championship of England (1839). He usually wore a rough fur cap which came to be called 'a bendigo'. A town in Australia was named after him. Weekley (1912) said that a correspondence then going on in a Nottinghamshire newspaper on the origin of the nickname stated in one version that Thompson was one of triplets which 'a jocular friend of the family nicknamed Shadrach, Meschach and Abed-Nego, the last of which was the future celebrity.' It is at any rate certain that his first challenge (*Bell's Life*, 1835) was signed 'Abed-Nego of Nottingham'. He retired in 1851 to become an evangelist and so was nicknamed The *Reformed Pugilist*.

BENDOR

i) Hugh Lupus Grosvenor, 1st Duke of Westminster (1825–1900).

ii) Hugh Richard Arthur Grosvenor, 2nd Duke of Westminster (1879–1958); so called after the *azure à bend or* in the Grosvenor coat-of-arms.

• Bend Or was the name of a racehorse

which won the 1880 Derby, owned by the Duke and ridden by Archer (the *Demon*).

BENEFACTOR, THE Morgan Mwynfawr (fl. 730), King of Morgannwg, Glamorgan.

- Morgannwg is the ancient name for Glamorganshire, but once it comprised almost the whole of Wales from Neath to the Wye. It means 'the country of Morgan', as Glamorgan = *gwlad Morgan*, 'the land of Morgan'.

BENICIA BOY, THE John Camel Heenan (1835–73), boxing champion of America (1858–63) whose most famous match was in England (1860) with Tom Sayers (the *Little Wonder*). It lasted 2 hours 20 min and was declared a draw after spectators invaded the ring. Heenan lived in Benicia, California, once its capital (1853–54).

BENNY Alfred Hawthorne Hill (1925–   ), British variety comedian and TV star.

BERKSHIRE LADY, THE Frances Kendrick, daughter of Sir William Kendrick, Bart., whose father had been created a baronet by Charles II (the *Blackbird*) in 1679. She became famous after she fell in love with a poor lawyer, Benjamin Child. She challenged him, masked, to a duel for some fictitious wrong, met him (still masked) and said 'Either you fight me or marry me.' Child married her without seeing her and found himself possessed of a beauty and a fortune; so called in a contemporary ballad *The Berkshire Lady's Garland*.

BESSIE WITH THE BRAID APRON Elizabeth, wife of Lord William Howard (*Bauld Willie*). She was the daughter of Thomas, Lord Dacre.

BESS OF HARDWICK Elizabeth Talbot, Countess of Shrewsbury (1518–1608), daughter of Sir John Hardwick of Hardwick Hall, Derby. Through her four marriages, she became England's wealthiest woman.

BEST-ABUSED MAN IN ENGLAND, THE John Dennis, *Appius*; so called because both Swift (*Dr Presto*) and Pope (the *Bard of Twickenham*) attacked him. Dennis's venom had wounded Pope, but in the end they were reconciled.

BEST BATSMAN IN ENGLAND, THE
i) Fuller Pilch (1803–70), Kent cricketer who introduced forward play and helped to make Kent so powerful that it sometimes vanquished what passed for an English side. He was also a wicket-keeper.
ii) George Parr (1826–91), Nottinghamshire cricketer who captained his county and England. He went to America with the first cricket team to visit the USA (1859), and led the second English team to tour Australia (1863). Also the *Lion of the North*.

BEST-DRESSED BAD MAN IN TEXAS, THE William P. Raynor, gunfighter, shot (1885) in El Paso in a shoot-out with 'Cowboy' Bob Rennick, an affray witnessed by Wyatt Earp (1848–1929).

BEST DRESSED WOMAN IN THE WORLD, THE The Duchess of Windsor (1896–1986), formerly Mrs Wallis Simpson, who held the distinction for fifteen years (1938–53).

BETSEY BOWEN Eliza Jumel (1775–1865), who was Eliza Brown until she married Stephen Jumel, an American wine merchant. After his death she married Aaron Burr (1756–1836), Attorney-General and later a Senator.

BIBLIOMANIACAL HERCULES, THE The Rev. Clayton Mordaunt Cracherode (1730–99), English bibliophile; so called by Dibdin (the *Beau Brummell of Living Authors*). His book collection went to the British Museum.

BIDDENDEN TWINS or MAIDS, THE Misses Mary and Eliza Chulkhurst, joined at the shoulders and hips when they were born at Biddenden, Kent (*circa* 1550). When one died at the age of thirty-four, the other died six hours later.

BIDS Lieutenant-General Sir Thomas Myddleton Biddulph (1809–78), Master of the Household to Queen Victoria (*Drina*) and Keeper of the Privy Purse.

BIG Charlie Green (1900–36), American jazz trumpeter.

BIG, THE Niall O'Neill *Mor*, King of Ulster (1364–94).

- *Mor* is Gaelic for 'big', 'tall', or 'important'.

BIG AL

i) Alphonse (Al) Capone (1899–1947), Chicago gangster and bootlegger during the Prohibition era (1920–33). Also *Public Enemy No 1* and *Scarface*.

ii) Alec Victor Bedser (1918–), fast-medium bowler for Surrey and England; because of his powerful build. He took 236 wickets in 51 Test Matches, and has been called one of the great bowlers of our time. He was subsequently chairman of the England Selection Committee until 1985.

BIG BAMBINO, THE Frank Rizzo (1921–), Mayor of Philadelphia and a former Commissioner of police.

BIG BEAR, THE Charles Liston (1932–70), American heavyweight world boxing champion (1962–64) who lost to Cassius Clay (*Gaseous Cassius*) for the world title. Also *Sonny*.

BIG BEGGARMAN, THE Daniel O'Connell (1775–1847), Irish politician and agitator; so called by Irish landlords. Also the *Big O*, *The Great O*, the *Irish Agitator*, the *Liberator* and the *Uncrowned King of Ireland*.

BIG BEN Benjamin Brain (1753–94), English pugilist, champion of England from 1790 until his death; so called from his size.

BIG BILL

i) William Howard Taft (1857–1930), 27th President of the USA.

ii) William Tatem Tilden (1893–1953), American lawn-tennis player who won the men's singles at Wimbledon in 1920 – the first American success in the tournament – and again in 1921 and 1930. He was tall, and played a 'big' game. Also the *Blue Grizzly*, the *Grizzly* and *June*.

iii) William Hale Thompson (1869–1944), Republican Mayor of Chicago (1915–23). It was under his administration that gang warfare took hold. Also *Kaiser Bill*.

iv) William Lee Conley Broonzy (1893–1958), American country blues singer.

BIG BIRD Joel Garner (1952–), 6 ft 10 in tall West Indian cricketer from Barbados, considered by some (1980s) to be one of the best batsmen in the world; also a fast bowler for Somerset and the West Indies.

BIG BOY

i) Guinn Williams (1900–62), American film actor in Westerns and gangster movies.

ii) Arthur Crudup (1905–73), American blues singer.

BIG BREADWINNER HOGG Quintin McGarel Hogg, Baron Hailsham (1907–), Lord Chancellor; so called when he was Quintin Hogg, MP.

BIG BREN Brendan Foster (1948–), British international athlete.

BIG BROOCHY George Gunn (fl. 15th century), chief of the Gunn clan and hereditary Crowner of Caithness, with castles in the Thurso region of Scotland; so called because of the large brooch he wore (*am Bràisd Mor*).

● A Crowner in the 15th century was one with the right to crown.

BIG C Clive Hubert Lloyd (1944–) of Guyana, cricketer for West Indies and Lancashire, a powerful batsman. He made centuries in his first Test Matches against England and Australia. He retired in 1985 and became a British citizen. Also the *Cat*.

● Big C = Big Cat.

BIG CROCODILE, THE P.W. Botha (*Piet Wapen*); so called in South Africa.

BIG DADDY

i) Donald Glenn Garlits (1932–), American racing driver, an outstanding competitor in American drag racing and the first man to exceed 200 mph (1964). He set a terminal speed record of more than 243 mph (1972) in Florida.

ii) Shirley Crabtree (1936–), 24-stone (336 lb), British-heavyweight wrestler and TV personality.

iii) Idi Amin Dada (1924–), dictator President of Uganda (1971–9). Also the *Kampala Butcher*.

iv) Thomas (Tom) Donahue (1928–75), American blues singer; from his size.

BIG DO Reginald Frank Doherty (1874–1910), British lawn-tennis player who with his brother Hugh (*Little Do*), made early Wimbledon history. Reginald held the singles title from 1897 to 1901. Between them, the Dohertys won seventeen championships in ten years.

BIG ED Edward Walsh, American baseball pitcher in the Hall of Fame (1904–7).

BIG FELLOW, THE Michael Collins (1890–1922), Irish revolutionary leader and commander of the Irish Free State Army; killed in an ambush by republicans.

BIG FOOT

i) William Alexander Anderson Wallace (1817–99), a Virginian who became a Texas Ranger and a mail carrier.

ii) Derek Pringle (1958–), cricketer for Essex and England. He takes a size 12 shoe. Also *Longman*.

- Big Foot (died 1890) was chief of the Minneconjou Indians, killed at Wounded Knee.

BIGGLES

i) Prince Philip, Duke of Edinburgh (1921–), husband of Queen Elizabeth (*Brenda*); so called by the royal family. Also *Lieutenant Pog* and *Number-One-Fella-Belong-Missus-Queen*.

ii) Ian Pearson (1951–), footballer for Exeter FC; because of his love for flying.

iii) Carol Barnes (1944–), British ITN news-reader; after she had been granted a pilot's licence.

- Biggles is the airman hero of boys' stories by Captain W.E.F. Johns (1893–1988).

BIG H Henry MacKenny (1937–), 6 ft 4 in tall 'hit-man', killer of six people, sentenced at the Old Bailey, London (1980) to four terms of life imprisonment and recommended to serve at least twenty-five years.

BIG HARRY Harry Crawford (1835–1910), caddie for *Ben* Sayers and friend of *Old Tom* Morris. He was the professional at North Berwick, where he later ran a ginger-beer stall; a big man with a loud voice.

BIG or GREAT HEAD Malcolm III (Scottish: reigned 1054–93), *Canmore*, who became king after the death of Macbeth (1054). He was crowned at Scone in 1057. He married (1069) Margaret ('St Margaret'), sister of Edgar the *Aetheling*; and invaded England (1070) to support Edgar's claim to the throne.

- The Gaelic *ceann mor* means 'large-headed', but it could also have been a title: *ceann* = chief.

BIG JACK

i) John (Jackie) Charlton (1935–), footballer for Leeds United and England with 39 caps. He retired in 1973 and became manager for Middlesbrough and Newcastle; so called because of his skill, not his size. Now manager of the Republic of Ireland FC. Also *Giraffe*.

ii) Jack Zelig (1882–1912), professional New York killer and gangster.

BIG JIM

i) James Colosimo (1871–1920), boss of the Chicago underworld. During his control (1910–20), he raked in more than 500,000 dollars a year. He was murdered by *Big Al* Capone in the pay of a rival, Johnny Torrio (the *Father of Modern American Gangsterism*). Also *Diamond Jim*.

ii) James Fisk (1834–72), financial buccaneer with a notorious reputation: murdered by Edward Stokes (died 1880), a rival for the love of Josephine Mansfield (died 1931), Jim's mistress. Also *Jubilee Jim*, *Prince Erie* and the *Robber Baron*.

iii) James Larkin (1876–1947), Liverpool-born pioneer of Irish trade unions (post-1907).

BIG JOHN

i) Iain *Dubh* Cameron (hanged 1753), Highland bandit and cattle thief. Stories about him have a heroic lustre.

- *Dubh* =black in Gaelic.

ii) Eldine A.E. Baptiste (1960–), Kent and Leeward Islands cricketer.

BIG MAC

i) Michael McLaughlin (1942–), ex-milkman, chairman of the fascist British Movement, formed on the break-up of the National Front; son of an Irish Republican. He now runs a shop selling arms in North Wales.

ii) Laurie McMenemy (1936–), ex-guardsman, manager of Grimsby,

Doncaster, and Sunderland FCs until he lost the last job in 1988.

BIG MAL Malcolm Allison (1927–), manager of Manchester City, Crystal Palace and Middlesbrough clubs before he lost the latter job.

BIG MOMMA Laura Davies (1964–), British and US women's Open golf champion (1987). She is 5 ft 10 in and weighs 111/2 stone (161 lb).

BIG-NOSED KATE Kate Fisher (died 1881), prostitute and friend of *Doc* Holliday in the American West. She was shot in a saloon fight.

BIG O, THE

i) Daniel O'Connell, the *Big Beggarman*; so called by *Boney Cobbett*.

ii) Oscar Robertson (1938–), American baseball player who captained the US Olympic team (1960) when they won a gold medal. He became a professional with the Cincinnati Royals and later with the Milwaukee Bucks; so called because of his skill.

iii) Roy Orbison, (1936–88), American rock and roll singer, once described by Presley (*Elvis the Pelvis*) as 'the greatest singer in the world'.

BIG SAM Samuel MacDonald (1762–1802), 6 ft 10 in, former soldier and porter to the Prince of Wales (*Adonis of Fifty*) at Carlton House, London. Also the *Scottish Hercules*.

BIG SID Sidney Catlett (1910–51), American drummer and jazz composer.

BIG SHIP, THE Warwick Windridge Armstrong (1879–1947), cricketer for Victoria who captained Australia against England (1920–1). In fifty Test Matches he took 87 wickets and made more than 2,800 runs; so called from his size.

BIG SMOKE, THE Jack Johnson (1878–1946), American heavyweight boxer who was the first negro to win a world championship (1908–15). A 'smoke' was slang for a negro.

• His nickname engendered the name (World War I) for a heavy German shell which gave off dense smoke. The *Illustrated London News* (October

1914) referred to 'the gigantic projectile which on bursting makes black smoke, called "Jack Johnson".'

BIG SUMO Colin Smart (1951–), Newport and England Rugby Union prop. He took part in a mock wrestling match during the England tour of Japan.

• Sumo is the name of a Japanese style of wrestling.

BIG TIM Charles F. Murphy (died 1924), Tammany Hall sachem during whose rule many charges of corruption and fraud were made.

• Tammany Hall was a political organization in New York which not only influenced city government, but the national administration as well. Early American revolutionaries called themselves 'Sons of St Tammany', Tammany or Tammanend being an Indian chief noted for his love of liberty. The organization's chief was called the Grand Sachem (a Narragansett word for a chief).

BIG TRAIN Walter Perry Johnson (1887–1946), fast ball baseball pitcher for the Washington Senators (Hall of Fame, 1907–27); because of the power of his deliveries. In 1913 he pitched 56 consecutive innings without a run scored against him.

BIG YIN, THE William (Billy) Connolly (1942–), Scottish comedian and singer.

• Scottish dialect for 'The Big One'.

BILIOUS BALE John Bale (1495–1563), Bishop of Ossory, Ireland. He was a violent propagandist for protestantism, even in the reign of *Bloody Mary*, and escaped with difficulty from Ireland. He returned in the reign of Elizabeth (the *English Diana*) and became Prebendary of Canterbury. He wrote the first historical play in English, *Kynge Johan* (1538).

BILLINGSGATE Caroline Barry (fl. 1780s–90s), daughter of Richard Barry, 6th Earl of Barrymore. She married the Comte de Melfort (1799); because of her language.

• Cf *Cripplegate*, *Hellgate* and *Newgate*.

BILL POSTER KING, THE Clement Smith, British theatrical poster printer (late 19th century); his nickname was one which had been bestowed on him by the London evening newspapers.

BILLY

i) William Augustus, Duke of Cumberland (1821–65), 3rd son of George II (*Augustus*); so called by English troops at Culloden (1746). Also *Billy the Butcher*, the *Bloody Butcher*, *Butcher Cumberland*, the *Butcher of Culloden*, *Stinking Billy* and *Sweet William*. See the *Wicked Uncles*.

ii) Ruth, née Nilsson (died 1969), Swedish wife of Norman, 1st Baron Birkett, KC (1883–1962); her family nickname.

BILLY BLUE

i) Admiral Sir William Cornwallis (1744–1819). Bowen says he 'always kept the Blue Peter [the signal for imminent sailing] flying when weather drove him to shelter from the blockade of Brest'. Also *Billy-Go-Tight*, *Coachee* and *Mr Whip*.

ii) Admiral of the Fleet John Jervis, Earl of St Vincent (1735–1823). He was an Admiral of the Blue. Also *Hanging Jervis* and *Old Jarvie*.

BILLY BOO Emerson Boozer (1943–   ), American footballer.

BILLY-GO-TIGHT Admiral Sir William Cornwallis, *Billy Blue*, who had a florid complexion.

BILLY GRAHAM OF SELLING, THE John Fenton (1939–   ), British millionaire salesman credited with revolutionizing sales techniques in the UK.

  • Billy Graham (1918–   ), highly successful American evangelist with a reputed following of 60 million people and a trusted confidant of several American Presidents.

BILLY THE BUTCHER The Duke of Cumberland, *Billy*.

BILLY THE KID

i) William H. Bonney (1859–81), whose real name was Henry McCarthy or Antrim, outlaw and cattle-thief who killed 21 men before he was shot down by a sheriff. Frank Collinson, a Texas cowboy born in Yorkshire, who knew him, said in a 1963 book that his name was Henry Antrim but other sources give McCarthy.

ii) Craig McDermott (1965–   ), Australian fast bowler; so called when he was the 'baby' of the team touring England (1985).

BING Harry Lillis Crosby (1904–77), American singer and film star. As a child he was an enthusiastic reader of the adventures of Bingo, a boy with big ears in a comic paper called *The Bingville Bugle*. Also the *Groaner*.

BIOGRAPH GIRL, THE Florence Lawrence (1886–1938). In 1908, when screen players were anonymous, she became famous and was given the 'title' in lieu of personal publicity. Florence's fame, however, broke the restriction and she proceeded to emerge as Hollywood's first star. 'Biograph' was an early name for a cinema.

BIRD

i) Charlie Parker (1902–55), American jazz saxophonist; an abbreviation of *Yardbird*, which was his nickname in the 1930s.

ii) Albert Johnson (1910–   ), jazz composer and arranger.

BIRDIE Lieutenant Henry R. Bowers (1883–1912), Royal Indian Marine, a member of the Scott (*Scotty*) main party which died at the South Pole; from his beak-like nose.

BIRDMAN OF ALCATRAZ, THE Robert Franklin Stroud (1887–1963), American murderer who became an expert on canaries while awaiting execution at Alcatraz prison, California. His sentence (1916) was commuted, and he died of old age in prison.

BIRDY

i) Field-Marshal William Riddell, 1st Earl Birdwood (1865–1951), commander of the Australia and New Zealand Army Corps at Gallipoli (World War I), where he won the affection and regard of Australian troops.

ii) R.W.V. Robins (1906–68), Middlesex

and England cricketer who led his county to become champions (1947), and captained England (1937).

BIRMINGHAM DOCTOR, THE Samuel Parr (1747–1825), prebendary of St Paul's Cathedral, London, a Whig who modelled himself on the Tory Dr Johnson (**Blinking Sam**). In 1792, he published an article in which he claimed he had succeeded in dissuading dissenters in Birmingham from celebrating the Fall of the Bastille; so called by de Quincy (the **English Opium Eater**). Also the **Brummagem Doctor**, the **Man with a Wig** and the **Whig Johnson**.

BIRMINGHAM POET, THE John Freeth (1730–1808), a publican who sang his own songs to his customers.

BISCUIT PANTS Henry Louis (Lou) Gehrig (1903–41), baseball player for the New York Yankees, who played 2,130 consecutive games between 1923 and 1939, and is in the Hall of Fame for his performance. He was voted the Most Valued Player of 1936. Also **Columbia Lou, Iron Horse**.

BISH

i) Stanley Bishop (1885–1965), Fleet Street crime reporter for more than forty years, and so famous that a Bish club was formed with its own tie.

ii) Sylvester Bolam (died 1953), editor of the *Daily Mirror*, sent to prison for contempt of court over the reporting of the **Vampire Killer** case.

BISHOP, THE

i) Charles Kemp, Kent cricketer who captained Oxford (1844) when they beat Australia.

ii) John Whale (1932–   ), former editor of *The Church Times* and Head of BBC religious TV.

iii) Jess Yates (1920–   ), organist and once presenter of the BBC TV programme *Stars on Sunday*; because of its religious content.

BISHOP BUNYAN John Bunyan (1628–88), author of *A Pilgrim's Progress* (1678). He was a nonconformist imprisoned for preaching without a licence; so called after he had been chosen (1672) by the Bedford Baptist community as general organiser for a widespread area. Also the

Immortal Dreamer, the *Immortal Tinker* and the *Inspired Tinker*.

BISHOP OF FLEET STREET, THE Hannen Swaffer (1879–1962), newspaperman with a rather ecclesiastical air, a large black bow tie, a black homburg and a tendency to pontificate on such matters as public morals. He developed the gossip column in modern journalism. Also the *Dean of Fleet Street*, the *Pope of Fleet Street* and *Swaff*.

BISHOP OF HELL, THE Dr Gaynham or Garnham, an 18th century 'chaplain' of the Fleet Prison, London, notorious for its cruelty and its illicit marriages.

BISHOP TUTU Wilfred (Wilf) Slack (1955–1988), West Indian born cricketer for Middlesex and England who collapsed and died on the pitch during a match in the Gambia, West Africa. He was an opening batsman and a good all-rounder; so called by his team mates.

- The Most Reverend Desmond Tutu (1931–   ) is the anti-apartheid Archbishop of Johannesburg.

BISI VC Kulbir Thapa of the 3rd Gurkha Rifles who won the VC (World War I) by bringing in wounded under fire (1915).

BISON, THE Fox Maule Ramsay, Lord Panmure, later 11th Earl of Dalhousie (1801–74), Secretary of State for War (1846–52) and a difficult man to get on with. He had a habit of swaying his head to and fro as he talked. Sidney Herbert (1st Baron: 1810–61) once wrote to Florence Nightingale (the **Lady with the Lamp**) inviting her to take part in 'a combined attack on the Bison.'

BISON WILLIAM See **Buffalo Bill**.

BITCH, THE Robyn Smith (1945–   ), American champion woman jockey; because of her ruthless tactics. She married film star Fred Astaire (Frederic Austerlitz, 1899–1987) in 1980. She is a former Hollywood starlet.

BIX Leon Bismarck Beiderbeck (1903–31), American jazz composer, cornet and piano player, from 'Bismarck'.

BIZZER or BIZZA Lady Elizabeth Kerr (1954–   ), Countess of Dalkeith (1981).

She is the youngest daughter of the Marquis of Lothian.

BLACK, THE
i) Hewald, a monk (died 695), an early recorded example of a nickname. The Venerable Bede (the *Father of English History*) writes (*A History of the English Church and People,* 731): 'Two other priests of English race . . . shared the same name . . . with the distinction that, since their hair was of different colour, one was known as Hewald the Black and the other as Hewald the *White*.' They both followed St Willibrord (the *Apostle of the Friesians*) and were martyred, the Black dying by slow torture.
ii) Sir Hugh *Duv* or *Dubh* O'Donnell, lord of Tyrconnel (16th century). Hugh routed Shane O'Neill, the *Proud* (1565). His grandson was *Red Hugh*.
 • *Duv* or *dubh* means 'black' in Gaelic. See also Iain *Dubh* Cameron, *Big John*.
iii) John, 9th Baron Clifford (1436–61); for his deeds. Also *Bloody Clifford* and the *Butcher.*
iv) Sir Ewen Cameron, Lord of Lochiel (1629–1719), who was dark. Also the *Great Lochiel* and the *Ulysses of the Highlands*.
 • Lochiel is the title of the Chief of the Camerons; from Loch Eil.

BLACK AGNES Agnes, Countess of Dunbar (circa 1312–69), daughter of the 1st Earl of Moray and wife of the 10th Earl of Dunbar. She played a heroic part in the siege of Dunbar by the English under the Earl of Salisbury (1338); so called because of her dark complexion.

BLACK ARTHUR Arthur Forbes (died 1571), youngest son of the 6th Lord Forbes. He was killed in a battle against the Gordons at Tullieangua.

BLACK BARON, THE or THE BLACK BARON OF FOULIS Robert Monro of Foulis (died 1633), who served with the army of Gustavus Adolphus (1594–1632) in Germany, joining as a volunteer with a company of Monro clansmen.

BLACK BART
i) Charles E. Bolton (circa 1820– ?), American hooded stagecoach-robber, especially of the Wells Fargo vehicles in California. He disappeared (circa 1883) after a prison sentence.
ii) Captain Bartholomew Roberts (died 1722), Welsh mate of a merchant ship who turned pirate and raided far and wide. He was about forty years old when he was killed in action with a British man-of-war.

BLACKBEARD Edward Teach, Thatch or Thach (died 1718), notorious pirate along the American coast. Captain Johnson (Defoe) said that Teach, who was born in Bristol, 'assumed the cognomen of Blackbeard from the large quantity of hair, which, like a frightful meteor, covered his whole face and frightened America more than any comet that has appeared there a long time'.

BLACKBIRD, THE
i) Charles II (1630–85); so called in ballads by Ramsay (the *Scottish Theocrates*). He was dark-complexioned. Also the *Black Boy*, the *Bonny Black Boy*, *Flatfoot the Gudgeon-Taker*, the *Great Physician*, the *Merry Monarch*, the *Mutton-Eating King*, *Old Rowley*, the *Satyr*, the *Son of the Last Man* and *Young Tarquin*.
ii) Robert Southey, the *Ballad-Monger*.

BLACKBIRDY J.M.W. Turner, *Admiral Booth.* He chased small boys at Twickenham away from blackbirds' nests in his garden.

BLACK BOB
i) Major-General Robert Craufurd (1764–1812), who commanded the Light Brigade during the Peninsular War and was killed at Ciudad Rodrigo. He was a small, dark man of violent temper. Also *Teapot.*
ii) Sir Robert Scholey (1921–), chairman of the British Steel Corporation.

BLACK BOMBER, THE Frank Bruno (1961-), British ABA champion (1980) turned professional heavyweight boxer; his early nickname in boxing. He lost (1989) to *Iron Mike* Tyson for the world heavyweight title. Also *Blackwall Tunnel*.

BLACK BOY, THE Charles II, the *Blackbird*. He was swarthy even as a baby. The nickname was given to a number of English public-houses.

BLACK CAESAR John Caesar (shot 1796), West Indian escaped slave and London pickpocket, transported to Australia, where he became a bushranger (1789).

BLACK CHARLIE Admiral Sir Charles Napier (1786–1860), commander of the Channel Fleet (1846–48) and the Baltic Fleet (1854). He had a bad temper. Also *Old Charlie*.

BLACK COCK OF THE WEST, THE Sir James Colquhoun, 20th Baron Luss (1647–76), British MP.

• The family of the Chief of Clan Colquhoun have lived at Luss on Loch Lomond for more than seven hundred years and become very powerful.

BLACK COLIN Colin Campbell (fl. 14th century), Knight of Loch Awe and hero of the wars between England and Scotland. He was the subject of many myths.

BLACK COMYN or CUMMIN John Comyn, Cummin or de Comines (died 1300), claimant to the Scottish throne and chief of the Cummins. His son, *Red Cummin*, competed with Robert the *Bruce* for the crown, and was slain by him.

BLACK CUR or HOUND OF ARDEN, THE Guy de Beauchamp, 10th Earl of Warwick (1298–1315), one of the bitterest opponents of Piers Gaveston, Earl of Cornwall (died 1312), who gave him the nickname. Warwick played a large part in bringing about the death of Gaveston by kidnapping him after he had surrendered to the Earl of Pembroke (*Joseph the Jew*).

BLACK DAN Daniel Owen, alias Daniel Morgan (1830-65), Australian bushranger and ruthless killer; said to have been the 'original' of Ralph Boldrewood's central figure in *Robbery under Arms* (1888). Also *Down-the-River-Jack*.

BLACK DEATH Joseph Henry Blackburne (1841–1924), brilliant English chess master (circa 1876), described by the *Encyclopaedia Britannica* as 'in the van of the world's chess army.' He was one of those under whom English chess flourished.

BLACK DIAMOND, THE
i) Thomas (Tom) Crib or Cribb (1781–1848), pugilist and champion of England for many years (post-1809). He had been a coal porter.
• Egan the *Elder* spelt his name both 'Crib' and 'Cribb'.
ii) Peter Jackson (1861–1901), negro boxer who made his name in Australia, and was brought to England (1890s) by Lord Lonsdale (*England's Greatest Sportsman*). Also *Gentleman Jackson* and (in Australia) the *Black Prince of the Ring*.
iii) Eliza Westbrook, elder sister of Harriet, whom Shelley (*Ariel*) married. Eliza had a mass of raven-black hair.

BLACK DICK
i) Admiral Richard, 1st Earl Howe (1726–99) who, says Bowen, 'was said only to smile when there was a battle in imminent prospect'. His nickname was given because of his swarthy complexion, evident in the portrait by Gainsborough (the *Painter Patriot*).
ii) Richard Wright (died 1792), a dangerous criminal hanged for the murder of William Begbie, a porter to the British Linen Company Bank, Edinburgh, who was robbed of almost £5,000. Wright denied the crime.

BLACK DOUGLAS
i) Sir James Douglas (1286–1330), Lord of Douglas, lieutenant to Robert the *Bruce*. He plundered the north of England (1319) and his nickname was so feared that English mothers used it to frighten their children into obedience. He set out to take the heart of the *Bruce* to the Holy Land, but was killed fighting the Saracens on the way.
ii) Sir William 1st Earl of Douglas (*circa* 1327–84) who murdered his kinsman, William Douglas (the *Flower of Chivalry*). He was tall, his hair black and his complexion swarthy.
iii) Sir James, 9th Earl Douglas (1426–88).
• The name 'Douglas' means 'The Black Water' (Gaelic *dubh glas*: Reaney).

BLACK EARL, THE Thomas Butler, 10th Earl of Ormonde (1532–1614). In a campaign against the Desmonds, his army killed more than 4,800. Also ***Black Tom***.

BLACK FACE Charles (Charley) Bryant (fl. 1890s), American gunman and member of the Dalton and Doolin gangs of train-robbers; from the powder burns he received in a gun-fight.

BLACK FLASH, THE

i) Jesse Owens (1913–80), American, arguably the greatest track athlete of all time. In the 1936 Olympic Games he won four gold medals, equalling or breaking Olympic records. 'Jesse' was in fact a nickname since he had been christened James Cleveland, but was too shy at school to say that to his teacher. 'J.C.' thus became 'Jesse'. Also the ***Ebony Antelope.***

ii) Emmanuel McDonald Bailey (1920–), Trinidad-born athlete who held the 100 metres sprint record between 1946 and 1953 and won fourteen AAA sprint titles and two relay titles – at that time the greatest number of national AAA titles held by one man.

BLACK HARRY Augustus Henry Fitzroy, 3rd Duke of Grafton (1735–1811), British Prime Minister (as First Lord of the Treasury, 1766–70); descendant of an illegitimate son of Charles II (the ***Blackbird***). Grafton was dark-complexioned, and could be short-tempered and irritable.

BLACK HUNTER, THE John Wallace Crawford (1847–1917), American frontier scout and Indian agent of the Black Hills, S. Dakota. In later life he was famous as a lecturer, well-known for reciting his own verse. Also ***Black Rifle***, ***Captain Jack*** and the ***Poet Scout of the Black Hills***.

BLACK HUSSAR OF LITERATURE, THE Scott, the ***Ariosto of the North***; so called by his son-in-law Lockhart (the ***Aristarch of British Criticism***) after Scott had written to the publisher Ballantyne (the ***Jenson of the North***): 'I belong to the Black Hussars of Literature who neither give nor receive criticism' (1816).

• The Black or Death Hussars were Brunswickers who gave no quarter. They wore black uniforms.

BLACK JACK

i) General John Alexander Logan (1826–86), American Civil War soldier and politician; so called by his soldiers because of his long black hair and dark complexion. Also the ***Jack of Spades***.

ii) General John Joseph Pershing (1860–1948), C-in-C, American Expeditionary Force to Europe (World War I).

iii) John Philip Kemble (1757–1823), British Shakespearian actor with long black hair and a dark complexion.

iv) Thomas E. Ketchum (1862–1901), leader of a gang of outlaws and train-robbers. He was hanged at Clayton, New Mexico.

BLACK JAMES Sir James Ormonde (killed 1497), Lord Treasurer for Ireland.

BLACK JANE Jennie Jerome, Lady Randolph Churchill (1851–1921); so called by the Press. She had long black hair.

BLACK JOCK John (Johnnie) Armstrong (died 1529), leader of a gang of border reivers, captured with Adam Scott (the ***King of the Border***) and William Cockburn of Henderland. All were promptly executed. Records give 'Blak Jok'.

BLACK JOHN OF THE MAIL-COAT Iain MacGregor, killed (1603) in a battle between the MacGregors and the Colquhouns at Glenfruin when mail-coats were rare.

BLACK KNIGHT OF ASHTON, THE Sir Ralph de Ashton or Assheton (fl. 15th century); from his tyranny over his tenants, who eventually murdered him in the street at Ashton-under-Lyne, Lancashire. An annual ceremony was held there on Easter Monday until 1939 called 'The Riding of the Black Lad'. The effigy of a knight was paraded through the streets and pelted with stones and other missiles.

• Sir Ralph was Knight Marshal and Lieutenant of the Tower of London under Richard II (the ***Coxcomb***) and Sheriff of York in the reign of Edward IV (the ***Robber***). 'Riding' = a mock procession.

BLACK-LETTER TOM T.F. (Tom) Dibdin, the ***Beau Brummell of Living Authors***; because of his interest in black-letter books, a name for those in Gothic type (i.e. those printed before 1600) to distinguish them from those printed in Roman; so called in *Noctes Ambrosianae*.

• Cf the **Father of Black-Letter Lore**.

BLACK MARIA Maria Lee, a negress who kept a sailors' lodging-house in Philadelphia (circa 1838) and helped police to find and arrest lawbreakers. The nickname was given to a police van.

BLACK MICHAEL Michael Edward Hicks-Beach, 1st Earl of St Aldwyn (1837–1916), Chancellor of the Exchequer on two occasions between 1885 and 1902; from Black Michael in *The Prisoner of Zenda* (1894) by Anthony Hope. Also Mr **Hicks-Bitch**.

BLACK MIKE Michael Howe (1787–1818), leader of a gang of Australian bushrangers and a hero of Australian folk-lore. He had been a highwayman in England, and was transported (1812). He was clubbed to death by bounty-hunters while resisting arrest. Also the **Lieutenant-Governor of the Woods**.

BLACK-MOUTHED ZOILUS John Milton (1608–74), poet of *Paradise Lost* and author of a number of pamphlets against episcopacy and of *Eikonoklastes* (1649), a reply to *Eikon Basilike*, which was printed as the final meditations of Charles I (the **Ahab of the Nation**) before execution – 'The Royal Images' answered by 'The Image Breakers'. So called by John Hacket (the **Begging Bishop**). Also the **Blind Poet**, the **British Homer**, the **English Mastiff**, the **Great Gospel Gun**, the **Lady of Christ's College**, the **Prince of Poets** and the **Trader in Faction**.

• Zoilus (4th century BC) was a Greek philosopher who made bitter criticisms of Plato and Homer. 'Black-mouthed' in the 17th century meant 'slanderous'. 'Zoilus' became in the 16th century a term for someone unduly severe in criticism.

BLACK NAPOLEON, THE Musquito (hanged 1825), Australian aboriginal bushranger with a large gang.

BLACK PANTHER, THE Donald Neilson (1936–), whose real name is Donald Nappey, a masked robber, gaoled for life for the abduction and murder of the heiress Lesley Whittle (1975) and the murders of three sub-postmaster; self-applied because he wore a mask and was stealthy.

BLACK PEARL, THE Laurie Cunningham (1956–89), British footballer; so called in Spain where he played for three years for Real Madrid. Cunningham, who held six caps for England between 1979 and 1981, was killed in a car crash in Spain. He was also known as 'Black Magic'.

BLACK PIMPERNEL, THE Nelson Mandela (1918–), leader of the African National Congress in South Africa, when forced underground; captured and imprisoned (1963–90).

BLACK PRINCE, THE Edward (1330–76), eldest son of Edward III (the **Father of English Commerce**). He won his spurs at Crécy (1346) at the age of sixteen; so called either from the colour of his armour or, as Froissart says, 'because of the terror of his arms'. However, there is no evidence that he ever wore black armour. He is buried in Canterbury Cathedral. Also the **Invincible Soldier**.

BLACK PRINCE OF THE RING, THE Peter Jackson, the **Black Diamond**; his nickname in Australia.

BLACK RIFLE John Crawford, the **Black Hunter**.

BLACK ROBIN Robin *Ddu* (or *Du*) ap Siencyn Bledrydd, a 15th-century Welsh poet.

• *Ddu* or *du* = black in Welsh.

BLACK RUSSELL The Reverend John Russell (1740–1817) of Kilmarnock; so called by Burns (the **Ayrshire Poet**) in *The Holy Fair*.

BLACK STEWART Sir John Stewart, hereditary Sheriff of Bute (post-1385); natural son of Robert II (**Blear-Eye**).

BLACK TERROR, THE William (Billy) Richmond (1763–1829), the first American pugilist to make a name in boxing, described by Egan (the **Elder**) as 'a man of colour'. He was well-known as a fighter in the early 19th century. Also **Lily White**.

BLACK TOBY Tobias Gill, a negro drummer of the 4th Hussars, hanged (1750) for raping and murdering a young girl at Blythburgh Heath, Suffolk. His ghost is said to haunt the area.

BLACK TOM
i) Sir Thomas, 3rd Baron Fairfax of Cameron (1612–71), Civil War Parliamentary general.

ii) Thomas, Earl of Ormonde, the ***Black Earl***, Lord Deputy of Ireland in the reign of Elizabeth (the ***English Diana***), a sombre and uncouth man.

BLACK TOM TYRANT Sir Thomas Wentworth, Earl of Strafford (1593–1641); so called by the Scots after he had advocated severe repression when Scottish Puritans rebelled in what are called the Bishops' Wars. Also ***Thorough***.

BLACK WILL HERBERT William Herbert, Earl of Pembroke (1501–70), for his escapades when young, which included killing a sheriff at Bristol. He later became a notable politician.

BLACK WILLIAM Sir William Herbert, created Earl of Pembroke in 1468 and died 1469, a Yorkist who was captured by the Lancastrian Sir John Conyers and beheaded; so called by the Welsh (*Gwiliam ddu*).

• See ***Robin Mend-All***.

BLACKWALL TUNNEL Frank Bruno, the ***Black Bomber***. His nose is big, black and wide.

BLASHERS Lieutenant-Colonel John Nicholas Blashford-Snell, Royal Engineers (1936–), soldier-explorer.

BLASPHEMER, THE Oliver Cromwell, the ***Almighty Nose***. He defied the Divine Right of Kings by having Charles I (the ***Ahab of the Nation***) executed, and put personal judgements in place of dictation by priests.

BLASPHEMOUS BALFOUR Sir James Balfour, Lord Pittendreich (died 1583), Scottish judge and political intriguer implicated in the plot to assassinate Cardinal Beaton (*circa* 1494–1546) and in the murder of Lord Darnley, Lord Consort of Scotland (1567). Balfour was a follower of John Knox (the ***Apostle of the Scots***) and was imprisoned with him. Cardinal Beaton had crowned Mary,

Queen of Scots (the ***Mermaid***). Balfour after his release from prison (1549) turned his coat and entered the service of Mary of Guise in return for legal appointments. His career has been described as one of the blackest perfidy.

BLAZING BEN Benjamin William Hogan (1912–), American professional golfer rated one of the top players of all time. He was world champion (1951 and 1953); so called because of his style and success.

BLEAR-EYE Robert II of Scotland (1316–90). Also the ***Steward***.

BLENHEIM PIPPIN, THE Lord Randolph Henry Spencer Churchill (1849–94), English statesman and father of Winston (***Bricky***). A political nickname given to him because he was the son of the 7th Duke of Marlborough (1822–83), whose home was at Blenheim Palace. Ware dated it from 1883. The pippin is a small apple, and Lord Randolph was quite short. Also ***Gooseberry-Faced Churchill***, ***Randy*** and the ***Uhlan***.

BLESSED, THE Caedwalla, king of Wessex (reigned 685–8). He was regarded as a saint, and in 688 abdicated to go to Rome to be baptized, dying there a few days later.

BLESSED MARGARET Margaret Thatcher, ***Attila the Hen***; so called by Norman St John-Stevas (1929–), Leader of the House of Commons (1979–81) because he felt she would save the country from Socialism. Mr St John-Stevas was created a life peer (1987) as Baron St John of Fowsley.

BLEST SWAN Richard Crashaw (*circa* 1612–49), poet who wrote on religious subjects, e.g. *Steps to the Temple* (1646); so called by Cowley (the ***English Pindar***) in a poem on his death. Also the ***Divine***.

• The poet-god Apollo was identified with the swan which the Greeks believed could sing, especially when it was dying. Homer was called 'the Swan of Meander', on the banks of which he is said to have lived.

BLIND BEAK, THE or THE BLIND MAGISTRATE Sir John Fielding (1722–80), who in spite of having been born blind became magistrate at Bow Street, London.

He is said to have been able to recognize the voices of three thousand criminals.

- 'Beak' ? from 'beck' as in 'harman's beck' = a constable or the stocks (*Pedlars' French*, 1573).

BLIND BOY or **BLIND BOY FULLER** Fuller Allen (1903–40), American blues singer.

BLIND HARPER, THE John Parry (died 1782), Welsh harper who lived at Ruaben and published a collection of Welsh music. Also *Blind Parry*.

BLIND HARRY or **HARY** An anonymous Scottish minstrel (fl. 1470–92), probably from Lothian, who is thought to have died in 1492. He is the reputed writer of the great poem on Sir William Wallace (the *Hammer and Scourge of England*) which runs to more then 11,800 lines. Also *Harry* or *Henry the Minstrel*.

BLIND JACK OF KNARESBOROUGH John Metcalf (1717–1810), who lost his sight when four years old, but was a carrier between Knaresborough and York and acted as a guide in the forest. He also fought at Culloden (1746).

BLIND MECHANICIAN, THE John Strong (1732–88), a mechanical genius who was blind from birth.

BLIND PARRY John Parry, the *Blind Harper*.

BLIND POET, THE John Milton, *Black-Mouthed Zoilus*, who had become totally blind by May 1652.

BLIND PREACHER, THE William Henry Milburn (1823–1903), American Methodist minister, born in Philadelphia.

BLIND TRAVELLER, THE James Holman (1786–1857), a lieutenant in the Royal Navy, who lost his sight (1812) after having been invalided out. In spite of this, he travelled widely in Europe and (in 1822) the world. He wrote *A Voyage Round the World* (1834 5).

BLIND WILLIE William Johnson (1896–1949), American blues singer, blinded by his stepmother.

BLINKING SAM Dr Samuel Johnson (1709–84), lexicographer, writer and poet. Scrofula had affected his eyes, and indeed he was blind for a short time; so called after

Reynolds (the *Bachelor Painter*) had finished his portrait, a picture which Johnson disliked. Also the *Bolt Court Philosopher*, the *Cerberus of Literature*, the *Classic Rambler*, the *Colossus of English Philology*, *Dictionary Johnson*, the *English Socrates*, the *Giant of Literature*, the *Great Bear*, the *Great Caliban*, the *Great Cham of Literature*, the *Great Moralist*, the *Great Seer*, the *Incomprehensible Holofernes*, the *Last of the Tories*, the *Learned Attila*, the *Leviathan of Literature*, the *Literary Colossus*, the *Literary Whale*, the *Polyphemus of Literature*, *Pomposo*, the *Respectable Hottentot*, *Surly Sam*, *Ultimus Romanorum*, and *Ursa Major*.

BLINKINSON Robert Banks Jenkinson, 2nd Earl of Liverpool (1770–1828), British Prime Minister (1812–27); so called by Canning (*Aeolus*). He had a fidgety twitch of his eyelids. Also *Young Jenky*.

- Cf *Jenky*.

BLOBBO Jack William Nicklaus (1940–), American professional golfer who won the American Open three times and the British Open twice – in fact, he has won more major championships than any other golfer. He is powerfully built. Also the *Golden Bear* and *Ohio Fats*.

BLOND BOMBER, THE William (Billy) Walker (1949–), British boxer. UK heavyweight champion, he defeated eight out of ten opponents by knock-outs. Also called 'Billy the Quid', a pun on *Billy the Kid*.

BLONDE BLITZ, THE Betty Hutton (1921–), American film star with a dynamic personality. Her real name is Betty Thornberg. She now works as a cook in a Rhode Island rectory. Also the *Blonde Bombshell*.

BLONDE BOMBSHELL, THE

i) Jean Harlow (1911–37), American film star who was a sensation when she appeared on the screen, as in *Bombshell* (1933). She had silver-blonde hair. Her real name was Harlean Carpenter.

ii) Betty Hutton, the *Blonde Blitz*.

BLONDY George Standing, top rackets player who lost the world championship (1897) to Peter Latham (1865–1953).

BLOOD AXE or BLOODY AXE King Eirik or Eric *Blodöxe* of Norway and York (killed 955), son of Harald Fairhair. Eirik's death and the expulsion of the Norwegians ended the Norse line of kings in York.

BLOOD MAN, THE Charles I, the *Ahab of the Nation*. The Puritans thought his double-dealings brought about the second phase of the Civil War.
- Cf the *Man of Blood*.

BLOOD MONEY MAN, THE Stephen Macdaniel or M'Daniel, an 18th century thief-taker, sentenced to death (1756) for murder but reprieved and sent abroad as a soldier. The *Newgate Calendar* states that he and others conspired against the lives of innocent people.

BLOOD ORANGE Lieutenant-General Sir George Gorringe (1868–1945). Soldiers in World War I alleged that as a commander on the Western Front he made wasteful use of men's lives.

BLOODY ANGELO Angelo Genna (died 1925), one of the six Genna brothers, American gangsters, bootleggers and murderers. Angelo was president of the Unione Siciliane (post-1924). He was given a sensational gangster's funeral in Chicago.

BLOODY BALFOUR Arthur James, 1st Earl Balfour (1848–1930), British Prime Minister (1902–05); so called by Irish Nationalists when he was Chief Secretary for Ireland (1887–91) for the vigour of his policies. Also *Fanny*.

BLOODY BILL William Anderson (1840–64), the most vicious of the Quantrill Raiders, Confederate guerrilla troops led by William Clarke Quantrill (1837–65). Anderson took part in the infamous massacre at Lawrence, Kansas. Later, he was shot dead by Union troops.

BLOODY BUTCHER, THE The Duke of Cumberland, *Billy* ; sometimes the 'Barbarous Butcher'.

BLOODY CASTLEREAGH Robert Stewart, Viscount Castlereagh, who became 2nd Marquis of Londonderry (1769–1822); so called when Chief Secretary of Ireland, accused of atrocities after the Irish rising of 1798. Also the *Derrydown Triangle;*

Intellectual Eunuch; Swell-Foot Tyrant.

BLOODY CLAVER'SE or BLUIDIE CLAVERS James Graham of Claverhouse, Viscount Dundee (*circa* 1649–89); because of his terrorism against Covenanters (1679–80). Also *Bonnie Dundee*.

BLOODY or BLUIDY MACKENZIE Sir George Mackenzie of Rosenhaugh (1636–91), King's Advocate who took severe action against Covenanters. Also the *Noble Wit of Scotland*.

BLOODY CLIFFORD John, 9th Baron Clifford, the *Black*, who murdered Edmund, Earl of Rutland (died 1460), son of Richard, Duke of York (1411–60) after the battle of Wakefield.

BLOODY MARY Mary I (1516–58), who had almost 300 Protestants put to death during her reign.

BLOOMSBURY DICK Richard Rigby (1722–88), British politician who was associated with John Russell, 4th Duke of Bedford (1717–71) and the Bloomsbury Gang. He was secretary to the Duke when the latter was Lord-Lieutenant of Ireland. Also the *Brazen Boatswain*.
- The Bloomsbury Gang was a political faction started by the Duke of Bedford after the fall of the Grenville administration (1765), of which he had been a member.

BLOWTORCH, THE Robert (Bob) William Komer (1922–   ), American Under-Secretary for Defence in the Carter Administration (1977–81).

BLUE DICK OF THANET Richard Culmer (fl. 1660s), British fanatical divine and iconoclast who destroyed the great window of the north transept of Canterbury Cathedral with a pike. He wore blue when most others in a puritanical period wore black. Also *Blueskin Dick*.

BLUE GRIZZLY, THE William Tilden, *Big Bill*. He was a big man who wore a large teddy-bear pullover while knocking-up before a match.

BLUE RUIN Sir Richard John Cartwright (1835–1912), Canadian politician who had many nicknames because of his gloomy predictions. They included the *Knight of the Rueful Countenance*, the

Nestor of Canadian Liberalism and the *Rupert of Debates*.

BLUESKIN Joseph Blake (1696–1724), thief and accomplice of Jack Sheppard (1702–24). He was a highwayman, and made an unsuccessful attempt to kill Jonathan Wild (the *Great Thief Taker*); so called from his dark countenance.

BLUESKIN DICK Richard Culmer, *Blue Dick of Thanet*; so called for the same reason as above.

BLUE STOCKING Benjamin Stillingfleet (1702–71), a member of the assemblies (soirées) which were held by literary ladies for conversations with men of literature. He always wore blue stockings, and from them the meetings were sardonically called by Admiral Edward Boscawen (*Old Dreadnought*) the Blue Stocking Society.

● Cf the *Queen of Blue Stockings*. France had a Bas Bleu society for intellectuals in the 16th century.

BLUE STREAK, THE Marjorie Jackson (1931–   ), later Mrs Nelson, Australian sprinter who set ten world records and won an Olympic gold (1952). She ran 100 yards in 10.4 sec (Sydney, 1952) and retired from athletics at the age of twenty-two.

● A blue streak is Australian slang for something very fast (like the aborted missile!).

BLUEY David Bairstow (1951–   ), Yorkshire (captain) and England batsman and wicket-keeper.

BLUFF HAL King Henry VIII (1491–1547), because of his size and his hearty manner (often deceptive). Also *Bluff Harry*, *Bluff King Hal*, *Burly King Hal*, *Burly King Harry*, *Coppernose Harry*, *Old Coppernose*, *Old Harry* and *Stout Harry*.

BLUFF HARRY Henry VIII, above.

BLUFF KING HAL Henry VIII, above.

BLUM Ralph David Blumenfeld (1864–1948), editor of the *Daily Express* (1902–32); known to his staff as 'R.D.B.'

BLUNDERING BROUGHAM Henry Peter Brougham, 1st Baron Brougham and Vaux (1778–1868), Lord Chancellor, orator and jurist; so called by Byron (*Baby*) after Brougham had savaged his *Hours in Idleness* (1807) in *The Edinburgh Review*. Also *Dominie Harry*, the *God of Whiggish Idolatory*, *Harry Twitcher*, *Jupiter Placens* and *Wickedshifts*.

BOADICEA Mrs Thatcher, *Attila the Hen*; so called by Tory MPs.

● See the *Warrior Queen*.

BOANERGES Edward Irving (1792–1834), Scottish minister generally thought of as the founder of the Catholic Apostolic Church. He regarded himself as 'a man of power', and attracted great crowds whenever he preached in London; so called by de Quincey (the *English Opium Eater*). Also *Doctor Squintum* and *Son of Thunder*.

● John and James, sons of Zebedee, were called 'Boanerges', 'Sons of Thunder', by Jesus (Mark iii, 17). It is an Aramaic word.

BOAR, THE Richard III (1452–85). His coat-of-arms included a wild boar; so called by Shakespeare (the *Bard of All Time*). Also *Crookback* and the *Hog*.

BOAR OF THE FOREST, THE James Hogg (1770–1835), shepherd-poet of Ettrick, Selkirkshire, Scotland, when he was discovered and nicknamed by Scott (the *Ariosto of the North*); a pun on his name, rough manners and workplace. Also the *Ettrick Shepherd*.

BOATSWAIN SMITH George Charles Smith (1787–1863), English preacher and pamphleteer who had been pressed into the Royal Navy. He founded the first sailors' home.

BOBBIN BOY, THE Nathaniel Prentiss Banks (1816–94), American general and politician. He had worked as a boy in a cotton factory of which his father was superintendent. Also *Old Jack's Commissary-General*.

BOBBING JOHN John Erskine, 6th or 11th Earl of Mar (1675–1732), because of his change in politics from Stuart to Hanover (*circa* 1715); after an old song (*Bobbing Joan*).

● In 1426, the Earl of Mar resigned his title, and the King granted it back to him by a re-creation of the earldom.

BOBBITY Robert Arthur James Gascoyne-Cecil, 5th Marquess of Salisbury (1893–1972), from 'Robert'.

BOBBY Arthur d'Arcy Locke (1917–87), South African golfer, South African Open champion (1935, 1937–40, 1946, 1950–1 and 1955), Canadian Open champion (1947), British Open champion 1949–50, 1952 and 1957); rated as the greatest putter of all time.

BOBBY DOUGHNUT Robert Donat (1905–58), British stage and screen star; so called in the theatre, first given in the Frank Benson company (see *Pa*).

BOBO

i) William Beaumont, the *Amiable Geronimo*; so called on the 1980 British Lions tour of South Africa.

ii) Carl Olson (1928–   ), American boxer who lost to *Sugar Ray* Robinson in a world middleweight title fight in Chicago (1955). Olson was champion 1953–5.

iii) Margaret MacDonald (1905–   ), Scottish maid to the Queen, who has been in her service since the Queen was four years old.

BOBS Field-Marshal Frederick Sleigh, 1st Earl Roberts (1832–1914), popular hero and VC who won twenty-four mentions in despatches; C-in-C, British Army (1901–4). Also *Bobs Bahadur*, *Fighting Bobs* and *Roberts of Kandahar*.

BOBS BAHADUR Lord Roberts, see above.

• *Bahadur* is Hindi for a champion or a hero, or, as *Blackwood's Magazine* translated it (1922), 'a hell of a fellow'.

BOBUS SMITH Robert Percy Smith (1770–1845), Advocate-General, Bengal and elder brother of Sydney (*Diner-Out of the First Water*); nickname at Eton (a Latinization of 'Bob?') which lasted all his life.

BODGER, THE Dr Thomas James (1748–1804), headmaster of Rugby School (1778–94) and so all his successors.

BODY, THE

i) Vivian Neves (1948–   ), first British model to appear nude in a photograph in *The Times*.

ii) Victoria Principal (1945–   ), American actress; was especially well known in TV's *Dallas*.

iii) Marie McDonald (1923–65), early American film star: real surname Frye.

BOEHME OF ENGLAND, THE George Fox (1624–91), Quaker and mystic who left home to become a wandering preacher. Also the *Man with Leather Breeches*.

• Jakob Boehme (1575–1624) was a German mystic who claimed direct divine inspiration and wrote books on the character of God.

BOGEY Humphrey DeForest Bogart (1899–1957), American film star.

BOIL, THE Trevor Bailey, the *Barnacle*. When he was playing football in front of a Cockney crowd the spectators persistently shouted 'Come on, Boiley!' His friends turned it into The Boil.

BOILERMAKER, THE James Jeffries (1875–1953), American who beat Bob Fitzsimmons (the *Antipodean*) for the world heavyweight boxing title (1890) and held it until his retirement (1905). Also the *Californian Grizzly*.

BOJANGLES William (Bill) Robinson (1878–1949), American negro dancer and actor.

BOLD, THE Sir William de Douglas (died 1298). He defended Berwick castle (1296) against Edward I (the *Hammer of the Scots*) and later joined the rebellion of Wallace (the *Hammer and Scourge of England*). Douglas died a prisoner in the Tower of London. Also *Le Hardi*.

BOLD BEAUCHAMP Thomas de Beauchamp, 11th Earl of Warwick (1329–69), who at Hogges, Normandy (1346), with one squire and six archers, defeated a hundred armed French. He was Marshal of England (1344) and one of the original Knights of the Garter.

BOLD BUCCLEUCH Sir Walter Scott of Buccleuch (1565–1611), a famous reiver or Border fighter, noted for his rescue of *Kinmont Willie* (1596) from Carlisle castle. Also *Flagellum Dei*, *God's Curse* and *Wicket Wat*.

BOLD JACK John (Jack) Donahoe (1808–30), Australian bushranger, folk hero of ballads. He was transported for life (1824) for 'intent to commit a felony'. He was shot. Also the **Wild Colonial Boy.**

BOLINGBROKE Henry IV (1367–1413), son of John of **Gaunt**; born at Bolingbroke, Lincolnshire.

BOLT COURT PHILOSOPHER, THE Dr Johnson, **Blinking Sam**. He lived at Bolt Court, Fleet Street, London.

BOMBARDIER, THE or BOMBARDIER BILLY Billy Wells, **Battling Billy**. A big gun (World War I) was named after him.

BOMBARDIER BISHOP, THE Peter Mews (1619–1706), Bishop of Bath and Wells, wounded thirty-six times for the royalist cause in the English Civil War. He used his carriage horses at Sedgemoor (1685) to draw cannons to the forefront of the fighting.

• See **Absalom**.

BOMBER

i) Brian Douglas Wells (1930–   ), cricketer for Gloucestershire and Nottinghamshire.

ii) Herol Graham (1956–   ), British and Commonwealth middleweight boxing champion who won all his thirteen fights. He lost the world middleweight title (1989) to Mike McCallum (1957–   ).

iii) Paddy Browne (1965–   ), Irish professional snooker player; from the manner in which he pots the reds.

BOMBER HARRIS Marshal of the Royal Air Force, Sir Arthur Travers Harris (1892–1984), C-in-C, Bomber Command (World War II). Also **Butcher** and **Ginger**.

BON, LE James Graham, 2nd Marquis of Montrose (circa 1631–69). Also the **Good**.

BONANZA KING, THE William Shoney O'Brien, born in Ireland 1825 and emigrant to America, who amassed a fortune in the Comstock bonanza.

• See the **King of the Comstock**, **Old Pancake** and **Old Virginny**.

BONECRUSHER, THE James Smith (1953–), 6 ft 4 in, 17 stone (238 lb) American heavyweight who regularly broke opponents' bones when boxing as an amateur in the US Army.

BONELESS WONDER, THE James Ramsay

MacDonald (1866–1937), one of the founders of the British Labour Party and Prime Minister (1924 and 1929–35); so called by Churchill (**Bricky**) in 1931. MacDonald abandoned Labour principles, formed a National Government and so stayed Prime Minister. Also **Ramsay Mac**.

BONES

i) Jane Russell (1921–   ), American film star; nickname at school because she was so skinny. Also the **Sexpot of the Century**.

ii) Geoffrey (Geoff.) P. Howarth (1951–   ), cricketer for Surrey and New Zealand (captain).

BONEY Major-General John Frederick Charles Fuller (1878–1966), soldier and military writer; so called from his resemblance to Napoleon Bonaparte and his ideas on warfare.

BONEY COBBETT William Cobbett (1763–1835), writer (Rural Rides, 1830) who brought back to England the bones of Thomas Paine (1737–1809), supporter of the revolutions in France and America and advocate of one in England. Cobbett was also an admirer of Napoleon Bonaparte. Also the **Trumpeter of Pitt**.

BONNIE DUNDEE Lord Dundee, **Bloody Claver'se**. He raised the Scottish clans for the Jacobites when William III (the **Deliverer**) was proclaimed king. Dundee was killed at the Battle of Killiecrankie (1689); so called by his adherents.

BONNIE (or BONNY) EARL OF MORAY, THE

i) James Stuart, 2nd Earl of Moray (1567–91). He was killed by the Gordons, and an old painting of his corpse is in Darnaway castle. The name 'Moray' became 'Murray'. Also the **Good Earl**.

ii) James Stewart or Stuart, 2nd Earl of Moray (by 2nd creation by James VI: 1533–70). Stewart was Regent of Scotland (1567 until his murder). He was a natural son of James V (the **Goodman of Ballengeich**). Also the **Good Regent**.

BONNY PRINCE CHARLIE Charles Edward Louis Stuart (1720–88), eldest son of James Stuart (the **Old Pretender**). He raised the Jacobites in the 1745 rebellion. Also *Charlie Over the Water*, the *Highland Laddie*, the *King Over the Water*, the *Young Adventurer*, the *Young Chevalier* and the *Young Pretender*.

BONNY BLACK BOY, THE Charles II (the *Blackbird*); so called by Ramsay (the *Scottish Theocritus*).

BONNY BOBBY SHAFTO Robert Shafto (1732–97), MP for Durham and shipowner who was a man of fashion; so called in a song written for an election campaign.

BONZO

i) William (Billy) Bonds (1946–), West Ham footballer; player for 20 years.

ii) John Bonham (1947–80), drummer for the rock group 'Led Zeppelin'; wordplay on 'Bonham'.

BOO Evelyn Laye (1900–), English actress in musical comedies and revues, especially those staged by C.B. Cochran (*Cockie*). Her autobiography (1958) was entitled *Boo To My Friends*.

BOOFY Arthur Kattendyke Strange David Archibald Gore, 8th Earl of Arran (1910–83), British journalist, especially as columnist for the *Evening News*.

BOOK IN BREECHES, THE Lord Macaulay, *Babbletongue*; so called because of his wide knowledge by Sydney Smith (the *Diner-Out of the First Water*): 'There are no limits to his knowledge on small subjects as well as great; he is like a book in breeches.'

BOOKSTALL SMITH William Henry Smith (1825–91), son of the founder of W.H. Smith and Son. He originated the idea of bookstalls on railway stations. Also *Morality Smith* and *Old Morality*.

BOOMERANG WALKER Sir Gilbert Thomas Walker (1868–1959), Director-General of Indian Observatories who revolutionized weather forecasting; so called at Cambridge University, where he was an expert on the aerodynamics of boomerangs.

BOOMING BOB Robert Molesworth, 1st Baron Kindersley (1871–1954), politician who was President of the National Savings Committee. He had a resonant voice.

BOOM TRENCHARD Air-Marshal Hugh Montague, 1st Viscount Trenchard (1873–1956), Chief of Air Staff (1919–28) and later Commissioner for the Metropolitan Police; so called first at the Royal Flying Corps School, Upavon, Wiltshire, because of his loud voice. Also the *Father of the Royal Air Force*.

BOOTS Patricia Mallory (1913–58), American star of films in the 1930s.

BO-PEEP William Drummond, Laird of Hawthornden (1585–1649), Scottish poet and historian in whose memory the Hawthornden Prize for Literature was established (1919); so called by his friends Jonson (the *Bricklayer*) and Drayton (the *Golden-Mouthed*). Also the *Petrarch of Scotland* and the *Scottish Petrarch*.

BORDER FOX, THE Desmond (Dessie) O'Hare (1958–), Ulster-born, Irish National Liberation Army terrorist who operated along the border between the Irish Republic and Northern Ireland. He was alleged to have been responsible for twenty-six killings, including that of the Irish National Liberation Army chief Gerard Steenson (*Dr Death iv*). O'Hare was shot and captured in November 1987, and in April 1988 was sentenced to forty years imprisonment in Dublin. He had pleaded guilty to having kidnapped and tortured a Dublin dentist – a crime the judge described as 'barbaric'. It was the longest sentence given by an Irish court.

BORDER MINSTREL, THE or THE GREAT BORDER MINSTREL Sir Walter Scott, the *Ariosto of the North*. Many of his poems have associations with the Border, e.g. *Kinmont Willie*. Mentioned in his autobiography.

BORU Brian (*circa* 926–1014), King of Ireland; from the Irish *boroma*, 'tribute', because he forced other rulers, including Malachi the *Great*, High King of Ireland, to submit to him. He crushed the power of the Danes in Ireland.

● See *Silken Beard*.

BOSIE or BOSEY

i) Bernard James Tindal Bosanquet (1877–1936), cricketer for England, Middlesex and Oxford University. When touring with the English team in

Australia (1903–4) he invented the 'googly' (still known there as a 'bosie') which brought them victory.

ii) Lord Alfred Douglas (1880–1937), younger son of the 8th Marquess of Queensberry (1844–1937), whose relations with Oscar Wilde (1854–1900) were the subject of a court case in 1895 which resulted in Wilde being imprisoned for two years. From 'boysie' by a doting mother.

iii) Norman Douglas (1869–1952), British novelist, born Norman George Douglass.

BOSS, THE

i) William Marcy Tweed (1823–78), leader of the Tweed Ring in American politics, a ring which dealt in corruption and fraud. He was found guilty of embezzlement and imprisoned (1871).

ii) Sir Archibald Hector McIndoe (1900–60), New Zealand-born plastic surgeon who treated badly burned RAF men at East Grinstead Hospital, Sussex; so called by his patients.

iii) Thomas Collier Platt (1833–1910), Republican leader, an opponent of Theodore Roosevelt (the *Cowboy President*) for President (1900). Also *Me Too*.

iv) Bruce Springsteen (1949–   ), American pop singer.

v) Don Revie (1927–89), manager of Leeds FC, England and Dubai.

BOSS CAT The Princess Royal, Princess Anne (1950–   ); so called by the royal family.

• Boss Cat is an American cartoon character.

BOSS CROKER Richard Croker (1843–1922), Irish-born American politician. Head of Tammany Hall (post-1884). He retired to England, where he won the Derby (1907) with Orby.

• See *Big Tim*.

BOSS EYE Arthur Paul Boissier (1882–1953) on the staff of Harrow School for forty-three years, and headmaster from 1940 to 1942.

BOSTON SIEGE GUN, THE Jesse P. Guilford (1895–1962), American amateur golf champion (1921); because of his hitting

power. Also the *Great Excavator*.

BOSTON STRANGLER, THE Albert De Salvo (1933–73). He terrorized Boston, Massachusetts by the attacks in which he strangled thirteen women (1962–4). He was gaoled for life (1967), and stabbed to death by a fellow-prisoner. Also the *Green Man* and the *Measuring Man*.

BOSTON STRONG BOY, THE John L. Sullivan (1858–1918), the last of the bare-knuckled fighters to win the American title (1882) and the last bare-fisted world champion (1889). He lost with gloves, however, to J.J. Corbett (*Gentleman Jim*) in 1892. His nickname as a youth. He was usually called 'John L'. Also *Spiky Sullivan*.

BOSTON TAR BABY Sam Langford (1880–1956), American boxer who fought from featherweight to heavyweight over twenty-one years but never won a title.

• The Tar Baby is a character in the stories of Uncle Remus by Joel Chandler Harris (1848–1908), such as *The Tar Baby and other Rhymes of Uncle Remus* (1904).

BOSY or BOZZY James Boswell, the *Ambitious Thane*; so called by Johnson (*Blinking Sam*), from 'Boswell' (BLJ).

BOTH Ian Terrance Botham (1955–   ), Somerset all-round cricketer until he signed for Queensland, Australia and Worcestershire. At the age of twenty-four he was chosen to captain England (1980–1). By August 1986, he had played in 85 Tests and set a new record by taking 357 wickets at an average of 26.96 runs. In one match (Somerset v Warwickshire 1985) he scored 100 in 49 minutes off 50 balls, including 9 sixes and 10 fours. Also *Guy the Gorilla, Old Beefy*, and *Rambo*.

BOTTLED BEER Alexander Nowell (*circa* 1507–1602), Dean of St Paul's, London with Puritan views. When rector of Great Hadlam, Hertfordshire, he left a bottle of ale in the grass near the river Ash where he had been fishing, and was surprised a few days later to find it effervescing.

BOTTOMLESS LAMBERT Major-General John Lambert (1619–84), one of Cromwell's most brilliant generals. He was a major-general at twenty-eight, but never won the confidence of his contemporaries; so called, it is reputed, by Cromwell (the *Almighty Nose*).

- Bottomless = lacking in substance, has been recorded since 1563, and was included in Johnson's dictionary in that sense in 1755.

BOTTOMLESS PIT, THE William Pitt, the *Younger* (1759–1806), British Prime Minister (1783–1801 and 1804–6). He was tall and thin. Also *Great Billy*, the *Heaven-Sent Minister*, *Old Billy*, the *Pilot that Weathered the Storm* and the *Spotless Minister*.

BOUNCER Phillip Jennings (1953–   ), one of the three British 'monster killers' of the Boarded Barn mansion near Congleton, Cheshire (1979); sentenced to life imprisonment.

- See *Puss* and *Spiderman*.

BOUNDING BASQUE, THE Jean Borotra (1898–   ), French lawn tennis player who won the Wimbledon men's singles title first in 1924. He always wore a Basque beret, and had a lively style beloved by British crowds.

BOW, THE See the *Fiddle and the Bow*, below.

BOWED DAVIE David Ritchie (*circa* 1740–1816), a deformed brush-maker of Peebleshire, Scotland who was the prototype of Scott's Black Dwarf in *Tales of My Landlord* (1819). Scott met him in 1797.

BOWRAL BOY, THE Sir Donald (Don) George Bradman (1908–   ), New South Wales and Australian cricketer who first played the game for the Bowral school team. He holds the record for thirty-seven double centuries. Also *Braddles* and the *Don*.

BOY

i) Lieutenant-General Sir Frederick Arthur Montague Browning (1896–1965), Deputy Commander, 1st Allied Airborne Army (1944).

ii) Andrew Charlton (1908–   ), Australian swimmer who won five Olympic medals and created five new world records between 1923 and 1928.

iii) David (Dave) Green (1953–   ), British welterweight and light

middleweight boxing champion and later a trainer. Also the *Fen Tiger*.

iv) David (Dave) McAuley (1962–   ), Irish-born British featherweight boxing champion. In 1989 he won the IBF world flyweight title by outpointing Duke McKenzie (1963–   ).

BOY BACCALAUR, THE Thomas Wolsey (*circa* 1475–1530), later Cardinal Wolsey who graduated as a BA at fifteen (1490). Also the *Butcher's Dog* and *Mastiff Cur*.

- Baccalaur = *baccalarius* = a bachelor; now obsolete.

BOY BACHELOR, THE William Wotton, Doctor of Divinity (1666–1726), critic and historian, a BA at thirteen.

BOYCS or BOYKS Geoffrey William Boycott (1940–   ), Yorkshire and England cricketer who for a long time held the record of scoring more runs in Test Matches than any other man, 8,114 out of a total of 48,000. He made 150 centuries.

- See the *Guru of Indian Batsmen*.

BOY GENERAL, THE General G.A. Custer, *Autie*, a Brigadier-General of volunteers at twenty-four.

BOY PREACHER, THE Charles Hadden Spurgeon (1834–92), famous nonconformist divine at the Tabernacle, Newton Causeway, London. He began drawing crowds to his sermons when he was seventeen years old. Also *Brimstone Spurgeon*.

BOY VC, THE John Travers Cornwell (1900–16). He won the medal after he had stayed and died with his guns on the blazing HMS *Chester*, hit by German light cruisers at Jutland (1916).

BOZ

i) Augustus Dickens (1827–died ? in America), brother of Charles (the *Inimitable*), so called after Moses in *The Vicar of Wakefield* which, says Forster, 'being facetiously pronounced through the nose became Boses', and so Boz. Taken by Dickens as a pseudonym.

ii) William Royce Scaggs (1944), American rock singer and musician.

BOZO

i) Sterling Belmont Bose (1906–58),

American jazz trumpeter.

ii) Edward Abraham Miller (1909–) of California, the world's champion eater. He once ate twenty-six chickens at one sitting (1963).

BOZZY See *Bosy*.

BRAB John Theodore Cuthbert Moore-Brabazon, 1st Baron Brabazon of Tara (1884–1964), the first man to hold a pilot's licence from the Royal Aero Club (1910). He won the *Daily Mail* prize (1909) for the British circular mile flight.

BRACK Field-Marshal Sir Henry Brackenbury, 1st Baron Grenfell (1837–1914), Director of Military Intelligence (1890) and Director-General of Ordnance (1899–1904). He had been one of Wolseley's Ashanti Ring.

- The Ashanti Ring was a group of officers chosen by Wolseley (*Our Only General*) for their courage and ingenuity to serve in the Ashanti campaign (1873–4).

BRADDLES Sir Donald Bradman, the *Bowral Boy*.

BRAINBOX Lord George Philip Nicholas Windsor, Earl of St Andrews (1902–), son of the Duke of Kent (1935–). so called by his cousins. Also *Stan*.

BRAINS OF THE CONFEDERACY, THE Senator J.P. Benjamin, the *Beaconsfield of the Confederacy*.

BRANDY NAN Queen Anne (1665–1714); so called by Londoners (early 18th century). She was said to have had a fondness for spirits. Of her statue at St Paul's, they claimed it showed her with her back to the church and her face to the gin-shops. Also *Mrs Bull* and *Mrs Morley*.

BRAS CROCHÉ, LE John McDonald of Garth (?1774–1860), Scottish-born trader with the Canadian North-West Company. He had a withered arm.

BRAT, THE John McEnroe (1959–), American tennis champion who three times won the men's singles title at Wimbledon (1981, 1983, 1984). He accumulated a great number of nicknames because of his conduct on court, including the *Incredible Sulk*, *Junior*, *King Sneer*, the *Merchant of Menace*, *Potato Head*, the *Prince of Petulance*, *Rude Dude* and the *Superbrat*.

BRAVE BROKE Rear-Admiral Sir Philip Bowes Vere Broke (1776–1841), commander of HMS *Shannon* in the action with the American warship *Chesapeake* (1813). After a broadside, he led his men aboard and captured her.

BRAVE JERSEY MUSE, THE William Prynne (1600–69), Parliamentarian and Puritan who ran foul of the Star Chamber. He lost both ears and was branded S.L. (seditious liar). He was sent to Jersey, where he wrote against Popery; so called by Cowley (the *English Pindar*). Also the *Cato of His Age*, *Marginal Prynne*, *Voluminous Prynne* and *William the Conqueror*.

- The Star Chamber was a court which began operations in the 15th century and tended to deal tyrannically with those 'offences' for which normal laws had no provision. It was abolished in 1641.

BRAVO or BRAYVO HICKS Newton Tree Hicks (1811–73), British actor.

- 'Bravo' came into England in the early 18th century from the Italian *brave*, fine or accomplished.

BRAVO ROUSE Thomas Rouse (1784–1852), manager of The Grecian Saloon in the City Road, London. It was part of The Eagle tavern, and Rouse opened it (1832) for concerts of music and for dancing and small dramas, the seeds of the 19th-century music-halls. The catch-phrase 'Bravo Rouse' became popular all over London.

- 'The Eagle' was made famous by the song *Pop Goes the Weasel*. Rouse owned a brickfield on which it was built. See the *Publican*.

BRAZEN BOATSWAIN, THE Richard Rigby, *Bloomsbury Dick* who made a fortune in the South Sea Bubble (1720). Rigby was 'the brazen boatswain of the crew', i.e. the Bloomsbury Gang. He was a man of brazen audacity.

- A boatswain summoned men to duty with a pipe (a whistle).

BRAZEN BULLY, THE Sir James Lowther, 1st Earl of Lonsdale (1st creation) (1736–1802). He exercised enormous power in the House of Commons, where his nominees for nine seats were called 'Sir James's Ninepins'; so called by Wolcot (*Peter Pindar*). Also *Farthing James*, *Lord Seventy-Four* and *Wicked Jimmy*.

BRAZEN WALL AGAINST POPERY, THE Thomas Taylor (1576–1633), a Puritan preacher. Also the *Illuminated Doctor*.

- The allusion is to a passage from Horace (*Epistolae*): 'Let this be thy brazen wall of defence.'

BRAZILIAN BOMBSHELL, THE Carmen Miranda (1913–55), American film star who was born in Portugal, but played Brazilian roles. Her name was Maria de Carmo Miranda de Cunha.

BREADFRUIT BLIGH Admiral William Bligh (1754–1817). He discovered breadfruit on his voyage as sailing master in HMS *Resolution* (1772–4), and was sent as captain of HMS *Bounty* to introduce the fruit to the West Indies, but mutiny (1789) broke out to prevent it.

BREAKER OF ROCKS, THE Sir Henry Morton Stanley (1841–1904), Welsh-born American journalist and explorer who found David Livingstone (1813–73) and looked for the source of the Nile; so called (*Bula Mutari*) by East Africans who went with him; because of his thrusting methods of exploration.

BRECHIN POET, THE Alexander Laing (1787–1857), Scottish poet of *Wayside Flowers*. He had been a herd-boy and pedlar.

- Brechin is in Angus, Scotland.

BREECHES MARTYR, THE William O'Brien (1852–1928), Irish MP who with several others was imprisoned (1889) for incitement to revolt; and refused to wear prison garb.

BREEZY BILL William Terriss (1847–97), whose real name was William C.L. Lewin, a popular actor who appeared with Sir Henry Irving (1838–1905) and Ellen Terry (1847–1928). He was stabbed to death by a madman as he was entering the Adelphi Theatre, London. The murderer was Richard Prince, whose real name was Richard Archer, an actor known as *Mad Archer*.

BRENDA Queen Elizabeth II (1926–   ); nickname given by the magazine *Private Eye* who refers to the Queen and Prince Margaret as 'Brenda and Yvonne'. Also *Cabbage*, *Lilibet*, *Missus Queen*, *Queenie*, *Sausage and the Sov*.

- See *Princess Yvonne*.

BREWER, THE Oliver Cromwell, the *Almighty Nose*; so called by the royalists because he was said to have once helped his widowed mother to run a brewery.

BRIAREUS OF THE KING'S BENCH, THE James Scarlett, 1st Baron Abinger (1769–1844), English judge, who had been an MP and Attorney-General (1827). He was dictatorial and partial; so called by Maginn (the *Adjutant*). Also *Ex-Officio Jemmy*.

- Briareus was a hundred-handed giant of Greek mythology who helped the Olympians against the Titans. Shakespeare referred to him as 'many hands and no use', (*Troilus and Cressida*, i.2).

BRICKLAYER, THE Ben Jonson (*circa* 1573–1637), English dramatist whose stepfather was a master bricklayer. After leaving Westminster School, Jonson worked at that trade until he became a soldier; so called by his contemporaries. Also the *English Horace*, *Father Ben*, the *Father of Poets*, *Honest Ben*, the *Horace of England*, the *Juvenal of English Drama*, *Rare Ben Jonson* and the *Virgil of Dramatic Poets*.

BRICKY Sir Winston Leonard Spencer Churchill (1874–1965), WSC, British Prime Minister in war-time (1940–5) and in 1951–5, whose hobbies included bricklaying. Also *Ratcatcher Churchill* and *Winnie*.

BRIDES IN THE BATH KILLER, THE George Joseph Smith (1872–1915) who married women for their money and then drowned them in a bath. He was hanged.

BRIMSTONE SPURGEON Charles Haddon Spurgeon, the *Boy Preacher*. He constantly threatened the torments of hell to his congregations.

BRING 'EM BACK ALIVE BUCK Frank Buck (1888–1950), American explorer and big-game hunter, who brought wild animals from Africa for zoos; title of a film (1932).

BRISTOL BOY, THE Thomas Chatterton (1752–70), poet born in Bristol. Also the *Marvellous Boy*.

BRISTOL BULL, THE William (Bill) Neate (fl. 1820s), pugilist who beat Tom Hickman (the *Gas Man*) in the 18th round of a bout at Hungerford, Berkshire, December 1821.
- 'Neat' is an Old English word for an ox or a bullock.

BRISTOL MILKWOMAN, THE Anne Yearsley (1756–1806), Bristol poetess; pseudonym 'Lactilla'.
- *Lac* = Latin for 'milk', e.g. *Via Lactea* is the Milky Way, 'lactation' means suckling.

BRITAIN'S AMBASSADOR OF MUSIC Sir Malcolm Sargent (1895–1967), conductor of the BBC Symphony Orchestra, who travelled round the world. Also *Flash Harry*.

BRITAIN'S JOSIAH Charles I, the *Ahab of the Nation*; so called in royalist pamphlets.
- Josiah, 'the ideal king' of Judah, was killed in battle (2 Chronicles xxxv, 22–24). It was seen as the end of Judah's prosperity.

BRITAIN'S PUBLIC ENEMY NO 1 Walter Probyn, *Angel Face*.

BRITISH AMAZON, THE Mary Anne Talbot (1776–1808) who served as a drummerboy in Flanders (1792) and as a powdermonkey in HMS *Brunswick*. She was wounded in the battle of the Glorious First of June (1794), and her sex was discovered. She was rumoured to have been an illegitimate daughter of Earl Talbot.
- William, Earl Talbot (created 1761), Lord Steward to the Royal Household of George III (the *Button Maker*) was a rough diamond, proud of his strength and friend and patron of prize-fighters.

BRITISH ARISTIDES, THE Andrew Marvell (1621–78), poet and firm opponent of Charles II (the *Blackbird*). He refused all offers of advancement or bribes.
- Cf the *English Aristides*. Aristides (died *circa* 468 BC), called the Just,

was an Athenian of strict impartiality.

BRITISH BAYARD, THE Sir Philip Sidney (1554–86), poet, statesman and soldier, a man of great courage and courtesy. He died after the siege of Zutphen, Holland. Also the *English Petrarch*, the *Flower of Chivalry*, the *Illustrious Philip*, the *Marcellus of the English Nation*, the *Miracle of Our Age*, the *Phoenix of the World* and the *Zutphen Hero*.
- See the *Bayard of the Confederate Army*.

BRITISH CASSIUS, THE Algernon Sidney (1622–83), politician, son of the 2nd Earl of Leicester (1595–1677). He espoused the Parliamentary cause in the English Civil War. At the time of the Rye House Plot he was beheaded for high treason; so called by James Thomson (1700–48) in *The Seasons* (1726–30).
- The Rye House Plot (1683) was a conspiracy to assassinate Charles II (the *Blackbird*) and his brother James. The plotters met in Rye House Farm, Hertfordshire. See the *Plotter*.
- Gaius Cassius Longinus was a principal in the plot to assassinate Julius Caesar (44 BC).

BRITISH CICERO, THE William Pitt, Earl of Chatham, *Aeolus*.
- Marcus Tullius Cicero (106–43 BC) was an outstanding orator, philosopher and statesman.

BRITISH CUVIER, THE Sir Richard Owen (1804–92), biologist who following Linnaeus was a pioneer in precise anatomical nomenclature, and made a special study of extinct animals.
- G.L.C. Cuvier (1769–1832) was a distinguished French naturalist.

BRITISH GIANT, THE Henry Blacker (born 1724) of Cuckfield, Sussex, who was 7 ft 4 in tall.
- Cf the *Young English Giant*.

BRITISH HOMER, THE
i) Geoffrey Chaucer (*circa* 1340–1400), poet of *The Canterbury Tales*. Also the *English Ennius*, the *Father of English Poetry*, the *Flower of Poets*, the *Morning Star of Song*, *Tityrus* and the *Well of English Undefiled*.

ii) John Milton, the **Blind Poet**.

- Homer, the epic poet of Greece, was said to have lived at the time of the Trojan War (*circa* 1200 BC) and to have been blind – although details are disputed.

BRITISH JEREMIAH, THE Gildas or Gildus (516–70), Celtic monk, historian and author of *Lamentations over the Destruction of Britain;* so called by Edward Gibbon (1737–94). Also **Sapiens**, the **Wise** and the **Wisest of Bretons**.

- Jeremiah (fl. 626–612 BC), prophet who foresaw the destruction of Jerusalem.

BRITISH JUVENAL, THE Charles Churchill (1731–64), satirical poet, wrote *The Rosciad* (1761). Also the **Clumsy Curate of Clapham**.

- Cf the **English Juvenal**. Decimus Junius Juvenalis (fl. 127), of whose personal life little is known, was the greatest of Roman satirists.

BRITISH MARTIAL, THE John Owen (circa 1560–1662), Welsh author of several volumes of Latin epigrams. Also the **Epigrammatist**.

- Marcus Valerius Martialis (43–102), Roman epigrammatist.

BRITISH PALLAS, THE The Duke of Marlborough, **Anne's Great Captain**.

- Pallas, an Attic hero who in Greek legends opposed with his fifty sons Aegeus, king of Athens.

BRITISH PAUSANIAS, THE or THE PAUSANIAS OF BRITAIN William Camden (1551–1623), antiquary who published *Britannia* (1586). He wrote in Latin. Also the **British Pliny**, the **British Strabo**, the **Nurse of Antiquity**, **Schoolmaster Camden** and the **Varro of Britain**.

- Pausanias (fl. 150) was a Greek traveller and geographer who in his books gave descriptions of historical remains.

BRITISH PINDAR, THE Thomas Gray (1716–71), poet; on his epitaph in Westminster Abbey. Also **Orosmades** and the **Sweet Lyricist of Peterhouse**.

- Pindar (518–438 BC) was a Greek lyric poet.

BRITISH PLINY, THE William Camden, the **British Pausanias**.

- Gaius Plinius Secundus (circa 23–79), called Pliny the Elder, wrote *Naturalis Historia*. He perished in the eruption at Pompeii, which he had visited out of scientific curiosity.

BRITISH POUSSIN, THE Richard Cooper (*circa* 1730–1820), painter and engraver.

- Nicolas Poussin (1594–1664) was a French painter whose work had a lasting effect on painting.

BRITISH PUSSYFOOT, THE Sir Wilfred Lawson (1829–1906), teetotaller and temperance advocate.

- See **Pussyfoot**.

BRITISH ROSCIUS, THE

i) Thomas Betterton (1635–1710), actor, a great figure on the Restoration stage, highly regarded by Charles II (the **Blackbird**) and praised by Pepys (the **Father of Black-Letter Lore**). Pope (the **Bard of Twickenham**), Steele (**Little Dicky**) and Cibber (**King Coll**). Also **Roscius Britannicus**.

ii) David Garrick, **Atlas**. Fanny Burney (the **Old Lady**) records that Garrick used the term about himself in fun (see the **Great Roscius**).

- See the **African Roscius** and cf the **English Roscius**.

BRITISH SAMSON, THE Thomas Topham (1710–53), son of a London carpenter. He lifted (1741) two hogsheads of water (1836 lb) before a crowd. Also the **English Milo**.

- Samson was a Nazarite of great strength (Judges xiv–xvi).

BRITISH SOCRATES, THE See Francis Bacon, the **Father of Inductive Philosophy**.

BRITISH SOLOMON, THE

i) Henry VII (1457–1509), who tried to cut out bribery and corruption and by marriage united the warring houses of York and Lancaster. Also **Solomon the Second**.

- See the **Rose of York**. Solomon (*circa* 986–*circa* 937 BC) king of the Hebrews (after *circa* 972), was given wisdom by God (1 Kings iii, 12).

ii) James I (1566–1625). Also the *English Solomon*, the *Learned Fool*, the *Scottish Heliogabalus*, the *Scottish Solomon*, the *Solomon of England*, *Solomon the Second* and the *Wisest Fool in Christendom*. Some of these could have been half in jest.

BRITISH STRABO, THE William Camden, the *British Pausanias*.

- Strabo (*circa* 54 BC–21 AD) was a Greek historian and geographer.

BRITISH ST STEPHEN, THE St Alban (died *circa* 301), the first British Christian martyr, whose death is described by the Venerable Bede (the *Father of English History*).

- St Stephen was the first Christian martyr (died circa 35: Acts vii, 59–60).

BRITISH VARRO, THE Thomas Tusser (*circa* 1524–80), poet who wrote *Hundreth good pointes of husbandrie* (1557); so called by the poet Thomas Watson (circa 1557–92).

- Marcus Terentius Varro (116–27 BC) wrote, among other works, *Rerum rusticarum libri* (37 BC); cf the *Varro of Britain*.

BROADWAY JOE Joe Willie Namath (1943–   ) American college and professional football player; outstanding quarterback for the New York Jets of the American Football League (fl. 1960s); because he leads a 'swinging life'.

BROADWAY VITAS Vitas Gerulaitis (1954–   ), American tennis player who loves New York night life. Also the *Lithuanian Lion*.

BROCKTON BLOCKBUSTER or BOMBER, THE Rocco Francis Marchegiano, otherwise *Rocky* Marciano (1923–69), who was born at Brockton, Massachusetts. He was heavyweight champion of the world from 1952 until he retired unbeaten (1956). He was killed in a plane crash. Also the *Rock*.

BROKEN HAND Thomas Fitzpatrick (*circa* 1799–1845), Irish-born guide in the American West. He organized the first emigrant trains to California and Oregon; so called by Indians. He lost two fingers when a rifle burst.

BRONCHO BILLY Gilbert M. Anderson (1883–1971), whose real name was Max Aronson, first Western film-star in Hollywood, e.g. *The Great Train Robbery* (1903).

BRONTE Edward W. Nelson (1883– ?), marine biologist with Scott's Antarctic expedition (1910–13). He had many nicknames, including *Marie*.

- The Duke of Brontë (Sicily) was one of Nelson's titles.

BRONX BULL, THE Jacob (Jake) La Motta (1921–   ), American middleweight boxing champion (1949–51). He lost the world title to *Sugar Ray* Robinson (1951); sometimes 'The Raging Bull'.

BROOKHAM Air Chief Marshal Sir Robert Brooke-Popham (1878–1953), who influenced the formation of the RAF.

BROST BELY Henry de Lacy, 3rd Earl of Lincoln (?1249–1311), Regent of England in the absence of Edward II (*Carnarvon*); so called by Piers Gaveston, Earl of Cornwall (died 1312). It means 'burst belly'.

- 'Brosten' is still northern dialect for 'burst'.

BROTHER JONATHAN Jonathan Trumbull (1710–85), Chief Justice of Connecticut; a nickname given to him by Washington (the *American Cincinnatus*), who used to seek his advice. Whenever he had a problem he would say 'We must consult Brother Jonathan.' It came later to mean all Americans, but not every scholar accepts the connection with Trumbell.

BROWN, THE Robert Mackay (1714–71), Gaelic poet; from the colour of his hair.

BROWN BOMBER, THE Joe Louis (1914–81), whose real name was Joseph Louis Barrow, world heavyweight boxing champion (1937–49). He defended his title 25 times.

BROWN DEMON, THE Elizabeth Hitchener, a school-teacher of Hurstpierpoint, Sussex, friend of Shelley (*Ariel*), to whom she wrote for a year; so called by Shelley to his wife Harriet Westbrook.

BROWNIE

i) Walter Brown McGhee (1914–   ), American jazz guitarist.

ii) Bernard Carslake (1886–1941), Australian jockey who had six victories in British classic horseracing, but never won the Derby. He was dark-complexioned.

BROWN SUGAR Lucille Armstrong (died 1984); so called by her husband, Louis (*Dippermouth*).

BROWN WILLIAM William Christian (1608–63), *Illiam Dhone*, Manx politician who negotiated with Parliamentary forces and eventually became Governor of the island (1656). He was shot for treachery to the Lord of the Isle (the Earl of Derby), whose Receiver-General he had been.

BRUCE, THE Robert I, King of Scotland (1274–1329), son of Robert de Bruce, the 7th descendant of Robert de Brus, a follower of William I (the *Bastard*). He won a great victory at Bannockburn (1314) which confirmed his position as king (1306). He was formerly Earl of Carrick. Also *Robert the Liberator*.

BRUMMAGEM JOE Joseph Chamberlain, *Artful Joe*. He was closely associated with Birmingham and was its mayor and MP.

- 'Brummagem' is the local pronunciation of 'Birmingham'.

BRUMMAGEM JOHNSON, THE Dr Samuel Parr, the *Birmingham Doctor*, who wrote the Latin epitaph for Johnson (*Blinking Sam*) for St Paul's Cathedral; so called by *Blackwood's Magazine* (1819).

BRUTE, EL Charles Bronson (1921–), American 'tough guy' film actor; so called in Europe. His real surname is Buchinski.

BRUTUS John Felton (circa 1595–1629), assassin of the Duke of Buckingham (*Steenie*) (1628). D'Israeli states 'Felton, the assassin of the Duke of Buckingham by the growing republican party, was hailed as Brutus . . .' Also *Honest Jack* and *Little David*.

- Marcus Junius Brutus (circa 85–42 BC) took part in the assassination of Julius Caesar (44 BC).

BRUTUS OF OUR REPUBLIC, THE Sir Arthur Hesilrige, Haselrigge or Haselrig (died 1661), supporter of Cromwell (the *Almighty Nose*) and prosecutor of royalist sympathizers. Also *Fidus Achates*.

BRYLCREEM BOY, THE Denis Charles Scott Compton (1918–), cricketer for Middlesex and England and footballer for Arsenal and England, who was shown in advertisements displaying the sleek hairstyle promoted by that product. Also *Compo*.

BUBBA Thomas (Tommy) Facenda (1939–), American rock singer and dancer.

BUBBLE AND SQUEAK

i) Sir Charles Watkin Williams-Wynne (or Wynn), MP, 5th baronet (1772–1840), centre of a famous parliamentary case when he inherited from his father the stewardship of HM Lordship and Manor of Bromfield and Yale, and so was disqualified from membership of the House of Commons, which he contested. He was so called by James Gillray (1757–1815) in a cartoon because of his peculiar voice. When Wynne was proposed as Speaker of the House (1812) Canning (*Aeolus*) said he would be afraid of calling him 'Mr Squeaker'.

ii) Thomas Sheridan (1687–1738), Irish scholar and grandfather of the dramatist Richard Brinsley Sheridan (*Sherry*). Thomas was also nicknamed *Sherry*.

BUBBLES Patricia (Pat), Viscountess Rothermere (1935–), socialite, nickname given to her by the magazine *Private Eye* because of her love of parties.

BUBBLE-GUM KID, THE Sean O'Grady (1959–), American lightweight boxer from Oklahoma. He chews bubble-gum.

BUCK

i) James Buchanan Duke (1856–1925), American tobacco millionaire and father of the *Richest Girl in the World*; from 'Buchanan'.

ii) *Beau* Brummell's nickname at Eton.

iii) Wilbur Clayton (1911–), American jazz trumpeter and arranger.

iv) Ivan Marvin Barrow (died 1933), a thief, and brother of Clyde Barrow (the *Texas Rattlesnake*) of 'Bonnie and Clyde' fame. He worked with the Barrow gang.

v) A Nebraska cowboy named Taylor, broncho-buster and steer-wrestler in *Buffalo Bill's* Wild West Show which visited London in 1887 and gave that nickname to all British Taylors ever since. His first name does not seem to have been recorded. Also *King of the Cowboys.*

BUCKHORSE John Smith (fl. 1732–46), British pugilist. The word 'buckhorse' became slang for 'a smart blow or box on the ears', say Farmer and Henley, 'because Smith would, for a small sum, allow anyone to strike him with the utmost force on the side of the face'.

BUCKINGHAMSHIRE DRAGON, THE George Nugent Grenville, Baron Nugent (1788–1851), British statesman. He was the son of the Marquis of Buckingham (1753–1813); so called by Canning (*Aeolus*) and *Noctes Ambrosianae.*

BUCK JONES Charles Gebhard (1889–1942), Wild West show star who died in a fire while heroically rescuing people at the Cocoanut Grove, Boston, Massachusetts.

BUCKSHOT
i) William Edward Forster (1818–86), Liberal statesman. As Chief Secretary for Ireland (1880–2), he was accused of ordering the police to use buckshot when firing at crowds.
ii) Andrew L. Roberts (died 1876), cowboy killed by *Billy the Kid.*

BUCKSHOT BILL ROBERTS Jesse Andrews (died 1878), Texas Ranger whose left arm was maimed by a buckshot wound.

BUCKSKIN Frank Leslie (?1842–?1924), Western pioneer who always wore buckskins.

BUCKY Captain William Owen O'Neill (1860–98), commander of 'A' Troop of the Rough Riders, killed leading his men at the battle of San Juan Hill, Cuba. He was the central figure on an American postage stamp (1948).
• The Rough Riders were a volunteer cavalry unit raised by Theodore Roosevelt (the *Cowboy President*).

BUD
i) Marvin H. Ward (1913–1967),

American amateur golf champion (1939 and 1941).
ii) William Abbott (1895–1974), American comedian, partner in the Abbott and Costello cross-talk vaudeville act, and in their comedy films.

BUDDHA OF THE WEST, THE Ralph Waldo Emerson, the *American Montaigne*; so called by Oliver Wendell Holmes (1809–94).

BUDDY
i) Charles Bolden (1870–1931), American jazz trumpeter who started jazz in New Orleans (1880s), called by *Jelly Roll* Morton 'the blowingest man since Gabriel'. He led Bolden's Ragtime Band (1890s–1900s).
ii) Barnard Rich (1917–87), once drummer in Harry James's band.
iii) Charles Rogers, *America's Boy Friend.*
iv) Narcisse Christian (1895–1958), American jazz musician on banjo and piano.
v) Leonard Hackett (1924–), American actor and comedian.
vi) George Gard (1895–1950) who used the surname de Sylva; American lyricist and librettist, especially for George White's *Scandals.*
vii) Charles Hardin Holley (1936–59). He changed his surname to 'Holly'; founder with the Crickets (1950s) of rock and roll music which inspired the Beatles and the Rolling Stones; killed in a plane crash.
viii) Jacob Henry Baer (1915–), American boxer, brother to *Madcap Maxie.* He lost to Joe Louis (the *Brown Bomber*) for the heavyweight championship of the world (1941).
ix) Christian Rudolf Ebsen (1908–), American actor and dancer, latterly famous as a TV star.

BUDGE Canon John d'Ewes Evelyn Firth (1900–57), Master of the Temple
• The Temple, London, named after Solomon's Temple in Jerusalem, was founded by the Knights Templar at an unknown date, but Richard de Hastings was Master of the Temple in 1135. The Master is now the preacher

at Temple Church. The Temple has been occupied by lawyers since the 14th century.

BUDGET General Sir Henry Charles Loyd (1891–1973), Colonel of the Coldstream Guards, who commanded a division in France (1939–40).

BUFFALO BILL

i) William Frederick Cody (1846–1917), American frontier scout and Indian fighter who later organized a famous Wild West show (1883); from his job of slaughtering buffalo (bison) for men working on the Canadian-Pacific Railway. In eighteen months he killed 4,280; so called by Ned Buntline (Edward Zane Carroll Judson: 1823–86), dime novelist. The people of New York turned it into 'Bison William'. Also *Long Hair* or *Long Yellow Hair*.

ii) William Brooks (fl. 1870s), Indian scout in the American West, buffalo hunter, stagecoach driver and lawman in Dodge City, Kansas.

iii) William Comstock (fl. 1860s–1870s), Indian scout on the American frontier.

iv) William (Billy) Casper (1931–), American PGA Player of the Year three times and US Open golf champion twice; so called after he had been given a diet of buffalo meat to cure an allergy.

BUFFALO CHIPS WHITE An otherwise anonymous US cavalry scout (died 1876) and friend of *Buffalo Bill* (i). He was killed in a raid by US cavalry on one of *Crazy Horse's* villages at Slim Buttes, South Dakota.

BUGBEAR, THE William Wyndham Grenville, 1st Baron Grenville (1759–1834), British Prime Minister (1806–7), Foreign Secretary (1791–1801). He was strong-willed and opinionated; nickname *circa* 1787.

BUGS George Moran (1893–1947), American bootlegger and gangster with a wild temper. Also the *Shooting Fool*.

BUGSY Benjamin Siegal (1906–47), American racketeer and 'founder' of Las Vegas.

BULL

i) Colonel Arthur Simons (1918–79) of the American Rangers (Green Berets)

who led fourteen men into Iran (1979) to rescue two Americans from prison.

• From a game played by the Rangers called 'the Bull Pen', to find how many men it took to throw one man out of a six-foot pit. It took about four to eject Simons.

ii) Fleet Admiral William Frederick Halsey (1882–1959), American commander in the Pacific (World War II).

iii) Edward (Ed.) Asner (1926–), American film and television star, famous as 'Lou Grant'.

iv) John Bramlett (1941–), American footballer; so called after he ran through a wooden fence.

v) J.A. Cowrie (1912–), fast bowler for New Zealand.

vi) Harry Houston Alexander (1905–), fast bowler for Victoria and Australia. He played in the 1932–3 Tests against England.

BULL, THE

i) Field-Marshal Edmund Henry Hyndman, 1st Viscount Allenby (1861–1936), commander of British forces in Palestine (World War I); from his build, his voice and his bluntness.

ii) Brigadier-General Edwin Vose Sumner (1797–1863), American Civil War commander of the right wing of the Union army at Fredericksburg (1862); from his manner and the fact that a musket-ball did little to damage his skull. Also the *Bull of the Woods*.

iii) Colonel the Honorable H. Townshend (fl. early 19th century) of the Grenadier Guards from his blunt manner and lack of tact, as well as his fatness from over-eating.

iv) Steven (Steve) Denton (1956–), American ace tennis player; from the Bullhorns, Texas University football team of which he was a member.

BULLDOG OF ALL CIRCUMNAVIGATORS, THE Admiral George, Baron Anson (1697–1762). He commanded a squadron which sailed round the world (1741–4), during which voyage he showed unbreakable courage and perseverance; so called by Dibdin (the *Bard of the British Navy*). Also the *Father of the Royal Navy*).

• See the *Jonah of the Wager*.

BULLER OF BRAZENOSE, THE John Hughes (1677–1720) of Oriel College, Oxford University; so called in *Noctes Ambrosianae*.

• A buller is a college 'bulldog', one of those 'police' who accompany the Proctor on his tours of law-enforcement. 'Brazenose' was college slang for an impudent person in the 18th century. John Hughes (1790–1857) used it as a pseudonym.

BULL OF BROOKLYN, THE Edward J. Reilly (fl. 1920s–1930s), a flamboyant American lawyer who because of his unsuccessful defence of many alleged murderers was also nicknamed *Death-House Reilly*. His clients included Bruno Hauptmann, convicted (unjustly, many believe, in 1935) of the killing of *Buster* Lindbergh.

BULLET BILL William Dudley, American half-back for Virginia (1938–42), as well as for the Pittsburgh Steelers, Detroit Lions and Washington Redskins (1945–53); in the Hall of Fame.

BULL-FACED JONAS Sir William Jones (1631–82), Attorney-General, who conducted the prosecutions in the 'Popish Plot', generated by Titus Oates (the *Knight of the Post*). He was a rough, disagreeable man. Also *Jock Presbyter*.

• See the *First Tory* and the *Protestant Martyr*.

BULL OF THE WOODS, THE Brigadier-General E.V. Sumner, the *Bull*.

• 'Bull of the Woods' is equivalent to the English 'Cock of the Walk'.

BULL-RUN RUSSELL Sir William Howard Russell (1821–1907), war correspondent of *The Times;* so called in derision by Americans. They said that at the battle of Bull Run (1861) when Union troops retreated, Russell was the first to fly.

BULL SPEAKER, THE Ralph Amner (died 1664), English bass lay-clerk at Windsor and the Chapel Royal; nickname recorded by John Hilton (1599–1657) in his *Catch that Catch Can* (1652).

BULLY John Egan (1754–1810), Irish lawyer and MP, uncle of Pierce Egan (the *Elder*).

He owned Bully's Acre, three miles from Dublin. He was a fat man and a noted duellist.

BULLY DAWSON A 17th-century ruffian and card-sharper, mentioned by Addison (the *English Atticus*) in *The Spectator:* 'Sir Roger . . . kicked Bully Dawson in a public coffee-house for calling him a youngster'. Also spoken of by Lamb (the *Mitre Courtier*): 'Bully Dawson kicked by half the town and half the town kicked by Bully Dawson.'

BULWARK OF THE STATE, THE Sir Henry Pelham (1696–1754), English Prime Minister (1743–54) and Chancellor of the Exchequer, the first Chief Minister to get the 'feel' of the country and by his management of finance give it a sense of confidence; so called by Francis Fawkes (1720–77) in *A Vernal Ode*.

BULWIG Edward George Earle Bulwer-Lytton, 1st Baron Lytton (1803–73), statesman and novelist. He was Secretary of State for the Colonies (1858–9) and author of *The Last Days of Pompeii* (1834), *Rienzi* (1835) and *The Last of the Barons* (1843); so called by *Fraser's Magazine* (1830).

BUMPS Robert A. Blackwood (1918–), US rock musician; now manages Little Richard (Richard Penniman: 1935–).

BUNCH Nelson Keys (1887–1939), British singer and dancer; title of his biography (1941).

BUNCO KELLY Joseph Kelly (1838–1934), noted abductor of seamen in Portland, Oregon. Born in Liverpool, he was a seaman skilled in shangaing his fellows.

• 'Bunco' is American slang for a swindling scheme.

BUNGALOW BILL William Wiggins (1947–), American friend of Joan Collins (the *Queen of the Soaps*) in 1987.

• He was once a builder.

BUNGO Field-Marshal Julian Hedworth George, 1st Viscount Byng (1862–1935), distinguished for his capture of Vimy Ridge (1917). He was Governor-General of Canada (1921–6).

BUNGY Prince Andrew Albert Christian Edward, Duke of York (1960–), son of

Queen Elizabeth (**Brenda**), so called by the Duchess (**Carrot Top**). Also **H.** and **Randy Andy**.

• Bungy is a nickname in the Royal Navy, usually for a man named William.

BUNK William Gary Johnson (1879–1949), American jazz trumpeter.

BUNKEY BOO General Sir J.M.S. Bunker, Inspector of the Royal Horse Artillery and Royal Field Artillery (World War I).

BUNNY

i) Elizabeth Ryan (1892–1979), American lawn tennis champion who won nineteen Wimbledon titles (1914–34).

ii) Henry Wilfred Austin (1906–   ), British lawn-tennis star.

iii) Rowland Bernard Berigan (1909–42), American jazz trumpeter.

BUNS C.I. Thornton (1850–1929), cricketer for Eton, Cambridge University, Kent and Middlesex.

BUNTER

i) Thomas Alexander, 3rd Baron Hesketh (1950–   ), London socialite and motor-racing fan. He is chubby like the schoolboy magazine's Billy Bunter. Junior Environment Minister (1988–).

ii) Henry Somerset (1952–   ), Marquis of Worcester, heir to the Duke of Beaufort. He is lead singer with a pop group called 'the Business Connection', and a Mayfair estate agent.

BUNTY Mrs Francis Smith (1924–   ), British Ladies golf champion (1949 and 1954).

BUPS Lord Baden-Powell, **Bathing Towel**.

BURGER KING OF JOURNALISM, THE Keith Rupert Murdoch (1931–), Australian millionaire newspaper tycoon and owner of the London *Times*. Also the **Dirty Digger**.

BURGLAR BILL Michael (Mike) Harrison (1956–   ), Rugby Union winger for Wakefield and captain of England; so called after two tries described as 'outrageous' by the *Sunday Times*, scored off interceptions in the 1985 England tour of New Zealand. A Wakefield beer has been named after his nickname.

• Burglar Bill Sikes is a character in Dickens' *Oliver Twist*.

BURKE OF OUR AGE, THE Lord Macaulay, **Babbletongue**; so called in *Noctes Ambrosianae*.

• For Edmund Burke, see the **Dinner Bell**.

BURLINGTON HARRY Henry Flitcroft (1697–1769), British architect of churches. His patron was Richard Boyle, 3rd Earl of Burlington (1695–1753), himself an architect of some achievement.

BURLINGTON HAWKEYE MAN, THE Robert Jones Burdette (1844–1914), American newspaper editor; from his humorous writings for an Iowa journal.

BURLY KING HAL King Henry VIII, **Bluff Hal**.

BURLY KING HARRY King Henry VIII, **Bluff Hal**.

BURRITO Eugene R. Romero (1947–   ), American racing motor-cyclist.

BURROWING DUKE, THE William John Cavendish Bentinck-Scott, 5th Duke of Portland (1800–79). He spent a great deal of his life digging at his home Welbeck Abbey, Nottinghamshire, and its grounds to construct huge underground chambers and tunnels. One corridor was wide enough to hold two carriages side by side.

BUS Emil Mosbacher (1922–   ), American yachtsman, competitor in the America's Cup races.

BUSBY William Berkeley Enos (1895–1976), American dance director and choreographer as 'Busby' Berkeley of many film musicals with spectacular scenic effect. Also the **Wizard of the Chorus Line**.

BUSTER

i) General Sir James Browne (1839–96), British administrator and engineer in India, e.g. the Sind-Pishin railway.

ii) Joseph Francis Keaton (1896–1966), American film star of silent pictures; so called by Houdini (the **Handcuff King**), his godfather, after Keaton had fallen downstairs unhurt when he was six months old. Also the **Great Stone Face**.

iii) Commander Lionel Philip Crabbe, Royal Navy (1910–56), frogman (World War II) who disappeared during a visit of the Russian fleet to Portsmouth.

iv) Christopher Mottram (1955–), British lawn-tennis star.

v) Pauline Marianne Wehde (1866–83), Bavarian giantess who was billed on the London music-halls as the tallest woman of all time, alleged to have been more than 8 ft tall. In fact, she was 7 ft 4 in and weighed more than 25 stone (350 lb). Ware says she was called *Maid Marian* when she came to London (1882) and small boys in Leicester Square used to shout at fat women: ''Ere's a Maid Marian for yer.'

vi) Clarence Crabbe (1907–83), American who played *Tarzan* and Flash Gordon in films (1930s) after success as a swimmer.

vii) William C. Bailey (1902–67), American jazz clarinettist.

viii) Ronald Edwards (1931–), one of the Great Train Robbers (1963). He served nine years of a fifteen-year sentence.

ix) Frank Wortman (1903–70), American gangster.

x) Leo Vincent Brothers (1899–1951), Chicago gangster and murderer.

xi) Charles Lindbergh jnr., kidnapped and murdered at the age of twenty months (1932); so called by his father (*Lindy*).

BUSY SCOTS PARSON, THE Gilbert Burnet (1643–1715), Bishop of Salisbury and historian; so called by his opponents. Also the *English Eusebius* and the *Lying Scot*.

BUTCH

i) Ray Wilkins (1956–), midfield footballer for Manchester United and England.

ii) Jackie Jenkins (1937–), American child film-star, as in *National Velvet* (1944).

BUTCH CASSIDY Robert Leroy Parker (1866–?1937), outlaw of the American West and leader of the Wild Bunch. He had been a butcher, and took the name Cassidy from Mike Cassidy, an outlaw and neighbour of the Parkers, who taught the boy to shoot. It is said that Parker's

grave is somewhere in Nevada, where he died in 1937, and not in South America.

BUTCHER Colonel (later General) Sir Banastre Tarleton (1754–1833), British cavalry leader; so called by the Americans in the War of Independence, following the killing of Colonel Abraham Burford's troops after they had surrendered (1780).

BUTCHER, THE

i) Lord Clifford, the *Black* (iii); so called during the Wars of the Roses (1455–85) when he fought for Henry VI (*Ill-Fated Henry*).

ii) *Bomber* Harris, because of the saturation bombing raids on Germany.

iii) William Alexander Louis Stephen, 12th Duke of Hamilton (1845–95), an enthusiastic sportsman who always wore butcher-blue shirts and ties. One of his horses won the Grand National (1867).

BUTCHER CUMBERLAND The Duke of Cumberland, *Billy*.

BUTCHER OF BROADWAY, THE Alexander Woollcott (1887–1963), American theatre critic. He made savage attacks on shows he did not like. Also the *First Grave Digger*, *Mr Guppy* and *Old Vitriol and Violets*.

BUTCHER OF CULLODEN, THE The Duke of Cumberland, *Billy*.

BUTCHER OF ENGLAND, THE John Tiptoft or Tibetot, Earl of Worcester (?1427–70), for his savagery when Constable of England during the Wars of the Roses (1455–85). He introduced impalement to England. When he was executed he asked the executioner to give him three strokes in honour of the Trinity. Also the *Cruel Judge*.

BUTCHER'S DOG, THE Cardinal Wolsey, the *Boy Baccalaur*; so called by Skelton (the *Vicar of Hell*). Wolsey's father had been a butcher at Ipswich, Suffolk. Emperor Charles V (1500–58) had called Wolsey 'a butcher's cur'.

BUTTERFINGERS Thomas B. Moran (1892–1971), American pickpocket.

BUTTERFLY QUEEN, THE Thelma McQueen (1911–), American negro actress. She had danced in a butterfly ballet and later played Butterfly in *Brown Sugar* (1938). The name was later adapted to 'Butterfly McQueen'.

BUTTERFLY SPY, THE Lord Baden-Powell, ***Bathing Towel***. When he was an intelligence officer in the Boer War (1889–1902) he disguised himself as a butterfly collector to obtain information.

BUTTONED BUSHELL Thomas Bushell (1594–1674), a gentleman in the entourage of Bacon (the ***Father of Inductive Philosophy***), to whom he acted as his secretary. Aubrey says he wore more buttons than usual on his cloak.

BUTTON MAKER, THE George III (1738–1820), one of whose hobbies was using a lathe at Windsor Castle to make buttons. An anonymous cartoon (1770) shows George bargaining with the King of Spain and has the caption: 'The Button Makers adjusting their differences.' Also ***Farmer George***, the ***Farmer King***, ***German Georgie***, ***His Nobs***, the ***Patriot King***, ***Ulysses*** and ***Uncle George***.

BUZZ

i) Colonel (Dr) Edwin Eugene Aldrin (1930–   ), American astronaut who walked on the moon from Apollo XI spacecraft (1969).

ii) Mary Ann Goodbody (1946–75), first woman director of the Royal Shakespearian Company at Stratford-on-Avon, where there is a tree planted in her memory.

BUZZER Reginald E. H. Hadingham (1915–   ), chairman of the All-England Tennis Club (1984–   ), the body that controls Wimbledon.

BYRON OF THE OREGON, THE Joaquin Miller (circa 1841–1913), American poet and newspaper editor. He had been a horse-thief, lawyer, pony express rider and messenger. He always wore cowboy dress. His real name was Cincinnatus Hiner Miller; he called himself 'Joaquin' after he had written a biography of the Mexican bandit Joaquin Murietta.

• For Byron, see ***Baby***.

C

CABBAGE Queen Elizabeth, **Brenda**; so called by the Duke of Edinburgh (**Biggles**).
- Cf **Sausage**.

CACTUS JACK John Nance Garner (1869–1967), Vice President of the United States of America (1933–41); Speaker of the House of Representatives (1931–3). He was a Texas cattle rancher.

CADE, JACK John Mortimer (died 1450), leader of the Peasants' Revolt (1450), hunted down and killed after the rebellion. Cade said his name was Mortimer and he calls himself that in Shakespeare's 2 Henry VI (iv.6): 'Now is Mortimer lord of this city' (i.e. London). Also the **Captain of Kent** and **Jack Amend-All**.
- 'Cade' is an obsolete word for a keg or barrel (in use since at least 1337). Nash (the **English Aretine**) wrote (1599): 'The rebel Jack Cade was the first that devised to put Red Herrings in cades . . . ' A cade contained 600 red herrings (Halliwell).

CAIN OF LITERATURE, THE
i) John Henley (1692–1756), English clergyman. Also **Orator Bronze**, **Orator Henley**, **Orator Humbug** and the **Zany of His Age**.
ii) John Hill (*circa* 1716–75) who, because of a Danish honour, called himself 'Sir John'. He was a botanist, quack doctor, author and editor of *The British Magazine* (1746–50). He had many quarrels with literary men and was accused of plagiarism. Johnson (**Blinking Sam**) politely called him a liar. Also **Doctor Atall**, the **Janus-Faced Critic** and a **Literary Proteus**.

CAIN'S BROTHER William Abell, **Alderman Medium**; so called in contemporary broadsheets.

CAIRO FRED Omar Sharif (1932–), Egyptian-born American film actor. The nickname began when Peter O'Toole (1932–), Irish-born star who appeared with him in *Lawrence of Arabia*, once said 'No one has the name Omar Sharif; you're Fred.' Sharif's real name is Michael (Mike) Shalhoub.

CALAMITY JANE Martha Jane Burke, née Cannary (*circa* 1852–1903). She dressed as a man, was an excellent horsewoman, an outstanding shot and acted as scout in Indian wars. She was given the nickname – possibly because of the calamity she could bring by her gun – by a Captain Egan whose life she saved. In popular fiction, she was said to have married **Wild Bill** Hickok.

CALCULATING BOY, THE
i) Zerah Colburn (1805–40), an American with amazing powers. At the age of seven he gave an exhibition in London (1812) where he raised the number 8 progressively to the 16th power, among other feats, as *The Annual Register* of 20 August of that year reports.
ii) George Parker Bidder (1806–78) whose father, an English stonemason, exhibited him as a phenomenon when he was a boy. At the age of eleven (1818), he mentally divided 468,592,413,563 by 9,076 in less than a minute and gave the correct answer (51,629,838). He became an engineer.

CALCULATOR, THE Jedediah Buxton (1705–72), a farm labourer of Elmton, Derbyshire. He had an astonishing facility of calculation, although he could absorb no other education. His father was a schoolmaster. Jedediah gave a show in London (1754).

CALEDONIAN COMET, THE Scott, the **Ariosto of the North**; so called by J. Taylor in a book of that title (1810).

CALICO JACK Captain John (Jack) Rackham (died 1720), a pirate who married Anne Bonny or Bonney (?1700– ?), the famous woman pirate. Johnson (Defoe): 'Because his Jackets and Drawers were always made of Callico.' He was hanged.

CALIFORNIA GRIZZLY, THE James Jeffries, the *Boilermaker*.

CALIFORNIA JOE Moses Embree Miner (1829–76), army scout, friend of *Wild Bill* Hickok.

CALIFORNIA COMET, THE Maurice McLoughton, American tennis champion (1901–2), the first 'smash' server.

CAM Sihtric or Sigtryggr (fl. 10th century), chief of the Vikings who plundered Kildare (962).

• *Cam* = crooked in Gaelic. See *Gam*.

CAMBRENSIS (Giraldus); Gerald de Barri (*circa* 1146–*circa* 1220), Archdeacon of Brecon, medieval historian and author of *Itinerarium Cambriae*, a book on the topography of Wales. His nickname = 'Gerald the Welshman' (*Cambria* = Latinized *Cymry*).

CAMBRIAN or WELSH SHAKESPEARE, THE Edward Williams (1746–1826), Welsh poet.

CAMBRIDGE RAPIST, THE Peter Cook (1928–   ) who terrorized Cambridge (1974–5) with rapes and attempted rapes. He wore a mask with 'rapist' painted on it. He was gaoled for life (1975).

CANADA BILL William Jones (died 1877), English-born American gambler who worked the Mississippi riverboats. He had emigrated first to Canada.

CANADIAN DISRAELI, THE Sir John Alexander Macdonald (1815–91), first Prime Minister of the Dominion of Canada (1867). He was very much like Disraeli (the *Asian Mystery*) in appearance. Also *Old Tomorrow*.

CANADIAN KIPLING, THE Robert William Service (1874–1958), Canadian poet and novelist whose most popular poem is *The Shooting of Dan McGrew*. Also the *Poet of the Yukon*.

• For Kipling, see the *Bard of Empire*.

CANAL BOY, THE James Abram Garfield (1831–81), 20th President of the United States of America, who had been a hand on a canal barge as a boy. He was assassinated by Charles Guiteau.

CANAL DUKE THE Francis Egerton, 3rd and last Duke of Bridgewater (1736–1803). He financed and planned canals from Worsley to Manchester, the first in England, and from Manchester to Liverpool. Also the *Father of British Inland Navigation*.

CANIS William, 5th Duke of Devonshire (1748–1811). He was ugly, awkward and slouched, but married the beautiful Georgina Spencer (1757–1806) and was apparently cowed into dog-like devotion; family nickname. Also the *Prince of Whigs*.

CANMORE Malcolm III, *Big Head*: in Gaelic *ceann mor*.

CANNIBAL Julius Adderley (1928–75), American jazz saxophonist; later *Cannon Ball*. As a youth he had an insatiable appetite.

CANNIBALISTIC IDIOT, THE James, Earl of Drumlanrig (died 1715), son of the 2nd Duke of Queensberry (the *Union Duke*). The feeble-minded earl once killed and roasted a kitchen hand.

CANNONBALL KID, THE Roscoe Tanner (1951–   ), American Wimbledon-class tennis player. His service was timed at 155 mph.

CAP Adrian Anson (1851–1922), player-manager for the Chicago White Stockings, who led them to win the National Baseball League championship five times (1880–90).

CAPABILITY BROWN Lancelot Brown (1715–83), English landscape gardener, once gardener to George III (the *Button Maker*). He was accustomed to say: 'I can see great capability of improvement here.'

• Cf *Equality Brown* and *Sense Browne*.

CAPTAIN

i) James Whitney (?1660–1690), leader of a gang of English highwaymen. He was hanged. Also the *Jacobite Robber*.

ii) Matthew Webb (1848–83), first man to swim the English Channel (1875). He was drowned trying to swim the rapids of Niagara Falls.

CAPTAIN BARCLAY Robert Barclay Allardice (1799–1845), British officer and a notable walker. He once covered 1000 miles in 1000 hours (1809).

CAPTAIN BATS George Ransley, leader of a gang of ruthless Kentish smugglers in Romney Marsh (1821–26). He was transported to Australia. Bowen says his nickname came from his readiness to employ batmen or armed bullies to protect his runs from the Coast Blockade. 'Bats' were six-foot-long ash poles.

CAPTAIN BLOOD Jack Dyer (1913–   ), a legend in Australian Rules football. A Richmond packman (1941–8), he represented Victoria sixteen times, a controversial tough footballer and a formidable goal-kicker.

CAPTAIN CRACKERS John Leadstone (fl. 17th century), an ex-pirate who retired with his fortune to Sierra Leone, West Africa. He saluted pirate ships arriving there with cannon-fire from his park-like garden.

- 'Cracker' is obsolete slang for a pistol; cf 'barker', which could also mean a cannon.

CAPTAIN HARRY Henry Carter (1749–1829), Cornish smuggler, brother to the *King of Prussia*. He later took up farming and wrote his autobiography.

CAPTAIN JACK John W. Crawford, the *Black Hunter*.

CAPTAIN LIGHTFOOT Michael Martin (1775–1822), American highwayman who started his 'career' in Ireland. He was hanged at Cambridge, Massachusetts.

CAPTAIN MELVILLE Frank McCallum, alias Edward Melville (1822–57), Australian bushranger after he had been transported at the age of fourteen. He died in a cell, possibly murdered.

CAPTAIN MOONLITE Andrew George Scott (1842–80), Australian bushranger who had been a lay reader. He had been born in Ireland and travelled to the Australian gold-diggings before he turned to highway robbery. He was hanged.

CAPTAIN OF KENT, THE John Mortimer, *Jack Cade*.

CAPTAIN OF THE AGE, THE The Duke of Wellington, the *Achilles of England*.

CAPTAIN RAG Edmund Smith (1672–1710), English poet, because of his untidy appearance; so called in *The Gentleman's Magazine* (1780). Also the *Handsome Sloven*.

CAPTAIN SALLY Sally Louisa Tomkins (1833–1916). She founded and ran a hospital for the wounded of the Confederate Army in the American Civil War.

CAPTAIN SHRIMP Miles Standish (*circa* 1584–1656), one of the Pilgrim Fathers, captain of New Plymouth and assistant Governor of the colony; so called by Thomas Morton, a Cavalier who hated him. Standish was a little man. Longfellow wrote a poem about him (1858).

CAPTAIN STERNPOST The 6th Duke of Bolton, *Admiral Sternpost*.

CAPTAIN SWING The nickname of an anonymous rick-burner in Kent (1830–2).

CAPTAIN THUNDERBOLT Frederick Ward (1836–70), Australian bushranger, born in New South Wales. He was shot.

CAPTAIN WHIRLWIND Captain Edward Sterling (1773–1847), acting editor of *The Times* for a short period and its principal leader-writer for many years (*circa* 1812–43); so called by Carlyle (the *Censor of the Age*) in his biography of Edward's son John Sterling (1806–44). Carlyle said 'he thundered through the newspaper, shaking it to pieces'. Also the *Magus of the Times* and the *Thunderer*.

CAP THE KNIFE Caspar Willard Weinberger (1917–   ), American Secretary of State for Defense (1980–7) in the Reagan administration; because of his policies as Budget director (post-1972) to Richard Nixon (*Tricky Dicky*). After his retirement he was awarded an honorary knighthood by Britain (1988) and was nicknamed in America 'Knightcap'.

CAR Charles, 2nd Earl Grey (1764–1845), British Prime Minister (1830–4); so called by his wife, Mary Elizabeth.

CARDS Adrian Karl Quist (1913–   ), Australian tennis player who twice won the Wimbledon doubles title with J.H. Crawford. He is also very fond of bridge.

CARDINAL CARSTAIRS William Carstairs or Carstares (1649–1717), Scottish clergyman who was chaplain to William III (the *Deliverer*). He was an intelligence agent and adviser to the King as well as becoming Moderator of the General Assembly of Scotland and Principal of Edinburgh University.

CARLO KHAN Charles James Fox (1749–1806), British statesman after, it was rumoured, he introduced into Parliament (1783) a Bill affecting India, and that he intended to establish a personal dictatorship there. James Sayers (1748–1823) published a cartoon (1783) of Fox in oriental dress riding an elephant into Leadenhall Street. The Bill sought to have the Commissioners to govern India appointed by Parliament and not by the king. Also the *Last of the Romans*, the *Man of the People* and the *Young Cub*.

CARNARVON Edward II (1284–1327), murdered by Queen Isabella (the *She-Wolf of France*) and Mortimer. He was born in Carnarvon castle the first English Prince of Wales after its conquest (1283).

CARO Lady Caroline Lamb (1785–1828), wife of Lord Melbourne (*Lord M*). She was passionately in love with Byron (whom she called *Baby*). She met him in 1812. Her family nickname. Also *Your Laviship*.

CAROLINA GAME-COCK, THE Brigadier-General Thomas Sumter (1734–1832), handsome, brave, reckless leader of guerrillas against the British in North and South Carolina in the War of Independence. Also the *Gamecock*.

CARRIE RED Caroline, Duchess of Montrose (1809–94), wife of the 4th Duke (1799–1846). She was a racehorse-owner and a familiar figure on racecourses e.g. at Newmarket. She had red hair and used the name *Mr Manton* as a racehorse-owner. Also *Old Six Mile Bottom*.

CARROT TOP Sarah Ferguson (1959–), who married Prince Andrew, Duke of York (*Bungy*) in July 1986. She is the daughter of Major Ronald Ferguson (1931–), an old friend of the Royal Family and polo manager to the Prince of Wales; her school nickname, as she herself said in Australia (1988). She has red hair. Also *Chatterbox One*, *Coppernob*, *Duchess Dolittle*, *Fergie*, *Lollipop* and *Strawberry*.

CASEY Charles Dillon Stangel (1889–1975), American baseball player and manager; in the Hall of Fame for his work with the Brooklyn Dodgers and the New York Yankees.

CASEY JONES John Luther Jones (1864–1900), American railroad hero. He was killed in a crash after having made his fireman jump to safety.

CASH AND CARY Barbara Hutton (see *Poor Little Rich Girl*) and Cary Grant (1904–86); so called in Hollywood after their marriage (1947). Grant's real name was Archibald Leach.

CAT, THE
i) Sir John Catesby (died 1486), one of the followers of Richard III (the *Boar*). The nickname is perpetuated in the couplet:

The ratte, the catte and Lovell, our dogge,
Rule all England under an Hogge,

for which William Collingbourne was executed (1484).

• **See** also the *Dog*, the *Hog* and the *Rat*.

ii) Mathilde-Lucie Carré (1908–) of Fontainebleau; the name by which she was known to British Intelligence (World War II). Captured by the Germans (1941), she became a German agent, and after the war (1949) was sentenced to life imprisonment, but was released in 1954. Also the *Mata Hari of the Second World War*.

iii) Clive Lloyd, *Big C*.

iv) Peter Bonetti (1941–), goalkeeper for Chelsea FC and England; from his agility; now a coach.

CATILINE CROLY The Reverend George Croly (1780–1860), English clergyman, author and poet who wrote a tragedy *Catiline* (1822); so called by *Blackwood's Magazine* (1822). Also the *Reverend Rowley-Powley* and *St Bernard Croly*.

• Catiline (died 62 BC) was an unscrupulous conspirator against the consul Cicero.

CATO OF HIS AGE, THE William Prynne, the *Brave Jersey Muse*.

• **See** the *American Cato*.

CAT'S EYES Wing-Commander John Cunningham (1920–), British night-fighter pilot (World War II) whose successes were so attributed to cloak the use of radar.

CATTLE KATE Ella Watson (1862–89), alias Kate Averill and Kate Maxwell, who used her lovers in the American West to rustle cattle for her. She was lynched.
- See the *King of Cattle Thieves*.

CATTLE KING OF AMERICA, THE John Simpson Chisum (1824–84). He owned vast herds in Texas. He is reputed to have put his brand on between 150,000 and 175,000 calves in 1866–7. Also *King of the Pecos*.

CAUSTIC BAREBONES Thomas Bridges (fl. 1759–75), British playwright and parodist. He first used it (1762) as a pseudonym for his satires.

CAUTIOUS CAL Calvin Coolidge (1872–1933), 30th President of the United States of America (1923–9). His policies were founded on a resolution 'not to weaken future positions'. Also *Honest Cal* and *Silent Cal*.

CAVALIER COLONEL, THE Sir Winston Churchill (1620–88), royalist in the English Civil War, and father of John Churchill, Duke of Marlborough (*Anne's Great Captain*).

CAVALIER POET, THE John Cleveland (1613–58) who conducted the defence of Newark until the King ordered (1646) its surrender. His anger at the Scots for their capture of Charles is expressed in *The Rebel Scot*. He was MP for Cambridge (1640).

CAVE The Rev. Charles Kingsley (1819–75), novelist; school nickname because of his big mouth. Also the *Chartist Parson*.

CELATUS Robert Owen (1771–1858), pioneer of co-operation in industry. His *A New View of Society* (1813) revolutionized employers' ideas. He began a 'silent monitor' system to check work rates. Also the *Father of British Socialism*.
- From the Latin *celare*, to conceal; cf *celator*, one who conceals.

CELEBRATED, THE Colman Ui Neill, joint King of Ireland (598–604).

CELTIC HOMER, THE Ossian or Oisin, a half-legendary warrior and Gaelic poet who is said to have lived in the 3rd century. His 'work' was published by James Macpherson (1736–96), who had read some Gaelic fragments of it, but there is great controversy about its authenticity. Also the *Gaelic Homer*, the *Glory of Scotland* and the *Northern Dante*.

CENSOR-GENERAL OF LITERATURE, THE John Nichols (1745–1826), British editor of *The Gentleman's Magazine*; so called by Wolcot (*Peter Pindar*) because of the authority Nichols held by his sole control of the publication (1792-1821) and his critical works.

CENSOR OF THE AGE, THE
i) Thomas Carlyle (1795–1881), Scottish essayist and historian; from his censorious pronouncements. He scorned the electoral system and wanted a return to benevolent dictatorship. Also the *Chelsea Philosopher* and the *Sage of Chelsea*.
ii) William Gifford, the *Bear Leader*, a bitter and conservative critic.

CENTURY WHITE John White (1590–1645), nonconformist lawyer who wrote *First Century of Scandalous Malignant Priests, made and admitted into Benefices by the Prelates &c.* (1643).

CERBERUS OF LITERATURE, THE Dr Johnson, *Blinking Sam*.
- Cerberus was the dog that guarded the entrance to hell. He is sometimes described as a monster with fifty or a hundred heads, though he is usually only credited with three.

CHAMP James Beauchamp Clark (1850–1921) of Missouri, Speaker of the United States House of Representatives (1911–19); from 'Beauchamp'.

CHAMPAGNE CHARLIE
i) Charles, Viscount Althorp (1964–   ), heir to Earl Spencer (1924–   ) and brother to the Princess of Wales (1961–   ).
ii) Charles Townshend (1725–67), son of the 3rd Viscount Townshend; Chancellor of the Exchequer (1766). He thought the American protest over taxes 'perfect nonsense'; so called by the

Americans, for whom he typified British arrogance. One of his speeches is labelled by British historians 'the champagne speech'. Also the *Weathercock*.

iii) Henry Waysford Charles Plantagenet Rawdon, 4th and last Marquis of Hastings (1841–67), a notorious rake, man-about-town and spendthrift (1850s–1860s). He was ruined by a wrong bet on the 1867 Derby and died bankrupt soon after. In 1864, Hastings eloped with Lady Florence Paget (the *Pocket Venus*). Also the *King of Plungers*, *Mad Harry*, *Plantago* and the *Wicked Marquis*.

iv) George Leybourne (1822–84), whose real name was Joseph Saunders. He first sang *Champagne Charlie* (1866) dressed as a man-about-town and was said always to have drunk champagne. Also *Lion Comique*.

v) Charles Morton (1819–1904) who built an 'empire' of music-halls between 1849 and his death. Also *Father of the Halls* and the *Father of Variety*.

vi) Leslie Cairns (1947–), gaoled (1985) with *Champagne Jimmy* for a massive fraud involving the sale of luxury cars. He went everywhere in a bullet-proof chauffeur-driven Rolls Royce with champagne in the boot.

- The nickname is reputed to have come originally from a wine merchant who was generous with presents of champagne to his friends.

CHAMPAGNE JACK Charles Henry George Howard, 20th Earl of Suffolk and Berkshire (1906–41) with a reputation for firing his revolver to eject corks out of champagne bottles. He was killed trying to defuse a bomb.

CHAMPAGNE JIMMY James Neale (1947–), Colchester solicitor struck off by the Law Society for contravention of its accounting rules. His debts totalled £1,300,000, the biggest ever. He was said always to have had a case of champagne in the boot of his car. In 1985, he was sent to prison for three years for fraud with *Champagne Charlie* (vi).

CHAMPAGNE TONY Anthony David Lema (1934–66), American golfer killed in an air crash. In 1962 he won four tournaments, including the British Open and World Series. He always celebrated his victories with champagne.

CHAMPER W.S. Unwin (fl. 1880s), afterwards the Rev.; British amateur sculling champion.

- University slang for 'champion'.

CHAMPION Jack Dupree (1910–), American barrelhouse pianist, once a boxer.

CHAMPION,THE William Gilbert Grace (1848–1915), cricketer for Gloucestershire and England. He made 54,896 runs in his career, including 126 centuries, and took 2,876 wickets. He scored 1,000 runs in May 1985 and three times more than 300 runs in an innings.

- **See** also the *Three Graces*.

CHAMPION OF HUMAN LAW, THE John Selden (1584–1654), British lawyer, scholar and statesman. His *Titles of Honour* (1614) is still a very respected work; so called by Edward Arber (1836–1912) who showed that Seldon fought for humanity and decency in the application of law. Also the *Monarch of Letters* and the *Walking Library*.

- Edward Arber was killed in a taxi-cab accident in London.

CHAMPION OF WOMEN, THE Hereward the *Wake* (fl. *circa* 1040–75), a Saxon who led an uprising against William I (the *Bastard*) in the Ely area of southern England. It is claimed in legend that he slew a huge white bear, called the Fairy Bear, to save a twelve-year-old girl. Also *England's Darling*, the *Exile* and the *Last of the English*.

- The girl, Alftruda, the king's ward, was in the castle in Northumbria ('or beyond') of Earl Siward, who bore a bear on his crest. Legends of Hereward were recorded within eighty years of his death by Geoffrey Gaimar in his *Gesta Herewardii Saxonis* and *Estorie des Angles* (between 1147 and 1151).

CHANCELLOR OF HUMAN NATURE, THE Edward Hyde, 1st Earl of Clarendon (1609–74), Lord Chancellor and Chief Minister. He was kind, but a greater historian than a statesman; so called by Warburton (the *Colossus of Literature*).

65

CHANCER, THE Patrick Magee (1951–), Irish Republican Army bomber sentenced (1986) to eight terms of life imprisonment with a recommendation that he should serve not less than thirty-five years for having placed a bomb in the Grand Hotel, Brighton (1984) designed to kill the British Cabinet met for the Conservative conference. Five people were killed in what has been called the worst crime since the Guy Fawkes gunpowder plot. Magee was also convicted with four others of plotting a summer bombing campaign in Britain's seaside resorts. The four others were given life sentences. Patrick Magee won his nickname because of the risks he took.

CHARLES THE BAD Charles Haughey (1925–) of the Irish Fianna Fail party (= Soldiers of Destiny). He was Taoiseach (= Premier) 1979–81; 1982 (for a few months) and 1987– . He is a tough politician. Also the *Man They Cannot Sink*.
- Cf *Garrett the Good*.

CHARLES THE FIRST Charles Sackville, 6th Earl of Dorset (1638–1706). He preceded Charles II (the *Blackbird*) as a lover of *Nell of Old Drury*, who gave him the nickname. Also the *Grace of Courts* and the *Muse's Pride*.

CHARLEY'S AUNT Princess Margaret Rose (1930–), sister of Queen Elizabeth II and aunt of Prince Charles (*Fishface*); so called first by the Princess herself. Also *Princess Yvonne*.
- *Charley's Aunt* is the title of a famous stage farce.

CHARLIE B Admiral Charles William de la Poer, 1st Baron Beresford (1846–1919), friend of the Prince of Wales (the *Peacemaker*) until scandal parted them. He was a hero of the Egyptian campaign (1880); so called in the Royal Navy.

CHARLIE OVER THE WATER Charles Edward Stuart, *Bonny Prince Charlie*. In exile in Europe, he was regarded by the Jacobites as king, and toasted with this nickname.

CHARMER OF THE WORLD, THE Scott, the *Ariosto of the North*; so called by Horace Smith (1779–1849), who wrote *Brambletye House* (1826) in imitation of him.

CHARTIST, THE Thomas Cooper (1805– ?), English poet. In *Wise Saws and Modern Instances* he demanded radical changes in government.
- Chartists fought in the 19th century for political reform in Britain.

CHARTIST PARSON or CLERGYMAN, THE Charles Kingsley, *Cave*, whose *Alton Locke* (1850) was on a Chartist theme.

CHAT Robert (Bob) W. Taylor (1941–), wicket-keeper for Derbyshire and England in the England-Australia Tests, 1978–9, he caught 18 and stumped 2. He holds 57 England caps. He is now a public relations officer.

CHATTERBOX ONE The Duchess of York, *Carrot Top*; after she had become the first female royal pilot.

CHATTIE Charlotte Reinage Cooper (1871–1966), British Wimbledon tennis singles champion in 1895, 1896, 1898, 1901 and 1908. Latterly she played under the name of Sterry, her married surname.

CHAY (Sergeant) Charles Blyth (1940–), one of the two first Britons to row across the Atlantic (1966) which he did in a 20-foot Nova Scotia dory. The other oarsman was Captain John Ridgeway, then twenty-seven.

CHEAPSIDE KNIGHT, THE Sir Richard Blackmore (died 1729), politician and poet, as well as physician to Queen Anne (*Brandy Nan*). He lived in Cheapside, London. Also the *City Bard* and *Maurus*.

CHEGGARS Keith Chegwin (1957–), British pop star of TV's *Cheggars Plays Pop*.

CHELSEA (or BATTERSEA) GARDENER, THE Tom Oliver (1789–1864), British pugilist, once a gardener's boy.

CHELSEA PHILOSOPHER, THE Thomas Carlyle, the *Censor of the Age*.

CHEROKEE BILL Crawford Goldsby (1876–96), American hold-up man hanged for murder. His mother was Anglo-Cherokee.

CHERUB DICKY Richard Suett (1755–1805), English comedian, once a choir-boy in Westminster Abbey. Lamb (the *Mitre Courtier*) in *Essays of Elia* (1820–33): 'he would speak of his chorister days when he was "Cherub Dicky".' Also mentioned by Fitzgerald in his *New History of the English Stage* (1882). Also the **Robin Goodfellow of the Stage**.

CHEVALIER, THE John Taylor (1703–72), British travelling oculist, writer of a treatise on the eye, but generally regarded as a charlatan; so called by Churchill (the **British Juvenal**). Also **Liar Taylor**.

CHICAGO RED John Elroy Sanford (1922–   ), American comedian and fan of the Chicago White Sox baseball team. He later took the name Redd Foxx, after Jimmy Foxx (1907–67), a player.

CHICAGO SMITH George Smith (1808–99), Briton who founded the first bank in Chicago (George Smith & Co.) and retired to England worth £5,000,000 – £1,000,000 of which he gave away to friends and charities.

CHICKEN, THE Michael Angelo Taylor (1757–1834), British barrister. In his first speech, he said he was 'but a chicken in the profession of the law'; so called by Lord Eldor (**Old Bags**) circa 1810–12.

CHIEF Captain Mark Phillips (1948–   ), husband of Princess Anne (**Boss Cat**); nickname at Sandhurst military college. Also **Foggy**.

CHIEF, THE
i) Lord Wavell, **Archie**.
ii) Alfred Charles William Harmsworth, 1st Viscount Northcliffe (1865–1922), British newspaper magnate; the staff nickname on the *Daily Mail*; sometimes the **Great White Chief**. Also the **Colossus of Fleet Street**, **Mr X**, the **Napoleon of the Press** and the **Ogre of Printing House Square**.
iii) William Randolph Hearst (1863–1951), American newspaper tycoon – also 'W.R.' but his 70,000 employees spoke of him as 'The Chief'.
iv) Charles Bender (1883–1954), baseball pitcher for the Philadelphia Athletes; in the Hall of Fame (1903–25). He was a Chippewa Indian.
v) Benjamin Disraeli, the **Asian Mystery**; so called in the Conservative Party (post-1873).
vi) Eamon de Valera (1882–1975), Irish nationalist and President of Eire (post-1959). He was a violent opponent of British rule and was imprisoned (1918–19). Also **Dev**, the **Father of the Irish Republic**, the **Long Fellow** and **Val**.

CHIEF OF THE ENGLISH PROTESTANT SCHOOLMEN, THE Richard Baxter (1615–91), English clergyman, nonconformist and Puritan. He followed the Schoolmen in an age which scorned them; so called by Dean Arthur Stanley (1815–81) of Westminster Abbey. Also the **English Demosthenes**.
• The Schoolmen (fl. 14th century) tried to reconcile the teachings of Aristotle with the Scriptures.

CHIFFY See *Chippy* (ii).

CHILD OF THE AUSONIAN MUSE, THE Edmund Spenser (?1552–99), poet of *The Fairie Queene* (1589–96); so called by D'Israeli. Also the **Child of Fancy**, the **Fairy Singer**, the **King of Poets**, **Mother Hubbard**, the **Page of State to the Muses**, the **Poets' Poet** and the **Rubens of English Poetry**.
• The Ausones or Aurunci occupied a strip of the west coast of Italy in the 4th century BC; name used by poets as a synonym for Italy as a whole.

CHILD OF FANCY, THE Edmund Spenser (above).

CHILD OF HALE, THE John Middleton (1578–1623), of Hale, Cheshire, reputed to have been 9 ft 3 in tall. He defeated the King's wrestler at the Court of James I (the **British Solomon**). The village inn, The Childe of Hale, bears his portrait as a sign, and has on show a sketch of his hand said to have been 8 in wide and 17 in from wrist to fingertips.

CHILD OF NATURE, THE Oliver (Noll) Goldsmith (1730–74), poet, novelist and dramatist; so called because although he was talented, he was naive and gauche. Also **Common Sense**, **Goldy**, **Impenetrable Goodman Dull** and the **Inspired Idiot**.

CHILLY Christopher (Chris) Old (1948–   ), Yorkshire and England cricketer: from C. Old.

CHILLY CHARLIE Charles Clark (1806–80), topographer and satirist; a play on his initials. He wrote *September, or Sport and Sporting* (1856).

CHINESE GORDON General Charles George Gordon (1833–85), commander of forces against Taiping rebels (1863–4); later killed while Governor-General of the Sudan. Also the *English Bayard*, 'Gordon of Khartoum', and the *Uncrowned King of Egypt*.

CHINGFORD STRANGLER, THE Norman Tebbit (1931–), abrasive chairman of the British Conservative Party (1985–7). He has been described as 'a political street fighter'. MP for Chingford in Essex.

CHIP Charles Eustis Bohlen (1904–74), American diplomat, expert on Russian affairs.

CHIPPIE Bertha Hill (1905–56), American blues singer.

CHIPPY

i) Arthur G. Chipperfield (1905–), New South Wales and Australia cricketer. He scored 99 in his first Test Match (Nottinghamshire 1934); highest score 221 runs.

ii) Christopher Stuart Patterson jnr. (1075–1933), noted Philadelphia lawyer (post-1903); from his younger sister's pronunciation of 'Christopher' as 'Chiffy'.

CHIPS

i) Sir Henry Channon (1897–1959), British shipping magnate and friend of the famous; said to have introduced potato chips at one of his parties.

ii) Charles Hector Fitzroy, Baron Maclean (1916–), Lord Chamberlain (1971–84), former Chief Scout and 27th Chief of the Clan Maclean.

CHOCK Charles Arthur Floyd (1901–34), American bank-robber and murderer; from his love of Choctaw beer in Arkansas. Also *Pretty Boy* and the *Robin Hood of Cookson County*.

CHOCOLATE-COLOURED COON, THE George H. Elliott (1884–1962), black-faced music-hall star.

CHOIRBOY Walter (Wally) Swinburn (1962–), British jockey, a millionaire at twenty-five. He won the Derby on the ill-fated Shergar. In 1984 he had a record 99 wins, and in 1985 he had 85; from his boyish appearance.

CHOKER, THE Greg Norman (1955–), Australian champion golfer who won the British Open (1986). Also the *Great White Shark* and *Mr Muscles*.

CHOLERA JOHNSON Sir George Johnson (1818–96), physician extraordinary to the Queen. He wrote a history of the cholera controversy.

CHOO-CHOO Charles (Charlie) Boston (1962–), American middleweight boxer.

CHOP R.T. (Tim) Robinson (1958–), Nottinghamshire batsman who opened for England. He was the hero of the Test Match (1987) against Pakistan when he scored 166, including 16 fours, his fourth Test century. Also the *Michelin Man*.

CHOPPER William Arthur Henry Cavendish-Bentinck, 7th Duke of Portland (1893–1877).

CHOTA GENERAL, THE Major-General Sir Thomas Wynford Rees (1898–1959) who captured Mandalay (World War II) from the Japanese; so called by Indian troops. His many nicknames included *Pete* and the *Pocket Napoleon*.
- *Chota* = Hindi for 'small'.

CHRIS Arthur Christiansen (1904–63), editor of the *Daily Express* (post-1933).

CHRISTIAN ATTICUS, THE Reginald Heber (1783–1826), Bishop of Calcutta, poet and hymn-writer (creator of the lines: 'Though every prospect pleases, And only man is vile.')
- Titus Pomponius Atticus (109–32 BC) was a Roman publisher and patron of the arts, among other things. He was an Epicurean. Cf the *English Atticus*. Richard Heber was half-brother of Reginald.

CHRISTIAN GENERAL, THE Major-General Oliver Otis Howard (1830–1909), Union general in the American Civil War. He negotiated peace treaties with Indians, and had a great deal to do with founding Howard University, primarily for negroes. Also the *Havelock of the Wars*.

CHRISTIAN PHILOSOPHER, THE Dr Thomas Dick (1774–1858), Scottish theologian and scientist who attempted to reconcile all philosophy with Christianity.

CHRISTIAN SENECA, THE Dr Joseph Hall (1574–1656), Bishop of Exeter and of Norwich, who claimed to have been the first English satirist. He was impeached and imprisoned for his opinions. Thomas Fuller (1608–61) commented: 'He was commonly called our *English Seneca* for the purenesse, plainesse and fulnesse of his style. 'Christian' came later. Also the *English Persius*.

- Lucius Annaeus Seneca (*circa* 5 BC–65 AD), statesman and philosopher, tutor to the Emperor Nero, was a popular writer.

CHRISTIE'S WILL William Armstrong (?1602–58), border reiver (not *Kinmont Willie*); mentioned by Scott (the *Ariosto of the North*).

CHRONICLE OF THE STAGE, THE William Beeston (died 1682) whose father Christopher was a fellow actor with Shakespeare (the *Bard of All Time*) in the Lord Chamberlain's Men (at least in Ben Jonson's *Every Man in His Humour*); so called by Dryden (*Asaph*). One of those to whom he gave information was Aubrey (the *Little Boswell of His Day*).

CHRYSOSTOM OF CHRIST'S COLLEGE, THE Henry More (1614–87), theologian, philosopher and poet who was one of the leading figures in the Platonist movement at Cambridge University. Also the *Intellectual Epicure* and the *Man Mouse*.

- St Chrysostom (347–407), whose name means 'Golden-Mouthed', was a mystic 'accused' of following the banned teachings of Origen (*circa* 185–254), a man who had made a thorough study of Plato.

CHU Lean Berry (1910–41), American jazz saxophonist.

CHUBBY CHECKER Ernest Evans (1942–), American 'founder' of Twist music and so *Twist King*.

CHUCK
i) Captain (later Brigadier-General) Charles Elmwood Yeager, United States Air Force (1923–), who made the first supersonic flight. ('Chuck' is common for 'Charles' in America).
ii) Charlton Heston (1924–), American film star, e.g. in *Ben Hur*. His real name is Charles Carter.
iii) Leslie O'Brien Fleetwood-Smith (1910–71), dangerous left-armed bowler who played for Australia ten times in the 1930s.
iv) Charles Edward Anderson Berry (1926–), leading American rock 'n' roll musician (1950s–70s).
v) Charles Jones (1915–), American film animator.
vi) John William Wilson (1921–85), Victoria and Australia bowler. He took 230 wickets with an average of 30.52 in 78 matches; so called from his jerky left-handed delivery. He was no batsman.

CHUCKER Ian Meckiff (1935–), Australian cricketer who played in the 1959 Tests; from his habit of 'throwing' when bowling.

CHUNKY Colin Chapman (1928–82), British head of the Lotus car firm and motor-racing pioneer; from his stolid, sanguine attitude to events.

CICERO OF THE BRITISH SENATE, THE George Canning, *Aeolus*.

- Marcus Tullius Cicero (106–43 BC), orator, poet and consul of Rome.

CINCINNATUS OF THE WEST, THE General William Henry Harrison (1773–1841), 9th President of the United States of America; whose tactics were largely defensive. Also *Hard Cider*, *Log Cabin Harrison*, *Old Tip*, *Tippecanoe* and the *Washington of the West*.

- See the *American Cincinnatus*.

CINDERELLA MAN, THE James J. Braddock (1905–74), American heavyweight champion of the world (1935–7), defeated by Joe Louis (the *Brown Bomber*); because of his 'rags-to-riches' story after he, an unknown late substitute for a fight (1934), knocked out Corn Griffen in the 2nd round.

CIRCE OF CARLISLE HOUSE, THE Teresa Cornelys (died 1797), German-born show-woman who established a rendezvous for balls, masquerades and concerts at Carlisle House, Soho, London (1756), but went too far and died bankrupt. Her entertainments were said to have been irresistible temptations.

- Circe, who lived on the island of Aeaea, was an enchantress.

CISSY Eleanor Medill Patterson (1881–1948), publisher and editor of *The Washington Time-Herald*; childhood nickname by her brother, John Patterson (1878–1946), founder of *The New York Daily News*; from 'sister'. The name became general.

CITIZEN STANHOPE Charles, 3rd Earl of Stanhope (1753–1816); self-applied for his Jacobin sympathies; father of Lady Hester Stanhope (the *Little Bulldog*). Also the *Don Quixote of the Nation* and the *Minority of One*.

CITIZEN THELWALL John Thelwall (1766–1834), English political lecturer and reformer; from the French republican form of address; for his revolutionary ideas.

CITY BARD, THE Sir R. Blackmore, the *Cheapside Knight*; so called by Dryden (*Asaph*).

CITY LAUREATE, THE Elkanah Settle (1648–1724), minor dramatist appointed poet of London (1691).

CLASSIC RAMBLER, THE Dr Johnson, *Blinking Sam*, who ran a periodical *The Rambler* (1749–52); so called by Wolcot (*Peter Pindar*).

CLASSIC SHEFFIELD James Montgomery, *Alcaeus*; so called by Byron (*Baby*).

CLAY PIGEON, THE John Thomas Diamond (1896–1931), whose real name was John T. Nolan, American gangster (1920s); so called because he was shot at so often. Also *Legs*.

CLEMENCY CANNING Charles John, Earl Canning (1812–62), Governor-General, India during the Indian Mutiny (1857–8). In an effort to halt vengeance killings, he published an order that sepoys should not be punished without investigation.

CLERK, THE
i) John de Northalle (fl. 14th century), a skinner who was Sheriff of London (1336–7) and an alderman. His will

(1349) spoke of him as 'John de Northall called Clerk' (Reaney).
ii) William atte Noke (fl. 14th century), a butcher and Warden of Butchers, because he was literate (Reaney).

CLIO Thomas Rickman (1761–1834), British bookseller and reformer; nickname in his youth from his interest in history; later used as a pseudonym.

- Clio is the muse of history.

CLOG MAKER, THE Harry Gray, a noted pugilist (fl. 1740s).

CLONES CYCLONE, THE Barry McGuigan (1961–), Irish-born World Boxing Association of America featherweight champion (1985–6). His home is at Clones, Co. Monaghan, Northern Ireland. He retired (1989) after having been beaten in a non-title fight by Jim McDonnell (1961–), once European featherweight champion.

CLOTHES HORSE, THE Joan Crawford (1903–77), American film-star with a highly developed dress-sense. Even in the Depression (1929–30), she had a wardrobe full of exclusive gowns. Her real name was Lucille Le Sueur.

CLOUT, THE Colin Jones (1948–), British welterweight boxer. Also the *Welsh Dragon*.

CLUMSY CURATE OF CLAPHAM, THE Charles Churchill, the *British Juvenal*. He was an ordained priest (1756), but was forced to resign his living because of his conduct; so called by Foote (*Beau Nasty*).

- See *Proteus*.

COACHEE
i) Admiral Sir W. Cornwallis, *Billy Blue*, perhaps because of (ii), although a 'coach' was the state room of a warship.
ii) Jack Holmes, pugilist (early 19th century) who had been a coachman. He was known in the fighting world as 'a bit of stuff', says Egan the *Elder*.

COACHMAN, THE George Stevenson (fl. late 18th century), pugilist who fought Jack Broughton (the *Father of Boxing*). He was a man of great courage.

COAL-HEAVER PREACHER, THE William Huntingdon (1744–1813), nonconformist preacher of Kent, formerly a coal carrier. He believed that by prayer he could provide all his needs from the 'Bank of Heaven'. He certainly became wealthy. Also *Sinner-Saved Huntingdon*.

COBBER KAIN Flying Officer Edgar James Kain (1919–40), first New Zealand air ace of World War II.

- 'Cobber' is Australian and New Zealand slang for a friend. Partridge says it comes from the Jewish *chaber*, 'comrade'.

COBBETT OF HIS DAY, THE Marchmont Needham or Marchament Nedham (1620–78) British editor and pamphleteer who restarted the newspaper *Mercurius Britannicus* (1644). Also the *Goliath of the Philistines* and *Son of Belial*.

- For William Cobbett, **see** *Boney Cobbett*.

COBBLER LAUREATE, THE Robert Bloomfield (1766–1823), poet of *The Farmer's Boy* (1800). He had been a shoemaker under his brother George in London; so called by Byron (*Baby*).

COBBLING WONDER OF ASHBURTON, THE William Gifford, the *Bear Leader*; so called by Wolcot (*Peter Pindar*). He had been apprenticed to a shoemaker.

COBDEN OF SOUTH AUSTRALIA, THE Sir William Morgan (1829–83), a gold-digger of *Bendigo* who became Prime Minister of South Australia (1878–81).

- For Richard Cobden, **see** the *Apostle of Free Trade*.

COBRA Donald Curry (1961–) American World Boxing Association of America boxing champion (1984–6), from the speed of his punches.

COCK Rear-Admiral David Thomas Norris (1875–1937), Rear-Admiral i/c 1st Battle Squadron, Mediterranean Fleet (1925–7); so called in the Royal Navy. He was small, and as fiery as a fighting cock.

COCK-A-DOODLE-DOO COATES Robert Coates (1772–1848), a wealthy eccentric, son of a sugar-planter in Antigua. Robert drove round London in a pink curricle shaped like a kettledrum, with a large cock on a bar and the motto: 'While I live, I crow'. He was called 'The Amateur of Fashion'. Other nicknames were *Curricle Coates*, *Diamond Coates* and *Romeo Coates*.

COCKALORUM The nickname of successive Marquises of Huntly, heirs to the Dukedom of Gordon (the *Cock of the North*).

- A cockalorum is a young cock, a bantam.

COCK-EYE Benjamin Franklin Butler (1818–93), American general, politician and lawyer, who had a strabismus. He led Union forces which occupied New Orleans (1862). Also *Picayune Butler*.

COCKIE Sir Charles Blake Cochran (1872–1951), master showman and impresario who staged almost everything, from boxing matches and rodeos to lavish revues.

COCK OF THE NORTH, THE The Dukes of Gordon from the 1st to the 5th and last (1778–1836). George, the 5th Duke, raised the Gordon Highlanders and commanded them (1795–9).

- Cf *Cockalorum*. Cock of the North comes from a term for a champion fighting cock. Fuller (*Worthies*, 1684) says 'A Cock of the Game, being the only Man of Note and so "cock of the walk"'.

COEUR DE LION Richard I (1157–99), given in a 14th-century chronicle as 'Richard queor de lyoun'; because of his bravery in war. He was believed by the superstitious to have eaten the heart of a lion. Also *Dickon of the Broom*, the *Lion-hearted* and *Yea and Nay*.

COIN HARVEY William Hope Harvey (1851–1936), American writer on coins and bimetallism.

COKE OF NORFOLK Thomas William Coke, Earl of Leicester (1752–1842), English agriculturalist who, by experiments around Holkham, Norfolk, did much to improve contemporary thinking on the subject. Also *King Tom*.

COLD WAR WITCH, THE Mrs Thatcher, *Attila the Hen*; so called by the Russians.

COLCHESTER EXPRESS, THE Neil Foster (1962–), fast bowler for England and Essex. He took 6 wickets for 84 in the Test against Pakistan (1987); 11 wickets in the 1985 Tests in India. Also *Fozzy*.

COLKITTO Major-General Alastair Mac-donald, the *Younger*, of Colonsay, lieutenant to Montrose (the *Great Marquis*) in his rebellion against Charles II (the *Blackbird*) in 1644. He led a force of Macdonalds, many of them Irish gallo-glasses, but eventually surrendered at Badenoch.

- A galloglass or, more correctly, a *galloglach,* was a retainer of an Irish chief, from *gall,* a stranger, and *oglach,* youth, servant or warrior.

COLLIE O'Neill Gordon Smith (1933–59), West Indies cricketer (post-1954), a fast-scoring batsman who once made 117 in 55 minutes. He died after a road accident.

COLLIER POET, THE Joseph Skipsey (1832–1903). He worked in the pits at the age of seven, and taught himself to read and write. He published seven volumes of verse, and became custodian of Sha-kespeare's birthplace at Stratford-on-Avon (1889–91).

COLONEL Samuel Franklin Cody (1862–1913), American who made the first flight in the UK (1908). He held no military rank. He became a naturalized Briton.

COLONEL, THE
i) Kenneth (Ken) Frank Barrington (1930–81), Surrey and England cricketer; capped 82 times and a master batsman, scoring 31,714 runs in his career; so called after the English tour of India (1960–1) because of his roman nose and jutting jaw.
ii) George Alfred Kolhkurst (1897–1958), reader in Spanish at Oxford University; from his manner.
iii) Ronald Kray (1934–   ), one of the Kray twins gaoled for life (1969) for the murder of Jack the *Hat* McVitie (1933). In 1982 he was in Broadmoor.
iv) William Joseph Simmons (fl. 1915–1920s), organizer and Imperial Wizard of the Ku Klux Klan, founder of the modern version (1915).

COLONEL ANNE Lady Anne Mackintosh of Moy Hall (1752– ?), wife of The Mackin-tosh. She raised her clan for the Jacobites before Culloden (1746), although her hus-band was fighting for the King. At the age of twenty, she rode at their head. She had

been a Farquharson of Invercauld.

COLONEL GROGG Sir Walter Scott, the *Ariosto of the North*. He was a cornet in a Scottish volunteer unit, and had, says Lockhart, 'a remarkable pair of grogram breeches'. His nickname among youths.

COLONEL NARCOTIC John Elliott, a Lon-don brewer who was a candidate for Westminster in the 1806 Parliamentary elections. He was supported by the Estab-lishment, and was elected with Lord Cochrane (the *Devil*); so called because of the soporific policies he advocated.

COLORADO CHARLEY Charles Utter (fl. 1870s), partner and friend of *Wild Bill* Hickok, whose funeral he arranged.

COLOSSUS, THE Cecil John Rhodes (1853–1902), pioneer statesman of Rhodesia (now Zambia and Zimbabwe), which was named after him; a pun on the Colossus of Rhodes, one of the wonders of the ancient world. Also the *Great Amalga-mator*.

COLOSSUS OF CLOUT, THE *Babe* Ruth.

COLOSSUS OF ENGLISH PHILOLOGY, THE Dr Johnson, *Blinking Sam*; so called by Dibdin (the *Beau Brummell of Living Authors*) in tribute to his dictionary (1755).

COLOSSUS OF FLEET STREET, THE
i) Lord Northcliffe, the *Chief*.
ii) Peter Wilson (1913–81), sports writer for the *Daily Mirror*, by-lined 'The Man They Can't Gag'; so called by the BBC.

COLOSSUS OF INDEPENDENCE, THE John Adams (1735–1826), 2nd President of the United States of America; one of the orig-inal movers for independence (1760s). He helped to draft the Declaration of Inde-pendence and was said by Jefferson (the *Apostle of Liberty*) to have been 'the pil-lar of its support on the floor of Con-gress'. Also the *Colossus of the Revolution* and *Old Sink or Swim*.

COLOSSUS OF LITERATURE, THE Wil-liam Warburton (1698–1779), Bishop of Gloucester, literary critic and author, as well as producing an edition of Shakes-peare. Also the *Literary Bull-Dog*, the *Modern Stagirite*, the *Mountebank of*

Criticism, the *Poets' Parasite*, the *Scaliger of the Age* and the *Universal Piece-Broker*.

COLOSSUS OF THE REVOLUTION, THE John Adams, the *Colossus of Independence*.

COLUMBIA LOU See *Biscuit Pants*.

COLUMBUS OF THE SKIES, THE

i) Sir Isaac Newton (1642–1727), whose book *Philosophiae Naturalis Principia Mathematica* (1687) put forward the first ideas on the laws of motion and universal gravitation. Also the *Priest of Nature*.

ii) Sir William Herschel (1738–1822), astronomer who discovered Uranus (1781), as well as a great number of other stars and nebulae.

- Christopher Columbus (*circa* 1451–1506) discovered the New World (1492).

COLUMKILLE or COLUM OF THE CHURCH St Columba, the *Apostle of Caledonia*. His Irish name was Colum, and so he was called Columkille (*kille* = church).

COMMANDO KELLY Charles Kelly (1921–85), the first American enlisted man to win the Congressional Medal of Honor in World War II.

COMMODORE, THE Cornelius Vanderbilt (1794–1877), American industrialist. He controlled the majority of the steamboats in New York state. He left an estate of more than 100,000,000 dollars, having started at the age of sixteen with a sailing-boat in which he carried farmers' produce. Also the *King of Wall Street*.

COMMON SENSE Oliver Goldsmith, the *Child of Nature*; so called by newspapers.

COMPLETE SEAMAN, THE Admiral Sir Richard Hawkins (1562–1622); nickname he gave himself. He took part in Drake's expedition to the Spanish Main, and commanded a ship against the Armada (1588).

COMPO Denis Compton, the *Brylcreem Boy*.

COMUS OF POETRY, THE Lord Byron, *Baby*.

- Comus was the god of festive mirth. As a young man, Milton (*Black-Mouthed Zoilus*) wrote a masque (1634) *Comus* which was presented at Ludlow castle before the nobility of Wales.

CONDUCTOR OF THE UNDERGROUND RAILWAY, THE Harriet Tubman (*circa* 1820–1913), a slave. She escaped, and helped more than 300 American slaves to freedom. Also General Tubman and *Moses*.

CONFESSOR, THE Edward or Eadward (1004–66), King of England; after he had made an open declaration of his faith in Christianity; canonized (1161).

CONKEY The Duke of Wellington, the *Achilles of England*; so called by his troops and in satirical journals and caricatures because of his large nose.

- See *Old Conkey*.

CONN THE HUNDRED FIGHTER or CONN OF THE HUNDRED BATTLES Conn (died 157), King of Ireland (*circa* 123–7). Also the *Hero of a Hundred Fights*.

CONNIE MACK Cornelius McGillicuddy (1862–1956), American baseball player and team manager of the Pittsburgh Pirates (1894–6). He won nine American League championships and five world championships. His name is a legend in baseball.

CONQUEROR, THE William I, the *Bastard*.

CONSEQUENTIAL JACKSON William Jackson (1751–1815), Bishop of Oxford. Also *Poor Con*.

CONTENTIOUS, THE Henry O'Neill (died 1392), Irish chieftain called *Enri Aimbreidh;* son of Aedh the *Fat*. Henry, however, was a peace-lover.

CONVERSATION COOKE William Cooke (1766–1835), journalist who published *Conversations* (1807) in which he 'interviewed' members of a literary club in Soho, London.

CONVERSATION SHARP Richard Sharp (1759–1835), journalist, critic and noted conversationalist.

COOCHIE Gareth Chilcott (1957–   ), British 5 ft 9 in, 16 stone (234 lb) Rugby Union prop for Bath and England; from a childhood nickname 'Coochie Coo', picked up by Bath fans. Also the **Mad Axeman**.

COOGIE Xavier Cugat (1900–), American Latin-American dance band leader. Also the **Rhumba Romeo**.

COOL KID, THE Steve Davis (1957–), the youngest-ever (1981) world professional snooker champion. By 1989 he had won six world championships. Also the **Ginger Magician**, the **Guv'nor**, the **Nugget**, the **Romford Robot** and the **Surgeon**.
- Cf the **Whirlwind**.

COONSKIN CONGRESSMAN, THE David (Davy) Crockett (1786–1836), American frontiersman, a member of the Tennessee legislature between 1821 and 1836. He wore a coonskin cap as a hunter and trapper. Also the **Munchausen of the West**.

COOP Frank James Cooper (1901–61), American film-star who adopted 'Gary'; mentioned in the film *It's a Great Feeling* (1949).

COOTE BAHADUR Major-General Sir Eyre Coote (1726–83), C-in-C, India. It was the battle-cry of his Indian troops. He, however, called them 'blacks'.
- See **Bobs Bahadur**.

COOTIE Charles Williams (1908–), American jazz trumpeter, long associated with **Duke** Ellington.

COPERNICUS George Dyer, **Archimagus**.
- Nicolaus Copernicus or Kopernik (1473–1543) was a Polish astronomer.

COPPERFACE Oliver Cromwell, the **Almighty Nose**; so called by Needham (the **Cobbett of His Day**).
- 'Coppernose' was a slang term from the fifteenth to the seventeenth century for a red, swollen nose.

COPPERNOB The Duchess of York, **Carrot Top**; school nickname mentioned by her (1988).

COPPERNOSE HARRY Henry VIII, **Bluff Hal**. When the silver veneer of his alloyed coins wore off the King was left with a copper nose.

COPPERNOSE SAINT, THE Oliver Cromwell, above.

CORKSCREW KID, THE Charles McCoy (1873–1940), world welterweight boxing champion (1896) whose real name was Norman Selby. His sportsmanship was said to have created the term 'The Real McCoy'. Also **Kid McCoy**.

CORKY Edward Cornelius (1914–43), American jazz trumpeter.

CORNISH GIANT, THE Anthony Payne (fl. 17th century) of Stratton, near Bude, who was 7 ft 6 in tall. During the Civil War he was bodyguard to Sir Bevil Grenville (1596–1643). Payne fought at Lansdowne Hill, where Sir Bevil was killed commanding the royalists. Payne rallied the King's men by putting Grenville's son beside the standard and crying out that a Grenville still led them. The giant's body is in Stratton churchyard. Sir Geoffrey Kneller (1646–1723) painted Payne as a captain of guns.

CORNISHMAN, THE Robert Fitzsimmons, the **Antipodean**.

CORNISH, POET, THE John Harris (1820–84), miner who wrote *Lays from the Mine* (1853).

CORNISH WONDER, THE John Opie (1761–1807), English historical and portrait painter, born in Cornwall. When he started his career in London (1780), he was introduced with this appellation by Wolcot (**Peter Pindar**) to which he added 'a self-taught genius'.

CORN-LAW RHYMER, THE Ebenezer Elliott (1781–1849), poet of *Corn-Law Rhymes* (1828). Their popularity, it is alleged, paved the way for the repeal of the hated Corn Laws (1846). Also 'The Corn-Law Poet'.
- Corn Laws restricted the export and import of corn and so raised the price of bread.

CORONER TO THE STARS, THE Dr Tom Noguchi (1928–), Japanese-born American. For fifteen years he was the Chief Medical Examiner and coroner for the Los Angeles area. During that time he examined 10,000 bodies, including those of Marilyn Monroe, William Holden and Natalie Wood.

CORPORAL, THE Field-Marshal Edward Augustus, Duke of Kent (1767–1820), son of George III (the **Button Maker**) and father of Queen Victoria (**Drina**); so called by the Duke of Wellington (the **Achilles of England**), because of his rigid manner and his love of military show. Also **Joseph Surface**.

CORPORAL JOHN The Duke of Marlborough, **Anne's Great Captain**; so called by his soldiers.

CORSICA BOSWELL James Boswell, the **Ambitious Thane** who wrote an *Account of Corsica* (1768) after a visit there. He always said he jumped off a rock in Corsica 'into the middle of life'. There is an apocryphal story that when he appeared at the Shakespeare jubilee celebrations in Corsican dress his cap was labelled 'Corsica Boswell'.

CORYPHAEUS OF BOOKBINDERS, THE Roger Payne (1739–97), a celebrated London bookbinder who was nevertheless said to have been 'a filthy ragged ale-sodden creature'. His business was near Leicester Square.

- The coryphaeus was the leader of the chorus in Greek comedies.

CORYPHAEUS OF LEARNING, THE Richard Porson (1759–1808), British classical scholar who advanced the modern knowledge of the Greek language by his observations on Greek idiom and usage. Also **Devil Dick** and the **Norfolk Boy**.

CORYPHAEUS OF LETTER-FOUNDING, THE William Caslon (1629–1766), British engraver and type-founder, who designed a range of new typefaces in twelve different sizes. It was once the most popular type for book-printing. Also the **Elder**.

CORYPHAEUS OF MATHEMATICIANS, THE Thomas Allen or Alleyn (1542–1632) of Oxford University. He was so clever that he was thought of as a magician. Aubrey (the **Little Boswell of His Day**) said: 'In those dark times, astrologer, mathematician and conjurer were accounted the same things and the vulgar did verily believe him to be a conjurer.'

CORYPHAEUS OF MODERN LITERATURE, THE William Gifford, the **Bear Leader**; so called by D'Israeli.

COSTER KING, THE Alec Hurley (died 1913), music-hall singer who married (1904) Marie Lloyd (**Our Marie**); from his songs.

- 'Coster' is short for 'costermonger' (from costard = apple), a London street trader, usually from a barrow.

COSTER LAUREATE, THE Albert Chevalier, **Albert the Great**; because of his songs.

COTTAGE COUNTESS, THE or THE PEASANT COUNTESS Sarah Hoggins of Shropshire (1774–97), daughter of a small farmer. She married (1791) at the age of seventeen Henry Cecil, nephew and heir of the 9th Earl of Exeter. (She knew him as John Jones.) His succession to the title made her a countess. Henry Cecil, the 10th Earl (1754–1804), became the 1st Marquess of Exeter.

COUNT

i) **Beau** Nash; his nickname at the Inner Temple where he staged a masque on the accession of William III (the **Deliverer**); so called from his good manners and dress. He refused a knighthood from William.

ii) William Basie (1904–84), American jazz pianist and band-leader; so called by an American radio announcer who did not like plain 'Bill Basie' in an era of **Duke** Ellington and Earl Hines.

iii) Joseph Haines or Haynes (died 1701), British dancer and actor.

COUNT ECLIPSE 'Colonel' Dennis O'Keefe (?1720–87), owner of the most famous of all British racehorses, Eclipse (1764–89), an ancestor through the male line of all thoroughbred racehorses in the world. O'Keefe was an Irish adventurer; his nickname of 'Count' was given when he was in the Fleet prison, London for debt. 'Eclipse' came later after his horse 'Eclipse' was never beaten in the 1769–70 season.

COUP KING, THE Angus Hill (1940–   ) of Worcestershire, British professional gambler on racehorses. He once won £30,000 on a 16-1 winner.

COURT EVIL Raphael Courteville (died 1772), organist at St James's church, London, and a political writer, a supporter of Walpole (the **Grand Corrupter**); a pun on his name by his opponents.

COURTEOUS, THE Morgan Mwynvawr (fl. 10th century), Welsh prince and warrior, alleged to have lived for 129 years.

COURTEOUS CULLEN Robert, Lord Cullen (1740–1810), Edinburgh judge and author; Lord of the Justiciary (1799).

COWBOY PHILOSOPHER, THE Will Rogers (1879–1935), American humorist and film-star who began as a rope-spinning vaudeville act and became a political commentator and newspaper-writer; so called because his jokes made people think. He has been called 'America's Poet Lariat'.

COWBOY PRESIDENT, THE Theodore Roosevelt (1858–1919), 26th President of the United States of America, who was in love with the American West. He wrote *Hunting Trips of a Ranchman* (1885). Also the *Sage of Princeton*.

COW-COW or COU-COU Charles (Charlie) Davenport (1894–1955), American jazz musician, from his composition *Cow-Cow Blues*, which was said to have been the original boogie song.
- Cow-Cow is an American negro term for the Devil, or trouble generally.

COXCOMB, THE Richard II (1367–1400), son of the *Black Prince* and the *Fair Maid of Kent*. He was given to lavish extravagance in dress. Also *Tumbledown Dick*.

COXCOMB BOOKSELLER, THE John Murray (died 1793). He set up as a bookseller at 32 Fleet Street, London (1768) and began a publishing firm. Among his early publications were Walpole's *Castle of Otranto* and Isaac D'Israeli's *Curiosities of Literature*. He announced he would sell 'choicest editions, the best Print and richest Bindings' to libraries.
- 'Coxcomb' was used for a person vain of his accomplishments, as in *The Examiner* (1820): 'Some coxcombical bookseller introduced the fashion.' Murray was originally Lieutenant John M'Murray, Royal Navy.

COZY William Randolph Cole (1909–81), American jazz drummer whose record *Topsy* was the only drum solo to sell more than a million copies.

CRAFTY, THE Archibald Constable (1774–1827), Scottish publisher; mentioned in a letter from Campbell (the *Bard of Hope*) to Scott (the *Ariosto of the North*). Also the *Czar of Muscovy*.

CRAFTY COCKNEY, THE Eric Bristow (1957–   ), London-born world professional darts champion (1980s).

CRASH Ray Corrigan (1903–76), American film actor, mostly in Westerns. His real surname was Benard.

CRAWFIE Marion Crawford (1909–88), governess (1930s) to the Queen (then Princess Elizabeth) and Princess Margaret (*Charley's Aunt*). She won royal disapproval when she published her reminiscences.

CRAZY HORSE
i) Emlyn Hughes (1947–   ), footballer for England and captain of Wolverhampton; Footballer of the Year (1977–8). He was captain of Liverpool when it won the First Division championship (1979); so called after an incident in a match.
ii) Timothy John Foli (1950–   ), baseball star of the New York Mets.
- Crazy Horse was Tashunka Witko (*circa* 1849–77), military leader of the Sioux and Cheyenne at the battle of Little Big Horn (1876). He gave himself the name after dreaming of horses.

CRAZY JOE Joseph Gallo (1929–72), American Mafia chief, shot at his 43rd birthday party.

CRAZY SALLY Sarah Mapp (died 1737), British bone-setter who travelled the country with this nickname she had bestowed upon herself.

CRIPPLEGATE Henry Barry, 8th Earl of Barrymore (1776–1823), Irish peer born with a club foot.
- Cf *Billingsgate*, *Hellgate* and *Newgate*.

CROCKY William Crockford (1775–1844), proprietor of Crockford's Club (post-1827), London gambling establishment.

CROESUS OF THE SENATE, THE Senator James Couzens (1872–1935), a rich man and philanthropist. Also the *Poor Man's Friend*.

- Croesus, king of Lydia (560–46 BC) was so rich that he drew to his court all the wise men of Greece, including Solon.

CROMBO Arthur C.M. Croome (1866–1929), cricketer for Oxford and Gloucestershire, cricket correspondent for *The Times*.

CROMWELL OF NEW ENGLAND, THE Samuel Adams (1722–1803), cruel English governor of Massachusetts.

CROOKBACK Richard III, the *Boar*, whom tradition (and Shakespeare) alleges was deformed.

CROUCHBACK
i) Edmund, Earl of Lancaster (1245–96), second son of Henry III (died 1272).
ii) Alasdair, 8th chief of the MacLeod (1461–1547).

CROUCHER, THE Gilbert Laird Jessop (1874–1955), cricketer for Cambridge, Gloucestershire, and England, a batsman who made a century against Australia at the Oval (1902) in 72 minutes. He scored eleven centuries in an hour or less between 1897 and 1913. Once he scored a double century in 120 minutes; so called from his stance.

CROW, THE Robert (Bob) Lee Hayes (1942–), American 100 metres Olympic champion, who set a world record for the 100 yards (1963); bow-legged and pigeon-toed.

CROWE Thomas Hobbes, the *Atheist*; so called in his youth when he had black hair.

CROWN PRINCE OF BASEBALL, THE Al Schacht (1893–1984), American entertainer.

CRUEL COPPINGER Daniel Herbert Coppinger, an Irishman wrecked off the Cornish coast (1792) who became a notorious smuggler; died bankrupt in the King's Bench prison (1802).

CRUEL JUDGE, THE John Tiptoft, Earl of Worcester, the *Butcher of England*.

CRUSOE or ROBINSON CRUSOE R.C. Robertson-Glasgow (1901–65), Oxford and Somerset cricketer, and later a well-known writer on the game; a word-play on his initials.

CRUM-HELL Cromwell, the *Almighty Nose*; so called by Needham (the *Cobbett of His Day*). In Cromwell's lifetime his name was pronounced 'Crum-ell'.

CUBBY Albert Romolo Broccoli (1909–), Italian-American film producer, especially of the James Bond films. Also the *Godfather*.

CUDDLES S.Z. Sakall (1884–1955), American film-star whose real name was Eugene Garo Szakall.

CUDDY Admiral Cuthbert, 1st Baron Collingwood (1750–1810), who took over command of the fleet after the death of Nelson at Trafalgar (1805).

- 'Cuddy' is a familiar form of 'Cuthbert' in some parts of northern England. It is also slang for a donkey or a stupid person, which would not seem to apply since Collingwood was regarded with affection by his men.

CUMBERLAND JACK Ernst Augustus (1771–1851), Duke of Cumberland (1799), fifth son of George III (the *Button Maker*). He was unpopular in England. He became king of Hanover (1837).

- 'Jack' was used for an 'ill-mannered fellow' (*Oxford English Dictionary*) from at least the 16th century.

CUMBERLAND POET, THE
i) William Wordsworth, the *Bard of Rydal Mount*, born in Cumbria.
ii) Robert Southey, the *Ballad Monger*, who lived there.
iii) Samuel Taylor Coleridge, the *Alnaschar of Modern Literature*.

CUPID Henry John Temple, 3rd Viscount Palmerston (1784–1865), British Prime Minister (1855–8 and 1859–65). *The Times*, under the editorship of Barnes (the *Thunderer*), referred to Palmerston as 'that juvenile old Whig, nicknamed Cupid', which was followed by a cartoon 'Cupid in the Park' in *Punch*. In the words of Lytton Strachey (1880–1932), 'his private life was far from respectable'. Also *Fireband*, the *Judicious Bottle-Handler*, *Lord P*, *Old Pam*, *Pam* and *Pumice Stone*.

CURIOUS SCRAP-MERCHANT, THE James Boswell, the *Ambitious Thane*; so called by Wolcot (*Peter Pindar*).

CURLY BILL William Brocius (1851–82), American gunman and cattle-rustler, whose real name was William Graham; shot by Wyatt Earp (1848–1929) at Tombstone, Arizona.

CURLY JACK Jack McCall (1851–77), hanged for the killing of *Wild Bill* Hickok at Deadwood, South Dakota (1876).

CURLY TOP Shirley Temple (1928–   ), child film-star, a No. 1 box-office attraction (1936) and worth a million dollars before she was ten. Later, as Shirley Temple Black, she became an American diplomat. She had blonde, curly hair. Also *One-Take Temple*.

CURRICLE COATES Robert *Cock-A-Doodle-Doo Coates*. He drove strangely shaped curricles, one like a cockleshell.

- A curricle was a light two-wheeled carriage, usually drawn by two horses harnessed side by side.

CURTHOSE Robert II (*circa* 1054–1134), eldest son of William I (the *Bastard*). He rebelled against his father, and so became Duke of Normandy (but not King of England). He introduced a new fashion in hose, for hose had often formerly covered the feet and so formed a kind of shoe. (In 1000 it had been rendered as *caliga* = half boot.) Reaney translated 'Curthose' as 'short boot'. Also *Shorthose* and *Short Thigh*.

CURTMANTLE or CURTMANTEL Henry II (1133–89), king of England, who wore the Anjou mantle, shorter than the one generally worn then in England.

CUTLETS Reginald Koettlitz (1861– ?), doctor of Guy's Hospital, London, and a member of the Jackson-Harmsworth expedition to Franz Joseph Land (1894–5), and the Scott Antarctic expedition (1901–4), where he was given the nickname.

CUT-LUGGED WILLIE William Lithgow (1582–?1650), Scottish adventurer and traveller. His ears ('lugs' in Scotland or northern England dialect since the 15th century) were mutilated by the brother of a lady with whom he had had an affair.

CUTTEPURS Alan Cuttepurs (= 'cutpurse'), hanged by the Prior of Coventry for having stolen bread, 1262 (Ewen).

CUTTY Robert Dewess Cutshall (1911–68), American jazz trombonist.

CUVIER OF ENGLAND, THE Robert Edmond Grant (1793–1874), professor of comparative anatomy and zoology at London University.

- See the *British Cuvier*.

CY

i) Denton True Young (1867–1955), American baseball pitcher for Boston; in the Hall of Fame (1890–1911), renowned for his perfect game (1904) and for the most no-hitters of a lifetime (1897, 1904 and 1908). There is a Cy Young award.

ii) Melvin James Oliver (1911–88), American musician and composer.

CYPRIAN QUEEN, THE Mary, Duchess of Buckingham. She was the only daughter of Lord Thomas Fairfax (*Black Tom*) and married the 2nd Duke of Buckingham (*Alcibiades*); so called by Cowley (the *English Pindar*) to whom Buckingham was patron. She had to contend with her husband's many mistresses, one of whom Pepys called 'a whore'.

- 'Cyprian', from the island of Cyprus where Venus or Aphrodite was traditionally born, and where her worship in ancient times began. The expression meant 'licentious' or 'profligate', and was applied to courtesans. See the *Wicked Countess*.

CZAR OF ALL THE RUSHES, THE Louis B. Mayer (1885–1957), powerful American head of Metro-Goldwyn-Mayer; so called by B.P. Schulberg (1892–1957), production manager for Paramount. If not widely known, it deserves to be.

- The Czar's title was 'Czar (or Tsar) of All the Russias'. The 'rushes' are the first showings of film footage usually to studio executives to decide on acceptance or rejection of a day's work.

CZAR OF MUSCOVY, THE Archibald Constable, the *Crafty*, self-styled.

D

DADDIE James Ratcliffe, a character in Scott's *The Heart of Midlothian*. He was a real person, and Scott (the *Ariosto of the North*) says in *The Waverley Anecdotes* (1833) that his name may be found by examination of the criminal records of Scotland. Alexander Nicol, spoken of as 'an unfortunate bard', wrote a song *Ratcliffe's Farewell to the Tolbooth*.

DADDY Air-Commodore Harold Probyn (1891–   ), Britain's oldest former pilot, who lives in Kenya.

DADDY CRISP Samuel Crisp (1708–83), an old friend of Dr Charles Burney (1726–1814), father of the diarist Fanny Burney (the *Old Lady*). He was an unsuccessful playwright who encouraged her to write. She called him by this nickname.

DADDY HILL General Rowland, 1st Viscount Hill (1772–1842); so called by his troops. Also *Farmer Hill* and the *Waterloo Hero*.

DAFFY

i) Paul Dean (1913–81), pitcher for the St Louis Cardinals when they won the world baseball championship (1934). Brother of *Dizzy*.

ii) Philip DeFreitas (1966–   ), Leicestershire and England bowler; born in Dominica, West Indies.

DAISY Princess Margaret of Connaught (1882–1920), daughter of Arthur, Duke of Connaught (1850–1942). She married (1905) the Crown Prince of Sweden.

DALEY Francis Morgan Thompson (1958–   ), British Olympic champion and the world's greatest all-round athlete. He held that record for nine years, until 1987. Also the *Muhammed Ali of the Track*.

DALLY Herbert Henry Messenger (1883–1964), Australian Rugby League pioneer of the game in Sydney. In 1908 he made a place-kick of about 80 yards.

DALLY THE TALL Mrs Grace Dalrymple Elliott (?1758–1825), divorced wife of a rich doctor and mistress of George IV (*Adonis of Fifty*) when he was Prince Regent.

DAME Peter West (1920–   ), British television personality and cricket commentator.

DAMSEL OF BRITTANY, THE Eleanor of Brittany (died 1241), niece of King John (*Lackland*). After the alleged murder by John of her brother Arthur, she was heiress to the English throne. Taken prisoner by John, she was treated well and lived to a good old age. Also the *Fair Maid of Brittany*.

DANA Rosemary Brown (1951–   ), Irish winner of the European Song Contest and television and stage personality: her Gaelic nickname at school means mischievous.

DANBURY NEWS MAN, THE James Montgomery Bailey (1841–94), American Civil War newspaperman and *Father of the Humorous Newspaper Column*. His newspaper was published at Danbury, Connecticut.

DANCING CHANCELLOR, THE Sir Christopher Hatton (1540–91), Lord Chancellor. He first drew the interest of Queen Elizabeth (the *English Diana*) by his graceful dancing at a Court masque. Also *Mutton*.

DANCING DIVINITY, THE Jessie Matthews (1907–81), British singing and dancing star of revues and musical comedies; later famous as Mrs Dale in *Mrs Dale's Diary*, a long-running serial on British radio.

DANCING DUKE OF YORK, THE Edward Augustus (1739–67), brother of George III (the *Button Maker*). His passion for the ladies brought him an early death.

DANDY BISHOP, THE The Hon. George Pelham (1766–1827), who was Bishop of Lincoln.

DANDY GEORGE Admiral Sir George Cockburn (1772–1853), who took part in the battle of St Vincent (1797) and carried Napoleon to St Helena in the *Northumberland* (1815). Also the *Scourge of the Chesapeake*.

DANDY KILLER, THE *Beau* Brummell; so called by George IV (*Adonis of Fifty*), after they quarrelled.

DANDY NICK Sir Nicholas Hardwick Fairbairn (1933–   ), MP, former Solicitor-General for Scotland.

DANIEL BOONE OF THE ROCKY MOUNTAINS, THE James (Jim) Bridger (1804–81), Virginia-born pioneer fur trader and explorer. Also *Old Gabe*.

 • Daniel Boone (1734–1820), frontiersman and explorer of Kentucky.

DANNY Robert Dennis Blanchflower (1926–   ), captain of the United Kingdom football team which met the Rest of Europe (1955); Footballer of the Year, 1958 and 1961, played for Northern Ireland and Tottenham Hotspur.

DANNY THE BLARNEY Danny Gunnery (1933–   ) of Shepherd's Bush, London, *Gatecrasher No 1*; so called because of his ability to talk himself into high places.

DANTON OF MODERN POETRY, THE Robert Browning (1812–89); so called by Augustine Birrell (1850–1933), essayist, because of his audacity.

 • A saying of Jacques Danton (1759–94), French Revolutionary statesman, was *Toujours de l'audace*.

DAPHNE Sir William Davenant (1606–68), English dramatist and theatre manager, reputed to have been an illegitimate son of Shakespeare (the *Bard of All Time*). Also *Old Daph* and the *Poetical Rochefoucauld*.

DAPPER, THE Thomas Vaughan (fl. 1772–1820), minor British playwright; so called by Colman the *Younger*, with whom he had quarrelled.

DAPPER DAN Daniel Currie (1935–   ), American footballer.

DAPPER GEORGE George II, *Augustus*.

DAPPER JEMMY James Boswell, the *Ambitious Thane*; so called by Wolcot (*Peter Pindar*).

DA PREEM Primo Carnera, the *Ambling Alp*; his nickname in America.

DARBY David Hugh Monro (1913–66), Australian jockey who rode a record nine winners at the Australian Jockey Club's Sydney meeting (1940).

DARK DESTROYER, THE Nigel Benn (1964–   ), Commonwealth middleweight boxing champion, who had held his title by 23 straight wins by February 1989. He lost (1989) his Commonwealth title to Michael Watson.

DARK HORSE (PRESIDENT) This nickname refers to several unexpected candidates for the United States Presidency, but to the 20th President, James A. Garfield (1831–81) in particular. Garfield won the Republican ticket on a compromise in 1880. He was assassinated the following year.

 • Cf *The Canal Boy*.

DARKIE Frank Gardiner (1830– ?), Australian bushranger and folk hero, sentenced (1864) to thirty-two years hard labour, but released (1874) on condition that he never returned to Australia. He is thought to have died in a San Francisco tavern brawl at the turn of the century; because of his dark skin. Also the *Prince of High Toby Men*.

DARK LANTERN MAN, THE Oliver St John (1598–1673), MP, Chief Justice of Common Pleas.

 • A dark lantern (post-1650) was a lantern with a slide which could conceal the candle at will. By 1700 it was in the dictionaries (i.e. B.E's *Dictionary of the Canting Crew*) for someone who could be bribed.

DARKY Jack Underwood (shot 1832), Australian bushranger and companion to *Bold Jack*.

DARLING OF THE GODS, THE Tallulah Bankhead (1902–68), American-born actress who was very popular on the London stage. Also 'Tallu'.

 • 'The gods' has been slang for the gallery of a theatre since at least 1750, and is said to have been 'christened' by Garrick (*Atlas*) because the audience there were so near heaven.

DARLING OF THE NINE, THE Thomas Manning (1772–1840), British traveller, linguist and mathematician; so called by Lamb (the *Mitre Courtier*).

- There are nine muses.

DARWIN'S BULLDOG Thomas Henry Huxley (1825–95) who defended *The Origin of Species* (1859) by Charles Darwin (*Gas*), especially at the meeting of the British Association at Oxford (1860); nickname he gave himself.

DAUGHTER OF THE CONFEDERACY, THE Varina (Winnie) Davis (1864–89), born in the Confederacy executive mansion when her father, Jefferson Davis (1808–96), was Confederate President.

DAVID Admiral of the Fleet David, 1st Earl Beatty (1871–1936), C-in-C of the Grand Fleet (World War I). Although David was his first name, it was in such common use on the lower deck as to become a nickname.

DAVY JONES David Armstrong-Jones, Viscount Linley (1961–) son of Princess Margaret (*Charley's Aunt*); so called in the commercial circles he moves in. He is the chairman of David Linley Furniture Ltd.

DAYSTAR OF THE AMERICAN REVOLUTION, THE Andrew Hamilton (1676–1741), lawyer; so called by Gouverneur Morris (1752–1816) after Hamilton's speech (1735) in defence of John Peter Zenger (1697–1746), printer, whose acquittal from criminal libel laid the foundations for American freedom of speech.

DAZZY Arthur Vance, baseball pitcher in the Hall of Fame (1915–35) because of his 'dazzy ball' (his own name for his style).

DEADLY DEREK Derek Leslie Underwood (1945–), Kent and England left-handed bowler. Before he was twenty-six he had taken 1,000 wickets in first-class cricket.

DEADWOOD DICK Richard W. Clarke (1845–1910), English-born frontiersman in South Dakota; famous as an Indian fighter and guard for gold shipments from the Black Hills.

- Deadwood is the city in South Dakota where *Wild Bill* Hickok was shot: see *Curly Jack*.

DEAF CHARLEY O.C. (Camilla) Hanks (1863–1902), American train-robber, one of the Wild Bunch.

DEAF POET, THE William Pope (fl. 1760s), Welsh poet.

DEAN HARRY Henry Wilkinson (1616–90), Principal of Magdalen Hall, Oxford University, a Puritan and a Parliamentarian.

- Cf *Long Harry*, with whom he has no connection.

DEANIE Charles O'Bannion, the *Arch Killer of Chicago*.

DEAN OF AMERICAN ECONOMISTS, THE John Bates Clark (1847–1938), whose *Distribution of Wealth* (1899) influenced American economic thinking.

DEAN OF AMERICAN MAGAZINE EDITORS, THE Henry Mills Alden (1836–1919), who edited *Harper's Monthly* (1869–1919).

DEAN OF AMERICAN PUBLISHERS, THE George Haven Putnam (1844–1930), who expanded the firm founded (1837) by his father George Palmer Putnam, the oldest publishers in the United States of America. G.H. fought strenuously for international copyright.

DEAN OF CHICAGO GUNMEN, THE Walter Stevens (1867–1939), gangster and 'hit man'.

DEAN OF DRAMATIC CRITICS, THE Robert Burns Mantle (1873–1948), American dramatic critic of *The Denver Times* (post-1898).

DEAN OF FLEET STREET, THE Hannen Swaffer, also called *Bishop of Fleet Street*.

DEAN OF TRAVEL WRITERS, THE Sydney Clark (died 1975), American who wrote many authoritative books on various countries.

DEAR LIBERTY BOY, THE Thomas Hollis (1659–1731), English merchant, prominent Baptist and benefactor of Harvard University, so called in America. Also *Ultimus Romanorum*.

DEATH Stephen Oliver (fl. 1740s–1780s), British pugilist who took part in a series of bouts before the Prince of Wales (*Adonis of Fifty*) near Croydon (June 1788).

DEATH-HOUSE REILLY Edward Reilly, the *Bull of Brooklyn*.

DEATH VALLEY SCOTT Walter Scott (1875–1954), American prospector who suddenly became wealthy. He claimed the money came from a gold-mine in Death Valley, California, although not everyone believed him.

DEB Frank Debenham (1883–1965), New Zealand-born scientist of Scott's Antarctic expedition (1910), Professor of Geography at Cambridge University and founder-director of the Scott Polar Research Institute.

DECALOGIST, THE The Rev. John Dodd or Dod (1549–1645) who wrote a treatise on the Decalogue – the Greek word for the Ten Commandments.

DECEITFUL, THE Domnal Ui Neill, joint King of Ireland (563–6).

DEED-DOER, THE Edmund or Eadmund I, King of the English (?922–46) who acceded to the throne at the age of eighteen (*Anglo-Saxon Chronicle*). He drove the Vikings from Northumbria, and raided Strathclyde. Florence of Worcester (died 1118), a monk, called him the *Magnificent* in his chronicle: *Edmundus magnificus*. Edmund was one of the leaders of the English in the famous battle of Brunanburh (?937), mentioned in the A.S.Ch.

DEINOL OF THE BANGORS St Deinol, a 6th century abbot-bishop; from the two monasteries he is reputed to have founded: Bangor Fawr and Bangor Iscoed.
- Bangor Fawr (= 'great' in Welsh) was formerly the name of Bangor, where the cathedral is dedicated to St Deinol.

DEKE Donald Kent Clayton (1924–   ), American astronaut who was 51 when he went on the Apollo-Soyuz mission (1975); from his initials, D.K.

DELIVERER, THE William III (1650–1702), who married Mary, daughter of James II, and came with her from Holland to become joint monarchs (1688); because he rescued Britain from Catholicism. Also the *Dutch Bear*, the *Gallic Bully*, *Great Nassau*, *King Billy* and *Old Glorious*.

DELIVERER OF AMERICA, THE George Washington, the *American Cincinnatus*; so called by Count Vittorio Alfieri (1749–1803). He saved America from the British.

DELLA CRUSCA Robert Merry (1755–98), British writer of verse and an unsuccessful playwright who headed the Della Cruscan School, a group of poets who were savagely attacked by Gifford (the *Bear Leader*) in *The Baviad* (1791).
- The Accademia Della Crusca was founded in Florence in 1582. It sought the 'purification' of language. *Crusca* = bran.
- Thomas Nugent wrote in *The Grand Tour* (1756): 'They have' (in Italy) 'an academy called *La Crusca* (a word which signifies *bran*, alluding to the sifting of the flour.)'

DEMOCRITUS JUNIOR Robert Burton (1577–1640), author of *The Anatomy of Melancholy* who wrote of melancholy with mordant, scholarly humour.
- Democritus (*circa* 460–370 BC) was nicknamed 'The Laughing Philosopher'.

DEMON, THE
i) Frederick Robert Spofforth (1853–1926), Australian cricketer famous for his 'unplayable' bowling. Once he clean-bowled all ten wickets in both innings of a match (1881). In a Test March (1882) he took 14 wickets for 90 runs. *Punch* published a cartoon of *Spoff* as a demon.
ii) George Fordham (1837–87), English jockey who rode 2,587 winners in his career. He headed the list of winning jockeys 14 times between 1855 and 1871. Also the *Kid*.
iii) or the **DEMON JOCKEY**: Frederick Archer (1857–86), champion jockey of England for 13 years. Also the *Tinman*.
iv) George E. Palmer (1860–1910), medium-pace bowler for Victoria and Australia, who played in the first Test Match at Lord's (1880) and was the youngest Australian to take 10 wickets in a Test. Also *Joey*.

DEMON BOWLER, THE John Jackson (1833–1901), cricketer for Nottinghamshire and England. He visited the United States of America (1859) and Australia (1863); so called especially by John Leech (1817–1864) in *Punch*.

DEMON OF DARKNESS, THE William Gifford, the *Bear Leader*; so called by J. Morley (1792) in the *Gentleman's Magazine*.

DEMOSTHENES OF THE PULPIT, THE Dr Thomas Rennell (1753–1840), Dean of Westminster; so called by Pitt (the *Bottomless Pit*).

• Demosthenes (384–322 BC) was a brilliant orator with lucidity and a sense of purpose (chiefly warning against the growing power of Macedonia).

DENARIUS PHILOSOPHORUM John Thornborough (1551–1641), Bishop of Worcester. The nickname could be loosely translated as 'The Penny Philosopher' or 'The Philosopher of Pennies', for Thornborough used his office to raise money for the Crown by forced levies and other methods.

DERBY DILLY, THE Edward Geoffrey Smith Stanley, Lord Stanley and 14th Earl of Derby (1799–1869), three times British Prime Minister (1852, 1858–9 and 1866–8), who withdrew from the Tory party (1835) over the Irish question. At the next session of Parliament O'Connell (the *Big Beggarman*) quoted of him and his follower: 'Down the hill, romantic Ashbourn, glides/The Derby dilly carrying six insides.' Also the *Hotspur of Debates*, the **Rupert of Debates** and *Scorpion Stanley*.

• 'Dilly' was slang for a diligence. Ashbourn is a district of Derbyshire. The quotation is from J.H. Frere's *Loves of the Triangles* (1798): 'So down thy hill, romantic Ashbourn, glides/The Derby dilly, carrying Three Insides.' Frere (1769–1846) published it in *The Anti-Jacobin*.

DERRYDOWN TRIANGLE, THE Lord Castlereagh, *Bloody Castlereagh*. He represented Derry in Parliament. The nickname was given to him by William Hone (1780–1842), bookseller and political satirist in *The Sinecurist's Creed*

(1817) in parody of the Athanasian Creed.

• The triangle, according to Hone, is a thing of three sides, the meanest and most tinkly of all musical instruments, and machinery used in military torture.

DEV De Valera, the *Chief*.

DEVIL, THE

i) *El Diablo*, the Spanish nickname for Thomas, Lord Cochrane (1775–1860), later the 10th Earl of Dundonald, British admiral, who helped free Latin America from Spanish rule. As a lieutenant commanding the sloop *Speedy*, he captured the Spanish frigate *El Gamo* (1801). Also the *Liberator of Greece*, the *Sea Wolf* and the *South American Lafayette*.

ii) Robert I, Duke of Normandy (died 1035), father of William I (the *Bastard*). He was a brave but cruel fighter, and it was reputed that his childless mother promised to the devil the soul of any child she might have. He is the 'hero' of a French romance *Robert Le Diable*. Also the *Magnificent*.

DEVIL DICK Richard Porson, the *Coryphaeus of Learning*. Porson drank a lot, and became violent and bestial. He drank everything he could lay his hands on, including spirits of wine for the lamp.

DEVIL OF DEWSBURY, THE Richard Oldroyd (hanged at York, 1664), conspirator in the Farnley Wood plot (1663) to overthrow Charles II (the *Blackbird*).

• Dewsbury, Yorkshire, is nine miles south of Leeds.

DEVIL ON TWO STICKS, THE Senator Oliver Perry Morton (1823–77), whose legs were paralysed. He was 'war governor' of Indiana during the American Civil War. He was very violent in debates.

DEVIL'S HOOK, THE Richard Burke (fl. 16th century), wild sea captain of the Irish Burke family.

DEVIL'S PIPER, THE Michael Scot or Scott, *Auld Michael*; so called in Northumberland.

DEVONSHIRE POET, THE O. Jones, an uneducated journeyman wool-comber, writer of *Poetic Attempts* (1786).

DEY OF ALGIERS, THE John Ballantyne (1774–1821), Scottish publisher and brother of James (the **Jenson of the North**) who were subsidized by Scott (the **Ariosto of the North**) to start their business; so called by Archibald Constable (the **Crafty**), another Scottish publisher. Also **Jocund Johnny**.

DIAMOND Wayne Daniel (1956–   ), cricketer for the West Indies and Middlesex.

DIAMOND COATES Robert **Cock-a-Doodle-Doo-Coates**, leader of fashion, whose father left him a magnificent collection of diamonds.

DIAMOND DUKE, THE Charles Frederick William Augustus (1804–73), who was Charles II, Duke of Brunswick until his unpopularity forced him to leave. During his minority, his dukedom had been ruled by the Prince Regent (**Adonis of Fifty**). The Duke, who had once been a possible suitor for the hand of Victoria (**Drina**), lived in England during his exile.

DIAMOND JIM

i) **Big Jim** Colosimo, Chicago gangster (1920s) with a passion for diamonds. He wore a diamond belt-buckle, diamond shirt-studs, diamond rings and a set of diamond cuff-links.

ii) James Buchanan Brady (1857–1917), high-powered salesman and industrial magnate who rose from a job as a railway worker; because of his extravagant taste in jewellery. He often gave diamond brooches or watches worth £200 to guests at his parties. He is said to have walked down Broadway, New York, once with 2,548 diamonds and rubies as shirt-studs and tie pins.

DIAMOND JOE Joseph Esposito (1892–1928), Chicago gangster who wore a belt on which his name was written in diamonds.

DIAMOND PITT Thomas Pitt (1653–1726), grandfather of the 1st Earl of Chatham (**Aeolus**), an East Indian merchant and Governor of Madras. He obtained the famous Pitt diamond of 137 carats, which came from the Parteal mines on the Kistna, from an Indian merchant. He sold it for £135,000 to the Duke of Orleans, Regent of France (1717). It was once set in the hilt of Napoleon's sword, and is still among the state jewels of France.

DIAMOND QUEEN, THE Celia Whipple Wallace (fl. 1880s–1916), wealthy Chicago widow with a passion for jewels. Because of her generosity, she died in poverty.

DIANA OF THE STAGE, THE Anne Bracegirdle (?1663–1748), one of the first English actresses. She was a friend of William Congreve (**Ultimus Romanorum**), and helped him to make his plays popular. She was suspected of having been secretly married to him; so called in Percy Fitzgerald's **New History of the English Stage** (1882).

• See the **English Diana**.

DICK Arthur Frederick Lilley (1867–1929), Warwickshire cricketer.

DICKIE

i) Louis Francis Albert Victor Nicholas, 1st Earl Mountbatten (1900–79), murdered by IRA terrorists; so called by the royal family, especially the Queen to whom he was 'Uncle Dickie'. Also **Lordy** and **Supremo**.

ii) Harold Bird (1933–   ), British Test Match cricket umpire; from 'dicky bird'.

DICK OF ABERDARON Richard Robert Jones (1780–1843), an eccentric Welsh scholar and linguist who lived in England. He has been described as 'a half crazy wanderer'.

• Aberdaron, 'the Land's End of Wales', is at the extreme tip of the Lleyn peninsula.

DICKON OF THE BROOM Richard I, **Coeur de Lion**; the broom plant was the symbol of his family.

• Cf **Plantagenet**.

DICKY SCRUB Henry Norris (1665–1725), British comedian; so called in **The Spectator**. Also **Heigh-Ho** and **Jubilee Dicky**.

DICTATOR OF WALL STREET, THE J. Pierpont Morgan (1867–1943), son of **Morgan the Magnificent** because of his amazing financial manipulations. He once organized a bankers' syndicate for $100,000,000 to help New York City.

DICTIONARY JOHNSON Samuel Johnson, *Blinking Sam*; his nickname for a time after the publication of his dictionary (1755), which established him as a literary figure and, says G.M. Trevelyan (*English Social History*: 1944), brought 'the settlement of spelling by rules now insisted on among educated people'.

DIDDY David Hamilton (1938–   ), British disc-jockey and television announcer. He is quite small.

- 'Diddy' is a dialect word for 'little', especially in the Liverpool area and its general popularity was created on television by the comedian Ken Dodd (1928–) in the 1970s. 'Diddy' began its life in the nursery and its present use may spring from the fact that 'diddy' is an archaic word for a nipple or a teat.

DIDEROT OF AMERICA, THE Isaiah Thomas, the *Baskerville of America*, printer, editor and publisher of Worcestershire, Massachusetts, whose publications included *The Massachusetts Spy* (1770–1904), a newspaper which helped the revolutionary cause, and *The Royal American Magazine* (1774–84), 'A Universal Repository of Instruction and Amusement'.

- Denis Diderot (1713–84) was a French encyclopaedist who attempted to summarize all human knowledge.

DIGNIFIED, THE Aedh Ui Neill, High King of Ireland, 797–819.

DIMPLED DANE, THE Carl Brisson (1895–1958), Danish-born star of British films and musical comedies, e.g. *Wonder Bar* (1930). His real name was Carl Pedersen. Also the *White Gardenia Man*.

DINER-OUT OF THE FIRST WATER, THE Sydney Smith (1771–1845), canon of St Paul's Cathedral, London, a brilliant conversationalist and wit who helped to found *The Edinburgh Review* (1802); so called by *The Quarterly Review*, a wordplay on 'a diamond of the first water'. Smith called Canning (*Aeolus*) 'a diner-out of the highest lustre'.

DINGUS Jesse Woodson James (1847–82), American train-robber and outlaw who had ridden with Quantrell's guerrilla force in the American Civil War; so called after he shot away the tip of one finger by accident and exclaimed, 'If that ain't the dingus-dangasted thing!'

DINNER-BELL, THE

i) Edmund Burke (1729–97), British MP (1765–94) who, says Timbs, 'wearied his hearers with those longer speeches which obtained for him the name of the "Dinner-bell".' Also *Paddy Burke*, the *Scientific Statesman* and the *Shakespeare of Orators*.

ii) David Hartley (1731–1813), British MP for Hull (1774–80 and 1782–4) whose rising to speak 'operated like a dinner-bell' (Timbs). The Earl of Liverpool (*Jenky*), who was an MP as Charles Jenkinson, said he once left the House of Commons when Mr Hartley rose to speak at 5 p.m. (1779), took a walk in the country, went home and dined, and returned to the House at about 9 p.m. When he asked what had happened he was told Mr Hartley was still speaking.

DINNY John Cole Reedman (1867–1924), cricketer for South Australia and Australia.

DINO John Dennis (1951–   ), Italian-born world heavyweight boxer.

DINTON HERMIT, THE John Bigg (1629–96), clerk to Simon Mayne (1612–61), one of the signatories to the death warrant of Charles I (the *Ahab of the Nation*). After the Restoration, Bigg lived for more than 30 years in a cave at Dinton, Buckinghamshire.

DIPPERMOUTH Louis Armstrong (1900–71), American jazz trumpeter and band leader. While playing with *King* Oliver's band he was the only one who could put a drinking-water dipper into his mouth. Also *Pops*, *Satchelmouth* and *Satchmo'*.

DIRECTOR OF STUDIES, THE Dr John Freind (1675–1728), physician and pamphleteer; so called by Bishop Berkeley (the *Irish Plato*) sardonically during the Boyle–Bentley controversy. As a student at Oxford University, Freind had picked the wrong side and supported Boyle.

- See *Phalaris Junior*, and the

Aristarchus of Cambridge.

DIRTY DEAN, THE The Very Reverend William Corbet Le Breton (1815–88), Dean of Jersey (1850s); so called on the island because of the scandalous reputation of his daughter **Lillie** Langtry (the **Jersey Lily**), although she said of him that he couldn't be trusted 'with any woman anywhere'.

DIRTY DICK Nathaniel Bentley, the **Beau of Leadenhall Street**, wealthy London miser who rarely washed. The contents of his hardware shop in Leadenhall Street were bought after his death for a public-house in Bishopsgate given the name of 'Dirty Dick's' and later 'the D.D. Cellars'. Bentley had once been an elegant dandy, but never recovered from the death of the girl he was to have married, who died on the day of their engagement.

DIRTY DIGGER, THE Rupert Murdoch, the **Burger King of Journalism**; so called by *The Daily Mirror*.

- 'Digger' is slang for an Australian from the Australian word (1850s) for a miner.

DIRTY DUKE, THE Charles Howard, 11th Duke of Norfolk (1746–1815). He had a dislike for soap and water, and his servants washed him when he was drunk. Also the **Drunken Duke** and the **Jockey**.

DISCO DICK Richard Hatfield (1931–   ), bachelor Prime Minister of New Brunswick, Canada, who has shown a love for New York night-clubs.

DISCO KID, THE Sandeep Patil (1957–   ), Indian cricketer who created a Test record (1982) by scoring six fours in a seven-ball over; so called after he had said he almost gave up cricket to become a pop singer.

DISMAL, THE Heneage Finch, Earl of Nottingham (1621–82), Lord Chancellor; from his appearance. Also the **Father of Equity** and the **Silver-Tongued**.

DISMAL JIMMY Admiral of the Fleet James, 1st Baron Gambier (1756–1833), C-in-C Channel Fleet who missed the chance to destroy the French fleet in the Basque Roads (1808); so called for his incompetence, his attempt to make women boarding ships produce marriage certificates and his opposition to drinking.

DISMEMBER FOR GREAT BRITAIN, THE William Ewart Gladstone (1809–98), British Prime Minister (1868–64, 1880–5, 1886 and 1892–4); so called (1886–7) after his ardent sponsorship of Irish Home Rule and his proposal to create an Irish Parliament. Also the **Eloquent Old Man**, **Mr G**, the **G.O.M.**, the **Grand Commoner**, the **Grand Old Man**, the **Great Commoner**, the **Napoleon of Oratory**, **Old Gladeye**, **Old Man Eloquent**, the **People's William** and **WEG**.

DISTRESSED STATESMAN, THE William Pitt, **Aeolus**, forced to resign as Secretary of State (1761) following his defeat over his determination to go to war with France and Spain, overthrown by the accession of George III (the **Button Maker**) and the advent of Lord Bute (**Jack Boot**). The Treaty of Paris (1763) followed.

DIVINE, THE

i) Richard Crashaw, **Blest Swan**, who wrote many sacred poems.

ii) Shakespeare, the **Bard of All Time**; so called by Dryden (**Asaph**) and Pope (the **Bard of Twickenham**).

DIVINE ASTRAEA, THE Mrs Aphra Behn (1640–89), British poetess and novelist; self-applied.

- Astraea, daughter of Zeus, was the goddess of justice in a golden age. It means 'star maiden'. The nickname was used by Pope (the **Bard of Twickenham**) in *Imitations of Horace* (1734).

DIVINE MISS M Bette Midler (1944–   ), American entertainer.

DIVINE ONE, THE Sarah Vaughan (1924–   ), American jazz singer. Also **Sassie**.

DIVING JENNY or JENNY DIVER Jane Webb (died 1740), whose real name was Mary Young, executed for picking pockets; from her skill.

- Thomas Dekker (?1570–1632) says in *The Guls Hornebooke* (1609) that a diver was someone who stole by pushing a small boy through a window; later it came to mean a pickpocket.

DIXIE Dean Coney (1964–   ), striker for Fulham F.C.; from *Dixie Dean*.

DIXIE DEAN William Ralph Dean (1907–80), footballer for Everton and England, who scored 17 goals in international matches between 1927 and 1932. He scored 60 goals in 39 league games in one season.

DIXIE DERRICK, THE Paul Anderson (1933–   ), American weightlifter. His amazing feats of strength included a back-lift of 6,270 lb (2,844 kg), the greatest weight ever lifted by a man (1957). He was 1956 Olympic champion.

DIZZY

i) Benjamin Disraeli, Earl of Beaconsfield, the *Asian Mystery*. In his early days as a novelist he called himself 'D'Israeli the Younger', since his father, Isaac D'Israeli (1766–1848), was a well-known writer. The 'D'Israeli' was shortened familiarly to 'Dizzy'.

ii) John Birks Gillespie (1917–   ), American jazz trumpeter, one of the originators of 'Bop' (1948–9); from his eccentric behaviour when young. Also *It*.

• See the *High Priest of Bop*.

iii) Jerome Dean (1911–74), pitcher for the St Louis Cardinals; in the Hall of Fame (1930–47); won the Most Valued Player award (1934); from a coach's remark 'This kid makes you dizzy.' Brother of *Daffy*.

iv) Roy Edward Carlyle (1900–56), American minor league baseball player.

DO Either Reginald Frank Doherty (1872–1910) or his brother Hugh L. (1875–1919), British lawn tennis players who helped to make the game popular. Reggie was *Big Do* and Hugh *Little Do*. Reggie was All-England singles champion at Wimbledon (1897–1900) and his brother from 1902 to 1906. They were also doubles champions.

DOC

i) John Henry Holliday (1852–87), American card-sharper and friend of Wyatt Earp (1848–1929). He took part in the gunfight at the O.K. Corral, Tombstone, Arizona (1881). He was a dentist.

ii) Adolphus Anthony Cheatham (1905–   ), American jazz trumpeter who had several relatives in the medical profession.

iii) Charles Cooke (1891–*circa* 1956), American pianist and arranger.

iv) Arthur Barker (1898–1939), American murderer and bank-robber of the Barker gang; sometimes 'Dock'. Killed trying to escape from Alcatraz.

v) James Edward Counsilman (1920–   ), oldest man to swim the English Channel (1979); coach to the United States Olympic team (1976).

vi) William Frank Carver (1840– ?), famous as a marksman in the *Buffalo Bill* Wild West Show; from his experience as a dentist.

DOC, THE Thomas (Tommy) Docherty (1928–   ), manager of Queen's Park Rangers Football Club and other clubs.

DOCKERS' K.C., THE Ernest Bevin (1881–1951), Assistant Secretary of the British Dockers Union and later Foreign Secretary (1945–51); because of his brilliant advocacy of their case.

DOCTOR, THE

i) William Maginn, the *Adjutant*.

ii) Henry Addington, 1st Viscount Sidmouth (1757–1844), British politician; partly because he was the son of Dr Anthony Addington of Reading and partly because during the illness of George III (the *Button Maker*) he prescribed a pillow of hops as a soporific for the King. Canning (*Aeolus*) gave him the nickname and Cruikshank (the *Prince of Caricaturists*) developed the idea by a cartoon of Sidmouth with a clyster hanging out of his pocket.

iii) James Watson (died 1820), eccentric British author and publisher of Salford, Lancashire, editor of The Salford Gleaner (post-1806).

DOCTOR ATALL John Hill, the *Cain of Literature*. Everyone came in for his criticism.

DOCTOR BLACK John Black (1783–1855), editor of the *Morning Chronicle*; because of his love of argument. Also the *Flying Scotsman* or *Scotchman* and the *Professor of Logic*.

DOCTOR COWHEEL John Cowell (1554–1611), English jurist and expert on common law; so called by Coke (the *Oracle of the Law*) who prosecuted him before the House of Commons for exaggeration of the King's prerogative.

DOCTOR DEATH

i) John Goundry (1932–80) of Braintree, Essex, who said he had developed a three-second death-pill for old and decrepit people. He was found dead surrounded by pill bottles and capsules.

ii) Sydney Noble (1929–   ), British confidence trickster imprisoned (1978) for ten years. He had posed as a doctor, and drugged old ladies before ransacking their homes. He escaped (1985), and after recapture was imprisoned for six life sentences (1986) for similar offences during his six months of liberty.

iii) Gerard Anthony Steenson (1958–87), Irish National Liberation Army commander; so called by INLA gunmen. He was gaoled in Belfast for six life sentences but successfully appealed. He was killed in an INLA feud.

• INLA is marxist. See the *Border Fox*.

DR DOOM Dr Henry Kaufman (1928–   ), chief economist for Salomon Brothers, United States brokers. He accurately forecast the dangers in many money-market situations.

DR DUPLICATE Dr Francis Willis (1718–1807), English clergyman with a medical degree from Oxford University treated George III (the *Button Maker*); so called by the medical profession. The nickname arose because the king had had many previous doctors, and Willis worked with his son, Dr John Willis. Also the *Mad Doctor*.

DOCTOR   EVANGELICUS   or   THE EVANGELIC DOCTOR John Wyclif, Wickcliffe or Wycliffe (*circa* 1324–84), English religious reformer, forerunner of the Reformation. Also the *Father of English Prose*, the *Gospel Doctor* and the *Morning Star of the Reformation*.

• Church Latin evangelium = 'good news'.

DOCTOR EVIL EYES Brian Harris (1937–   ), British optician struck off after accusations of having drugged women patients to have sex with them; gaoled for life (1985) for the murder of his wife.

DOCTOR FUNDATUS William Varro, a 13th century English minorite and philosopher; translated (Latham) *Thorough Doctor*.

DOCTOR INKPOT John Standish (?1501–70), Archdeacon of Colchester who wrote many tracts.

DOCTOR INVINCIBILIS or THE INVINCIBLE DOCTOR William of Occam or Ockham (*circa* 1270–1349). English Nominalist philosopher and Franciscan monk, famous for 'Occam's Razor'. He was a pupil of Duns Scotus (*Doctor Subtilis*), and a formidable debater. Also *Doctor Singularis et Invincibilis*, the *Intellectual Doctor*, the *Singular Doctor* and the *Unique Doctor*.

• Occam's Razor was *Entia non sunt multiplicanda praeter necessitatem*, which the *Oxford English Dictionary* explains as: 'Things not known to exist should not, unless absolutely necessary, be postulated as existing', with which he dissected every problem. He helped to end the Scholastic school.

DOCTOR IRREFRAGABILIS or the IRREFUTABLE DOCTOR Alexander of Hales (1175–1245), English theologian who wrote *Summa Theologiae*, considered to be indisputable. He was born at Hales in Gloucestershire. The nickname is mentioned by Camden (1605). Also the *Fountain of Life*.

DR JIM Sir Leander Starr Jameson (1853–1917), famous for the Jameson Raid (1895–6) and Prime Minister of Cape Colony (1904–8). He was a doctor of medicine.

DOCTOR MIRABILIS or ADMIRABILIS Roger Bacon, the *Admirable Doctor*.

DOCTOR MY-BOOK John Abernethy (1764–1831), an English surgeon who wrote *Surgical Observations on the Constitutional Origin and Treatment of Local Diseases* (1809), to which he referred very often.

DOCTOR OF HYPOCRISIE Dr Andrew Perne, *Andrew Ambo*; so called by *Ape Gabriel* Harvey.

DOCTOR PLANUS ET PERSPICUUS Walter Burleigh or Burley (1274-5–*circa* 1345), an English Schoolman and pupil of Duns Scotus (*Doctor Subtilis*). Also the *Plain and Perspicuous Doctor*.

- See the *Chief of the English Protestant Schoolmen*.

DOCTOR PRESTO Jonathan Swift (1667–1745), Dean of St Patrick's, Dublin, author of *Gulliver's Travels* (1726); so called by the Duchess of Shrewsbury, daughter of the Marquis Paleotti of Bologna. *Presto* is the Italian for 'swift'. Swift liked the nickname and used it in his *Journal to Stella*. Also the *English Rabelais*, the *Impious Buffoon*, the *Mad Parson, Martin*, the *Prince of Journalists*, and the *Rabelais of Good Society*.

DOCTOR PROFUNDUS or THE PROFOUND DOCTOR

i) Thomas Bradwardine (*circa* 1290–1349), Archbishop of Canterbury (1349), who wrote a number of important theological works. He was a Schoolman. Also the *Solid Doctor*.

ii) Richard Middleton (died 1304), an English Franciscan Schoolman. Also the *Solid Doctor*.

DOCTOR ROGUERY Thomas Smith (1638–1710), one of the clergymen who refused to take the oath of allegiance to William III (the *Deliverer*) and Mary; an orientalist. Also *Rabbi Smith* and *Tograi Smith*.

DOCTOR SINGULARIS ET INVINCIBILIS William of Occam, *Doctor Invincibilis*. It means 'the unique and unconquerable doctor' (from Vulgar Latin *invincibilis*).

DOCTOR SLOP Sir John Stoddart (1773–1856), acting editor of *The Times* (1812–16), who wrote a great deal of bombastic nonsense which earned him the nickname, given by the satirist William Hone (1780–1842). It ended Stoddart's career in journalism. Sir John was a medical man.

- Dr Slop is a narrow-minded, choleric doctor in Sterne's *Tristam Shandy* (1760–7).

DOCTOR SMUG Dr David Anthony Llewellyn Owen (1938–   ), former Labour Foreign Secretary and leader of the Social Democrat Party; so called in Parliament.

DOCTOR SQUINTUM

i) The Rev. George Whitefield (1714–70), religious leader who worked with John Wesley (1703–70); so called by Foote (the *English Aristophanes*) in *The Mirror* (1760).

- See the *Whitefield of the Stage*.

ii) Edward Irving, *Boanerges*, a noted preacher who squinted; so called by Theodore Hook (the *Little Pet of the Green Room*).

DOCTOR SUBTILIS or THE SUBTLE DOCTOR John Duns Scotus (*circa* 1265–*circa* 1308), an English Franciscan monk, author of many works of philosophy and metaphysics. He was a Scholastic theologian, and because of his arguments – and those of his followers – against the new thinking the word *dunce* (from Duns) arose. He was born at Duns, Scotland. Also the *Wise*.

DOC WOOD John B. Wood (died 1884), American printer and journalist. Also the *Great American Condenser*.

DODD George Osborne (1903–57), skipper of the trawler *Girl Pat* who in 1936 'disappeared' after having sailed his ship out of Grimsby. He turned up in British Guiana three months later and was arrested. George Dodd served 18 months hard labour for theft.

DODGER, THE W.W. Whysall (1887–1930), cricketer for Nottinghamshire and England.

DODO

i) Edward Frederick Benson (1867–1940), author, after the success of his novel *Dodo* (1893).

ii) Doris Day (1924–   ), American film star, especially of musicals. Her real surname is Kappelhoff.

DOG, THE Francis, Viscount Lovell (1454–?87), English politician and adherent of Richard III (the *Boar*) which earned him inclusion in the rhyme which brought about Collingbourne's execution.

- See *Cat*.

DOG James H. Kelly, mayor of Dodge City, Kansas (1878).

- See *Spike (ii)*.

DOGA Richard Pentreath (fl. end 18th century) of Mousehole, Cornwall, a renowned smuggler.

DOG JENNINGS Henry Constantine Jennings (1731–1819), an eccentric collector, who bought in Rome the famous marble dog which is now in Duncombe Park, Yorkshire. He sold it for 1,000 guineas.

DOLLY Basil d'Oliveira (1931–   ), South African-born English Test cricketer (1966–72); now coach for Worcestershire Cricket Club.

DOLLY DIMPLES Celesta Geyer (1901–   ), American fat lady, 4 ft 11 in tall and once weighing 39 stone 5 lb (555 lb). She wrote a book telling how she lost 400 lb in fourteen months.

DOMESTIC POET, THE William Cowper, the *Bard of Olney*.

DOMINA ANGLORUM Matilda (1102–1167), daughter of Henry I (*Beauclerc*) and wife of Emperor Henry V of Germany. The appellation *Domina Anglorum* was given to her by the Council of Winchester (1141). Also the *Lady of England*.

DOMINIE HARRY Lord Brougham and Vaux, *Blundering Brougham*, Lord Chancellor and jurist; so called in *Noctes Ambrosianae*. He was enthusiastic about promoting popular education and helped to found London University. He told the House of Commons (1828) that he trusted the schoolmaster more than the soldier to expand liberty.

• A dominie is a Scottish schoolmaster.

DOMINIE LEGACY PICKEN Andrew Picken (1788–1833), Scottish author of *The Dominie's Legacy*; so called in *Fraser's Magazine*.

DON, THE
i) Sir Donald Bradman, the *Bowral Boy*; so called by C.B. Fry (1872–1956).
ii) Carlos Wesley Byas (1912–   ), American jazz saxophonist.

DON CARLO Charles Fitzcharles, Earl of Plymouth (1657–80), illegitimate son of Charles II (the *Blackbird*) by Catherine Page.

DON QUIXOTE OF THE NATION, THE

Lord Stanhope, *Citizen Stanhope*; for his eccentricities.

DON VITTONE Vito Genovese (1897–1968), American Mafia's chief murderer.

DONZEL DICK *Astrological Richard* Harvey, younger brother of *Ape Gabriel* Harvey.

• A donzel was a gentleman, not yet knighted, a squire or a page; from Italian *donzello*, Old French *donsel*, a young man, from late Latin *domnicellus*, a young master.

DOODLES Winstead Sheffield Weaver (1911–83), American film comedian, e.g. 'the growing sailor' in *The Navy Steps Out* (1941).

DOOG, THE Derek Dougan (1939–   ), centre-forward for Wolverhampton FC and Northern Ireland.

DOOMSDAY BELL William Bell (fl. mid-18th century), an ex-Life Guardsman who caused a panic when he predicted after an earthquake in London (8 February 1750) that the next tremor would mean the end of the world. He was put in Bedlam (the Bethlehem Hospital). Also *Mad Bell*.

• Aaron Hill (1685–1750), author and minor poet, a great organizer of unsuccessful schemes, died the minute the earthquake began.

DOOMSDAY SEDGWICK William Sedgwick, the *Apostle of the Isle of Ely*, a fanatical preacher who declared he had had a vision of Doomsday.

DOUBLE DICK Richard Richards (1787–1860), British lawyer, Chief Baron of the Court of Exchequer.

• See *Green Park*.

DOUBLE DUCHESS, THE
i) Louise Fredericke Augusta (died 1911), widow of William Drogo, 7th Duke of Manchester (*Kim*) who married (1892) Spencer Compton, 8th Duke of Devonshire (*Harty-Tarty*). Also *Lottie* and *Ponte Vecchio*.
ii) Elizabeth, née Gunning (1724–90), widow of the 6th Duke of Hamilton, who married (1759) John, 5th Duke of Argyll (1723–98). She was created (1776)

Baroness Hamilton of Hambledon.

DOWN-THE-RIVER JACK Daniel Owen, alias Morgan, *Black Dan*, i.e. the Murray river.

DRACULA

i) Ray Reardon (1932–   ), Welsh professional snooker player; six times world champion; from his 'satanic' appearance and prominent eye-teeth.

ii) David (Dave) Whitcomb (1954–   ), British professional darts player. He won the World Masters in 1982.

- Dracula is the fictional vampire created (1897) by Bram Stoker (1847–1912).

DRAGON, THE

i) *El Dracone* or *El Draco*, the Spanish nickname for Sir Francis Drake (*circa* 1540–96), English admiral who often 'singed the King of Spain's beard'. Also *England's Neptune* and *Warrior Drake*.

ii) Robert Harley, 1st Earl of Oxford, the *Backstairs Dragon*; so called by Swift (*Dr Presto*) by reversal of ideas: Harley was mild.

- *Draco* is the Latin for 'dragon' and the ancestor of the Old English 'drake', as in 'fire-drake', a dragon portrayed breathing fire.

DRAGON LADY Nancy Reagan (1921–   ), wife of Ronald Reagan (*Dutch*), 40th President of the United States of America; because of the strong hand she was said to have applied to White House affairs after the Iran arms scandal (1986). So called first by Donald Regan (*Reagan's Prime Minister*). Also *Ice-Station Zebra*, *Mousey Davis* and *Queen Nancy*.

- Nancy is a stage name. Her real name is Anne Frances Robbins Davis Reagan.

DRAPER OF BRITAIN, THE Hugh, 1st Baron Fraser of Allander (1903–66). He controlled a number of department stores which mostly sold clothes, e.g. Harrods, John Barker, Derry and Tom's, Pontings.

DREAMER OF WHITBY, THE Caedmon, the *Anglo-Saxon Milton*, a monk of Whitby, Yorkshire, who said he was told in a dream to write of the Creation.

DRINA Queen Victoria (1819–1901), whose first name was Alexandrina. Also the *Faery*, the *Grandmother of Europe*, *Mary Collins*, the *Mother of Her Country*, *Mrs Brown*, *Mrs Melbourne*, *Ouma*, the *Quagger*, *She* and the *Widow of Windsor*.

DRINO Alexander, Marquess of Carisbrooke (1886–1960), son of Prince Henry of Battenberg (1858–96), and grandson of Victoria (*Drina*).

DROMEDARY, THE Thomas Campbell, the *Bard of Hope*; so called in *Noctes Ambrosianae*, a pun on 'camel' and 'Campbell'.

DRUNKEN BARNABY Robert Braithwait (1588–1693), writer of *Barnabee's Journall* (1638), the 'hero' of which has also been called 'Drunken Barnaby'.

DRUNKEN DUKE, THE The 11th Duke of Norfolk, the *Dirty Duke*.

DRURIOLANUS Sir Augustus Harris, *Augustus Druriolanus*; also Drury Lane Theatre, London.

DRUSUS William Cartwright (1611–43), English playwright and renowned preacher; so called by Kingsley (*Cave*).

- Marcus Livius Drusus (fl. 91–98 BC) was a famous orator.

DRY GINGER Admiral of the Fleet Sir Michael Le Fanu (1913–70). He was First Sea Lord when rum was abolished in the Royal Navy. Also *Lef* and *Leffy*.

DRYSALTER Mr Justice Arthur Clavell Salter (1859–1928), the judge who sentenced Bottomley (*England's Recruiting Sergeant*); from his manner.

DUBLIN or HIBERNIAN ROSCIUS, THE Gustavus Vaughan (1818–58). He appeared on the Dublin stage at the age of fourteen and toured England with this nickname.

- See the *African Roscius*.

DUCHESS DOLITTLE The Duchess of York, *Carrot Top*; after criticisms (1988–9) that she liked holidays and the good life more than duty.

DUCHESS OF DOWNING STREET, THE Marcia Williams, Baroness Falkender (1932–   ), secretary to Harold (later Lord) Wilson (1916–   ), Labour Prime Minister (1964–70; 1974–5). Also the *First Lady of Westminster*.

DUCHESS OF KENSINGTON, THE Diana Willis (1943–   ), London high-society drug-dealer sentenced to four years imprisonment (1985). Her clients included at least one titled person.

DUCHESS OF NORTH STAR, THE Jane Makim, née Ferguson (1957–   ), elder sister of the Duchess of York (*Carrot Top*). She married Alex Makim of North Star Farm on the borders of Queensland and New South Wales, Australia.

DUCKER Douglas Maclean, president of the Oxford University Boat Club (1885–6).

DUCKY
 i) Princess Victoria Melita of Coburg (1876–1964), granddaughter of Victoria (*Drina*). She married Prince Ernest of Hesse.

 ii) Clarence Nash (1905–85), American voice of the cartoon character Donald Duck (post-1934).

DUDE PRESIDENT, THE Chester Alan Arthur (1830–86), 21st President of the United States of America (1881–5), from his courtly manner and dandified dress which belied an efficient and courageous official. Also the *First Gentleman of the Land*, the *Gentleman Boss* and *Prince Arthur*.

DUGOUT DOUG General of the Army Douglas MacArthur (1880–1964), C-in-C Philippines and the Pacific (World War II) who lost command in Korea (1951) after a policy disagreement with President Harry Truman (*Give 'Em Hell Harry*); so called by American GIs who said he had a great concern for his personal safety.

DUG-UP DANDY, THE Samuel Rogers, the *Banker Poet*; so called in London clubs because of his funereal appearance. He was once asked 'Why don't you keep your own hearse? You can well afford it.'

DUELLIST, THE Beauchamp Bagenal (1741–1820) of Dunleckny, Ireland, a fire-eater said to have fought more than twenty duels, one of them as an old man sitting in a chair (from which he escaped unhurt). Also *King*.

DUKE
 i) Edward Kennedy Ellington (1899–1974), American jazz composer and pianist; so called as a boy because he was so well dressed. His father was a butler at the White House.

 ii) John Wayne (1907–79), American film-star whose real name was Marion Michael Morrison; so called after a pet dog he had as a boy.

 iii) Nduka Odizor (1958–   ), Nigerian Wimbledon-class tennis-player.

 iv) John Bond (1932–   ), manager of Birmingham FC (1986–   ) and formerly manager of Manchester City (1980–3). He played for West Ham for 16 years.

 v) David Nicholson (1939–   ), British racehorse trainer.

 vi) Michael S. Dukakis (1933–   ), Democratic presidential candidate in the 1988 elections. He is Governor of Massachusetts.

DUKE or COUNT COMBE William Combe (1741–1823), author of *The Three Tours of Doctor Syntax* (1809); from his dress and the way he lived. A note in Murray's reprint (1871) says reports represented Combe as having been born to wealth, but dying in poverty. At one time he kept two carriages, several horses and many servants.

DUKE DANGERFIELD Thomas Dangerfield (*circa* 1650–85), English adventurer involved in the Meal-Tub Plot (1679), a pretended conspiracy to assassinate the Duke of York (the *King Over the Water*). Papers he said proved the conspiracy were found in a meal-tub in the house of Mrs Cellier (the *Popish Midwife*), but they had been 'planted'. Dangerfield – proved to be a liar – died in custody. He was so called by John Smith in a pamphlet (1685) which declared that Dangerfield claimed to represent the Duke of Monmouth (*Absalom*), and had assumed the title of duke in Cornwall.

DUKE OF DARNICK, THE Scott, the *Ariosto of the North*; so called by the villagers of Abbotsford, Selkirkshire, Scotland, where he lived.
 • Darnick Tower is an old border peel near Abbotsford.

DUKE OF SHOREDITCH, THE An archer named Barlow of Shoreditch, one of the guards of Henry VIII (*Bluff Hal*), who gave such a dazzling performance at an archery contest at Windsor that the King awarded him the 'title'. The 'honour' continued until about 1682 with the captaincy of London archers until they were merged with the Artillery Company.

DULEEP Prince Kumar Shri Duleepsinhji (1905–59), Indian cricketer for Cambridgeshire and England between 1924 and 1932. He scored 173 against the Australians (1930). He was the nephew of *Ranji*. Also *Smith*.

DULL, THE Hugh Douglas (1294– ?), a churchman in a family of fighters. Hugh inherited the Douglas lands, but surrendered them to David II of Scotland (reigned 1324–71), who granted them to William, 1st Earl of Douglas (*circa* 1327–84).

DUM DUM John Stonehouse (1925–88), ex MP and former Postmaster General, sentenced at the Old Bailey (1976) to seven years imprisonment for theft, forgery and fraud. He 'faked' his own death to cover debts of about £800,000; so called by Sheila Buckley, his mistress, who later (1981) became his wife. Stonehouse served three years of his sentence.

DUMMY Admiral of the Fleet Sir Henry Francis Oliver (1865–1965), who was shrewd but said very little. The DNB suggests that the nickname came from 'Dumby' because of his 'verbal economy'. Also the *Father of Modern Navigation*.

DUMONT OF LETTERS, THE William Hazlitt (1778–1830), essayist and critic; so called by Bulwer Lytton (*Bulwig*). Also *Pygmalion Hazlitt*.

- Dumont was the name of a family of famous French artists.

DUNCAN OF THE KILN Colonel Duncan Macpherson of Cluny (1748–1817), who commanded a battalion of the 71st, or Fraser's Regiment, in America. He was born in a corn-kiln while his Jacobite parents were hiding after the 1745 rebellion.

DUNCE Duns Scotus, *Doctor Subtilis*. The name 'Duns' was first applied to 'whoso surpasseth others in cauilling or subtile philosophie' as Richard Stanyhurst wrote in 1577. 'Duns' became 'Dunce'. Few understood the subtlety of Duns Scotus, a scholastic theologian. Those who attacked the new way of thinking soon became 'dunces', incapable of learning.

DUNNIE WASSAIL Alexander Campbell (1764–1824), writer and music-master; so called by Scott.

DUNS SCOTUS Sir Walter Scott, the *Ariosto of the North*; so called by some young people around Abbotsford where he lived. It was an old college nickname from his love of antiquities, revived by them.

- After John Duns Scotus, *Doctor Subtilis*.

DURABLE DANE, THE O.M. Nelson, *Battling Nelson*.

DUSTBIN Dustin Hoffman (1937–), American film star; his school nickname.

DUSTY

i) Mary O'Brien (1940–), British singer who took her stage name Springfield from the Springfields when she was a member of that group.

ii) William Henry Hare (1952–), Rugby Union player for Nottingham, Leicester and England. He scored 6,319 points between 1971 and 1986. He holds 26 caps for England.

DUTCH

i) Ronald Wilson Reagan (1911–), 40th President of the United States of America (1981–8) and former film actor; his nickname as a boy allegedly from his Dutch bob hair style, although another version (said to come from Reagan himself) is that his father commented on baby Ronald that he looked like 'a little fat Dutchman'. After his retirement he was created (1989) a Knight of the Bath. Also the *Gipper*, the *Great Communicator*, *Ramblin' Ron* and the *Teflon President*.

ii) Ernest Joe Harrison (1910–), American golfer; Canadian Open champion (1949); All-American Open champion (1956).

iii) Cornelius Warmerden (1915–), American record pole jumper.

iv) Henry G. Dehnert (1896–1979), American basketball player in the Hall of Fame (1968). He played for the Celtics and is credited with originating pivot play.

DUTCH BEAR, THE William III, the *Deliverer*. Englishmen resented the way the best jobs went to William's Dutch friends and grumbled about the 'Dutch Bear'. While Dutchmen sat down to eat with the King, men like the Duke of Marlborough (*Anne's Great Captain*) had to stand.

DUTCH HENRY Henry Borne (died 1930s), horse-thief in the American West (1870s).

DUTCH JOHN John Wagner (hanged 1864), gold-train robber in the American West.

DUTCH SAM Samuel Evans (fl. early 19th century), a pugilist who had the reputation of being unbeatable. His height – about 5 ft 6 in – prevented him from becoming champion of England. He had, nevertheless, says Egan (the *Elder*), 'vanquished some of the best 10 or 12 stone bruisers in the country'. He fought Tom Belcher to a standstill in the 57th round (1806).

DUTCH SCHULTZ Arthur Flegenheimer (1902–35), German-born bootlegger of the New York gangster era (1917–30s). He made a fortune from the numbers racket, but was a brutal paranoic miser; of the Frog Hollow gang.

- 'Dutch' = Deutsch = German. See also *Dutchy*.

DUTCH THOMSON Richard Thomson (died 1613), British biblical scholar and divine.

DUTCHY

i) Franz Sigel (1824–1902), German-born American general during the American Civil War.

ii) Marlene Dietrich (1901–   ), German-born American film actress; so called by her Hollywood friends because she had been born in Berlin. Her pre-film name was Maria Magdalene von Lorsch.

- Cf *Dutch Schultz*.

DWARF GIANTESS, THE Mary Jane Youngman, an Australian (19th century) who was 35 in tall at fifteen, but was 3 ft 6 in round the shoulders and 4 ft 3 in round the waist.

DYING TITAN, THE Robert Greene, the *Ape of Euphues*, overshadowed by Shakespeare (the *Bard of All Time*); so called by J.A. Symonds (1840–93) in *Shakespeare's Predecessors*.

- Titans in Greek mythology were a race of giants banished from heaven by Zeus. The name came to mean someone of great intellectual stature.

DYLAN Robert (Bob) G.D. Willis (1949–   ), cricketer for Surrey, Warwickshire, and England (captain), awarded an MBE for his services to cricket. He took 325 Test Match wickets – 128 of them in 35 Tests against Australia. He retired in 1984; name adopted by him from the singer Bob Dylan (1941–   ). Also *Goose* and *Harold*.

DYNAMITE DICK Dan Clifton (died 1896), American cattle rustler and train-robber in Oklahoma, a member of the Doolin gang.

E

EAGLE, THE Edward (Eddie) Edwards (1963–), Cheltenham plasterer who was the darling of the crowds at the 1988 Winter Olympics in Calgary, Canada, when he was the sole British competitor in the ski jump. He came last but set a new British record with a jump of 71 metres. He appeared on the Johnny Carson show in America before he returned home and then on British television.

  • See the *Prince of Darkness* (iii).

EARL BEARDIE Alexander Lindsay, 4th Earl of Crawford (died 1454), a doughty fighter who earned another nickname, the *Tiger Earl*. In the mid-15th century he was the most powerful man in the east of Scotland, and arranged with the earls of Ross and Douglas to divide the country between them, but the rebellion was frustrated and they submitted (1452).

  • 'Beardie' is the Scottish name for the three-spined stickleback or bearded loach, a fierce defender of its territory.

EARL-BISHOP, THE Frederick Augustus Hervey (1730–1803), 4th Earl of Bristol; Bishop of Derry.

EARL OF EARLSTON, THE Alexander Smith (1587–1654), a Covenanter of Earlston who opposed the ecclesiastical plans of Charles I (the *Ahab of the Nation*). The King gave him the nickname.

  • Earlston, Scotland was the home of *Thomas the Rhymer*.

EARL PATE Patrick Stewart, 2nd Earl of Orkney (died 1614), son of Robert Stewart (died 1592) and cousin of James IV (the *Star of the Stewart Line*). Patrick defied royal authority in the Orkneys, and in 1609 was arrested and imprisoned. He was later hanged, and his honours were forfeited.

  • 'Pate' is the Scottish abbreviation of Patrick.

EASY ETHEREGE Sir George Etherege (?1635–91), English dramatist and poet, rake, dandy and wit, friend of Lord Rochester (*Virgin Modesty*). He was also called *Gentle George* because of his tolerant manner.

EBONY William Blackwood (1776–1834), publisher of *Blackwood's Magazine* (1817) which received the same nickname, given by Hogg (the *Ettrick Shepherd*).

EBONY ANTELOPE or EXPRESS, THE Jesse Owens, the *Black Flash*, from his speed.

EDDY Prince Albert Victor, Duke of Clarence (1864–92), eldest son of the Prince of Wales (the *Peacemaker*). He might have been King had he lived longer.

EDGEWORTH BESS Elizabeth Lyon, a prostitute who frequented The Black Lion in Newton Street, London, and was friend and accomplice of Jack Sheppard (1702–24). She helped him to escape on two occasions, once from the condemned cell. Soon after Sheppard's execution, she was transported for theft.

EDWARD'S FRENCH LADY Thérèse-Bernardine Mongenêt, known as Mlle Julie de St Laurent, mistress of Edward Augustus, Duke of Kent the *Corporal*, father of Queen Victoria (*Drina*), for twenty-five years before he was married.

EGGHEAD, THE Adlai Edward Stevenson (1900–65), American lawyer and Presidential candidate (1952 and 1956), American Ambassador to the United Nations (1961–5); from his intelligence.

EIGHTPENCE Osbert Huit Deniers, Justiciar of London (1141), a rich merchant who employed as a notary his kinsman, Thomas à Becket (1118–70) between 1140 and 1142 before he took Holy Orders; a nickname which became his surname.

  • A notary in those days was a clerk or secretary. 'Denier' was a French coin, a word used for an English penny. Justiciar was roughly equivalent to the present Lord Mayor.

EIGHT-STRING JACK John Colledge (fl. 1770s), a boy pickpocket.

- Cf *Sixteen-String Jack*.

ELDER, THE

i) Edward or Eadward, King of England (Wessex: reigned 901–24), second son of Alfred the *Great*.

- 'Elder' in this context would appear to be the *ealdor* = the chief of the clan, and so is a rank and not a family relationship.

ii) Thomas Howard, Earl of Surrey, and later 2nd Duke of Norfolk (1444–1524), Earl Marshal of England (1513–24).

iii) Edmund Calamy (1600–66), English clergyman who opposed the execution of Charles I (the *Ahab of the Nation*).

iv) George Colman (1732–94), British dramatist and essayist, who wrote *The Jealous Wife*, an adaptation of Fielding's *Tom Jones*. Also *George the First*, and the *Temple Leech*.

v) Pierce Egan (1772–1849), sporting writer and author of the *Life in London* books, works on pugilism (e.g. *Boxiana*) and the first British sports editor. Also *Fancy's Child*, *Glorious Pierce*, the *Great Lexicographer of the Fancy*, the *Immortal Pierce*, *Pippy* and the *Veteran Historian of the Ring*.

vi) John Crome (1768–1821), British landscape painter. Also the *English Hobbema* and *Old Crome*.

vii) William Pitt, Earl of Chatham, *Aeolus*.

viii) Thomas Boston (1677–1732), Scottish calvinist minister. Also the *Marrow Man*.

ix) William Caslon, the *Coryphaeus of Letter-Founding,* who began as a gun-engraver. His son (1720–98) was also William.

ELECTRIC HEELS or 'LECTRIC HEELS Stanley (Stan) Mortensen (1921–   ), Blackpool, Wales and England footballer, famous in the 1950s for his speed on the field. He holds 26 caps for England. During the war he survived a crash in an RAF bomber. Also 'Morty' and *Thunderboots*.

ELECTRIC SPARK, THE Lillie Langtry, *Baby*.

ELEPHANT, THE

i) Edward Law, 1st Earl of Ellenborough (1790–1871), Governor-General of India (1841–4). A word-play on his title and the fact that he was an aggressive man and a powerful speaker. He also had a love of pageantry and personally supervised the paintings of elephants for a fantastic military spectacle at Ferozepur; nickname mentioned in *Punch* (March 1856).

ii) Charlotte von Kilmannsegge (1675–1725), mistress of George I (the *Turnip-Hoer*). She was fat and ugly. Walpole (the *Autocrat of Strawberry Hill*) said she had 'two acres of cheeks' and a swollen neck.

ELEPHANT BILL Lieutenant-Colonel James Howard Williams (1897–1958), in charge of elephant companies with the Fourteenth Army in Burma (World War II).

ELEPHANT MAN, THE Joseph Carey Merrick (1862–90), a Leicestershire man who suffered from neurofibromatosis, which gravely disfigured him. He was exhibited in a travelling freak show until he was rescued by Frederick Treves (1853–1923; later Sir), a British surgeon and professor of anatomy at the Royal College of Surgeons. Treves wrote *The Elephant Man and Other Reminiscences* (1923). There was a notable film (1980) starring John Hurt.

ELLA Elizabeth, Princess of Hesse (1864–1918), granddaughter of Queen Victoria (*Drina*). She married the Grand Duke Serge of Russia.

ELOCUTION WALKER John Walker (1732–1807), British lexicographer and teacher of elocution, author of *The Pronouncing Dictionary*.

ELOQUENT OLD MAN, THE W.E. Gladstone, the *Dismember for Great Britain*.

- Cf *Old Man Eloquent*.

EL TEL Terence (Terry) Venables (1943–   ), former manager of Queen's Park Rangers Football Club and coach to Barcelona FC (1984–7); so called in Spain. He became manager of Tottenham Hotspur in 1987.

ELVIS THE PELVIS Elvis Aron Presley (1935–77), American pop singer (1960s);

because of his hip movements when singing. Also *King* and *King of Rock 'n' Roll*.

EMERALD PIMPERNEL, THE James McCann (1940–   ), Irish, linked with the Irish Republican Army; so called for his amazing adventures in drugs and arms smuggling. He escaped from a gaol when charged with arson. Also the *Fox*.

EMIR DYNAMITE Colonel Thomas Edward Lawrence (1888–1935), British agent who helped the Sharif of Mecca in his revolt against Turkish rule (World War I); so called by the Arabs, who also knew him as 'El Aurans'. He used dynamite to blow up Turkish railways. Also 'Lawrence of Arabia' and the *Uncrowned King of Arabia*.

EMPEROR, THE William Stebbing (died 1869), British bookmaker with a close resemblance to the Emperor Louis Napoleon of France.

EMPEROR AUGUSTUS, THE Augustus Harris, *Augustus Druriolanus*.

EMPEROR OF BOWLERS, THE Alfred Shaw (1842–1907), Nottinghamshire cricketer; so called by Richard Daft (1835–1900), also of Nottinghamshire, who captained an All-England XI (1872). In 1878 Shaw took 201 wickets for an average of 10.96 runs. He played in an All-England XI, and with other players took four teams to Australia in the 1880s.

EMPEROR OF THE WEST, THE John Murray, the *Anak of Publishers*; so called by Constable (the *Crafty*) after Murray had moved from Fleet Street to the West End of London.

EMPIRE BUILDER, THE James Hill (1838–1916), American steamship and railway magnate who built the Great Northern Railway and so helped to develop agriculture and trade in the north-west of America. He also contributed to the building of the Canadian Pacific Railway.

EMPIRE JIM Captain (later Colonel) James Foley (1887–1947); because of his great interest in and contribution to the development of British West Africa. Also the *Father of the RWAFF* and *Ruwan Zafi*.

EMPRESS OF EMOTION, THE Elissa Landi (1904–48). Austrian-Italian actress in American films. Her real name was Elizabeth Kuhnelt.

EMPRESS OF THE BLUES, THE Bessie Smith (1894–1937), American blues singer. Earlier in her career she had been *Queen of the Blues*.

'ENERY Henry William Cooper (1934–   ), British heavyweight boxer, especially in ''Enery's 'Ammer', his favourite punch; because of his Cockney background. He was British champion 1959–69 and 1970–1, and once knocked down Muhammed Ali (*Gaseous Cassius*).

ENGLAND'S DARLING

i) Alfred the *Great* (849–901), King of Wessex. As a resistance leader, he defeated the Vikings and united the West Saxons and the Mercians; nickname recorded in the 13th century by Layamon (the *English Ennius*). Also the *Father of English Prose*.

ii) Hereward, the *Champion of Women* who fought a long rearguard action against the Normans (*circa* 1070). Both 'England's Darling' and the 'Wake' were latter-day nicknames.

ENGLAND'S GREATEST SPORTSMAN Hugh Cecil, 5th Earl Lonsdale (1857–1944). He took part in and promoted all manner of sports including boxing and horse-racing. He once met J.L. Sullivan (the *Boston Strong Boy*) in the ring and knocked him out. He is best remembered for the Lonsdale Belt awards, which he created in 1909 when he was President of the National Sporting Club. Also *Lordy* and the *Yellow Earl*.

ENGLAND'S NEPTUNE Sir Francis Drake, the *Dragon*, admiral and circumnavigator with a long list of victories over the Spanish, including action against the Armada (1588); so called in the poems of Richard Barnfield (1574–1627).

• Neptune was the Roman sea god.

ENGLAND'S NESTOR Sir John Hawkins (1532–95), admiral who introduced slave-trading to England and fought against the Armada; so called by Barnfield (above).

• Nestor, King of Pylos, was one of those who sailed against Troy, and was renowned for his wisdom, justice and knowledge of war.

ENGLAND'S PRIDE AND WESTMINSTER'S GLORY Sir Francis Burdett (1770–1844), British agitator for reform against abuses, and the most popular politician of his day. Also *Old Glory* and the *Piccadilly Patriot*.

ENGLAND'S RECRUITING SERGEANT Horatio Bottomley (1860–1934), MP and confidence trickster, a financial wizard who was co-founder of the *Financial Times* (1888) and owner and editor of *John Bull* (1906). He was imprisoned for seven years for a Victory Bond swindle (1920); from his patriotic speeches and articles during World War I. Also the *Great Horatio*, the *Houdini of the Courts*, the *Man of Millions* and the *Napoleon of Finance*.

ENGLISH ACHILLES, THE

i) John Howard (1408–35), because of his distinction in the French wars. He became Earl of Arundel (1433).

ii) John Talbot, Earl of Shrewsbury, the *Achilles of England*.

iii) Robert Devereux, 2nd Earl of Essex (*circa* 1567–1601), English admiral and Earl Marshal of England. He distinguished himself at Zutphen (1586), and commanded a successful expedition against Cadiz (1596). In 1601 he led a protest 'rebellion' in London, and was executed for treason.

• See also the *Achilles of England*.

ENGLISH ALEXANDER, THE Henry V (1387–1422). He scored a series of victories against the French, including Agincourt (1415). Also *Monmouth*.

• Alexander III, the Great (356–323 BC), king of Macedon (336–323 BC) created an empire which extended to the Punjab. Fluellen in Shakespeare's *Henry V* says: 'If you mark Alexander's life well, Harry of Monmouth's life is come after it indifferent well.'

ENGLISH ANACREON, THE Alexander Brome (1620–66), English poet; so called in Edward Phillips' *Theatrum Poetarum Anglicorum* (1675).

• See *Anacreon Moore*. Phillips (whose name is also spelt 'Philips') was Milton's nephew.

ENGLISH ARETINE, THE Thomas Nash or Nashe (1567–1601), poet and dramatist; so called by Thomas Lodge (?1558–1625), traveller, lyric poet and author. Nash wrote the first English adventure story, *The Unfortunate Traveller, or the Life of Jacke Wilton* (1594). Also the *Young Euphues* and the *Young Juvenal*.

• Pietro Aretino (1492–1556), Italian author at the court of Giovanni de Medici, wrote satires, comedies and poems.

ENGLISH ARISTOPHANES or THE MODERN ARISTOPHANES Samuel Foote, *Beau Nasty*. He invented the word 'panjandrum'. Counsel in a libel action likened his client to Socrates, and Foote to Aristophanes.

• Aristophanes (*circa* 450–*circa* 385 BC) wrote a number of plays, including *The Clouds* and *The Wasps* which were caricatures of contemporary life. *The Clouds* satirized the Greek love of litigation.

ENGLISH ARISTIDES, THE John Pym (1584–1643), republican and promoter of the impeachments of Lord Strafford (*Black Tom Tyrant*) and Archbishop Laud (**Hocuspocus**). Also *King Pym*.

• See the *British Aristides*.

ENGLISH ATTILA, THE Oliver Cromwell, the *Almighty Nose*.

• See *Attila the Hen*.

ENGLISH ATTICUS, THE

i) Joseph Addison (1672–1719), essayist, poet and editor; so called by Pope (the *Bard of Twickenham*). Also the *Literary Machiavel*.

ii) Richard Heber (1773–1833), bibliomaniac. So called by Dibdin (the *Beau Brummell of Living Authors*). Also *Magnificent Heber*.

• See the *Christian Atticus*.

ENGLISH BACH, THE Johann Christian Bach (1735–1782), who lived in London (1759–82). He was the eleventh son of J.S. Bach. For twenty years he was the most popular musician in London.

ENGLISH BAYARD, THE George *Chinese Gordon*.

• See the *Bayard of the Confederate Army*.

ENGLISH CLAUDE, THE Richard Wilson (1714–82), British landscape painter, an original member of the Royal Academy.
- Claude Lorrain (1600–82), French classical painter in the classical Italian tradition.

ENGLISH DEBUSSY, THE Cyril Scott (1879–1970), composer and concert pianist.
- Claude-Achille Debussy (1862–1918), was a French impressionist composer.

ENGLISH DEMOSTHENES, THE Richard Baxter, the *Chief of the English Protestant Schoolmen*; so called by Philip Dodderidge (1702–51), a celebrated nonconformist and hymn-writer.
- See the *Demosthenes of the Pulpit*.

ENGLISH DIANA, THE Queen Elizabeth I (1533–1603). Also *Gloriana*, the *Glory of Her Sex*, *Good Queen Bess*, the *Great Eliza*, the *Maiden Queen*, the *Miracle of Time*, *Nature's Glory*, *Oriana*, *Queen Bess*, the *Queen of Shepherds*, the *Queen of the Northern Seas*, the *Untamed Heifer*, the *Virgin Queen* and the *World's Wonder*.
- Diana was the Roman goddess of the Moon, the chase, chastity and children, equated with Artemis, the Greek goddess.

ENGLISH ENNIUS, THE
i) Layamon or Lawemon (fl. 1200), a priest who wrote *Brut* (*circa* 1205), a chronicle of England from the time of the supposed arrival of Brutus to Cadawalader or Ceadwalla (689), based on Wace's *Roman de Brut*.
- See Caedwalla, the *Blessed*.
ii) Geoffrey Chaucer, the *British Horace*.
- Quintus Ennius (239–169 BC), 'Father of Roman Poetry', wrote *Annales,* a history of Rome from the earliest times to his own.

ENGLISH EPICURUS, THE Bertrand Arthur William, 3rd Earl Russell (1872–1970), British philosopher.
- Epicurus (*circa* 342–*circa* 271 BC), Athenian philosopher, taught that the greatest good was the greatest pleasure, but he meant by that peace of mind and freedom from fear.

ENGLISH EUSEBIUS, THE Bishop Gilbert Burnet, the *Busy Scots Parson*, who wrote *The History of the Reformation in England* (1679–81).
- Eusebius, Bishop of Caesarea (*circa* 275–340) wrote *A History of the Christian Church* (*circa* 325) and was called 'The Father of Church History'.

ENGLISH HERCULES, THE Guy, Earl of Warwick, hero of a verse romance (early 14th century). He was tall and very strong, fought the Saracens, slew a dragon and the Dun Cow of Dunsmore. The Beauchamp earls claim descent from Guy.
- Hercules, one of the heroes of Roman and Greek legend, performed twelve labours given to him by Eurystheus, ruler of Argos, whom he served.

ENGLISH HERMIT, THE Roger Crab (1621–80) of Bethnal Green, London. He lived on 3*s*.3*d* (about 17p) a year, eating herbs and roots. He had served in the Parliamentary army, and had had his skull cloven by a sword. He was said to have been almost a skeleton when he died. Also the *Mad Hatter*.

ENGLISH HIPPOCRATES, THE Thomas Sydenham (1624–89), physician in the Cromwellian army. He discovered a cooling remedy for smallpox and revived the holistic idea of Hippocrates. He was in fact the founder of modern clinical medicine. A London suburb was named after him.
- Hippocrates (*circa* 469–399 BC), established by his non-philosophic approach the scientific attitude to medicine.

ENGLISH HOBBEMA, THE John Crome, the *Elder*, leader of the Norwich School of painters, whose last words were reported as 'O Hobbema, Hobbema, how I do love thee.'
- Meyndert Hobbema (1638–1709) was a Dutch landscape artist.

ENGLISH HOMER, THE William Warner (?1558–1609), poet of *Albion's England*; so called by Ascham (the *Father of English Prose*).
- See the *British Homer*.

ENGLISH HORACE, THE or THE HORACE OF ENGLAND

i) Ben Jonson, the *Bricklayer*; so called by Thomas Dekker (*circa* 1570–1623) who worked with him on a play.

ii) Alexander Pope, the *Bard of Twickenham*.

ENGLISH JOAN OF ARC, THE
Mary Ambree, who is reported to have taken part in the siege of Ghent (1584) when it was held by the Spanish. She fought to avenge her lover's death, says the ballad of which she is the heroine. She is mentioned in Percy's *Reliques* (1765), by Beaumont and Fletcher (*The Scornful Lady*: 1610) and several times by Jonson (the *Bricklayer*).

- Joan of Arc (1412–31) raised the siege of Orleans and helped Charles VII to regain the French throne from the English. She was burnt at the stake but later canonized.

ENGLISH JUSTINIAN, THE
Edward I (1239–1307), who influenced the development of land laws and the summoning of parliamentary assemblies; so called by Edward Jenks in a book title (1902). Also the *Hammer of the Scots*, *Longshanks* and the *Scourge of Scotland*.

- Justinian I (483–565), East Roman or Byzantine emperor, consolidated the laws of the Roman empire and turned chaos into order.

ENGLISH JUVENAL, THE

i) John Oldham (1653–83), poet and satirist of *Satires Against Virtues* and *Satires Against the Jesuits* (1681), who took Juvenal as his model; so called by Scott (the *Ariosto of the North*). Also the *Marcellus of Our English Tongue*.

ii) George Wither (1588–1667), imprisoned for his satires *Abuses stript and whipt* (1613). He was, however, a bad poet.

- See the *British Juvenal*.

ENGLISH LITERATURE'S PERFORMING FLEA
Sir Pelham Grenville Wodehouse (1881–1975), comic novelist and creator of Jeeves; so called by Sean O'Casey (1880–1964), Irish playwright. Also *Plum*.

ENGLISH MARCELLUS, THE
Henry Frederick, Prince of Wales (1594–1612), son of James I (the *British Solomon*), whom he disliked; so called by D'Israeli (1766–1848).

- Three members of the Marcellus family were bitter enemies of Caesar; the greatest was Marcus Claudius Marcellus, consul (51 BC).

ENGLISH MARIVAUX, THE
Samuel Richardson (1689–1761), novelist best remembered for *Clarissa Harlowe* (1747–8). Also the *Founder of the English Domestic Novel* and the *Shakespeare of Prose Fiction*.

- Pierre Marivaux (1688–1763), French novelist whose brilliant dialogue added the words *marivaudage* and *marivauder* to the French language.

ENGLISH MASTIFF, THE
John Milton, *Black-Mouthed Zoilus*; so called by the German writer Gerhard Johann Vossius (1577–1649), who visited England in 1629.

ENGLISH MERLIN, THE
William Lilly (1602–81), astrologer whose almanacs received serious attention, particularly from members of the Long Parliament (1640–53). He published two pamphlets under the name of *Merlinus Anglicus*. Also the *Last Astrologer*.

- Merlin was the legendary magician and bard in stories of King Arthur.

ENGLISH MERSENNE, THE
John Collins (1625–83), mathematician and physicist.

- Marin Mersenne (1586–1648) was a well-known contemporary French mathematician.

ENGLISH MESSIAH, THE

i) James Naylor (*circa* 1618–60), Cromwellian soldier and Quaker who declared he was the incarnation of Jesus Christ. He was convicted of blasphemy (1656) and sentenced to be whipped through the streets, branded on the forehead with a B, have his tongue bored through with a red-hot iron and serve two years in prison.

ii) Richard Brothers (1757–1824), an ex-Royal Navy officer and religious fanatic who proclaimed himself (1793) 'the Nephew of the Almighty, and Prince of the Hebrews, appointed to lead them to the land of Canaan'. He was imprisoned as a criminal lunatic after he had prophesied the end of the British monarchy.

iii) John Nichols Tom (1799–1838), a religious fanatic who thought his body housed the Holy Ghost. He was imprisoned as a criminal lunatic (1833–7), and on his release led a band of followers in Kent. He was killed in a skirmish with soldiers near Canterbury.

iv) The Reverend Henry James Prince (1811–99), founder of the Agapemonites, who declared he was the personification of the Holy Ghost. Letters to him were addressed to 'Our Holy Lord God'. He died at the Agapemone he founded at Spaxton, near Bridgewater, Somerset.

v) The Reverend John Hugh Smyth-Pigott (1852–1927), who became leader of Agapemonites after the death of (iv). He also announced that he was the Christ (1902).

- An *agape* (a Greek word meaning 'brotherly love') was a love feast held by early Christians before the erection of churches and associated with the Lord's Supper. The *agapai* were not originally occasions of physical love, although that could not be said of the Victorian versions.

ENGLISH MESSOFANTI, THE Edward Craven Hawtrey (1789–1862), headmaster and Provost of Eton (1834–52); because of his command of languages. Also *Priscian*.

- Giuseppe Caspar Mezzofanti (1774–1849) was a cardinal and a linguist who spoke 27 languages fluently.

ENGLISH MILO, THE Thomas Topham, the *British Samson*.

- Milo of Crotona was a renowned athlete (fl. 511 BC). He is reputed to have carried a four-year old heifer on his shoulders through the stadium at Olympia and to have eaten it in a single day.

ENGLISH MOLIERE, THE John O'Keefe or O'Keeffee (1747–1833), dramatist, an actor in Dublin before he went to London. He specialized in farces and light operas. Hazlitt (the *Dumont of Letters*)

gave him this rather unjustified nickname, considering he was Irish and his work is little remembered.

- Jean Baptiste Poquelin de Molière (1622–73), one of the greatest of French dramatists.

ENGLISH MONTESQUIEU, THE John Louis de Lolme (?1740–1807), who wrote a book on the English constitution (English edition 1775).

- Baron Charles Louis de Secondat de Montesquieu (1689–1755), social philosopher, wrote *De l'Esprit des Lois* (1748).

ENGLISH MOZART, THE Sir Henry Rowley Bishop (1786–1855). He wrote operas, cantatas, songs and incidental music to Shakespeare's plays. He was the first musician to be knighted.

ENGLISH OPIUM-EATER, THE Thomas de Quincey (1785–1859), after the publication of his *Confessions of an English Opium-Eater* (1822).

ENGLISH PAGANINI, THE Henry Hayward (1814–84), a remarkable violinist.

- Niccolo Paganini (1782–1840), Italian violinist of amazing virtuosity.

ENGLISH PALESTRINA, THE Orlando Gibbons (1583–1625), organist and composer. Also the *Greatest Finger of the Age*.

- Giovanni Pierluigi de Palestrina (*circa* 1525–94), Italian composer.

ENGLISH PALLADIO, THE Inigo Jones (1573–1651), architect who designed the Banqueting Hall, Whitehall, London, a façade of St Paul's Cathedral and the piazza at Covent Garden, among other things. Also the *English Vitruvius* and the *Master Surveyor*.

- Andrea Palladio (1508–80), Italian architect, adapted and developed the classical style of building.

ENGLISH PERSIUS, THE Bishop Joseph Hall, the *Christian Seneca*, a satirist.

- Aulus Persius Flaccus (34–62), Roman poet and satirist, has been described as the forerunner of Christian apologists.

ENGLISH PETRARCH, THE Sir Philip Sidney, the *British Bayard*; so called by Raleigh (the *Knight of the Cloak*).

- Francesco Petrarch (1304–74), humanist, patriot and poet, precursor of the Italian Renaissance.

ENGLISH PINDAR, THE Abraham Cowley (1618–67), who began to write poetry at the age of ten. His *Pindarique Odes* (1656) introduced a fashion admired and imitated by poets from Dryden to Gray (who was nicknamed the *British Pindar*). Also the *English Virgil* and the *Horace of England*.

ENGLISH PLATO, THE The Reverend John Morris (1657–1711), a follower of Plato and Descartes. He wrote *Essay towards the Theory of an Ideal and Intelligible World* (1701–4).

- Plato (428–347 BC), the great Greek philosopher, was a disciple of Socrates. He wrote *The Republic* and the *Dialogues*.

ENGLISH POMPADOUR, THE Elizabeth, Marchioness Conyingham (1774–1861), wife of Henry, 1st Marquess Conyingham (1766–1832) and last mistress of George IV (the *Adonis of Fifty*). She took over from Isabella, Marchioness of Hertford (the *Sultana*) in 1821; so called because of her vigorous interference in State matters. She was also mean and greedy. Also the *Lady Steward* and the *Vice-Queen*.

- Jeanne Antoinette Pompadour (1721–64), mistress of Louis XV, wielded great influence over the government of France.

ENGLISH RABELAIS, THE

i) Jonathan Swift, *Doctor Presto*; so called by Voltaire (1694–1778).

ii) Laurence Sterne (1713–68), author of *Tristram Shandy* (1760–7) and *A Sentimental Journey* (1768); so called by Warburton (the *Colossus of Literature*).

iii) Thomas Amory (?1691–1788), author of *The Life of John Buncle Esq* (1756–66).

- François Rabelais (1490–1553) was the author of *Pantagruel and Gargantua* (1532–3). Cf the *Modern Rabelais*.

ENGLISH RAPHAEL, THE Thomas Stothard (1755–1834), painter, engraver and book-illustrator.

- Raffaello Sanzio (1483–1520), Italian painter, was known as Raphael.

ENGLISH ROCHEFOUCAULD, THE or THE LA ROCHEFOUCAULD OF ENGLAND Philip Dormer Stanhope, 4th Earl of Chesterfield (1694–1773), statesman and wit, famous for his letters to his son (1774). Also the *Maecenas and Petronius of His Age*, the *Prince of Wits* and the *Tea-Table Scoundrel*.

- François, duc de la Rochefoucauld (1613–80), French politician, published *Moral Maxims and Reflections* (1665).

ENGLISH ROSCIUS, THE Richard Burbage, *Another Roscius*.

- See the *African Roscius*.

ENGLISH ST SEBASTIAN, THE St Edmund (841–69), *Martyr* king murdered by the Danes with arrows.

- St Sebastian was put to death in a similar way (288).

ENGLISH SALVATOR ROSA, THE John Hamilton Mortimer (1741–79), historical painter.

- Salvator Rosa (1615–1673) was an Italian painter who specialized in battle scenes, soldiers and bandits.

ENGLISH SAPPHO, THE Mary Robinson (née Darby) (1758–1800), actress, novelist and poet, who became the mistress of the Prince of Wales (the *Adonis of Fifty*) after he had seen her as Perdita in *The Winter's Tale*; sometimes 'The Lame Sappho', after an illness which left her with a limp. Also the *Fair Perdita*.

- Sappho (*circa* 612–? BC), renowned Greek poetess of Lesbos. **See** the *Tenth Muse*.

ENGLISH SENECA, THE Joseph Hall, Bishop of Exeter, the *Christian Seneca*.

ENGLISH SOCRATES, THE Samuel Johnson, *Blinking Sam*; so called by Boswell (the *Ambitious Thane*), e.g. in *A Journal of a Tour to the Hebrides with Dr Samuel Johnson* (1785).

- Socrates (*circa* 470–399 BC), Greek philosopher of Athens, wrote nothing and is known only through the works of Plato and others.

ENGLISH SOLOMON, THE James I, the *British Solomon*.

ENGLISH TENIERS, THE George Morland (1763–1804), painter of landscapes and animals, as well as scenes of the life of the poor.

- David Teniers (1610–90), of the Flemish School, was a painter of landscapes and drinking scenes.

ENGLISH TERENCE, THE or THE TERENCE OF ENGLAND Richard Cumberland (1732–1811), prolific dramatist and novelist; so called by Goldsmith (the *Child of Nature*). Also the *Man Without a Skin*.

- Publius Terentius Afer (*circa* 190–159 BC) was a Roman comic poet and dramatist praised by Julius Caesar as a polished playwright.

ENGLISH TINTORETTO, THE or THE TINTORETTO OF ENGLAND William Dobson (1610–46), painter of portraits and historical subjects; so called by Charles I (the *Ahab of the Nation*). Also the *English Van Dyck*.

- Jacopo Rubusti, nicknamed 'Tintoretto' (a little dyer) (1518–94) was a Venetian painter of many richly coloured canvases.

ENGLISH VAN DYCK, THE William Dobson, see above.

- Sir Anthony Van Dyck (1599–1641) was a great Flemish portrait-painter who became an Englishman.

ENGLISH VIRGIL, THE

i) Lord Tennyson, the *Bard of Arthurian Romance*.

ii) Abraham Cowley, the *English Pindar*; so called by Sir John Cotton (died 1752), MP, wit and antiquary.

- Publius Vergilius Maro (70–19 BC), Roman poet of *The Aeneid*.

ENGLISH VITRUVIUS, THE Inigo Jones, the *English Palladio*.

- Marcus Vitruvius Pollio (fl. 1st century BC) was a Roman architect and military engineer under Augustus (63 BC–14 AD).

ENGLISH XENOPHON, THE John Astley (died 1595), courtier and Master of the Jewel House, who wrote a book on horsemanship (1584); so called by *Ape Gabriel* Harvey.

- Xenophon (*circa* 430 BC) was a pupil of Socrates. He wrote treatises on horses and hunting.

ENSIGN, THE William Maginn, the *Adjutant*. He wrote under the pseudonym of 'Ensign Doherty'; so called in *Noctes Ambrosianae*.

EPIC RENEGADE, THE Robert Southey, the *Ballad Monger*; so called by Byron (*Baby*). Southey, who had been expelled from Westminster School for an essay on flogging, was attacked in the House of Commons as 'a renegado' after his drama *Wat Tyler*, filled with republican sentiments, had been printed (1817).

EPIGRAMMATIST, THE John Owen, the *British Martial*.

EQUALITY BROWN Timothy Brown (1744–1820), a supporter of Queen Caroline (1768–1821) in her conflict with George IV (*Adonis of Fifty*).

EREMITE OF TIBBALS, THE William Cecil, Baron Burghley (1520–98), statesman under Queen Elizabeth (the *English Diana*) who gave him the nickname because he had a house at Theobalds. 'Eremite' is an old spelling of 'hermit' and 'Tibbals' is a diminutive of 'Theobalds' (others are 'Tibble' and 'Tibbles'). Burghley spent a lot of time at and money on the house. Also *Machiavel*.

- Theobalds Park, Hertfordshire, once belonged to Cardinal Wolsey (the *Boy Baccaleur*). James I (the *British Solomon*) died there.

EREWHON BUTLER Samuel Butler (1835–1902), author of *Erewhon* (1872); so called to distinguish him from *Hudibras Butler*.

'ER INDOORS Margaret Thatcher, *Attila the Hen*.

- The nickname of the never-seen wife of Arthur Daley in the British television series *The Minder*. One play in the series contained the line '"'Er Indoors" at No 10.'

EST-IL-POSSIBLE? Prince George of Denmark (1653–1708), consort of Queen Anne (*Brandy Nan*). Every time in 1699 when Prince George heard of someone deserting his father-in-law, James II (the

King Over the Water), he exclaimed *Est il possible?* When James at last missed Prince George he commented 'So *Est-il possible?* is gone too', and the nickname stuck.

E.T. Sir Kenneth Newman (1926–   ), Commissioner of the Metropolitan Police (1982–7).
- E.T. was an extraterrestrial figure, centre of a film (1982).

ETHIOPIAN BRUCE James Bruce, *Abyssinian Bruce*.

ETTERICK SHEPHERD, THE James Hogg, the *Boar of the Forest*.

EUROPE'S LIBERATOR The Duke of Wellington, the *Achilles of England*; so called by Byron (*Baby*).
- But what Byron wrote was: 'Called "Saviour of the Nations" – not yet saved, / And "Europe's Liberator" – still enslaved.'

EVANGELIC DOCTOR, THE John Wyclif, *Doctor Evangelicus*.

EVANS OF THE BROKE Admiral Edward Ratcliffe Garth Russell Evans, 1st Baron Mountevans (1881–1957), who gained fame (World War I) when he commanded HMS *Broke* (**see Brave Broke**) by defeating six German destroyers. This was in a Channel action when *Broke* was in the company of the destroyer HMS *Swift*. The engagement developed into hand-to-hand fighting with cutlasses and revolvers.

EVENING STAR OF STEPNEY, THE William Greenhill (died 1677), who drew large crowds by his lectures in Stepney, London.
- Cf the *Morning Star of Stepney*.

EVER-MEMORABLE, THE John Hales (1584–1656), scholar and Arminian divine who was said by Marvell (the *British Aristides*) to be 'one of the cleverest heads . . . in Christendom'. He was chaplain to Archbishop Laud (*Hocuspocus*). Also the *Walking Library*.
- Arminians followed the doctrines of Jacobus Arminius (1560–1609), Dutch opponent of the Calvinistic philosophy of predestination.

EXCHEQUER OF ELOQUENCE, THE Sir John Cheke (1514–57), Greek and Latin scholar and statesman. He founded Greek studies at Oxford University and was an MP (1547–53); so called by Nash (the *English Aretine*).

EXILE, THE Hereward, the *Champion of Women*. He was banished by Edward the *Confessor* for his unruly conduct as a young man, but returned at the time of the Norman Conquest.

EX-OFFICIO JEMMY Lord Abinger, the *Briareus of the King's Bench*; so called by Maginn (the *Adjutant*). Abinger gathered 'ex-officio' data to use against newspaper editors.

EXOTIC BOOKSELLER, THE James Edwards (1757–1816), London bookseller and bibliographer; so called because of the material he sold: rare books which he travelled widely to buy.

EXPOUNDER OF THE CONSTITUTION, THE
i) Daniel Webster (1782–1852), American lawyer and Secretary of State. He studied the United States constitution from childhood, and in a famous speech (1830) put it into common-sense terms for the ordinary man, making a major contribution to American unity.
ii) John Marshall (1755–1835), Chief Justice of the United States of America from 1801 until his death.

EXTRA BILLY William Smith (1797–1887). He imposed extra charges on packages carried on the stage-line he established in Virginia and the Carolinas. He became Governor of Virginia and a Brigadier-General for the Confederates.

F

FACE THAT SANK A THOUSAND SCHO-LARSHIPS, THE Lady Florence Horsbrugh (1889–1969), Tory Minister of Education (1950s); because of her tough cost-cutting measures. She was the first Conservative woman Cabinet Minister.

FACTORY KING, THE Richard Oastler (1789–1861) of Bradford. His campaign against labour conditions – and particularly child employment – ended in improvements by the Ten Hours Bill.

FAERY, THE Queen Victoria, *Drina*, a high-powered piece of flattery by Lord Beaconsfield (the *Asian Mystery*) between 1874 and 1880. The term derives from Spenser's *Faerie Queene* (1589–96) with the inference of *Gloriana*. In a letter to a friend (1876), he wrote of the Faery being created Empress of India.

FAIR, THE

i) Edwy or Eadwig (*circa* 940–59), King of the English, who for a time shared the kingdom with his brother Eadgar. On Edwy's death, Eadgar (the *Peaceful*) united the country.

ii) Eochaid (died 630), King of Dalriada, a kingdom in the West of Scotland, colonized by Scots from Ireland. It means 'Riada's portion'. Riada was grandson of Conn, the *Hundred Fighter*.

• Eochaid was another nickname of the Celtic god Dagda: Eochaid Ollathair, 'Eochaid, the Father of All'.

iii) Edith or Eadgyth, mistress of King Harold (the *Last of the Saxons*). She identified his body after the battle of Hastings (1066), searching the battlefields for his mutilated corpse. Also *Swan-Neck* or *Swan-Necked*.

FAIR EURYALUS George John West, 5th Earl De La Warr (1791–1869); so called by Byron (*Baby*) in *Childish Recollections*.

• Euryalus was a Trojan, a close friend of Nisus who gave his life to rescue him during a Rutulian raid on their camp.

FAIR GERALDINE, THE Lady Elizabeth Fitzgerald (*circa* 1528-89), youngest daughter of the 9th Earl of Kildare and reputed mistress of Henry Howard, Earl of Surrey (*circa* 1518-47), who gave her that nickname in a number of poems.

FAIR–HAIRED, THE Duncan Macintyre (1724–1812), Gaelic poet.

FAIR MAID OF ANJOU, THE Lady Edith Plantagenet (fl. 1200) of the House of Anjou, a kinswoman of Richard I, *Coeur de Lion*. She married David, Prince Royal of Scotland.

FAIR MAID OF BRITTANY, THE Eleanor, the *Damsel of Brittany*.

FAIR MAID OF GALLOWAY, THE Margaret, only daughter of the 5th Earl of Angus (*Bell-the-Cat*). She married her cousin William, who became Earl Douglas in 1443.

FAIR MAID OF KENT, THE Joan (1328–85), daughter of Edmond Plantagenet, Earl of Kent, and wife of Edward, the *Black Prince*. She was the mother of Richard II (the *Coxcomb*).

FAIR MAID OF NORWAY, THE or THE MAID OF NORWAY Margaret (1283–90), daughter of Eric II of Norway and granddaughter of Alexander III of Scotland (1241–85). Recognized as the heiress to the throne of Scotland, she set sail but died of sea-sickness on the way.

FAIR MAID OF PERTH, THE Catherine Glover (fl. late 14th century), made famous by Scott's novel and Bizet's opera.

FAIR MISS FRIGIDAIRE, THE Grace Kelly (1928–82), American film star; so called by Sinatra (the *Guv'nor*). She became Princess Grace of Monaco. Reports after her death allege this to have been a grotesque understatement.

FAIR PERDITA Mary Robinson, the *English Sappho*. After the Prince of Wales (*Adonis of Fifty*) had seen her in *The*

Winter's Tale she received a lock of his hair with a note 'To the adorable Perdita–Florizel, to be redeemed'. The two became well-known as 'the Fair Perdita' and *Florizel*.

FAIR QUAKERESS, THE Hannah Lightfoot (died 1765), mistress and, some say, morganatic wife of Prince George (later George III, the *Button Maker*). He had seen her in her uncle's draper's shop in St James's Market, London in 1756. It is claimed they were married in Kew Chapel (1759). Her uncle was a Quaker.

FAIR ROSAMUND, THE Rosamund Clifford (died *circa* 1176), daughter of Walter, Lord Clifford of the family of Fitz-Ponce, and mistress of Henry II (*Curtmantle*). She is the subject of many legends; mentioned in Percy's *Reliques* (see the *Father of Poetical Taste*).

FAIRY SINGER, THE Edmund Spenser, the *Child of the Ausonian Muse*; so called by Nash (the *English Aretine*). Spenser wrote *The Faerie Queene* (1589–96).

FAITHFUL ALLY, THE The Nizam of Hyderabad (1896–1967), reputed to have been the richest man in the world, who was a staunch friend of Britain.

FAME'S DUCKLING *Ape Gabriel* Harvey; so called by Nash (the *English Aretine*) in 1596.

FANCY'S CHILD
i)Shakespeare, the *Bard of All Time*; so called by Milton (*Black–Mouthed Zoilus*).
ii) Pierce Egan, the *Elder*. 'The Fancy' was the world of pugilism in the late 18th–early 19th century, and Egan was recognized as its great expert.

FANG Edgar Rosenberg (1924–87), husband and manager of Joan Rivers (*Joan the Mouth*); so called by his wife.

FANNY
i) Lord Balfour, *Bloody Balfour*. Winston Churchill (*Bricky*) said he was 'deemed by his critics to be a ladylike dilettante dialectician'.
ii)F. Walden (1888–1949), Tottenham Hotspur footballer, cricketer for Northamptonshire and lastly a cricket umpire.

• See also *Lord Fanny*.

FARMER, THE or FARMER DENNING Alfred Thompson, 1st Baron Denning (1899–), Master of the Rolls (1962–82); because of his accent.

FARMER GEORGE George III, the *Button Maker*. He had a great interest in agriculture, and made a profit out of his farm at Windsor. (George comes from the Greek for 'farmer'.)

FARMER HILL Lord Hill, *Daddy*.

FARMER KING, THE George III (above); both nicknames were propagated, if not invented, by Wolcot (*Peter Pindar*) who depicted the King wondering how apples got into dumplings.

FARMER WHITE J.C. White (1891–1961). Somerset and England cricketer who was also a farmer. He played in the 1928–1929 Test series.

FARMERS' FRIEND, THE Richard, 2nd Duke of Chandos and Buckingham (1797–1861), author of the 'Chandos Clause' in the Reform Bill of 1832, extending franchise to tenant farmers. Also because of his opposition to the repeal of the Corn Laws.

FARTHING JAMES Sir James Lowther, Earl of Lonsdale, the *Brazen Bully*. He was a mean man. He once went back to a London coffee-house to say a halfpenny he had been given was bad and demanded another in exchange.
• A farthing was a quarter of a pre-decimal penny, and a halfpenny was a half.

FARTHING POET, THE Richard Horne (1803–84), British poet and critic. His principal work, *Orion* (1843), was published at one farthing to mock the supposed poverty of the poetry-buying public. Also *Orion Horne*.

FASTEST MAN ON EARTH, THE Sir Harold Maurice Abrahams (1899–1978), British sprinter, after he had won the 100 metres in the Olympics in Paris (1924) defeating the then *World's Fastest Human*, Charley Paddock. Abrahams was until 1988 the only Briton ever to win the Olympics 100 metres and he was the central figure of the film *Chariots of Fire*.

FASTEST WOMAN ON EARTH, THE Florence Griffith-Joyner (1960–), American champion sprinter who won a gold medal at the Seoul Olympics (1988) for the 100 metres which she covered in 10.54 seconds. In trials in the USA that year she did the same distance in 10.49 seconds. She retired in 1989. Also *Flojo* and the *Joan Collins of the Track*.

FASTING WOMAN OF TUTBURY, THE Ann Moore (1761–?). Forced by poverty to fast, she lost all desire to eat (1806). She claimed she could live without food and crowds flocked to Tutbury, Staffordshire, to see her. In 1813 she confessed she was an imposter. She was last heard of a little later in prison for theft.

FAT, THE
i) Aedh, King of Northern Ireland (reigned 1196–1230).
ii) Aedh, *Reamhar*, Irish king (died 1346). Also the *Stout*.
• See *Aedh of the Ague*. *Reamhar* is Irish for stout or fat.

FAT ADONIS, THE See the *Adonis of Fifty*.

FATHA or FATHAR Earl Hines (1905–83), American jazz pianist.

FAT JACK
i) A man buried at Esher (1772) was entered in the parish register as: Bacchus, alias Hogtub alias Fat Jack alias John, who came from Claremont (Ewen),
ii) John Pritt Harley (1786–1858), British comedian and singer who appeared at Drury Lane, London and with W.C. Macready (the *King Arthur of the Stage*) at Covent Garden (1838); so called because he was very thin.

FATHER or FARVER Captain Graham Edwards, Royal Navy, of the Dover Patrol (WWI) who commanded the flotilla leader *Hoste* and frequently made the signal 'Follow Father'.

FATHER ABRAHAM Abraham Lincoln (1809–65), 16th President of the USA. Also the *Great Emancipator*, *Honest Abe*, *Honest Old Abe*, the *Illinois Baboon*, the *Martyr President*, *Old Abe* and the *Rail Splitter*.

FATHER BEN Ben Jonson, the *Bricklayer*, so called by Dryden *(Asaph)*.
• 'Father Ben' has been a pseudonym of

Franklin, the *American Socrates*.

FATHER GREYBEARD William Howlett or Hewlett (fl. 1640–61), a Parliamentarian who voted for the execution of Charles I (the *Ahab of the Nation*).

FATHER OF AMERICA, THE
i) Samuel Adams, the *American Cato*.
ii) George Washington, the *American Cincinnatus*.

FATHER OF AMERICAN ANTHROPOLOGY, THE Lewis Henry Morgan (1818–81) who, from a casual interest in the Iroquois Indian, came to write *Systems of Consanguinity and Affinity of the Human Family* (1871).

FATHER OF AMERICAN DEMOCRACY, THE Thomas Hooker (1586–1647), English-born Congregationalist pastor at Cambridge. Massachusetts. He took his whole congregation to found the colony of Connecticut (1636), where his thinking moulded the constitution.

FATHER OF AMERICAN FOOTBALL, THE Walter Chauncey Camp (1859–1925), a major factor in turning football in America from a type of rugby into a distinctive game of its own. From 1899, he trained an All-American team.

FATHER OF AMERICAN HISTORY, THE William Bradford (1590–1657), Englishman who went to America on the *Mayflower* and became Governor of Plymouth. He wrote *The History of the Plimmoth Plantation* (published 1856).

FATHER OF AMERICAN GEOGRAPHY, THE Jedediah Morse (1761–1826). His *Geography Made Easy* (1784) was the first book on the subject published in America.

FATHER OF AMERICAN GOLF, THE John Reid (1840–1916), Scottish-born founder of the St Andrew's Golf Club (1888) and one of the founders of the US Golf Association, notable as one of the 'Appletree Gang', a group of early golfers who used an apple-tree as a 'clubhouse'.

FATHER OF AMERICAN MINSTRELSY, THE Thomas Dartmouth Rice (1808–60), the original 'negro minstrel' who popularized that type of show. Also *Jim Crow*.

FATHER OF AMERICAN MUSIC, THE
Charles Ives (1874–1954), who won a
Pulitzer Prize for his Third Symphony.

**FATHER OF AMERICAN NEWSPAPERS,
THE** Benjamin Harris (*circa* 1673–1716),
English-born bookseller and publisher of
Boston. In 1690, he issued *Publick Occur-
rences, Both Foreign and Domestick*. It
was not licensed, and was immediately
suppressed by the Government, but it
was the first newspaper in America.

FATHER OF AMERICAN POETRY, THE
William Cullen Bryant, the *American
Wordsworth*.

FATHER OF AMERICAN SURGERY, THE
i) Philip Syng Physick (1768–1837)(,
professor of surgery at Pennsylvania
University (1805–19), who introduced
new methods of surgery.
ii) Dr William Stewart Halstead
(1852–1922).

**FATHER OF AMERICAN UNIVERSALISM,
THE** John Murray (1741–1815), English-
born pastor who left Wesleyanism for
Universalism and led the Boston Univer-
salist Society (1793–1809).

FATHER OF AMERICAN YACHTING, THE
John Cox Stevens (1785–1854), part of
the movement in the early 19th century
to popularize small-boat sailing and who
headed a syndicate to produce the
schooner-yacht *America*. In 1851, Commodore Stevens of the New York Yacht
Club aboard the *America* won a race
round the Isle of Wight, which began the
America's Cup competition.

**FATHER OF AMERICAN WOOD ENGRAV-
ING, THE** Alexander Anderson, the
American Bewick. Self-taught, he made
his first engravings at the age of twelve.
Eventually he did book illustrations.

FATHER OF ANGLING, THE Izaak Walton
(1593–1683) who wrote *The Compleat
Angler* (1653).

FATHER OF ASSYRIOLOGY, THE Sir
Henry Creswicke Rawlinson (1810–95),
British soldier who became interested in
the then undeciphered cuneiform script
while serving in Persia, copied the Behis-
tun inscriptions which he then deci-
phered and interpreted (published 1846)

and so opened the way for the study of
Assyrian history.

FATHER OF AUSTRALIA, THE Sir Ed-
mund Barton (1849–1920), first federal
Australian Prime Minister
- Cf the *Father of the Australian
  Commonwealth*.

FATHER OF AVIATION, THE Sir George
Cayley (1773–1857). At the age of 22
(1726), he constructed a small helicopter-
type machine with two feather wind-
mills. It was not until 1853 that he built
one in which he could persuade his
coachman to fly a short way. The coachman's name is thought to have been John
Appleby.

FATHER OF BASEBALL, THE General
Abner Doubleday (1819–93) who is said
to have devised the game at Coopers-
town, New York (1839), but, of course,
the game was played in England and
America before that. Oliver Wendell Holmes (1809–94) declared he played baseball at Harvard (1829). It is mentioned by
Jane Austen (the *Shakespeare of Prose*)
in *Northanger Abbey* (*circa* 1818).

FATHER OF BASKETBALL, THE James
Naismith (1861–1961), Canadian-born
professor of Physical Education at Kansas
University. He thought of the game at the
International Y.M.C.A. Training College,
Springfield, Massachusetts (1891).

**FATHER OF BLACK–LETTER COLLEC-
TORS, THE** Dr John Moore (1662–1714),
Bishop of Norwich (1691) and Ely (1707–
14); the earliest to collect black–letter lit-
erature. He amassed 30,000 volumes.
- See *Black–Letter Tom*.

FATHER OF BLACK–LETTER LORE, THE
Samuel Pepys (1633–1703), Secretary for
the Affairs of the Admiralty of England
(1684) and diarist who collected books
and ballads. Also the *Prince of Gossips*
and the *Weatherglass of His Time*.
- His collection, the largest and most
  complete of its kind, he had bound
  into five volumes. It is housed in the
  Pepysian Library at Magdalene
  College, Cambridge.

FATHER OF BOXING, THE
i) Jack Broughton (1704–89), English

champion (1734–50) who drew up the first set of rules and introduced 'mufflers', the forerunners of boxing-gloves.

- Cf *George the Barber*.

ii) James Figg, the *Atlas of the Sword*; first British boxing champion (1719).

FATHER OF BRITAIN'S CANALS, THE James Brindley (1716–72) who had been a millwright's apprentice and built the first canal.

- See the *Canal Duke* (below).

FATHER OF BRITISH INLAND NAVIGA-TION, THE The Duke of Bridgewater, the *Canal Duke*. He worked with Brindley (above).

FATHER OF BRITISH MILITARY HY-GIENE, THE or THE FATHER OF THE ROYAL ARMY MEDICAL CORPS Sir James McGrigor (1771–1858), Inspector–General of Hospitals, and Wellington's Principal Medical Officer in the Peninsular War. He was knighted (1819) for his work in improving conditions. Later he was Director General of the Army Medical Department.

FATHER OF BRITISH MUSIC PUBLISH-ING, THE John Playford (1623–86). He and his son were the biggest publishers of music in the second half of the 17th century. They were the first to make music publishing a separate business.

FATHER OF BRITISH SOCIALISM, THE Robert Owen, *Celatus*. His ideas led to the establishment of socialised agricultural communities and he sponsored the Grand National Consolidated Trades Union (1833–4). Followers of Owen met in 1864 with French workmen to found the International Working-men's Association.

FATHER OF BUSINESS EFFICIENCY, THE Frederick Winslow Taylor (1856–1915), American engineer, pioneer of scientific management which he promoted by writing and lecturing.

FATHER OF CANADA, THE Jacques Cartier (1491–1557), French navigator who, looking for the north–west passage to China, discovered Canada and the St Lawrence river (1534).

FATHER OF CHEMISTRY, THE Robert Boyle (1627–91), Irish–born scientist, son of the *Great Earl of Cork*. He was the creator of Boyle's Law. i.e. that the volume of gas varies inversely to the pressure. He invented the air pump and introduced new ideas and attitudes to science.

FATHER OF CHICAGO, THE

i) Jean Baptiste Pointe Du Sable (died 1818), Haitian Indian trader, son of a black mother and white sailor, and well educated. He established the first settlement on the Chicago river in about 1773. He had a Potawatamie wife. As well as a large farm in Chicago, he had a house in Peoria.

ii) John Kinzie (1763–?1860), the first white settler in Chicago (1804),.

FATHER OF CONFEDERATION, THE Senator J.C. Chapais (1811–85) of Canada.

FATHER OF COUNTRY MUSIC, THE James (Jimmie) Charles Rodgers (1897–1933), American singer and guitarist who began singing country music in the mid–20s. Also the *Singing Brakeman*.

FATHER OF COURTESY, THE Richard de Beauchamp, 13th Earl of Warwick (1382–1439) who was captain of Calais at the time of Agincourt (1415) and received the Emperor Sigismund with such magnificent display (1416) he bore the nickname ever afterwards. Also the *Good*.

FATHER OF DAYLIGHT SAVING, THE William Willett (1856–1915), Englishman who conceived the idea (*circa* 1907) and began to campaign for altering clocks in spring and autumn to give more daylight working hours. The system was not adopted until 1916.

FATHER OF DEMOCRACY IN VIRGINIA, THE Thomas Ritchie (1778–1854), editor of *The Richmond Examiner*, later *The Richmond Enquirer*, with unequalled influence as a Democratic organ (1820–45).

FATHER OF ECONOMICS, THE Adam Smith (1723–90), Scottish author of the 5-vol. *The Wealth of Nations* (1776) which had enormous effect on Government thinking in Britain and on the shape of economic policies ever since.

FATHER OF ENGLISH BOTANY, THE William Turner (1520–86). In 1544 he published a commentary on the birds in Aristotle and Pliny, and was one of the best-known internationally of herbalists.

FATHER OF ENGLISH CHURCH MUSIC, THE Thomas Tallis (?1505–85), composer, one of the Gentlemen of the Chapel Royal. He raised the whole standard of English church music by his compositions. With his pupil, William Byrd (1542/3–1623), he won the right to print music.

- Cf the *Father of British Music Publishing*.

FATHER OF ENGLISH COMMERCE, THE Edward III (1312–77). He protected the cloth trade and helped foreign bankers to settle in London. He assisted merchants in establishing businesses (see the *Beloved Merchant*). Also the *King of the Sea*.

FATHER OF ENGLISH DEISM, THE Edward, Baron Herbert of Cherbury (1583–1648), soldier, diplomat, historian and religious philosopher.

- Deists oppose revelation in religion and advocate belief in God through reason. Theism, on the other hand, does not reject revelation. See the *Bacon of Theology*.

FATHER OF ENGLISH DRAMATIC POETRY, THE Marlowe, the *Atheist Tamburlan*, whose *Tamburlaine* (circa 1587) preceded Shakespeare's first play by about four years.

FATHER OF ENGLISH FOOTBALL, THE Sir Stanley Rous (1895–1986). He was a referee (1920–34) and controlled the FA Cup match between Portsmouth and Manchester City (1934). He was Secretary of the Football Association, and President of FIFA (1961–74).

FATHER OF ENGLISH GEOLOGY, THE William Smith (1769–1839), the first man to map the rock strata of England, and identify the fossil layers of each. Also *Strata Smith*.

FATHER OF ENGLISH GRAMMAR, THE Lindley Murray (1745–1826), American whose *Grammar of the English Language*

(1795) was a standard work in England, and America for many years.

FATHER OF THE ENGLISH HEXAMETER, THE *Ape Gabriel* Harvey; self-bestowed.

FATHER OF ENGLISH HISTORY or ENGLISH LITERATURE, THE The Venerable Bede or Baeda (673–735). He finished his *Historia Ecclesiastica Gentis Anglorum* (*A History of the English Church and People*) in 731.

FATHER OF ENGLISH NATURAL HISTORY, THE John Ray or Wray (1627–1705) who wrote *Methodus planatarum nova* (1682) and *Historia plantarum* (3 volumes, 1686, 1688 and 1704). A Ray Society was founded in his honour.

FATHER OF ENGLISH NUMBERS, THE Edmund Waller (1606–87), poet; so called by Dryden (*Asaph*). Also the *Inimitable*.

- 'Numbers' is a term for metrical periods of verse, e.g. 'But most by Numbers judge a poet's work' (Pope).

FATHER OF ENGLISH PANTOMIME, THE John Rich (*circa* 1692–1761), actor who first appeared as Harlequin in 1716 and then developed the idea into an annual pantomime. Also the *Father of Harlequins, Lun* and the *Prince of Harlequins*.

FATHER OF ENGLISH POETRY, THE Geoffrey Chaucer, the *British Homer*.

FATHER OF ENGLISH POTTERY, THE Josiah Wedgwood (1730–95), creator of pottery as a fine art in England. Also the *Father of the Potteries*.

FATHER OF ENGLISH PRINTING, THE William Caxton (1422–91), the first English printer. He set up a press at Westminster and issued books from 1477 to 1491.

FATHER OF ENGLISH PROSE, THE
i) King Alfred, *England's Darling.* He translated Latin texts into Old English and inspired the Anglo–Saxon Chronicle.
ii) John Wyclif, *Doctor Evangelus*.
iii) Roger Ascham (1515–68) was Queen Elizabeth's tutor. He wrote a treatise on archery (1538) in English, when most scholars wrote in Latin. His influential

The Schoolmaster was published posthumously, in 1568.

FATHER OF ENGLISH SONG, THE Caedmon, the *Anglo–Saxon Milton*.

FATHER OF ENGLISH UNITARIANISM, THE John Biddle (1615–62). He denied the deity of the Holy Spirit and fought a lifelong battle with authority. After 1652 his followers met regularly and were called Biddellians, Socinians or Unitarians. Cromwell (the *Almighty Nose*) befriended him and sent him to the Scilly Isles, but he returned to London, where he was arrested and fined. Since he could not pay, he was sent to prison where he died.

FATHER OF ENGLISH WATCHMAKING or CLOCKMAKING, THE Thomas Tompion (?1639–1713), whose inventions made possible the creation of a flat watch.

FATHER OF ENGLISH WATER-COLOUR PAINTING, THE Alexander Cozens (died 1786), said to have been the son of Peter the Great of Russia and an English woman from Deptford. His son, John Robert Cozens (*circa* 1752–97), was an even greater landscape painter in water–colours.
- Cf the *Father of Modern Water–Colour Painting*.

FATHER OF EUROPE, THE Jean Monnet (1888–1979), French member of the European Coal and Steel Community and founder and President of the Action Committee for a United States of Europe. In 1950 he proposed a plan for the European Community. He was made a Companion of Honour (1972). Also the *Father of the Common Market*.

FATHER OF EQUITY, THE The Earl of Nottingham, the *Dismal*. He was the first Lord Chancellor to accept the enactments of his predecessors. Lord Eldon (*Old Bags*) followed him, and consolidated the practice.
- Equity is that part of law which derives from decisions of the old Court of Chancery.

FATHER OF FOUR-IN-HANDS, THE The Honourable Tommy Onslow, Lord Cranley and later the 2nd Earl of Onslow (1755–1864), an eccentric with a passion for driving four-in-hands. Also *Little T.O.*.

FATHER OF FROZEN FOOD, THE Clarence Birdseye (1886–1956), American inventor and industrialist. He devised a technique for deep-freezing food. His first Birdseye packs were marketed in 1929, but Clarence Birdseye held more than two hundred other patents.

FATHER OF GEOMORPHOLOGY, THE William Morris Davis (1850–1934), American geographer and geologist who among other things discovered the cycle of erosion of land masses.

FATHER OF GREYHOUND RACING, THE Brigadier-General Alfred Cecil Critchley (1890–1964), who built and operated the first track at Belle Vue, Manchester (1926).

FATHER OF HARLEQUINS, THE John Rich, the *Father of English Pantomime*. D'Israeli: Rich had the glory of introducing Harlequin on the English stage, which he played under the feigned name of *Lun'*.

FATHER OF HIS COUNTRY, THE George Washington, the *American Cincinnatus*, 1st President of the USA (1789–97). The nickname was first used in Francis Bailey's *Nord-Amerikanische Kalender* (1779), but was common in Pennsylvania before that.

FATHER OF HISTORICAL CRITICISM, THE William of Newburgh or Newbridge (?1136–98). He wrote *Historia Rerum Anglicarum*, covering the period from 1066 to 1198; so called by Edward Freeman (1823–92), the historian. Also *Gulielmus Parvus*.

FATHER OF IMMUNOLOGY, THE Edward Jenner (1749–1823), English doctor who discovered the smallpox vaccine after investigating 'an old wives' tale' that dairy women who caught cowpox never caught smallpox.

FATHER OF INDIAN NATIONALISM, THE Dababhai Naoroji (1825–1917), who in 1906 claimed the right of India to self–government, or *swarajya*. He was the first Indian member of the House of Commons. Also the *Grand Old Man of India*.

FATHER OF INDIAN RAILWAYS, THE Sir Rowland Macdonald Stephenson (1808–45). He built the first railway (from Calcutta to Benares), and became managing director of the East Indian Railway Company.

FATHER OF INDUCTIVE PHILOSOPHY, THE Francis Bacon, Viscount St. Albans (1561–1626). In his writings he led people away from the old rigid standards of Scholasticism (which sought links between philosophy and Christian ethics) to endeavour to find a relation between the natural world and human conduct, so as to universalize knowledge. In *Novum Organum* (1620) he maintained that induction from experience was the 'right' way. The DNB says that he 'might well be called the 'British Socrates'. Also the *Great Verulum* and the *Secretary of Nature*.

FATHER OF JESTS, THE Joseph Miller (1684–1738), British comic actor whose jokes were collected into *Joe Miller's Jest Book, or the Wits' Vade Mecum* (1739). Miller in reality was so solemn that he reportedly never made a joke, and the book was a piece of opportunism by John Mottley (1682–1750), a not very successful playwright.

FATHER OF JURISPRUDENCE, THE Ranulf de Glanvill, Glanvil or Glanville (died 1190), Chief Justiciar of England (post 1180). Courts were reorganized and circuit judges introduced. Glanvil wrote or supervised the first coherent code of laws in England (first printed 1554).

● For Justiciar, see *Roger the Great*.

FATHER OF LEGAL JOURNALISM, THE Robert Maugham (1788–1862). He wrote *Treatise on the Law of Attornies* (1825), was co-founder of the Law Society and founded *The Legal Observer* (1830); grandfather of W. Somerset Maugham (1874–1965).

FATHER OF LINE ENGRAVING, THE James Heath (1756–1834), associated engraver of the Royal Academy (post 1791).

FATHER OF LONDON, THE Sir John Barnard (1685–1764), an eminent merchant and Lord Mayor (1737) as well as author of *A Present for an Apprentice* (1740). Also the *Great Commoner*.

FATHER OF LOUISIANA, THE Jean-Baptiste Le Moyne, sieur de Bienville (1680–1768). He founded the city of La Nouvelle Orleans when he was French Governor of Louisiana.

FATHER OF LOUISIANA JURISPRUDENCE, THE François Xavier Martin (1762–1846), Attorney-General for the new state of Louisiana (post 1813) and eventually presiding judge of the state's supreme court. He published a digest of the state's laws and reports of court decisions, sorting out a tangle of French, Spanish and English laws.

FATHER OF MANAGEMENT EDUCATION, THE Joseph Wharton (1826–1909), American who established the Wharton School in the University of Pennsylvania,

FATHER OF MODERN AMERICAN GANGSTERISM, THE John (Johnny) Torrio (1882–1957), bootlegger, brothel-keeper and killer who took over the 'empire' of *Big Jim* Colosimo after he had been shot by Al. *Scarface* Capone.

FATHER OF MODERN ENGLISH CRIMINOLOGY, THE Dr Hermann Mannheim (1889–1974), German-born Briton who established the study of criminology.

FATHER OF MODERN COMMENTATORS, THE Zachary Grey (1688–1766), British antiquarian and editor of *Hudibras*.

● See *Hudibras Butler*.

FATHER OF MODERN DENTISTRY, THE Dr Greene Valadiman Black (1836–1915), American who invented new techniques in dentistry.

FATHER OF MODERN LAWN TENNIS, THE

i) William Charles Renshaw (1861–1904). With his brother Ernest, he popularized the game after the creation of the rectangular court for the first Wimbledon championships (1877).

ii) Major Walter Copton Wingfield (1833–1912) who devised the game of 'Sphairistike' introduced in 1873–4. It had an hour–glass court, superseded four years later.

FATHER OF MODERN PROSE FICTION, THE Daniel Defoe (*circa* 1661–1731), author of *Robinson Crusoe, Moll Flanders,* etc. Also the **Sunday Gentleman**.

FATHER OF MODERN NAVIGATION, THE Admiral of the Fleet Sir Henry Oliver, **Dummy**.

FATHER OF MODERN WATER–COLOUR PAINTING, THE Thomas Girtin (1775–1802), British, friend of Turner (**Admiral Booth**) who said at his early death 'If Tom Girtin lived, I should have starved'.

- Cf the **Father of English Water–Colour Painting**.

FATHER OF MONKS, THE St Ethelwold or Aethelwold (*circa* 908–84), Bishop of Winchester who founded or reformed a number of monasteries. He introduced the strict Benedictine Order and wrote or translated the regulations and customs of the Order: *Regularis Concordia*.

FATHER OF MUSICAL COMEDY, THE James T. Tanner (1858– ?). He composed with Andrew Moss a musical farce entitled *In Town* staged at the Prince of Wales Theatre, London (1892), produced by George Edwardes (**Gaiety George**).

FATHER OF NUCLEAR PHYSICS, THE Ernest, 1st Baron Rutherford (1871–1939), New Zealand physicist who in the early 1920s split the atom and laid the foundations of modern atomic theory. He won a Nobel Prize (1908) for his work on alpha particles.

FATHER OF OHIO, THE Rufus Putnam (1738–1824), American soldier and pioneer who with others founded the Ohio Company of Associates and eventually was a member of the Ohio State Constitutional convention.

FATHER OF ORNITHOLOGISTS, THE George Edwards (1693–1773). He wrote a *History of Birds* (4 volumes, 1743–51) and *Gleanings of Natural History* (1758–64). He also published an index of names supplied by the Swedish botanist Linnaeus (1707–78).

FATHER OF OTTAWA, THE Philemon Wright (1760–1839), American founder of a settlement on the Quebec side of the Ottawa river (1800). He came from Woburn, Massachusetts. Part of the city is called Wrightville in his honour.

FATHER OF PENGUIN PAPERBACKS, THE Sir Allen Lane (1902–70), British publisher who issued the first six in 1935. His real name was Allen Williams.

FATHER OF PHILOSOPHY, THE Roger Bacon, the **Admirable Doctor**.

FATHER OF POETICAL TASTE, THE Thomas Percy (1728–1811), Bishop of Dromore who assembled and edited *The Reliques of Ancient Poetry* (1765), which did a great deal to awaken interest in older English poetry.

FATHER OF POETS, THE Ben Jonson, the **Bricklayer**, so called by William Cartwright (1611–43).

FATHER OF PUBLISHED RAGTIME, THE Irving Berlin (1888–1989), American composer whose real name is Israel Baline. He issued *Alexander's Ragtime Band* in 1911.

FATHER OF RAGTIME, THE Scott Joplin (1886–1917), American jazz pianist and composer who wrote music in the 'cakewalk' idiom, a dance among negroes in the early 20th century. Also the **King of Ragtime**.

FATHER OF RAILWAYS, THE George Stephenson (1781–1848), British engineer who built the famous *Rocket* locomotive and constructed the first passenger railway line from Stockton to Darlington (1825).

- Cf the **Father of the Locomotive**.

FATHER OF REFORM, THE John Cartwright (1740–1824), English radical politician who advocated parliamentary reform from 1776.

FATHER OF SCOTTISH LANDSCAPE ART or PAINTING, THE

i) Alexander Nasmyth (1758–1840) who worked mainly on landscapes, although he did paint a portrait of Robert Burns (the **Ayrshire Bard**).

ii) John Thomson of Duddington (1778–1840).

FATHER OF SCOTTISH POETRY, THE John Barbour (?1316–95), Archdeacon of Aberdeen, the first. In about 1375 he composed the poem *The Brus*, an epic describing the deeds of King Robert the **Bruce** and Sir James Douglas (**Black Dou-**

glas) in the Scottish struggle for independence.

FATHER OF STEAM, THE James Watt (1736–1819), British engineer who patented a working steam-engine (1769).

FATHER OF SUNDAY NEWSPAPERS, THE John Bell (1745–1831) who began *The Weekly Messenger* in 1796. Egan the *Elder* worked with him on *Bell's Life in London*. Although the *Messenger* was not the first, it was the most popular and famous.

FATHER OF TELEVISION, THE John Logie Baird (1888–1946), Briton. He invented a set on which he gave the first demonstration of pure TV in January 1926.

FATHER OF WESTERNS, THE Thomas Ince (1882–1924) American film producer who introduced motion pictures of the Far West to the film industry. He died mysteriously on board W.R. Hearst's (*Chief*) yacht *Oneida*. Some allege he was shot, and the crime was hushed up by Hearst's power. Ince produced *Custer's Last Fight* in 1912.

FATHER OF THE AMERICAN NAVY, THE

i) Joshua Humphroys (1751–1838). He designed the frigate *Constitution*, one of the first three naval vessels built by the USA, and launched in 1797. He designed other ships used in the war of 1812.
ii) John Barry (1745–1803), the first under a commission of Congress, and under the Grand Union flag, to fight a battle with a British warship and make it strike its colours.
iii) John Paul Jones (1747–92), Scottish-born sailor, the first to raise the American flag on a warship.

- This point is, however, fiercely debated,and there are other candidates for the honour.

FATHER OF THE AMERICAN NOVEL, THE William Hill Brown (1765–93) who published anonymously *The Power of Sympathy* (1789), the first American novel.

FATHER OF THE AMERICAN RING, THE Jacob Hyer of New York who defeated Tom Beasley in the first prize-ring bout (1816) in America. It was his only fight.

FATHER OF THE ANTHEM, THE Christopher Tye (?1497–?1572), Master of the Choristers at Ely cathedral and Court musician to Edward VI (the *Josiah of England*).

FATHER OF THE ATOMIC BOMB, THE Dr Robert Oppenheimer (1904–67) American physicist who worked on the details for making an atomic bomb and supervised its construction during World War II. (He was director of the Los Alamos laboratory, 1945–7.)

FATHER OF THE AUSTRALIAN COMMONWEALTH, THE Sir Henry Parkes (1815–96), statesman and Prime Minister of Victoria, who devoted a great part of his life to the problems of Australian federation and was largely responsible for the constitution discussed at the Federal Convention, Melbourne (1890), which he inaugurated.

- Cf the *Father of Australia*.

FATHER OF THE BLUES, THE William Christopher Handy (1873–1958), American composer of *Memphis Bues* (1909) and later the *St Louis Blues*. His autobiography was entitled *Father of the Blues* (1941)

FATHER OF THE CHIN, THE Major–General Sir John Bagot Glubb (1897–1987), commander of the Arab Legion in Transjordan (1938–56), known to his men as *Abu Hunait* and 'Glubb Pasha'. He lost part of his chin when he was wounded in the face.

FATHER OF THE COMIC STRIP, THE Richard Fellow Outcault (1863–1928), American artist of *The Yellow Kid*, which began to make its appearance in the 1890s.

FATHER OF THE COMMON MARKET, THE Jean Monnet, the *Father of Europe*.

FATHER OF THE CONSTITUTION, THE James Madison (1751–1836), 4th President of the USA who was instrumental in calling the Federal Constitutional Convention (1787) which framed the American constitution.

FATHER OF THE COWBOYS, THE Charles Goodnight (1836–1929), American pioneer cattleman. He began as a cowboy in the 1850s and died owning 20 million acres of Texas cattle country.

FATHER OF THE DETECTIVE STORY, THE Edgar Allan Poe, the *American Richard Savage*, author of *The Murders in the Rue Morgue* (1841), the first of the genre.

- See *Grandfather of the Detective Story*.

FATHER OF THE ENGLISH GENERAL BAPTISTS, THE James Smyth (died 1610).

FATHER OF THE ENGLISH NOVEL, THE

i) Henry Fielding (1707–1754), author of *Tom Jones* (1749); so called by Scott (the *Ariosto of the North*). Also the *Hogarth of Novelists*, the *Prince of Novelists*, the *Prose Homer of Nature* and the *Shakespeare of Novelists*.

ii) Sir Walter Scott, the *Ariosto of the North*.

FATHER OF THE ENGLISH TURF, THE Tregonwell Frampton (1641–1727) who supervised the racehorses at Heath House, Newmarket. Egan, the *Elder* says in his *Book of Sports* (1832) that Frampton was 'the oldest and, as some say, the cunningest jockey in England' in the reign of Queen Anne (*Brandy Nan*).

FATHER OF THE FACTORY SYSTEM, THE Sir Richard Arkwright (1732–92) who set up the first English factory – for textiles – in Nottingham (1769).

FATHER OF THE FLEET, THE Admiral the Honourable Sir Henry Keppel (1809–1904), husband of the *White Lady*. Also the *Little Admiral*.

ii) Admiral of the Fleet Sir Provo William Parry Wallis (1791–1892), Canadian-born; so called in the Royal Navy. His name was on the active list until he died at over a hundred years old.

FATHER OF THE FOUR–LETTER WORD, THE Henry Miller (1891–1980), author of *Tropic of Cancer* (1934) and *Tropic of Capricorn* (1938); because of the blatant sexuality of his books.

FATHER OF THE GAME OF WHIST, THE Edmond Hoyle (1672–1769), Briton who wrote a *Short Treatise on Whist* (1742) and later compiled the laws of whist

which controlled the game for more than a hundred years.

FATHER OF THE GOSSIP COLUMN, THE Walter Winchell (1897–1972), American newspaperman. He began his first column when he worked for Hearst (the *Chief*) in 1929. He was said to have had a readership of 25 million people a day.

- See the *Bishop of Fleet Street*.

FATHER OF THE HALLS, THE Charles Morton, *Champagne Charlie (v)*, who opened the first music-hall in London, the Canterbury (1849) and then built up an 'empire'.

FATHER OF THE HAUSAS, THE Captain (Sir) John Hawley Glover (1829–85). He started the para-military force in West Africa which became known as 'Glover's Hausas'. Also *Golobar*.

FATHER OF THE HELICOPTER, THE Igor Sikorsky (1889–1972), who was a naturalized American, and who invented the machine (1910).

FATHER OF THE HOUSE OF COMMONS, THE

i) Charles Pelham Villiers (1802–98), British M.P for 63 years, the longest unbroken record; returned at 16 elections at Wolverhampton.

ii) David Rhys Grenfell (1881–1968), Labour M.P from 1922 to 1959.

iii) Colonel Henry Cecil Lowther (1790–1867). He was an M.P. for fifty–five years (post 1812), but never made a speech. He was the second son of the 1st Earl of Lonsdale (*William the Good*). Also *Lowther the Silent* and the *Silent Colonel*.

FATHER OF THE HUMOROUS NEWS-PAPER COLUMN, THE J.M. Bailey, the *Danbury News Man*.

FATHER OF THE INDIAN ARMY, THE Major–General Stringer Lawrence (1697–1775), commander of the East India Company's troops (post 1748).

FATHER OF THE IRISH REPUBLIC, THE Eamon de Valera, the *Chief*.

FATHER OF THE KING'S AFRICAN RIFLES, THE Frederick John Dealtry, 1st Baron Lugard (1858–1945), explorer for the British East African Company, and Governor of Nigeria (1912–1919). He raised the KAR (1891) and the West African Frontier Force.

FATHER OF THE LOCOMOTIVE, THE Richard Trevethick (1771–1833), Cornish mining engineer, the first man to build a steam locomotive (1800). In 1802 his engine pulled the first passengers by steam.

- Cf *Father of Railways*.

FATHER OF THE MILITARY SUBMARINE, THE John Philip Holland (1841–1914), Irishman who in his teens designed his first submarine. His first adult design (1875) sank, but he did succeed in 1898. He won a contract from the US Navy (1900).

- Cf the *Father of the Submarine* (below).

FATHER OF THE PONY EXPRESS, THE William Hepburn Russell (1812–72), the *Napoleon of the West*.

FATHER OF THE POOR, THE Bernard Gilpin, the *Apostle of the North*.

FATHER OF THE POTTERIES, THE Josiah Wedgwood, the *Father of English Pottery*. He set up the Etruria pottery works in Hanley, producing fine white English earthenware and copies of classical Greek vases and plates. The area of North Staffordshire called 'The Potteries' grew up round it.

FATHER OF THE ROYAL AIR FORCE, THE Lord Trenchard, *Boom*.

FATHER OF THE ROYAL NAVY, THE Lord Anson, the *Bulldog of Circumnavigators*. He reduced many of the hardships of life in the Royal Navy and, as First Lord of the Admiralty (post 1745), did a great deal to raise the standards of the service from the depths of corruption into which they had fallen.

FATHER OF THE ROYAL WEST AFRICAN FRONTIER FORCE, THE Captain Foley, *Empire Jim*.

FATHER OF THE SKYSCRAPER, THE

i) William Le Baron Jenney (1832–1907), American architect who used steel in the construction of tall buildings, e.g. the Manhattan building in Dearborn Street, Chicago.

ii) Cass Gilbert (1859–1934). He designed the Woolworth building in New York and many other tall buildings.

FATHER OF THE SUBMARINE, THE David Bushnell (1742–11824) American inventor of 'The Bushnell Turtle' the first submarine. He was ridiculed and gave up.

- Cf the *Father of the Military Submarine* (above).

FATHER OF THE TELEPHONE, THE Alexander Graham Bell (1847–1922), Scottish–born American inventor and teacher of the deaf. He evolved the apparatus in his research into the techniques of speech.

FATHER OF THE THIRTEENTH AMENDMENT, THE Lyman Trumbell (1813–96), American proposer of the amendment to the constitution which abolished slavery in the USA.

FATHER OF THE TWENTIETH AMENDMENT, THE Senator George Norris (1861–1944) who advocated the amendment that the inauguration of the President should take place on 20th January instead of 4 March (1933). Also the *Gentle Knight*

FATHER OF THE UNITED NATIONS, THE Cordell Hull (1871–1955), American Secretary of State (1933–43). His idea at the Moscow conference (1943) led to the formation of the United Nations and the award of a Nobel Peace Prize (1945).

FATHER OF UTILITARIANISM, THE Jeremy Bentham (1748–1832), English philosopher. He put forward the idea that the good or evil of any action should be judged by its contribution to the happiness of the greatest number of people. Also *Jerry the Old Screw* and the *Queen Square Hermit*.

FATHER OF VARIETY, THE Charles Morton, *Champagne Charlie* (qv) who as well as starting music–halls managed the London Palace of Varieties.

FATHER OF VERTU IN ENGLAND, THE Thomas Howard, 2nd Earl of Arundel (1586–1646), art patron and discoverer of the Parian slab recording events in Greek history (at Oxford University since 1667).

- Vertu or virtu is a love of works of art or curios.

FATHER OF WAR CORRESPONDENTS, THE A writer signing himself William Richardson who gave an eye–witness account in *The Daily Post* (1740) of the capture of Portobello (1739) by Admiral Vernon (*Old Grog*).

FATHER PROUT Francis Sylvester Mahony (1804–66), dismissed priest and British journalist; Rome and Paris correspondent for *The Globe* (post 1846); from his contributions ('Prout Papers') to *Frazer's Magazine* (*circa* 1834).

FATHER SMITH Bernhardt Schmidt (*circa* 1630–1708), German-born organ-maker who became a celebrity in England after his arrival (1660). He made the organ at Durham Cathedral.

FATHER TAYLOR Edward Thomas Taylor (1793–1871), American minister and former seaman who established a mission to help sailors.

FAT TONY or FATS Anthony Salerno (1911–), head of the Lucchese Mafia family, given a 100 year sentence for drug trafficking and gangsterism (1987).

FATS

i) Thomas Waller (1904–43), American jazz pianist and composer.

ii) Antoine Domino (1928–), New Orleans pianist after the success of his song *The Fat Man* (1950).

iii) Theodore Navarro (1923–50), American jazz trumpeter.

FATTY

i) Roscoe Arbuckle (1887–1933), American film star in early Hollywood days, when he weighed 23 stone (322 lb). Although he was cleared of manslaughter, the scandal ruined him.

ii) Willie J. Foulke (1874–1916), England goalkeeper, 6ft 3 in tall who weighed 21 stone 7 lb (311 lb). He played for Sheffield United, Bradford City and England.

iii) Alfred William Moore (1823–1882), London surgeon. He discovered a new diet by which he lost 3 stone (42 lb).

FEARLESS, THE Richard, Duke of Normandy (died 996), son of William *Longsword*, whom he succeeded as a minor when the Duke was assassinated (942).

FEMALE BILL HART, THE *Texas* (Mary Louise) Guinan (1884–1934), Canadian-born American entertainer. She began in a rodeo, was a cowgirl in films, became a Broadway star and then turned to nightclubs to win the 'title' of the *Queen of the Night Clubs*.

- William S. Hart (1870–1946) was the first great Western star in silent films.

FEMALE HOWARD, THE Elizabeth Fry (1780–1845), British prison and asylum reformer (post 1813).

- John Howard (1726–90), British prison reformer, wrote *The State Prisons* (1777).

FEMALE MAECENAS, THE Lady Mary Wortley Montagu (1689–1762), *Sappho*, was daughter of a Duke and wife of the wealthy British Ambassador to Constantinople. The name was ironic, since her husband, Mr Edward Wortley Montagu, was a miser, and she made an enemy of Pope (the *Bard of Twickenham*).

- C. Cilnius Maecenas (died 8 BC) was a patron of the arts, especially of Virgil and Horace. Edith Sitwell wrote (*Alexander Pope*, 1930): 'I do not, however, know one instance of kindness or generosity of the straight-backed Lady Mary Wortley.'

FEMALE PHIDIAS, THE The Honourable Anne Seymour Damer (1749–1865), British sculptress; so called by Wolcot (*Peter Pindar*).

- Phidias (490-432 BC), one of the greatest sculptors in Ancient Greece.

FEMALE PSALMANAZAR, THE Mary Wilcox (1795–1865), a Devon girl who posed as the 'Javasu princess Caraboo' and invented a Javasu language. She also used the name Baker, and was married to a Mr Davidson.

- George Psalmanazar (?1679–1763) was an impostor who published a catechism in 'Formosan,' which he created. He knew Johnson (*Blinking Sam*), who thought highly of him. The name he used was adapted from Shalmaneser (2 Kings xviii 9).

FEMALE SOLDIER, THE or THE FEMALE MARINE Hannah Snell (1723–92) of Worcestershire, She enlisted to find her husband, who had deserted her. She was wounded at Pondicherry (1748). She also served in ships, and ran a public-house at Wapping, London.

- Modern British Wrens (Women's Royal Naval Service) with the Royal Marines are often called 'Hannahs'.

FENELON OF SCOTLAND, THE Robert Leighton (1613–84), Archbishop of Glasgow,

- François de Salignac de la Mothe Fénelon, Archbishop of Cambrai (1651–1715). A French moralist and theologian, he had a concern for the poor in France.

FEN TIGER, THE Dave *Boy* Green.

FERGIE The Duchess of York, *Carrot Top*.

FIDDLE AND THE BOW, THE Oliver Hardy (1892–1957) and Stan Laurel (1890–1965), American film comedians. The real name of Laurel, born in Britain, was Arthur Stanley Jefferson. Hardy was fat.

- See *Babe*, vii.

FIDDLER A. W. Goodwill (1911–), British jockey and trainer. When he began as an apprentice jockey, he took a violin with him.

FIDDLING CONYERS Dr Conyers Middleton (1683–1750), British theologian and amateur musician.

FIDDLING KNIGHT, THE Sir John Hawkins (1719–89), lawyer and author of a history of the Academy of Ancient Music (1770) and a *General History of the Science and Practice of Music* (1776).

FIDUS ACHATES Sir Arthur Hesilrige, the *Brutus of the Republic*, a Parliamentarian who raised a troop of horse for Sir William Waller (*William the Conqueror*), who gave him the nickname.

- Achates was the faithful friend of Aeneas and a Trojan hero. Hesilrige's unit became the Royal Horse Guards.

FIELDING OF DRAMA, THE George Farquhar (1678–1707), British actor who became a famous, but poor, playwright. *The Beaux' Stratagem* (1707) was written after a gift of 20 guineas from an actor named Robert Wilks. Farquhar heard of the success of the play just before he died. Also the *Smollett of the Stage*.

- For Fielding, see the *Father of the English novel*.

FIEND, THE John James Ferris (1876–1900), Australian bowler who took 220 wickets in the 1880 Test Matches. He and Turner (the *Terror*) bowled 20,000 balls and took 534 out of the 663 wickets that fell.

FIERCE, THE Alexander I of Scotland (*circa* (1078–1124), fourth son of *Canmore*. Also the *Proud*.

FIERY John Carey, one of the best known of early golf caddies. He carried for Willie Park (1864–1925), British Open champion (1887 and 1889); from his weather-beaten face.

FIERY FACE James II of Scotland (1430–60), who had a red spot in his face.

FIERY FRED Frederick Sewards Trueman (1931–), cricketer for Yorkshire and England; because of his fast bowling. He was the first bowler to take 300 Test Match wickets, and by the end of 1965 has taken 307 at an average of 21.57.

FIFI Fiore Buccieri (1904–73), American gangster, 'executioner' for the Chicago syndicate.

FIGHTING ADMIRAL, THE
i) Sir William Nathan Wrighte Hewett (1834–1888). He won the VC (1854) and fought in the Crimean and Ashanti wars.
ii) Rear-Admiral Robley Dunglison Evans (1846–1912), American given his nickname for his aggressive attitude to Chile. He fought in the Spanish-American war (1898).

FIGHTING BOB Robert Fitzsimmons, the *Antipodean*.

FIGHTING BOBS Lord Roberts, *Bobs*.

FIGHTING CHAPLAIN, THE Samuel Newel (died 1688), He served with the Massachusetts troops in *King Philip's* War (1675–76).

FIGHTING FITZGERALD George Robert Fitzgerald (?1748–86), British dandy and notorious duellist and gambler. A fine shot and an expert swordsman, he would fight a duel on the slightest provocation. He was executed for murder.

FIGHTING FRED Thomas Frederick, 1st Baron Peart (1914–88), British Labour Minister of Agriculture and Lord Privy Seal. Leader of the Opposition in the House of Commons in the 1970s.

FIGHTING IRISHMAN OF SOUTH BOSTON, THE John W. McCormack (1892–1980), the Speaker of the House of Representatives and a Democratic contender for the US Presidency,

FIGHTING JACK General John Mackenzie (1763–1860). At the time of his death he was the oldest serving officer in the British Army.

FIGHTING JARVEY, THE William Wood (fl. 1810–30), British pugilist.

- A 'jarvey' was slang for a hackney coachman.

FIGHTING JOE or FIGHTING JOE HOOKER General Joseph Hooker (1814–79), American who distinguished himself in the Mexican War and the American Civil War. He won his nickname at the battle of Williamsburg (1862); so called first by newspapers.

FIGHTING MAC

i) Major-General Sir Hector Archibald Macdonald (1852–1903). He rose from the ranks to become a general with a command in India. Also *Old Mac*.

ii) Major-General Sir WIlliam MacPherson (1853–1927), Director-General of Medical Service, 1st Army (World War I) and Deputy Director-General at General Headquarters. He was mentioned several times in despatches.

FIGHTING McCOOK Major-General Alexander McDowell McCook (1831–1903), who fought in the Indian wars, at Bull Run (1861) and Chickamauga (1863). His family was known as 'the Fighting McCooks'.

FIGHTING NAT Nathaniel Fitz-Randolph, a courageous American soldier in the War of Independence (1775–83).

FIGHTING PARSON, THE

i) William Gannaway Brownlow (1805–77), American journalist and politician, originally a wandering Methodist preacher. He fought for pro-Union, anti-slavery principles in the South, where he was imprisoned and later driven out. Also *Parson Brownlow*.

ii) Sir Henry Dudley Bate (1745–1824), a clergyman who became a sporting journalist and later editor of *The Morning Post*. He was notorious as a duellist. Also 'Fighting Parson Bate' and ' Parson Bate'.

iii) The Reverend Mr Frith, who was chaplain to the 5th Division of the Peninsular War. He rescued many wounded under fire.

iv) Colonel John Minton Chevington (1821–94), a former American Methodist minister who was responsible for the infamous 'battle' of Sand Creek (1894) in which he attacked an Indian camp flying the white and American flags and killed or mutilated about 200 Indians, including women and children.

v) Thomas Allen (1743–1811) of Pittsfield who led a force of men from western Massachusetts to help sway the battle of Bennington in Vermont (1777).

FIGHTING PHIL General Philip Kearney (1815–62), American soldier who lost an arm in a magnificent cavalry charge at Churubusco in the Mexican War (1846–8). He had raised the company at his own expense. He was in Paris when the American Civil War broke out, but returned immediately to command an infantry division. Also the *One-Armed Devil* and 'One-Armed Phil'.

FIGHTING PREACHER, THE Trevor Berbick (1953–), Jamaican–born World Boxing Council heavyweight boxing champion defeated (1986) by *Iron Mike* Tyson. He is an ordained minister.

FIGHTING PRELATE, THE Henry le Despenser, Bishop of Norwich (*circa* 1341–1406) in the reign of Richard II (the *Coxcomb*). He put down the East Anglian rising during the Wat Tyler rebellion (1381). He carried a large two–handed sword, and had once been a soldier. Also the *Warlike Bishop*.

- See the *King of the Commons*.

FIGHTING QUAKER, THE
i) William Willis (fl. 1740s), a pugilist who used that nickname in a challenge to Thomas Smallwood in *The Daily Advertiser* (April, 1742). Smallwood won the fight.
ii) Thomas Cumming (died 1774), merchant in the African trade and a friend of Johnson (***Blinking Sam***). He was a well-known drunkard. As a private merchant, he fought the French to protect his trade routes.

FILCHER Charles Montague, 1st Earl of Halifax (1661–1715), English statesman and poet, whose run of brilliant financial successes while Chancellor of the Exchequer were attributed in the House of Commons to corruption. The nickname was shouted across the House. As a result, he had to resign. Also ***Maecenas***.

FILL CHAISE Philip Hayes (1738–97), British musician with a very bad temper; a pun on 'Phil Hayes', presumably meaning that people rushed to their carriages to get away from him.

- A chaise was a carriage having one of several shapes, usually a low, four–wheeled open vehicle with one or two horses.

FINALITY JOHN or JACK John, 1st Earl Russell (1792–1878), British statesman, orator and author. He always spoke of the Reform Bill (1832) as 'a finality'. Also ***John Finality*** and the ***Lycurgus of the Lower House***.

FINGO John Henry Webb Fingleton (1908–81), New South Wales and Australia cricketer and journalist; first man in Test history to make four successive centuries.

FIREBALL Edward Glenn Roberts (1929–64), American motor-racing champion, who, ironically, died of burns in an accident in North Carolina.

FIREBRAND Lord Palmerston, ***Cupid***; because of his gunboat diplomacy.

FIREBRAND OF FRANCE, THE Prince John of Lancaster, Duke of Bedford (1389–1435), third son of Henry IV (***Bolingbroke***). John was Regent of England and France on the death of his father and the absence of his brother, Henry V (the ***English Alexander***). Joan of Arc was burnt under his command. Also ***John With the Leaden Sword***.

FIREBRAND OF HIS COUNTRY, THE John Knox, the ***Apostle of the Scots***.

FIREMAN OF THE EXCHANGE TELEGRAPH, THE Alan Whicker (1925–), journalist and British TV personality; so called in *World's Press News* (July 1953).

- A 'fireman' in Fleet Street jargon is a correspondent (in this case of a news agency) sent to all the hot spots of the world.

FIRST ENGINEER IN EUROPE, THE Thomas Telford (1757–1834), Scottish civil engineer who built the Menai bridge and the Caledonian canal. He also built roads in Britain. A new English town has been named after him.

FIRST GENTLEMAN IN EUROPE, THE The Prince Regent, the ***Adonis of Fifty***.

FIRST GENTLEMAN OF THE LAND, THE Chester Arthur, the ***Dude President***.

FIRST GENTLEMAN OF THE SCREEN, THE George Arliss (1868–1946), English-born actor in American silent films; because of his elegance and his monocle. His real name was George Augustus Andrews. Also the ***Grand Old Man of the Stage***.

FIRST GRAVE-DIGGER, THE Alexander Woollcott, the ***Butcher of Broadway***; nickname among actors and actresses of New York. He stopped a number of shows by his reviews.

- The grave-diggers are characters in Shakespeare's *Hamlet* (Act 5).

FIRST LADY OF AMERICAN TENNIS, THE Hazel Hotchkiss, Mrs George Wightman (1886–1974), US singles champion (1909–11 and 1919) and Wimbledon doubles champion (1924). She was the donor of the Wightman Cup.

FIRST LADY OF BROADWAY, THE Katherine Cornell (1893–1974), renowned American actress.

FIRST LADY OF FLEET STREET, THE Jean Rook (1933–), chief columnist and assistant editor of *The Daily Express*.

FIRST LADY OF HOLLYWOOD, THE
i) Norma Shearer (1902–83); Canadian-born; sometimes 'First Lady of the Screen'.
ii) Greer Garson (1908–).
iii) Irene Dunne (1904–).

FIRST LADY OF HOLLYWOOD FASHION, THE Edith Head (1907–81), designer of costumes for films. She won eight Oscars for her creations.

FIRST LADY OF THE STAGE, THE Helen Hayes (1900–), American actress who won an Oscar (1932), an Emmy (1954) and a Tony (1958). Also 'the First Lady of the American Theatre'. Her real name is Helen Brown.

FIRST LADY OF WESTMINSTER, THE Marcia Williams, the *Duchess of Downing Street*; so called when she was private secretary to Prime Minister Harold Wilson.

FIRST MAN OF LETTERS IN EUROPE, THE Robert Southey, the *Ballad Monger*.

FIRST SCOTTISH REFORMER, THE Patrick Hamilton (1504–28), Scottish priest burnt at the stake for having preached Lutheran ideas.

FIRST TORY, THE Sir Roger L'Estrange (1616–1704), royalist pamphleteer and newspaper editor. In *The Observator* (1679), he took the stand of a Tory when he attacked Titus Oates (the *Knight of the Post*) in the campaign which unmasked the 'Popish Plot'. Also *Oliver's Fiddler*.

- 'Tory', which means an Irish brigand or outlaw, was applied (*circa* 1700) to the political party which grew out of the royalists (Conservatists *circa* 1830). It was given by the Whigs as an insult.

FISHFACE The Prince of Wales, Prince Charles Philip Arthur George (1948–); so called by his wife, Princess Diana (1961–). Also *Number-One-Piccaninny-Belong-Missus-Queen*.

FIVE P's, THE William Oxberry (1784–1824), British printer, publisher, poet, publican and player, i.e actor.

FLAGELLUM DEI Sir Walter Scott, *Bold Buccleugh*, the *Scourge of God*.

FLAHERTY or FLAITHBHERTACH OF THE PILGRIM'S STAFF Flaherty, King of Ailech in West Ireland (reigned 1004–1030 and 1033–1036). He went on a pilgrimage to Rome (1030). Aedh the *Handy* ruled while he was away.

FLAMBARD Ranulf (died 1128), Bishop of Durham (post-1099), Chief Minister to William *Rufus*; so called by the barons who hated him since he was the King's agent for tax-extortion from all classes, and a mischief-maker. The name means 'flaming torch', from OF *flambe*. Dauzat gives *flambart* (1285). A medieval monastic document gives him another nickname, *passeflabere*. It is apparently a play on his name and suggests handing on the torch.

FLAMINGO Virginia Hill (1918–66), American call-girl after whom *Bugsy* Siegal named his first gambling casino in Las Vegas (1946). Also the *Queen of the Mobs*.

FLANDERS MARE, THE Anne of Cleves (1515–57), fourth wife of Henry VIII (*Bluff Hal*). After riding down to Rochester to meet her, he exclaimed sourly that she was no better than a Flanders mare. He divorced her a few months after the marriage.

FLANNELFOOT Edward Vicars (fl. 1933–6), British housebreaker throught to have covered his feet with cloth. Scotland Yard set up a special unit to capture him.

FLASH, THE Norman Cowans (1961–), Jamaican-born fast bowler for Middlesex and England. He grew up in London. In the 1982 Test series he took 6 for 69. Also *Persil*.

FLASH BILLY William Tobin (1951–), British gunman, gang boss and lavish spender, sentenced (1981) to sixteen years for his part in a raid on a security van.

FLASH HARRY Sir Malcolm Sargent, *Britain's Ambassador of Music*; from his dapper appearance, Sir Malcolm said it referred to him flashing round the world.

- 'Flash' has been an English slang word for someone of smart bearing since the 17th century, e.g. 'flash kiddy', a dandy.

FLATFOOT THE GUDGEON-TAKER Charles II, the *Blackbird*; so called by Rochester (*Virgin Modesty*).

- Flatfoot was the name of a horse the King raced at Newmarket and Charles was an enthusiastic fisherman.

FLAT or BIG NOSE George L. Curry (1841–82), cattle rustler and bandit with the Wild Bunch, originally nicknamed 'Big Nose'. His real name was said to have been George Parrott.

- See *Kid Curry*.

FLAT JACK John (Jack) Simmons (1941–), Lancashire spin bowler; from 'flat spin'.

FLEA Alan P. E. Knott (1946–), wicket-keeper for England and Kent, responsible for a record 269 dismissals. He is small. He was the first man to make 200 Test catches.

FLINT JACK Edward Simpson (1815–? 67) of Whitby, Yorkshire, who sold spurious stone celts and arrow–heads. His forgeries were so good that experts gave him unlimited orders. He disappeared soon after he came out of prison for theft (1867).

FLOGGING JOEY Captain Joseph McCulloch, Royal Navy, founder of the Coast Blockade to restrict smuggling (early 19th century). Bowen says the name arose 'because of the enormous number of men from land stations who were sent on board [HMS *Ramillies*] to be flogged, often on the simple recommendation of a petty officer.' He was also called 'Old Jock McCulloch.'

FLOJO Florence Griffith-Joyner, the *Fastest Woman on Earth*.

FLOGSTER, THE The Duke of Clarence (1765–1837), afterwards William IV; his nickname in the Royal Navy. His opposition to 'whipping' is mentioned in a contemporary song, *Duke William's Frolic*. Also *Our Billy, Pineapple Head*, the *Sailor King*, *Sailor William* and *Silly Billy*.

FLORIZEL George, Prince of Wales (*Adonis of Fifty*). Florizel is the lover of *Fair Perdita* in *The Winter's Tale*. Egan the *Elder* helped to popularize the nickname by *The Mistress of Royalty or the Loves of Florizel and Perdita* (1814).

FLOS REGNUM or THE FLOWER OF KINGS King Arthur; so called by John of Exeter (died 1268), Bishop of Winchester.

FLOSS John Lloyd (1954–), British champion tennis-player; winner of the Wimbledon doubles (1983), once married to Christine Evert (the *Ice Maiden*); so called in the tennis world. Also *Legs*.

FLOWER OF CHIVALRY, THE

i) Sir William Douglas (*circa* 1300–53) who retook Hermitage castle, Liddesdale from the English; so called by David II (1324–71). Also the *Knight of Liddesdale*.

ii) Sir Philip Sidney, the *British Bayard*.

FLOWER OF HADDINGTON, THE Jane Baillie Carlyle, née Welsh at Haddington (1801–66); for her wit and beauty. She married Thomas Carlyle (the *Censor of the Age*) in 1826. She is rated one of the best letter-writers in England.

- Haddington, Scotland is in East Lothian (once called Haddingtonshire).

FLOWER OF POETS, THE Chaucer,. the *British Homer*.

FLOWER OF STRATHEARN, THE Carolina Oliphant, Baroness Nairne (1766–1845), Scottish poetess. She wrote Jacobite songs, e.g. *Will ye no' come back again* and *Charlie is my darling*; from *Lays from Strathearn* published 1846.

FLUFF Alan Freeman (1912–), British disc jockey. He rejoined the BBC (1989). He had previously been with them for 19 years from 1960. Freeman says the nickname came from an old fluffy pullover he wore, but 'to fluff' is stage slang for making mistakes or missing cues.

FLY Admiral Sir William F. Martin (1801–95), Commander–in–Chief, Mediterranean Fleet; his nickname in the Royal Navy, says Bowen, for Martin took evolutions to such a pitch 'that it was generally believed that...he regularly hoisted a general signal "Bury your Dead" after the Monday forenoon drill'. He commanded the *Fly* sloop (1823). Also *Pincher*.

- 'Fly' is slang for someone knowing,

artful and up to every dodge.

FLYING DUCHESS, THE Mary, 11th Duchess of Bedford (1865–1937). She took up flying at the age of sixty, and for eleven years made flights all over the world. She was lost on one of them.

FLYING DUSTMAN, THE Charles Fox, convicted at the Middlesex Sessions (1812) of assault after having been accused of 'pirating' the collection of dust and ashes, for which a man named Lacock had a contract.

FLYING DUTCHMAN, THE John Peter Wagner (1874–1955), American baseball batter with Louisville and Kansas in the National League; in the Hall of Fame (1897–1917). Also *Honus*.

FLYING GHOST, THE Katerina Sengilwoman, alias dicta (=called) Keterina the flying ghost, Surrey (1492). 'Sengilwoman = ? the woman living by the burnt clearing' (Ewen/Reaney); from the records of the King's Bench, High Court.

FLYING GRANDMOTHER, THE Mrs Gerry Mock of Ohio, who set up a new record for the longest non–stop flight by a woman (1966). In thirty–one hours she covered 4,500 miles from Honolulu to Colombus, Ohio.

FLYING HIGHWAYMAN, THE. William Harrow (executed 1763) who leapt turnpikes to escape capture when pursued.

FLYING MOUTH, THE Francis Lee Bailey (1933–), American attorney who flies his own jet plane to various regions to represent clients in court.

● 'Mouth' or 'mouthpiece' = a lawyer.

FLYING PEACEMAKER, THE Henry Alfred Kissinger (1923–), American Secretary of State (1973–7); so called for his air journeys to trouble spots, e.g. the Middle East.

FLYING SCOTSMAN (or SCOTCHMAN), THE

i) John *Doctor Black*, a fast walker and a rapid notetaker.
ii) Ronald Flockhart (1923–62), Scottish motor–racing driver killed in an air crash.

iii) (or SCOT): Eric Liddell (1902–45), Scottish athlete who set a new world record and won an Olympic gold medal in the 1/4 mile (1924). He died, a missionary, in a Japanese prison camp.

FOGGY Captain Mark Phillips, *Chief*; his reputed nickname at Sandhurst, although Captain Phillips vehemently denies it. 'Fog' is allegedly used by the Prince of Wales.

FOGHORN

i) Senator William Allen (1806–79), because of his voice, Also the *Ohio Gong*.
ii) George Wenslow (1946–), American actor with a 'big' voice. His real name is George Wenzleft.

FOO Felicity Kendal (1946–), British stage, TV and screen actress; a relic of a childhood nickname 'Fatty Foo'.

FORCES' SWEETHEART, THE Dame Vera Lynn (1917–), British singer who broadcast to and visited British Servicemen during World War II. Her real name is Vera Lewis, née Welch.

FORKBEARD Sweyn, Danish King of England for about 40 days (1013–14). He was killed by a fall from his horse at Gainsborough, Lincolnshire – frightened, it is said, by a vision of Edmund (the *English St Sebastian*). Sweyn = Danish Svein.

FORK-CARRYING TRAVELLER, THE Thomas Coryate (?1577–1617), Briton who visited Greece, the Holy Land, Persia and India, among other places, and was thought to have introduced the fork into England; so called by contemporary playwrights.

● A 'silvir forke for grene gyngour' is, however, included in a will of 1463, and a fork has been found in a Saxon tumulus.

FOUL-WEATHER JACK

i) Vice-Admiral the Honourable John Byron (1723–86), reputed never to have experienced a fine-weather passage anywhere. He was the father of *Mad Jack* Byron, and grandfather of the poet. Also the *Jonah of the Wager*.
ii) Admiral of the Fleet Sir John Norris (1660–1749), Commander-in-Chief,

Spithead. His whole fleet was once driven back by bad weather when blockading a French port.

FOUNDER OF ENGLISH COMMERCIAL LAW, THE William Murray, 1st Earl of Mansfield (1705–93). He brought commercial law from a chaos of unselected decisions to an exact science. He was Lord Chief Justice (1756–88).

FOUNDER OF THE ENGLISH DOMESTIC NOVEL, THE Samuel Richardson, the *English Marivaux*.

FOUNTAIN OF LIFE, THE Alexander of Hales, *Doctor Irrefragibilis*.

FOUR–EYED GEORGE Major-General George Gordon Meade (1815–72), American who wore spectacles. He fought in the Mexican War (1846–8), and in the battles of Bull Run (1861) and Antietam (1862) in the American Civil War.

FOX, THE
i) Edward Hickman (1907–28), American executed for the murder of Marion Parker (12), daughter of a Los Angeles banker; self-applied in a ransom note.
ii) Arthur Hutchinson (1941–), Briton sentenced to life imprisonment at Durham (1984) for the wedding day murders of a bride's parents and brother. He was also sentenced for rape and robbery; self-applied during the hunt.
iii) Malcolm Fairley (1952–), British hooded rapist and burglar who terrified an area of Bedfordshire, Hertfordshire, and Buckinghamshire, labelled 'the triangle-of-terror' (1985); sentenced to six terms of life imprisonment. He built a 'lair' in the house of an intended victim.
iv) James McCann, the *Emerald Pimpernel*.

FOXY
i) William Corder (1804–28), hanged for the murder of Maria Marten. His crime was the theme of a British film *Maria Marten or Murder in the Red Barn* (1935).
ii) Graeme Fowler (1957–), Lancashire and England cricketer, one of the first two batsmen to make more than 200 in an innings in a Test Match. The other was Mike Gatting, *Panda*.

FOZZY Neil Fowler, the *Colchester Express*.

FRANK James Thomas Harris (1856–1931), Irishman and a notorious journalist. He was an editor in America and England. His *My Life and Loves* (1923–7) was a sensation.

FRANKLIN OF THEOLOGY, THE Andrew Fuller (1754–1815), English Baptist preacher. His writings helped Baptists towards a less rigid point of view.
• Franklin, the *American Socrates*, was a man of tolerance and common sense.

FRANK SINATRA OF SHAKESPEARE, THE Richard Burton (né Jenkins: 1925–84), British Shakespearian actor; so called by his wife, Elizabeth Taylor (1932–).
• For Sinatra, see the *Guv'nor*.

FREEBORN JOHN John Lilburne (*circa* 1613–57), leader of the Levellers (an English republican movement who demanded his rights 'as a freeborn Englishman' when he was taken before the infamous Star Chamber. He was so contentious that it was said if he were alone in the world 'Lilburne would quarrel with John and John with Lilburne'. Also *Sturdy John*.
• For Star Chamber, see the *Brave Jersey Muse*.

FRECKLED, THE
i) Brian Ballach (1395–1425), Prince of Clannaboy.
• See *French John*, below.
ii) Walter Ballach, Earl of Menteith (died 1282).
• *Breac-bhallach* or *balach* means 'freckled' in Gaelic or Irish.

FRECKLED FREAK, THE Robert Fitzsimmons, the *Antipodean*. When he started to box he was lanky and freckled, and thought to be no good.

FRED, Omar Sharif, *Cairo Fred*.

FRED, THE Lord Frederick Windsor (1977–), younger son of the Duke and Duchess of Kent; so called by the Royal Family.

FRENCH JOHN John O'Neill (died 1739), son of the last Lord of Clannaboy. He came from Paris to build the Clannaboy tomb at Shane's castle, Ireland.

- Henry O'Neill became prince or lord of *Clann Aodhe Buidhe* (Clannaboy or Clanaboy) in the 14th century.

FRENCHIE Herbert Charles Denton Nichols (1913–), British National Hunt jockey, born in France.

FRIEND OF SINNERS, THE Nathaniel Hawthorne (1804–64), American novelist who studied criminals; so called by James Freeman Clarke (1810–88), Unitarian and liberal.

FRIEND OF THE JEWS, THE Robert Grant (1785–1838), M.P. who tried in Parliament with the help of Macaulay (*Babbletongue*) to establish equality for Jews in Britain. His Bill was passed by the Commons but rejected by the Lords (1833).

FRITZ

i) Frederick Edward Grey Ponsonby, 1st Baron Sysonby (1867–1935), equerry to Queen Victoria (*Drina*) and assistant private secretary to Edward VII (the *Peacemaker*).

ii) Walter Frederick Mondale (1928–), Democratic Vice-President, USA under President Carter (1924– :1976–81) and unsuccessful Presidential candidate (1984).

iii) Professor Friedrich August von Hayek (1899–), a naturalized Briton, expounder of the economic theory of monetarism.

- Monetarism (in over-simplification) is a policy to expand the real national income (rather than to borrow) to raise the standard of living, allied with an anti-inflation policy to keep money stable.

FROG Dallas Elmer Chambers (1897–*circa* 1952), American jazz trumpeter. Also *Ruffle Jaws*.

FROGMAN Clarence Henry (1937–), American rock singer; after he had imitated frog noises in the song *Ain't Got no Home*.

FRUITY Major Edward Dudley Metcalf (died 1957), Irishman, of the 3rd Skinner's Horse, equerry and close friend of Edward, Prince of Wales (*Sardine*). Metcalf married Lady Alexandra Curzon, daughter of the Viceroy of India.

FRY Jo Ann Prentice (1933–), American golfer.

FUBBS Louise de Kéroualle, Duchess of Portsmouth, *Bathsheba*; from her childlike beauty.

- 'Fubbs' is an old word for 'chubby', from 'fub', a fat child (Bailey's dictionary, 1757).

FUHRER, THE Nicola Martin (1951–), creator and boss of the Bucks Fizz pop group; so called by members of the group.

- *Führer* – leader in German.

FUM THE FOURTH George IV (*Adonis of Fifty*); so called by Byron (*Baby*) in *Don Juan* (xi 78).

- The fum (the phoenix) was a legendary bird of China, symbolic of royal dignity.

FUSE, THE Brian Donald Hume (1919–), murderer of Stanley Setty (1948) and Arthur Maag (1959), sentenced to life imprisonment in Switzerland (1959); his nickname in Dartmoor from his trade as an electrician. Found insane, he was repatriated and sent to Broadmoor (1976).

FUSS AND FEATHERS or OLD FUSS AND FEATHERS General Winfield Scott (1786–1866), who fought in the war of 1812 and the Mexican War (1846–8). He was fussy and self-important, loved military display and insisted on strict military etiquette. Also *Old Chapultepec*.

FUZZY

i) J. Forrest Knight (1901–76), American cabaret star and film actor in Westerns e.g. *The Trail of the Lonesome Pine*.

ii) Al. St John (1893–1963), American film comedian, celebrated in silent movies from 1913.

G

GABBY

i) George Hayes (1885–1969), American film actor, mostly in Westerns.

ii) Charles Leo Hartnett (1900–72) of the Chicago Cubs baseball team, the Most Valued Player of 1935, who made the strike to win the 1938 game with Pittsburgh Pirates and so the National League pennant; in the Hall of Fame (1922–41) and the Chicago Historical Museum; so called because he talked a lot.

GAELIC HOMER, THE Ossian, the *Celtic Homer*.

GAFFER, THE Sir Basil Henriques (1890–1961), chairman of magistrates at the East Ham Juvenile Court and a founder of the Bernard Bairn Settlement.

- A gaffer (from 'godfather') is an old English dialect word for someone elderly or in authority, usually used affectionately.

GAIETY GEORGE George Edwardes (1855–1915), English theatre manager, especially of the Gaiety, London (post 1886) where his musical comedies established 'The Gaiety Girl'. Also the *Guv'nor*.

- See the *Father of Musical Comedy*.

GALLANT, THE Major John Pelham (1838–1863) of the Confederate Army; so called by Lee (the *Bayard of the Confederate Army*) after Fredericksburg (1862).

GALLANT HARRY OF THE WEST Henry Clay, the *Apostle of Liberty*. He worked for western expansion in America and the emancipation of slaves.

GALLANT YOUNG JUVENAL Francis Meres (1565–1647), British clergyman and author who published *Palladis Tamia, Wits' Treasury* (1598) which dealt critically with all writers from Chaucer to his own time. He listed Shakespeare's works and praised him for 'mightily' enriching the English language. So called by Nash (the *English Aretine*).

- See the *British Juvenal*.

GALLIARD, THE William Johnstone (fl. 16th century) of Whamphrey, a Scottish freebooter.

- A galliard is a man of spirit or courage.

GALLIC BULLY, THE William III, the *Deliverer*.

GALLOPER SMITH Frederick Edwin Smith, 1st Earl of Birkenhead (1872–1930), Lord Chancellor; so called for his part in organizing the Protestant resistance to Home Rule in Ireland (1914).

GALLOPING DICK Richard Ferguson (hanged 1800), a celebrated highwayman who displayed courageous riding when pursued.

GALLOPING GHOST, THE

i) Harold Grange (1903–), American footballer and All-American half-back. He played for the Chicago Bears and the New York Yankees between 1925 and 1937; in the Hall of Fame. He scored 31 touchdowns in three seasons of college football, including 5 against Michigan (1924). Also *Red*.

ii) William (Bill) Wheatley (1909–), American amateur basketball player and coach.

GALLOPING GOURMET, THE

- i) Graham Kerr (1934–), British TV cook, whose programmes were shown world-wide until 1975, when he retired to live in Washington.
- ii) Dale Lyons (1957–); so called at the Birmingham College of Food after he had run a marathon race tossing a pancake.

GALLOPING HEAD Sir Francis Bond Head (1793–1875), British soldier and colonial Governor; author of *Rough Notes of Journeys to the Pampas and the Andes* (1827).

GALLOPING JACK Brigadier-General John Robinson Royston (1860–1942) of the Imperial Light Horse in the South African war (1899–1902). He formed his own regiment, Royston's Horse (1906).

GALLOPING MAJOR, THE Sir Trevor Dawson (1933–83), former Guards officer, City banker and London nightclubber; so called because he was always 'galloping off' to race-meetings; from the music-hall song *Here comes the galloping major*.

GALLOPING O'HOGAN Captain O'Hogan, an Irish raparee (irregular), guide to General Patrick Sarsfield (later the Earl of Lucan) at the siege of Limerick (1690–1691).

GALLOWAY POET, THE William Nicholson (?1782–1849), verse–writing pedlar encouraged by Hogg (the **Boar of the Forest**).

GAM David (Davyddab) ab Llewelyn (died 1415), a Welsh esquire (?knighted) who with three knights joined Henry V (the **English Alexander**) in France, and was killed at Agincourt; so called because he squinted. He is said to have been the original of Captain Fluellen in Shakespeare's *Henry V*.

- 'Gam' is a Welsh word for 'crooked' or 'twisted', and is still used in English slang, e.g. 'gammy–eyed' means a person with some defect. Cf. the Gaelic **cam** as in 'Campbell,' 'crooked mouth'; and see the preface.

GAME CHICKEN, THE Henry Pearce (fl. 18th–early 19th century), champion of England (1805). He defeated John Gully (**Poor Gully**) in a bout before the Duke of Clarence (the **Flogster**) in 1805; so called as a pun on 'Hen', from 'Henry'.

GAMECOCK, THE Brigadier-General Thomas Sumter, the **Carolina Gamecock**.

GAMECOCK OF THE WILDERNESS, THE Danforth Marble (1810–49), American actor; from his success in a play of that name.

GARBO Marlon Brando (1924–), American film actor.

- Greta Garbo (1905–), Swedish-born American film star, was renowned for wanting to be alone. Her real surname is Gustafsson.

GARIBALDI'S ENGLISHMAN John Whitehead Peard (1811–80), well-known as a rower, boxer and shot, who joined Giuseppe Garibaldi (1807–82), the Italian patriot, in his fight to free Italy from Austrian rule. Peard distinguished himself at the battle of Melazzo (1860). He became a colonel commanding the English Legion; so called throughout England.

GARRET MORE Gerald Fitzgerald, 8th Earl of Kildare (from 1477 to 1513), Deputy Governor of Ireland (post 1481). Under him the powers of the Kildares reached almost royal status. Also the **Great Earl**.

- *Garret* = Gerald. *More* = great.

GARRET OGE Gerald Fitzgerald, 9th Earl of Kildare (from 1513 to 1534); also Deputy Governor of Ireland. Through the influence of the Ormondes, he was accused of treachery and supplanted. Also **King of Kildare** and the **Younger** = Oge.

GARRET THE GOD Garret Fitzgerald (1926–), Taoiseach (= Premier) of Ireland (1981–82, 1982–87), leader of the Fine Gael party (named after a tribe of ancient Gaul). He is a respected politician and academic. After defeat (1987) he resigned from leadership.

- Cf **Charles the Bad**.

GARVE James Louis Garvin (1868–1947), British editor, e.g. of *The Observer* (1908–42).

GARYGOAL Gary Lineker (1960–), British striker for Everton, Tottenham Hotspur and England; so called in Spain, when he played for Barcelona FC, from his accuracy in shooting for goal. His transfer is rated at £2 million. He was the top goalscorer in the 1986 World Cup matches. Also **Smiler**.

GAS Charles Robert Darwin (1809–82), British naturalist and author of *On the Origin of Species*...(1859), when a young man; from his chemical experiments with his brother under the influence of Professor John Henslow. Also the **Sage of Down House**.

GASEOUS CASSIUS Muhammed Ali (1942–), American world heavyweight boxing champion (1964, 1974, 1978), whose original name was Cassius Clay, renowned for bombastic claims. Also the **Greatest** and the **Louisville Lip**.

GAS MAN, THE, GAS or THE GAS LIGHT MAN Thomas (Tom) Hickman (1785–1823), British pugilist as brilliant as the gas-lighting introduced in 1807. He was killed in a drag-cart accident, i.e. a cart without wheels
- 'Drag' became slang for a coach and eventually the road, e.g. 'the main drag').

GATECRASHER NO 1 Danny Gunnery, *Danny the Blarney*, who by his uninvited presence at various functions met Pope Paul VI, Henry Kissinger, President Jimmy Carter, the Queen–Mother and Princess Margaret. He 'retired' in 1980.

GATEMOUTH Clarence Brown (1924–), American blues guitarist.

'GATOR LOVER, THE Joseph (Joe) Ball (1892–1938), a tavern-keeper of Elmendorf, Texas, where he kept a pond of alligators. After he had made his waitresses pregnant he is believed to have fed them to the reptiles. He committed suicide after the stories became public.

GAUNT John, Duke of Lancaster (1340–99), third son of Edward III (the *Father of English Commerce*) and father of Henry IV (*Bolingbroke*); born at Ghent.

GAWKY SQUIRE, THE Richard Granville-Temple, 1st Earl Temple (1711–79), First Lord of the Admiralty (1766). Walpole (the *Autocrat of Strawberry Hill)* said he was ridiculously awkward. Also *Lord Gawky, Squire Gawky, Tiddy-Doll* and the *Water-Gull.*

GAY LOTHARIO OF POLITICS, THE Lord Beaconsfield, the *Asian Mystery*; so called by *Tay Pay* O'Connor.
- Lothario is the heartless libertine of Nicholas Rowe's *The Fair Penitent* (1703). Beaconsfield wrote a novel called *Lothair* (1870).

GAZZA Paul Gascoigne (1967–), British footballer for Newcastle United transferred (1988) to Tottenham Hotspur for £2 million.

GEE
i) Gertrude Lawrence (1898–1952), English musical comedy actress. Her real name was Alexandra Dagmar Lawrence-Klausen.

ii) Lady Georgina Dorothy Cavendish (1763–1858), who married (1801) George Howard, Viscount Morpeth and 6th Earl of Carlisle (1773–1848). Also the *Rat.*

GEM OF NORMANDY, THE Emma Aelgifu (died 1052), daughter of Duke Richard the *Fearless* of Normandy. She was wife of Ethelred the *Unready*, and, after his death, to Canute the *Great.* Her marriage to Ethelred paved the way for the Norman Conquest (1066).

GENE James Joseph Tunney (1897–1978), American undefeated world heavyweight boxing champion (1926–8), a business executive when he left the ring.

GENERAL BACKACHER Major-General Sir William Forbes Gatacre (1843–1906), divisional general in the South African War (1899–1902). Conan Doyle (*The Great Boer War, 1900)*: '..he had been criticised, notably during the Soudan campaign, for having called upon his men for undue and unnecessary exertion. "General Backacher" they called him.' He commanded a brigade there.

GENERAL BOTHER General Louis Botha (1862–1919), Commander–in–Chief, Boer forces in the South African War (1900–1902) and 1st Prime Minister of the Union of South Africa; because that is what he caused to British troops.

GENERAL LEE'S WAR HORSE Lieutenant-General James Longstreet (1821–1904), Confederate general who held high office for a long time in the Army of Virginia. He often led his troops into action personally. Lee (the *Bayard of the Confederate Army*) called him 'My Old War Horse.' Also *Lee's Old War Horse.*

GENERAL or CAPTAIN LUDD Ned Ludd of the English machine–breakers in the Midlands (1811–16) called the Luddites; although historians are not absolutely sure he was a real person. One version says he was a man of weak intellect who lived in a Leicestershire village in about 1779 and broke stocking–makers' machines. The Luddites, usually masked, worked at night. Also *King Lud.*

GENERAL MAFIA Don Calogero Vizzini (1877–1947), head of the Mafia in Sicily at the time of the Allied invasion (1943) who helped to ease the situation in their favour, at the request, it is said, of *Lucky* Luciano; so called by Allied troops.

GENERAL RIP VAN CREALOCK Major–General Henry Hope Crealock, commanding the 1st Division in the Zulu War (1879–80), because of his slow advance against Cetywayo (1879). It took his column ten hours to cover three miles.

• Rip Van Winkle is the central character in a story in *The Sketch Book* (1819–1820) by Washington Irving (the *American Addison)*. He slept for 20 years.

GENERAL TOM THUMB Charles Sherwood Stratton (1837–83), celebrated American dwarf in Barnum's show (see the *Prince of Humbugs)*. When twenty-five years old, Stratton was 31 in high. He married Lavinia Warren, five years younger but the same height. Also *Tom Thumb.*

• Tom Thumb is the hero of a nursery tale, first mentioned in 1579. Richard Johnson published *The History of Tom Thumb* (1621).

GENERAL TUBMAN Harriet Tubman, the *Conductor of the Underground Railway*; so called by John Brown *(Old Brown of Ossawatomie)*

GENEVA BULL, THE Stephen Marshall (c 1594–1655), British Presbyterian divine and one of the authors of *Smectymnuus* in which five clergymen pamphleteers attacked episcopacy; so called because he was a Calvinist and roared like a bull, but also probably as a pun on Papal Bull.

GENERAL GEORGE George Elliott, K.C. (1860–1916), popular London barrister. He defended (1903) George Chapman, the Whitechapel poisoner, hanged in 1903, one candidate for *Jack the Ripper*.

GENTLE BEN Ben Crenshaw (1953–), American golfer, winner of the US Masters (1984).

GENTLE GEORGE Sir George Etherege, *Easy Etherege*; so called by Sir John Suckling (1609–52).

GENTLE GIANT, THE William John Charles (1932–), centre-half for Leeds United and Cardiff, who played for Wales for 18 years and helped them to the World Cup finals (1958).

GENTLE JUDGE, THE Christmas Humphreys (1901–83), English judge noted for his consideration. He was a founder of the Buddhist Society, London (1924).

GENTLE KNIGHT, THE Senator George Norris, the *Father of the Twentieth Amendment.* He helped to create the Tennessee Valley Authority; so called by Roosevelt (the *Barrymore of the White House)*. He 'christened' Norris 'The Gentle Knight of Progressive Ideals'.

GENTLE LOCHIEL, THE Donald Cameron (died 1748), chief of the clan Cameron, whose title comes from Loch Eil. He pledged everything to support the *Young Pretender* (1745) and, wounded in both ankles, was carried with the prince into exile in France, where he died. His father was Lord Lochiel in the Jacobite peerage. He was so called because he was very much a gentleman.

• See the *Black* (iv).

GENTLEMAN BOSS, THE Chester Arthur, the *Dude President*.

GENTLEMAN BOXER, THE Richard Humphries (fl. 1780s–1790s) who beat Dan Mendoza (the *Light of Israel)* and whose match with Martin, the Bath butcher (1786) was watched by the Prince of Wales. (*Adonis of Fifty)* the Duke of York (the *Soldiers' Friend)*, the Duke of Orleans and most of the French nobility in England at the time. Egan the *Elder* says Humphries got his nickname from his 'genteel' appearance and behaviour.

GENTLEMAN BUSHRANGER, THE William Westwood (1821–46), an English-born Australian bushranger who had been a prisoner on the dreaded Norfolk Island. Also the *Gentleman Convict* and *Jacky-Jacky*.

GENTLEMAN COACHMAN, THE Henry Stevenson (fl. early 18th century), an amateur stagecoach driver, or 'swell dragsman' in the slang of the time.

GENTLEMAN CONVICT, THE

i)Matthew Brady (1799–1826), a Tasmanian hanged as a bushranger. He was an intelligent and well-educated man, transported for forgery. He once offered a reward for the capture of the Governor.

ii) William Westwood, the **Gentleman Bushranger.**

GENTLEMAN CRACKSMAN, THE Bertram (Bert) Redvers Holliday (fl. 1932–49) who committed a series of burglaries in the British Home Counties and lived a life of luxury at Wraysbury-on-Thames. He was found shot through the head (1949) when Scotland Yard were closing their net on him.

GENTLEMAN FROM NORTH CAROLINA, THE Andrew Jackson Joyner (1861–1943), American racehorse trainer.

GENTLEMAN FROM VIRGINIA, THE Randolph Scott (1903–87), American film star, mainly of Westerns; born there, His real name was Randolph Crance.

GENTLEMAN GEORGE
i) Senator George H. Pendleton (1825–89), American politician from Ohio.
ii) George Barrett (1794–1855), English-born actor, the best light comedian in America.

GENTLEMAN HIGHWAYMAN, THE James M'Lean, Macleane, Maclane, Maclean or Maclaine (1724–50) son of a Presbyterian minister of Northern Ireland. He once robbed Horace Walpole (the **Autocrat of Strawberry Hill)** (1749). He lived a life of elegance in St James's, London, and was reputed to have had an estate in Ireland. He was hanged at Tyburn.

GENTLEMAN JACK John Bannister (1760–1836), British actor encouraged by Garrick (**Atlas**). It was said that few men on the stage had more solid virtue and unblemished character. Lamb (the **Mitre Courtier**) talks of his 'sweet good-natured moral pretensions'.

GENTLEMAN JACKSON
i) John Jackson (1769–1845). He beat Dan Mendoza (the **Light of Israel**) to become champion of England (1795–1803). He raised the standards of boxing in Britain. At the coronation of George IV (**Adonis of Fifty**), he provided a royal bodyguard

of famous prizefighters. Also **Gentleman John.**
ii) Peter Jackson, the **Black Diamond**.

GENTLEMAN JIM
i) Lieutenant-Colonel James Skinner (1778–1841), British soldier in India who raised Skinner's Horse.
ii) James John Corbett (1866–1933), American who took the world's heavyweight boxing championship (1892) from Sullivan (the **Boston Strong Boy**) in his first title fight with gloves. He was champion for five years before he lost to the British Bob Fitzsimmons (the **Antipodean**); so called after he popularized the new gentlemanly style under the Marquess of Queensberry rules.
iii) Jim Reeve (1925–64), American country and Western singer killed in a plane crash.

GENTLEMAN JOHN John Jackson, **Gentleman Jackson**.

GENTLEMAN JOHNNY General Sir John Burgoyne (1722–92), soldier, playwright, politician and wit. He was forced by the Americans to surrender at Saratoga (1777). He was chairman of a Select Committee which inquired into the conduct of Clive (the **Heaven-Sent General**) in India. Also the **Martial Macaroni** and **(Sir) Jack Brag.**

GENTLEMAN JONES Richard Jones (1779–1851), English actor and dramatist who became a famous teacher of elocution in Belgrave Square, London.

GENTLEMAN LEWIS William Thomas Lewis (circa 1749–1811), best known as a comedian, an actor with polish and cordiality. Also the **Mercutio of Actors.**

GENTLEMAN PALMER John Palmer (1728–1768), English actor, a vain man who dressed well and who had an excellent reputation on the stage.

GENTLEMAN SMITH William Smith (1730–1819). a handsome and elegant British actor, coached by Spranger Barry (the **Irish Roscius**) and the first to play Charles Surface in The School for Scandal (1777) by Sheridan (**Sherry**). He had fine manners, and married an heiress.

GENTLE SHEPHERD, THE George Grenville (1712–70), Chancellor of the Exchequer (1763–5). The nickname followed a quotation by his brother–in–law, William Pitt (*Aeolus*) during the debate in Parliament on the unpopular tax on cider imposed in 1763: 'Gentle shepherd, tell me where.'
- It is a quotation from Samuel Rogers (1710–82), a writer of popular songs.

GEORGE John Brian Statham (1932–), captain of Lancashire cricket team, who took 252 wickets for England in Test Matches (1950s). Also the *Quiet Man of Cricket.*

GEORGE RANGER George William Frederick, Duke of Cambridge (1819–1904), cousin of Queen Victoria *(Drina)*, a Field-Marshal in the British Army. He was made ranger of Hyde Park and St. James's Park (1852) and of Richmond Park (1857). Also *Royal George.*

GEORGE THE BARBER George Taylor (fl. 1740s–1750s), a pugilist who ran a booth in Tottenham Court Road, London outshone by the Amphitheatre in the Oxford Road, kept by Broughton (the *Father of Boxing*) for which he drew up a set of boxing rules. Taylor was beaten twice in the ring by Broughton.

GEORGE THE FIRST George Colman, the *Elder*. His son of the same name was also a successful dramatist (see below).

GEORGE THE GREATER George IV as Prince of Wales (*Adonis of Fifty*) when he was a friend of *Beau* Brummell.
- See *George the Lesser.*

GEORGE THE GRINNER George Colman (1762–1836), playwright who wrote *Broad Grins*; so called in North America. Also the *Younger*.
- Cf *George the First.*

GEORGE THE LESSER George *Beau* Brummell when he was friends with the Prince of Wales
- Cf *George the Greater.*

GEORGIA DEACON, THE Tiger Flowers (1894–1926), American middleweight champion of the world (1926).

GEORGIA PEACH, THE Tyrus Raymond Cobb (1886–1961), outstanding baseball player for the Detroit Tigers and the Philadelphia Athletes. He made a record 2,244 runs , 4,191 hits in more than 3,000 major league games. He held the highest lifetime batting average (0.367).

GERMAN GEORGIE George III, the *Button Maker*; so called by American colonists, especially at the time of the War of Independence.

GERMAN PRINCESS, THE Mary (Moll) Carleton (1642–73), a Kentish adventuress and thief who pretended to have been born in Germany, but in fact was the daughter of a lay clerk in Canterbury Cathedral named Meders. John Carleton was one of her several husbands. She was twice acquitted of polygamy. She was hanged for having returned from transportation.

GERRY Franz C. M. Alexander (1928–), captain of West Indian cricket team (1959–60).

GERSCHY Margaretha Gertrud Zelle (1876–1917), courtesan spy known as Mata Hari (the 'Eye of the Morning' in the Malay language of Java); nickname as a child.

GHOST, THE Garry Garrison (1944–)., American footballer.

GHOST WITH A HAMMER IN HIS HAND, THE James (Jimmy) Wilde (1892–1969), British world featherweight boxing champion (1916–23), probably the hardest–hitting featherweight ever to go into the ring, and once described as the greatest boxer who ever lived. Also the *Mighty Atom*.

GIANTESS OF GENIUS, THE Hannah More (1745–1833), English playwright who wrote *Percy* (1777) and *The Fatal Falsehood* (1779), both produced by Garrick (*Atlas*): so called by Wolcot (*Peter Pindar*): Also the *Tenth Muse.*

GIANT HAYSTACKS Luke McMasters (1946–). 6ft 11 in British wrestler. His weight varies between 41 stone (574 lb) and 43 stone (602 lb). He is the heaviest man in Britain.
- Cf *Happy Humphrey.*

GIANT OF LITERATURE, THE Dr Johnson, *Blinking Sam.*

GIANT OF THE LAW, THE Chief Justice Theophilius Parsons (1750–1813) of Massachusetts; so called in irony by his enemies.

GIANT SQUIRE, THE Jacob Butler (died 1766), a barrister of the Old Abbey House, Barnwell, Cambridge, who was 6ft 4 in tall.

GILDEROY Patrick Macgegor (?1620–58), a man of good family in Perthshire who murdered his father and mother and burned his sister and a maid to death by setting fire to the house, He became a Highland bandit, but fled to France, where he robbed Cardinal Richelieu. He returned, and with a gang made his name feared throughout West Scotland. He once hanged a judge. When he was executed his gibbet was 30 ft. high.

• 'Gilderoy' is formed from the Gaelic *gille ruadh*, 'the red fellow'.

GILLYFLOWER OF LIVERPOOL, THE William Roscoe (1753–1831), British politician and writer, born in Liverpool, son of a market-gardener. He welcomed the French Revolution as a promise of liberty; so called in *Noctes Ambrosianae*.

• The gillyflower was an emblem of falsehood, but perhaps there may be also a reference to *The Winter's Tale* (iv. 3):'...gillyvors, which some call nature's bastards.'

GINGER
i) Marshal of the Royal Air Force Sir Arthur Harris, ***Bomber Harris***.
ii) Virginia McMath (1911–). American film star who married John Rogers (1920). She added her childhood nickname to his surname to become Ginger Rogers.
iii) Paul Johnson (1928–), British journalist, former editor of *The New Statesman*.
iv) John Robson Welby, known as G. C. Evans (1940–64), hanged for the murder of a van-driver. He and Peter Allen (1943–64) guilty of the same crime, were the last persons to be hanged in Britain.

GINGER BOYLE Admiral of the Fleet William Henry Dudley Boyle, 12th Earl of Cork (1873–1967), Commander-in-Chief, Home Fleet (1922–34); so called in the Royal Navy.

GINGER MAGICIAN, THE Steve Davis, the ***Cool Kid***.

GINNY Jane Bunford (1895–1922), 7ft 7 in tall. Her skeleton is in the Anatomical Museum at Birmingham University.

GIPPER, THE
i) George Gipp (died 1920), football back for Notre Dame who helped (ii) to make it the best-known college team. He became a legend after his death, when Rockne used the phrase 'One for the Gipper' to encourage his team in difficult situations.
ii) Knute Rockne (1888–1931), American football player and coach; by reflection from (i). Also the ***Rock of Notre Dame***.
iii) President Reagan, ***Dutch***, who played George Gipp (i) in a film.

GIOVANNI ACUTO Sir John Hawkwood (died 1394), leader of the English mercenaries (the White Company) who fought in Italy; nickname meaning 'John the Far-sighted,' or 'Cunning', given to him by Machiavelli (see ***Little Machiavel***).

• Since Hawkwood's name is variously spelt in Italian 'Haccoude', 'Acutus', 'Acud', and 'Aguto', it is possible that *Acuto* is Italian word-play. *Acuto* is linked with the American 'cute'.

GIPSIES' FRIEND, THE The Reverend James Crabb (1774–1851), missionary working among them in Hampshire. He wrote *The Gipsies' Advocate*.

GIPSY Rodney Smith (1860–1947), British evangelist with a gipsy background.

GIRAFFE Jackie Charlton, ***Big Jack***.

G.I'S GENERAL, THE General of the Army Omar Nelson Bradley (1893–1981), Commander-in-Chief, 12th Army Group which captured Cherbourg (WWII). He tried to win battles without great loss of life. He served a record sixty-nine years on the active service list.

GIRL WHO IS TOO BEAUTIFUL, THE Barbara La Marr (1900–26), American film star brought to Hollywood by Douglas Fairbanks (1883–1939) for his film *The Three Musketeers* (1921).

● She was 'too beautiful to be true'.

GIRL WITH THE BEE-STUNG LIPS, THE
Mae Murray (1889–1965), American film
star and former star of the Ziegfeld Follies. Her real name was Maria Adrienne
Köning.

GIVE 'EM HELL HARRY Harry S. Truman
(1884–1972). 33rd President of the USA
(1945–72) with a reputation for stern
dealing (he once discharged General
MacArthur: *Dugout Doug*), but Truman
himself said in an interview on CBS TV
(February 1958): 'I never did give anybody hell. I just told them the truth and
they thought it was hell.' (It was of course
Truman who authorized the use of the
atomic bomb on Japan.)

GLADYS Gladstone Cleophas Small (1961–
),. Warwickshire and England cricketer,
born in Barbados; from his first name. He
took 5 wickets for 63 in the 5th Test
Match at Sydney (1986), including 4 for
22 in 32 balls.

GLADYS HACKSAW Margaret Thatcher,
Attila the Hen; so called in Australia.

GLENN Alton Miller (1904–44), American
band leader who won the first Golden
Disc.

GLITTER Paul Gadd (1944–), British pop
star who added 'Gary' to his nickname.

GLOOMY DEAN, THE The Very Reverend
William Ralph Inge (1860–1954) who
wrote a column for *The Evening Standard* for a very long time (1930s) and did
not find much to be happy about. He was
Dean of St Paul's, London (1911–34).

GLORIA Ernest William Swanton (1907–),
cricketer for Middlesex and writer on the
game; from the film star Gloria Swanson
(1899–1983). Also *Jim*.

GLORIANA
i) Elizabeth I, the *English Diana*; from
the name of the *Faerie Queene* in the
poem of that name (1589–96) by Spenser
(the *Child of the Ausonian Muse*).
● Cf the *Faery*.
ii) Mrs Thatcher, *Attila the Hen*; so
called by besotted Tories.

**GLORIFIER OF THE AMERICAN GIRL,
THE** Florenz Ziegfeld (1869–1932),
American theatre producer who staged
lavish spectacles. He used the slogan
'Glorifying the American Girl'. Also *Ice
Water* and *Ziggy*.

GLORIOUS, THE Aethelstan or Athelstan
(895–940), King of the West Saxons and
Mercia, grandson of Alfred the *Great*.
Through his energetic harassing of his
enemies, he was the first king who could
make any claim to rule over all England
and to have brought the country into
close touch with Europe.

GLORIOUS HONEYBUN Gloria Hunniford
(1940–), British TV and radio personality with a notable Sunday afternoon TV
chat show.

GLORIOUS JOHN
i) John Dryden (*Asaph*); so called by
Scott (the *Ariosto of the North*).
ii) John Murray, the *Anak of Publishers*;
so called by George Borrow (1803–81).
iii) Sir John Barbirolli (1899–1970),
English conductor.

GLORIOUS PIERCE Pierce Egan, the *Elder*.

GLORIOUS VILLAIN, THE Cromwell, the
Almighty Nose; so called by Lord Clarendon (the *Chancellor of Human Nature*).

GLORVINA Lady Sydney Morgan (circa
1783–1859), Irish novelist, after the heroine of *The Wild Irish Girl* (1806). Also
the *Irish de Staël*.

**GLORY AND REPROACH OF SCOTLAND,
THE** Robert Burns, the *Ayrshire Poet* because of his poetry and his love of re-
velry.

GLORY AND SCANDAL OF HIS AGE, THE
Samuel Butler (1612–80) who wrote
Hudibras (1663–78); so called by John
Oldham (the *English Juvenal*). Also
Hudibras Butler.

GLORY OF HER SEX, THE
i) Queen Elizabeth I, the *English Diana*;
so called by Voltaire (1694–1778).
ii) Anne Bradstreet (1612–72), British
poetess; so called in *Noctes
Ambrosianae*. Also the *Mirror of Her
Age*.

GLORY OF SCOTLAND, THE Ossian, the *Celtic Homer*.

GLORY OF THE ENGLISH STAGE, THE William Shakespeare, the *Bard of All Time*; so called by Edward Phillips in *Theatrum Poetarum Anglicorum* (1675).

GLORY OF THE HUMAN INTELLECT, THE Shakespeare, the *Bard of All Time*; so called by de Quincy (the *English Opium Eater*).

GLORY OF THE MUSES, THE Sir Thomas Smith (1513–77), British statesman, scholar and author; so called by his friend *Ape Gabriel* Harvey.

GLOSSATOR, THE Aldred, a tenth–century priest, writer of two Anglo-Saxon glosses for the Lindisfarne Gospels; so called to distinguish him from Archbishop Aldred (died 1069) of York.

GNOME K.W.R. Fletcher (1944–   ), Essex cricketer who once captained England and was also captain of his county. Fletcher, who holds 59 caps, is small.

GOAT, THE David, 1st Earl Lloyd–George (1863–1945), British Prime Minister (1916–22); so called because of his extra marital adventures. Also the *Great Commoner* and the *Welsh Wizard*.

GODFATHER, THE
i) Harry Oppenheimer (1908–   ). South African diamond magnate; chairman of De Beers and the Anglo-American Corporation.
ii) Albert Broccoli, *Cubby*.

GODFATHER OF PUNK, THE Malcolm McLaren (1946–   ). British creator of the Sex Pistols, a punk rock group and instigator of the punk revolution (1970s), an iconoclastic movement in fashion, music and manners.

GOD OF WHIGGISH IDOLATRY, THE Lord Brougham and Vaux, *Blundering Brougham*; so called by Scott (the *Ariosto of the North*). He was a man of almost magical personality as an orator, and although not the leader of the party, was dictatorial and arrogant.

GOD'S CURSE Sir Walter Scott, *Bold Buccleugh*.

GOLDEN BALL Edward Hughes Ball (1799–1863), a handsome man who made a sensation in London society after he had inherited a fortune from his uncle Admiral Sir Edward Hughes (1720–94).

GOLDEN BEAR, THE Jack Nicklaus, *Blobbo*. He is 6ft tall and powerfully built and once had golden hair.

GOLDEN FARMER, THE William Davis (1627–90), a Gloucestershire farmer who got his nickname from always paying his debts in gold. It was thought he made a great deal of money from his farm, but it was eventually discovered that he had been a highwayman for 42 years. He had been captain of a gang which included *Old Mobb*. Davis was hanged.

GOLDEN KNIGHT, THE Sir Henry Cromwell, great-uncle of Oliver (the *Almighty Nose*). He was reputed to have ridden between Hinchingbrooke and Ramsey, Huntingdonshire, where he had houses, tossing out handfuls of coins. He was knighted in 1563. He was an MP and Sheriff for Cambridgeshire and Huntingdon.

GOLDEN MOUTHED, THE Michael Drayton (1563–1631), English poet who wrote *Polyolbion* (1622), a long work which glorified England; so called by Meres (the *Gallant Young Juvenal*) and by Charles Fitzgeffrey (?1576–1638) in a poem on Drake.

GOLDEN MOUTH Laurence Anderton (or Scroop) (1577–1643), British Jesuit; because of his eloquence; sometimes 'Golden-Mouthed Anderton'.

GOLDEN RULE JONES Samuel Milton Jones (1846–1904), Welsh-born Mayor of Toledo, Ohio (1897–1904). He was a manufacturer who introduced business methods into city affairs and won his nickname by his insistence on reforming rules in his factory and city administration.

GOLDEN VOICE OF THE GREAT SOUTHWEST, THE Bruce Phillips (1935–   ), American folk–singer. Also *U–Utah*.

GOLDFINGER
i) Sir James Goldsmith (1933–   ), international financier, whose wealth is

estimated at £1 billion.

ii) Harvey Michael Rose (1940–), British investment 'shark', sentenced to 14 years imprisonment (1988) at Leeds for frauds involving millions of pounds. He pleaded guilty to 25 charges of theft, and admitted 143 others. More than 700 investors lost a total of £5.5 million. He lived a life of fast cars, aircraft and champagne, and had to be extradited from Uruguay.

- *Goldfinger* is a novel by Ian Fleming (**Lady Rothermere's Fan**).

GOLDILOCKS Michael Heseltine, **Action Man**; from his profusion of fair hair which gave him another nickname, **Veronica Lake**.

GOLD KING, THE William Pritchard Morgan, Welshman, who discovered gold in Merioneth (1888) and controlled the Gwynfynnd and Prince Edward mines.

GOLDSMITH OF THE BAR, THE Peter Burrowes (1753–1841), Irish judge and politician. He had a weak voice.

- For Goldsmith, see the **Child of Nature**.

GOLDWYN'S FOLLY Anna Sten (1908–), Russian-born film actress promoted unsuccessfully by Samuel Goldwyn (1882–1974) to outshine Greta **Garbo** (1906–). Her real name is Anjuschka Stenski Sujakevitch.

GOLDY Oliver Goldsmith, the **Child of Nature**; so called by his friends, including Johnson (**Blinking Sam**). *The Percy Anecdotes* records its use at a meeting of the Literary Club.

GOLIATH OF FEDERALISM, THE Senator James A. Bayard (1767–1805). He claimed descent from the Seigneur de Bayard (see the **Bayard of the Confederacy**).

- Federalism was a policy advocating the establishment of a strong central government, as opposed to autonomous state governments.

GOLIATH OF THE PHILISTINES, THE Marchmont Needham, the **Cobbett of His Day**; so called by Wood (the **Ostade of Literary Criticism**).

GOLOBAR Captain (Sir) John Hawley Glover, the **Father of the Hausas**; from the pronunciation of his name by West Africans.

G.O.M., THE W.E. Gladstone, the **Dismember for Great Britain**; acronym for the **Grand Old Man**. It was first used (1882) by Lord Rosebery (the **Orator of Empire**).

GOOD, THE

i) Albert, Prince Consort (1819–61), husband of Queen Victoria (**Drina**), usually 'Albert the Good'.

ii) James Graham, 2nd Marquis of Montrose, usually **Le Bon**.

iii) Richard, Duke of Normandy (996–1026).

iv) Sir James Douglas (1286–1314), killed at Bannockburn.

v) Sir James Douglas, 2nd Earl of Douglas and Mar (*circa* 1358–88), the 'Erle Douglas' of the ballad *Chevy Chace*.

vi) Richard de Beauchamp, 13th Earl of Warwick, the **Father of Courtesy**.

vii) Hywel **Dda** (916–50), King of Wales from 943 to 950 who unified Wales and drew up a code of laws. He visited Rome (928).

- *Da* or *Dda* = 'good' in Welsh.

viii) Matilda (1080–1118) whose true name was Edith, daughter of Margaret and Malcolm **Canmore**, King of Scotland. She was the wife of Henry I (**Beauclerc**).

ix) Sigebert or Sebert (died ?660), King of the East Saxons; so called for his Christian piety. (He is said to have founded the original Westminster Abbey.)

- See also **Benjamin the Good** and **William the Good**.

GOOD DUKE, THE Edward Seymour, 1st Duke of Somerset (*circa* 1506–52), Lord Protector of England on the death of Henry VIII (**Bluff Hal**).

GOOD DUKE HUMPHREY, THE Humphrey Plantagenet, Duke of Gloucester (1391–1447), patron of learning. He was the son of Henry IV (**Bolingbroke**); so called because of his devotion to the Church and his encouragement of the poet John Lydgate (the **Monk of Bury**) and the theologian and historian John Capgrave (1393–1464).

GOOD EARL, THE

i) Archibald Douglas, 8th Earl of Angus (died 1588).

ii) Anthony Ashley Cooper, 7th Earl of Shaftesbury (1801–85), philanthropist who founded the Shaftesbury Homes.

iii) the 2nd Earl of Moray, the *Bonnie Earl of Moray*.

GOOD EARL JOHN John, 5th Earl of Sutherland (1609–63), a Covenanter who fought against Montrose (the *Great Marquis*).

GOOD EARL OF KINGSTON, THE Robert Pierrepoint, 1st Earl of Kingston (1584–1643); he helped the poor in the difficult times of the English Civil War.

GOOD FRIDAY Alfred Bunn (1798–1860), English theatre manager. He made a brave attempt to establish English opera, but, trying to control both Drury Lane and Covent Garden, went bankrupt. He was bumptious and quarrelsome; a word-play on *Hot Cross Bun*; so called by Madame Maria Malibran (1808–36), the French opera singer. Also the *Napoleon of Drama* and *Poet Bunn*.

GOOD GRAY POET, THE Walt Whitman. the *Bard of Democracy*; first applied to him by William Douglas O'Connor (1832–89) who wrote a book of that title (1866) to defend the poet after he had been dismissed from a government clerkship on the grounds that *Leaves of Grass* (1855) was an immoral book.

GOOD JOHN OF ISLAY John Macdonald or Eoin of Islay, Lord of the Isles (post 1354).

- The Lords of the Isles regarded themselves as autonomous rulers.

GOOD LORD COBHAM Sir John Oldcastle (died 1417) who married the Cobham heiress. He was a leader of the Lollards and was executed, the first martyr of a noble family. He was the original of Shakespeare's 'Sir John Falstaff', the 'old lad of the castle'.

- The Lollards were followers of John Wyclif (*Doctor Evangelicus*): 'Lollard' = mumbler (Dutch).

GOODMAN OF BALLENGEICH or GUDE-MAN OF BALLINBREICH, THE James V of Scotland (1512–42) who went round Edinburgh periodically in disguise – as he did in other parts of Scotland – to learn what his subjects were saying and thinking. Also the *King of the Commons*.

- Ballengeich was a steep pass behind Stirling castle. *Goodman* = tenant, a respectable householder. It was sometimes abbreviated to *Goody*.

GOOD QUEEN BESS Elizabeth I, the *English Diana*.

GOOD REGENT, THE James Stewart, the *Bonny Earl of Moray* (ii).

GOOD SIR JAMES Sir James Douglas, *Black Douglas* (i).

GOOD SIR JOHN Signor Giovanni Andres Battista Gallini (1728–1805), owner and manager of the Assembly Rooms, Hanover Square, London. The Pope gave him a knighthood of the Order of the Golden Spur and he became known as Sir John Gallini. He married Lady Elizabeth Bertie, daughter of the 3rd Earl of Abingdon.

GOOD TIME WALLY Wallace Reid (1802–1923), handsome popular film star, thought of as the typical American hero, whose 'good time' with drink, drugs and girls led to his death from drug addiction at the age of thirty. Also *King of Paramount*.

GOODY NEWCASTLE Thomas Pelham-Holles, 1st Duke of Newcastle (3rd creation) (1693–1768), British Prime Minister (1754–56 and 1757–62); nickname mentioned by Walpole (the *Autocrat of Strawberry Hill*) in his memoirs. Also *Hubble-Bubble* and *Permis*.

- 'Goody' was an abbreviation of 'goodman'.

GOODY PALSGRAVE Elizabeth Stuart (1596–1662), daughter of James I (the *British Solomon*) and wife of Frederick V, Elector Palatine (1596–1632). Her husband was nicknamed 'Goodman Palsgrave'. She was buried in Westminster Abbey. Also the *Snow Queen* and *Winter Queen*.

- A 'goody' (= goodwife) was a

respectable housewife and 'palsgrave', was a version of 'palatine' (German *pfalzgraf*).

GOOSE

i) Mrs Augusta Leigh (1783–1851), Byron's half-sister, who married Colonel George Leigh. It was the nickname given to her by Byron (**Baby**): 'Augusta' clipped to 'Gus' and turned into 'Goose'.

ii) Robert (Bob) G. D. Willis, **Dylan**.

iii) Adrian Moorhouse (1964–), British swimmer who won a gold medal at the Seoul Olympics (1988) for the 100 metre breast stroke. Moorhouse, Commonwealth and European champion, had been the first to break the 1 min record for the breast stroke 100 metres (29.75 seconds, 1987); so called by his team mates after his name appeared on a programme as 'Mongoose'.

GOOSEBERRY-FACED CHURCHILL Lord Randolph Churchill, the **Blenheim Pippin**; his school nickname.

GOOSEY Lady Albertha (Bertha: died 1932), wife of Lord (George) Blandford (1844–92), heir to the 7th Duke of Marlborough. Lord Blandford was involved in the Aylesford scandal.

• See **Sporting Joe**.

GOOSEY GODERICH Frederick John Robinson, Viscount Goderich (1827) and 1st Earl of Ripon (1833). Robinson (1782–1859) was Prime Minister (1827–8), Chancellor of the Exchequer (1823–7) and Secretary of State for the Colonies (1827–33); so called by **Boney Cobbett** with the analogy of 'Goosey, Goosey Gander, whither dost thou wander?' Goderich was a fussy, timid politician. Also **Little Goody Two-Shoes** and **Prosperity Robinson**.

GORGEOUS GEORGE

i) George Anthony Geoffrey, Lord Howard (1920–84) of Castle Howard, Yorkshire, and chairman of the BBC (1980–83); because of his life-style.

ii) George Galloway (1955–), Labour MP for Glasgow Millhead and a former secretary of the charity 'War on Want'.

GORGEOUS GUSSIE Gussie Moran, American tennis player who caused a sensation at Wimbledon by wearing frilly panties which were much displayed. They had been designed by Teddy Tinling (1910–), Wimbledon fashion expert.

GORILLA MURDERER, THE Earle Leonard Nelson (1892–1928). He killed 22 women in America and Canada, mostly landladies; from his powerful hands. He was hanged.

GOSPEL DOCTOR, THE John Wyclif, **Doctor Evangelicus**.

GOSPEL QUEEN, THE Mahalia Jackson (1911–72), American jazz singer who specialized in gospel songs.

GOVERNESS OF THE TIMES, THE Theodore Bernstein (1904–79), head of the copy desk (a post equivalent to the English Chief Sub–Editor), of *The New York Times*. He set standards of style for the newspaper and gave directions on the use of English. He wrote a number of books on journalism and language.

GOVERNOR-GENERAL, THE Charles George Macartney (1886–1958), cricketer for New South Wales and Australia, because of his powerful batting and clever slow bowling, with the implication that he was more skilful than most.

• Cf the **Guv'nor** (i).

GRACE DARLING OF AMERICA, THE Ida Lewis, Mrs W. H. Wilson (1842–1911), keeper of the Lime Rock Lighthouse, Rhode Island, who saved many lives from wrecks.

• Grace Horsley Darling (1815–42), with her father, rescued survivors from a wreck in dangerous seas (1828) off the Farne Islands, Northumberland.

GRACE DARLING OF CANADA, THE Bertha Grace Boyd (1861–1944), daughter of a lighthouse-keeper on the Sainte Croix river, New Brunswick, Canada, who at the age of twenty-one saved two men from drowning (1882). She became keeper until she died.

GRACE OF AUSTRALIA, THE George Giffen (1859–1927), all-round cricketer for Australia and South Australia. In the 1894–5 Test series, he scored 475 runs and took 34 wickets.

- See the *Champion* and of the *W. G. Grace of Australia*.

GRACE OF COURTS, THE The Earl of Dorset, *Charles the First*; so called in his epitaph by Pope (the *Bard of Twickenham*).

GRACIE FIELDS OF THE PSYCHIC WORLD, THE Doris Stokes (1920–87), British internationally famous medium who toured a road show called 'An Audience with Doris Stokes'. So called in theatrical circles.

- See *Our Gracie*.

GRAMMARIAN, THE

i) James Henry (1789–1876), Irish classical scholar; from his pedantry.

ii) Geoffrey (alias Starkey) (fl. 1400), British Dominican friar and lexicographer.

GRAMMATICUS Aelfric (circa 955–1020), English abbot who wrote a Latin grammar for his pupils, and other works regarded as the beginnings of English literature.

- *Grammatica* meant learning in general and thus *Grammaticus* a learned man

GRAND, LE William Le Grand (1109–1210), a Norman French; nickname meaning 'big' or 'tall', but which could have meant 'elder'. The *grand* evolved into the surname 'Grant' and became a clan name (Reaney).

- Cf *Grandius*.

GRAND COMMONER, THE W. E. Gladstone, the *Dismember for Great Britain*; from his skill in the House of Commons.

- Cf The *Great Commoner*.

GRAND CORRUPTER, THE Sir Robert Walpole, 1st Earl of Orford (1676–1745). He used corruption to win and maintain his position as the first Prime Minister (1721–42). Macaulay (*Babbletongue*) in *The Edinburgh Review* (1833) said that 'Walpole governed by corruption because in his time it was impossible to govern otherwise'. Also the *Leviathan*, the *Norfolk Gamester*, *Robin Bluestring* and the *Triumphant Exciseman*.

GRANDFATHER OF THE DETECTIVE STORY, THE William Godwin (1756–1836). He wrote *Caleb Williams* (1793–4) which included murder and detection. Also the *Sage of Skinner Street*.

GRANDIUS Gilbert Grant (1183), a Norman-French nickname.

- See *Le Grand* (above).

GRANDMA James Buchanan (1791–1868), 15th President of the USA. He lacked self-confidence, particularly in the North–South issue. Also *Old Buck*, the *Old Public Functionary* and *Ten Cent Jimmy*.

GRANDMA MOSES Anne Mary Robertson (1860–1961), Mrs A. M. R. Moses, American primitive painter who did not begin to paint until she was seventy-eight and was still painting at a hundred.

GRANDMOTHER OF EUROPE, THE Queen Victoria, *Drina*.

- Cf the *Uncle of Europe*.

GRAND or GREAT NASH *Beau* Nash.

GRAND OLD MAN, THE

i) W. E. Gladstone, the *Dismember for Great Britain*, so called by Labouchère (*Labby*) in June 1880 in the tea–room of the House of Commons in conversation with Charles Bradlaugh (*Our Charley*) after Bradlaugh, a free-thinker, had refused to take the oath. Bradlaugh later used the term in a speech in Northampton, and it gained currency (cf *G.O.M.*).

ii) George Frederick Handel (1658–1759), German-born British composer; nicknamed by Walter Farquhar Hook, Dean of Chichester (1789–1875). Also the *Orpheus of the 18th Century*.

iii) Theodore, Archbishop of Canterbury (602–90), reformer and peace-maker; nicknamed by Hook (above).

iv) Henry Clay, the *Apostle of Liberty*.

v) Senator Thaddeus Stevens (1773–1868), chairman of the committee to draft the articles of impeachment (1868) against Andrew Johnson, 17th President of the USA (1808–75). Also *Old Thad*.

GRAND OLD MAN OF EMPIRE, THE Donald Alexander Smith, 1st Baron Strathcona and Mount Royal (1820–

1914), Governor of the Hudson Bay Company, Canada. Also *Silver Cloud*.

GRAND OLD MAN OF INDIA, THE Dadabhai Naoroji, the *Father of Indian Nationalism*.

GRAND OLD MAN OF TENNIS, THE Edward James Johnson (1879–1970), lifelong British professional.

GRAND OLD MAN OF THE STAGE, THE

i) George Arliss, the *First Gentleman of the Screen*.

ii) C. Aubrey Smith, *Round-the-Corner Smith*.

iii) Cyril Maude (1862–1951), English actor–manager. He started his career in America and later appeared with Sir Henry Irving (1838–1905).

GRAND YOUNG MAN, THE Joseph Chamberlain, *Artful Joe*; as a riposte to the *Grand Old Man* (i); Chamberlain's nickname came into use *circa* 1885.

GRANITE WOMAN, THE Ruth Snyder (1895–1928), American electrocuted in Sing Song prison for the murder with Henry Judd Gray (1983–1928) of her husband. She was described as 'a cold–blooded Swedish-Norwegian vampire.'

GRANNY

i) Henry Grantland Rice (1880–1954), American sports writer who nicknamed Dempsey the *Manassa Mauler*.

ii) Norman Gifford (1940–), left–arm spinner; cricketer for England and Warwickshire. He played the game for 23 years.

GRANNY MAFIA Barbra Mouzin (1939–), gaoled for 25 years (1983) in Los Angeles for deals in cocaine worth millions of dollars. She was the leader of a gang of eight women who made the transactions in between visits to their grandchildren.

GRAY FOX, THE Brigadier-General George Crook (1829–90), American commander of a column which marched against the Sioux (1876) after the Battle of Little Big Horn; so called by the Indians.

GRAYSTONE SAGE, THE Samuel Jones Tilden (1814–86), New York lawyer and politician who helped to destroy the Tweed (*Boss*) Ring; from the name of his house.

GREAT, THE

i) Malachi, Maelsechlainn or Mael Sechnaill II of Ireland (reigned 980–1022) who restored the High Kingship of Ireland.

ii) Alfred, *England's Darling*. He defeated the Danes, founded the British Navy, restored law and order and opened schools.

iii) Canute, Cnut or Knut (*circa* 995–1035), King of England, Denmark and Norway, who brought order and security to England after the Viking raids.

iv) Hugh O'Neill, 2nd Earl of Tyrone (circa 1540–1616), chief of the O'Neill clan; because of his daring raids on English forts after he had broken with England, and been declared a traitor. Also the *Great Earl*.

v) Rhodri *Mawr* (reigned 844–78), founder of the princely house of Gwynedd and Deheubarth in South Wales, and ruler of all Wales except Dyfed.

- *Mawr* = Welsh for 'great'; cf Gaelic *mor* (below).

vi) Llywelyn *Fawr*, Welsh king (reigned 1194–1240).

- *Fawr* is also Welsh for 'great'.

vii) Roger de Montgomery (*circa* 1030–94), who accompanied William the *Conqueror*, fought at Hastings (1066) and was later made Earl of Shrewsbury, and so virtual sovereign over parts of West England.

viii) Captain Alexander Gunn of Badenloch (died 1763), known as *Alasdair Mor*, head of the Gunn clan, the 7th Mac Seumas.

ix) E. W. Mackney (1825–1909), 'black–faced minstrel' of the British music–halls.

- See *Roger the Great*.

GREAT AGNOSTIC, THE Colonel Robert Green Ingersoll (1833–99), American lawyer and politician. He campaigned for free-thinking, and gave anti-religious lectures. Also the *Illustrious Infidel*.

GREAT AMALGAMATOR, THE Cecil Rhodes, the *Colossus*; because of his many amalgamations, both political and commercial, e.g. the Consolidated Goldfields of South Africa.

GREAT AMERICAN CONDENSER, THE John *Doc Wood*. He remorselessly used a blue pencil as an editor.

GREAT AMERICAN FARO BANKER, THE Reuben Parsons (died 1875). He ran a string of gambling houses in and around New York.

GREAT AMERICAN NAVEL, THE Cher (1946–), pop star and film actress who won an Oscar in 1988. Her flamboyant dresses usually show her navel. Her full name is Cherilyn Sarkassian Le Piere Bono Allman. Also the *Queen of Flash*.

GREAT AMERICAN TRAVELLER, THE Daniel Pratt (1809–87), an eccentric living on charity who travelled round the USA, giving lectures; self–bestowed.

GREAT BEAR, THE Dr Johnson, *Blinking Sam*; so called by Gray (the *British Pindar*)
- See the *Bear Leader* and cf *Ursa Major*.

GREAT BEAST, THE Aleister Crowley, *Boast 660*.

GREAT BILLY William Pitt, the *Bottomless Pit*.

GREAT BOHUNKUS, THE Ian Mackay (1898–1952), columnist for the *News Chronicle*; Fleet Street nickname which means 'The Great Bohemian'.
- From. American slang 'bohunk', a bohemian or a foreigner; originally someone from Bohemia.

GREAT CALIBAN, THE Dr Johnson, *Blinking Sam*. Boswell (the *Ambitious Thane*) in his life of Johnson: 'Being told that Gilbert Cooper [1723–1769] called him the Caliban of literature, "Well," said he, "I must dub him the Punchinello." When Hogarth (the *Juvenal of Painters*) first saw Johnson (1753), he thought he was an imbecile until Johnson spoke to him. Wolcot (*Peter Pindar*) added the 'great'.

GREAT CHAM OF LITERATURE, THE Dr Johnson, *Blinking Sam*; so called by Smollett (*Smelfungus*) in a letter to Wil-

kes (*Squinting Jack*) in 1759.
- 'Cham' is a variation of 'khan', applied to Mongol rulers.

GREAT COLLABORATOR, THE George Simon Kaufman (1889–1961), American playwright. He wrote several plays with someone else, e.g. Marc Connelly (1850–1961) and Edna Ferber (1885–1968).

GREAT COMMONER, THE
i) William Pitt, *Aeolus*; because of the eloquence of his speeches in the House of Commons. He was the only commoner in the Cabinet in 1783.
ii) W. E. Gladstone, the *Dismember for Great Britain*. He refused a peerage.
Cf the *Grand Commoner*.
iii) Henry Clay, the *Apostle of Liberty*.
iv) Sir John Barnard, the *Father of London*; so called by Walpole (the *Grand Corrupter*).
v) David Lloyd George, the *Goat*.

GREAT COMMUNICATOR, THE President Ronald Reagan, *Dutch*. He was helped in the delivery of his speeches by his background as an actor.

GREAT COMPROMISER, THE Henry Clay, the *Apostle of Liberty*. He made great efforts to bring about reconciliation between the North and the South.

GREAT DESMOND, THE Thomas Fitzgerald, 8th Earl of Desmond, (died 1467). He governed Ireland as Lord Deputy (1463–7) and maintained English rule.

GREAT DUKE, THE The Duke of Wellington, the *Achilles of England*.

GREAT EARL, THE
i) Ulick de Burgh Clanricarde, Earl of St Albans (1604–57) who tried to bring about unity in Ireland.
ii) Hugh O'Neill, the *Great* (iv)
iii) Donough O'Brien, 4th Earl of Thomond (died 1624), president of Munster (1605)
iv) The 8th Earl of Kildare, *Garrett More*.

GREAT EARL OF ANGUS, THE Archibald Douglas, 5th Earl of Angus, *Bell-the-Cat*.

GREAT EARL OF CORK, THE Richard Boyle, 1st Earl of Cork (1566–1643), Lord

Treasurer of Ireland (post 1631); because of his estates and palaces.

GREAT EARL OF DERBY, THE James Stanley, 7th Earl of Derby (1607–51), sent to the Isle of Man by Charles I (the *Ahab of the Nation*) to put down a threat of revolt. He took a firm hold and tried to help farmers and workers. When General Henry Ireton (1611–51) demanded the surrender of the island, Stanley refused and took 300 Manxmen to join the royalist army. He was later captured and executed. Also the *Great Stanley*.

GREAT EARL OF OXFORD, THE Edward de Vere, 17th Earl of Oxford (1550–1604), Lord Chamberlain of England, a man of wealth who, says Aubrey, spent £40,000 a year when he was travelling and lived in Florence in more grandeur than the Duke of Tuscany.

GREAT ELIZA, THE Queen Elizabeth I, the *English Diana*.

GREAT ELTCHI or ELCHEE, THE Stratford Canning, Viscount Stratford de Radcliffe (1786–1880), British Ambassador to Turkey (post 1824). Canning won favour with Sultan Mahmud II, and the nickname was given to him by the Turks.
- *Eltchi* is Turkish for 'ambassador'.

GREAT EMANCIPATOR, THE Abraham Lincoln, *Father Abraham*. In 1862 he issued the famous Emancipation Proclamation freeing all slaves in Confederate areas.

GREAT EPIGRAMMATIST, THE John Heywood (1494–1580), dramatist; so called by Camden (the *British Pausanias*). Also *Merry John*.

GREATEST, THE Muhammed Ali, *Gaseous Cassius*; self-bestowed.

GREATEST FINGER OF THE AGE, THE Orlando Gibbons, the *English Palestrina*. His nickname (1624) refers to his dexterity in keyboard fingering.

GREATEST ATHLETE IN THE WORLD, THE James (Jim) Francis Thorpe (1888–1953), American Indian world-class player in football and baseball and an outstanding track athlete, the first to win the decathlon and pentathlon; so called by the King of Sweden. Thorpe was voted (1950) the best athlete in the first half of the 20th century.

GREATEST SWIMMER OF THE HALF–CENTURY, THE John (Johnny) Weismüller (1903–84), winner of five Olympic gold medals (1924). He set up 67 world records and won 52 national championships. Later he was famous as *Tarzan* in films.

GREATEST WHIP IN THE WEST, THE Charlie Parkhurst (died 1879), American stagecoach driver who was found at the end of 'his' life to be a woman.

GREAT EXCAVATOR, THE Jesse P. Guilford, the *Boston Siege Gun*.

GREAT GANDER OF GLASGOW, THE John Galt (1779–1839), Scottish novelist who once worked in the Customs-house at Glasgow; so called in *Noctes Ambrosianae*.

GREAT GEORGE George Augustus Selwyn (1719–91), M.P. and wit with a taste for corpses and executions; so called by Walpole (the *Autocrat of Strawberry Hill*).

GREAT GOD PAN, THE Wordsworth, the *Bard of Royal Mount* who wrote a good deal about nature.

GREAT GOSPEL GUN, THE Milton, *Black–Mouthed Zoilus*. He published a number of pamphlets against episcopacy, and engaged in a long controversy with the Bishop of Exeter (the *Christian Seneca*); so called in *Noctes Ambrosianae*.

GREAT GRETSKY, THE Wayne Gretsky (1961–), American hockey player who twice won the most-valued player award.

GREAT GUN OF WINDSOR, THE Thomas (Tom) Cannon (1790–1858), a bargee of Windsor who became a British pugilist, once champion of England. He shot himself.

GREAT HISTORIAN OF THE FIELD, THE Charles James Apperley (1777–1843), English sports writer who used the pseudonym 'Nimrod'. He wrote (1837) a book on Mytton (*Mad Jack*).

GREAT HORATIO, THE Horatio Bottomley, *England's Recruiting Sergeant*.

GREAT IMPOSTER, THE Ferdinand Waldo

Demara, junior (1921–82), American who posed as a doctor during the Korean war (1950–3) and as a school-teacher, a naval surgeon and a Trappist monk.

GREAT IMPROVER, THE George Granville Leveson-Gower, 2nd Marquess of Stafford (1758–1833). He became the 1st Duke of Sutherland after his marriage (1785) to the Countess of Sutherland (*Banzu Mohr Ar Chat*). His 'improvements' often tended to drive tenants off their land so that they could be used for grazing sheep. Also the *Leviathan of Wealth*.

GREAT INDEPENDENT, THE Cromwell, the *Almighty Nose*; so called by Robert Baillie (1599–1662).

GREAT ISOLATIONIST, THE Senator William Edgar Borah (1865–1940), lawyer. He led the opposition to America joining the League of Nations. Also the *Lone Lion*.

GREAT KNIT, THE Roger Moore (1927–), British film star famous as James Bond. In the 1950s he appeared on the covers of knitting magazines modelling sweaters.

GREAT LADY OF THE CAT, THE The Countess of Sutherland, *Banzu Mohr ar Chat*.

GREAT LAKER, THE William Wordsworth, the *Bard of Rydal Mount*. He was one of the Lake School of Poets; so called in *Noctes Ambrosianae*.

- See the *Aristarchus of the Edinburgh Review*.

GREAT LEVIATHAN OF MEN, THE Cromwell, the *Almighty Nose*.

GREAT LEXICOGRAPHER OF THE FANCY, THE Pierce Egan, the **Elder**. He wrote a great deal about the prize-ring.

- See *Fancy's Child*.

GREAT LITTLE ROBSON Frederick Robson (1822–64), English comedian famous for his songs such as *Villikins and his Dinah* (1840s–1850s). These songs were also sung by Samuel Cowell (the **Young American Roscius**). Robson's real name was Thomas Robson Brownbill.

- 'Villikins and his Dinah' was originally a cockney street song (circa 18th century) and published as a broadside. Dinah = girl (from *dona*, a sweetheart in Parlyaree, theatrical slang based on Italian).

GREAT LITTLE TILLEY Vesta Tilley (1864–1952), British music-hall male impersonator whose real name was Matilda Bowles. She was famous for her song *Burlington Bertie*. Also the **London Idol**.

GREAT LOCHIEL, THE Sir Ewen Cameron, Lord of Lochiel, the **Black** (iv), who fought against Cromwell (the *Almighty Nose*) for the King and was the last Highland chief to continue the fighting. He is said to have killed the last wolf in Scotland.

- Lochiel is the title of the chief of the clan Cameron, from Loch Eil.

GREAT LOVER, THE Charles Boyer (1899–1978), French-born American film star.

GREAT MAGICIAN OF THE NORTH, THE Scott, the *Ariosto of the North*; so called by John Wilson (the **Admiral of the Lake**).

GREAT MAKE-BATE OF ENGLAND, THE John Ap Henry or Penry (executed 1593), Welsh Puritan convicted for writing the Martin Marprelate pamphlets; so called in a pamphlet by Nash (the **English Aretine**).

- See the **Untamed Heifer** Make-bate = someone who breeds strife, from 'bate', to fight (e.g. as in 'debate').

GREAT MARQUIS, THE James Graham, 1st Marquis of Montrose and 5th Earl (1612–50). He fought for the royalist cause in the English Civil War and was made Captain-General and Lord-Lieutenant of Scotland. Charles II (the **Blackbird**), however, abandoned him to his enemies, and he was hanged as a traitor.

GREAT MASTER IN THE SCIENCE OF GRIMACE, THE Henry Woodward (1717–77), British actor; so called by Churchill (the **British Juvenal**).

GREAT MINSTREL, THE Scott, the *Ariosto of the North*; so called in *The Edinburgh Review*.

GREAT MORALIST, THE Dr Johnson, *Blinking Sam*. Boswell (the *Ambitious Thane*) in *The Tour of the Hebrides* refers to him as 'the Great English Moralist.'

GREAT NASSAU, THE William III, the **Deliverer**.

- William the Silent (1533–84) and his descendants were called princes of Orange-Nassau, but the line became extinct when William III died.

GREAT O, THE Daniel O'Connell, the **Big Beggerman**; so called by Bulwer Lytton (**Bulwig**).

GREAT O'NEILL, THE

i) Sir Niall *Og*, King of Ulster (reigned 1394–1403), called 'le Grand O'Nel' by Froissart (?1337–1410), knighted by Richard (the **Coxcomb**) in 1394. Also the **Young** (*Og*).

ii) Sir Felim O'Neill, *Ruadh* (died 1653), Lord-General of the Catholic Army who led an uprising (1641) and was executed. Also the **Red** (*Ruadh*).

GREAT PACIFICATOR, THE Henry Clay, the **Apostle of Liberty**. He brought about a reconciliation which smoothed the way for the Missouri Compromise, held up by a dispute over slavery.

- The Missouri Compromise (1820) enabled Missouri to form a state government.

GREAT PATRON OF MANKIND, THE George II, **Augustus**.He accepted democratic ideas which eventually penetrated Germany; so called by Pope (the **Bard of Twickenham**). George was pushed by events into agreeing to loss of royal power, but managed in a large degree to continue directing affairs. George was Elector of Hanover, a position of authority paramount in his mind.

GREAT PHYSICIAN, THE Charles II, the **Blackbird**: so called by Cowley (the **English Pindar**).

GREAT PRONCONSUL, THE Warren Hastings (1732–1818), first Governor of India. who devoted himself to the welfare of the Indians and evolved a system of civil administration which was the foundation of later government. He was impeached for corruption but acquitted. He was given the nickname by Macaulay (**Babbletongue**).

GREAT PROFILE, THE John Barrymore (1882–1942), the **World's Greatest Actor**. American actor and film-star, one of the **Royal Family of Broadway**.

GREAT PROPHET OF TAUTOLOGY, THE Thomas Shadwell (?1642–92), British poet-laureate and playwright; so called by Dryden (**Asaph**). Shadwell had attacked Dryden after the publication of *Absalom and Achitophel* (1681) in which Shadwell had been called 'Og': 'For every inch that is not fool is Rogue.' Also the **True Blue Protestant Poet**.

GREAT RED DRAGON OF COLEMAN STREET, THE John Goodwin (?1594–1665), British Nonconformist clergyman, republican and enemy of Presbyterians who gave him the nickname. He was expelled from Parliament for his attacks on them. He was vicar of St Stephen's, Coleman Street, London (1633–45).

GREAT ROSCIUS, THE David Garrick, **Atlas**. It was a nickname he used himself. Fanny Burney (the **Old Lady**) reports him as saying of a maid 'Egad, sir! She does not know the Great Roscius'.

- See the **African Roscius**.

GREAT SCHNOZZOLA, THE Jimmy Durante (1893–1980), Italian-born American comedian and film star. Also **Schnozzle**.

GREAT SEDUCER, THE Jack Nicholson (1937–), American film star; so called in the 1950s by his friends, as he himself as said.

GREAT SEER, THE Dr Johnson, **Blinking Sam**.

GREAT SOUTHERN LAND PIRATE, THE James Copeland (died 1857), American highwayman and professional killer who helped land-grabbing families in the Mississippi area.

GREAT STAFFORDSHIRE IRONMASTER, THE James Wilkinson (1728–1808). He built the large iron foundries in the British Midlands and helped to design and cast the first iron bridge.

GREAT STANLEY, THE James Stanley, 7th Earl of Derby, the **Great Earl of Derby**.

GREAT STONE FACE, THE Buster Keaton, for his expressionless 'acting' face.

GREAT TEACHER OF GARDENING, THE
John Abercrombie (1726–1806).

GREAT THIEF TAKER, THE Jonathan Wild
(1682–1725) who in fact ran a huge
racket for the 'recovery' of goods stolen
by his own thieves. He was hanged.

GREAT UNBOWLABLE, THE William Mal-
don Woodfull (1897–1965), Australian
batsman who captained Australia during
the 'body-line' Tests (1932–3); because of
his skill. He scored 49 centuries and
2,300 runs in Test cricket. Also the *Rock*,
the *Unbowlable* and *Old Steadfast*.

- 'Body-line' bowling is that in which,
  says John Arlott (1914–), 'fast rising
  balls are directed at or just outside the
  leg stump to a packed leg-side to make
  ordinary scoring strokes either
  impossible or especially hazardous.'
  See *Lol*.

GREAT UNKNOWN, THE Scott, the *Ariosto
of the North*. The Waverley novels (post
1814) were published anonymously and
Scott did not reveal his authorship until
1827; so called by his publishers Ballantyne (the *Jenson of the North*).

GREAT VERULAM, THE Francis Bacon, 1st
Baron Verulam and later Viscount of St.
Albans, the *Father of Inductive Philosophy*. He was Lord Chancellor (1618–21)
and was called by a contemporary 'the
eloquentest man in England'.

GREAT WHITE CHIEF, THE Lord Northcliffe, the *Chief*.

GREAT WHITE SHARK, THE Greg Norman,
the *Choker*, Australian golfer, who used
to fish for shark off Brisbane.

GREAT WHORE, THE Anne Boleyn or Bul-
len (circa 1507–36), wife of Henry VIII
(*Bluff Hal*). She was alleged to have had
many lovers, including her own brother,
was imprisoned in the Tower of London
and executed for adultery and high treason.

GREAT WITCH OF BALWERY, THE Margaret Aiken (fl. late 16th century), Scot
accused of witchcraft who informed on
others.

GREAT WIZARD OF THE NORTH, THE
John Henry (1814– ?), Scottish magician,
first to pull a rabbit out of a hat.

GREAT W.T., THE William (Willie) Thorne
(1954–), British world-class snooker
champion, with more maximum breaks
than any other player. Also *Mr Maximum*.

GRECIAN WILLIAMS Hugh William Williams (1733–1829), British landscape
painter; so called after he published etch-
ings of a tour of Italy and Greece (1820):
mentioned by Lockhart (the *Aristarch of
British Criticism*).

GREEK THOMSON Alexander Thomson
(1817–75), Glasgow architect influenced
by Greek styles.

GREEN GODDESS, THE Diana Moran
(1940–), callisthenics teacher on BBC
breakfast TV. She wears a green cat-suit.

GREEN MAN, THE
i) Henry Cope (*circa* 1735–1806),
eccentric of Brighton, Sussex, who wore
green clothing and put green powder on
his face; mentioned in the *Annual
Register* of 1806.
ii) Albert de Salvo, the *Boston Strangler*.
He wore green overalls in his attacks on
women.

GREEN PARK James Parke, 1st Baron Wensleydale (1782–1868), Baron of the Court
of Exchequer; so called to distinguish
him from Mr Justice James Alan Park,
who was called 'St James's Park'.

- Barons of the Court of Exchequer were
  until 1875 six judges who dealt with
  revenue cases. Green Park is off
  Piccadilly, London.

GREGOR OF THE GOLDEN BRIDLES Gregor (fl. 14th century), first chief of the
McGregor clan.

GREGOR THE BEAUTIFUL Gregor McGregor, Laird of Inverdine (fl. 1730s–1740s).
His grandson, Sir Gregor McGregor, set
himself up as the 'Prince of Payais' and
organised a great land swindle (1820s).

GREYCLOAK Geoffrey of Anjou, *Le Bel*;
nickname mentioned by Camden (*British
Pausanias*).

GREY COLIN Colin Campbell of Glenorchy
(fl. late 16th century).

GREY HOUND, THE St Kentigern (died
circa 612), a Briton of Strathclyde, said to

have been of royal descent; called by Goidelic-speaking Celts *In Glaschu*, with the nickname of *Mungo*.

GREY JOHN John Campbell, 1st Earl of Breadalbane (*circa* 1635–1717). He persuaded Jacobites to swear allegiance to William III (the *Deliverer*), and was paid £12,000 for them which he is alleged to have kept. He also helped to organize the massacre of Glencoe (1692). His Gaelic nickname was *Iain Glas*. Also *Slippery John*.

GREY STEEL

i) Archibald, 3rd Earl of Douglas (*circa* 1328–1400), warden of the western marches; so called by James V (the *Goodman of Ballengeigh*). Also the *Grim*.

ii) Alexander Montgomerie, 6th Earl of Eglinton (1588–1661: Sir Alexander Seton), a Covenanter who fought against the King at Marston Moor.

iii) Archibald Douglas, Earl of Angus, *Bell-the-Cat.*

GRIFF Thomas Griffith Taylor (1881–1963), Australian scientist with the Scott Antarctic expedition (1910–13) and Professor of Geography at Sydney University (1921–8).

GRIM, THE

i) Archibald, 3rd Earl of Douglas, *Grey Steel*.

ii) Donald Macdonald, chief of Sleat (fl. late 16th century).

GRIM-ALL-DAY Giuseppe Grimaldi (died 1788), ballet master at Drury Lane to Garrick (*Atlas*) from 1758 until his death and father of Joseph (the *Michelangelo of Buffoonery*). Giuseppe was a bad-tempered, cruel man.

GRINDER, THE Cliff Thorburn (1948–), Canadian former world snooker champion, so called because of his methodical style.

GRIZZLED ROBERT Robert Duncanson, 3rd Chief of the Donnachaidh clan (late 15th century).

GRIZZLY, THE W. T. Tilden, *Big Bill*, from Blue *Grizzly*.

GROANER, THE *Bing* Crosby.

GROCER Edward R. G. Heath (1916–), British Prime Minister (1970–4); nicknamed by the magazine *Private Eye* (1962) when as Secretary of State for Trade and Industry he was negotiating British entry into the Common Market and so was discussing prices of eggs, butter, bacon etc.; picked up enthusiastically by the *Guardian*.

GROS, LE

i) Raymond or Redmond Fitzgerald (died *circa* 1182), sent by *Strongbow* to Ireland, where he became acting Governor. He may have been fat, but was a brave man.

ii) William Fitz–Odo (died 1180), prior of the British Black Canons who founded Thornton Abbey, Lincolnshire (1139).

iii) Hugh of Avranches (died 1101), 2nd Earl of Chester (post 1071). He fought in Wales and Normandy and contributed to the foundation of a monastery at Chester (1092), whose church developed into the cathedral. Also *Lupus*.

GROSS, THE James, 7th Earl of Douglas (1371–1444), fat, indolent and peace-loving (Dawson). A contemporary chronicle said he had 'four stane of taulch' [tallow] and mair'.

GROSVENOR'S COBBLER William Gifford, the *Bear Leader*. His first patron was the 1st Earl of Grosvenor. The son of a poor family, he had been apprenticed at the age of fifteen to a Presbyterian shoemaker; so called by Wolcot (*Peter Pindar*).

GRUMACH GILLESPIE Archibald Campbell, 1st Marquis and 8th Earl of Argyll (1607–61), chief of the Campbell clan and a powerful Covenanter. He was executed for treason by Charles II (the *Blackbird*). Also the *Presbyterian Ulysses*.

• *Grumach* in Gaelic means 'gloomy, sullen or forbidding' and the Earl had a squint ('Gley'd Argyll') and was generally unsmiling although some found charm in him. He was certainly forbidding. *Gillespie* = 'bishop's servant' and Argyll was a fanatic.

GRUMPY Allan Border (1955–), cricketer for New South Wales, Gloucester, Queensland, Essex and Australia (captain 1985–)

In 1985 he scored four consecutive centuries; so called in Australia.

GUBBY Sir George Oswald Browning Allen (1902–89), Middlesex and England cricketer. He captained England in 1936–7; from his initials. He was knighted in 1986.

GUITAR SLIM Edward (Eddie) Jones (1926–1959), American blues and soul musician.

GULIELMUS PARVUS William of Newburgh, the *Father of Historical Criticism*; so called at the Augustinian Priory in Yorkshire where he was a canon. It means 'Little William'.

GULLY Guy Oliver Nickalls (1899–1974), President of the Oxford University Boat Club (1923), oarsman and coach; Olympic silver medallist (1920 and 1928).

GUNBOAT SMITH Edward Watson Smyth (1883–1951), American cruiserweight boxer who knocked out (1914) Arthur Pelkey in 15 mins and met Georges Carpentier (1894–1975), French light-heavyweight champion. He was later a referee.

GUNNER Richard Gunstone, steward of the Junior Common Room, Magdalen College, Oxford University (1880–1904).

GUNNER, THE Sir William Skeffington (died 1535), Master of the Ordnance and Lord Deputy of Ireland.

GUNPOWDER PERCY Alexander Pope, the *Bard of Twickenham*. His satire often provoked explosive reactions from high places, e.g. Lord Hervey (*Lord Fanny*) and Lady Mary Wortley Montagu (the *Female Maecenas*); so called by Sir C. Hanbury Williams (1708–59), diplomat and satirist.

GURRAH Jacob Shapiro (fl 1930s), American gangster and killer for Murder Incorporated. He made 'Get out of here' sound like 'gurrah'.

GURU OF INDIAN BATSMANSHIP, THE Sunil Gavaskar (1949–), Indian cricketer who (1983) equalled the record of Bradman (the *Bowral Boy*) by making 29 Test Match centuries; so called by the *Observer*. He beat Boycott's record by scoring 10,122 runs in 125 Tests. Before he retired in 1987 he made 188 in the MCC match v the Rest of the World. Also the *Little Master* and *Sunny*.

GUSTI Prince Augustus of Saxe-Coburg-Kohary (1818–81), cousin of Albert the *Good*.

GUTO-NYTH-BRAN Griffith Morgan (1700–37), Welsh cross-country runner who dropped dead after a record run (alleged to be twelve miles in fifty-three minutes!). He was born on Nyth Bran (Crow's or Raven's Nest) farm.

GUV'NOR, THE

i) Robert Abel (1857–1936), cricketer for Surrey and England. He carried his bat for 132 in a Test Match in Sydney, Australia.

ii) George Edwardes, *Gaiety George*, theatre manager who virtually invented musical comedy.

iii) Francis (Frank) Albert Sinatra (1915–), American singer. Also *Ol' Blue Eyes* and the *Voice*.

iv) Bertram Mills (1873–1938), British circus proprietor who staged the annual show at Olympia, London for many years.

v) James (Jimmy) Tarbuck (1940–), British comedian. Also 'Tarby'.

vi) Steve Davis, the *Cool Kid*.

GUY THE GORILLA Ian Botham, *Both*, for his powerful physique; cut down to 'Guy'.

• Guy was a gorilla in the London zoo for thirty years (post 1947).

GYPSY, THE or THE SWAFFHAM GYPSY James (Jem) Mace (1831–1910). British boxer once recognized as the heavyweight champion of the world. In 1861 he was heavyweight champion of England, and is thought of as the creator of scientific boxing. He had been a travelling tinker in his youth but denied having any Romany blood. Also *Pride of the Fancy*.

H

H Prince Andrew *(Bungy)*, from H.R.H.; his nickname in the Royal Navy; especially when he served with the Falkland Islands Task Force (1982).

HACKNEY MONSTER, THE William Cooper, gaoled (1805) for offences against women.

- Cf the *Monster*. Hackney was formerly a fashionable London suburb.

HAIG, THE Walter C. Hagen (1892–1969), American Open golf champion (1914 and 1919), and British Open champion (1928–9), a man whose career has had a lasting effect on the game. In the PGA Hall of Fame (1940).

HAIR BUYER, THE Henry Hamilton (died 1796), British lieutenant colonel in command of the fort at Detroit; so called by Americans. He instigated Indian raids in which frontier settlers were scalped during the American War of Independence (1775–83).

HAIR-TRIGGER DICK Richard Martin (1754–1834), British M.P. who fought cruelty to animals. As a young man, he had a passion for duelling. Also *Humanity Dick* or *Humanity Martin*.

HAIRY BROGUES Olaf, King of Northumberland (941–4 and 948–52). King of York and Dublin (945–48 and 953–81). He died a monk on Iona (981).

HAIRY MONSTER, THE Dave Lee Travis (1945–), British disc jockey and TV personality. He has a beard.

HALF-HANGED MEG Margaret Dickson of Musselburgh, Scotland, who was hanged in 1728 but did not die until 1753. She was sentenced for the murder of her illegitimate child which she steadfastly denied. Her body was cut down and handed over to her friends. On the way home, they stopped for a drink at Peffer Mill, near Edinburgh. While they were there they saw the coffin-lid move and Half-Hanged Meg sat up. A few days later she married another man, since under Scottish law a marriage is dissolved by a sentence of execution. Her Scottish nickname is 'Half-Hanget Maggy Dickson'.

HALF-HANGED SMITH John Smith, convicted (1705) for robbery. His reprieve came 15 minutes after the execution had begun. He was cut down and bled so that he revived. He was indicted twice later for similar offences, but circumstances each time prevented him from being executed.

HAM Leonard Davis (1904–57), American jazz trumpeter.

HAMMER, THE (of the Underworld). Sir David Blackstock McNee (1925–), Commissioner of the Metropolitan Police (1977–82); so called for his vigorous crime-fighting as Chief Constable of Glasgow (1971–5).

HAMMER AND SCOURGE OF ENGLAND, THE Sir William Wallace (*circa* 1270–1305), Scottish hero who tried to drive the English under Edward I (the *English Justinian*) out of Scotland, and almost succeeded after the battle of Stirling (1297). He was later betrayed and executed.

HAMMERIN' HANK Henry Louis Aaron (1934–), American negro baseball star, outfielder for Milwaukee and Atlanta. He exceeded *Babe* Ruth's record (755 home runs, as against Ruth's 700). He also holds the records for runs batted (2,297).

HAMMERING HENRY Henry Armstrong (1912–), the only man to hold three world boxing championships simultaneously (light, middle and heavy); because of his fierce attacks at great speed. He later became the Reverend Harry Jackson. Also *Homicide Hank*, the *Human Buzzsaw*, *Hurricane Henry* and *Perpetual Motion*.

HAMMER OF THE MONKS, THE Thomas Cromwell, Earl of Essex (?1485–1540) who under Henry VIII (*Bluff Hal*) carried out the dissolution of the English monasteries (1525 and 1535). Also ***Malleus Monachorum*** and the ***Maul of the Monks***.

HAMMER OF THE SCOTS, THE Edward I, the ***English Justinian***, who defeated Sir William Wallace (the ***Hammer and Scourge of England***) at Falkirk (1298). The words *Edwardus Longus Scotorum Malleus hic est* are inscribed on his tomb in Westminster Abbey.

HANDCUFF KING, THE Harry Houdini (1874–1926) whose real name was Ehrich Weiss, American escapologist who pioneered underwater escapes.

HANDS Johnny Lee Bench (1947–), American baseball star for Cincinnati (1970s) and TV personality; from his skill in using them as a catcher.

HANDSOME, THE

i) Aedh Ui Neill, King of Ireland (reigned 734–43).

ii) Geoffrey, Count of Anjou, ***Le Bel***.

HANDSOME CONWAY William Augustus Conway (1789–1828), English actor. He played Hamlet and Othello in London, but was so excessively sensitive that he committed suicide.

HANDSOME ENGLISHMAN, THE The Duke of Marlborough, ***Anne's Great Captain***.

HANDSOME FEILDING Robert ***Beau*** Feilding; nickname given to him by Charles II (the ***Blackbird***).

HANDSOME JACK

i) The Duke of Marlborough (above); his nickname at the English Court.

ii) Jack Tanner (1889–1965), President for fifteen years of the Amalgamated Engineering Union.

HANDSOME SLOVEN, THE Edmund Smith, ***Captain Rag***; so called in *The Gentleman's Magazine* (1780).

HANDSOMEST MAN IN THE WORLD, THE Francis X Bushman (1883–1966), Hollywood star of silent films, e.g. *The Magic Wand* (1912).

HANDY, THE Aedh, King of Ailech (reigned 1030–3).

- See ***Flaherty of the Pilgrim's Staff***.

HANGING HAWKINS Sir Henry Hawkins, Lord Brampton (1817–1907), British judge. *Punch* called him 'the Master of Hard Sentences', and he was said to have been regarded even by barristers as unfair, hard-hearted and brutal. Also the ***Hanging Judge***.

- 'Awkins' became Cockney slang for a severe man.

HANGING JERVIS Lord St Vincent, ***BIlly Blue***, who (Bowen) 'did not believe in gentle methods of enforcing discipline'. His strictness caused him to be hated by his officers, and one indeed challenged him to a duel, but his sternness raised standards of discipline and efficiency in the Royal Navy.

HANGING JUDGE, THE

i) Sir Henry Hawkins, ***Hanging Hawkins***.

ii) Isaac Parker (1838–96), American judge in Fort Smith, Arkansas.

iii) Mr Justice John Toler, 1st Earl of Norbury (1745–1831), who is reported to have joked with prisoners when passing sentence of death. He was Chief Justice of Common Pleas in Ireland (post 1800).

iv) Sir Francis Page (*circa* 1661–1741), English judge; so called by contemporaries.

v) Mr Justice Avory, the ***Acid Drop***.

vi) Robert Macqueen, Lord Braxfield (1772–99), Scottish judge who tried William Brodie and George Smith (1788). Also the ***Jeffreys of Scotland***.

- Brodie was the 'original' of R. L. Stevenson's 'Jekyll and Hyde'.

vii)'Judge' Roy Bean (?1821–1902), self–appointed 'justice west of the Pecos' in America (1890s).

HANGMAN, THE Lieutenant-Colonel Henry Hawley (*circa* 1679–1759); nickname given to him by his troops who hated him because he was violently abusive and cruel. He was in command of the cavalry at Culloden (1745), and caused ruthless butchery afterwards.

HANG-THEOLOGY ROGERS William Rogers (1819–96), Prebendary of St Paul's Cathedral, London and a member of the London School Board who advocated secular education.

HANK Angelo Luisetti (1916–), American basketball player, famous for his 'jump shot', which revolutionized the game. In the Hall of Fame (1959).

HANOI JANE Jane Fonda (1937–), American film star, for her passionate support for the Communist North in the Vietnam war (1957–75).

● Hanoi was the capital of North Vietnam.

HAP General of the Army Henry Harley Arnold (1886–1950), Chief of the US Army Air Force.

HAPPY

i) Margaretta Rockefeller (1928–), wife of Nelson Rockefeller (1909–79), Vice-President (1974–7) and Governor of New York (1958–1973). She won this nickname in spite of having lung cancer.

ii) Fanny Fields (1881–1961), American-born British music-hall star (late 19th-early 20th century).

iii) Albert Caldwell (1903–), American jazz saxophonist.

HAPPY HUMPHREY William J. Cobb (1926–), American professional wrestler of Macon, Georgia, who weighed 57 stone 4 lb (802 lb) in 1965, the heaviest sportsman of all time. In three years he lost 40 stone 10 lb, but then went back to 46 stone 4 lb (650 lb) in 1973.

● Cf *Giant Haystacks*.

HAPPY JACK George Ulyett (1851–98), cricketer for Yorkshire (1873–93), one of the best batsmen in England.

HAPPY WARRIOR, THE Alfred Emanuel Smith (1873–1944), Governor of New York, defeated by Herbert Hoover (1874–1964) in the 1928 Presidential election.

HARD CIDER W. H. Harrison, the *Cincinnatus of the West*. His campaign for President (1840) was called 'the Log Cabin and Hard Cider campaign'. He was a frontier hero who said he lived in a log cabin, and that cider and not wine had been served at the family's table. It helped him to beat van Buren (the *Little Magician*). He had in fact been born in a mansion.

HARDI, LE Sir William de Douglas, the *Bold*. The French word can mean 'bold',

'rash', or 'hardy'.

HARDY, THE Kenneth, son of Alpin (and so MacAlpine: died 858), first King of Alba (reigned 843–58). He was buried on Iona. He had been king of the Scots of Dalriada.

● 'Alba' was an early name for all Scotland. See the *Fair* (ii).

HAREFOOT Harold I (died 1040), King of England from 1035; son of Canute the *Great*. It was (Reaney) an anglicization of the Old Norse *harfótr*, a nickname for a swift runner.

HARE LIP Thorgils (died 967), Norwegian, who with his brother Kormak raided Britain. They were the first to fortify Scarborough, Yorkshire (*circa* 965), named from Thorgils' Norse nickname *Skarthi* (Harelip): 'Skarthi's burg'. (Ekwall, from the *Kormak Saga*).

HARLEQUIN The Earl of Oxford, the *Backstairs Dragon*; a pun on 'Harley'.

HAROLD Bob Willis, *Dylan*.

HARRY Kenneth Clarke (1940–), Minister of Trade and Industry and later Secretary of State for Health (1988–).

HARRY OF THE WEST Henry Clay, the *Apostle of Liberty*, representative of Kentucky in the Senate.

HARRY or HENRY THE MINSTREL *Blind Harry*.

HARRY TWITCHER Lord Brougham and Vaux, *Blundering Brougham*, with a facial twitch.

HART William, Marquis of Hartington (1790–1858), later 6th Duke of Devonshire. Also the *Maecenas and Lucullus of His Island*.

HARTY-TARTY Spencer Compton Cavendish, Marquis of Hartington (1833–62), later 8th Duke of Devonshire.

HARY-O Lady Henrietta (Harriet) Elizabeth Cavendish (1785–1862), later wife of Lord Grenville (*Antinous*).

HARYANA HURRICANE, THE Kapil Dev Nikhanj (1959–), cricketer for Northants and India, who made a century from 83 balls in a Test Match against England (1982).

HASIMOVA Alla Nazimova (1879–1945), American film star of the silent days; a pun on her name in the catch-phrase (especially among schoolboys); 'She puts out her foot and Hasimova' (or 'and Nazimova'.) She was born in Romania and had the name Alla Nazimoff Rassia.

HAT, THE Jack McVitie (1929–67), Briton for whose murder Ronald (the *Colonel*) and Reginald Kray were sent to prison for not less than thirty years (1969). They had a long history of crime. McVitie always wore a hat to hide his baldness.

HAUL DOWN THE FLAG JONES Alfred Gilpin Jones (1824–1906), Canadian politician who opposed federation of the British provinces in Canada and made an angry speech after the British refusal to repeal portions of the British North America Act.

HAVELOCK OF THE WAR, THE Major–General Oliver Otis Howard, the *Christian General*. During the Civil War, he served with great bravery and was twice wounded, losing his right arm.
- General Sir Henry Havelock, the *Young Varmint*, Indian Mutiny hero.

HAWK, THE Ernest Rupolo (died 1964). New York gangster.

HAWKIE William Cameron (died *circa* 1785), Scottish street orator and seller of chapbooks and ballads, a patterer; from 'hawker'.
- A patterer was a 'cheap jack' who spoke glibly at speed; from one who recites Paternosters swiftly, without thought. A chapbook was a tract or a pamphlet of popular tales, from OE *ceap*, 'market' etc (as in 'Cheapside' or 'cheap jack').

HAWK'S-EYE Lieutenant-Colonel Henry Somerset, eldest son of Lord Charles Somerset, and a descendant of John of *Gaunt*. After having served with the 10th Hussars in the Peninsular War, he went to South Africa, where he commanded the Cape Mounted Rifles, mostly Hottentots, during the 6th Frontier War (1835). He was a nephew of Lord Raglan (1788–1855). His nickname among the Africans.

HEADSMAN CLARKSON James Sullivan Clarkson (1842–1918), Assistant Postmaster General under President Benjamin Harrison (1833–1901:1889–93). A Republican, he 'chopped' almost 32,000 Democrats from Post Office jobs when he took office; so called by Democrats.

HEAD WAITER, THE Harry Wragg (1902–), British jockey who was a master of pace and could judge exactly how long to wait before moving forward to win. He won the Derby three times (1928, 1930 and 1942).

HEART-BREAK HILDA Hilda Sperling, née Krahwinkel, German tennis star (1930s); because of her ability to return the 'unreturnable' during the 1936 finals at Wimbledon. She was long-legged, and ran well. She was French champion 1935, 1936–7.

HEAVEN-BORN GENERAL or HERO, THE Robert, 1st Baron Clive (1725–74), the man who created the Indian empire; so called by Pitt (*Aeolus*) in tribute to his victories at the age of twenty-seven. Also *Sabut Jung*.

HEAVEN-SENT MINISTER, THE William Pitt, the *Bottomless Pitt*. He took office as Prime Minister (1738) in time to save England from Napoleon.

HEAVEN-SENT PLOUGHMAN, THE Robert Burns, the *Ayshire Poet*, who had little education.

HEAVY HORSEMAN, THE Edward Quillinan (1791–1851), British poet who had served in the Dragoon Guards in Spain; so called in *Noctes Ambrosianae* with apparent reference to his verse.

HEAVY VILLAIN, THE Raglan Somerset (1885–1956), editor of *The Granta* at Cambridge University and famous later as a journalist and critic, who became a Q.C; his nickname at Cambridge, which stayed with him.

HECTOR OF STATE, THE John Maitland, 2nd Earl of Lauderdale and 1st Duke (1616–82); because of his ferocious methods as Secretary of State for Scotland (post 1660).
- Hector, the chief hero of the Trojan War, has given a word to the English language meaning to bully or intimidate.

HECTOR OF THE WEST, THE Murketagh Ui Neill, King of Ailech, West Ireland (reigned 938–43), one of the great Irish commanders who defeated the Danes. He was killed at the battle of Ardee against the King of Dublin. His deeds are recorded in the Book of Leinster, compiled in the 12th century by Finn macGorman, Bishop of Kildare. Also *Murketagh of the Leather Cloaks*.

HE-FACE Colonel Valentine Baker (1827–87), 'Baker Pasha', who commanded the Egyptian gendarmerie in the Sudan (1883); his school nickname which persisted. Also the *Man on the White Horse*.

- 'He' is given by Partridge as slang for 'cake'.

HEFF Hugh Hefner (1926–   ), American founder of the *Playboy* magazine and clubs.

HEIGH-HO Henry Norris, *Dicky Scrub*; from the repetition of the expression in a soliloquy in *The Rehearsal*, (printed in 1672).

HELL-FIRE DICK Richard Owen (died 1822), driver of *The Cambridge Telegraph*, the stage–coach that served the university.

HELL-FIRE FRANCIS Sir Francis Dashwood, Baron le Despenser (1708–81), originator of the Hell–Fire club called the Monks of Medmenham, whose members included Sterne (the *English Rabelais*), Lord Sandwich (*Jemmy Twitcher*) and Wilkes (*Squinting Jack*). Dashwood was Chancellor of the Exchequer (1762–3).

HELLGATE Richard Barry, 7th Earl of Barrymore (1769–93), Irish peer; because of his notorious life as a rake. He shot himself after frittering away a £300,000 fortune.

- Cf *Cripplegate*, *Newgate* and *Billingsgate* (his sister). See *Tinman*.

HELL-RAISER, THE Terence (Steve) McQueen (1930–80), American film actor labelled 'superstar'; because of his lifestyle.

HEMANS OF AMERICA, THE Lydia Huntley Sigourney (1791–1865), American poetaster who wrote sentimental and pious verse.

- Mrs Felicia Hemans (1793–1835), British poetaster whose *Casablanca* was very popular in America.

HENDERS Ralph Bushill Henderson (1880–1958), headmaster of Alleyn's School, Dulwich, London (1920–40).

HENGEST One of the two brothers who were leaders of the first German people – apart from those who lived under late Roman rule – to settle in Britain (*circa* 450–5) Hengest (died ?488) was a war–name = 'stallion'.

- Cf *Horsa*.

HENRY Philippe (Phil) H. Edmonds (1951-), cricketer for Cambridge University and England. He is a left-arm spinner. He was christened Philippe Henri. His mother was Belgian.

HENRY OF THE BATTLEAXES Henry Fitzgerald, Earl of Kildare (died 1597), killed fighting the rebels of Tyrone, Ireland.

HENRY THE MINSTREL *Blind Harry*.

HERMIT OF GRUB STREET, THE Henry Welby (1554–1638), an eccentric British recluse. It was said that for 47 years he was never seen by anyone, except, in cases of great need, by an old female servant. He lived on bread, oatmeal, water–gruel, milk, vegetables and, on special occasions, the yolk of an egg. A portrait (1794) depicts him as a man with a very long beard wearing a type of monk's robe and open-toed sandals, leaning on a stick. His daughter married a Yorkshire gentleman, Sir Christopher Hildyard, but she never saw her father after he became a hermit.

- Water-gruel, see the *Water-Gruel Bard*.

HERMIT OF HAMPOLE, THE Richard Rolle de Hampole (?1300–49), recluse and author who wrote many scriptural commentaries and meditations in Latin and English. He cured another recluse, Margaret Kirby, of a seizure and dedicated some of his works to her.

- Hampole is a village in west Yorkshire, near Doncaster.

HERMIT OF HULL, THE Philip Larkin (1922–85), British poet described as 'the best Poet Laureate we never had'. He was librarian at Hull University and was alleged to have shunned publicity and a gregarious life.

HERMIT OF LITERATURE, THE Thomas Baker (1656–1740), British scholar and antiquary. He spent most of his life at St. John's College, Cambridge. His best known work is *Reflections on Learning* (1709–10).

HERMIT OF NEWTON-BURGOLAND, THE William Lole (1800–74), self-applied because of his passion for freedom, although he was not strictly a recluse.

● Newton-Burgoland is near Ashby-de-la-Zouch, Leicestershire.

HERMODACTYL The Earl of Oxford, the *Backstairs Dragon*.

● Hermodactyl, Hermes' finger, is a bulbous plant used in medicine, but is also applied to the Snake's–head Iris.

HERODOTUS OF OLD LONDON, THE John Stow (1525–1605), author of *The Survey of London* (1598), the greatest description of a medieval city.

● Herodotus (?484–440 BC), Greek historian, has been called 'The Father of History' (and also 'The Father of Lies').

HERO OF A HUNDRED FIGHTS, THE

i) The Duke of Wellington, the *Achilles of England*; so called by Tennyson (the *Bard of Arthurian Romance*) in his *Ode on the Death of the Duke of Wellington* (1825).

ii) Horatio, 1st Viscount Nelson (1758–1805). Also the *Hero of the Nile*.

iii) Conn, the *Hundred Fighter*.

HERO OF ALIWAL, THE Sir Henry George Wakelyn Smith (1787–1860), who preferred to be known as Sir Harry Smith, and after whose wife Ladysmith was named. As a general in the Sikh War, he smashed the Sikhs at Aliwal on the Sutlej river (1846). Lord Brougham (*Blundering Brougham*) wrote in his diary (1848) that Smith was a celebrity on his return to London, 'He spoke of himself without scruple as "The hero of Aliwal," but gave all the credit to his mentor, the Duke of Wellington'.

HERO OF CHÂTEAUGUAY, THE Lieuten-

ant-Colonel Charles-Michel d'Irunberryde de Salaberry (1778–1829). He was a British officer who raised the Canadian Voltigeurs, defeated an American force (1813) and halted an invasion of Lower Canada.

HERO OF THE HUMBER, THE John Ellerthorpe (1806–68), foreman of the Humber Dock Gate who in forty years saved 39 people from drowning. He was a very courageous swimmer.

HERO OF THE NILE, THE Lord Nelson, the *Hero of a Hundred Fights*. Nelson destroyed the French fleet at Aboukir Bay (1798) and left Napoleon's troops stranded in Egypt.

HERO OF THE PENINSULA, THE The Duke of Wellington, the *Achilles of England* who drove the French out of Spain.

HERO OF THE YANGTZE, THE Commander John Kerans (1915–85), DSO. He brought the British frigate HMS *Amethyst* down the Yangtze river under fire from Chinese artillery (1949) after its captain had been killed.

HERO OF UPPER CANADA, THE Sir Isaac Brook (1769–1812), British soldier and administrator who defended Upper Canada against invasion by the Americans in the war of 1812. He was killed at the battle of Queenstown Heights.

HERTFORDSHIRE HERMIT, THE James Lucas (1813–74), whose mind was affected by the death of his mother, and who afterwards lived in one room of a big house (with rats as his friends) at Great Wymondley, Hertfordshire.

HESIOD COOKE Thomas Cooke (1703–56) translator of Hesiod into rhymed couplets (1728–9). Dr Johnson (*Blinking Sam*) said that Cooke lived for twenty years on subscriptions for a translation of Plautus which never appeared.

● Hesiod (?fl. 8th century BC) was one of the earliest of Greek poets.

HIBERNIAN ROSCIUS, THE Gustavus Vaughan, the *Dublin Roscius*.

● See the *African Roscius*.

HICKORY General Andrew Jackson (1767–1845), 7th President of the USA. After he had led his men through 500 miles of wilderness, they said he was as 'tough as hickory' (1812 war). He was nicknamed both **Tough** and **Hickory**. The **Old** was added when he was regarded with affection by his men. Also **Old Hero** and **Sharp Knife**.

HIGH CHURCH TRUMPET, THE Dr Henry Sacheverell (1674–1724), English churchman and politician who became the idol of the Tories after he had attacked the Whigs in several sermons for neglecting the Church. He was prosecuted for 'malicious, seditious and scandalous libels', and was such a public hero that Queen Anne (**Brandy Nan**) attended his trial. He was suspended from preaching for three years, and his sermons were publicly burnt. Also the **Pulpit Physician** and the **Zealous Doctor**.

- See also **Volpone**.

HIGHLAND LADDIE, THE Prince Charles Stuart, **Bonny Prince Charlie**.

HIGHLAND MARY Two sweethearts of Robert Burns, the **Ayrshire Poet**.

i) Mary Campbell (died 1786), daughter of a Glasgow skipper. Burns wrote *To Mary In Heaven* for her.

ii) Alison Begbie (Mary Morison), who rejected him.

HIGH–METTLED MARY Henry St John, 1st Viscount Bolingbroke (1678–1751), Secretary of State (1710–14) under Harley (the **Backstairs Dragon**); but he was a confirmed Jacobite, dismissed on the accession of George I (the **Turnip Hoer**). He fled to France to become Secretary of State to the **Young Pretender**. Later he returned to England. His mother was Mary Rich, daughter of the 2nd Earl of Warwick (1587–1658). Also **Mercury**, the **Patriot King** and **Proud Bolingbroke**.

HIGH POCKETS George Kelly (1895–1984), American baseball player for New York (1915–32); in the Hall of Fame.

HIGH PRIEST OF BOP, THE Thelonious Monk (1920–1982), American jazz pianist.

- Bop is 'a linear conception of jazz, developed in the 1940s and typified by improvisations on a basic melody' (*Radio Times*).

HIGH PRIEST OF MUSIC, THE Arturo Toscanini (1867–1957), Italian-born American conductor who controlled orchestras of the National Broadcasting Company, New York, La Scala, Milan and the Metropolitan Opera House, New York.

HILLSIDE STRANGLER, THE Kenneth Bianchi (1951–), a security guard at Bellingham, Washington State. He terrorized Los Angeles and Hollywood for five months (1977), and killed ten women. Later he killed two girls in Bellingham. He was tried (1984) with his cousin Angelo Bono (1934–), and both were sent to life imprisonment without parole. The dead women were dumped on a hillside. Bianchi pleaded guilty after having failed to fake a multiple personality.

HIMSELF Eamonn Andrews (1922–87), Irish-born TV personality and presenter of the programme *This is Your Life*.

HIPPO Jim Fuller (1757–1834), an MP who weighed more than 20 stones (280 lb). Also **Mad Jack**.

HIS NOBS George III, the **Button Maker**; his nickname among courtiers and palace staff.

- 'Nob' may be a shortening of **nabob** e.g. Nob Hill, San Francisco, where the nabobs lived. **Nobby** has been slang (post 1788) for being smart and elegant like the 'nobs', the rich people caricatured by Foote (the **English Aristophanes**) in *The Nabob* (1772). The theory that it derived from 'nob; written in early university rolls against a student who was a noble is rejected by the OED. Cf **Nobs**.

HIS NOSESHIP Cromwell, the **Almighty Nose**; so called by Marchmont Needham (the **Cobbett of His Day**) because of his large nose.

HITCH Sir Alfred Hitchcock (1899–1980), British film-maker. Also **Mr Suspense**.

HIT MAN, THE Thomas Hearns (1959–), American World Boxing Association of America light–heavyweight champion (1987), also welterweight and middleweight champion.

H.M. Mrs Thatcher, **Attila the Hen**. She has been known to use the royal 'we', e.g.

'We have become a grandmother' (TV news, March 1989).

HOAGY Everett Hoagland Carmichael (1899–1981), American jazz pianist and composer.

HOARY BARD OF NIGHT, THE Edward Young (1683–1765),.poet of *Night Thoughts* (1742–5); so called by Beattie (the *Bard of the North*).

HOBBIT Ann Hobbs (1959–), British Wimbledon-class tennis player.

- A Hobbit is one of the imaginary race of people, a small variation of the human race, invented by Professor J.R.R. Tolkien (1892–1973), author of *The Lord of the Rings* (1954–5).

HOBO Major-General Sir Percy Hobart (1884–1957), British expert on tank warfare, seen by some as a genius.

HOCUSPOCUS Archbishop William Laud (1573–1645), beheaded for high treason. He supported Strafford (*Black Tom Tyrant*) and showed extreme royalism at a time of struggle between King and Parliament. He acknowledged the Roman Catholic Church as *a* true church, while denying it was *the* true church. Also the *Little Vermin* and the *Urchin*.

HOD Glenn Hoddle (1957–), striker for Tottenham Hotspurs F.C., rated a £1,000,000 player.

HOG, THE Richard III, the *Boar*.

- See also the *Cat*, the *Dog* and the *Rat*.

HOGARTH OF NOVELISTS, THE Henry Fielding, the *Father of the English Novel*.

- For Hogarth, see the *Juvenal of Painters*.

HOLY AUTOLYCUS John Tetzel (1470–1519), an English Dominican monk sent to Germany to sell indulgences.

- Autolycus (maternal grandfather of Odysseus), master-thief of Greek legend, was called by Shakespeare (the *Bard of All Time*) 'a snapper-up of unconsidered trifles' (cf a character of that name in *The Winter's Tale*).

HOLY HORATIO Horatio Alger (1832–99), American author. He became a Unitarian minister but left to be a writer; famous for his 'Ragged Dick' series (1867 on) which inspired boys to strive to succeed. He was thought to be overmoralizing and self-righteous in his style.

HOLY JOE
i) James (Jim) Orson Bakker (1940–), American millionaire televangelist ordained by the Assembles of God (1964). Unfrocked for alleged sexual offences with men and a woman, he was back on TV by 1989, but in the same year was sent to a prison mental hospital by Judge 'Maximum Bob' Potter, having been found guilty of fraud and conspiracy and later jailed for 45 years.
ii) Joseph Radcliffe (fl. 1860s–1870s), British racehorse owner whose Salvanos won the Cesarewitch in 1871. He died in poverty.

HOLY MAID OF KENT, THE Elizabeth Barton (*circa* 1506–34), a British religious imposter admitted to a convent after a feigned trance in which she made prophecies against the King and the Roman Catholic Church. She later confessed and was hanged. Also the *Maid of Kent* and the *Nun of Kent*.

HOLY VIPER, THE Sarah Junner, Lawrence or Chapman (1861–1959), mother of T. E. Lawrence (*Emir Dynamite*). She was the common-law wife of Thomas Chapman, who took the name of Lawrence. She was a strong-minded woman with puritanical views and ruled the family with great severity. Her family nickname; also the *Vinegar Queen*.

HOLY WILLIE 'General' the Reverend William Booth (1829–1912), founder of the Salvation Army. Also the *Publican*.

HOMER OF DRAMATIC POETS, THE Shakespeare, the *Bard of All Time*; so called by Dryden (*Asaph*).

- See the *British Homer*.

HOMER OF WOMEN, THE Robert Greene, the *Ape of Euphues*; so called by Nash (the *English Aretine*). His best poetry is about women.

HOME RUN John Franklin Baker (1886–1955), American baseball batting star (in the Hall of Fame, 1908–22).

- A home run (*Enc. Brit.*) is a hit beyond

the reach of fielders which entitles the batter to run as he pleases around the bases to score a run at the home plate.

HOME RUN KING, THE *Babe* Ruth. He made 714 home runs in twenty–two years of major League games. In 1927 he made 60.

● But see *Hammerin' Hank*.

HOMICIDE HANK Henry Armstrong, *Hammering Henry*.

HONEST ABE or HONEST OLD ABE Abraham Lincoln, *Father Abraham*.

HONEST ALLAN Allan Cunningham (1784–1842), Scottish poet and author; mentioned by Lockhart.

HONEST BEN Ben Jonson, the *Bricklayer*.

HONEST CAL Calvin Coolidge, *Cautious Cal*. His probity promoted confidence, which led to business prosperity in the USA just before the Depression of the 1930s.

HONEST ED Ed. Mirvisch (1914–   ), Canadian millionaire department store-owner who bought the Old Vic Theatre, London (1983).

HONEST GEORGE
i) George Monk, Duke of Albemarle, *Abdael*. He showed honesty of purpose in difficult times.
ii) George Graham (1675–1751), British watchmaker and inventor; pupil of Tompion (the *Father of English Watchmaking*); because of his sincerity.

HONEST HARRY Henry Meiggs (1811–77), railway builder who went to San Francisco in the gold rush days and ran up debts of a million dollars which he could not immediately meet. He paid them all off, however, before his death.

HONEST JACK
i) John Charles, 3rd Earl Spencer (1782–1845), better known as Lord Althorp, his title as heir. He was a man of truthfulness and integrity, completely trusted by his friends and colleagues. Also *Honest John*.
ii) John Felton, *Brutus*. D'Israeli comments that he was nearly 'sainted' before he reached London, after the

assassination of Buckingham (*Steenie*) in 1628, and his health was the reigning toast among republicans. (He was executed, all the same.)
iii) John Lawless (1773–1837), Irish agitator.

HONEST JOHN
i) Lord Spencer, *Honest Jack*.
ii) John, 1st Viscount Morley (1838–1923), journalist for *The Saturday Review* and *The Fortnightly Review* and an English statesman.
iii) John Burns (1858–1943), English radical politician who held a portfolio in the Liberal Government (1905). He was often spoken of as a 'cough-drop', i.e. a 'character'. (*The Referee*, 1895).
iv) John Phelps (1805–90), judge in the Oxford and Cambridge boat–races. It was he who declared a dead heat after one of the Oxford crew broke an oar near the finish (1877).
v) John Barham Day (1794–1860), English jockey (1830s) and later a trainer (1850s–1860s), with a record 146 wins in one season (1867); ironic: he was a ruthless rogue.
vi) John Biffen (1930–   ), leader of the House of Commons (1980s); his nickname in Parliament.
vii) John Kelly (1821–86), successor (1870s) to *Boss* Tweed at Tammany Hall; ironic.

HONEST OLD ABE Abraham Lincoln, *Father Abraham*.

HONEST OLD ZACH Senator Zachariah Chandler (1813–79), American politician, active in the reorganization of the Republican Party. He was a rich merchant and Mayor of Detroit.

HONEST SKIPPON Sergeant-Major-General Philip Skippon (died 1660), Privy Councillor (1653 and 1655), one of the commanders of military districts in the Commonwealth. Also *Stout Skippon* and the *Pious* (*q.v.* for Sergeant-Major-General).

HONEST STANLEY Stanley, 1st Earl Baldwin (1867–1947), three times British Prime Minister (1922, 1924–9 and 1935–7). Also *Old Sealed Lips*.

HONEST TOM Thomas, 1st Marquess of Wharton (1648–1715), leader of the Whigs, Lord–Lieutenant of Ireland and author of the political ballad *Lilliburlero*, which helped to drive James II (the *King Over the Water*) off the throne. Ironic: Swift (*Dr Presto*) thought him ' the most universal villain I ever knew'.

- 'Lilliburlero' was said to have been the password of the Irish Roman Catholics in their massacre of Protestants (1641), an anglicization of the Irish *Buaro–a–lo* or *Bull–a–lo*, 'the day of victory'. *Lo* is the poetic version of *latha*, 'day'. A street ballad of the time had the line: 'Now *Lero, Lero* is the only song.'

HONEY BEAR Eugene Sedric (1907–1963), American tenor saxophonist and clarinettist with *Smack* Henderson; from the coat he wore.

HONEY FITZ John F. Fitzgerald (1863–1951), Mayor of Boston and grandfather of J. F. Kennedy (1917–63: 35th President of the USA). He was honey-tongued and dapper.

HONOURABLE MEMBER FOR AFRICA, THE Fenner, 1st Baron Brockway (1889–1988); for his advocacy – often passionate – of independence for African countries during his term as a Labour MP; so called in the House of Commons.

HONOUR AND GLORY GRIFFITHS Captain Griffiths (fl. 1830s) of the Royal Navy. He addressed all his despatches to 'Their Honours and Glories at the Admiralty'.

HONUS J. P. Wagner, the *Flying Dutchman*.

HOODED MAN, THE John Williams (1884–1913), British cat burglar executed for the murder of police-inspector Arthur Walls in Eastbourne, Sussex. His face was covered on his journeys to and from court. His real name was George Mackay, son of a Scottish clergyman, and he did not want his father to know.

HOOKY
i) Admiral Sir Montagu Edward Browning, Royal Navy (1863–1947), after losing a hand.
ii) Admiral Sir Harold Thomas Coulthard Walker (1891–1975). He had a

brass hook instead of one hand.

HOOKY or HOOKEY WALKER John Walker (fl. 18th century) who, says Brewer (1898 edition), quoting Jon Bee (1823), was an outdoor clerk at Longman, Clementi & Company, Cheapside, London, noted for his eagle nose. His job was to report on workmen to his principals. Also *Old Hooky*.

- 'Hooky Walker' is an obsolescent expression for an untrustworthy tale. *Hooker* is Romany for a lie: 'Yes, with a hook' = it is false.

HOOSIER SCHOOLMASTER, THE Victor Eddington Aldridge (1894–1973), American baseball star who had been a schoolmaster before entering the game.

- Indiana is the Hoosier state, from the demand by early settlers to night callers: 'Who's yere?' (*The Naming of America*, by Allan Wolk, 1981).

HOOT Edward Richard Gibson (1892–1962), American cowboy actor in silent films. He had a boyhood love of hunting owls.

HORACE OF ENGLAND, THE
i) Abraham Cowley, the *English Pindar*; so called by the 2nd Duke of Buckingham (*Alcibiades*) who was his patron.
ii) Ben Jonson, the *Bricklayer*.
- See the *English Horace*.

HORSA One of the two 'Saxons' who led the first post-Roman German settlers in England. They were probably Jutes. Horsa is said to have died in 455.

- See *Hengest*. The nickname means 'horse' with, it has been suggested, the idea of 'mare'.

HORSE Alan Ameche (1933–), American star footballer for Baltimore; rusher of the year (1955).

HOSTEST WITH THE MOSTEST, THE Perle Mesta (1889–1975), White House hostess and American Ambassador to Luxembourg (1949–53), the subject of a Broadway musical, *Call Me Madam*. Also *Madam*.

HOT CROSS BUN Alfred Bunn, *Good Friday*; so called by *Punch*, with whom he engaged in a dispute.

HOT GOSPELLER, THE
i) Edward Underhill (fl. 1539–62), prominent British protestant imprisoned for a ballad against Papists.
ii) Aimée Semple McPherson, the **Barnum of Religion**. Her name before marriage was Aimée Elizabeth Kennedy.
• See **Ma**. 'Hot Gospeller' was a nickname (1560s) for an over–zealous Puritan. Some preached under an elm on Hampstead Heath, London.

HOTPANTS Senator Gary Hart (1936–), contender for the Democrat nomination for the American Presidential elections (1984); so called at school. His real surname is Hartpence, and he has been described as a ' womanizer'.

HOTSPUR Sir Henry Percy (1364–1403), son of the 1st Earl of Northumberland; so called because of his hot temper and his furious riding. He appears in Shakespeare's *Henry IV* and is the hero of the ballads of *Chevy Chace* and *Otterburn*.

HOTSPUR OF DEBATES, THE Lord Derby, the **Derby Dilly**.

HOUDINI David Martin (1948–84), who escaped from police custody (Christmas Eve 1982) while held on a charge of shooting a policeman. He was skilful in picking locks and undoing handcuffs. He was recaptured (1983) and sentenced to a total of forty years imprisonment, of which he would serve at least twenty–five years. He hanged himself in his cell.
• For Houdini, see the **Handcuff King**.

HOUDINI OF THE COURTS, THE Horatio Bottomley, **England's Recruiting Sergeant** who though untrained conducted his own defences in complicated financial cases. He often confounded eminent lawyers, counsel, and sometimes judges.

HOUDINI OF THE HARDWOOD, THE John Townsend (1916–), American All-State basketball star, noted for his brilliant passing.

HOUDINI OF THE UNDERWORLD, THE Walter Probyn. **Angel Face**, expert at prison breaking.

HOUR-GLASS GIRL, THE Anna Held (1873–1918), American Ziegfeld Follies girl of the late 19th century; because of her figure. She had an 18in waist: the record figure is 13 in for an adult woman.

HUBBLE-BUBBLE The 1st Duke of Newcastle, **Goody Newcastle**, who was energetic and fussy.
• 'Hubble-Bubble' in the 18th century meant the confused noise made by a person who spoke so quickly it was difficult to understand what was said or meant.

HUDIBRAS BUTLER Samuel Butler, the **Glory and Scandal of His Age,** who wrote *Hudibras* (1663–78); to distinguish him from **Erewhon Butler**.

HUGE DEAL Hugh D. McIntosh (fl. early 20th century), boxing promoter; from his initials and the big fights he staged.

HUGE FOOT Sir Hugh Mackintosh Foot, 1st Baron Caradon (1907–) who was Chief Secretary in Nigeria, Governor of Jamaica and Cyprus and Ambassador to the United Nations; so called in West Africa.

HUGH LITTLEJOHN Hugh John Lockhart (died 1831); so called by his grandfather, Scott (the **Ariosto of the North**). He was the son of John Lockhart (the **Aristarch of British Criticism**). The boy, who died young, was the dedicatee of *Tales of a Grandfather* (1827–9), a history of Scotland, originally designed for him.

HUGO Henry Yarnold (1917–74), Worcestershire wicket-keeper who stumped six batsmen in one innings (1951).

HUM Alfred Edward Lynam (1873–1956), associated with the Dragon preparatory school, Oxford, from 1883 (as a pupil) until his death as headmaster; the nickname first given by his sister stayed with him all his life; in fact his wife Mabel became 'Mrs Hum'.

HUMAN BUZZSAW, THE Henry Armstrong, **Hammering Henry**.

HUMAN HAIRPIN, THE Carlton Phillips (died 1942), card manipulator and magician on British music–halls (early 20th century). He was tall and thin.

HUMANITY DICK or HUMANITY MARTIN Richard Martin, **Hair-Trigger Dick**, who, as an MP helped to promote the Animals Protection Act (1822) and was part-founder of the Royal Society for the Prevention of Cruelty to Animals; so called by George IV (the **Adonis of Fifty**).

HUMANITY LAWSON John Lawson (1866–1920), British actor who toured the music–halls with a sketch *Humanity* (post 1896) which proved a sensation.

HUMAN WINDMILL, THE or THE PITTS-BURGH WINDMILL Edward Henry (Harry) Greb (1894–1926), American world middle weight champion (1923–6) who died following an eye operation just after he had lost his title.

HUMBLE AND HEAVENLY-MINDED, THE Dr Richard Sibbes (1577–1635), British Puritan clergyman. Walton (the **Father of Angling**) wrote of him: 'Heaven was in him before he was in Heaven'. Sibbes refused the Provostship of Trinity College, Dublin.

HUMPH Humphrey Lyttleton (1921–), British jazz trumpeter and band leader.

HUMPTY-DUMPTY Dr William King (1663–1712), British journalist and satirist. King was founder-editor of *The Examiner* (1710), a Tory journal to which Swift (**Doctor Presto**) contributed. He had attacked Richard Bentley (the **Aristarchus of Cambridge**) who replied with this nickname.

* 'Humpty-Dumpty was a short, dumpy, round-shouldered person, usually clumsy as well, e.g. Grose (1785): 'a short clumsey person of either sex'.

HUNCHBACKED, THE Donald Gunn (died 1723) of Killearnan, 6th Chief of the Gunn clan.

HUNK, THE Victor Mature (1917–), beefy American star of innumerable films.

HURRICANE, THE Alex Higgins (1949–), Irish-born world professional snooker champion (1972 and 1982). In two years he won six major events out of thirteen and was runner-up in five; because of his style. Also **Kerrygold**.

HURRICANE HENRY Henry Armstrong, **Hammering Henry**.

HURT THE CURT William Hurt (1950–), American film and TV star, e.g. *Gorky Park*; so called in his younger days as an actor.

HUTCH
i) Leslie Hutchinson (1900–69), West Indian-born London cabaret entertainer for forty years.

ii) David Soul (1944–), American actor and singer; from his role in the long-running TV series *Starsky and Hutch*. His real name is David Solberg.

HYPOCRITE, THE Stephen Lobb (died 1699), British non-conformist clergyman caught up in the Rye House Plot. After being acquitted of any participation in the affair, he was one of those who presented an address of thanks to James (the **King Over the Water**) for his declaration of conscience (1687), i.e. the Declaration of Indulgence.

* See the **British Cassius**, the **Jesuit** and the **Plotter**.

I

IAIN GLAS Lord Breadalbane, *Grey John*.
- *Glas* is Gaelic for a lock or a muzzle as well as 'grey'.
- *Iain* = John.

IANTHE Jane Digby, *Aurora*. 'Ianthe' is the Greek version of 'Jane'; self-applied when she was young, and the more enduring nickname.

ICEBERG, THE Sherman Adams, the *Abominable No-Man*. A cold, distant autocrat in his job.

ICE-CREAM KID, THE Kirk Stevens (1958–), Canadian-born professional snooker player (1980s); from his white cars and the white suits he wears.

ICE MAIDEN, THE Christine (Chris) Evert (1954–), American tennis champion once married to John (*Floss*) Lloyd, because of her unruffled manner when playing. Also *Miss Frigidaire*.

ICE STATION ZEBRA Nancy Reagan, *Dragon Lady*; so called by American newspapermen from Alastair Maclean's novel of that name.

ICE WATER Florenz Ziegfeld, the *Glorifier of the American Girl*. It was said that he never laughed at the comedians in his shows and they included W. C. Fields (1879–1946) and Eddie Cantor (*Banjo Eyes*).

IDEAL WARD William George Ward (1812–82) of the Oxford Movement, He published *The Ideal of a Christian Church* (1844) and lost his degree from Oxford University for heresy. His book said that the only hope for the Church of England was to rejoin the Roman Catholic Church.
- The Oxford Movement, begun in the 19th century, aimed at taking the Church of England back to the early Church and restoring the High Church movement of the 17th century.

IDOL OF THE RABBLE, THE William Penkethman (died 1725), British comedian who kept a theatrical booth at St Bartholomew Fair, London. Also *Pinkey*.

IKE Dwight David Eisenhower (1890–1969), Supreme Allied Commander (World War II) and the 34th President of the USA (1953–61). It was his childhood nickname. Also the *Kansas Cyclone*.

IKE MARVEL or IK MARVEL Donald Grant Mitchell (1822–1908), American author. The nickname resulted from a misprint of his pseudonym, J. K. Marvel, which he used for contributions to *The Morning Courier* and *The New York Enquirer*.

ILL-FATED HENRY Henry VI (1421–71) who was a well-meaning but unlucky king; so called by Pope (the *Bard of Twickenham*). Also the *Martyr King* and the *Saint*.

ILLINOIS BABOON, THE Abraham Lincoln, *Father Abraham*; so called by the Confederates in the Civil War, and by *The Times*, London.

ILLUMINATED DOCTOR, THE Thomas Taylor, the *Brazen Wall against Popery*.

ILLUSTRIOUS DOCTOR, THE Adam Marsh or de Marisco (?1200–58), English Franciscan monk, scholar and theologian, tutor to Roger Bacon (the *Admirable Doctor*). He had a considerable influence at the English Court.

ILLUSTRIOUS INFIDEL, THE Robert G. Ingersoll, the *Great Agnostic*.

ILLUSTRIOUS PHILIP Sir Philip Sidney, the *British Bayard*; so called by *Ape Gabriel* Harvey.

ILL WILL William Armstrong (fl. 1520s), Scottish border reiver, grandfather of *Kinmont Willie*.

ILLY Raymond (Ray) Illingworth (1932–), cricketer for England, Yorkshire and Leicestershire. He made more than 1,800 runs in Test Matches, and took more than 120 wickets.

IMMATERIALITY BAXTER Andrew Baxter (1686–1750), British metaphysician and 'bear-leader' (*qv*) to Wilkes (***Squinting Jack***). His *An Inquiry into the Nature of the Human Soul* (dedicated to Wilkes) held that the human body was moved by an immaterial force and the soul, being immaterial, was immortal.

IMMORTAL BARD, THE William Shakespeare, the ***Bard of All Time***.

IMMORTAL DREAMER, THE John Bunyan, ***Bishop Bunyan***.

IMMORTAL PIERCE Pierce Egan, the ***Elder***.

IMMORTAL REBEL, THE Oliver Cromwell, the ***Almighty Nose***; so called by Byron (***Baby***).

IMMORTAL TINKER, THE John Bunyan, ***Bishop Bunyan***.

IMMORTAL TRAMP, THE Sir Charles (Charlie) Spencer Chaplin (1889–1977), English-born comedian of American silent films; from his characterization of that role in his career.

IMPENETRABLE GOODMAN DULL Oliver Goldsmith, the ***Child of Nature***.

* 'Goodman' used as a mock title and cf. Holofernes in Shakespeare's *Love's Labour's Lost* (Act iv.sc.ii): 'Dictynna, goodman Dull'. [Dictynna was a name for the Cretan goddess Britomartis, identified with Artemis.]

IMPIOUS, THE Oliver Cromwell, the ***Almighty Nose***; so called by Cowley (the ***English Pindar***).

IMPIOUS BUFFOON, THE Jonathan Swift, ***Doctor Swift***; so called by Blackmore (the ***Cheapside Knight***) in his *Essays* (1717).

IMPUDENT, THE Sir Constantine Phipps (1656–1723), Lord Chancellor of Ireland with Jacobite sympathies. Phipps, a barrister, was reprimanded by the Lord High Steward in the House of Lords for beginning to speak without permission when he was defending George Seton, 5th Earl of Wintoun (died 1749) for treason by taking part in the 1745 rebellion, Wintoun escaped from the Tower of London.

INCOMPARABLE, THE William Shakespeare, the ***Bard of All Time***; so called by Dryden (***Asaph***) in his preface to *Troilus and Cressida* (1679).

INCOMPREHENSIBLE HOLOFERNES, THE Dr Johnson, ***Blinking Sam***. Not everyone understood him. 'Sir,' he once said to a man who did not,' I have found you an argument; I am not obliged to find you an understanding'.

* Holofernes is a pedantic schoolmaster in Shakespeare's *Love's Labour's Lost* – thought to have been a caricature of John Florio (?1553–1625), the lexicographer and translator of Montaigne.

INCREDIBLE SULK, THE John McEnroe, the ***Brat***, American Wimbledon tennis champion (1981).

* A pun of the name of the TV series *The Incredible Hulk*.

INDIAN BRADMAN, THE Cottari Kanakayia Nayudu (1895–1967), who was a brilliant batsman.

* For Bradman, see the ***Bowral Boy***.

INDIAN WARNER 'Thomas' Warner (?1630–47), 'Governor' of Dominica. He was the illegitimate son of Sir Thomas Warner (died 1648) by an Arawak woman. His half–brother Colonel Philip Warner, Governor of Antigua, was tried in England for Thomas's murder but acquitted.

INFANT ROSCIUS, THE or THE YOUNG ROSCIUS William Henry West Betty (1791–1874) who caused a sensation in London when he appeared on stage at the age of eleven. The House of Commons once adjourned on a motion by Pitt (the ***Bottomless Pit***) to see him as Hamlet. He retired from the stage at the age of thirty-three.

* See the ***African Roscius***.

INIMITABLE, THE
i) Charles Dickens (1812–70), novelist of *David Copperfield* (1849–50) and *The Pickwick Papers* (1836–7).
ii) Edmund Waller, the ***Father of English Numbers***; so called by George Granville (1667–1735).

INSPIRED IDIOT, THE Oliver Goldsmith, the ***Child of Nature***; so called by Walpole (the ***Autocrat of Strawberry Hill***) because of his ungainly, blundering ways and his reputation as a fool. Garrick (*Atlas*) wrote in a mock epitaph: 'Here lies Nolly Goldsmith, for shortness called Noll./Who wrote like an angel but talked like poor Poll.'

INSPIRED TINKER, THE John Bunyan, *Bishop Bunyan*, son of a village tinsmith, he was taught his father's trade.

INTEGRITY HARRIS Jean Harris (1924–), headmistress of an American girls' school in Virginia, convicted (1981) of murdering her lover, Dr Herman Tarnower (1910–80) in New York state and sentenced to a minimum of fifteen years in gaol; nickname by her pupils because she used the word so often.

INTEGRITY MOUNTAIN Kenesaw Mountain Landis (1866–1944), judge of the Federal Courts of Chicago, boss of 'clean baseball' after the 1919 World Series was found to have been 'fixed'.

INTELLECTUAL EPICURE, THE Dr H. More, the *Chrysostom of Christ's College*.

INTELLECTUAL EUNUCH, THE The Marquis of Londonderry, *Bloody Castlereagh*, who was Secretary of State for war (1805–9); so called by Byron (*Baby*) in *Don Juan* (1819–24). His speeches in Parliament were often unintelligible.

INVINCIBLE DOCTOR, THE William of Occam, *Doctor Invincibilis*.

INVINCIBLE SOLDIER, THE Edward, the *Black Prince*.

IRISH AGITATOR, THE Daniel O'Connell, the *Big Beggarman*, who fought to bring about the repeal of the Act of Union between England and Ireland. He has been credited with inventing mass agitation to achieve a purpose.

IRISH ANACREON, THE Turlogh O'Carolan (1670–1738), a blind Irish poet who wandered about the Irish countryside, receiving food and lodgings for his songs. Also the *Last True Bard of Ireland* and the *Orpheus of the Green Isle*.
- See *Anacreon Moore*.

IRISH ATTICUS, THE George Faulkner (1700–75), bookseller and friend of Swift (*Doctor Presto*); so called by Chesterfield (the *English Rochefoucauld*) when he was Lord-Lieutenant of Ireland (1744–6); almost certainly ironic since Faulkner was engaged in a ridiculous newspaper 'war' over the piracy of the novels of Richardson (the *English Marivaux*).
- See the *Christian Atticus*.

IRISH-BORN JOHN John Erigena, Eriugena or Scotus (*circa* 815–877), a medieval scholar and philosopher, a teacher at the Court of King Charles the Bald, Holy Roman emperor (823–77), John was a pioneer of Scholastic philosophy. Also *John the Scot*, the *Last of the Platonists* and *Scotus the Wise*.
- See the *Chief of the English Protestant Schoolmen*.

IRISH CRICHTON, THE John Henderson (1757–88), an eccentric student, poet and essayist.
- See the *Admirable Crichton*.

IRISH DE STAËL, THE Lady Sidney Morgan, *Glorvina*.
- Anne Louise Germaine de Staël (1766–1817) wrote two romances centred on her love for Benjamin Constant (1767–1830), philosopher and politician.

IRISH FAIRY, THE Mrs Catherine Kelly (1756–85) who stood 34 in tall and weighed 22 lb.

IRISH GIANT, THE
i) Patrick Cotter O'Brien (1760–1806). 8ft. 6 in. tall. His skeleton is in the Royal College of Surgeons, London. He was born at Kinsale, County Cork.
ii) Ned O'Baldwin (1840–75), Irish-born American boxer 6ft 5 in tall.

IRISH JOHNSON, THE John Henry Johnson (died 1826), impersonator of Irish characters; so called in *Noctes Ambrosianae*.

IRISH PLATO, THE Dr George Berkeley (1685–1753), Bishop of Cloyne, philosopher who used the platonic method of presentation, e.g. in *Alciphron* (1732).

IRISH ROSCIUS, THE Spranger Barry (1719–77), actor who challenged the popularity of Garrick (*Atlas*). Also the *Silver-Tongued*.

- See the *African Roscius*.

IRISH SMOLLETT, THE Charles James Lever (1806–72), novelist of military life and Irish hunting society, e.g. *Charley O'Malley* (1840).

- Smollett, see *Smellfungus*.

IRISH TARTAR, THE Tom Johnson, trick rider who opened the first circus in England at Islington, London (1758).

IRISH TOMMY or TOM Thomas J. Ranahan (fl. 1860s), pioneer stagecoach driver of the American West. He drove his coach over the South Pass, near Fort Laramie, Wyoming.

IRKSOME DIRKSON Senator Everett Dirkson (1896–1969); so called for his tactics. Also the *Wizard of Ooze*.

IRON BUTT General Custer, *Autie*; so called by his men because of his strictness.

IRON BUTTERFLY, THE Jeanette MacDonald (1907–1965) American concert singer who turned to film musical comedy and operettas, frequent partner of the *Singing Capon*.

IRON DUKE, THE The Duke of Wellington, the *Achilles of England*. In one of his despatches (1789), he wrote 'We now have that iron frontier' which may have influenced the thought.

IRON GLOVES Rodney Marsh (1947–), Australian wicket-keeper; retired in 1984.

IRON HORSE Lou Gehrig, *Biscuit Pants*, for his 2,120 consecutive games.

IRON KING OF WALES, THE Robert Thomas Crawshay (1817–1879), head of Merthyr Tidfil iron works.

IRON LADY, THE Margaret Thatcher, *Attila the Hen*; so called first by the newspaper *Red Star*, because of her adamant stand against Communism; sometimes turned into 'The Iron Mädchen'.

IRON MAGNOLIA, THE Eleanor Rosalynn Carter (1927–), born in Georgia, wife of President Jimmy Carter (the *Peanut Politician*), a determined and forceful personality in the White House, as well as a profound influence on his campaigning.

IRON MAN, THE
i) Joseph McGinnity, American baseball player in the Hall of Fame (1899–1908).

- 'Iron Man' is a baseball term for a man who pitches every innings of both games in a double-header and is the winning pitcher of each.

ii) Edward (Ted) Drake (1912–), centre-forward for England and Arsenal (for whom he scored 136 goals); now a manager. Also *Never Say Die Drake*.

iii) Graham Roberts (1960–), footballer for England and Tottenham Hotspur.

iv) John (Johnny) Seagrave (1932–), top British jockey on whom falls seem to have little effect.

IRON MAN OF SOCCER, THE Thomas (Tommy) Smith (1946–), full-back for Liverpool FC.

IRON MIKE Michael (Mike) Tyson (1966–), American WBC world heavyweight boxing champion (1986–90), the youngest ever. Fifteen of his twenty-seven fights (pre November 1986) did not go beyond the first round. By 1987 he had twenty-seven knock-outs out of thirty fights. Also *Typhoon*.

IRONSIDE or IRONSIDES
i) Edmund or Eadmund II (980–1016), King of England, son of Ethelred the *Unready*; a strong man who always wore a complete suit of armour. Camden (the *British Pausanias*) says the nickname was for his valour. Edmund was king for only seven months after his father's death.

ii) Oliver Cromwell, the *Almighty Nose*. The nickname was first given to him by Prince Rupert (the *Mad Cavalier*) because of his iron breastplate, and was later transferred to his soldiers.

IRREFUTABLE DOCTOR, THE Alexander of Hales, *Doctor Irrefragabilis*.

IT J.B. Gillespie, *Dizzy*.

ITALIAN NIGHTINGALE, THE Angelica Catalini (1780–1849), Italian soprano opera singer who first appeared in England in 1806.

ITALIAN SMITH John Smith (1749–1831), British water-colour painter who went with his patron, the Earl of Warwick, to Italy (*circa* 1783). Also *Warwick Smith*.

ITALIAN STALLION, THE Sylvester Stallone (1946–), Italian–born American film star and writer; so called in America after the film *Rocky*. He is known to his friends as 'Sly'.

IT GIRL, THE Clara Bow (1905–1965) American film star and sex symbol. 'It' later became 'sex appeal'. She played the lead in the film *It* (1927); so called by Elinor Glyn (1864–1943), who wrote *It and Other Stories*, when she saw her on a Paramount film set.

IVAN THE TERRIBLE Ivan Lendl (1960–), Czech-born champion tennis player living in America. He reached the Wimbledon singles final (1986). He rarely smiles on court.

- Ivan IV (1530–84), Grand Duke of Moscow who took the title of Tsar of Russia (1547) was nicknamed 'The Terrible' for his ruthless cruelty. He killed his own son, the Tsarevich, in 1581.

J

JABBO Cladys Smith (1908–), American jazz musician who once competed with Louis Armstrong (*Dippermouth*) as top jazz player.

JACK

i) Harvey Leader (1894–1972), English racehorse trainer and former jockey.

ii) Dr Harry Schmitt (1935–), 12th man on the moon (from Apollo XVII). He stayed there for more than 72 hours (1972).

iii) Joseph Alfred Slade (1824–1864), American stagecoach superintendent and gun-fighter; hanged by vigilantes for murder in Virginia City. Also *Killer*.

iv) Weldon Teagarden (1905–64), American trombonist who played with Louis Armstrong (*Dippermouth*).

v) Sir Trevor Gould (1906–), Justice of the Fiji Court of Appeal (post 1965).

JACK AMEND-ALL Jack Mortimer, *Jack Cade*, who promised by his revolt to remedy all abuses.

JACKANAPES See *Jack Napes*.

JACK BOOT

i) John Stuart, 3rd Earl of Bute (1713–92), English P.M. (1762–3) who was so much disliked that angry mobs burnt jack-boots in the streets; a pun on his title. One boot was seized from a mob by Thomas Harley, Lord Mayor of London (1768). Also *Sawney the Scot* and the *Wire Master*.

ii) Henry Compton (1632–1713), Bishop of London (post 1675). He had been a foot soldier in Flanders, and became a cornet in the Royal Horse Guards.

JACK BRAG or SIR JACK BRAG Sir John Burgoyne, *Gentleman Johnny*. He was the subject of a street ballad called *Jack Brag*. Walpole (the *Autocrat of Strawberry Hill*) referred to him as 'General Swagger'.

- 'Jack Brag' is given in John Withal's dictionary (1602) as 'a vaunter, a cracker', i.e. a boaster.

JACKER Colonel the Honourable Francis Stanley Jackson (1870-1947) who played cricket for Harrow, Cambridge, Yorkshire and England. In 1898 he scored 1,566 runs and took 104 wickets. He was later Governor of Bengal (1927).

- See the *Tagger Ragger of St Pagger Le Bagger*.

JACK KETCH, KITCH or CATCH ??Richard Jacquett (fl. 1603-86), a hangman at Tyburn, London, an executioner of such barbarity that his nickname became a byword and was applied to all later hangmen. He owned Tyburn Manor in which the gallows stood and began his work in 1663. He executed Monmouth (*Absalom*) with several blows.

- Cf the *Two Gregories*.

JACK FOR KING Sir John Arundell (1576-?1656) of Trerice, royalist soldier, M.P. and Sheriff for Cornwall, a grandson of *Jack of Tilbury*.

JACK NAPES or JACKNAPES The Duke of Suffolk, *Apeclogge*. The first spelling of it was Iac Napes. In a poem of 1450, there is a line: 'Jack Napys with his clogge Hath tiede Talbot, oure gentille dogge...'

- See *Talbot, our Good Dog*. A clog was a log attached to a prisoner's foot or leg. Talbot's successes in France were thought to have been nullified by Suffolk's treason.

JACKO Anthony (Tony) Jacklin (1944-), British professional golfer; British Open champion (1969); US Open champion (1970). He retired as England's captain in 1989 after his team had held the Ryder Cup for three years.

JACK OF CLUBS, THE Philip Henry Sheridan (1831-86), Union cavalry general of the American Civil War, noted for 'Sheridan's Ride'. While he was in conference at his headquarters his troops were engaged in battle. He made a mad dash to turn defeat into victory. Also *Little Phil*.

JACK OF NEWBURY John Winchcombe, alias Smalwoode or Smallwood (died 1520), a wealthy clothier who equipped 100-200 men at his own expense to help Henry VIII (*Bluff Hal*) against the Scots at Flodden (1513).

JACK OF NORFOLK Sir John Howard (*circa* 1420-85), the first Howard to become Duke of Norfolk (1483); killed at Bosworth, where he led the archers. He figures in Shakespeare's *Richard III* in which his other nickname the *Jockey of Norfolk* is mentioned (Act v, Scene iii).

JACK OF SPADES, THE General J. A. Logan, *Black Jack*; so called by his troops in the American Civil War.

JACK OF TILBURY Vice-Admiral Sir John Arundell (1495-1561) of Trerice, Sheriff of Cornwall. He died attempting with a force to wrest St Michael's Mount from the *Great Earl of Oxford*.

JACK SPOT Jack Comer (1909-), London crook and black marketeer who vanished for a long period after being slashed in Soho (1955) in a feud with other gang chiefs. He was left for dead and needed 300 stitches. Also the *King of Aldgate*.

JACK THE DRIPPER
   i) Sir John Dalzell Rankine (1907–), Governor of the west region of Nigeria (1954-60). Also *Jolly Jack.*
   ii) Jackson Pollock (1912-56) American abstract painter; so called by *Time* magazine. He dripped paint over a large canvas.

JACK THE RIPPER An unknown person who committed a series of murders in Whitechapel, London (August–November 1888). Self-applied in a letter to the police, In another he called himself 'Saucy Jacky'. One school of thought believes he was George Chapman, executed (April 1903) for the murder of Maud Marsh. He lived in Whitechapel at the time.
   • Cf the *Yorkshire Ripper* and the *Ypsilanti Ripper*: see *Genial George*.

JACKY Admiral of the Fleet John, 1st Baron Fisher (1841-1920), First Sea Lord (1904-10). His flagship as Commander-in-Chief, Mediterranean, HMS *Renown*, was called 'Jacky's yacht'.

JACKY-JACKY William Westwood, the *Gentleman Bushranger*.

JACOBITE ROBBER, THE *Captain* James Whitney.

JACOB OMNIUM Matthew James Higgins (1810-88), British journalist: the pseudonym he used for his first article, which became a nickname.

JAFSIE Dr John F. Condon, intermediary in the Lindbergh kidnapping (see *Buster* xi) 1932-34; from J.F.C. He was seventy-two, a retired Brooklyn schoolmaster.

JAGUAR JON Jon D. Arnett (1934-), American footballer, because of his speed.

JAI Lieutenant-General Sawai Man Singh, Maharajah of Jaipur (1912-70).

JAKE John K. Lever (1949-), Essex, Natal and England bowler; from J.K.

JAMAICA JOHN John Campbell of Knockbury (died 1838), born in Jamaica.
   • See *Old Knockbury*.

JAMES THE LAME James Butler, Viscount Thurles (died 1546).

JAMES THE WHITE James Butler, 12th Earl and 1st Duke of Ormonde (1610-80), Irish soldier and statesman with long fair hair.

JANUS-FACED CRITIC, THE John Hill, the *Cain of Literature*.
   • Janus, a Roman god, had two faces, one looking forward and one backward.

JAPANESE BOWES James Lord Bowes (1834-99), Liverpool wool-broker, an expert on Japanese culture. He kept a museum of Japanese art in London and published works on the subject; so called in Europe, America and Japan.

JARRIN' JAWN John Kimbrough, American footballer for Texas (1938-40), All-American (1940s); from the Southern pronunciation of 'Jarring John'.

JAUNTING CARR Sir John Carr (1772-1832), British barrister, traveller and author; a pun on the Irish jaunting-car, a light two-wheeled vehicle to carry four, two back-to-back. He published books on France, Holland and Spain.

JAWS

i) Prince Edward Anthony Richard Louis (1964-), son of Queen Elizabeth II; so called at Gordonstoun School when he had a brace on his teeth.

ii) Joseph (Joe) Jordan (1961-), centre-forward for Southampton F.C. In 1988 he became player-manager for Bristol City; so called after his teeth had been damaged in a match against Coventry.

- 'Jaws' = titles of films about man-eating sharks (1975 on)

JAZZ WONDER CHILD, THE Lil Armstrong (1903–), American singer.

JEB James Ewell Brown Stuart (1833-1864), Confederate General and cavalry leader in the American Civil War. He was mortally wounded in the Wilderness campaign; so called from his initials.

JEDGE, THE Heneage Finch, 7th Earl of Aylesford (1849-85) who owned 40,000 acres of cattle country in Wyoming (1870s). His American nickname. Also **Sporting Joe**.

JEFFREYS OF SCOTLAND, THE Robert Macqueen, Lord Braxfield, the **Hanging Judge**. The Lord Chief Justice Lord Cockburn (1802-80) said 'his very name makes people start'. Macqueen earned his nickname during the political trials of 1794. He sentenced an Edinburgh lawyer to fourteen years transportation to Botany Bay because he had advocated Parliamentary reform and the widening of the franchise.

- For Judge Jeffreys, see the **Western Hangman**.

JEHU Sir John Lade (1759-1838), a rich landowner and one of the best whips in England, professionals included. He married the adventuress Laetitia Smith, once mistress of **Sixteen-String** Jack Rann. Lade was a rake and a colourful sporting character. Lord Thurlow (**Tiger**) once said of him that his proper place was on the coach-box of the Prince of Wales (**Adonis of Fifty**) and not at his dinner-table.

- Jehu was king of Israel, described in Kings (ix. v 20) as a man who 'driveth

furiously'; and so was used for coachman or gentlemen drivers.

JEKKER, THE Miss Henrietta Jex-Blake (1863-1953), Principal of Lady Margaret Hall, Oxford University for forty years (post 1909).

- See the **Tagger Ragger of St Pagger Le Bagger**.

JELLY Frank Nash (1892-1933), American friend and associate of **Pretty Boy** Floyd; from the knowledge he possessed of explosives. Nash was shot in the Kansas City massacre.

- Jelly = gelignite.

JELLY ROLL MORTON Ferdinand LaMenthe (1885-1941), American jazz pianist. He wrote **Jelly Roll Blues**. Also **Mr Jelly Roll**.

- 'Jam Roll' is the English equivalent of 'jelly roll'.

JEMMY TWITCHER John Montagu, 4th Earl of Sandwich (1718-92) who in the House of Lords attacked Wilkes (**Squinting Jack**) for obscene libel, although they had both been members of the Hell-Fire Club at Medmenham Abbey, notorious for its excesses.

- See **Hell-Fire Francis** and **Malagrida the Jesuit**. Jemmy Twitcher is a character in John Gay's **The Beggar's Opera** who betrays his friend: 'That Jemmy Twitcher should 'peach me, I own surprised me'.

JENKY Charles Jenkinson, 1st Earl of Liverpool (1729-1808), Secretary at War (1782-6). His eyelids twitched and fluttered like those of his son **Blinkinson**.

JENNY or THE SPINNING JENNY Sir Robert Peel (1788-1850), British Prime Minister (1834, 1841-5 and 1845-6). He was the son of a small farmer who made a fortune out of the cotton industry (see **Parsley Peel**); and the nickname carries the implication of changing political opinions. Also **Judas**, the **Leonidas of His Day, Moral Surface, Orange Peel,** the **Runaway Spartan** and the **Spinning Spoon**.

JENSON OF HIS DAY, THE John Baskerville (1706–75), British printer and typefounder; so called by Dibdin (the **Beau**

Brummell of Living Authors).

- Nicolas Jenson, a Frenchman, perfected the Roman type (1470) in Venice, where he printed from 1470 to 1480.

JENSON OF THE NORTH, THE James Ballantyne (1772–1833), Scottish printer and publisher; so called by Dibdin.

JERRY Flight-Lieutenant P.E.G. Sayer (killed 1942) who made the first jet flight in the UK (1941).

JERRY THE OLD SCREW Jeremy Bentham, the *Father of Utilitarianism*; so called in *Noctes Ambrosianae*.

- A 'screw' has been slang for a prison warder since the beginning of the 19th century, but it could also mean a stingy, miserly person.

JERSEY Harry Flegg (1878–1960), pioneer of Australian Rugby League football; president of the New South Wales League for thirty-two years, and champion of the Australian Rugby League.

JERSEY JOE
i) Joe Walcott (1914–), American who won the world's heavyweight boxing title (1951). His real name is Arnold Raymond Cream. At thirty-eight, he was the oldest man ever to win the championship. He was born in New Jersey.

- Cf the *Barber's Demon*.

ii) Joseph (Joe) Morris (1961–), American footballer for the New York Giants.

JERSEY LILY, THE *Lillie* Langtry (1852–1929), actress and friend of the Prince of Wales (the *Peacemaker*): because of her beauty and the fact that she was the daughter of William Corbet Le Breton, Dean of Jersey (the *Dirty Dean*) (as Emilie Charlotte Le Breton). She also posed as the model for the painting *The Jersey Lily* by Sir John Millais (1829–96). Also *Mr Jersey*.

JERUSALEM WHALLEY Thomas Whalley (fl. end of 18th century), a rich Irish gentleman who received the nickname from having won a bet by making a journey to Jerusalem on foot (except for a

time spent on sea passages). He wore on the trip a long blue coat, top-boots and buckskin breeches.

JESSAMY BRIDE, THE Mary Horneck (1753–1840), with whom Goldsmith (the *Child of Nature*) fell in love; so called by Goldsmith. Boswell (the *Ambitious Thane*) said she was a 'very pretty girl'. Her father was Captain Kane Horneck.

- 'Jessamy' was a name for a jasmine perfume, and also for a dandy. See *Little Comedy*.

JESUIT, THE William Penn (1644–1718), Quaker who preached in favour of James II and his Declaration of Indulgence (1687–8). Penn was the founder of Pennsylvania.

- The Declaration of Indulgence gave religious freedom to Roman Catholics and Dissenters.

JESUIT OF BERKELEY SQUARE, THE William Petty Fitzmaurice, 2nd Earl of Shelburne (1737–1805) British Prime Minister (1782–3), a statesman who was not trusted as he was thought to be 'jesuitical' in his arguments. One writer (Frank O'Gorman) said: 'an aura of secrecy and sinister mystery surrounded Shelburne'. He lived in Berkeley Square, London. Also *Malagrida the Jesuit*.

JEUNE CUPIDON, LE Count Alfred Guillaume Gabriel D'Orsay (1801–1852), son of *Beau* D'Orsay. He was a famous dandy with considerable accomplishments, and was a friend and correspondent of Byron (*Baby*) who gave him the nickname. D'Orsay married Lady Harriet Gardiner (1827), a daughter of Lady Blessington. Also the *Last of the Dandies and the* and the *Prince of Dandies*.

- *Cupidon* = French for 'cupid', was used in England for a beau or Adonis.

JEWEL OF BISHOPS, THE John Jewel (1522–71), Bishop of Salisbury, a puritanical cleric who fled to Germany at the time of *Bloody Mary*, but returned after her death. He made the first reasoned statement of the position of the Church of England vis-à-vis the Roman Catholic Church in his *Apologia ecclesiae Anglicanae* (1562).

JIM E.W. Swanton, *Gloria*.

JIMBO James (Jimmy) Connors (1952–), American tennis star; Wimbledon singles champion (1974 and 1982).

JIM CROW or JIM CROW RICE Thomas D. Rice, the *Father of American Minstrelsy*. The nickname, from a song he sang, became a 'generic' term for a negro.

- Rice is reputed to have heard a negro singing *Jump Jim Crow* and concocted a song from that whose success was so enormous that there were Jim Crow needles and pins and rum and gin everywhere. The original Jim Crow was said to have been a runaway Indian slave (a Crow?: died 1809) who became a street entertainer. His rendering of this song included amazing physical gyrations.

JIMMY Sir John Neall (1890–1975), scholar of the Elizabethan period; because he was always so happy; from *Sunny Jim*.

JIMMY THE WEASEL (or THE WEASEL): Aladino Fratiannio (1913–), American Mafia 'hit man', and head of the Mafia in Los Angeles. Also 'The Squealer' after he talked to the FBI (1980). He confessed to 11 contract killings.

JINGLE Franklin Engelmann (1900–72), BBC announcer and radio personality; a joke pronunciation of 'Engel'.

JINGO Lord Beaconsfield, the *Asian Mystery* seen as the representation of British imperialism.

- 'By Jingo' was an expression (17th century) used later in a music hall song written by G. W. Hunt (*circa* 1829–1904), which became a nickname for Beaconsfield and those who supported his readiness to fight Russia (1878) after the outbreak of war between Russia and Turkey (1877). See *Lion Comique* (iii).

JIX Sir William Joynson-Hicks, 1st Baron Brentford (1865–1932), Home Secretary (1926–30).

JOAN COLLINS OF THE TRACK, THE Florence Griffith-Joyner, the *Fastest Woman on Earth*, glamorous US sprinter.

- For Joan Collins, see the *Queen of the Soaps*.

JOAN MAKEPEACE Joan, Queen of Scotland (*circa* 1321-62). Her marriage as a child to David II (1324–71) was among the conditions of the treaty between Scotland and the English at Northampton (1328). She was the sister of Edward III (the *Father of British Commerce*) and was born in the Tower of London. Also *Joan of the Tower*.

JOAN OF KENT Joan Bocher, Boucher or Butcher of Canterbury (died 1550), an Anabaptist martyr, burned for heresy.

- Anabaptists insisted on adult baptism and the extremists in the sect coupled the idea with social reorganization.

JOAN OF THE TOWER See above.

JOAN THE MOUTH Joan Rivers (1933–), sardonic, acid-tongued American comedienne.

JOCK

i) Professor A. J. Marshall (1911–67), Australian conservationist and zoologist.

ii) Earl Malcolm Carruthers (1910–), American jazz saxophonist and singer.

iii) Sir Henry Delves Broughton (1884-1942), sportsman, acquitted of the murder of Lord Erroll (the *Passionate Peer*) in Kenya (1941). He committed suicide in a Liverpool hotel a year later.

iv) Sir John Macpherson (1898–1971), Permanent Under-Secretary for the Colonies (1956–9) and former Governor of Nigeria (1948).

JOCKEY, THE The 11th Duke of Norfolk, the *Dirty Duke*; a pun on 'riding' as he was Lord-Lieutenant of the West Riding of Yorks.

JOCKEY OR NORFOLK, THE Sir John Howard, *Jack of Norfolk*.

- 'Jockey' is a diminutive of 'Jack' or 'Jock'.

JOCK PRESBYTER Sir William Jones, *Bull-Faced Jonas*.

JOCULAR SAMSON, THE George Canning, *Aeolus*, a wit who became a notable Foreign-Secretary (1807–12 and 1822–7); so called by Sydney Smith (the *Diner-Out of the First Water*).

JOCUND JOHNNY John Ballantyne, the *Dey of Algiers*; so called by Scott (the *Ariosto* *of the North*) whose books he published.

JOE

ii) Giuseppe Venuti (1904–78), American jazz violinist.

ii) Mohammed Yusuf Daar, Britain's first full-time coloured policeman sworn in at Coventry (1966). 'Yusuf' is the Arabic equivalent of Joseph.

JOE ADONIS Joseph Doto (1902–72), a specialist in political and labour rackets in the American Crime Syndicate; self-applied. Also *Joey A*.

JOE BANANAS Joseph Bonnano (1905–), New York Mafia chief and a powerful figure in American crime. He published his autobiography in 1983.

JOE BATTERS Anthony Joseph Accardo (1906–), Chicago gangster. He was clever in assaults with a baseball bat. Also *Tough Tony*.

JOE THE BOSS Joseph Masseria (shot 1931), top Mafia man in New York and leader of the gang of which *Lucky* Luciano was a member.

JOEY G.E. Palmer, the *Demon*.

JOEY A Joseph Doto, *Joe Adonis*.

JOHN BASS John Spreull (1657–1722), Scottish Presbyterian imprisoned on the Bass Rock for nonconformity.

JOHN-BOY Richard Thomas (1951–), American film star and TV actor; name of his part in the long-running TV series *The Waltons* (1970s–1980s).

JOHN BULL FIGHTER, THE Joshua (Josh) Hudson (1797–1835), pugilist whose greatest fight was when he was beaten by Jem Ward, later British champion. Hudson was a man of courage.

JOHN FINALITY Lord John Russell, *Finality John*.

JOHNNY

i) General Sir Ian Standish Monteith Hamilton (1853–1947), commanding the Mediterranean Expeditionary Force, Gallipoli (World War I).

ii) Air-Vice-Marshal James Edgar Johnson, Battle of Britain ace who brought down 38 enemy planes (World War II). He won two bars to his DSO and one to his DFC.

iii) Amy Johnson (1903–41), the first woman to fly solo from Britain to Australia (1930). She was lost while serving as a ferry pilot in World War II. Also the *Queen of the Skies*.

iv) Group-Captain Adolphus Gysbert Malan (1910–63), 3rd highest-scoring RAF ace in the Battle of Britain (1940) with 35 enemy planes to his credit. Also *Sailor*.

JOHNNY ALLGOOD John Goodall (1863–1942), English international footballer who also played for Preston FC.

JOHNNY APPLESEED John Chapman (1774–1847). He roamed 100,000 miles around America, planting apple trees.

JOHNNY BLOOD John McNally (fl. 1930s), American footballer, half-back for the Green Bay Packers in the National Football League.

JOHNNY WON'T HIT TODAY John William Henry Tyler Douglas (1882–1930), slow-scoring English batman; his nickname in Australia, from his initials. He was a good all-rounder and a noted amateur boxer. He was drowned in the SS *Oberoon*.

JOHN O'CATARACT John Neal (1793–1896), American novelist; first a nickname (because of his impetuosity) and then a pseudonym.

JOHN O'GROATS Jan de Groot, a Dutchman who worked the Orkney ferry (15th century). He settled on the extreme tip of Caithness, Scotland, in the reign of James IV (the *Star of the Stuart Line*).

JOHNSON'S ZANY James Boswell, the *Ambitious Thane*, friend of Dr Johnson (*Blinking Sam*); so called by Horace Walpole (the *Autocrat of Strawberry Hill*).

• A zany was a clown who imitated his master's acts. Walpole used it in the sense of a hanger-on.

JOHN THE CHIEF John Ormond (fl. late 18th-early 19th century), son of a Liverpool trader and a chief's daughter in the Rio Pongas area of West Africa. He set up as a slave trader and became very wealthy. Also *Mungo* or *Mongo John* and the *Mulatto Trader*.

JOHN THE PAINTER James Hill or Aitken (1752–77), British arsonist who is said to have been paid by Silas Deane (1737–89), American agent to destroy British dockyards and shipping. He was hanged at Portsmouth.

JOHN THE SCOT or JOHANNES SCOTUS ERIGENA John Erigena, *Irish Born John*.
- In earlier times, a 'Scot' meant an Irishman.

JOHN WITH THE LEADEN SWORD John of Lancaster, Duke of Bedford, the *Firebrand of France*. In 1417 he marched against the Scots, and it was a Scot, the Earl of Douglas, (the *Tineman*) who gave him the nickname.

JOKER, THE William (Willie) Carson (1942-), British champion jockey (1972–3). On Nashwan he won his third Derby (1989).

JOLLY JACK Sir John Rankine, *Jack the Dripper*.

JOLLY JIM James Prior (1927–), Secretary of State for Employment (1979–81) and Secretary of State for Northern Ireland (1981–4), later chairman of GEC. He was created a peer in 1987 (Baron Prior of Brampton). Also *Peaches Prior*.

JOLLY JOHN or JOLLY John Nash (1828–1901), British music-hall comedian who once appeared before Edward VII (the *Peacemaker*).

JOLLY SOOPER Jilly Cooper (1937–), British author and star writer for *The Sunday Times*. 'Jilly' is short for Gillian.

JOLTIN' JOE Joseph (Joe) Paul Di Maggio (1914–), one of the greatest baseball stars in the Hall of Fame (1936–51); because of his batting skill. Also the *Yankee Clipper*.

JONAH A.O. Jones (1872–1914), Cambridge and Nottinghamshire cricketer.

JONAH OF THE WAGER, THE Vice-Admiral the Honourable John Byron, *Foul-Weather Jack*. He was a midshipman on HMS *Wager*, which should have gone with Admiral Lord Anson (the *Bulldog of All Circumnavigators*) round the world (1740–4), but was wrecked on the coast of Tierra del Fuego (1741).
- Jonah, son of Ammittai, was on his

way to Ninevah via Tarshish, when a storm blew up. The sailors chose him by lot to be thrown overboard as the cause of all their troubles. He was swallowed by 'a great fish' (Jonah i 4-17).

JONJO John O'Neill (1952–), British jockey who rode 149 winners in one season (1977–8). He retired in 1986.

JOPLIN GHOST, THE Horton Smith (1908–63), American golfer in the Hall of Fame (1958). He was rated American top golfer in 1936.
- Joplin is a city in south-west Missouri.

JOSEPH SURFACE Edward Augustus, Duke of Kent, the *Corporal*; nicknamed by his sisters.
- Joseph Surface is a young hypocrite in Sheridan's (*Sherry*) *School for Scandal* (1777).

JOSEPH THE JEW Aymer de Valence, 6th Earl of Pembroke (*circa* 1265–1324); so called by Piers Gaveston, Earl of Cornwall, because he was tall, thin and pale. As a result, Pembroke did not attempt to stop the Earl of Warwick (the *Black Cur of Avon*) from kidnapping Gaveston while Pembroke held him prisoner.

JOSIAH OF ENGLAND, THE Edward VI (1537–53). Despite his age, he saw the need to remedy the defects in the administration of Britain. Also the *Pious* and the *Saint*.
- Josiah, King of Judah, eradicated the profligacy and idolatry he found when he came to the throne at the age of eight (2 Chron xxxiv 3).

JOVE OF JOLLY FELLOWS, THE John van Buren (1810–66), American lawyer, Attorney-General for New York and son of Martin van Buren (*King Martin the First*). Also the *Jupiter Tonans of His Party* and *Prince John*.
- Jove was another name for Jupiter, the supreme god of the Romans.

JOVE OF THE MODERN CRITICAL OLYMPUS Leigh Hunt, *Bacchus*. He wrote many volumes of criticism, and went to prison for his criticism of the Prince Regent (*Adonis of Fifty*).

JOVE'S POET Samuel Lover (1797–1868), British song-writer, novelist and poet, e.g. *Handy Andy* (1842) and *Songs and Ballads* (1839).

JOVIAL TOPER, THE Walter Map or Mapes, the *Anacreon of the 12th century* who wrote a famous drinking song (*Meum est propositum*).

JOWLER, THE Benjamin Jowett, (1817–93), Master of Balliol college, Oxford, an industrious worker for university reform and a great moral teacher ('the first rule in life is never explain').

● See the *Tagger Ragger of St Pagger Le Bagger*.

J.R. Larry Hagman (1931–   ), American actor, because he played the villain (J.R. Ewing) in the successful TV serial *Dallas* (1970s–1980s). He is the son of stage and screen star Mary Martin (1913–   ).

JUBILEE DICKY Henry Norris, *Dicky Scrub*; from his performance in *The Constant Couple* (1700) which had the subtitle 'A Trip to the Jubilee'.

JUBILEE JIM James Fisk, *Big Jim*.

JUBILEE JUGGINS, THE A Mr Juggins who is reputed to have thrown away an entire fortune in racecourse betting in the 1880s. (See below for an alternative explanation).

● A 'Juggins' is slang for a simpleton.

JUBILEE PLUNGER, THE Ernest Benzon, a wealthy young man who squandered a fortune on reckless gambling on racecourses in two years, the first of them being the Jubilee year (1887) of Queen Victoria (*Drina*). He wrote a book entitled *How I Lost £250,000 in Two Years*.

JUDAS

i) Sir Robert Peel, *Jenny*. He betrayed the Tories by the repeal of the Corn Laws, over which he had his first big clash with Disraeli (the *Asian Mystery*); so called in *Noctes Ambrosianae*.

ii) Dr Andrew Perne, *Andrew Ambo*.

JUDAS OF THE WEST, THE Henry Clay, the *Apostle of Liberty*. Clay had been a candidate for the Presidency with Andrew Jackson (*Hickory*), John Quincy Adams (*Old Man Eloquent*) and W. H. Crawford.

He appeared to oppose Adams and favour Jackson. When Adams was elected (1825), Clay accepted a post as secretary of State. Jackson became a bitter enemy, accused Clay of corruption, and gave him this nickname.

JUDGE, THE George D. Hay (died 1968), who helped to make the Grand Ole Opry in Nashville, Tennessee famous. As an announcer on WSM radio station he called himself 'the Solemn Old Judge' when he originated the National Barn Dance competition.

JUDGE GRIPUS. Philip Yorke, 1st Earl Hardwicke (1690–1764), Lord Chancellor (1737); because of his greed.

● 'Gripulous' is an obsolete word for 'avaricious' (from 'gripple = grapple = grasping).

JUDICIOUS BOTTLE-HOLDER, THE Lord Palmerston, *Cupid*. A bottle-holder in a prize-fight was a man who gave comfort and advice to a fighter, and Palmerston considered himself the bottle-holder of oppressed European states. *Punch* printed (1851) a cartoon of Palmerston as 'the Judicious Bottle-Holder', holding a sponge labelled 'Protocol'.

JUDICIOUS HOOKER Richard Hooker (*circa* 1553-1600), theologian; because of the wisdom of his judgements. The adjective is inscribed on his monument at Bishopsbourne, Kent. He wrote *Of the Laws of Ecclestical Politie* (1594–1648: 8 vols) which contains discussion of the origin and nature of law in general and Church law in particular, demonstrating a liberal point of view.

JUG Harold Spaden (1908–), American golfer; Canadian Open champion (1939).

JUICE, THE Orenthal James (usually O. J.) Simpson (1931–   ), American footballer for the Buffalo Bills and something of a national hero. He was voted America's best college player (1968) and was the first runner in professional football to rush 2,000 yards in a season; he was so called because he squeezed out of tight places.

JUMBO

i) Field-Marshal Maitland, 1st Baron Wilson (1881–1964),

Commander-in-Chief of the 9th Army (World War II). He was a very large man.

ii) 2nd-Lieutenant (later Captain) Alfred Oliver Pollard (died 1960) of the Hon.Artillery Company, who won the VC, MC and bar and DCM (World War II); also a big man.

iii) James Elliott (1914–81), American athletic coach who led the Wildcats to eight national collegiate championships and trained five Olympic gold medallists.

iv)Floyd Cummings (1953–), American heavyweight boxer; because of his size.

- Jumbo was the name of a very large African elephant which gave rides to children in the London Zoo, sold in 1882 to Barnum (the *Prince of Humbugs*). 'Jumbo' is Swahili for 'chief'.

JUMPING JACK FLASH Paul McNamee (1954–), Wimbledon-class tennis player; so called in Australia where he is No. 1.

- A jumping jack is the figure of a man made to jump by pulling strings. It was formerly made out of a wishbone. 'To cut a flash' is Australian slang for making a show, from the English slang 'flash', to make a show to attract a crowd.

JUMPING JOE.

i) Joseph Lorrison (died 1792), English highway robber who was clever at jumping in and out of moving carts and wagons to steal whatever packages he could lay his hands on.

ii) Joseph Anthony Dugan (1897–), American baseball player. He changed clubs many times.

JUMPING SOLDIER, THE John Francis (fl. 1740s), British pugilist.

JUNE *Big Bill* Tilden: short for 'junior'. He had the same name as his father and 'junior' was added. Tilden, tired of 'June', called himself 'the Second' instead.

JUNGLE JIM James Loscutoft (1930–), American basketball player for Boston Celtics.

JUNIOR John McEnroe, the *Brat*.

JUPITER CARLYLE The Reverend Alexander Carlyle (1722–1805), Scottish minister at Inveresk. His head, it was said,

could have served as a model for that of Jupiter Tonans. Scott (the *Ariosto of the North*) described him as 'the greatest demigod I ever saw'.

- Jupiter Tonans was the title of the Romans' supreme god as the deity of thunder, lightning and storm.

JUPITER PLACENS Lord Brougham and Vaux, *Blundering Brougham*; 'the Pleasant Jupiter' as a contrast to the 'Thundering Jupiter'. Brougham was a powerful orator.

JUPITER TONANS Thomas, 1st Baron Erskine (1750–1823), Lord Chancellor, a man of impassioned eloquence and skilful argument, considered the greatest advocate the English Bar has ever seen. He was Attorney-General before he became Lord Chancellor.

- See above at *Jupiter Carlyle*.

JUPITER TONANS OF HIS PARTY, THE John van Buren, the *Jove of Jolly Fellows*.

JUVENAL OF ENGLISH DRAMA, THE Ben Jonson, the *Bricklayer*; so called by D'Israeli.

- See the *British Juvenal*.

JUVENAL OF PAINTERS, THE William Hogarth (1697–1764) British painter and engraver. Also *Painter Pug* and the *Pensioned Dauber*.

JUVENILE LEAD, THE Robert Anthony Eden, 1st Earl of Avon (1897–1977), British Foreign Secretary (1935–8 and 1940–5) and Prime Minister (1955–7); so called by Aneurin Bevan (*Nye*). Eden was handsome and debonair.

K

KAFFIR KING, THE Barnett (Barney) Isaacs Barnato (1852–97) who made a fortune in the diamond mines of Kimberley and Johannesburg, South Africa in speculation in stocks called 'The Kaffir Circus'.

KAISER BILL W.H. Thompson, *Big Bill*.

KAISER WILLIAM Ambrose Everett Burnside (1824–81), *Rhody*, American general and senator of Rhode Island. He was an incompetent who managed to turn victory into defeat.
- 'Kaiser' was the title of the German emperor (post-1871). Kaiser William (1797–1888) lost almost every 'battle' with Bismarck (1875–98).

KAMIKAZE KID, THE G. M. Wood (1956–), Western Australia and Australia batsman.
- Kamikaze (= god wind in Japanese) was a name given to suicide Japanese pilots (World War II) who crashed bomb-laden planes on to vessels such as aircraft carriers.

KAMPALA BUTCHER, THE Idi Amin Dada, *Big Daddy*; because of his atrocities in Kampala, capital of Uganda.

KANGA Dale Elizabeth, 3rd Baroness Tryon, (1948–), wife of Anthony, Baron Tryon (1940–) so called by the Prince of Wales (*Fishface*) for her Australian background.
- 'Kanga' is a character in A. A. Milne's *Winnie the Pooh*.

KANGAROO Major-General Sir Henry Frederick Cooke who was private aide-de-camp to the Duke of York (the *Soldiers' Friend*) and in the latter part of his life a dandified man-about-town. He was the brother of Sir George Cooke, commander of the 1st Guards Division at Waterloo (1815).
- ?from the name association with Captain James Cook (1728–79), discoverer of New South Wales, the land of kangaroos.

KANGAROO KID, THE Jim Pollard (1922–), American basketball star in the Hall of Fame (1977).

KANSAS CYCLONE, THE President *Ike* Eisenhower when he was a footballer. He came from Abilene, Kansas, although he had been born in Texas.

KEEKS Lady Carina Fitzalan-Howard (1953–), daughter of the Duke of Norfolk; wife of David Frost (*Mr TV*).

KENNY B. Sir Kenneth Barnes (1878–1957), President of the Royal Academy of Dramatic Art; so called by students.

KENTISH SAMSON, THE Richard Joy (1657–1724).

KENTUCKY KID, THE Steven (Steve) Cauthen (1960–), American champion jockey after he won the Kentucky Derby at the age of eighteen. He won the English Derby in 1985, and was champion jockey (England) in 1987.

KENTUCKY ROSEBUD, THE Walter Edgeton (1853– ?), American boxer. At the age of sixty-three (1916), he knocked out John H. Johnson (then forty-five) in four rounds.

KERRYGOLD *Hurricane* Higgins after he had been suspended for six months (1987) for having butted an official at a snooker tournament.
- Kerrygold's slogan is 'Ireland's best butter'. Higgins is Irish.

KESWICK IMPOSTER, THE John Hatfield (1759–1803), British forger who tricked Mary Robinson (the *Beauty of Buttermere*) into marriage. He was executed for forgery.

KEYBOARD CONMAN, THE Leslie Allen (1922–), Britain's most wanted confidence trickster who made a small fortune by posing as a doctor to defraud lonely widows. He was caught and gaoled in 1980. He got his nickname as a talented pianist.

KHAKI ROBERTS Geoffrey Dorling Roberts (1886–1967), Recorder of Bristol and former England rugby footballer; one of the prosecution team at the Nuremberg Trials (1945–6); so called first at school. He had a brick-dust complexion.

KICK Kathleen Hartington Kennedy (1920–48), sister of President J.F. Kennedy and widow of the Marquis of Hartington (killed 1944, six weeks after his marriage). She was abandoned by her Roman Catholic family when she agreed to bring up any children as Anglicans. She was killed in an air crash.

KID

i) Edward Ory (1886–1973), American trombonist and New Orleans band leader, whose players included Louis Armstrong (*Dippermouth*) and *King* Oliver.

ii) Charles McCoy, the *Corkscrew Kid*.

iii) Ted Lewis (1894–1970), British world junior welterweight boxing champion (1915, 1917–1919). His real name was Geriston Mendeloff.

iv) Jack Berg (1909–), British world junior welterweight boxing champion (1930–1). His real name is Jacob Bergman. Also the *Whitechapel Windmill*.

v) Charles Nichols, American baseball pitcher in the Hall of Fame (1890–1906).

vi) George Lavigne (1869–1928), British, world lightweight boxing champion (1896–9)

vii) David Allen Jensen (1950–), Canadian-born British disc-jockey who started to broadcast at the age of eighteen.

KID CURRY Harvey Logan (died 1903), ruthless killer in the Wild Bunch and an associate of *Butch Cassidy* and the *Sundance Kid*. Logan took his nickname from George Curry (*Flat Nose*), a cattle-rustler he admired.

KID DROPPER

i) Louis Kaplan, American featherweight boxing champion (1926–7).

ii) Nathan Kaplan (1891–1923), shot by *Legs* Diamond's men. He was an expert at the dropped wallet confidence trick; pretending to have found a wallet (stuffed with counterfeit money) which

he 'returned' for a reward.

KIDDER FROM KIDDERMINSTER, THE Sir Gerald Nabarro, the *Barrow Boy*: M.P. for Kidderminster (1950–64); from his persistent questioning in the House of Commons, not always taken (or, indeed, perhaps intended) seriously.

• To kid has, since at least 1811, meant to hoax or deceive.

KID PUNCH or PUNCH Ernest Miller (1901–), American jazz trumpeter.

KID, THE George Fordham, the *Demon*. He had a trick of 'pulling' his horse in a race to deceive other jockeys into thinking he had given up. They would relax and Fordham would win.

KID TWIST

i) Abraham Reles (1907–41), one of the 'executioners' for Murder Incorporated. He confessed when held for murder, but before he could be charged, he fell from a sixth-floor window.

ii) Max Zwerbach (1882–1908), New York gangster; because he was so crooked.

KILL General Judson Kilpatrick (1836–1908), Union commander in the American Civil War.

KILLER

i) Marshal of the RAF Sir Thomas Geoffrey Pike (1906–), Chief of Air Staff (1960–1963) and Deputy Supreme Commander, Europe. He commanded fighter squadrons in World War II.

ii) *Jack* Slade.

iii) Kevin Sheedy (1960–), midfield player for Everton FC with a lethal goal kick.

KILLER, THE Jerry Lee Lewis (1936–), American-born 'wild man' of Rock and Roll. He has been married six times. He has said the nickname came from his youth (*circa* 13 years old) when 'we called everyone we knew "Killer".'

KILLER RUNCIE The Most Reverend Robert Alexander Kennedy Runcie (1921–), Archbishop of Canterbury (1980–); so called as a tank commander (World War II) when he won the MC while serving with the Scots Guards: mentioned by *Time* magazine (1987).

KILTIE Stewart Maiden (1886–1948), American professional golfer who taught Bobby Jones (1902–71), the great American golfer; so called from his Scottish ancestry.

KIM

i) Harold Adrian Russell Philby (1912–88), British journalist and Soviet spy who fled to Russia (1963): born in the Punjab, he was nicknamed after the boy in Kipling's book of that name (1902). Also the *Third Man*.

ii) William Drogo, 7th Duke of Westminster (1823–90).

- See the *Double Duchess*.

KING

i) Joseph Oliver (1885–1938), American jazz trumpeter, founder of the Creole Jazz Band; nickname given to him by *Kid* Ory. Also the *King of Jazz*.

ii) Elvis Presley, *Elvis the Pelvis*; *King of Rock and Roll*.

iii) Nathaniel Cole (1919–65), American singer. Also *Mr Velvet Voice*.

iv) Beauchamp Bagenal, M.P. for Carlow (1780s), the *Duellist*.

v) Sir Richard Mayne (1796–1868), one of the first two Commissioners of the Metropolitan Police, London (1829). He had supreme power after the death of the other, Sir Charles Rowan (1852). Also the *Satrap of Scotland Yard*.

vi) Viscount Allen (died 1843), a famous dandy who had distinguished himself at Talavera (1809) as an ensign in the Guards in the Peninsular War; so called from his majestic deportment.

vii) Sumner Leslie Edwards (died *circa* 1950), American jazz tuba and bass player.

viii) Robert Carter, who owned 300,000 acres and 1,000 slaves in Virginia (1720s).

ix) Barry John (1945–), Welsh rugby fly-half. He scored 90 points in twenty-five games, and 180 for the British Lions against New Zealand.

x) Leonard Matchan (1911–), American multi-millionaire accountant to the theatrical profession. Also *Vaudeville's Godfather*.

KING ARTHUR

i) Arthur Halliwell (1911–1980), columnist for *The Sunday People* for many years and a well-known Fleet Street figure and film critic.

ii) Arthur Scargill (1938–), former President of the Yorkshire Miners' Union and President of the National Union of Mineworkers (post 1982).

KING ARTHUR OF THE STAGE, THE William Charles Macready (1793–1873). As an actor and theatre manager, he tried to raise the standards of the English theatre.

KING BILLY

i) William III, the *Deliverer*, especially among the Irish Protestants.

ii) William (Billy) Bremner (1944–), Scottish international footballer. He played for Leeds United (1960s–1970s) and became its manager.

KING COHN Harry Cohn (1891–1958), American film producer, head of Columbia Pictures for many years; the title of a biography.

KING COLL or COL Colley Cibber (1671–1757), British actor-dramatist who became poet-laureate (1730). Also *King of Dullness, King of Dunces* and the *Spagnolet of the Theatre*.

KING COLE Cole Porter (1893–1964), American composer, because of his great success.

KING DICK

i) Admiral of the Fleet Sir Frederick William Richards (1833–1912), First Sea Lord (1893–9) and so 'king of the Navy'.

ii) Richard John Seddon (1845–1906), English-born Prime Minister of New Zealand (post 1893).

KING DOWAGER, THE Louis Duras, 2nd Earl of Feversham (1640–1709), Lord Chamberlain to Queen Catherine of Braganza (1680). The influence of the queen-dowager saved him after James II (the *King Over the Water*) fled. He had been his Commander-in-Chief.

KINGFISH Huey Pierce Long (1893–1935), ruthless American dictator of Louisana, where he was Governor (1920s–1930s).

- The kingfish has been described as

'the most voracious and destructive of all fish'.

KING FREDDIE Sir Edward Frederick Mutesa (1924–69), the Kabaka of Buganda and London socialite; his nickname in London society.

KING JOG John George Lambton, 1st Earl of Durham (1792–1840), English statesman; so called by Thomas Creevey (1768–1838), a Whig MP, after Lambton had said 'one might jog along with £40,000 a year'. Also *Radical Jack*.

KING JOHN

i) The Duke of Marlborough, *Anne's Great Captain*. The power he had as commander-in-chief, plenipotentiary and prince (of the small principality of Mindelheim, Bavaria) was enormous; so called in London society.

ii) John Edward Redmond (1856–1918), Irish politician who amalgamated the two Irish nationalist parties under his leadership (1910), and held the balance of power in the House of Commons. Also the *Uncrowned King of Ulster*.

KING KELLY Michael Joseph Kelly (1857–94), American baseball player for the Chicago White Stockings and the Cincinnati Red Stockings. Also the *Ten Thousand Dollar Beauty*.

KING KEV Kevin Keegan (1952–), British footballer. He retired as a rich man in 1984 after sixteen years in the game during which time he rose from a small club, Scunthorpe, to captain England (1980s). He also played for Newcastle United. He holds 63 caps. Player of the Year (1982). He became coach to an African team in South Africa (1988). Also the *Mighty Mouse*.

KING KHAMA Sir Seretse Khama (1921–80), President of Botswana (1966–80), chief of the Bamangwato tribe, who married Ruth Williams, a London typist (1948). He was the first Prime Minister of Bechuanaland (1965–6). His ancestors were kings.

• See *Moatlodhi*.

KING LEIGH Leigh Hunt, *Bacchus*; so called in *Noctes Ambrosianae*.

KING LUD See *General Ludd*.

KINGMAKER, THE Richard Neville, Earl of Warwick (*circa* 1428–71). He first supported Henry VI (*Ill-Fated Henry*) and then Edward IV (the *Robber*), and so helped each to the throne; so called by John Major (the *Last of the Schoolmen*) in a *History of Greater Britain, England and Scotland* (1521). Also the *Last of the Barons* and *Richard Make-a-King*.

KING MARTIN THE FIRST Martin van Buren (1782–1862), 8th President of the USA. He was the leading member of the Albany Regency which controlled New York politics and influenced those of all America. He had a great many political nicknames, including the *Little Magician, Little Van*, the *Northern Man with Southern Principles*, the *Political Grimalkin*, the *Red Fox of Kinderhook,* the *Weasel, Whisky Van* and *Young Hickory*.

KING MONMOUTH The Duke of Monmouth, *Absalom*; so called because he aspired to the throne. He was actually 'crowned' in Taunton market-place.

KING OF ALDGATE, THE *Jack Spot* Comer; so called in the 1950s. He called himself 'King of the Underworld'.

• Aldgate is a district of London just north of the Tower of London.

KING OF THE BANK ROBBERS, THE George Leonidas Leslie (1838–84), American thought to have stolen $12,000,000 from various banks; so called by the New York police.

KING OF BATH, THE Richard *Beau* Nash. For more than forty years, he was Master of Ceremonies at the fashionable Assembly Rooms there and, by a rigid code of conduct, caused a revolution in British manners.

KING OF BLARNEY Michael Terence (Terry) Wogan (1938–) British TV and radio personality with an almost daily chat show (BBC). Also *Tel*.

• Blarney ranges from cajolery to downright effrontery and is supposed to be given to a person's tongue by kissing the Blarney Stone in a castle near Cork, Ireland.

KING OF BOOK COLLECTORS, THE The Earl of Oxford, the *Backstairs Dragon*.

His great collection of books and manuscripts is in the British Museum (the Harleian).

KING OF CHARACTER ACTORS, THE Paul Muni (1896–1967), Polish-born American film actor; so called first in *The Picture Show Annual* (1939). His real name was Muni Weisenfreund.

KING OF CLOWNS, THE Dan Rice (1828–1900), American whose real name was Daniel McLaren. He dressed in red, white and blue and was the original 'Uncle Sam'.

KING OF CARRICK, THE Gilbert Kennedy, 4th Earl of Cassillis (*circa* 1541–76). A Protestant, he fought for Queen Mary (*Bloody Mary*); from his estates and power. Also the *Uncrowned King of Carrick*.

- Carrick is in Ayrshire, Scotland, south of the river Doon.

KING OF CATTLE THIEVES, THE James Averill (lynched 1889), lover of *Cattle Kate* who sometimes took his name. Many did not believe him guilty.

KING OF COCOS, THE Captain John Clunies Ross, a Scot. In 1827, he established the first permanent settlement on the Keeling Islands, often called the Cocos, in the Indian Ocean. His family were rulers until 1946 and his descendants are still there.

KING OF COMEDY, THE Mack Sennett (1880–1960), Hollywood producer of comic films, e.g. the Keystone Kops. He discovered Charles Chaplin (the *Immortal Tramp*).

KING OF DEPRAVITY, THE Aleister Crowley, *Beast 666*.

KING OF DIRECTORS, THE David Wark Griffith (1875–1948), American setter of standards for film production in the early days of Hollywood. His films included *The Birth of a Nation* (1914). His real name was Llewelyn Wark Griffith. Also the *Master*.

KING OF DULLNESS, THE Colley Cibber, *King Coll*; so called by Pope (the *Bard of Twickenham*). Cibber, when in charge of Drury Lane Theatre, London, refused to stage *The Beggar's Opera* by John Gay

(the *Aesop of England*), later a huge success when it was first produced in 1728.

KING OF DUNCES, THE
i) Lewis or Louis Theobald (1688–1744) who issued *Shakespeare Restored* in 1726. Edith Sitwell (1887–1964), the poet, said he was 'a learned bore'. So called by Pope (the *Bard of Twickenham*) who was angry at the book. Also *Margites*.

ii) Colley Cibber, *King Coll*; so called by Pope (above) in *The Dunciad* (1712).

KING OF EXETER 'CHANGE, THE Thomas Clark (1737–1817). He took a stall at the Exeter Exchange, London (1765) with £100 lent to him by a stranger and died worth almost £500,000. He was, however, a notorious miser who lived in Belgrave Place, Pimlico, but never spent more than 1s. (5p) on a meal.

- Exeter Exchange, erected in 1676, was demolished in 1829. There were stalls for milliners, seamstresses and ironmongers (of which Clark was one).

KING OF FARCE, THE Sir Brian Rix (1924–), British actor; so called after a run of successful comedies at the Whitehall Theatre, London. Knighted for his services to the mentally handicapped.

KING OF FIRE, THE Sir Benjamin Thompson (1735–1814), founder of the Royal Institution, London, the first man to determine that heat is a mode of motion; so called by Wolcot (*Peter Pindar*).

KING OF FOLLY, THE Roger Mortimer (?1287–1330); so called by his son, because of his affectation of royal splendour.

KING OF FORGERS, THE Ralph Cooper, who had a long history of forgery, gaoled for fifteen years (1888) for having forged a cheque for £3,670 on the London and Westminster Bank.

KING OF HEARTS, THE Charles Talbot, 12th Earl and only Duke of Shrewsbury (1660–1718), explained by the description of him by Swift (*Doctor Presto*) as the 'favourite of the nation'.

KING OF HOLLYWOOD, THE Clark Gable (1901–60), American film-star, idol of millions of women; so called after a poll by Edward Sullivan (1902–74), New York newspaper columnist.

KING OF INATTENTION, THE Dr John Arbuthnot (1667–1735), physician to Queen Anne (**Brandy Nan**). He wrote *The History of John Bull* (1712) which created the prototype caricature of an Englishman; so called by Swift (**Doctor Presto**).

KING OF IRELAND, THE John Beresford (1738–1805), Irish statesman who became Earl of Tyrone (1746). His father married the heiress. John wielded great power in Ireland as First Commissioner of Revenue.

KING OF KILDARE, THE Gerald Fitzgerald, 9th Earl of Kildare, **Garret Oge**.

KING OF JAZZ, THE
i) Paul Whiteman (1890–1967), American jazz violinist and band leader (1920s), although his 'title' is disputed by some because of the big band element. Also **Pops**.
ii) Joseph **King** Oliver.

KING OF LAGOS, THE William McKoskry, British vice-consul and Acting Governor of Lagos, Nigeria (1860s). The 'honour' was not only given to him by Africans in Lagos, but by many tribes farther down the West African coast.

KING OF MADAGASCAR, THE Captain John Avery, the **Arch Pirate**.

KING OF MELTON, THE Seymour John Grey, 4th Earl of Wilton (1839–1913), sportsman and race-horse owner. Also the **Wicked Earl**.
• Melton Mowbray, Leicestershire, is a celebrated fox-hunting area of England.

KING OF MISSOURI, THE Kenneth McKenzie (1797–1861), factor for the American Fur Company at Fort Union (1830s–1840s) after whom Fort McKenzie is named. He was related to Sir Alexander McKenzie (*circa* 1764–1820), the explorer of the Canadian river (1789) which bears his name.

KING OF NORFOLK AND SUFFOLK, THE Robert Kett (died 1549), a tanner of Wymondham, Norfolk. With his brother William, a butcher, he led a revolt against landowners who enclosed common land. He gave himself the nickname and 'ruled'

for twenty-seven days. He was hanged in chains in Norwich castle. Also **King Robert**.

KING OF PANTO, THE Emile Littler (1904–85), British theatrical impresario noted for his many pantomimes.
• See the **Father of Pantomimes**.

KING OF PARAMOUNT, THE Wallace Reid, **Good Time Wally**: i.e Paramount Pictures.

KING OF PIMPS, THE Charles Luciano (Salvatore Lucania: 1897–1962), American Mafia gangster, head of the prostitution rackets in New York. Also **Lucky**.

KING OF PLUNGERS, THE Lord Hastings, **Champagne Charlie** (iii). He was an inveterate gambler and lost £120,000 on the 1867 Derby, which contributed to his early death.
• 'Plunger' is colloquial for a reckless gambler.

KING OF POETS, THE
i) Edmund Spenser, the **Child of the Ausonian Muse**; so called by his contemporary, Richard Barnfield (1574–1627),
ii) William Hayley (1745–1820); nicknamed by his friend Southey (the **Ballad Monger**).

KING OF PORN, THE Paul Raymond (1926–), British promoter of erotic clubs and revues and sexy plays at the Whitehall Theatre, London. His real name is Geoffrey Anthony Quinn.

KING OF PULP WRITERS, THE Max Brand (1892–1944), American author of about 530 books, including many westerns and the Dr Kildare stories. He died as a war correspondent.

KING OF PRACTICAL JOKES, THE William Horace de Vere Cole (1881–1936), Briton who, in a lifetime of practical jokes, organized a party to act as the Emperor of Abyssinia and his staff to visit a Royal Navy flagship – and got away with it!

KING OF PRUSSIA, THE John Carter (fl. end of the 18th century), was a Cornish smuggler of Prussia Cove, and the most famous of the Carter gang. He is said to have been 'an honest smuggler'. His nickname arose from the 'I'm the king of the castle' game played by the Carter children: ' I'm the king of Prussia Cove'.

- See *Captain Harry*.

KING OF RAGTIME, THE Scott Joplin, the *Father of Ragtime*. He won a Pulitzer prize (1976) for his opera *Tremonisha* (1916).

KING OF REGGAE, THE Robert (Bob) Nesta Marley (1945–81), Jamaican-born musician and Rastafarian.

- Reggae is a type of West Indian rock-jazz. Rastafarians are members of a West Indian sect who are expected to work out their ideas of religion themselves, and look to Ethiopia and the Lion of Judah for their spiritual inspiration.

KING OF ROADS, THE John Louden Macadam (1756–1836). It was he who invented tar macadam as a road surface; a pun on 'Rhodes'.

KING OF ROCK 'N' ROLL, THE
i) Elvis Presley, *Elvis the Pelvis*.
ii) William (Bill) Hayley (1925–81) who, with the Comets, recorded *Rock Around the Clock* (1954) and sold more than 22,000,000 copies.

KING OF ROCK 'N' SOUL, THE Solomon Burke (1936–), American soul singer.

KING SEARS Isaac Sears (1729–85) of Norwalk, Connecticut, a rich merchant who stood with the Sons of Liberty, the organisation that protested in America against the Stamp Act and so precipitated the Revolution.

- See the *American Cato*.

KING OF SCHLOCK ART, THE Morris Katz (1932–), American who paints cheap portraits. By 1982 he had painted – it is estimated – 110,600 pictures.

- 'Schlock' is American slang for an inferior product.

KING OF SCOTLAND, THE Archibald Campbell, 3rd Duke of Argyll (1682–1761), Keeper of the Privy Seal, given the management of affairs in Scotland (1721).

KING OF SCOTS FIDDLERS, THE Neil Gow (1727–1807), weaver and noted violinist and composer.

KING OF SKIFFLE, THE Anthony James Donegan (1931–), British pop singer and guitarist who led the skiffle world in the 1960s. Also *Lonnie*.

- Skiffle is a type of music dominated by guitars and a washboard 'scrubbed' rhythmically.

KING OF SOHO, THE William (Billy) Hill (fl. 1920s–1950s), gang boss in London.

KING OF SWING, THE
i) Benny Goodman (1909-86), American jazz clarinettist who started it.
ii) Ted Heath (1902-69), British band leader. Also *Mr Music*.

- Swing has been described as 'commercialized jazz'. Its main period was 1935–46.

KING OF THE BEGGARS, THE Bamfylde-Moore Carew (1693–c 1770), famous English vagabond who was elected *King of the Gypsies*. He was transported to America, but escaped to return to England. He became a trooper for the *Young Pretender* (1745), following him to Derby. Also called 'King of the Mendicants'.

KING OF THE BIZARRE, THE Stephen King (1940–), American horror novelist, e.g. *Carrie* (1974).

KING OF THE BORDER, THE Adam Scott (died 1529) of Tushielaw, robber and outlaw whose gang infested the border country during the wars between England and Scotland under Robert the *Bruce*. James V (the *Goodman of Ballengeigh*) took strong action, and Scott was arrested and beheaded. Also *King of the Thieves*.

KING OF THE CHEROKEES, THE Sir Alexander Cumming (died 1775), who was made a chief of the Cherokee Indians, and took six of them to England to visit George II (*Augustus*) at Windsor; so called in London.

KING OF THE COMMONS
i) James V of Scotland, the *Goodman of Ballengeigh*.
ii) Geoffrey Litser (died 1381), leader of the Norfolk Peasants' Revolt (1381). He was a dyer.

- See the *Fighting Prelate*.

KING OF THE COMSTOCK, THE William Sharon who brought up shares in the Comstock Lode near Virginia City, Nevada (1860–70) when they were seemingly worthless before the silver bonanza (1873).

- See the *Bonanza King, Old Pancake* and *Old Virginny*.

KING OF THE COTSWOLDS, THE Grey Brydges, 5th Baron Chandos (1580–1621), Lord-Lieutenant of Gloucester. He lived a life of luxury at Sudeley Castle.

- The Cotswold Hills run through Gloucestershire and Oxfordshire.

KING OF THE COWBOYS, THE

i) *Buck* Taylor.

ii) Roy Rogers (1912–), American film star of Westerns, whose real name is Leonard Slye.

iii) Tom Mix (1880–1940), early cowboy film hero, star of more than 400 westerns.

KING OF THE FEDS, THE Alexander Hamilton (1757–1804), American statesman, principal author of *The Federalist* (1787–8), a series of essays on the constitution of the USA. He died as the result of a duel with Aaron Burr (1756–1836).

- See the *Goliath of Federalism*.

KING OF THE GYPSIES, THE

i) Bamfylde-Moore Carew, the *King of the Beggars*.

ii) Samuel Cooper (?1794–1856), a tinker who took over from his father.

KING OF THE JUKES, THE Perry Como (1912–), American singer whose records were played constantly on juke-boxes. His first name is actually Pierino. Also *Mr Relaxation*.

KING OF THE LOBBY, THE Samuel Ward (died 1884), powerful manipulator in the American legislature.

KING OF THE KOP, THE Kenneth (Kenny) Dalglish (1951–), player-manager for Liverpool FC; so called after Liverpool won the FA Cup and League championship (1986).

- The Kop is Liverpool's ground at Anfield Road from Spion Kop, a Boer War battle (1900) in which Liverpool regiments took part.

KING OF THE ONE-LINERS, THE Henny Youngman (1906–), English-born comic in America, with a torrent of one-line jokes. On British TV (1989), he said he had ben in show business for sixty years.

KING OF THE PAPER STAGE, THE Robert Greene, the *Ape of Euphues*; so called by *Ape Gabriel* Harvey, because his plays were more 'written' than acted. Harvey and Greene were bitter enemies and Harvey published an attack on Green immediately after his death.

KING OF THE PEAK, THE Sir George Vernon (died 1567), whose daughter Dorothy (died 1584) eloped with Sir John Manners (died 1611). Sir George thereby acquired Haddon Hall, Derbyshire, in the Peak District; because of his hospitality. Dorothy by her marriage became the ancestress of the Dukes of Rutland.

KING OF THE PECOS, THE John Chisum, the *Cattle King of America*.

- The Rio Pecos runs through east New Mexico and west Texas.

KING OF THE POOR, THE William Fitz-Osbert (died 1196), English crusader who on his return devoted himself to work for the poor. Accused falsely of plotting a revolt, he was executed with great cruelty and hanged in chains with some of his 'followers'. Also *Longbeard*.

KING OF THE SEA, THE Edward III, the *Father of English Commerce*; so called after the defeat of the French at Sluys (1340) and the Spanish at Winchelsea (1350).

KING OF THE SOAPS, THE Aaron Spelling (1928–), American film magnate behind *Dynasty, Hotel, The Colbys*, etc.

- See the *Queen of the Soaps*.

KING OF THE STAKES RIDERS, THE Eddie Arcaro, *Banana Nose*.

KING OF THE THIEVES, THE Adam Scott, the *King of the Border*.

KING OF THE TURF, THE Sir Charles Bunbury (1740–1821), president of the English Jockey Club for more than forty years. His horse Diomed won the 1780 Derby. In 1791 he had the Prince Regent (*Adonis of Fifty*) warned off the course at

Newmarket because of the irregular riding of his jockey Sam Chifney (1755–1807).

KING OF THE TWELVE-STRING GUITAR, THE Huddie Ledbetter (1888–1949), American jazz musician and folk singer. Also *Leadbelly*.

KING OF THE UNDERTAKERS, THE Howard Hodgson (1950–), British millionaire who handled one out of every twenty funerals in Britain in the 1970s by owning 118 undertakers in the country. He is negotiating for 2,500 more. Also *Mr Death*.

KING OF THE WEST, THE John Pyne, a regicide indemnified by the Bill of 1660–1.

KING OF WESTERN SWING, THE Robert (Bob) Wills (1905–75), American songwriter and leader of the Texas Playboys whose heyday was in the 1940s.

KING OF THE FAIRIES, THE Thomas Crofton Croker (1798–1854), author of *Fairy Legends and Traditions* (1825–8) and other books of antiquarian interest. He was admired by Scott (the *Ariosto of the North*) who gave him the nickname.

KING OF WALL STREET, THE Cornelius Vanderbilt, the *Commodore*.

KING OLIVER Oliver Cromwell, the *Almighty Nose*. Evelyn (1657): 'The Protector Oliver, now affecting King-ship, is petition'd to take the title on him...but dare not...'

KING OVER THE WATER, THE
i) James II (1633–1701) after he had been succeeded by William III (the *Deliverer*) and was living in France; nicknamed by the Jacobites. Also the *Popish Duke*.
ii) James Francis Stuart (1688–1766), son of James II (above) and so Prince of Wales. He was recognized by Pope Innocent XIII and the Jacobites as James III. Also the *Old Pretender* and the *Warming-Pan Hero*.
iii) *Bonny Prince Charlie*, the *Young Pretender*, son of the above.

KING PHILIP Metacomet (*circa* 1639–76), chief of the Wampanoag Indians, New England, who fought the English settlers (1675–6) in what is called 'King Philip's War'; so called by the settlers who nick-named his brother Wamsutta 'Alexander'.

KING PYM John Pym, the *English Aristides*, with great influence as a parliamentary leader.

KING RICHARD Richard Petty (1937–), American racing driver and stock-car hero; NASCAR national champion eight times and Daytona 500 winner seven times.

KING ROBERT Robert Kett, the *King of Norfolk and Suffolk*.

KING'S DWARF, THE Sir Jeffrey Hudson (1619–82), said to have been 18 in at thirty, but later 3 ft 6 in. Once a page to Queen Henrietta (the *Little Queen*), he was served up in a pie to Charles I (the *Ahab of the Nation*). Hudson was carried round in the pocket of William Evans, a royal porter 8ft tall, so they say. Also *Lord Minimus* and *Strenuous Jeffrey*.

KING'S JESTER, THE Dan Leno (1860–1904), British music-hall comedian whose real name was George Galvin (fl. 1880s-1890s). He gave a command performance before King Edward VII (the *Peacemaker*) at Sandringham (1901).
• Cf the *Queen's Jester*.

KING'S MURDERER, THE John Bradshaw (1602–59), English lawyer and fanatical anti-monarchist. Lord President of the court which sentenced Charles I (the *Ahab of the Nation*) to death. At the Restoration his corpse was exhumed and exposed on the Tyburn gallows, and later his head was cut off and exhibited in Westminster Hall.

KING SNEER John McEnroe, the *Brat*, an analogy with *King Lear*.

KING STEPHEN Sir James Stephen (1789–1859), Permanent Under-Secretary for the Colonies (1836–47). He had, however, been associated with colonial policy since 1825, and virtually ran the colonial service. Also *Mr Mother Country* and *Mr Over-Secretary*.

KING TOM
i) Thomas Coke, Earl of Leicester, *Coke of Norfolk*, because of his estates.
ii) Sir Thomas Osborne, 1st Earl of Danby and 1st Duke of Leeds (1631–1712). He held important

positions of state, and during the absence of William III (the *Deliverer*) in Ireland, was adviser to Queen Mary II (1662–94). Also *Tom the Tyrant* and the *White Marquis of Carmarthen*.

KINMONT WILLIE William Armstrong (fl. 1580s–1590s) famous border reiver or moss trooper celebrated by Scott (the *Ariosto of the North*) in the ballad *Kinmont Willie* in *Border Minstrelsy* (1802–3); so called after his castle of Kinmont in Canonby, Dumfriesshire.

KIPPER

i) Michael Colin Cowdray (1932–), English cricket captain, who played for Oxford University and Kent. He scored 42,719 runs, including 107 centuries, and played in 114 Test Matches.

ii) John Lynch (1940–), English top jockey (1979–1980).

KIPPY Christopher Smith (1959–). South African-born cricketer for Hampshire and England.

KISSING POET, THE Robert Herrick (1591–1674), English cavalier poet who mentions the word very often in his poems, e.g. in his lyrics in *Hesperides* (1684).

KISS ME HARDY Captain Thomas Masterman Hardy (1769–1839), Nelson's flag-captain at the battle of Trafalgar (1805), to whom Nelson (the *Hero of a Hundred Fights*) is reported to have said 'Kiss me, Hardy' before he died in the cockpit of the *Victory*; so called in the Royal Navy.

KIT-CAT POET, THE Sir Samuel Garth (1661–1719), best remembered for *The Dispensary* (1699). He was a member of the Kit-Cat Club (early 18th century).

• The club met at a house of a cook named Christopher Cat (or Katt) whose mutton-pies were called 'kit-cats'. Pope was one of the members.

KLASSIE Nicolaas Christian Havenga (1882–1957), South African statesman; leader of the Afrikaner Party.

KLONDIKE William O'Donnell (fl. 1920s), one of the O'Donnell gang of Chicago.

KNICKERS Richard Francis Needham, 6th Earl of Kilmorey (although he does not use the title: 1942–). He once worked in the ladies underwear department of Marks and Spencers to study workers' conditions. Minister for Northern Ireland.

KNIGHTCAP See *Cap the Knife*.

KNIGHT IN BUCKSKINS, THE Jedediah Smith (1799–1831), Bible-reading, clean-living explorer and mountain man,

• See *Old Gabe*.

KNIGHT OF LIDDESDALE, THE Sir William Douglas, the *Flower of Chivalry*.

KNIGHT OF SOHO SQUARE, THE Sir Joseph Banks (1743–1820), pioneer patron of exploration and scientist; President of the Royal Academy (1778–1820); so called by Wolcot (*Peter Pindar*).

KNIGHT OF THE CLEAVER, THE Jack Slack, butcher-pugilist who defeated Broughton (the *Father of Boxing*) and held the British championship for 10 years (1750–60).

KNIGHT OF THE CLOAK, THE Sir Walter Raleigh (*circa* 1552–1618), courtier, author, explorer; reputed to have laid his cloak across a puddle for Queen Elizabeth (the *English Diana*). Also the *Ocean Shepherd* and *Shepherd of the Ocean*.

KNIGHT OF THE POST, THE Titus Oates (1649–1705), informer on the 'Popish Plot'; convicted of perjury, he was given savage floggings to try to kill him, but he survived. Also the *Light of the Town*.

• A 'knight of the post' earned a living by giving false evidence. Nash (1592): 'a fellow who will swear you anything for twelve pence'. See the *First Tory* and the *Protestant Martyr*.

KNIGHT OF THE RUEFUL COUNTENANCE, THE Sir Richard Cartwright, *Blue Ruin*

• Nickname for Don Quixote (Miguel de Cervantes: 1547–1616): *El Caballero de la triste Figure*.

KNIGHT OF THE TURF, THE Sir Gordon Richards (1904–86), champion British jockey twenty-six times (1925–53). He rode 4,870 winners, 269 of them in 1947; first jockey to be knighted.

KNOCKY

i) John Williams (1918–), white

American jazz pianist; professor Texas university.

ii) William H. Walker (1898–1964), centre-forward, England and Aston Villa.

KNUCKLE John Emburey (1952–), Middlesex and England cricketer, labelled the No.1 off-break bowler. At Sydney in the 5th Test Match, he took 7 wickets for 78 (4 for 10 in one spell; 1987). Captained England (1988). Also 'Embers'.

K OF K Field-Marshal Herbert Horatio, 1st Earl Kitchener of Khartoum (1850–1916). He crushed the Mahdi's army and recaptured Khartoum (1898).

KOO Kathleen Norris Stark (1956–), film actress and friend of Prince Andrew (**Bungy**). As a child in America, she imitated the call of doves: 'koo, koo, koo'. Also **Princess Koo**.

KORTIE Charles Jess Kortright (1871–1952), English cricketer, thought by many to have been the fastest bowler ever. He also played for Middlesex.

KRUPPS OF THE CONFEDERACY, THE Brigadier-General Joseph Red Anderson (1813–92). He made guns at Tredegar Iron works for the Confederate army.

- The Krupps family made armaments at Essen for German armies from Bismarck to Hitler.

L

LABBY Henry Du Pre Labouchère (1831–1912), British Member of Parliament. He started and edited *Truth* which exposed frauds, and was political opponent of Lord Rosebery (the **Orator of Empire**) and Joseph Chamberlain (**Artful Joe**).

LACKLAND King John (1167–1216), youngest son of Henry II (**Curtmantle**). He received no grants of land in the European provinces as other sons did. Camden (the **British Pausanias**) gives it (1605) as 'Sans-terre'. Also **Softsword**.

LADDIE Percy Belgrave Lucas (1915–   ), Member of Parliament, chairman of the Greyhound Racing Association Property Trust Limited, the world's biggest track group and champion amateur golfer. He was a fighter pilot in World War II.

LADIES OF LLANGOLLEN, THE Lady Eleanor Butler (?1746–1829) and Miss Sarah Ponsby (?1746–1831), called 'the most celebrated virgins in Europe'. They left Ireland together to escape the fashionable world (1778), dressed as men and settled in a small Welsh town. They are said never to have left it for a single night for more than fifty years. Eleanor was sister to the 17th Earl of Ormonde and Sarah cousin to the Earl of Bessborough. Also the **Platonists**.

LADY, THE or DAVY THE LADY David Armstrong (died 1525), border reiver, brother to **Sym**.

LADY BETTY BESOM Juliana Papjoy (?1711–77), Bath seamstress, mistress to **Beau** Nash. She was nicknamed by the people of Bath after she had been seen riding with a whip of many thongs given to her by Nash. After his death (1761), she became eccentric and lived in a hollow tree.

LADYBIRD Claudia Johnson, née Taylor (1912–   ), wife of President Lyndon Baines Johnson, 'LBJ' (1908–73: in the White House, 1963–8); childhood nickname after a nurse had exclaimed 'She's as pretty as a lady bird'.

LADY BLARNEY
i) Henrietta Spencer, Countess of Bessborough (1758–1821), mother of Lady Caroline Lamb (**Caro**); so called by Byron (**Baby**). Also the **Queen-Mother**.
ii) Marguerite, Countess of Blessington (1789–1849). She published *Conversations with Lord Byron* (1834); so called by Byron.
● Lady Blarney is one of the 'fine ladies' in the *Vicar of Wakefield* by Goldsmith (the **Child of Nature**).

LADY CHEAT'EM Hesther Pitt, Countess of Chatham (1721–1803). Her husband, the Earl of Chatham (**Aeolus i**), had been paid £3,000 a year after he had been pushed out of office by the Earl of Bute (**Jack Boot**), the King's favourite.

LADY DAY Billie Holliday (1915–59), American singer with – among others – Paul Whiteman's (the **King of Jazz**) band. Her real name was Eleanor Gough McKay. Billie is from Billie Dove, American film star; so called by Lester Young (**Pres**).

LADY FREEMASON, THE The Honourable Elizabeth St Leger (died 1773), daughter of Alfred St Leger, 1st Viscount Doneraile (died 1727), and niece of Colonel Anthony St Leger (*circa* 1759–1821), founder of the St Leger horse-race. She hid in an empty clock-case in her father's house to watch lodge proceedings and when discovered was forced to become a member (circa 1713). She became the Honourable Mrs Richard Aldworth.

LADY LEWSON Jane Lewson (?1700–1816), a rich, eccentric Londoner who, although she never washed, wore extravagant clothes in Queen Anne style all her 116 years.

LADY LINDY Amelia Earhart (1898–1937), American flier, the first woman to cross the Atlantic solo by air (1928). She was lost on a round-the-world flight.
● After Charles Lindbergh, **Lindy**.

LADY OF CHRIST'S COLLEGE, THE John Milton, *Black-Mouthed Zoilus* when at Cambridge University.

- Milton himself commented on it in *Vacation Exercises* (1628): 'Some people have lately nicknamed me the Lady. But do I seem to them too little of a man? I suppose because I have never had the strength to drink off a bottle of beer like a prize-fighter; or because my hand has never grown horny with holding a plough-handle; or because I was not a farm-hand at seven, and so never took a midday nap in the sun – last perhaps because I never show my virility the way these brothellers do'.

LADY OF ENGLAND, THE Matilda, *Domina Anglorum*.

LADY OF THE MERCIANS, THE Aethelflaed or Ethelfleda (died 918), daughter of Alfred the *Great*. She married Aethelred, Earl of Mercia (*circa* 886), and after his death in 911 she controlled Mercia until her death.

- The Old English title *Hlafdige* (*hlaf* = loaf; *dige* = knead) which became 'lady' was used for a queen.

LADY OF THE SUN, THE Alice Perrers or Perers (died 1400), mistress of Edward III (the *Father of English Commerce*). She dominated the Court and country after Queen Philippa died (1368); from her title as queen of the lists at the great tournament at Smithfield (1376). She toured London in that character.

LADY OF WALES, THE Joan or Joanna (died 1237), illegitimate daughter of John (*Lackland*) and wife of the powerful Prince Llywelyn ap Iorworth (1194–1240).

LADY ROTHERMERE'S FAN Ian Lancaster Fleming (1908–64), British novelist, creator of James Bond (007), so called in Fleet Street when he was courting Anne Rothermere, divorced wife of the 2nd Viscount Rothermere. They married in 1945.

- *Lady Windermere's Fan* (1892) is a play by Oscar Wilde (1854–1900).

LADY STEWARD, THE Lady Conyingham, the *English Pompadour*, who meddled in State matters.

LADY WASHINGTON Martha Washington (1732–1802), wife of the 1st President of the USA (the *American Cincinnatus*).

LADY WITH THE LAMP, THE Florence Nightingale (1820–1910), English nurse and hospital reformer. She carried a lamp round the wards of Scutari hospital which she had organized (1854–7) during the Crimean War; so called by wounded soldiers; attributed to Tennyson (the *Bard of Arthurian Romance*) in 1858.

LAIRD OF THE HALLS, THE Sir Harry Lauder (1870–1950), first music-hall performer to be knighted, remembered for his song *Roamin' in the Gloamin'*.

LAIRD'S JOCK Johnny Armstrong, cattle thief of Liddesdale (2nd half of the 16th century).

LA LOLLO Gina Lollobrigida (1927), Italian-born American star, so called in Hollywood.

LAMBETH POISONER, THE Dr Thomas Neill Cream (1850–92), Scottish-born physician in North America; hanged in Britain for having poisoned four women in London. He said on the gallows 'I am Jack the ...', assumed to have been *Jack the Ripper*.

LAME, THE

i) Eoin, King of Man (died 1317).

ii) Conn O'Neill *Bacach* (died 1559), King of Ulster (1519–42) and 1st Earl of Tyrone (1542), leader of the Irish against the English.

- See also *James the Lame*. *Bacach* = lame or crippled in Gaelic.

LANCASHIRE GIANT, THE Robert (Bob) Gregson (1778–1824), pugilist who fought John *Poor Gully*, losing twice to him, and once met Tom Cribb, champion of England (the *Black Diamond*). He was 6 ft 2 in tall and very broad. Later he was proprietor of 'Bob's Chop House' in Holborn, London, where fights were staged. Also the *Poet Laureate of the Ring* and the *Poet Laureate of Pugilists*.

LANCASHIRE HOGARTH, THE John Collier (1708–1786), author and painter.

- For Hogarth, see the *Juvenal of Painters*.

LANCASHIRE TOREADOR, THE George Formby junior (1906–61), Lancashire comedian, who was noted for his songs which he accompanied himself on his ukelele.

LANDLORD OF NEW YORK, THE William Backhouse Astor (1792–1875), from his property holdings.

L'ANGLAIS Hilaire Belloc (1870–1953), British writer born in France; nickname in the French Army during his military service. He had a French father and an English mother notable in the suffragette movement. Belloc became a naturalized Briton.

LANKY Bennet Langton (1737–1801), a Lincolnshire squire, so called by his friend Johnson (*Blinking Sam*) with the alternative (on at least one occasion) of 'Langton Longshanks'.

LANNY Terry Wadkin (1949–), American amateur golf champion (1970).

LANSDOWNE LAUREATE, THE Thomas *Anacreaon Moore*. He was a friend of the 3rd Marquis of Lansdowne (1780–1863). Moore lived at Sloperton Cottage, Wiltshire, near Devizes, the country house of the Marquis.

LAPLAND WILLIE William (Bill) Weaver (died 1954), American gunman, member of the Barker gang (1930s), imprisoned for life in Alcatraz.

LAST ASTROLOGER, THE William Lilly, the *English Merlin*. He issued almanacs with predictions. His nickname would, however, appear a little premature.

LAST ENGLISH MAECENAS, THE Samuel Rogers, the *Banker Poet*. He helped many poets, including Wordsworth (the *Bard of Rydal Mount*).
- See the *Female Maecenas*.

LAST MAN, THE Charles I, the *Ahab of the Nation*; so called by Parliamentarians who thought he would be the last king of England (but whose sensibilities would not allow them to say 'king').
- Cf the *Son of the Last Man*.

LAST MINSTREL OF THE ENGLISH STAGE, THE James Shirley (1596–1666), a leading dramatist when the Puritans shut the playhouses (1642). He died of terror and exposure in the Great Fire of London.

LAST OF THE BARONS, THE Warwick the *Kingmaker*; the title of a novel by Lord Lytton (*Bulwig*). He represented the last of the feudal barons whose powers were as great as, and sometimes surpassed, those of the King.

LAST OF THE DANDIES, THE Count Alfred D'Orsay, *Le Jeune Cupidon*.

LAST OF THE ENGLISH, THE Hereward the *Wake*, a Saxon who fought against the Normans in the fenlands of East Anglia. The subject of many legends, he is mentioned in the Domesday Book (1086–7).

LAST OF THE PATROONS, THE Stephen Van Rensselaer (1764–1839), American politician and Major-General. He was fifth in descent from Killian Van Rensselaer, the original patroon of Rensselaerwyk, New York (1595–1644).
- A patroon was the owner of land given by the Dutch West India Company to members who founded colonies (1029).

LAST OF THE PLATONISTS, THE John Scotus Erigena, *Irish-Born John*.

LAST OF THE PURITANS, THE Samuel Adams, the *American Cato*; so called by Edward Everett (1794–1865) in 1825.

LAST OF THE RED-HOT MOMMAS, THE Sophie Tucker (1884–1966), American vaudeville star who specialized in 'red hot' singing. Her family name was Kalish; she adopted the first name of Abuza.

LAST OF THE ROMANS, THE
i) C J Fox, *Carlo Khan*; so called by Congreve (*Ultimus Romanorum*).
ii) Horace Walpole, the *Autocrat of Strawberry Hill* .
- See also *Ultimus Romanorum*. In a world soaked in classical culture, they seemed the embodiment of Roman virtues.

LAST OF THE SAXONS, THE Harold II Godwinsson (1022–66), Saxon king who died fighting the Normans.

LAST OF THE SCHOOLMEN, THE John Major or Mair (1469–1550), Scottish doctor of theology who wrote many commentaries on religious subjects.

- See the *Chief of the English Protestant Schoolmen*.

LAST OF THE STUARTS, THE Henry Benedict Maria Clement Stuart (1725–1807), usually known as Cardinal York, younger son of the *Old Pretender* and last of the royal house. He was created Duke of York by his father, and once gave Lord Cloncurry a medal inscribed *Henricus nonus dei Gratia Rex* (Henry 9th, by the grace of God, King).

LAST OF THE TORIES, THE Dr Johnson, *Blinking Sam*; so called by Carlyle (the *Censor of the Age*). Johnson defined in his dictionary (1755) a Tory as 'one who adheres to the ancient constitution of the state ...' whereas 'Whig' was 'the name of a faction'.

- See the *First Tory*.

LAST TRUE BARD OF IRELAND, THE Turlogh O'Carolan, the *Irish Anacreon*.

LA STUPENDA Dame Joan Sutherland (1926–), Australian soprano; so called by Milan audiences.

LATE MAN, THE Charles I, the *Ahab of the Nation*; so called by Parliamentarians after his execution.

LATHE PAINTED TO LOOK LIKE IRON, THE Robert Arthur Talbot Gascoyne-Cecil, 3rd Marquess of Salisbury (1830–1903), British Prime Minister (1885–6, 1886–92 and 1895–1902); so called by Bismarck (1815–98), 'The Iron Chancellor' of Germany, in reference to the Berlin Conference · (1878) which Salisbury attended as Foreign Secretary. He was tall and thin. Also *Solly*.

LAUGHING HANGMAN, THE Jack Hooper, who hanged Sarah Malcolm (1733) for murder. He tried to make the last moments of a condemned person bearable by little jokes. He is depicted in Hogarth's engraving of the execution of the Idle Apprentice. Also 'Laughing Jack'.

LAUGHING KILLER, THE Ralph Jerome von Braun Selz (1909–), American imprisoned for life for murder (1936). He laughed and danced on his victim's grave.

LAUREATE OF THE NURSERY, THE William Brighty Rands (1823–82), Briton who wrote poems and fairy stories for children, a book of which was entitled *Lilliput Levee*.

LAW-GIVER, THE James I of Scotland (1394–1437), who introduced a code of statutes; called *Rex Legifer* by his barons. Also the *Orpheus of Scotland*; the *Second Solomon*.

LAY BISHOP, THE Sir Henry Savile (1549–1622) who helped to found the Bodleian Library, Oxford University. He was one of the scholars commissioned to prepare the authorized translation of the Bible, and published an edition of St Chrysostom (8 volumes 1610–13).

- See the *Chrysostom of Christ's College*.

LAZY-ARSED KING, THE Aedh Ui Neill, *Macaemh Tóinlensg*, King of Cenal Eoghan (1176–7), royal heir of Ireland.

LEADBELLY Huddie Ledbetter, *King of the Twelve-String Guitar*.

LEANDER John Jones (1575–1636), Welsh Benedictine monk and scholar. He took the religious name *Leander a Sancto Martino* (Leander = Greek 'lion-man').

LEAN JACK John Yeoman (flourished mid 18th century), Cornish smuggler of Mousehole.

LEAN JIMMY JONES Senator James C Jones (1809–59) of Tennessee.

LEARNED ATTILA, THE Dr Johnson, *Blinking Sam*.

- See *Attila the Hen*.

LEARNED BLACKSMITH, THE Elihu Burritt (1811–79), American blacksmith, linguist and social reformer. He ran a newspaper and travelled America lecturing. He translated the poems of Longfellow (the *Poet of the Commonplace*) into Sanskrit. He could read about fifty languages.

LEARNED CABBAGE-EATER, THE Joseph Ritson, the *Antiquary of Poetry*, one of the first vegetarians; so called by Scott (the *Ariosto of the North*).

LEARNED FOOL, THE James I, the *British Solomon*. The Duc de Sully (1560–1641) called him the *Most Learned Fool in Christendom*. James was studious, and somewhat of a pedant. He boasted of his kingcraft, playing one faction against another – a policy which brought disaster.

LEARNED KNIGHT, THE Sir Thomas Elyot (?1499–1546), English author of *The Governour* (1531), which discussed education and politics. He also translated a number of classics; so called by Wood (the *Ostade of Literary Criticism*).

LEARNED PRINTER, THE William Bowyer (1699–1777), printer to the House of Commons, the House of Lords, the Royal Society and the Society of Antiquaries. He wrote *The Origins of Printing* (1774) and printed an edition of the New Testament in Greek with notes.

LEARNED TAILOR, THE

i) Henry Wild, the *Arabian Tailor*.

ii) Robert Hill (1684–1734) who taught himself Latin, Greek and Hebrew while working at his trade.

LEE Wladziu Valentino Liberace (1919–87), American pianist and entertainer. Also *Mr Showmanship*.

LEE'S OLD WAR HORSE Lieutenant-General James Longstreet, *General Lee's War Horse*. Lee (the *Bayard of the Confederacy*) called him 'My old war horse'.

LEF or LEFFY Admiral of the Fleet Sir Michael Le Fanu, *Dry Ginger*.

LEFTY

i) Vernon Gomez, pitcher for New York, in the Hall of Fame (1930–43).

ii) Robert Grove (1900–75), pitcher for Boston, in the Hall of Fame (1925–41).

iii) Wilburn Stackhouse (1911–), American golfer.

LEGION HARRY Lieutenant Colonel Henry Lee (1756–1818), commander of 'Lee's Legion' and father of General Robert E Lee (the *Bayard of the Confederacy*). Henry Lee gave the funeral oration for Washington (the *American Cincinnatus*). Also *Light-Horse Harry*.

LEGS

i) J T Diamond, the *Clay Pigeon*;

because he was so expert as a youngster at running away from the police after small-time thefts in New York.

ii) John Lloyd *Floss*; so called by his girl fans.

LEGS, THE Betty Grable (1916–1973), American film star and World War II 'pin up girl'. Her legs were insured at Lloyds for £250,000.

LELY Captain van der Faes or Vander Vaas, father of Sir Peter Lely (1618–80), English painter. Both father and son had the nickname from the sign of the lily (*lelie* in Dutch) on their house in Westphalia. Peter took it as his surname.

LENCHEN Princess Helena (1846–1923), daughter of Queen Victoria (*Drina*). She married Christian, Prince of Schleswig-Holstein (1831–1917).

LEONIDAS GLOVER Richard Glover (1712–85), British merchant, poet and dramatist who wrote *Leonidas* (1737), a blank-verse poem in nine books.

• Leonidas, king of Sparta (491–480 BC) was killed with his men guarding the pass at Thermopylae against the Persians

LEONIDAS OF HIS DAY, THE Sir Robert Peel, *Jenny*, who made a stand against his critics, including Disraeli (the *Asian Mystery*) over the repeal of the Corn Laws (1846), although a coalition defeated him.

• But see *Judas*.

LEPKE or LITTLE LEPKE Louis Buchalter (1897–1944) whose real name was Louis Bookhouse; ruthless killer and head of Murder Incorporated; electrocuted in Sing Sing.

LEVELLER IN POETRY, THE Francis Quarles (1592–1644), Englishman who wrote much religious verse; his *Emblems* (1635) was very popular; so called by Dryden (*Asaph*).

• For Levellers, see *Ahab of the Nation*.

LEVIATHAN, THE Sir Robert Walpole, the *Grand Corrupter*.

• The Leviathan was a large creature (at present unidentified) mentioned in the Book of Job, the Psalms and Isaiah.

LEVIATHAN BOOKMAKER, THE John Stephenson (died 1869), leader of the English betting ring, who committed suicide.

- 'Leviathan' was nineteenth-century slang for someone who 'plunged' heavily on backing horses.

LEVIATHAN OF BOOK COLLECTORS, THE Thomas Rawlinson (1681–1725), whose collection of manuscripts is in the Bodleian Library, Oxford University. It took several auctions to dispose of his enormous book collection. Also *Tom Folio*.

LEVIATHAN OF LITERATURE, THE Dr Johnson, *Blinking Sam*.

LEVIATHAN OF WEALTH, THE The 1st Duke of Sutherland, the *Great Improver*, so called by George Grenville (the *Gentle Shepherd*) because of his vast estates. He owned 1,500,000 acres.

LIAR TAYLOR John Taylor, the *Chevalier*. No-one believed the story he wrote of his life and adventures.

LIBBIE Elizabeth Bacon (1842–1933) of Monroe, Michigan, who married General Custer (*Autie*).

LIBERATOR, THE Daniel O'Connell, the *Big Beggerman*. He formed the Catholic Association (1823), led the successful campaign for Catholic Emancipation (1829) and battled in the House of Commons for the repeal of the Act of Union.

LIBERATOR OF GREECE, THE Lord Cochrane, the *Devil* who entered the service of Greece in 1825.

LIBERATOR OF MISSOURI, THE General Gideon Johnson Pillow (1806–78). He commanded Confederate troops which occupied New Madrid, Missouri (1861); self-applied.

LIBERATOR OF THE NEW WORLD, THE Benjamin Franklin, the *American Socrates*. He helped the new states of Latin America to draft their constitutions.

LIEUTENANT-GOVERNOR OF THE WOODS, THE Michael Howe, *Black Mike*.

LIEUTENANT POG Prince Philip, Duke of Edinburgh (*Biggles*); so called by his shipmates in the Royal Navy.

- Pog = Prince of Greece.

LIFERS' MOUTHPIECE, THE Helen Mehan (1908–1984) of Massachusetts, lawyer with a reputation for defending convicts; so called by newspapers.

LIGHT-HORSE HARRY

i) Lieutenant Colonel Henry Lee, *Legion Harry*.

ii) Henry (Harry) Cooper (1904–), English-born American golfer, Canadian Open champion (1932, 1937).

LIGHTNIN' Samuel Hopkins (1912–82), American guitarist and blues singer. In 1946, he played in a duo 'Thunder Smith and Lightning Hopkins'.

LIGHT OF ISRAEL, THE Daniel Mendoza (1764–1836), British boxer who won the prize-ring championship (1795). Egan (the *Elder*) said he was a pugilist of no ordinary merit. His name, he added, resounded from one part of the kingdom to the other.

LIGHT OF THE HAREM, THE Emmeline Free, 12th wife of Brigham Young (the *Lion of the Lord*), Mormon leader who was survived at his death (1877) by 17 wives out of – it is said – 27.

LIGHT OF THE TOWN, THE Titus Oates, the *Knight of the Post*.

LILY WHITE Billy Richmond, the *Black Terror*.

LILIBET Queen Elizabeth II, *Brenda*; her family nickname, given by Princess Margaret (*Charley's Aunt*) as a child when she was unable to say 'Elizabeth'.

LILLIE Lillie Langtry, the *Jersey Lily*, her family nickname as a child; from 'Emilie?'

LIMB OF SHAKESPEARE, THE John Fletcher (1597–1625), English dramatist; so called by Dryden (*Asaph*). He was a disciple of Shakespeare (the *Bard of All Time*) and succeeded him as the poet of the King's Men. Fletcher's name is linked forever with that of Francis Beaumont (1584–1616). Fletcher may have collaborated with Shakespeare in the writing of *Henry VIII*. Also the *Muses' Darling*.

LIME AND MORTAR KNIGHT, THE Sir William Chambers (1726–96), English architect. He laid out the gardens at Kew, and designed the pagoda there. He was also the architect of Somerset House, London; so called by Wolcot (*Peter Pindar*).

LIMPING OLD BARD, THE Sir John Denham (1615–69), son of the Lord Baron of the Exchequer of Ireland. He was a poet, and wrote *Cooper's Hill* (1652), described by Dryden (*Asaph*) as 'the exact standard of good writing', but it was he who gave Denham the nickname. Denham had a limp towards the end of his life.

- See *Green Park*.

LINDY

i) Charles Augustus Lindbergh (1902–74), American airman who made the first solo crossing of the Atlantic (1927), later Brigadier Lindbergh. Also the *Lone Eagle* and *Lucky Lindy*.

- See *Buster* (xi).

ii) Fred Charles Lindstrom (1905–81), baseball player for the New York Giants (1924–32), the Pittsburgh Pirates (1933–4), the Chicago Cubs (1935) and the Brooklyn Dodgers (1936). His batting average was .311. In the Hall of Fame (1976).

LINEN COOK Robert Cook (?1646–?1728), whom Dawson describes as an eccentric vegetarian of Ipswich and Bristol.

LINGUIST JONES Sir William Jones, the *Admirable Crichton of His Day*. He spoke many languages, including Hindi, Arabic and Sanskrit as well as Latin and Greek.

LINNAEUS OF HOGARTH, THE John Ireland (died 1808). He classified the works of Hogarth (the *Juvenal of Painters*) and wrote a biography (1798).

- Linnaeus was Carl Linné (1707), Swedish botanist who devised a system of botanical classification.

LION William (Willie) Smith (1897–1973), American jazz pianist; from his bravery in World War I.

LION, THE or THE LION OF SCOTLAND William, King of Scotland (1142–1214) who chose a red lion for his device, the origin of the arms of Scotland.

LION COMIQUE

i) George Leybourne, *Champagne Charlie* (iv); nickname given to him by J J Poole (1826–82), manager of the Metropolitan music-hall, London and proprietor from 1875; after he had heard *Champagne Charlie* first sung by Leybourne at the New Canterbury music-hall (1867).

ii) Alfred Peck Stevens (1840–89), 'The Great Vance', British music-hall singer of cockney songs, who also wore top-hat and tails.

iii) Gilbert Hastings Farrell (1845–1901), 'The Great Macdermott', famous for his song 'We don't want to fight, but by *jingo* if we do'. *The Daily Telegraph* (May 1901) said that 'Macdermott's death snapped the last link with the Lion Comique'.

- Pierce Egan (the *Elder*) mentions in his *Book of Sports* (1832) that John Reeve (1799–1838) was the great comic lion after his success in the burlesque *Lions of Mysore*. Leybourne's nickname may have been given because of his parody of a social lion.

LION-HEARTED, THE Richard I, *Coeur de Lion*.

LION HUNTER, THE Roualeyn George Gordon-Cummings (1820–66), second son of Sir William Gordon-Cummings. He hunted in Bechuanaland and the Limpopo valley for five years. His trophies were shown at the Great Exhibition (1851).

LION OF JUSTICE, THE Henry I, *Beauclerc*.

LION OF KASHMIR, THE Sheikh Mohammed Abdullah (1905–82), Chief Minister of Jammu and Kashmir (post-1975).

LION OF KENT, THE Alfred Mynn, *Alfred the Great*.

- Cf the *Lion of the North*.

LION OF THE FOLD OF JUDAH, THE John MacHale (1791–1881), Archbishop of Tuam, Ireland; so called by his friend O'Connell (the *Big Beggerman*) whom the Archbishop succeeded as leader.

- The allusion is to Revelations v.5 where the Lion of the Tribe of Judah is seen as Jesus Christ.

LION OF THE LORD, THE Brigham Young (1801–77), American Mormon leader who founded a settlement in Utah.

LION OF THE NORTH, THE George Parr, the *Best Batsman in England*, who played for Nottinghamshire.
- Cf the *Lion of Kent*.

LION OF THE PUNJAB, THE Maharajah Ranjit Singh (1708–1839). He tried to form a Sikh empire at the time of British expansion in India, and was the owner of the Koh-i-Noor diamond now in the Imperial crown.

LIPPY Leo Ernest Durocher (1906–), baseball manager for Brooklyn, New York when they were National League winners (1954). He is flamboyant and outspoken.

LIPSIAN DICK *Astrological Richard* Harvey; so called by Nash (the *English Aretine*).
- ?after Justus Lipsius (1547–1606), Dutch scholar (Joeste Lips) whose knowledge of Greece and Rome was limited, although he translated Tacitus (1575). Richard took part in the Marprelate controversy (see the *Great Make-Bate of England*) and offended Nash's friend Greene (the *Ape of Euphues*). Tarleton (*Roscius Britannicus*) made jests about Richard, and Nash called him 'an asse'.

LIQUORICE George Jones (1786–1869), British painter and engraver who exhibited 221 paintings at the Royal Academy; from the colour of his sepia drawings.

LITERARY ANVIL, THE The Reverend Dr Henry Mayo (1733–93), a Dissenting minister and friend of Johnson (*Blinking Sam*). Boswell (the *Ambitious Thane*), says he never flinched under Johnson's reiterated blows in argument; and so obtained the nickname, often wrongly attributed to Johnson himself.

LITERARY BAKER, THE Caleb Jeacock (1706–86), British baker, author and orator.

LITERARY BULLDOG, THE Bishop Warburton, the *Colossus of Literature*, who was thought of as an arrogant bully in his writings.

LITERARY COLOSSUS, THE Dr Johnson, *Blinking Sam*.

LITERARY LEATHER-DRESSER, THE Thomas Dowse (1772–1856), a currier of Massachusetts. He was also a book collector and was given an LL.D by Harvard University.

LITERARY MACHIAVEL, THE Joseph Addison, the *English Atticus*. While praising Pope's *Iliad* he was preparing a rival translation.
- 'Machiavel' is one spelling of the name of Niccolò Machiavelli (1469–1527), writer of *The Prince*, a text-book of political opportunism.

LITERARY PROTEUS, THE John Hill, the *Cain of Literature*. He had many activities: quack doctor, newspaper contributor, translator, compiler, botanist and editor.
- Proteus, the Greek old man of the sea, assumed various shapes when anyone tried to catch him.

LITERARY SINBAD, A Captain Basil Hall, *Argonaut*.

LITERARY SYCOPHANT, A Richard Hurd (1720–1808), Bishop of Worcestershire and friend of Warburton (the *Colossus of Literature*). He made a flattering comment on Warburton in his preface to the 1749 edition of his translation of Horace, and Warburton helped him in his rise to a bishopric; so called by D'Israeli.

LITERARY TAILOR, THE Theophilius Brown (1811–*circa* 1879). His shop in Worcester, Massachusetts was a rendezvous for literary figures, including Henry Thoreau (1817–62) and Emerson (the *Buddha of the West*). Brown's letters were published in 1879.

LITERARY WHALE, THE Dr Johnson, *Blinking Sam*; so called by Wolcot (*Peter Pindar*).

LITHUANIAN LION, THE Vitas Gerulaitis, *Broadway Vitas*, of Lithuanian ancestry.

LITTLE, THE

i) John of Salisbury (*circa* 1115–1180),

ecclestiastical scholar and Bishop of Chartres, who was present at the murder of Thomas à Becket (1170). His Latin nickname was *Parvus*.

• See *Eightpence*.

ii) Suibne O'Neill, King of Ireland (615–28).

iii) Sigebert (flourished 626), King of the East Saxons.

LITTLE ADMIRAL, THE Admiral of the Fleet Sir Henry Keppel, the *Father of the Fleet*; a small man.

LITTLE ALEC Alec C Bannerman (1854–1924), cricketer for New South Wales and Australia who played in 28 Test Matches, including those of 1882. He was overshadowed by his famous brother, Charles Bannerman, who virtually won what is regarded as the first Test Match (1877) with a score of 165.

LITTLE AUGIE Jacob Urgen (died 1927), New York gangster for whom *Legs* Diamond worked.

LITTLE BEAGLE, THE Robert Cecil, 1st Earl of Salisbury (*circa* 1565–1612), Lord Treasurer. On the death of Lord Burghley (the *Eremite of Tibbals*), he became Chief Minister of State. He corresponded secretly with James of Scotland, and aided him to the English throne. He was small and hunchbacked; so called by James I (the *British Solomon*). Elizabeth (the *English Diana*) had called him *Pygmy*. Also the *Weasel*.

• A 'beagle' in the 16th century was a spy or an informer.

LITTLE BILL William Johnston (fl. 1920s–1930s), American lawn-tennis player; so called to distinguish him from *Big Bill* Tilden who took the US championship from him in 1920.

LITTLE BOSWELL OF HIS DAY, THE John Aubrey (1626–97), British antiquary, famous for his *Brief Lives* which he began in 1679. Also the *Wiltshire Antiquarian*.

• For James Boswell, see the *Ambitious Thane*.

LITTLE BRITCHES Jennie Stevens (1878–?), American outlaw of Oklahoma, always in men's clothes.

LITTLE BROWN HEN, THE Bette Davis (1908–89), American film star, so called at the beginning of her career; mentioned by her in a British TV interview (1987).

LITTLE BULLDOG Lady Hester Stanhope (1776–1839); so called by Ernest Augustus, Duke of Cumberland (*Cumberland Jack*) because of her pugnacious attitudes. Also the *Queen of the Arabs* (or *the East* or *Palmyra*).

LITTLE CAESAR

i) Abe Saperstein (1901–66), English-born basketball player who founded the Harlem Globetrotters; nicknamed by team members.

ii) Joseph Vincent di Varco (1911–), gangster in Las Vegas and Chicago.

LITTLE CHOCOLATE George Dixon (1870–1909), American boxer who held both bantamweight (1890) and featherweight (1891) world titles. He was the first negro boxer to become a champion and fought 33 or 34 bouts between 1890 and 1901, a record figure.

LITTLE COMEDY Catherine Horneck (1750–*circa* 00), sister of the *Jessamy Bride*, so called by Goldsmith (*Child of Nature*). She and her sister were painted by Sir Joshua Reynolds (the *Bachelor Painter*).

LITTLE DASHER H H Graham (1870–1911), Australian cricketer for Victoria and Australia. He secured two Test centuries, one (170) in his Test debut.

LITTLE DAVID John Felton, *Brutus*; so called by the people after the assassination of Buckingham (*Steenie*: 1628). D'Israeli said that an old woman called out as Felton passed her in London after his arrest: 'God bless thee, little David'.

LITTLE DAVY David Garrick, *Atlas*.

LITTLE DICKY Sir Richard Steele (1672–1729), British essayist and journalist who was editor of *The Spectator* with Addison (the *English Atticus*) and founded *The Tatler* (1709–11).

LITTLE DO Hugh Lawrence Doherty (1876–1919), champion British lawn tennis player who was also called 'H.L.'

LITTLE DOCTOR, THE William Aubrey (1529–95), British statesman; so called by Elizabeth (the **English Diana**). He was a Doctor of Civil Law. 'He was not tall in stature' (Aubrey, his great-grandson).

LITTLE DRUMMOND Malcolm of Drummond (fl. 13th century), Seneschal of the Lennox (post 1225) and ancestor of the Drummond clan; called *Maelcolum Beag* in Gaelic (*beag* = little).

LITTLE DUKE, THE The Duke of Monmouth, **Absalom**.

LITTLE EGYPT Fareeda Mahzar (1873–1916), a Syrian or Armenian near-nude dancer who performed during the Columbian Exposition, Chicago (1893); still remembered in the city.

LITTLE EMPEROR, THE Sir George Simpson (1787–1860), Governor-in-Chief of the Hudson Bay territories, Canada (post-1839). He was small and forceful.

LITTLE FERRET, THE William Adkins (fl. early 19th century), was a Bow Street Runner who became Governor of the House of Correction, Coldbath Fields, London, which was known as 'Adkins Academy'.

LITTLE FLOWER Fiorello La Guardia (1882–1947), a reform Mayor of New York (1934–45); from his Christian name, a diminutive of the Italian for 'flower'.

LITTLE FREE Admiral the Honourable Sir Edward Fremantle (1836–1929) who as Captain Fremantle commanded the naval detachment in the Ashanti War (1873–4).

LITTLE GEM, THE Anne Diamond (1954–), British TV presenter; a pun on diamond – she is small.

LITTLE GENERAL, THE Sir James Outram, the **Bayard of India**.

LITTLE GEORGE COCKING George Onslow (1731–92), British politician and Lieutenant-Colonel in the 1st Foot Guards; so called by the newspapers.

LITTLE GIANT, THE Stephen Arnold Douglas (1813–61), American statesman; small with a powerful intellect.

LITTLE GIRL WITH THE GOLDEN CURLS, THE Mary Pickford, **America's Sweet-**

heart; an early nickname.

LITTLE GOODY TWO-SHOES Lord Ripon, **Goosey Goderich**.

- *Little Goody Two-Shoes* was a nursery tale which first appeared in 1765 and was assumed to have been written by Goldsmith (the **Child of Nature**).

LITTLE JIMMY Thomas James Matthews (1864–1943), cricketer for Williamstown and Australia, who scored a double hat-trick at Manchester in a match against South Africa (1912).

LITTLE JOCK or LITTLE JOCK OF THE PARK Jock Elliott, a border outlaw of Liddesdale. He was said to have died of wounds after he tried to kill the Earl of Bothwell (*circa* 1536–78). The Earl is reputed to have shot him off his horse.

LITTLE JOHN An English outlaw said to have been named Nailor, a companion of **Robin Hood**. When his alleged grave was opened at Hathersage (1784), a thigh-bone $29\frac{1}{2}$ in long was found.

- Ritson (the **Antiquary of Poetry**) identified him as John Nailor and his burial at Hathersage in the High Peak district east of Sheffield. He said Nailor's descendants were living at Hathersage 'to this day' (i.e. the late 18th century).

LITTLE KEPPEL Admiral Augustus, Viscount Keppel (1725–86) who went round the world, with Anson (the **Bulldog of All Circumnavigators**) and became First Lord of the Admiralty; great-uncle of the **Little Admiral**.

LITTLE LEPKE Louis Buchalter, **Lepke**.

LITTLE LOOIE Luis Aparicio (1934–), shortstop for the White Sox, Chicago baseball team; in the Hall of Fame; now in the insurance business.

LITTLE LYNDON Senator Robert (Bobby) Baker (1928–), aide in the American Senate to Lyndon Johnson (1908–83; President 1963–73), until he parted company with him (1963).

LITTLE MAC General George Brinton McClellan (1826–85), Union Commander in the American Civil War, whose success brought him great popularity. Also the *Little Napoleon*, the *Modern Belisarius* and the *Young Napoleon*.

LITTLE MACHIAVEL, THE Lord Shaftesbury, *Achitophel*; so called by Dryden (*Asaph*) because of his machinations during the English Civil War and the Restoration.

- See the *Literary Machiavel*.

LITTLE MAGICIAN, THE Martin van Buren, *King Martin the First*, after he showed skill in operating the 'spoils system' which rewarded campaign workers with public offices.

LITTLE MAN OF TWICKENHAM, THE Pope, the *Bard of Twickenham*; so called by James T Field (1817–81), his American publisher.

LITTLE MASTER, THE

i) Sunil Gavaskar, the *Guru of Indian Batsmanship*.

ii) Clive Churchill (1927–85), one of Australia's greatest Rugby League full backs. From 1950 to 1955 he captained the Kangaroos, Australia's national team, for whom he was coach after he retired (1959).

LITTLE MISS DYNAMITE Brenda Lee (1944–), British pop singer (fl. 1960s): an international star at sixteen.

LITTLE MISS MOFFITT Billie Jean King, née Moffitt (1943–), American tennis champion, US singles champion four times and Wimbledon singles champion four times; in fact over the years she won fourteen titles. From the nursery rhyme *Little Miss Muffet*.

LITTLE MISSY or MISSIE Annie Oakley (1860–1926), whose real name was Ann Mozee and who became Mrs Frank Butler; markswoman with *Buffalo Bill's* Wild West Show; so called by *Buffalo Bill*. Also *Little Sure Shot*.

LITTLE MO Maureen Catherine Connolly (1934–69), later Mrs Norman Brinker; American who was the first woman to win all four major tennis titles; US (1951–52), England (1952), Australia (1953) and France (1963).

LITTLE NAPOLEON

i) General Brinton McClellan, *Little Mac*.

ii) General Pierre Gustav Toutant Beauregard (1818–93), Confederate general who opened fire on Fort Sumter (1860). Also *Old Bory*.

iii) Kevin Mulgrew (1955–), sentenced to a total of 963 years (1983) for 84 IRA murders and attempted murders. He won an appeal in Belfast (1986) and was released.

LITTLE NAPOLEON OF THE COAST BAR, THE Delphin Delmas (1844–1924) of California, who defended Harry Thaw (1871–1947) in 1908, and almost certainly saved him from a death sentence.

LITTLE NEW YORK Louis Campagna (1900–55), American gangster and bodyguard to *Big Al* Capone, who gave him the nickname.

LITTLE NIGHTINGALE, THE Alexander Pope, the *Bard of Twickenham*; nickname from his youth.

LITTLE PALE STAR OF GEORGIA, THE Alexander H Stephens (1812–83), American Congressman, so called by Confederate President Jefferson Davis (1808–89), because of his advocacy of union between the South and the North. Also the *Nestor of the Confederacy*.

LITTLE PEPPER Sir Richard Pepper Arden (1745–1804), Master of the Rolls (1796); so called by Thomas J Mathias (the *Nameless Bard*) in *Pursuits of Literature* (1794).

LITTLE PET OF THE GREEN ROOM, THE Theodore Hook (1788–1841), English author and journalist, son of a composer who exhibited the boy in the green rooms of theatres as a musical prodigy. The boy, however, abandoned music and later in life started *John Bull* (1820).

LITTLE P.F. Helen Newington Wills (1905–), later Mrs Helen Wills Moody, American tennis star who won the singles championship in America (1923–5), France and England (1927–30). 'P.F.' is an abbreviation of *Poker Face*, from her impassive manner of playing. She was also called *Queen of Wimbledon*.

LITTLE PHIL General Philip H Sheridan, the *Jack of Clubs*.

LITTLE PICKLE Dorothy or Dorothea Jordan (1762–1816), Irish actress (née Bland)

and mistress of William IV (the *Flogster*) when he was Duke of Clarence. Also *Miss Romp*.

- Little Pickle was a character in a farce *The Spoiled Child*, popular in the late 18th century.

LITTLE POET, THE Prydydd y Bychan (1200–70), whose real name is unknown.

LITTLE QUEEN, THE

i) Henrietta Maria (1609–69), Queen to Charles I (the *Ahab of the Nation*). Pepys (the *Father of Black-Letter Lore*) described her (1660) as 'Very little'.

ii) Isabella of Valois (1389–1409), who married (1396) Richard II (the *Coxcomb*) at the age of seven and was a widow in four years.

LITTLE RED Charles Starkweather (executed 1959), nineteen-year-old American mass murderer of ten people in a week of terror in Nebraska. He was small with red hair and 'modelled' himself on the film star James Dean (1931–55).

LITTLE RED FOX, THE Alexander II (Scottish) (1198–1249), son of William the *Lion*. He fought with the English barons against John (*Lackland*) , and two years later invaded England. Also the *Peaceful*.

LITTLE SID

i) The Honourable Henry Sidney, who became Earl Russell (1688) and Lord Lieutenant of Ireland. He was the brother of Algernon Sidney (the *British Cassius*); so called by Dryden (*Asaph*).

ii) Sir Charles Sedley (*circa* 1639–1701), Restoration wit, dramatist and notorious rakehell. He was also a generous patron of literature.

LITTLE SIR JOHN WITH THE GREAT BEARD Sir John Byron who took possession of the priory and lands at Newstead, Nottinghamshire in 1540. He was knighted by Elizabeth (the *English Diana*), and was an ancestor of the poet.

LITTLE SURE SHOT Annie Oakley, *Little Missy*; so called by Sitting Bull (?1834–90).

LITTLE TICH Harry Relph (1867–1928), British music-hall comedian with long-toed boots; from his supposed likeness to the Tichborne Claimant. This was Arthur Orton who said he was Sir Roger Tichborne, but later confessed he was an impostor. All small men in Britain have run the risk of being called *Tich* after him.

LITTLE T.O. Tommy Onslow, the *Father of Four-in-Hands*.

LITTLE VAN Martin van Buren, *King Martin the First*.

LITTLE VERMIN Archbishop Laud, *Hocuspocus* who persecuted Puritans. He was ugly, bad-tempered and harsh.

LITTLE VILLAIN Henry Jarvis Raymond (1820–69), American newspaperman who worked with Horace Greeley (the *Napoleon of Essayists*), but then stood against him – and defeated him – on the nomination for Lieutenant-Governor of New York; so called by Greeley himself.

LITTLE WHIG, THE Anne, Countess of Sutherland (died 1716), second daughter of Duke of Marlborough (*Anne's Great Captain*). Her mother went over to the Whigs and earned the hatred of her friend, Queen Anne (*Brandy Nan*).

LITTLE WONDER, THE

i) Tom Sayers (1826–1865) British prize-fighter who, although only 5 ft 8 in, won the championship of England (1851). He became a national hero after his fight with Heenan (the *Benicia Boy*).

- Sayer's right hand was known as 'The Auctioneer'. 'To deliver an auctioneer' was to knock someone down.

ii) John Wisden (1826–84), cricketer for Sussex and England; a fast bowler. He once claimed all ten wickets in a North–South match (1850). He left *Old Clarke's* All-English XI and began the United English XI. In 1864 he founded *Wisden's Cricketer's Almanac*. He was not very tall.

iii) Charles Blondin (1824–1897), whose real name was Jean François Gravelet, French acrobat and tight-rope walker who crossed Niagara Falls on a tight-rope. He was buried in London. His nickname as a child.

LIVELY POPE Jane Pope (1742–1818), English actress who was the original Mrs Candour in *The School for Scandal*

(1777). At fourteen, she acted with Garrick (*Atlas*).

LIVERY MUSE, THE Robert Dodsley (1703–64), publisher, writer and editor, who had once been a footman. He wrote *The Footman's Friendly Advice to his Brothers of the Livery* (1729). Thomas Warton (1728–90), poet laureate (1785) wrote a book about him entitled *The Muse in Livery*.

LIVERPOOL LANDSEER, THE William Huggins (1821–84), a noted British painter.

● Sir Edwin Landseer (1802–73) was England's most famous animal-painter.

LOG CABIN HARRISON or LOG CABIN AND HARD CIDER HARRISON W H Harrison, the *Cincinnatus of the West*. He was in fact born in the family mansion in Virginia.

LOGGERHEAD OF LONDON, THE The Earl of Chatham, *Aeolus*. He stubbornly pursued policies that seemed fated, convinced that by them he could save England.

● A loggerhead was someone thought to be 'thick' or stupid.

LOL

i) Harold Larwood (1904–), cricketer for Nottinghamshire and England, centre of the 'body-line' controversy in the 1932–3 Test Match series.

● See the *Great Unbowlable*.

ii) Sue Lawley (1946–), BBC personality. As a child, she was given ice-cream lollies from her father's shop for her school-friends. She became a freelance in 1988. Also the *Queen Bee*.

LOLLIPOP The Duchess of York, *Carrot-Top*; her nickname as Sarah Ferguson when she worked with the Graphic Company, Mayfair, London.

LONDON IDOL, THE Vesta Tilley, the *Great Little Tilley*, British male impersonator who first appeared on the London music-hallls in 1868. She later became Lady de Frece.

LONDON LITTLE-GRACE Edmund Bonner (1500–69), the last Roman Catholic Bishop of London; because of his severity

in the persecution of 'heretics' during the reign of *Bloody Mary*. On her accession, Elizabeth (the *English Diana*) refused to allow him to kiss her hand; so called by the Rev. Thomas Bryce (1559).

LONE CAT, THE Jesse Fuller (1897–1976), American jazz musician and 'one-man-band'.

LONE EAGLE, THE Charles Lindbergh, *Lindy*; so called by American newspapers.

LONE LION, THE W E Borah, the *Great Isolationist*.

LONELY, THE Art, High King of Ireland (flourished 3rd century), son of *Conn the Hundred Fighter*; so called after the death of his brother Connla. He was the father of Cormac MacArt (the *Magnificent*).

● Art = Arthur in Gaelic.

LONESOME Dave Peverett (1950–), American member of the blues and boogie band 'Foghat', a 'child' of the Savoy Brown band.

LONESOME CHARLEY Charles Alexander Russell (?1842–76), American soldier, hunter and probably the greatest of all army scouts in the West. He was the guide to *Autie* Custer's Black Hills expedition (1876) and was shot in the retreat from Little Big Horn.

LONESOME GEORGE George Gobel (1920–), American comedian.

LONG, THE

i) John of Wykeham, father of William of Wykeham (?1323–1404), Lord Chancellor of England and Bishop of Winchester.

ii) Fercher *Fada* (died 697), King of Dalriada, west Scotland, sometimes called Ferchardus II. He tried to drive out the Britons and Angles (*circa* 678).

● See the *Fair* (ii). Fercher = Farquhar. *Fada* = long.

LONGBEARD William Fitz-Osbert, *King of the Poor*.

LONG BEN Captain John Avery, the *Arch Pirate*.

LONGBOW John Philpot Curran (1750–

1817), Irish judge and politician, Master of the Rolls (post-1806); so called by Byron (*Baby*) who said he was 'rich in imagination'. Also *Orator Mum*.

- Drawing the long bow = making exaggerated claims (since the 17th century).

LONG FELLOW, THE

i) De Valera, the *Chief*.

ii) Lester Piggott (1935–), English champion jockey nine times between 1960 and 1971; so called because at 5 ft 7 in he was considered too big to be a jockey. In 1984, he equalled the record of Frank Buckle (the *Pocket Hercules*) by riding 27 classic winners, and then beat it by riding his 28th. He retired in 1985 to become a trainer. Also *Old Stoneface*.

LONG HAIR
General *Autie* Custer; so called by the Sioux Indians. Also *Buffalo Bill Cody*.

- Cf *Long Yellow Hair*.

LONG HARRY
Henry Wilkinson (1610–75), Professor of Divinity at Oxford University, and a member of the Westminster Assembly (1643–53) to advise Parliament on the new form of Church government.

- Cf *Dean Harry*, a different man.

LONG HEAD

i) Fergus *Cennfada* (fl. *circa* 425), the son of Conall, King of Tir Conaill (Tyrconnell).

ii) Muircheartach *Cennfada* (fl. 14th century), the Prince of Clannaboy (1369–95).

- See *French John*. *Cenn* = head; *fada* = long in Gaelic.

LONG JOHN
John Wentworth (1815–88), 6 ft 6 in tall. He was an editor and arguably the greatest Mayor of Chicago.

LONGLEG
Sir William de Douglas (died *circa* 1288), father of the *Bold*.

LONGMAN
Derek Pringle, *Big Foot*.

LONG MEG OF WESTMINSTER

i) A noted – and obviously tall – bawd and virago in the time of Henry VIII (*Bluff Hal*). She assumed men's clothing, served as a soldier and then set up an alehouse in London. A life of Long Meg was published in 1635, but she was mentioned in pamphlets and ballads of 1582–94. Other than that, her existence cannot be proved.

ii) Peter Branan, aged 104 and 6 ft 6 in tall when he was mentioned in *The Edinburgh Antiquarian Magazine* of September 1769. The nickname seems to have been given to many people of unusual height. There is a proverb 'As long as Meg of Westminster'.

- A stone circle, 100 yards in diameter, in Cumberland is known as 'Long Meg and Her Daughters' and has long been believed by the superstitious to be a ring of petrified witches. 'Long Meg', tall and thin, is reputed to bleed if chipped.

LONG SCRIBE, THE
Vincent George Dowling (1785–1852), British sportsman and journalist, an authority on sport of every kind. He was very tall. He worked with *The Observer* and was a 'scoop-hunter' of Regency days.

LONGSHANKS
Edward I, the *English Justinian*; so called in a fifteenth-century chronicle and on his tomb in Westminster Abbey (*Edwardus Longus*). He had long, spindly legs.

LONG SIR THOMAS or LONG TOM
Sir Thomas Robinson (?1700–77), Governor of Barbados and Commissioner of Excise, who was very tall and thin; so called to distinguish him from Sir Thomas Robinson, 1st Lord Grantham (1695–1770), who was short and plump.

LONG TOM
Thomas Jefferson, the *Apostle of Liberty*, who was tall and thin.

LONGSPÉE or LONGSWORD

i) William, Duke of Normandy (died 942: reigned 927–42), great-great-grandfather of William I (the *Bastard*).

ii) William (died 1226), natural son of Henry II (*Curtmantle*) and 3rd Earl of Salisbury.

LONGITUDE HARRISON
John Harrison (1693–1776), British inventor of the chronometer which enabled sailors to calculate longitude.

LONG WILL
William Langland (?1330–?1440), Middle English poet, principally

of *The Vision concerning Piers Plowman* (?1360–99); nickname mentioned by him in that poem. Langland was tall and thin.

LONGY Abner Zwillman (1899–1959), head of the Jewish gangsters in New York (1920s). He was 'long' on talk. He was found hanged.

LONG YELLOW HAIR William Cody, *Buffalo Bill*; nickname given to him by Chief Yellow Hair (1874), *Pahaska* in Sioux.

- Cf *Long Hair*.

LONNIE A J Donegan, the *King of Skiffle*; self-applied after the American guitarist Lonnie Johnson (1900–70).

LORD

i) Timothy Dexter (1747–1806), merchant of Newburyport, Massachusetts, who gave himself the 'title'.

ii) John Sangar (1816–89), British circus proprietor with his brother George (1825–1911), who also used the honorific. They adopted the distinction because *Buffalo Bill* was always called 'the honourable' and they decided to go one better.

LORD-ALL-PRIDE John Sheffield, 3rd Earl of Mulgrave and 1st Duke of Normanby and Buckingham (1648–1721). He built (at the end of the Mall, London) Buckingham House which was bought by George III (the *Button Maker*) for his daughter.

LORD BLACKOUT Julius S Elias, 1st Baron Southwood (1873–1946), chairman of *The Daily Herald*. Also called 'J.S.E'.

LORD BLUFF George Brudenell, 4th Earl of Cardigan (1712–90); so called by Wolcot (*Peter Pindar*).

LORD BLUSTER Henry Richard Fox, 3rd Baron Holland (1773–1840); so called in *Noctes Ambrosianae*.

LORD CROP Lord George Gordon (1751–93), third son of the Duke of Gordon. He led the Gordon riots (1780) designed to persuade the Government to repeal the 1778 Act which gave relief to Catholics.

- A Newgate crop was the prison hairstyle. Lord George spent the last years of his life in Newgate, and in fact died there.

LORD DOGGO John Maynard, 1st Baron Keynes (1883–1946), British economist who was British Treasury representative at the Versailles Peace Conference (1919) and leader of the British delegation to the Bretton Woods Conference (1944). His room at the Treasury was opposite that of Lord Catto (1879–1959).

LORD EDWARD Edward (Ted) Ralph Dexter (1935–), cricketer for Cambridge, Sussex and England, which he captained in 25 Test Matches. He is a fearless batsman and once scored 70 against fierce West Indian bowling. In 62 Test Matches, he made 4,502 runs, including nine centuries, and took 66 wickets; chosen (1989) as chairman of the English Selectors.

LORD EXPORT Donald Gresham, 1st Baron Stokes (1914–), former manager of Leylands which he joined as an apprentice. His export deals became legendary.

LORD FANNY John, Baron Hervey of Ickworth (1696–1743), British statesman, vice-chamberlain to the royal household and writer of memoirs of the Court of George II; so called by Pope (the *Bard of Twickenham*) in *The Dunciad* (1728) in scorn for his ineffeminate habits. He bathed in asses' milk ('that mere white curd of Ass's milk' says Pope) to avoid epilepsy and used rouge on his face. Also *Sporus*.

LORD FREDDY Frederick Swindell (1812–85), British racehorse owner, bookmaker and gambler, for whom Archer (the *Demon* iii) won the Lincoln (1874). Also the *Napoleon of the Turf*.

LORD GANNEX Joseph, 1st Baron Kagan (1916–), founder of the Gannex group of companies which manufacture raincoats. He was imprisoned (1980) after admitting taking £189,000 from his company.

LORD GAWKY Lord Temple, the *Gawky Squire*. Walpole (the *Autocrat of Strawberry Hill*) said he was ridiculously awkward; so called in contemporary works.

LORD GNOME

i) Peter Cook (1937–), British comedian and major shareholder in *Private Eye*, the satirical magazine.

- 'Lord Gnome' is the mythical

proprietor of *Private Eye* often mentioned in the magazine. 'Gnome' is a columnist.

ii) Richard Ingram (1937–), former editor of *Private Eye* (pre-1986).

LORD HAW-HAW William Joyce (1906–46), British fascist who broadcast for the Nazis (World War II) and was hanged as a war criminal; from his drawling, affected accent; so called first by Jonah Barrington in *The Daily Mail*.

LORD HIGH EXECUTIONER, THE Albert Anastasia (1903–57), head of Murder Incorporated, and 'hit man' for the Mafia; from the Gilbert and Sullivan character (*The Mikado*). Also the *Mad Hatter of Crime*.

LORDLY, THE Duncan MacGregor (fl. 16th century) of Ardchoille, who led the Gregor clan on a raid on Balquihidder (1543).

LORD M William Lamb, 2nd Viscount Melbourne (1779–1848), Prime Minister (1834 and 1835–9); nicknamed by Queen Victoria (*Drina*) to whom he was friend and confidant.

LORD MINIMUS Sir Jeffrey Hudson, the *King's Dwarf*.

LORD NELSON Byron Nelson (1912–), American Open golf champion (1939), one of the game's greatest players.

LORD OF CRAZY CASTLE, THE John Hall-Stevenson (1718–85), author of *Crazy Tales*. He named his home at Skelton castle, near Gainsborough, Lincolnshire, 'Crazy Castle'.

LORD OF THE SPIES, THE Thomas (Tom) Edward Neil Driberg, Baron Bradwell (1905–76). Fleet Street journalist as 'William Hickey' of the *Daily Express*. He had associations with MI5 and other intelligence organizations; mentioned by Chapman Pincher of *The Daily Express*.
- See *Pickle*. Sir William Golding has written a novel *Lord of the Flies*.

LORD P Lord Palmerston, *Cupid*.

LORD PICCADILLY William Douglas, 4th Duke of Queensberry (1724–1810), sportsman and voluptuary, Vice-Admiral of Scotland and a Lord of the Bedchamber.

He lived in Piccadilly, and some of his activities earned him the nickname of the *Piccadilly Ambulator*. He was called 'Degenerate Douglas' by Wordsworth (the *Bard of Rydal Mount*). Also *Old Q* and *Old Tick*.

LORD PORN Francis Aungier Pakenham, 7th Earl of Longford (1905–). He campaigned against pornography.

LORD SEVENTY-FOUR Lord Lonsdale, the *Brazen Bully*; so called by Byron (*Baby*) after he had offered to build and man a 74-gun warship during the War of Independence (1775–83).

LORD SPAM Samuel George Armstrong, 3rd Baron Vestey (1913–), head of the Dewhurst chain of butcher shops and producers of canned meat.

LORD WIBBLY-WOB Harold Sidney Harmsworth, 1st Viscount Rothermere (1868–1940), British newspaper proprietor and brother to Lord Northcliffe (the *Chief*); so called by the *Morning Post*, which alleged political instability.

LORDY

i) Lord Mountbatten, *Dickie*; so called in the Romsey area of Hampshire where he lived.

ii) Lord Lonsdale, *England's Greatest Sportsman*.

LOTTIE The 8th Duchess of Devonshire, the *Double Duchess* (i).

LOUIE Princess Marie Louise of Schleswig-Holstein (1872–1957), grand-daughter of Queen Victoria (*Drina*). She married Albert, Prince of Anhalt (1864–1933).

LOUISA Major-General Lewis Wallace (1827–1905), American statesman, lawyer and author of *Ben Hur* (1880); so called by Union troops in the American Civil War; from 'Lewis'.

LOUISCHEN Princess Louise Marguerite of Prussia (1860–1917), wife of Arthur, Duke of Connaught (1850–1942).

LOUISVILLE LIP, THE Cassius Clay, *Gaseous Cassius*, born in Louisville, Kentucky, later Mohammed Ali.

LOVE GODDESS, THE Rita Hayworth (1918–87), American film star of romantic pictures; so called in the 1940s. Her real name was Margarita Cansino.

LOVELY GEORGIUS George Washington, the *American Cincinnatus*; so called by British soldiers during the American War of Independence (1775–83) [Frey, Boston, 1888].

LOVE ROUSER, THE *Buddy* Rogers, *America's Boy Friend*.

LOWER MACWILLIAM, THE Edmund de Burgh or Burke, Earl of Mayo who, on the murder of the 3rd Earl of Connaught (1333), became an Irish chieftain as Mac-William Lochtair or Oughter (Gaelic *hugh-daich* = lesser).

- Cf the *Upper MacWilliam*.

LOWTHER THE SILENT Colonel Henry Cecil Lowther (1790–1867), the *Father of the House*, a MP who never made a speech.

LOYAL, THE Richard de Lucy (died 1179), Chief Justiciar of England. He was the first of the supporters of Henry II (*Curtmantle*) to be excommunicated after the murder of Thomas à Booket (1170).

- For Justiciar, see *Roger the Great*.

LUCKNOW KAVANAGH Thomas Henry Kavanagh (1821–82), Assistant Commissioner of Oudh, stationed in Lucknow during the siege (1857). He made his way out disguised as an Indian scout to guide in the relief forces of Sir Colin Campbell. He had been in the service of the East India Company for sixteen years. He was awarded the Victoria Cross, one of the only four civilians ever to receive it.

LUCKY

i) Richard John Bingham, 7th Earl of Lucan (1934–?74) who disappeared after the murder (1974) of his children's nurse; because he was lucky in gambling. Some reports put him in South Africa.

ii) Harold Lewis Lasseter (died 1930), American-born prospector alleged to have found a gold treasure near Alice Springs, the legendary Lasseter's Reef, but he died of thirst in the desert.

iii) Lieutenant-General Sir Miles Christopher Dempsey (1896–1969), commander of the 2nd Army (World War II).

iv) Salvatore Lucania, known as Charles Luciano, the *King of Pimps*. He escaped alive after having been tortured and left for dead.

LUCKY BARONET, THE Sir Joseph Hawley, Bart. (1814–75), British racehorse owner who won the Derby four times (1851, 1858, 1859 and 1868), as well as other classic races. He won £100,000 on Beadsman, the Derby winner of 1858.

LUCKY LINDY Colonel Lindbergh, *Lindy*.

LUCKY LODER Major Eustace Loder (1867–1914). He bought Spearmint for 300 guineas, and with it won the Derby and the Grand Prix de Paris, both in 1906. He also owned Pretty Polly, a filly which won 22 out of 24 races, including the Oaks and the St Leger and took more than £37,000 in stake money.

LUCULLUS Samuel Bernard (1651–1739), a rich English gourmet who lived in lavish style.

- See the *Maecenas and Lucullus of His Island*.

LULU David Ivon Gower (1957–), cricketer for Leicestershire (captain) and England (captain 1984–86 and 1989) who had played in 25 Test Matches before he was twenty six. By 1988 he had scored 7,000 Test runs. He has a mass of fair, curly hair. Also *Stoat*.

LUN John Rich, the *Father of English Pantomime*; so called by Garrick (*Atlas*).

- See the *Father of Harlequins*.

LUPO THE WOLF Ignazio Saietta (fl. 1900s), one of the leaders of the American Black Hand gang and later of the *Unione Siciliane*; because of his cruelty.

LUPUS The 2nd Earl of Chester, *Le Gros*.

LUSTY PAKINGTON Sir John Pakington (1549–1625), prominent as one of the courtiers of Queen Elizabeth (the *English Diana*). He lived in great luxury.

LUSTY STUCLEY Sir Thomas Stucley (*circa* 1525–78), English soldier of fortune, said to have been an illegitimate son of Henry VIII (*Bluff Hal*); so called at Court.

LYCURGUS OF THE LOWER HOUSE, THE Lord John Russell, *Finality John*; advocate of Parliamentary reform.

- Lycurgus (*circa* 825 BC) was a Spartan legislator who maintained that only he could cure the nation of its evils.

LYING DICK TALBOT Richard Talbot, Jacobite Earl of Tyrconnel (1630–91), an agent in many intrigues, one of them being an attempt to ruin Anne, Duchess of York (née Hyde) whom James had married secretly. Talbot was Lord-Lieutenant of Ireland (1686–9) for James III (the *King Over the Water*) and fought against William III (the *Deliverer*).

LYING OLD FOX, THE Horace Walpole, the *Autocrat of Strawberry Hill*; so called in *Noctes Ambrosianae*.

LYING SCOT, THE Gilbert Burnet, the *Busy Scots Parson*, who wrote *The History of My Own Times* (1724–34). He was accused of misrepresentation. Johnson (*Blinking Sam*) thought it not so much lying as prejudice.

LYING TRAVELLER, THE Sir John Maundeville or Mandeville (1300–72) whose *Travels* (published 1568) contained some fantastic stories. They were, however, thought to have been compiled by Jean d'Outremeuse of Liège, described as 'an artistic liar'.

M

MA

i) Gertrude Rainey (1886–1939), pioneer American jazz singer, whose real name was Gertrude Melissa Pridgett before she married 'Pa' Rainey. Also the *Mother of the Blues*.

ii) Arizona Donnie Clark Barker (1872–1935), leader of the American Barker gang of thieves and train-robbers. Killed in a shoot-out with the police.

iii) Minnie Kennedy, mother of Aimée McPherson (the *Hot Gospeller*).

MA COUTTS Harriott Mellon (1777–1837), Irish actress of poor parents, widow of Thomas Coutts (1735–1822), a banker believed to have been the richest man of his day, who left her his entire fortune. In 1827, at the age of fifty, she married William Aubrey de Vere Beauclerk (aged twenty-six), the 9th Duke of St Albans. Also *Old Mother Coutts*.

MABON William Abraham (1842–1922), MP for Glamorgan, and President of the South Wales Miners' Federation. The nickname was first adopted by him for an eisteddfod.

- Mabon was the Celtic sun-god.

MACARONI PAINTER, THE Richard Conway (1740–1821), a British miniaturist.

- A macaroni was a fop or a dandy (*circa* 1760), derived, it seems, from members of the Macaroni Club who liked that food and affected extravagant fashions.

MACARONI PARSON, THE

i) Dr William Dodd (1729–77), Prebendary of Brecon, King's chaplain and Shakespearean scholar, who was executed at Tyburn for forgery.

ii) John Horne Tooke (1736–1812), curate at New Brentford, philologist and supporter of Wilkes (*Squinting Jack*). David Hume (1711–76) the philosopher once commented on his 'gay apparel'. Also the *Philosopher of Wimbledon*.

MACDALEK Ian Macdonald (1936–   ),

Ministry of Defence spokesman at press conferences (1982) during the Falklands Islands conflict; so called by Fleet Street and TV men. Some newspapers called him 'The Braille Speaker'.

- The Daleks with monotonous electronic voices were figures in the TV series *Dr Who*.

MACDONELL SCOTUS John Macdonell (1728–1810) of the Canadian North-West Company, also *Spanish John*.

MACHIAVEL William Cecil, Lord Burghley, the *Eremite of Tibbals*; so called by D'Israeli.

- See the *Literary Machiavel*.

MACHINE GUN

i) George R Kelly (1897–1954), Chicago gangster who coined the term 'G Man' for a member of the FBI.

ii) Jack McGurn (1904–36), Chicago gangster; real name Jack Vincenzo de Mora.

MACHITO Frank Grillo (1908–84), Cuban-born Afro-Cuban band leader in America, whose style was adopted by *Dizzy* Gillespie and Charlie *Bird* Parker.

MAC THE KNIFE

i) Harold Macmillan (1894–1986), British Prime Minister (1957–63). He sacked seven Cabinet Ministers. He became 1st Earl of Stockton (1984). Also *Supermac* and *Wondermac*.

ii) Sir Ian MacGregor (1912–   ), American-born chairman of the British Steel Corporation (1980–3); because of his cuts in the organization to attain profitability; later chairman of the British Coal Board (1983–   ); so called by *King Arthur* Scargill.

- Mac the Knife is a character in *The Threepenny Opera* (Berlin 1928; London 1956) by Kurt Weill (1900–50).

MACVEINUS NASO Macveigh Napier, the *Bacon Fly*, who, seemingly, had a veined nose; so called in *Blackwood's Magazine*.

- Naso was the cognomen of Ovid (cf Latin *nasus* = nose).

MACWILLIAM OF THE HEADS Ulick de Burgh, 1st Earl of Clanricarde (died 1544) who made a mound of dead men's heads after a battle and covered it with earth. The Irish version of his nickname was *Na-gCeann* or *Ne-gan* (*ceann* = head).

- The ancient Celts were head-hunters. See the *Upper MacWilliam*.

MADAM

i) Violet Melnotte (1856–1935), English actress and theatre manageress with flamboyant ways. Also *Mad Melnotte*.

ii) Perle Mesta, the *Hostess with the Mostest*.

MADAM CAREWELL The Duchess of Portsmouth, *Bathsheba*; a pun on her name 'Kéroualle'.

MADAME DU DEFFAND OF THE ENGLISH CAPITAL, THE Elizabeth Robinson Montagu (1720–1800), a leader of London society and a *blue stocking*. She gave breakfast parties and evening conversaziones at which there was much stimulating and intelligent talk. Also the *Queen of the Blue Stockings*.

- Madame Marie Anne de Vichy-Chamrond, Marquise du Deffand de la Lande (1697–1780), held a salon at which Voltaire, Montesquieu, D'Alembert and the Encyclopaedists were regular visitors.

MAD ANTHONY Brigadier-General Anthony Wayne (1745–96), American soldier in the War of Independence, famous for his daring exploits. The Indians called him 'The Chief who never sleeps'.

MAD AXEMAN, THE Gareth Chilcott, *Coochie*; from his wild tactics as a young player.

- The original Mad Axeman was Frank Mitchell who escaped from Dartmoor prison in December 1965 and vanished. The Krays (see *Colonel* iii) were believed to have murdered him but they were acquitted and Mitchell is officially still on the run, his 'murder' never having been solved.

MAD ARCHER Richard Miller Archer (1858– ?), an actor known as Richard A Prince; so called in theatrical circles. After his killing of *Breezy Bill* Terriss, he was sent to Broadmoor (1898).

MAD BELL William Bell, *Doomsday Bell*.

MAD BOMBER, THE George Peter Metesky (1903–), sent to an asylum after having planted bombs in New York for revenge; released 1973.

MAD BUTLER, THE Archibald Hall (1924–), the *Monster Butler* gaoled for life (1978) for five murders, including that of the Labour MP Walter Scott-Elliott to whom he was butler. He began a hunger strike in prison but gave it up (1980).

MADCAP MAXIE Max Baer (1909–59), American world heavyweight boxing champion (1934–35); from his crazy behaviour.

MAD CAVALIER, THE Prince Rupert of Bavaria or the Rhine (1619–82), nephew of Charles I (the *Ahab of the Nation*) for whom he fought in the English Civil War; a man of reckless courage. Also the *Prince Robber*.

MAD COLIN Colin Campbell of Glenlyon (fl. 1580s).

MAD DANNY Daniel (Danny) McCann (1958–88), Belfast-born IRA terrorist shot by the SAS in Gibraltar with two others. They were there to try to blow up a ceremonial parade by the Royal Anglian Regiment.

MAD DOCTOR, THE Dr Francis Willis, *Dr Duplicate*, who treated George III (the *Button Maker*) for insanity. Captain R H Gronow says 'it was said, and I believe with truth, that the poor king could not hear Dr Willis's name spoken without shuddering'.

MAD DOG

i) Vincent Coll (1909–32), New York gangster (1920s) and murderer, called 'the mad dog killer' by American newspapers.

ii) Dominic McGlinchey (1956–), leader of the INLA, wanted for thirty murders and two hundred shootings, bombings and kidnappings; sentenced to life imprisonment (1984) in Belfast. The sentence was quashed by the Belfast Appeal Court (October 1985) and he was released, but immediately re-arrested for offences in the Irish Republic; sentenced to ten years imprisonment in Dublin (1986) for having shot a policeman to resist arrest.

MAD DUCHESS, THE

i) Margaret, née Lucas (circa 1625–73), wife of the Duke of Newcastle (1592–1676), called by Charles II (the *Blackbird*) 'the crackbrained Duchess of Newcastle'. Pepys (the *Father of Black-Letter Lore*) declared she was 'a mad, conceited, ridiculous woman'. Also *Mad Madge of Newcastle*.

ii) Her daughter Elizabeth, wife of the 2nd Duke of Albemarle (1653–88).

MAD FRANKIE Frank Fraser (1927–), described as Britain's most violent man; 'enforcer' for the Richardson torture gang in South London. He spent 32 out of his first 58 years in gaol.

MAD FRED Frederick Bayley Deeming (*circa* 1854–92), Australian confidence trickster and murderer. He 'confessed' on the scaffold that he was *Jack the Ripper*.

MAD HARRY Lord Hastings, *Champagne Charlie* (iii).

MAD HATTER, THE Roger Crab, the *English Hermit*. He gave away hats to the poor when he could not make his shop at Chesham, Buckinghamshire, pay.

MAD HATTER OF ASCOT, THE Mrs Gertrude Shilling, a company director who wears extravagant fantastically designed (by her son David) hats each year to the Ascot race-meeting. By 1989, she had attended 28 Ascots wearing them, but after that race-meeting, she said she had 'retired, as I don't have my heart in it now'.

MAD HATTER OF CRIME, THE Albert Anastasia, the *Lord High Executioner*, said to have had an insane desire to kill.

MAD JACK

i) Captain John Byron (1756–91), father of the poet and son of *Foul-Weather Jack*. He was a libertine and gambler and died in poverty in Paris.

ii) John Hall, executed (1716) after the 1715 Jacobite Rising.

iii) John Mytton (1796–1834), who once set fire to his night-shirt to cure himself of hiccups.

iv) John Fuller, *Hippo*. He built several follies.

MAD LIZZIE Lizzie Webb (1948–), British dance and exercise teacher on TV.

MAD MADGE OF NEWCASTLE Margaret, Duchess of Newcastle, the *Mad Duchess* (i).

MAD MAJOR, THE Major James Stewart (1589– ?) of Ardvorlich who served with Montrose (the *Great Marquis*). In a rage, Stewart murdered (1644) his friend Lord Kingpoint, the son of the Earl of Monteith.

- A Major Hutchins of the Machine Gun Corps was nicknamed 'The Mad Major' for his reckless bravery in World War I.

MAD MARQUIS, THE Joseph Henry De La Poer Beresford, 5th Marquis of Waterford (1844–95) who had a great reputation for practical jokes in questionable taste. He once put a donkey into the bed of a stranger at an inn and spread aniseed on the hoofs of a clergyman's horse so that he could hunt him with bloodhounds. He shot himself. Also known as *Spring-Heeled Jack*.

MAD MELNOTTE Violet Melnotte, *Madam*; so called after she had decided to build a theatre in a slum area – St Martin's Lane, London – but the venture was a great success.

MAD MIKE Colonel Michael Hoare (1919–), mercenary soldier, particularly in the Congo (1964–7). He was sentenced in South Africa (1982) to ten years imprisonment for a kidnap attempt in the Seychelles, and released (1984) under a Christmas amnesty.

MAD MITCH Lieutenant-Colonel Colin Mitchell (1926–), after his bravery in Crater Town, Aden (1967) as a major in the Argyll and Sutherland Highlanders.

MAD MULLAH, THE Muhammed bin Abdullah (died 1921), Somali rebel who conducted a long campaign against the British (post-1899).

MAD MYRA Myra Hindley (1942–), one of

204

the **Moors Murderers**, imprisoned for life; so called in the open prison Cookham Woods, Rochester, Kent (1980s). She was said to live in a fantasy world.

MAD PARSON, THE

i) Jonathan Swift, **Dr Presto**; so called in London clubs because of his eccentricity.

ii) John Edward Allen (1912–), convicted murderer who escaped from Broadmoor Criminal Lunatic Asylum (1947) wearing a clergyman's collar he had used in a concert party. He was recaptured (1949) and released (1951).

MAD POET, THE

i) Nathaniel Lee (?1653–92), British poet and playwright of *The Rival Queens* (1677). He was in an asylum for five years.

ii) Macdonald Clarke (1798–1842), American who died in an asylum.

iii) William Collins (1721–59), insane in the last years of his life.

MAD PRIEST OF KENT, THE

John Ball (died 1381), a leader of the English Peasants' Revolt (1381) with Wat Tyler and Jack Straw. He advocated the principles of Wyclif (**Doctor Evangelicus**) and made famous the text: 'When Adam delved and Eve span, who was then the gentleman?' so called by Froissart (?1337–1410): 'They had been greatly encouraged by a mad priest of Kent called John Ball'.

• See the **King of the Commons** (ii).

MADRE, LA

Jane Elizabeth Coke (1777–1863), Viscountess Andover (1796) and later wife of Admiral Digby (the **Silver Captain**): mother of Jane Digby (**Aurora**). It was her family nickname.

MAD RIDER, THE

Sir Claude Champion de Crespigny (1847–1935); nickname as a steeplechaser.

MAD SHELLEY

P B Shelley, **Ariel**; nickname at Eton because of his revolt against authority.

MAD WINDHAM

William Frederick Windham (1840–66); so called at Eton. There were fears that this might be literally true, but a commission (1861) found him sane. *Punch* (January 1862) said that Windham, the heir to a large property in Norfolk, was 'considered to be insane by his guardian and an inquiry occupied the law courts for nearly a month'. Costs were enormous.

MAECENAS

i) The Earl of Halifax, **Filcher**; so called by the playwright Nicholas Rowe (1674–1718) in 1715 at the time of the Earl's death.

ii) William Blount, 4th Lord Mountjoy (died 1534) who commanded the forces that put down the rebellion of Perkin Warbeck (the **White Rose of England**) in 1485; statesman and patron of learning. Fuller described him as 'one of the chief revivers of learning in England'. He was a friend of the philosopher Erasmus (1467–1536).

• See the **Female Maecenas** and the **Last English Maecenas**.

MAECENAS AND LUCULLUS OF HIS ISLAND, THE

The 6th Duke of Devonshire, **Hart**; so called by Emerson (the **American Montaigne**).

• Lucius Licinius Lucullus (*circa* 117–56 BC) lived the last years of his life in luxury and indolence.

MAECENAS AND PETRONIUS OF HIS AGE, THE

Lord Chesterfield, the **English Rochefoucauld**.

• Gaius Petronius (died *circa* 66), companion of Nero and director of his pleasures, wrote the *Satyricon*.

MAGNIFICENT, THE

i) Edmund I, the **Deed-Doer**; so called by Florence of Worcester (died 1118); *Edmundus magnificus*.

ii) Cormac MacArt (reigned 250–300), the most illustrious of the pagan kings of Ireland, grandson of **Conn the Hundred Fighter**. Legends give him the wisdom of Solomon and credit him with having founded schools for history, law, literature and military science at Tara. He is said to have become a Christian after abdicating on the loss of an eye, since no pagan with a physical blemish could rule.

• See Art the **Lonely**.

iii) Robert of Normandy, the **Devil**.

iv) Sir John Arundell (died *circa* 1433), MP and Sheriff of Cornwall.

- See also *Morgan the Magnificent* and *Old Magnificent*.

MAGNIFICENT HAYES Rear-Admiral John Hayes (1775–1838) who in the Basque Roads (1814) when the 74-gun vessel *The Magnificent*, of which he was Captain, was in danger of being driven ashore by a violent storm, club-hauled her. (This meant that he tacked the ship and then let down the lee anchor as soon as the wind was out of the sails, so bringing her round into the wind as soon as she paid off, cut the cables and trimmed the sails to the other tack.) This whole process has been described as being as dangerous as the most delicate operation in surgery.

MAGNIFICENT HEBER Richard Heber, the *English Atticus*; so called for his wine cellar and his library (said to have consisted of 500,000 volumes).

MAGNIFICENT WILDCAT, THE Pola Negri (1899–1987), tempestuous American film star, born in Poland, the title of one of her films. Her real name was Appolonia Chalupek.

MAGNIFICO Henry, 1st Viscount Chaplin (1840–1923), statesman and lifelong friend of Edward VII (the *Peacemaker*); his nickname at Oxford University where he lived in great style. He was something of a rake. He won the Derby with Hermit (1867), and so contributed to the ruin of *Champagne Charlie* (iii).

MAGUS OF THE TIMES, THE Edward Sterling, *Captain Whirlwind*; so called by Carlyle (the *Censor of the Age*) who in his biography of John Sterling (1851) wrote 'His father ... the Magus of the *Times*, had talk and argument ever ready'.

- See *Archimagus*.

MAGWITCH Clive Vivian Leopold James (1939–), Australian-born London journalist and TV personality.

- Abel Magwitch in Dickens' *Great Expectations* was transported to Australia.

MAIDEN, THE or **MALCOLM THE MAIDEN** Malcolm IV, King of Scotland (1141–65), from his gentle disposition. He came to the throne at the age of eleven.

MAIDEN QUEEN, THE Elizabeth I, the *English Diana*. She never married.

MAID MARIAN

i) Matilda or Marian, daughter of Richard, Baron Fitzwalter. She is reputed to have fled to Sherwood Forest to avoid the attention of King John (*Lackland*) and to have married *Robin Hood*, but there is no evidence.

ii) Pauline Marianne Wehde, *Buster* (v).

MAID OF BATH, THE Eliza Ann Linley (1754–92), English actress. She married Sheridan (*Sherry*) after he had fought two duels (1772) with a Major Matthews who had caused a paragraph detrimental to her to be printed in a newspaper.

MAID OF BUTTERMERE, THE Mary Robinson, the *Beauty of Buttermere*; so called by Wordsworth (the *Bard of Rydal Mount*) in *The Prelude* (1799–1805).

MAID OF KENT, THE

i) Elizabeth Barton, the *Holy Maid of Kent*.

ii) Caroline Heathorne (1784–1888), died aged 104 at Maidstone, Kent.

MAID OF THE OAKS, THE Elizabeth (née Farren), Countess of Derby (?1759–1829), former actress.

- The Oaks is a classic race for fillies (post-1779) named after the shooting-box of the 12th Earl of Derby (died 1834), her husband.

MAIN-DE-FER Henri de Tonti (?1650–1704), French officer who explored the Niagara and Illinois rivers and built Fort Saint Louis de Illinois. He also started the first settlement in Arkansas. He lost a hand fighting in Sicily.

MAJOR BOB Robert Astles (1921–), aide to Idi Amin (*Big Daddy*). He was charged with two murders in Uganda (1981), but was never tried. He was released in 1985 and returned to Britain. He holds no commission in the British Army.

MAJOR MITE William E Jackson (1864–1900). In 1880 he stood 21 in tall and weighed 9 lb. He was a New Zealander and died in New York.

MAKER OF STARS, THE Jessie Bonstelle (1872–1932), American actress and theatre manageress. Among the stars she discovered was Katherine Cornell (1898–1974).

MAKEPEACE See *Joan Makepeace*.

MALAGRIDA THE JESUIT The Earl of Shelburne, the *Jesuit of Berkeley Square*. D'Israeli says 'Malagrida the Jesuit and *Jemmy Twitcher* were nicknames which made one of our ministers [Lord Shelburne, he points out in a footnote] odious and the other contemptible'. So called by *The Public Advertiser* (1767). James Gillray (1757–1815) published a cartoon (1782) of Shelburne captioned 'Malagrida and conspirators'.
- Gabriel Malagrida (1689–1761) was a Jesuit charged with conspiracy against the King of Portugal and burned as a heretic.

MALCOLM X Malcolm Little (1925–65), assassinated leader of the American negro separatist movement.
- Cf *Michael X*.

MALIGNANT AND FILTHY BABOON, THE John Williams (1761–1818), better known as Anthony Pasquin. He was an English satirist and critic, but the reaction to his vitriolic writings forced him to emigrate to America; so called by Macaulay (*Babbletongue*).

MALLEUS MONACHORUM Thomas Cromwell, minister to Henry VIII, and the *Hammer of the Monks*.

MALMESBURY PHILOSOPHER, THE Thomas Hobbes, the *Atheist*; so called by Aubrey (the *Little Boswell of His Day*), from his birthplace.

MAMIE Mary Geneve Doud (1896–1972) who married (1918) the future President Eisenhower (*Ike*).

MANAGER TOM Thomas Sheridan (1719–88), father of R B Sheridan (*Sherry*); actor and playwright; so called in Ireland where he had once been manager of the Theatre Royal, Dublin. Also *Sherry* and *Sherry-Derry*.

MANASSA MAULER, THE Jack Dempsey (1895–1983), whose real name was William Harrison Dempsey, world heavyweight boxing champion (1919–26); so called first because of his savage punching by Grantland Rice (*Granny*). Dempsey had been born in Manassa, Colorado.

MANKATA or MANKRATA Sir Charles MacCarthy (1770–1824), British Governor of the West African Settlements (1822–4). He was killed at the battle of Adamanso in a campaign which is known to the Ashantis as the *Mankatasa* (or MacCarthy War); from the African pronunciation of his name.

MANCHESTER POET, THE Charles Swain (1803–74), born in Manchester.

MANCHESTER PROPHET, THE Ellison or Elisha Hall (*circa* 1502–64), British religious fanatic who called himself 'The Carpenter's Son'.

MAN MOUNTAIN Dr George Cheyne (1671–1743), physician of Bath and friend of *Beau* Nash. He weighed 32 stone (448 lb), and found it difficult to walk upstairs. He dieted, and as a result wrote *An Essay on Health and Long Life*; so called by the people of Bath.

MAN MOUSE Dr Henry More, the *Chrysostom of Christ's College*; so called by Thomas Vaughan (*Anthroposophus*) in retaliation for More's comments on his book.

MANNY
i) Emmanuel, 1st Baron Shinwell (1884–1986), British Labour statesman; from 'Emmanuel'. He had the longest Parliamentary career of all time. Also *Sinbad the Tailor*.

ii) Emmanuel Lionel Mercer (1930–59), British jockey killed when his horse fell during a race at Ascot.

MAN OF BATH, THE Ralph Allen (1694–1764), English philanthropist and friend of Pope (the *Bard of Twickenham*). He lived at Prior Park, and Pope was a constant visitor there. Allen, one of the richest men in England, revolutionized the postal service and helped to build modern Bath. He was the original of Squire Allworthy in *Tom Jones* (1749) by Fielding (the *Father of the English Novel*), another visitor to Prior Park, to whom Allen was patron.

MAN OF BLACK RENOWN, THE William Wilberforce (1759–1833), British MP who worked for the abolition of slavery; so called by Byron (*Baby*).

• See the *Son of the Saint*.

MAN OF BLOOD, THE

i) Charles I, the *Ahab of the Nation*; so called by Thomas Harrison (1606–60) when he opposed Parliamentary proposals for negotiations with the King (1647). Macaulay (*Babbletongue*) in *The Battle of Naseby*: 'And the Man of Blood was there ...'

ii) Thomas Simmons, British murderer executed (March 1808) at nineteen for two killings.

MAN OF BRASS Harry Mortimer (1902–), British brass band conductor and festival organizer.

MAN OF FEELING, THE Henry Mackenzie, the *Addison of the North*, from his most famous novel (1771), written in the style of Addison (the *English Atticus*); mentioned by Lockhart (the *Aristarch of British Criticism*).

MAN OF MILLIONS, THE Horatio Bottomley, *England's Recruiting Sergeant*; so called by *The Financial Times* of which he was co-founder.

MAN OF ROSS, THE

i) John Kyrle (1637–1724), who lived most of his life at Ross, Herefordshire, and, although he had little money, affected great improvements in the town; so called by Pope (the *Bard of Twickenham*).

ii) Stephen Higginson (1770–1834), a rich American merchant and steward of Harvard University, famed for his philanthropy: nickname after (i).

MAN OF SIN, THE Oliver Cromwell, the *Almighty Nose*; so called by the Fifth Monarchy Men, a religious sect in the Commonwealth. They believed Cromwell was preparing a monarchy when Jesus Christ would reign on earth. Disappointed, they attacked him.

MAN OF THE PEOPLE, THE C J Fox, *Carlo Khan*; so called after a satire by George Colman (*George the Grinner*).

MAN OF THE REVOLUTION, THE Samuel Adams, the *American Cato*; so called by Jefferson (the *Apostle of Liberty*) in 1825.

MAN OF THE TOWN MEETING, THE Samuel Adams (above) influential in local politics before he entered national affairs.

MAN ON THE WHITE HORSE, THE Colonel Valentine Baker, *He-Face*, of the 10th Hussars. The white charger he rode was a present from the Prince of Wales (the *Peacemaker*) also of the 10th.

MAN THEY CANNOT SINK, THE Charles Haughey, *Charles the Bad*, after he had survived a 1960 gun-running scandal that might have ruined another man politically.

MAN THEY COULDN'T HANG, THE John Lee (1865–1933), whom executioner James Berry made three attempts to hang in Exeter Gaol (1885). He had been found guilty of murdering a woman who employed him as a footman. The death sentence was commuted, and Lee died in America.

MAN THEY LOVE TO HATE, THE Mick McManus (1927–), British wrestler seen a lot on TV. His unorthodox tactics in the ring brought him screams of rage, but inevitably victory. He is now a referee.

MAN WHO ALMOST INVENTED ARCHERY, THE Dr Robert Potter Elmer (1878–1951), champion of America eight times and president of the American Archery Association. He did an immense amount of research on archery and wrote several books on the subject.

MAN WHO BROKE THE BANK AT MONTE CARLO, THE Joseph Jagger (died 1892). In 1875, he won two million francs in eight days. A Yorkshire mill-worker, he noticed a defect in one machine. He became famous anonymously in the Victorian music-hall song.

MAN WHO WOULDN'T TAKE A DARE, THE Steve Brodie, an American who jumped off Brooklyn Bridge, New York, on 23 July 1886. He died.

MAN WITH or OF A THOUSAND FACES, THE Lon Chaney (1883–1930), American film star with an amazing talent for make-up. His first name was Alonzo.

MAN WITH A WIG, THE Dr Samuel Parr, the **Birmingham Doctor**; so called in *Noctes Ambrosianae*. Parr wore a full-bottomed wig which Sydney Smith (the **Diner-Out of the First Water**) said 'swells out into boundless convexity of frizz, the *magna thauma* [great wonder] of barbers and the terror of the literary world'. Parr was a Whig in politics.

MAN WITHOUT A SKIN, THE Richard Cumberland, the **English Terence**. He was so sensitive he could not stand the slightest criticism; so called by Goldsmith (the **Child of Nature**).

MAN WITHOUT FEAR, THE Captain William (Billy) Avery Bishop, VC (1894–1956), Canadian air ace (World War I) who shot down 72 planes; so called by Rickenbacker (the **Ace of Aces**). Bishop was an Air Marshal in World War II.

MAN WITH LEATHER BREECHES, THE- George Fox, the **Boehme of England**, founder of the Quakers, who always wore them.

MAN WITH THE OILCAN, THE Clarence Decatur Howe (1886–1960), Canadian politician with a knack of resolving difficulties. Also 'C.D.'

MAN YOU LOVE TO HATE, THE Erich von Stroheim (1885–1957), Austrian-born player of villains in American films. His real name was Hans Erich Maria Stroheim von Nordenwall.

MANX GIANT, THE James Arthur Caley (1817–60), born at Sulby, west of Ramsey, he stood 7 ft 11 in tall and weighed 14 stone (616 lb). He was exhibited in the Barnum and Bailey show.

- For Barnum, see the **Prince of Humbugs**.

MANX POET, THE Thomas Edward Brown (1830–1897). He wrote poems and tales in the Manx language, e.g. *Fo'c'sle Yarns*.

MAORI Air Marshal Sir Arthur Coningham (1895–1948), born in Brisbane, Australia, but educated in New Zealand. He served (World War I) in the New Zealand Army, but was an airman in World War II. Often misunderstood, mispronounced and written **Mary**.

MAOU or THE MAOU Prince Michael George Charles Franklin of Kent (1942–), cousin of the Queen, and husband of **Our Val**; so called by the Royal Family.

MAPS John Nicholson (1730–96), Cambridge bookseller. His portrait is in the University Library. He would shout 'Maps' to announce himself when visiting a customer. He began the first circulating library in Cambridge.

MARCELLUS OF OUR TONGUE, THE John Oldham, the **English Juvenal**; so called by Dryden (**Asaph**).

- See the **English Marcellus**. Marcus Claudius Marcellus was a great orator and rhetorician, who was praised by Cicero.

MARCELLUS OF THE ENGLISH NATION, THE Sir Philip Sidney, the **British Bayard**; so called by Wood (the **Ostade of Literary Criticism**).

MARCH KING, THE John Philip Sousa (1854–1904), American composer who at one time was bandmaster of the US Marine Corps; his nickname in England. Also the **Pied Piper of Patriotism**.

MARCO POLO OF THE DRUGS TRADE, THE Dennis Howard Marks (1946–), British Oxford graduate, accused (1988) of masterminding a multi-million pound worldwide drugs syndicate, the world's biggest. He was reputed to have a personal fortune of £14 million; he was so called by the American anti-drugs organization.

- Marco Polo (*circa* 1254–1324), Venetian trader and traveller, made journeys to the Far East and lived for years in China.

MARCUS SUPERBUS Wilson Barrett (1847–1904), English actor who played that part in *The Sign of the Cross*, which he wrote himself (see below).

MARCUS SUPERFLUOUS Wilson Barrett (above). After Barrett's success, a variety artist Louie Freear invented this nickname in a show *The Gay Parisienne*.

MARGINAL PRYNNE William Prynne, the **Brave Jersey Muse**; so called by Milton (**Black-Mouthed Zoilus**).

MARGITES Louis or Lewis Theobald, the

King of Dunces; so called by Warton (*Honest Tom*).

- Pope (the **Bard of Twickenham**) in *The Dunciad* (1728), of which Theobald was at first the 'hero', wrote: 'Margites ... whom Antiquity recordeth to have been dunce the first ...' The word means 'a mad idiot', and was the subject of a poem (*circa* 700 BC) ascribed to Homer.

MARIA OF THE WEST Maria Cowen Brooks (*circa* 1794–1845), American poet of Massachusetts; so called by Southey (the **Ballad Monger**).

MARIE Edward Nelson, **Bronte**.

MARK THE MACHINE Mark McCormack (1931–), American millionaire promotor and impresario. He lives his life on a strict regime he himself designed.

MARROW MAN, THE Thomas Boston, the **Elder**. He was a Scottish Calvinist who opposed the General Assembly of the Church of Scotland in its condemnation (1720) of *The Marrow of Modern Divinity by E F* (1645). His followers were called Marrow Men. E F may have been Edward Fisher (flourished 1627–65), and his book was a collection of opinions of Reformation clergy on the doctrine of grace.

MARSE HENRY Henry Watterson (1840–1921), American, editor of *The Louisville Courier Journal* and looked on as a typical Southerner. He used his nickname as the title of his autobiography (1919): from the American negro pronunciation of 'Master'.

MARSHAL OF THE ARMY OF GOD, THE Robert Fitzwalter (died 1235), Lord of Dunmow and of Baynard's Castle, London; leader of the barons in their opposition to King John (**Lackland**). He was elected Marshal of the Army of God and Holy Church (1215) when hostilities broke out. He was one of the twenty-four appointed to see that the clauses of the Magna Carta (1215) were carried out.

MARTIAL MACARONI, THE General Sir John Burgoyne, **Gentleman Johnny**; so called by John Trumbull (1750–1831), an American lawyer who was a member of a literary group called 'the Connecticut Wits'.

- See the **Macaroni Painter**.

MARTIN Jonathan Swift, **Dr Presto**; so called at Oxford University after the bird; later it became 'Martin Scriblerus', used by Swift as the name of a club (post-1714).

MARTYR, THE

i) Edward, King of England (*circa* 963–78), murdered at Corfe Castle by order of his step-mother Aelfthryth who wanted her son Aethelred to be king. *Anglo-Saxon Chronicle:* 'No worse deed for the English was ever done'.

- Aethelred II, the **Unready**, reigned from 978 until his death in 1016 when Canute the **Great** became king.

ii) Edmund, the **English Saint Sebastian**, murdered by the Danes.

iii) Prince Kenelm (died *circa* 811), a saint, whose shrine was at Winchcombe, Gloucestershire. He was a prince of Mercia and his murder was arranged by his sister Quonthryth, it is said, although he may have died in battle. His name is also spelt 'Cynehelm'.

MARTYR KING, THE

i) Henry VI, **Ill-Fated Henry**. He died violently – almost certainly at the hands of Richard of Gloucester – after the battle of Towton (1461) between the armies of York and Lancaster.

ii) Charles I, the **Ahab of the Nation**.

MARTYR OF THE SOLWAY, THE Margaret Wilson (1667–85), Scot, judicially drowned with Margaret Maclachlan at Wigtown Bay, Stirling. They refused to conform to episcopacy, remaining faithful to the Covenant.

- The General Assembly of the Church of Scotland abolished episcopacy in 1581, a cause of conflict with Charles I (the **Ahab of the Nation**).

MARTYR PRESIDENT, THE Abraham Lincoln, **Father Abraham**, assassinated by Wilkes Booth (the **South's Avenging Angel**).

MARVELLOUS BOY, THE Thomas Chatterton, the **Bristol Boy**.

MARVELLOUS MARVIN Marvin Hagler (1952–), American world (World Boxing

Association of America and World Boxing Council) heavyweight champion (1980–7) who got record purses for his fights; lost (1987) to *Sugar Ray Leonard*.

MARY Air-Marshal Sir Arthur Coningham, *Maori*.

MARY COLLINS Queen Victoria, *Drina*; her nickname in Irish-speaking Munster, from *Maire Ni Choileàn*. Her family name of Guelph was thought to be 'whelp' and translated *coilean*, *Ni Choilean* or *Cuilean*. *Cuilean* was used by Scottish kings. One of that name was killed in a battle at Lothian (971).

MARY OF ARNHEM Helen Sensburg, a Nazi broadcaster whose seductive voice tried to persuade Allied troops at Arnhem (World War II: 1944) to surrender.

MARY OF THE GAEL, THE St Brigid or Bride, Abbess of Kildare (*circa* 450– *circa* 523). Also the *Pearl of Ireland*.

MASH-TUB Alderman Combe, a brewer who was Lord Mayor of London (1799–1800). Its use by *Beau* Brummell is recorded at Brooke's Club.

MASSACHUSETTS MADMAN, THE John Quincy Adams (1767–1848), 6th President of the USA; so called by his opponents for his fanatical support for the principle of independence. He became a Federalist, but their leader found him 'too unmanageable'. He was born in Massachusetts. Also *Old Man Eloquent* and *Second John*.

MASTER Henry Hugh Arthur Fitzroy, 10th Duke of Beaufort (1900–84), because he was Master of the Horse in the Royal Household.

MASTER, THE
i) Sir John (Jack) Berry Hobbs (1882–1963), cricketer for Surrey and England, one of the greatest batsmen in the game. He scored 61,237 runs and 197 centuries; nickname given by John Arlott (1914–) BBC commentator.
ii) John Corlett (1841–1915), proprietor and editor of *The Sporting Times* ('The Pink'Un') between 1874 and 1912.
iii) Sir Noel Pierce Coward (1899–1973), British actor, playwright and composer.
iv) Captain John Pender, Resident of

Benin, Nigeria (1940s), a member of the Colonial Service in Nigeria for many years.
v) Joseph Chamberlain, *Artful Joe*; his nickname at the Colonial Office after he became Colonial Secretary at his own request (1869).
vi) D W Griffith, the *King of Directors*, a great pioneer.

MASTER GRAFTER, THE Samuel Allan Taylor (1838–1913), leader of the Boston Gang producing forgeries of postage stamps. He also issued *The Stamp Collector's Record* (40 issues from 1864).

- A 'grafter' is a person who schemes to make an illegal profit as, for example, in America by payments to public officials for special privileges or 'blind eyes'. In English slang, it is someone who works a pitch at a fair. 'Graft' has been slang for work since at least the 1870s.

MASTER OF THE ROLLS, THE John (Jack) Martin (1769–?1868) well-known pugilist who was a baker. He won nine of his fourteen fights.

- The Master of the Rolls is, of course, an English legal dignitary.

MASTER SURVEYOR, THE Inigo Jones, the *English Palladio*; so called by Jonson, the *Bricklayer*.

MASTIFF CUR, THE Cardinal Wolsey, the *Boy Baccaleur*; so called by Skelton (the *Vicar of Hell*).

- See the *Butcher's Dog*.

MATA HARI OF THE SECOND WORLD WAR, THE Mathilde-Lucie Carré, the *Cat*.

- See *Gerschy*.

MATCHLESS, THE Shakespeare, the *Bard of All Time*; so called by Pope (the *Bard of Twickenham*).

MATCHSTICK, THE Lesley Hornby (1949–), later Mrs Michael Witney, model, actress and TV personality. She was very slim when she was a star model (1960s). See also *Oxfam*, *Skinny*, *Sticks* and *Twiggy*.

MATE, THE Sir John Dugdale Astley, baronet (1828–94), well-known sporting character, was a bearded giant of a man and one of the founders of the body which became the National Sporting Club (1891). He served in the Guards in the Crimea.

MATT Thomas Carey (1891–1948), American jazz trumpeter.

MATT MEDLEY Anthony Aston (fl. 1703–30), Irish actor reputed to have been the first British entertainer on the American continent (*circa* 1713). His form of show was a medley. Also *Trusty Anthony*.

MAUL OF THE MONKS, THE Thomas Cromwell, the *Hammer of the Monks*.

MAURUS Sir Richard Blackmore, the *Cheapside Knight*; so called by Dryden (*Asaph*).

• *Maurus* is Latin for a blackamoor.

MAVERICK OF CAPITOL HILL, THE Senator Wayne Morse (1900–74), an argumentative individual.

MAY

i) Princess Mary Victoria of Hesse (1874–8), grand-daughter of Victoria (*Drina*).

ii) Princess Mary of Teck (1867–1953) who married the prince who became George V (the *Ordinary Fellow*).

MAYFLOWER MADAM, THE Sydney Biddle Barrows (1952–), American society girl whose ancestors were among the first to be landed from the *Mayflower* (1620). She ran a call-girl agency, 'Cachet', in New York. It was closed in 1984 after a raid by the police. She pleaded guilty in court and was fined $5,000 and had to pay $300,000 in costs. She wrote *The Mayflower Madam* to help to raise the money for the debt; so called first by a reporter named Peter Fearon.

MAYPOLE, THE Ehrengarde, Duchess of Kendal (1667–1743), mistress of George I (the *Turnip Hoer*). She had been Ehrengarde Melusina von der Schulenburg and was tall and thin.

MEAN DOE Joseph Greene (1946–), American footballer for the Pittsburgh Steelers; a hard, fast player.

• 'John Doe' is a fictitious name used in American legal and commercial

papers. Its use dates from 1768 in England.

MEAN MACHINE, THE Frederick (Freddie) Foreman (1931–), British 'enforcer' for the Kray gang, arrested by the British police for questioning over the raid on the Security Express depot in East London (1983) when £6 million pounds was stolen. When living in Spain he was known as 'The Godfather of the Costa del Crime.'

• For Kray, see the *Colonel* (iii).

MEASURING MAN Albert de Salvo, the *Boston Strangler*. One of his confidence tricks was to pretend he was a tailor so that, measuring, he could run his hands over women's bodies.

MECHANICAL MAN, THE Charles (Charley) Leonard Gehringer (1903–), American baseball batter for the Detroit Tigers; so called from his steady batting. In the Hall of Fame (1924–42).

MEDICINE PAINT George Catlin (1796–1872), American painter of Indian life; nickname given to him by the Indians. Also *White Medicine Painter*.

MEKON, THE Mrs Thatcher, *Attila the Hen*.

• The Mekon is a dictatorial monster in the TV series *Dr Who*.

MELONS Lady Helen Windsor (1964–), daughter of the Duke and Duchess of Kent; after she had appeared topless on a Corfu bathing beach.

MEMORY CORNER THOMPSON John Thompson (1757–1843), grocer of St Giles, London, with an astounding local knowledge. He once drew from memory a correct plan of the parish of St James's. He could also read a newspaper over night, and repeat any portion of it verbatim next morning.

MEMORY MAN, THE Leslie Welch (1908–80). He could answer from memory on the music-hall stage, TV or radio any question, particularly those on sport.

MEMORY WOODFALL William Woodfall (1745–1803), British Parliamentary reporter who without taking notes (they were then forbidden in the House of Commons), could write down the debates word for word. He established *The Diary* in which for the first time Parliamentary debates were reported the day after they had happened.

MEMPHIS SLIM Peter Chatman (1916–), American blues pianist and singer.

MENDICANT BARD, THE Stuart Lewis (1756–1818), a wandering Scottish poet.

MERCHANT OF MENACE, THE John McEnroe, the **Brat**, by analogy with *The Merchant of Venice*.

MERCHANT OF VENICE, THE Joseph Smith (1682–1770), British Consul at Venice who sold his art collection to George III (the **Button Maker**) for Buckingham Palace. Also called 'Consul Smith'.

MERCHANT PRINCE, THE Samuel Mendel (1814–84), rich Manchester merchant and shipper.

MERCURY Viscount Bolingbroke, **High-Mettled Mary**; because of the speed with which he did things.

• Mercury was the Roman messenger of the gods, usually equated with the Greek Hermes.

MERCUTIO OF ACTORS, THE William Lewis, **Gentleman Lewis**.

• Mercutio is Romeo's gallant friend in *Romeo and Juliet* who challenges Tybalt to protect Romeo.

MERE DANDINI, THE George IV, the **Adonis of Fifty**; so called by John Doran (1807–78).

• Dandini is the court attendant in the pantomime story of Cinderella who takes the glass slipper to find its owner.

MERLIN OF SCOTLAND, THE Thomas Learmont of Ecildoune or Erceldoune (flourished 1255–1300), Border poet and seer who predicted the battle of Bannockburn (1314). Also the **Rhymer**, **Thomas the Rhymer** and **True Thomas**.

• Merlin was King Arthur's magician and seer.

MERMAID, THE Mary Queen of Scots (1542–87). At the time of the murder of Darnley (1567), a placard appeared on the streets of Edinburgh showing Mary as a mermaid, naked to the waist with a crown on her head. Also **La Reine Blanche** and the **White Queen**.

• 'Mermaid' was then cant for a strumpet.

MERRY ANDREW Andrew Borde or Boorde (1500–49), physician to Henry VIII (**Bluff Hal**). He was an eccentric who went to fairs and made humorous speeches to amuse the crowds. Thomas Hearne (1678–1735) says in his preface to *Benedictus Abbas* (1735) that this was so, but the *Oxford English Dictionary* states that Hearne had neither evidence nor intrinsic probability for the assertion. Borde did, however, have a reputation for buffoonery. In *A Compendyous Regyment or a Dietary of Helth* (1542) he did say 'rise with mirth ... and go to bed ... with mirth'.

MERRY DROLL, THE Thomas Killigrew (1612–83), English dramatist and wit; so called by Pepys (the **Father of Black-Letter Lore**). Killigrew, a sort of unofficial royal jester, used the king's name to borrow money. He was indeed sometimes called "King Charles' Jester."

• Cf the **Scriptural Killigrew**.

MERRY JOHN John Heywood, the **Great Epigrammatist**. He wrote *A Dialogue concerning Witty and Witless*. He was a spirited early playwright.

MERRY MONARCH, THE Charles II, the **Blackbird**; because of his wit, good humour, love of sport and his many mistresses; so called by Rochester (**Virgin Modesty**) in 1676.

MERTHYR MATCHSTICK, THE John (Johnny) Owen (1956–1980), British European and Commonwealth bantamweight boxing champion. He died of a brain injury after twelve knockdowns in a world championship fight in Los Angeles. He was thin, and his home was in Merthyr Tidfil, Wales.

MERVE THE SWERVE (1962–) Mervyn Hughes, Australian, from his style of bowling.

MESSALINA OF THE PUNJAB, THE Mahrani Jindan, wife of Ranjit Singh (the **Lion of the Punjab**) and mother of Duleep Singh. She was described (1845) by Sir Henry Lawrence (1806–57) as 'a strange mixture of prostitute, the tigress and Machiavelli's Prince'.

- Valeria Messalina, wife of Emperor Claudius (reigned 41–54), infamous for her profligacy and licentiousness.

ME TOO T C Platt, *Boss*, regarded as an echo of other men's thoughts.

MEXICAN SPITFIRE, THE Lupe Velez (1910–44), temperamental star of American films. She first appeared with Douglas Fairbanks (1883–1939) in *The Gaucho*. Her real name was Guadeloupe Velez de Villalobos; so called from a film of that name (1939).

MICHELANGELO OF BUFFOONERY, THE Joseph Grimaldi (1779–1837), the world's greatest clown, whose nickname 'Joey' has become a traditional name for all his successors.

- Michelangelo Buonarotti (1475–1564), giant of the Renaissance as painter, sculptor, poet and architect.

MICHAEL X Michael Abdul Malik (1933–75), whose real name was Michael de Freitas; leader of the Black Power in Britain, executed for murder in Trinidad.

- Cf *Malcolm X*.

MICHELIN MAN, THE Tim Robinson, *Chop*, after he wore heavy padding against fierce West Indian bowling (1986).

- The Michelin Man is a padded figure advertising rubber tyres.

MICHIGAN ASSASSIN, THE Stanley Ketchel (1886–1910), American middleweight boxing champion (1907–1910), for the fury of his attacks. He lost his title to Billy Papke (the *Thunderbolt*) in 1908, but regained it within three months.

MICK Captain (acting Major) Edward Mannock (1887–1918), VC, who shot down 73 German planes (World War I).

MICKEY

i) Mary Kathryn Wright (1935–), American golf champion. She won more than 80 tournaments, including 13 in 1963; chairwoman of the Women's Professional Golf Association (1980s). Her father had decided his 'son's' name should be 'Michael'.

ii) Carol Michelle Walker (1952–), British golfer; Ladies champion (1971–2).

iii) Edward Patrick Walker (1901–81), American who won the world welterweight title (1922) and middleweight (1926–41) boxing title. Also the *Toy Bulldog*.

MICKLE OR MUCEL Ethelred, Earl of Gaini (fl. 9th century) because he was so big.

- 'Mickle' or 'muckle' are Scottish words for a great size (Old English = *mycel*).

MICROCHAP, THE Sir David Martin Scott Steel (1938–), leader of the Liberal Party until its amalgamation with the Social Democratic Party; from 'microchip'. He decided to become a backbencher in May 1988. Also *Peter Pan*.

MIDDLESEX OWL, THE Professor Herbert Mayo (1796–1852), surgeon at the Middlesex Hospital, London.

MIDNIGHT COWBOY, THE Thomas (Tom) McEvoy (1945–), world champion poker player. He wears a black 'ten-gallon' hat while playing.

MIE-MIE Maria Fagninai (1771–1856), illegitimate daughter of the 4th Duke of Queensberry (*Lord Piccadilly*); so called by *Great George* Selwyn who adopted her. Maria married (1798) the 3rd Marquess of Hertford (*Red Herrings*).

- *Mie* is an abbreviation of *mon ami*. Molière used *ma mie*.

MIGHTY ATOM, THE

i) Patrick Gallagher (1894–1953), small but powerful Irish-born footballer. He played the game for twenty years (Glasgow Celtic was among his clubs).

ii) Jimmy Wilde, the *Ghost with a Hammer in His Hand*.

MIGHTY LEVIATHAN, THE Thomas Hobbes, the *Atheist*, writer of 'The Leviathan' (1651), a study of sovereign power that shocked Charles II (the *Blackbird*) into forcing Hobbes into exile; so called by D'Israeli.

- See the *Leviathan*.

MIGHTY MIDGET, THE William (Willie) Carlin (1940–), mid-field footballer for Leicester City, Sheffield United and Derby County. At 5ft 4 in, he was thought at first to be too small to be a good footballer but proved everyone wrong.

MIGHTY MINSTREL, THE Scott, the *Ariosto of the North*; so called in *Noctes Ambrosianae*.

MIGHTY MOUSE, THE
i) Kevin Keegan, *King Kev*. He is not very tall.
ii) Ian McLauchlan (1942–), schoolmaster and Rugby Union player, banned for life by the Scottish Rugby Union for having broken the amateurism rule by having written about the game.

MIKE Maurice Joseph Micklewhite (1933–), British film star who turned his nickname into 'Michael' and added 'Caine' (from *The Caine Mutiny*). Also the *Professor*.

MIKE THE BIKE Stanley Michael Bailey Hailwood (1940–81), English racing motor-cyclist, star of the Brands Hatch circuit. He won ten world championships between 1961 and 1967. He was killed in a road accident.

MILK SNATCHER, THE Margaret Thatcher, *Attila the Hen*. She cut school milk while Minister of Education in the Heath Government (1970–4); rhyme with 'Thatcher'.

MILK-WHITE GOSSET The Reverend Dr Isaac Gosset, the *Younger* (1745–1812), British bibliographer; so called by Mathias (the *Nameless Bard*) in *Pursuits of Literature* (1794). Gosset's books were bound in white vellum.

MILKY BAR KID, THE Keith Deller (1960–), British world darts champion (1983); from the TV advertisement. He prefers milk to beer. Also *Mr Cool*.

MILL BOY OF THE SLASHES, THE Henry Clay, the *Apostle of Liberty*. As a boy he worked in a mill in a swampy district known as 'The Slashes', in Harrison, Virginia.

MILLIONAIRE HOBO, THE James Eads How (1868–1930), who became a vagrant and wanted to use the family fortune to help hoboes in the USA.

MILLIONAIRE SHERIFF, THE Anderson Yancey Baker (1876–1930). Although a millionaire, he acted as sheriff of Hidalgo County, Texas (1912–30).

MILLION DOLLAR FACE, THE Fiona Fullerton (1956–), beautiful British actress.

MILWAUKEE PHIL Felix Anthony Alderisio (1922–71), Chicago gangster.

MINDER, THE Patrick Murray (1944–); former British Commando and IRA bomber. He acted as bodyguard to Patrick McGee (the *Chancer*).

MINIATURE FOR SPORT, THE The Honourable Colin Berkeley Moynihan (1955–), son of Baron Moynihan; the far from tall Minister of Sport in the Thatcher Government; so called in Parliament. Also *Noddy*.

MINETTE Princess Henriette-Anne, Duchess of Orleans (1644–70), daughter of Charles I (the *Ahab of the Nation*). It is alleged that she was poisoned.

MING THE MERCILESS Sir Robert Gordon Menzies (1894–1978), Prime Minister of Australia (1939–41 and 1941–66): because of his hard-hitting tactics in Parliament.
- The Scottish pronunciation of 'Menzies' is 'Minges'.

MINNESOTA FATS Walter R Wanderone (1913–), famed American pool player, born at St Paul's, Minnesota.

MINORITY OF ONE, THE The Earl of Stanhope, *Citizen Stanhope*, the only voice to support a motion he introduced into the House of Lords (1795) to express sympathy with the French Revolution. He was chairman of the Revolutionary Society.

MINSTREL BOY, THE Sir Alfred Scott-Gatty, York Herald (1886) and Garter King-at-Arms (1904). He wrote songs.
- From Thomas *Anacreon Moore's* poem *The Minstrel Boy*.

MINUS MILLIONAIRE, THE James Slater (1929–), British Stock Exchange speculator with an empire of companies worth £20,000,000 which collapsed (1975), leaving him with debts of £1,000,000, all of which were paid.

MIRACLE OF OUR AGE, THE Sir Philip Sidney, the *British Bayard*; so called by Camden (the *British Pausanias*).

MIRACLE OF OUR TIME, THE Queen Elizabeth I, the *English Diana*; so called in 1591.

MIRANDOLA OF HIS AGE, THE Sir Kenelm Digby (1603–65), British naval commander, author and diplomat. He was well versed in all kinds of learning (Aubrey).

- Count Giovanni Pico della Mirandola (1463–94), Italian philosopher.

MIRROR OF HER AGE, THE Anne Bradstreet, the *Glory of Her Sex*; so called by *Noctes Ambrosianae*.

MISS FLOGGIE Margaret Thatcher, *Attila the Hen*; so called by Denis Healey, the *Beast*.

MISS FRIGIDAIRE Chris Evert, the *Ice Maiden*.

MISS GLAM VAM Ingrid Pitt (1944–), British star of horror films, e.g. *The Vampire Lover*. Her real surname is Petrov. A shortening of 'vampire' and 'glamour'.

MISS IMPACT Britt Ekland (1942–), Swedish-born British and American film star who, in her early days, was determined to 'make an impact'. She was a Bond girl in *The Man with the Golden Gun* (1974).

MISS NANCY Anne Oldfield (1683–1730), famous and beautiful British actress; from her most popular characterization. Her other nickname *Nance* provided a word for a homosexual.

- 'Miss Nancyism' is given by Farmer and Henley (1905) as effeminancy.

MISS NANCY KING Senator William Rufus Devane King (1786–1853), of Alabama, because he was a prim and proper bachelor.

MISS RHYTHM Ruth Brown (1928–), American rock and blues singer.

MISS ROMP Dorothy Jordan, *Little Pickle*, renowned for playing tomboy parts, such as Priscilla Tomboy in *The Romp* (although 'tomboy' dates from the 16th century). George Romney (1734–1802) painted her in the part.

- 'Romp' and 'rompish' were favourite words in the 18th century for a woman with liberal sexual ideas.

MISSUS QUEEN Queen Elizabeth, *Brenda*; her pidgin English nickname, e.g. in New Guinea and Tonga.

MISSY Princess Marie (1875–1938), daughter of the Duke of Edinburgh (1844–1900) and grand-daughter of Victoria, (*Drina*). She married King Ferdinand of Romania (1856–1927).

MR and MRS See after Mou.

MITCHAM MONSTER, THE Eriel Ennis (1958–), gaoled for fourteen years (1983) for rape and attacks on women. At home he was a model husband, and at night he was a robber and rapist.

- Cf the *Hackney Monster*.

MITRE COURTIER, THE Charles Lamb (1775–1834), British essayist under the pseudonym of 'Elia' who once lived in Mitre Court, Fleet Street, London; so called by Hazlitt (the *Dumont of Letters*). Also *Upright Truth Esq.*

MITRED DULLNESS Dr Samuel Parker (1640–88), Bishop of Oxford; so called by his political opponents. He changed his religious views under James II (the *King Over the Water*) to get preference. He wrote long, elaborate dissertations on Church history and political science.

MOANING MATTY Madison Bell, American football coach between 1919 and 1949.

MOATLODHI Joseph Chamberlain, *Artful Joe*; so called when he was Colonial Secretary by King Khama, chief of the Bamangwato (fl. 1870s) and other South African chiefs. It means 'He who gets things done'.

MODERN ADMIRABLE CRICHTON, THE Sir Richard Francis Burton (1821–90), British explorer, linguist, translator, author, soldier and diplomat. Also *Ruffian Dick*.

- See the *Admirable Crichton*.

MODERN ARISTOPHANES, THE Samuel Foote, the *English Aristophanes*.

MODERN BELISARIUS, THE General Brinton McClellan, *Little Mac*.

- Belisarius (?505–65), a Roman general who, under the Emperor Justinian, overthrew the Vandals in North Africa (531) and the Goths in Italy (552).

MODERN HOGARTH, THE George

Cruikshank (1792–1876), British artist and caricaturist who illustrated some of the books of Charles Dickens (the *Inimitable*). Also called the *Prince of Caricaturists*.

- For Hogarth, see the *Juvenal of Painters*.

MODERN K.O. KID, THE George D Chaney (1893–1958), American boxer credited with 86 knock-outs.

MODERN MESSONIER OF BRITISH DOMESTIC ART, THE Charles Spencelayh (1865–1958), figure and portrait painter.

- Jean Louis Ernest Messonier (1815–91) was a French painter of meticulous care and attention to detail.

MODERN METHUSELAH, THE Henry Jenkins (?1501–1670), of Ellerton-Swale, Yorkshire. He claimed to have taken arrows to Flodden (1513) when he was ten or twelve years old. He was said to have been 169 years old when he died, but his age cannot be verified.

- Methuselah, son of Enoch, lived 969 years (Genesis v.27).

MODERN MIDAS, THE Ernest Terah Hooley (1860– ?), British financier and share-pusher who dealt in millions; imprisoned for three years for conspiracy in the Jubilee Cotton Mill fraud (1922). He was involved with Bottomley (*England's Recruiting Sergeant*). Hooley bought the Prince of Wales's yacht *Britannia* for £10,000.

- Midas, king of Phrygia, was granted a wish that everything he touched should turn to gold, but he repented of it when his daughter and his food did so.

MODERN PICT, THE Thomas Bruce, 7th Earl of Elgin (1766–1841), from whom the British Government bought the Elgin Marbles (now in the British Museum) which he had brought from Greece; so called by Byron (*Baby*).

MODERN RABELAIS, THE William Maginn, the *Adjutant*.
- See the *English Rabelais*.

MODERN STAGIRITE, THE William Warburton, the *Colossus of Literature*; so called by D'Israeli.

- Samuel Butler (*Remains* 1759): 'The Stagyrite, unable to explain the Euripus, leapt into it and was drowned'. The Euripus was the ancient name for the channel between Euboea and the Greek mainland. A Stagirite was a native of Stagira, where Aristotle was born.

MODEST BOB Robert (Bob) Geldof (1954–), Irish-born singer with the Boomtown Rats (1980s); modesty is not reputed to be one of his qualities. He became an international hero after his Live-Aid project to relieve African famine (1985), and was given an honorary knighthood by the Queen (1986). Also *Saint Bob*.

MOGA Nicholas (Nick) G B Cook (1956–), cricketer for Leicestershire and England. He took 5 wickets for 18 in a Test Match against Pakistan (1984).

MOGODON MAN, THE Sir Richard Edward Geoffrey Howe (1926–), Chancellor of the Exchequer (1979–83) and Foreign Secretary (1983–9). Deputy Prime Minister and Leader of the House of Commons (1989–). Also 'Geoffrey Who?' on occasions.

- Mogodon is a soporific.

MOLE, THE Anthony Blunt (Sir, before he was stripped of his knighthood: 1907–83) former Surveyor of the Queen's Pictures, discovered to have been a Soviet spy in the 1960s who helped Burgess, Maclean and Philby (*Kim*) to escape from Britain; so called because he remained 'underground' until he was needed by his masters.

- See the *Third Man*.

MOLL CUTPURSE Mary Frith (*circa* 1585–1659), an English thief who got her nickname from cutting purses (then hanging from waistbands by thongs). She was very ugly, and dressed like a man. For a time she was a 'highwayman'. She was the central figure of *The Roaring Girl* (1611) by Thomas Middleton (?1570–1627) and Thomas Dekker (1570–1632).

MOLLY PITCHER Mary L Hays or Heis McCauley (1754–1832) who carried pitchers of water to American soldiers during the battle of Monmouth (1778) in great heat and became a legendary figure in American folklore.

MOLAUG St Lughaidh (died 592) who founded the Colombian monastery on the island of Lismore, Argyllshire (562) after he had crossed from Ireland. He was also known as St Molaug (= 'shining light' in Gaelic).

MOMO Samuel Giancana (1908–75), head of the Chicago Mafia and gangster (1920s–1930s), a variation of 'Mooney', descriptive of his strange personality.

MONARCH OF CROSBITERS, THE *Ape Gabriel* Harvey; so called by Greene (the *Dying Titan*) in 1592.

- A 'crosbiter' (modern 'crossbiter') was a cheat or a swindler, but could also mean someone who attacked or criticized without mercy.

MONARCH OF LETTERS, THE John Selden, the *Champion of Human Law*; so called by Jonson (the *Bricklayer*).

MONARCH OF MONT BLANC, THE Albert Richard Smith (1816–60), British writer and humorist who lectured at the Egyptian Hall, London on his ascent of Mont Blanc.

MONEYBAGS Neil Simon (1927–), American playwright; so called by his friends after the success of his plays brought him wealth.

MONGOOSE Archie Moore (1913–), American world heavyweight boxing champion (1952 and 1962). His real name is Archibald Lee Wright.

MONKEY
i) Sir Henry Monck-Mason Moore (1887–1964), Colonial Governor and Deputy Under-Secretary of State for the Colonies (1939); from 'Monck'.
ii) A N Hornby (1847–1925), Lancashire cricketer.

MONKEY, THE Charles (Charlie) Frederick Peace (1832–79), a picture framer who became a notable British burglar and by his exploits earned the reputation of the *Vanishing Cracksman*. He was hanged for the murder of a former neighbour, Arthur Dyson, but admitted in the condemned cell the murder of a policeman, Nicholas Cock, for which another man had been sentenced to death. Peace was a very agile cat burglar. Also the *Napoleon of the Jemmy*.

MONKEY ON A STICK, THE Tod Sloan (flourished 1890s–1900s), American jockey who, at the turn of the century, revolutionized horse-racing in England by his crouching style of riding; so called by his critics.

- He was so popular eventually in England that his first name went into slang: 'On your Tod' = on your own, (rhyme with 'Sloan'). Tod Sloan, however, was very much on his own with his at first unacceptable manner of riding.

MONK LEWIS Matthew Gregory Lewis (1775–1818), British novelist and playwright whose fame rests on one book, *The Monk* (1796). Also the *Prince of Dandies*.

MONK OF BURY, THE John Lydgate (?1370–?1451), poet who spent most of his life at the monastery at Bury St Edmunds, Suffolk. His works include *Troy Book* (1412–20) and *The Story of Thebes* (printed 1513).

MONK OF WESTMINSTER, THE Richard of Cirencester (?1335–1401), a member of the Benedictine Order of St Peter's, Westminster, a historian who compiled the *Speculum Historiale de Gestis Angliae (447–1066)*.

MONMOUTH Henry V, the *English Alexander*. He was born there.

MONOCLE MAN, THE Harold Doran Trevor (1897–1942), British petty thief executed for the murder in London of a 65-year-old lady during a robbery. He wore a monocle, and used such names as Sir Charles Warren and Commander Crichton; so called by the police.

MONOCLED MUTINEER, THE Private Francis Percy Toplis (?1897–1920). He deserted from the British Army in 1917 and was alleged to have come out of hiding to join the mutiny at the training camp at Etaples, France (1917). He is said to have passed as an officer wearing a monocle. He was shot dead in the Lake District after a police hunt when he was wanted on charges of having shot two police-officers and a taxi-driver at Andover, Hampshire. A monocle was found on the body. He had a long criminal record, but was turned into a folk hero by a TV mini-series (1986), most of which was fiction.

MONSTER, THE Renwick Williams, convicted (January 1790) of attacks on young women who, as *The Newgate Calendar* observes, 'had been secretly wounded in different parts of their bodies'. He became the universal terror of the female population of London before he was captured and sent to prison.

• Cf the *Hackney Monster*.

MONSTER BUTLER, THE Archibald Hall, the *Mad Butler*.

MONTY

i) Field-Marshal Bernard Law, 1st Viscount Montgomery of Alamein (1887–1976), commander of the Eighth Army which defeated Rommel, and military commander of the troops in the invasion of Normandy (1944); so called by the troops under his command in the Western Desert (post-1942) and eventually by the world.

ii) Sir Edward Montague Compton Mackenzie (1883–1972), British novelist, notably of *Sinister Street* (1913–14).

MOON Neil Reagan (1909–), brother of President Ronald Reagan (*Dutch*).

MOONDYNE JOE Joseph Bolitho Johns (1831–1920), Australian bushranger, hero of folk ballads. He was transported (1853) and escaped. He worked in the Moondyne Hills, north-east of Perth.

MOONLIGHT MURDERER, THE American sex-maniac killer and rapist at full moon in Texarkana, Texas (1946), never traced in spite of a massive police hunt. He was thought to have been an unidentified man who committed suicide by leaping under a train that same year.

MOONRAKER Detective-Superintendent George Smith (1905–70), British spy-catcher; so called at Scotland Yard. *The Times* said at his death no-one remembered why. He lived in Wiltshire.

• 'Moonraker' has been a nickname for a Wiltshireman since at least 1787 when

Grose observed that some Wiltshire men tried to pull the reflection of the moon out of a pond with a rake.

MOOR, THE Tom Molineaux (1784–1858), American negro pugilist.

MOORS MURDERERS, THE Ian Brady (1938–), and his mistress, Myra Hindley, *Mad Myra*, imprisoned for life (1966) for the murders of five or more young people, whose bodies were buried on the Yorkshire moors.

MORAL BYRON, THE Byron Walter Proctor, *Baby Cornwall*.

MORAL GOWER John Gower (*circa* 1325–1408), English poet of *Confessio Amantis* and *Vox Clamantis*. The latter poem dealt largely with the Peasants' Revolt of 1381, telling of the corruption of society; so called by his friend Chaucer (the *British Homer*) in *Troilus and Criseyde* (*circa* 1386).

MORALITY SMITH W H Smith, *Bookstall Smith*.

MORAL SURFACE Sir Robert Peel, *Jenny*; so called by his political opponents.

• See *Joseph Surface*.

MORETTA Princess Victoria (1866–1929) of Prussia, daughter of the Princess Royal (*Pussy*) and grand-daughter of Queen Victoria (*Drina*). Also *Young Vicky*.

MORGAN THE MAGNIFICENT John Pierpont Morgan (1837–1913), American millionaire with a fortune in banks, railways, coal and steel. His company supplied the US Government with $62,000,000 to restore Treasury gold reserves to $100,000,000.

• Cf the *Dictator of Wall Street*.

MORNING STAR OF SONG, THE Chaucer, the *British Homer*; so called by Tennyson (the *Bard of Arthurian Romance*).

MORNING STAR OF STEPNEY, THE Jeremiah Burroughs (1599–1646) who drew great crowds by his eloquence; so called by Hugh Peter (the *Pulpit Buffoon*).

• Cf the *Evening Star of Stepney*.

MORNING STAR OF THE REFORMATION, THE John Wyclif, *Doctor Evangelicus*.

MOSES Harriet Tubman, the *Conductor of the Underground Railway*.

MOSES OF THE MIDDLE CLASSES, THE- Howard Arnold Jarvis (1902–), who led a tax revolt in California (1978–80).

MOSSY Princess Margaret (1872–1954), daughter of the Princess Royal (*Pussy*).

MOST METHODICAL DOCTOR, THE John Bassol (died 1347), Scottish theologian and pupil of Duns (*Dunce*) – Latin *Doctor Ordinatissimus*, also used as his nickname.

MOSQUI Lady Muriel Lowther, née Farrer, wife of Anthony Lowther (died 1949). Once at a dinner-party she said that she had seen mosquitoes as big as dinner-plates.

MOTHER St Hilda or Hild (614–80), grand-niece of King Edwin of Northumberland and abbess of a convent at Hartlepool, Durham, because of her grace and goodness.

MOTHER ANN Ann Lee, *Ann the Word*.

MOTHER BICKERDYKE Mary Bickerdyke (1817–1901), volunteer nurse and welfare worker with the Union Army. She 'mothered' the soldiers.

MOTHER BRICKBAT The Reverend Mother Frances Bridgeman, superior of a congregation of Irish nuns who helped Florence Nightingale (the *Lady with the Lamp*) at Scutari but refused to accept her authority; so called by Miss Nightingale.

MOTHER DAMNABLE Jinny Bingham (flourished under George III), daughter of Jacob Bingham, a bricklayer of Kentish Town, London, hanged with his wife for murder and witchcraft. Jinny was tried for, and acquitted of, the murder of her husband. She was a fortune-teller and a 'witch'. Also *Mother Red Cap*.

- 'Mother Damnable' was a term for a brothel-keeper.

MOTHER GOOSE Elizabeth Goose (1665– ?), nèe Foster of Boston, Massachusetts, whose name is also given as Vergoose and Vertigoose. Her son-in-law, Thomas Fleet, a printer, is said to have published *Songs for Children or Mother Goose Melodies for Children* (1719).

MOTHER HUBBARD Edmund Spenser, the *Child of the Ausonian Muse*; so called after writing *Mother Hubbard's Tale* (1590), a satire on Church and Court, by *Ape Gabriel* Harvey (1592).

MOTHER JONES Mary Harris Jones (1830–1930), American Labour leader (1871–1923).

MOTHER OF HER COUNTRY, THE Queen Victoria, *Drina*.

MOTHER OF KINDERGARTEN, THE Susan Elizabeth Blow (1843–1916), American who inaugurated the system in St Louis, Missouri after having seen it work in Germany.

MOTHER OF METHODISM, THE Barbara Huckle Heck (1734–1805), Irishwoman whose zeal helped to establish Methodism in Canada and the USA.

MOTHER OF QUAKERISM, THE Margaret Fell (1614–1702), a leading advocate, converted by Fox (the *Boehme of England*), whom she married (1669).

MOTHER OF THANKSGIVING, THE Sarah Josepha Hale (1788–1879), American, whose writings for the magazine *The Lady's Book* are alleged to have created the movement to celebrate Thanksgiving Day which was first celebrated by a holiday in 1864.

MOTHER OF THE BLUES, THE *Ma* Rainey.

MOTHER OF THE NAVY, THE Dame Agnes Weston (1840–1918), English founder of rest-homes for sailors in three British naval ports; called 'Aggie' by Royal Navy seamen. Also the *Sailors' Friend*.

MOTHER OF THE SALVATION ARMY, THE Catherine Booth, née Mumford (1829–90), wife of 'General' William Booth (*Holy Willie*).

MOTHER OF WALES, THE Catherine Tudor of Berain (1534/5–91), because of the number of children she had by her four husbands.

MOTHER RED CAP Jinny Bingham, *Mother Damnable*.

MOTHER ROSS Christiana or Kit Cavanagh (1667–1739), later Mrs Davies, who went (1692) to find her husband, who was a soldier in France. She joined the 2nd

Royal North Dragoons (Scots Greys), and fought at Ramillies (1706) where she was wounded and her sex discovered. She found her husband, who was then killed at Malplaquet (1709). She subsequently became the mistress of Captain Ross. She was afterwards a pie-seller in Westminster, and is buried in a corner of the churchyard of St Margaret's there; so called by Defoe (the *Father of Modern Prose Fiction*). Also the *Pretty Dragoon*.

MOTHER SHIPTON Ursula Southill, Sowthiel or Southiel (?1486–?1561), 'witch' and prophetess who married a Yorkshire builder Tobias Shipton. There is, however, no reliable information about her, although her alleged prophecies have had a dramatic impact. Their earliest printing was in 1641.

MOTOR CITY'S MOST FAMOUS MOUTH, THE Lee Iacocca (1932–), chairman of the Chrysler Corporation of America; so called by *The Wall Street Journal*.

• Detroit is America's Motor City, or Motor Town (as in 'Motown').

MOUNTAIN JIM James Nugent (shot 1874), Canadian-born Irishman, celebrated scout and guide who had an affair with Isabella Bird (1831–1904), English traveller and authoress. He was also known as *Rocky Mountain Jim*.

MOUNTEBANK OF CRITICISM, THE Bishop William Warburton, the *Colossus of Literature*. Johnson (*Blinking Sam*) once commented: 'The worst of Warburton is that he has a rage for saying something when there's nothing to be said'.

MOUSE

i) Alvin Burroughs (1911–1950), American jazz drummer.

ii) Michael Roberts (1954–), South African jockey who had ridden 2,400 winners before he came to Britain where he rode 20 by June 1987. He is very small.

iii) Henry Bellingham (1956–) MP, barrister, farmer and amateur steeplechase jockey.

MOUSEY DAVIS Nancy Reagan, *Dragon Lady*; her nickname as a schoolgirl in Chicago.

MOUTH, THE Michael Parkinson (1913–),

British TV chat-show personality; so called in Australia when he went to work there. Also *Parky*.

MOUTH OF THE SOUTH, THE Robert Edward (Ted) Turner (1938–), American yachtsman and owner of a baseball team. He won the America's Cup races (1977).

MOUTHY Robert Southey, the *Ballad Monger*, so called by Byron (*Baby*) and *Noctes Ambrosianae*. By assonance with 'Southey?'

MUESSEL-MOU'D CHARLIE Charles Leslie (died 1782 at the reputed age of 105), a Jacobite ballad-singer known to Scott (the *Ariosto of the North*). Charlie was a seller of broadsides in Aberdeen.

• A broadside is a sheet of paper printed on one side only and used for political propaganda and popular songs. 'Muessel' is an Aberdeen term for 'loud'.

MR A Lieutenant-General H H Shri Maharajah Hari Singh Bahadur, Maharajah of Jammu and Kashmir (1895–1961), centre of a sensational case of blackmail and embezzlement (1924). The initial was used in court to mask his identity.

MR ACKER Bernard Stanley Bilk (1929–), British jazz clarinettist.

• 'Acker' is a friendly appellation in Somerset.

MR ALL-GOLD Terence (Terry) Lawless (1934–), British top boxing manager.

MR B William (Billy) Eckstine (1914–), American singer. Also the *Sepia Sinatra*.

MR BEAUTIFUL John Taylor (1961–), handsome pop star of Duran-Duran; so called by girls.

MR BIG

i) Arnold Rothstein (1882–1928), American gambler and gangster who backed a gang led by Jack *Legs* Diamond. He was shot by an unknown gangster.

ii) Alexander (Terry) Sinclair (1945–83), New Zealand millionaire 'emperor' of an international drug smuggling ring; imprisoned for life (1981) for murder and drug-trafficking. His real name was Terence Clark.

• See *Australian Bob*.

iii) Paul Castellano (1916–85), head of the Gambino Mafia family accused of twenty-five murders as well as extortion and drug-trafficking. He was arrested in 1984, and was murdered in New York while on bail for fear of the information he might give to the police. Also 'Big Paul'.

MR BLACKPOOL Reginald Dixon (1905–85), British organist at Blackpool's Tower. He made more than two thousand radio broadcasts during his twenty-nine years there.

MR BOFFIN John (Jack) Rayner, a British Post Office research scientist of Muswell Hill, London. In 1943 he worked with a man who gave all his colleagues Dickensian nicknames. He called Rayner's assistant (and future wife) 'Mrs Boffin' from *Our Mutual Friend*. Raynor became 'Mr Boffin' and was so addressed by his associates when they visited Bomber HQ during World War II; thought to have been the origin of 'Boffin' for any egg-headed scientist.

MR BROADWAY

i) George Abbott (1887–), American playwright and Broadway producer for more than eighty years.

ii) George M Cohan (1878–1942), American song-writer and producer who staged eighty Broadway shows between 1901 and 1940, many of which he wrote. His most famous song, *Yankee Doodle Dandy*, almost became a nickname for him.

MR COOL Keith Deller, the *Milky-Bar Kid*.

MR CORNWALL David Penhaligon (died 1986 aged 42 in a car crash), Liberal MP for Truro; so called from his deep involvement in Cornish affairs. Also the *Voice of Cornwall*.

MR DEATH Howard Hodgson, the *King of Undertakers*.

MR FITZ James Fitzsimmons (1874–1966), American racehorse trainer who retired on his 89th birthday.

MR FIVE-BY-FIVE James (Jimmy) Rushing (1903–72), American blues singer.

MR FIVE PER CENT

i) Calouste Gulbenkian (1869–1955), Armenian millionaire financier who operated in Britain. He charged 5 per cent commission on his deals, mostly in Middle East oil, eg the Iraq Petroleum Company, of which he was founder.

ii) Nubar Gulbenkian (1896–1972), his son, for the same reason.

MR FLASH Ronald (Ron) Atkinson (1939–), manager of Manchester United Football Club (pre-1986), West Bromwich Albion (1987–8), El Atletico, Madrid (1988–9) and Sheffield United (1989–). He wears ultra-smart suits and gold bracelets.

MR GUPPY Alexander Woollcott, the *Butcher of Broadway*; family nickname. When he was born, his brothers, sisters and cousins were reading Dickens' *Bleak House* which contains the line: 'A young gentleman has arrived whose name is Mr Guppy.'

MR HEART-THROB David Hughes (1929–72), handsome pop star and later opera singer.

MR HICKS-BITCH Sir Michael Hicks-Beach, *Black Michael*, Colonial Secretary (1878–80); so called especially by Wolseley (*Our Only General*) who despised him as 'feminine' in politics.

MR JELLY ROLL *Jelly-Roll* Morton.

MR JERSEY Lillie Langtry, the *Jersey Lily*, a turf nickname to hide her identity as a woman.

MR JOHNSON King George VI, *Bat Lugs*, when a midshipman in HMS *Collingwood*.

MR LASERBEAM Phil Donahue (1936–), American TV interviewer who earns $10 million a year. By the means of penetrating questions, he cajoles people into disclosing secrets.

MR MADONNA Sean Penn (1960–), American actor once married to Madonna (the *Queen of the Pops*).

MR MANTON The Duchess of Montrose, *Carrie Red*, as a racehorse owner.

• Manton, Leicestershire, stable for racehorses. See *Wizard of Manton*.

MR MAXIMUM Willie Thorne, the *Great W T.*, British snooker star, because he was always reaching the maximum – at least fifty-nine times by early 1986.

MR MOONLIGHT Frankie Vaughan (1928–), TV and theatre entertainer; from his song *Give Me the Moonlight*, the title of his autobiography (1983).

MR MOTHER COUNTRY Sir James Stephen, *King Stephen*; so called in Canada by Charles Buller (1806–48), British Liberal statesman who went to Canada with Lord Durham (*King Jog*).

MR MUSIC Ted Heath, the *King of Swing*.

MR MUSCLES Greg Norman, the *Choker*, once a lifeguard in Australia.

MR NASTY
i) Ilie Nastase (1946–), Romanian tennis star; so called because of his bad temper on court, especially at Wimbledon; a pun on his name.
ii) Donald Pleasance (1919–), British actor in British and American films; not from his character but from the parts he plays.

MR OVER-SECRETARY Sir James Stephen, *King Stephen*, who as Under-Secretary for the Colonies virtually ruled the British Empire.

MR PIANO Joe Henderson (1920–80), British pianist and entertainer.

MR PLASTIC FANTASTIC Walter Cavanagh (1943–), of Santa Clara, California, who has the world's biggest collection of credit cards (1,196 in 1987).

MR RELAXATION Perry Como, the *King of the Jukes*; from his singing manner.

MR REPUBLICAN Senator Robert Alphonse Taft (1889–1953), of Ohio, a conservative who worked on the Taft-Hartley Labour Act; son of President Taft (*Big Bill*).

MR ROMANCE Engelbert Humperdinck (1936–), British singer with an international reputation for romantic songs, which include *The Last Waltz*. He likes to be called 'Enge' by his friends. His real name is A. George Dorsey.

MR SHOW JUMPING Dorian Williams (1914–85), BBC TV show-jumping commentator for thirty years.

MR SHOWMANSHIP W V Liberace, *Lee*.

He wore a sequin-studded jacket and had a candelabrum on the piano for his act.

MR SPORT Denis H Howell (1923–), Britain's first Minister of Sport (Labour Government 1970s). He began the Sports Aid Foundation; called the outstanding sports politician of the past ten decades. By 1989, he had been an MP for thirty-five years.

MR SUSPENSE Sir Alfred Hitchcock, *Hitch*, a master of producing suspense films.

MR TV
i) David Paradine Frost (1939–), British world TV personality.
ii) Jackie Pallo (1926–), British wrestler. His flamboyant style in the ring attracted a large following on TV.
iii) Peter Cushing (1913–), British film, stage and TV actor, for his outstanding success in TV plays in the 1950s.

MR VELVET VOICE Nat *King* Cole.

MR WHIP Admiral Cornwallis, *Billy Blue*. He was always swift to take disciplinary action.

MR WONDERFUL Sammy Davis Junior (1925–), American singer, dancer and comedian. It was the title of a Broadway show in which he starred.

MR X Lord Northcliffe, the *Chief*, to hide his identity when he was negotiating to buy *The Times* (1907–8). For a time, he called himself 'The Admiral', after the Kaiser, who styled himself 'Admiral of the Atlantic'.

MRS AINTREE Mrs Mirabel Topham (1892–1980), owner for many years of the racecourse at Aintree, near Liverpool, on which the Grand National steeplechase is held annually.

MRS BANG Mary Bertram, a Brighton bathing-cabin attendant and mistress of Henry Fauntleroy, the forger (1784–1824). She was 'bang-up' in fashion and well known in elegant circles there. Fauntleroy was executed for having forged securities worth £170,000.

MRS BROWN Queen Victoria, *Drina*; because of her apparent devotion to her gillie, John Brown (died 1883) in her later life.

MRS BULL Queen Anne, *Brandy Nan*; so called in the *History of John Bull* (1712) by her physician, Dr Arbuthnot, (the *King of Inattention*).

MRS FEATHER Jeanne de Casilis (1898–1966), British stage, screen and radio actress who created the part in the long-running radio series of that name.

MRS FREEMAN Sarah Jennings, Duchess of Marlborough (1660–1744), a name used by her in her friendship and correspondence with Queen Anne (*Brandy Nan*). Also *Old Sarah, Queen Sarah*, the *Viceroy* and the *Wise Duchess*.

• Cf *Mrs Morley*.

MRS MELBOURNE Queen Victoria, *Drina* who showed partisanship for Lord Melbourne (*Lord M*) in the Bedchamber crisis (1839) and displayed hatred for Peel (*Jenny*).

MRS MORLEY Queen Anne, *Brandy Nan*; used in her correspondence with the Duchess of Marlborough (*Mrs Freeman*).

MRS PRESIDENT Abigail Adams, née Smith (1744–1818), wife of President John Adams (the *Colossus of Independence*); the only woman to have been the wife of one President and the mother of another (J Q Adams, the *Massachusetts Madman*). She was well educated and intelligent and helped both men's careers. A US Postal Service publication said she 'played a major role in the development of the emerging nation'.

MRS PRO Mrs Jean Grant (1729–88), wife of Duncan Grant (1743–1825), Provost of Forres, Scotland, and mother of four distinguished sons: Sir James Grant, Wellington's senior medical officer in the Waterloo campaign; Colonel Alexander Grant; Lieutenant-Colonel Lewis Grant and Lieutenant-Colonel Colquhoun Grant, Wellington's intelligence chief in the Peninsular campaign.

MRS WORLD Julia Morley (1940–), British boss of the Miss World beauty competition. She is the wife of Eric Morley.

MS HAIRPERSON Harriet Harman (1950–), Labour's Shadow Minister of Health.

MUDDY WATERS McKinley Morganfield (1915–83), American blues singer. He was brought up in the Mississippi Delta, a river known as the 'Old Muddy'.

MUFFIE Mabel Brandon (1925–), Social Secretary to President Reagan (*Dutch*) for two and a half years and wife to Henry Brandon of *The Sunday Times*, London.

MUGSY Francis Joseph Spanier (1906–67), white jazz cornettist with a 'homely' face. He played with *King* Oliver's band.

MUHAMMED ALI OF THE TRACK, THE *Daley* Thompson; so called in America.

• See *Gaseous Cassius*.

MULATTO TRADER, THE John Ormond, *John the Chief*.

MULE Perry Bradford (1895–1970), American jazz pianist and composer.

MUL-SACK John Cottington (1640–85), chimney-sweep, highwayman and murderer. He fled abroad, and was introduced at the Court of Charles II (the *Blackbird*) in exile, but believing the Commonwealth would pardon him, he returned to England, was captured and executed. Cottington loved mulled sherry (sack).

MUNCHAUSEN OF THE WEST, THE David (Davy) Crockett, the *Coonskin Congressman*. He told many tall stories, as in his disputed autobiography *A Narrative of the Life of David Crockett of the State of Tennessee* (1834).

• Baron Karl von Munchausen (1720–97) built up a reputation for incredible stories. Some were published by Rudolf Raspe (1785) in England.

MUNCHKIN Eleanor Weightman (1965–), girl-friend of Prince Edward (*Jaws*).

• The Munchkins are characters in *The Wizard of Oz* (1939).

MUNGO

i) St Kentigern, the *Grey Hound*; so called by St Servanus.

• *Munghu* in Gaelic means 'dearest' or 'aimable'.

ii) Jeremiah Dyson (1722–76), British politician; so called after the ubiquitous slave in Isaac Bickerstaffe's (d ?1812) play *The Padlock* (1768).

iii) Flight-Lieutenant John Henry Park (died 1941), fighter pilot in the Battle of Britain (World War II); from Mungo Park (1771–1806), explorer in West Africa.

MUNGO or MONGO JOHN John Ormond, *John the Chief*.

- Mungo = a slave merchant, from *Mango*, which was a dealer or salesman in Latin.

MURDERER OF THE CENTURY, THE Dennis Andrew Nilsen (1948–), sentenced to eight terms of life imprisonment (1983) for six murders and two attempted murders in London. He admitted fifteen or sixteen killings, but the police believe there are more. All were young men; self-applied.

MURKETAGH OF THE LEATHER CLOAKS Murketagh Ui Neill, the *Hector of the West*; after the dress of his force which made the Circuit of Ireland (941).

MURT E J O'Donaghue (born New Zealand 1901), first snooker player to make a break of 147. (Australia 1932).

MUSCLES Kenneth (Ken) Ronald Rosewell (1934–), Australian tennis player and Wimbledon finalist.

MUSES' DARLING, THE John Fletcher, the *Limb of Shakespeare*; so called by the poet, James Shirley (the *Last Minstrel of the English Stage*).

MUSES' PRIDE, THE The Earl of Dorset, *Charles the First*; so called in an epitaph by Pope (the *Bard of Twickenham*). He was a poet and courtier as well as a generous patron of other poets.

MUSICAL SMALL-COAL MAN, THE Thomas Britton (1644–1714), a charcoal dealer of Clerkenwell, London, who was a self-taught musician and organized concerts in the loft over his shop which were attended by celebrities including Handel (the *Grand Old Man*). Britton was frightened to death by the first ventriloquist he heard: 'Talking Smith', whose real name was Honeyman.

MUTTON Sir Christopher Hatton, the *Dancing Chancellor*; so called by Queen Elizabeth (the *English Diana*): a word-play on 'Hatton'.

MUTTON-EATING KING, THE Charles II, the *Blackbird*; so called by Rochester (*Virgin Modesty*).

- A 'mutton-monger' in the slang of those days was, in the definition of Cotgrave (1611), 'a cunning solicitor of a wench'. Mutton = a loose woman.

MUTTONLEG Theodore Donnelly (1912–58), American jazz trombonist.

MYRON OF THE AGE, THE George Garrard (1760–1826), British scholar, painter and sculptor; so called by Wolcot (*Peter Pindar*).

- Myron (flourished *circa* 480–445 BC), was one of the six great sculptors of Greece, famous for his *Discobolus*.

MYSTERIOUS DAVE David Mather or Mathers (1844– ?), American gunman and suspected train-robber who appeared and disappeared mysteriously in Dodge City, Kansas (1880s).

MYSTERIOUS MONTAGUE John Montague (1906–72), American golfer who had a hatred of photographers. Later it was found out that he was wanted for robbery in New York (1930).

MYSTERY MAN OF EUROPE, THE Sir Basil Zaharoff (1850–1936), armaments manufacturer. He had to remain anonymous and hidden from the possibility of assassination. A reward of £20,000 was once offered to anyone who could kill him. His name as a boy in Greece was Basileios Zacharias.

MYSTERY V.C., THE Captain (later Vice-Admiral) Gordon Campbell (1886–1953) who commanded the famous Q-ship *Farnborough*. *The London Gazette* in announcing the award cloaked the details of his exploits. When he went to Buckingham Palace to receive the medal, the Guards' band played *Hush! Hush! Here comes the Bogey Man*.

- A Q-ship was a merchantman equipped as a warship in anti-submarine warfare (World War I), but appearing unarmed.

N

NAB Sir Gerald Nabarro, the **Barrow Boy**. His cars bore number-plates NAB 1 to NAB 5.

NABOB, THE

i) Sir George Shee, Baronet (fl. 1780s) who served in India, cousin to Sir Martin Archer-Shee who was President of the Royal Academy (1830–50). William Hickey (**Pickle**) met him at a dinner-party in Calcutta when he was plain Mr Shee.

ii) George Gray (1738– ?), born in India, he made a fortune in Bengal. He went home to Scotland for his education and was a schoolfellow of Boswell (the **Ambitious Thane**). Gray may have been to 'blame' in part for 'The Nabob' by Foote (**Beau Nasty**).

• See **His Nobs**.

NAILER, THE William (Bill) Stevens (fl. 1760s), champion British pugilist who lost prestige by 'throwing' a fight against George Meggs, a Bristol collier, so called for his punishing style.

• A 'nailer' in 18th–19th century slang meant an exceptional person or someone exceptionally good at something.

NAMBY-PAMBY Ambrose Philips (?1675–1749), a minor British poet whose work was ridiculed by Pope (the **Bard of Twickenham**) and Henry Carey (circa 1690–1749). Philips wrote some verses for the children of Lord Carteret, and Carey commented 'So the nurses get by heart Namby-Pamby's little rhymes'. The nickname was immediately picked up by Pope and made famous. 'Namby' is the supposed childish pronunciation of 'Ambrose', and 'Pamby' is for the first letter of Philips's name.

• Carey wrote *Sally in Our Alley*.

NAMBY-PAMBY WILLIS Nathaniel Parker Willis (1807–67), American poet and journalist. He was talented, but assumed the manners of a dandy, which led Oliver Wendell Holmes (1809–94) to say he was 'something of a remembrance of the Count D'Orsay' (**Le Jeune Cupidon**) 'and an anticipation of Oscar Wilde' (1856–1908). Willis' initials N. P. brought the analogy.

NAMELESS BARD, THE Thomas James Mathias (1750–1835), author of *Pursuits of Literature* (1794).

NANCE Anne Oldfield, **Miss Nancy**.

NAPOLEON OF DRAMA, THE Alfred Bunn, **Good Friday**, lessee of the Drury Lane Theatre, London (1819–26) and Covent Garden, where he tried to reinstate English opera.

NAPOLEON OF DRURY LANE, THE Robert William Elliston (1774–1831), British actor who became manager of the Drury Lane Theatre, London, and of several provincial theatres. He staged Edmund Kean (1787–1833) in *King Lear* but like Bunn (above) he went bankrupt. Lamb (the **Mitre Courtier**) wrote. 'Wherever Elliston walked, sate or stood still, there was the theatre'; so called by Fitzgerald in *A New History of the English Stage* (1882).

NAPOLEON OF ESSAYISTS, THE Horace Greely (1811–72), founder and editor of *The New Yorker* (1834–1941) and essayist, best remembered for his phrase 'Go west, young man'. Also the **Sage of Chappaqua**.

NAPOLEON OF FINANCE, THE

i) Jabez Spencer Balfour (1849–1916), British politician and financier gaoled for fourteen years (1895) for financial conspiracy and fraud.

ii) Horatio Bottomley, **England's Recruiting Sergeant**; so called by James Judd (1890s).

NAPOLEON OF LIVERPOOL FINANCE, THE Morris Ranger (died 1883), who speculated in millions.

NAPOLEON OF NIGHT CLUBS, THE Harry Andrews, who ran several night-clubs in London in the 1920s.

NAPOLEON OF THE JEMMY, THE Charlie Peace, the *Monkey*.

- American for 'Jemmy' = 'Jimmy'.

NAPOLEON OF ORATORY, THE

i) W E Gladstone, the *Dismember for Great Britain*.

ii) William Pitt, *Aeolus*.

NAPOLEON OF THE INDIANS, THE Chief Joseph, whose real name was Heinmot Tooyalaket (1831–1904); leader of the Nez Percés of Oregon in the Snake River campaign (1877). He outgeneralled the American troops several times, and won the respect of General Miles (*Bear Coat*).

NAPOLEON OF THE PRESS, THE Lord Northcliffe, the *Chief*.

NAPOLEON OF THE RING, THE Jem Belcher (1781–1811) who won the bare-knuckle boxing championship of England (1800). He introduced refinements of ringcraft and looked like Napoleon Bonaparte. He gave his name to a large spotted handkerchief.

NAPOLEON OF THE STUMP, THE James Knox Polk (1795–1849), 11th President of the USA; because of his success as a speaker at political meetings. Also *Young Hickory*.

- The stump in America is the platform on which political speeches are made.

NAPOLEON OF THE TROTTING TURF, THE Hiram Woodruff (1817–61), hero of American trotting (harness racing) for thirty years.

NAPOLEON OF THE TURF, THE

i) Lord William George Frederick Cavendish Bentinck (1802–48), son of the 4th Duke of Portland. He introduced to racecourses many of the practices now standard. He was a politician, but he was better known in sporting circles.

ii) Frederick Swindell, *Lord Freddy*.

NAPOLEON OF THE WEST, THE

i) William Hepburn Russell, the *Father of the Pony Express*. He began by organizing the carriage of army supplies to the American West and then introduced wagon-trains. With Alexander Majors (*Ol' Gospel*), he started the Pony Express and stagecoaches.

ii) Ben Holladay (1819–87). He took over the Central Overland Pacific and Pike's Peak Line (1861) and made it pay. He built an 'empire' from Missouri to San Francisco. Also the *Stagecoach King of the West*.

NAPPER Stanley Joseph McCabe (1910–68), Australian batsman who played three memorable innings in Test Matches before World War II. He made 11,949 runs in 252 innings, 20 of them not out; from his likeness to Napoleon.

NATURE'S DARLING Shakespeare, the *Bard of All Time*; so called by Thomas Gray (the *British Pindar*) in *The Progress of Poesy* (1754).

NATURE'S GLORY Queen Elizabeth I, the *English Diana*; so called in 1591.

NAVIGATOR, THE St Brendan, Brandon or Brandan of Clonfert (*circa* 484–578), Irishman, reputed to have been the first man to cross the Atlantic (*circa* 565–573). The story is in the 9th century *Navigatio Sancti Brendani*. Also the *Voyager*.

NEAGLE THE BEAGLE Neagle Cathcart (1954–), British hair transplant specialist; so called after his persistent pursuit of Gloria Hunniford (*Glorious Honeybun*) had come to public attention.

NEEDLE-WATCHER, THE William (Will) Adams (1564–1620) of Gillingham, Kent, England, navigator, the first Englishman to reach Japan, where he was retained in honour for the rest of his life; so called by the Japanese because he used a compass. The original of Blackstone in *Shogun*.

NED Wayne Larkins (1953–), English and Northamptonshire cricketer.

NELL OF OLD DRURY Eleanor (Nell) Gwynn (1650–87), orange-seller at Drury Lane Theatre, London, and later an actress and mistress of Charles II (the *Blackbird*); so called by Pepys (the *Father of Black-Letter Lore*). Also *Pretty Witty Nell*.

NERVOUS NELLY Frank B Kellogg (1856–1937), American Secretary of State (1925–29) in the Coolidge (*Cautious Cal*) administration. He negotiated the Kellogg–Briand Pact (1928) to outlaw war. The nickname was given to him by isolationists.

NESTOR OF CANADIAN LIBERALISM, THE Sir Richard Cartwright, *Blue Ruin*.

- Nestor, King of Pylos, ruled over three generations. A hero of *The Iliad*, he was famous for his wisdom, eloquence and justice and was renowned as a veteran.

NESTOR OF CANADIAN POLITICS, THE Robert Baldwin (1804–58). He resigned from a number of bodies (e.g. the Executive Council) because of a tender conscience.

NESTOR OF ENGLISH AUTHORS, THE Samuel Rogers, the *Banker Poet* who was ninety-two when he died.

NESTOR OF THE CHEMICAL REVOLUTION, THE Dr Joseph Black (1728–1799), born in France of Scottish parents. In his thesis *De humore acido a cibis orto et magnesia alba*, for his doctorate (1754), he anticipated – but did not develop – many of the findings of Antoine Lavoisier (1743–94) who gave him the nickname.

NESTOR OF THE CONFEDERACY, THE A H Stephens, the *Little Pale Star from Georgia*. Although he led the Southern secessionists, he worked to prevent its realization.

NESTOR OF THE HOUSE OF COMMONS, THE Edward Ellice, the *Bear*, an MP from 1818 to 1863.

NESTOR OF THE PLAINS (or the ROCKY MOUNTAINS), THE Christopher (Kit) Carson (1809–68), American frontiersman on the Santa Fé Trail and Brigadier-General in the army.

NEVER-SAY-DIE DRAKE Ted Drake, the *Iron Man*.

NEWGATE The Honourable and Reverend Augustus Barry (1773– ?), son of the 6th Earl of Barrymore; because that was the only prison in London he had not been in. He was a reckless gambler and a wild character.

- Cf *Billingsgate* and *Cripplegate*.

NEW HERESIARCH, THE John Toland (1670–1772), British deist theologian, whose writings, it was thought, founded a new religious heresy. His *Christianity Not Mysterious* (1696), published anonymously, caused him to be denounced and prosecuted. He later declared the book 'a youthful indiscretion'. See *The Father of English Deism*.

NEWK John Newcombe (1944–), Australian tennis player; so called in Australia.

NEW KIM NOVAK, THE Melanie Griffith, *Baby Monroe*.

- Kim Novak (1933–), American film star.

NEWSBOY Joseph Moriarty (1911–79), American gambling boss of New Jersey, convicted of a gambling conspiracy (1973).

NEWTON OF CHEMISTRY, THE The Honourable Henry Cavendish (1731–1810) who in a wide range of experiments determined the specific gravity of hydrogen and carbon dioxide as well as the composition of water.

- For Sir Isaac Newton, see the *Columbus of the Skies*.

NEWT THE BEAUT John (Jack) Newton (1949–), Australian golfer who won the Australian Open Golf Tournament (1979) and the British Open (1975). He had an arm torn off in an aeroplane accident (1983).

NEW YORK'S QUEEN OF THE NIGHT Dianne Brill (1961–), 6 ft 1 in men's fashion designer, partygoer and nightclubber; so called by newspapermen (especially in *The New York Times*).

NIALL BLACK KNEE Niall Ui Neill, *Glundubh* (which means 'black knee' in Gaelic), High King of Ireland (reigned 916–919). He was killed in battle against the Norse King of Dublin (in what is now Phoenix Park). A lament for his death was written by the poet Gormliath and included in the Book of Lismore (*circa* 15th century), where the king was referred to as 'Black-kneed Nial'.

NIALL OF THE NINE HOSTAGES Niall Ui Neill, *Noigiallach*, High King of Ireland (379–405) who took the Irish Kingdom to the height of its power. His descendants from fourteen sons are named O'Neill. One of these was St Columba (the *Apostle of the Highlanders*).

NIALL OF THE SHOWERS Niall, High King

of Ireland (763–70) who died a monk on Iona where the O'Neills were hereditary abbots.

NICKS John Nevison, a highwayman (late 17th century) mentioned by Defoe (the *Father of Modern Prose Fiction*) in his *A Tour Through England and Wales* (1724–6). His nickname was originally 'Nicks', but was changed to *Swiftnicks* after he had ridden from Gad's Hill, Kent, to York (1676), appearing on the bowling-green and discussing the time with the Lord Mayor. Defoe did not give the name; that attribution came later in the *Encyclopaedia Britannica*.

NIFTY NEVILLE Neville Kenneth Wran (1926–   ), Australian Labour Premier, New South Wales (1976–1986), the longest serving Premier of that State; so called because of his political adroitness which often caused raised eyebrows.

NIGER Wlfricus Niger or Black (flourished *circa* 1080) who is said to have received this nickname (Reaney) from the fact that he went unrecognized among his foes with his face blackened with charcoal.

NIGHTINGALE OF TWICKENHAM, THE Alexander Pope, the *Bard of Twickenham*; so called in *Noctes Ambrosianae*.

- Cf the *Little Nightingale*.

NIGHT TRAIN Richard Lane (1928–   ), American National Football League all-time leader for interception. He studied with a friend who seemed always to be playing the record of that song when he arrived (and rhyme with 'Lane?').

NIKAL SEYN John Nicholson (1822–57), British political officer on the Punjab frontier and later Deputy Commissioner of Bannu where he became a legend among the Punjabis for his bravery. They worshipped him as a god under the name 'Nikal Seyn'. He was a Brigadier-General when he was killed in the Indian Mutiny.

NINE DAYS QUEEN, THE Lady Jane Grey (1537–54), grand-daughter of Henry VIII (*Bluff Hal*). She was manoeuvred into taking the crown on the death of Edward VI (the *Josiah of England*) in 1553 by her father, the Duke of Suffolk and her father-in-law, the Duke of Northumberland. She was executed for high treason after having been overthrown by *Bloody Mary*.

NIP Clarence Edward Pellew (1894–1981), Australian wicket-keeper (1920s).

NIPPER

i) Frank Nicholson (1910–82), wicket-keeper for South African cricket team.

ii) Lupino Lane (1892–1959), British comedian, especially in *Me and My Girl*. His real name was Henry George Lupino.

iii) Detective-Superintendent Leonard Read (1925–   ), of Scotland Yard. He became Assistant Chief Constable of Nottinghamshire.

- A 'nipper' is one who catches or arrests; from 'nip', to catch since about 1560. 'Nippers' was 19th century slang for handcuffs or policemen. 'Nipper' for a boy is said to derive from the lads who nipped the running anchor cables of a ship.

NITRATE KING, THE Colonel John Thomas North (1841–96), of Eltham, South London, who made a fortune by speculation in nitrates.

NOB, THE George IV, *Adonis of Fifty*.

- See *His Nobs*.

NOBBY

i) Admiral Charles Ewart, who, when Captain of HMS *Melpomene* (1859–62), was renowned for his neat personal appearance and for his insistence on everything being spick and span in his ship.

- See comment at *His Nobs*.

ii) Norbert Stiles (1942–   ), right-half for Manchester United and Middlesbrough at a transfer fee (1971) of £20,000. He played in the 1966 World Cup team. When he played in Spain for a time, he was nicknamed 'El Bandito'. Coach for West Bromwich.

NOBLE WIT OF SCOTLAND, THE Sir George Mackenzie, *Bloody Mackenzie*; so called by Dryden (*Asaph*).

NOBS George IV (see above), who was a dandy.

NODDY Colin Moynihan, the *Miniature of Sport*; so called by Dennis Skinner (the *Beast of Bolsover*).

- Noddy is a character in children's stories by Enid Blyton.

NOD-NOLL Oliver Cromwell, the *Almighty Nose*; so called by Needham (the *Cobbett of His Day*).

NO FLINT or GENERAL NO FLINT Major-General Charles, 1st Earl Grey (1729–1807). He preferred bayonets to musketry in the American War of Independence.

NOIR, LE

i) Alan Niger (*circa* 1040–89), a Breton kinsman of William (the *Bastard*). He took part in the Norman Conquest (1066).

ii) Alan Niger (*circa* 1045–93), Breton in the Norman Conquest (1066) who became Duke of Richmond in succession to his brother *Le Roux*.

- Cf *Niger*.

NONPAREIL, THE

i) Jack Randall (fl. early 19th century), a British pugilist noted for his courtesy in the ring.

ii) Frederick William Lillywhite (1792–1854), cricketer for Sussex and England; pioneer of round-arm bowling: sometimes the 'Nonpareil Bowler'.

NONSUCH, THE Mrs Ann Hutchinson (?1590–1643), religious fanatic and founder of Antinomianism in New England; an anagram of part of her name.

- Antinomianism, which first appeared in Germany in 1535, was the faith of a sect which held that moral law was not binding upon Christians.
- A nonsuch or nonesuch is someone without equal (post-1590).

NORFOLK B. C. (Chris) Broad (1957–), Gloucestershire, Nottinghamshire and England cricketer; from Norfolk Broads. He made 162 runs in the 2nd Test Match in Australia (1986) and 116 in the 3rd. He was chosen Cricketer of the Year (1986) after a total score of 993 runs in Australia.

NORFOLK BOY, THE Richard Porson, the *Coryphaeus of Learning*; so called at Eton. It stuck. He was the son of the parish clerk at East Ruston, near North Walsham.

NORFOLK GAMESTER, THE Sir Robert Walpole, the *Grand Corrupter*; so called

in ballads. He was born in Norfolk and was MP for King's Lynn in the same county.

NORFOLK GIANT, THE Robert Hales (1814–63) who was 7 ft 6 in tall. He was born at Somerton, Norfolk, and was exhibited by Barnum (the *Prince of Humbugs*) and at the Great Exhibition (1851). He was presented to the Queen. His father was 6 ft 6 in tall and his sister Mary was 7 ft 2 in.

NORTHAMPTONSHIRE PEASANT POET, THE or THE NORTHAMPTONSHIRE POET John Clare (1793–1864), son of a Northamptonshire labourer.

NORTHERN DANTE, THE Ossian, the *Celtic Homer*; so called by Henri van Lann.

- Dante Alighieri (1265–1321) was the poet of *Divina Commedia*, written *circa* 1300.

NORTHERN MAN WITH SOUTHERN PRINCIPLES, THE Martin van Buren, *King Martin the First*; so called in *The Charleston Courier*, because of his political stances.

NORTHUMBERLAND PIPER, THE James Allen (flourished 1770s) whose *Life* (1828) recounted his adventures in Europe, Asia and Africa.

NOSE ALMIGHTY Oliver Cromwell, the *Almighty Nose*. He had a large nose.

NOSEGAY NAN Frances Abington (1737–1815), British actress, daughter of a soldier; née Fanny Barton. Her nickname as a flower-seller and street singer before she went on the stage. She was eighteen years at the Drury Lane Theatre, London, with Garrick (*Atlas*) and was the first to play Lady Teazle in *The School for Scandal* (1777).

NOSEY

i) The Duke of Wellington, the *Achilles of England*.

ii) Oliver Cromwell, the *Almighty Nose*.

iii) Matthew Parker (1504–75), chaplain to Henry VIII (*Bluff Hal*) and later Archbishop of Canterbury (1559). He had a large nose and a reputation for poking it into many church matters which did not concern him.

iv) Richard Parker, born 1767 and

hanged for his part in the mutiny at the Nore (1797); possibly because of (iii).

v) Giacobbe Baseni (?1682–1783), famous violoncellist who adopted the name Cervetto before he came to London in 1738 or 1739. He was very popular at the Drury Lane Theatre where crowds in the balcony used to shout 'Play up, Nosey', which became a catch-phrase. He had a large nose.

NOTTINGHAM POET, THE Philip James Bailey (1816–1903), born at Old Basford, Nottinghamshire. He wrote a version of the Faust story entitled *Festus* (1839).

NOVELIST OF WESSEX, THE Thomas Hardy (1840–1928). He set most of his novels there.

- Wessex was an Anglo-Saxon kingdom in south and west England.

NUDGER Ernest Needham (1837–1936), half-back for Sheffield United and England.

NUGGET, THE Steve Davis, the *Cool Kid*.

NUMBER-ONE-FELLA-BELONG-MISSUS-QUEEN Prince Philip, Duke of Edinburgh, *Biggles*: a nickname given to him in New Guinea during a royal tour.

NUMBER-ONE-PICCANINNY-BELONG-MISSUS-QUEEN Prince Charles, Prince of Wales, *Fishface*; so called in pidgin English during a tour of Tonga.

NUNAWADDING MESSIAH, THE Andrew Fisher (flourished 1870s) of Nunawaddy, Victoria, Australia, who declared himself the Messiah (1871). His followers were polygamous.

NUN OF KENT, THE Elizabeth Barton, the *Holy Maid of Kent*; so called by Scott (the *Ariosto of the North*).

NURSE NOAKES James Noakes (died 1696), British actor who excelled in 'dame' parts; so called from his success as a nurse in Nevil Payne's *Fatal Jealousy*.

NURSE OF ANTIQUITY, THE William Camden, the *British Pausanias*. He gathered material for a history of Britain.

NUTCRACKER Vincent (Vinny) Jones (1965–), footballer for Wimbledon Football Club who has been sent off the field at least three times for violent tactics; mentioned by Tommy Smith (the *Iron Man of Soccer*). Also *Psycho*.

- A combination of 'nuts' and 'crackers'.

NYE Aneurin Bevan (1897–1960), British Labour statesman who created the National Health Service (1948); also called 'The Conscience of the Labour Party'; from 'An-nye-rin'.

O

OAKIE Lewis Delaney Offield (1893–1978), American film actor; school nickname to which he added 'Jack'. He came from Oklahoma.

OBADIAH AVE-MARIA Obadiah Walker (1616–99), a fervent Roman Catholic and Master of University College, Oxford who tried to convert the university to Catholicism.

OBBY Osborne de Vere Beauclerk, 12th Duke of St Albans (1875–1964).

OBO Prince Alexander Obolensky (1916–40), Oxford and England rugby wing three-quarters (1930s), with four caps for England. He died in an RAF plane crash.

OCEAN SHEPHERD, THE Sir Walter Raleigh, the *Knight of the Cloak*. He appears as 'the Shepheard of the Sea' in *Colin Clouts come home againe*, dedicated to him by Spenser (the *Child of the Ausonian Muse*).

OCEAN SWELL, THE Admiral Sir Bertram Ramsay (1883–1945), Commander-in-Chief, Allied Naval Forces in the invasion of Normandy (1944); from his smart appearance.

OFFICER IN THE TOWER, THE Lieutenant Norman Baillie-Stewart (1909–66) of the Seaforth Highlanders, held in the Tower of London before trial for acting as an agent for the Nazis (1933). He was sentenced to five years penal servitude. He became a German citizen and broadcast for the Nazis. He was sentenced (1946) to another five years penal servitude for that.

OGRE OF PRINTING HOUSE SQUARE, THE Lord Northcliffe, the *Chief*; his nickname for himself after he had bought *The Times* (1908).

- Printing House Square, London was where John Walters (1738–1812) established *The Times* (1785) as *The Daily Universal Register*. See *Mr X*.

OHIO FATS Jack Nicklaus, *Blobbo*. He was born in Columbus, Ohio.

OHIO GONG, THE Senator William Allen, *Fog Horn*.

OHIO ROSCIUS, THE Louis Aldrich (1843–1910), American actor who played Shakespeare in Ohio before going to New York.

- **See** the *African Roscius*.

OLD ABE Abraham Lincoln, *Father Abraham*.

OLD ANDREW TURNCOAT Dr Andrew Perne, *Andrew Ambo*, described in a sixteenth-century book as 'the notablest turnecoat in al this land'.

OLD ARBITRATOR, THE William (Bill) Klem (1874–1951), American National Baseball League umpire. In the Hall of Fame (1953).

OLD BAGS John Scott, 1st Earl of Eldon (1751–1838), Lord Chancellor for twenty-five years. He carried home with him a number of bags, each containing papers for a case which needed judgment. Also the *Stormy Petrel of Politics*.

OLD BALD HEAD Richard Stoddert Ewell (1817–72), American Confederate general who commanded a division under *Stonewall* Jackson; so called by his soldiers.

OLD BALDILOCKS Gerald Bernard Kaufman (1930–   ), Labour Shadow Foreign Secretary (1980s), who hasn't much hair; nickname by *Private Eye*.

- Cf *Goldilocks*.

OLD BEEFY Ian Botham, *Both*, mentioned by Gower (*Lulu*).

OLD BEESWAX Admiral Raphael Semmes (1809–77), commander of the *Alabama*, a Confederate battleship under the English flag which sank fifty-seven Northern ships and was the subject of the Alabama Claim against England. He had a habit of waxing his huge moustache.

OLD BILL William Miner (1847–1913), American stagecoach and train robber.

OLD BILLY William Pitt, the *Bottomless Pit*; so called by the Prince of Wales (*Adonis of Fifty*).

OLD BLOOD AND GUTS General George Smith Patton (1885–1945), American commander of the invasion forces in North Africa (1942) and the United States 3rd Army in France and Germany (World War II), a thrusting, fire-eating general. Also *Two-Gun Patton*.

OLD or OL' BLUE EYES Frank Sinatra, the *Guv'nor*.

OLD BOOTS Thomas Spence, known as Tom Crudd (died ?1702), bootcleaner at the Unicorn Inn, Ripon, Yorkshire, and a notable character. He had a long nose and a curved chin, so that he could hold a coin between them. The Unicorn Inn has a Tom Crudd bar.

OLD BORLUM Brigadier William Mackintosh of Borlum, who, at the age of about sixty, commanded the Highland infantry in the 1715 Jacobite Rising. After the rebellion he was imprisoned in Newgate, London, but escaped and went to France. Also the *Old Brigadier*.

OLD BORY General Pierre Beauregard, *Little Napoleon*; from 'beaure-'.

OLD BRAB (or sometimes **BWAB**) Major-General J.P. Brabazon, the *Beau Brummell of the Day*. He was unable to pronounce the letter r, making it sound like a w.

OLD BRAINS Major-General Henry Wager Halleck (1815–72), an American military theorist whose intervention in practical warfare was often disastrous; so called in derision by American soldiers.

OLD BRIGADIER, THE Brigadier Mackintosh, *Old Borlum*.

OLD BROWN OF OSSAWATOMIE John Brown (1800–59), famous figure of the song *John Brown's Body*, who incited slaves to rebel and was hanged. He moved from Ohio to Ossawatomie, Kansas, and operated his 'underground railway' from there. His raid on Harper's Ferry sparked off the Civil War. Also *Ossawatomie Brown*.

OLD BUCK James Buchanan, *Grandma*.

OLD BUENA VISTA Zachary Taylor (1784–1850), 12th President of the USA, and general at the victory of Buena Vista (1847) in the Mexican War which made him a national hero. Also *Old Rough and Ready* and *Old Zach*.

OLD BULLION Thomas Hart Benton (1782–1858), American Democratic senator who opposed the Bank of the United States of America and advocated bimetallism and 'hard money'.
- 'Hard money' = coins as opposed to paper money, cheques etc.

OLD CHAPULTEPEC General Winfield Scott, *Fuss and Feathers*. His capture of Fort Chapultepec (1847) led to the taking of Mexico City and the end of the Mexican War. He, like Taylor (above), became a national hero.

OLD CHARLIE Admiral Sir Charles Napier, *Black Charlie*.

OLD CHICH Admiral Sir Edward Chichester (1849–1906). Bowen says he was 'one of the most popular officers in the Royal Navy at the end of the 19th century'.

OLD CHICKAMAUGA General James Barrett Steedman (1818–83), American who distinguished himself at the battle of Chickamauga (1863). Also *Old Steadfast*.

OLD CHIEF Henry Clay, the *Apostle of Liberty*.

OLD CIA MA THA Sir Alan Cameron, first colonel of the 79th Cameron Highlanders, which became the Queen's Own Cameron Highlanders in 1881; from his habit of responding to salutes with the Gaelic *Cia ma tha?* (= How are you?).
- The regiment was nicknamed the Camarhas as a result (Fraser and Gibbons).

OLD CLARKE William Clarke (1798–1856), Nottinghamshire and England cricketer, an underarm bowler who helped to make cricket popular all over England with a touring All-England XI.

OLD CLOSE-THE-RANGE Admiral of the Fleet Lord Cunningham, *A.B.C.*. He always had a desire to get to close quarters with the enemy.

OLD CONKEY The Duke of Wellington, the

Achilles of England; so called in contemporary satirical papers and caricatures.

• See *Conkey*.

OLD COPPERNOSE Henry VIII, *Bluff Hal*; see *Coppernose Harry*.

OLD CREEPY Alvin Karpis (1907–79), American member of the Barker gang, train-robber and murderer; so called by Fred Barker (1902–35) who was in prison with him, because of his sinister appearance. Also *Public Rat No 1*.

• See *Ma* (ii).

OLD CROME John Crome, the *English Hobbema*.

OLD DAPH Sir William Davenant, *Daphne*.

OLD DAVEY, THE BENGAL TIGER Brevet Major-General David Emanuel Twiggs (1790–1862) who commanded in Texas (1857–61) until his quick surrender of Federal property to Texas secessionists brought him dismissal from the army and the nickname of *Traitor Twiggs*. He was bad-tempered and vindictive.

OLD DEMDIKE Elizabeth Southern or Sowthern (died 1612), head of a gang of 'witches' of Pendle Forest, Lancashire. She died in prison – aged eighty, it was said, and blind – after a trial at which ten others were condemned to death.

OLD DOURO The Duke of Wellington, the *Achilles of England*. He was created Marquis of Douro after one of his most famous victories in the Peninsula.

OLD DREADNOUGHT Admiral the Honourable Edward Boscawen (1711–61). At the age of twenty-eight with a party of seamen at the siege of Cartagena, he captured a battery of 15 guns under fire from another fort. Also *Wry-Necked Dick*.

OLD EAGLE EYE Jacob (Jake) Peter Beckley (1867–1918), American baseball star in the Hall of Fame as a batter (1888–1907).

OLD ENGLISH BARON, THE Byron (*Baby*); nickname at Harrow (1801–5), where he was labelled a snob.

OLD ERSKINE James Erskine of Mar, Scottish lawyer and friend of Boswell (the *Ambitious Thane*). He was Knight-Marshal of Scotland.

OLD EVERLASTING Thomas (Tom) Walker (1762–1831), Hambledon cricketer. He stayed at the wicket a long time when he was batting.

• In the 1760s and 1770s, Hambledon, Hampshire, fielded the finest cricket team in England and was vital in the genesis of the modern game.

OLD FAGIN Sir Charles James Napier (1782–1853), C-in-C, India, who conquered Sind; so called by his troops from his supposed resemblance to the Dickens character. Also the *Soldiers' Friend*.

OLD FATHER EPHRAIM The Reverend Ephraim Paget (died 1646), vicar of St Edmund's, Lombard Street, London (1601–46).

OLD FATHER PALINODE Dr Andrew Perne, *Andrew Ambo*.

• A palinode is a poet's recantation for something said earlier.

OLD FITZ Edward Fitzgerald (1809–83) who translated *The Rubaiyat of Omar Khayyam* (1859); so called (1885) by Tennyson (the *Bard of Arthurian Romance*) in his dedication to *Tiresias*.

OLD FOCUS Robert Smith (1689–1768), English mathematician who published *A Compleat System of Opticks* (1738).

OLD FOX, THE Simon Fraser, 12th Baron Lovat (*circa* 1667–1747), beheaded after the battle of Culloden (1746); from his plots, intrigues and lies for the Jacobites.

OLD FRENCH Count Casimir de Montrond, sent by the British on a secret mission to Vienna (1815); his nickname in London clubs (early 19th century). He was a French adventurer and spy.

OLD FUSS AND FEATHERS General Winfield Scott, *Fuss and Feathers*.

OLD GABE Jim Bridger, the *Daniel Boone of the Rocky Mountains*; nickname given by Jedediah Smith (the *Knight in Buckskins*), who said that Bridger reminded him of Gabriel spreading the word of God.

OLD GEORGE George Monk, *Abdael*.

OLD GLADEYE W.E. Gladstone, the *Dismember for Great Britain*; a pun on his name because of his campaign to rescue prostitutes. It was commonly believed that he always chose to rescue the prettiest.

OLD GLORIOUS William III, the *Deliverer*; so called in *Noctes Ambrosianae*.

OLD GLORY Sir Francis Burdett, *England's Pride*; so called by Conservatives.

OLD or OL' GOSPEL Alexander Majors (1815–1900), American pioneer trader along the Santa Fé Trail from Mississippi (post-1848). By 1854 he had some hundred wagons, and later joined with Russell (*Father of the Pony Express*) in the Pony Express and stage-coaches. He gave away Bibles to his customers.

OLD GROG Admiral Edward Vernon (1684–1757). He always wore a grogram cloak in bad weather. He gave orders (1740) for the sailors' rum to be diluted, and this mixture was called 'grog' after him. He is renowned for his capture of Portobello (1739).

OLD HARD-HEART Admiral of the Fleet Sir Arthur Knyvet Wilson, VC (1842–1921), Commander-in-Chief of the Home and Channel Fleets (1901–7) with a reputation for toughness. Also *Tug*.

- He won the VC for gallantry in hand-to-hand fighting with the Arabs at El Teb (1884) in the Anglo-Egyptian Sudan.

OLD HARRY Henry VIII, *Bluff Hal*.

OLD HARVE Harvey Bailey (1899–1963), American bank-robber, sentenced to life imprisonment for a kidnapping he did not commit.

OLD HERO Andrew Jackson, *Hickory*.

OLD HEWSON THE COBBLER Colonel John Hewson (died 1662 abroad), Parliamentary soldier who suppressed the riot of London apprentices. He had once been 'sometime an honest shoemaker in Westminster' (Wood: the *Ostade of Literary Criticism*). He was also satirized as 'one-eyed Hewson.'

OLD HICKORY Andrew Jackson, *Hickory*.

OLD HOOKY John Walker, *Hooky*.

OLD HORACE Horatio Walpole (1678–1757), brother of Sir Robert Walpole (the *Grand Corrupter*). He was created 1st Baron Walpole of Wolterton (1756).

OLD HOSKINS John Hoskins (died 1664), English miniature-painter. There was a younger painter of the same name.

OLD HOSS Charles Radbourne, American baseball pitcher in the Hall of Fame (1880–91).

OLD IMPERTURBABLE Charles Philip Mead (1887–1958), Hampshire and England cricketer who made a total of 55,060 runs in first-class cricket and 153 centuries. He was a calm and deliberate batsman.

OLD JACK General Thomas Jonathan Jackson (1824–63), also known as *Stonewall Jackson*; so called by his troops.

OLD JACK'S COMMISSARY-GENERAL Major-General Nathaniel Banks, the *Bobbin Boy*. In the American Civil War, he was twice defeated by *Stonewall* Jackson (above) and forced to leave behind great quantities of stores.

OLD JARVIE Lord St Vincent, *Billy Blue* whose name was Jervis; so called in the Royal Navy.

OLD JEW, THE Lord Beaconsfield, the *Asian Mystery*. He was Jewish by birth.

OLD JEW OF ETON, THE Francis Rous (1579–1659), English Puritan and an MP from 1625 until his death. He was Speaker of the Commons (1653), and was made a Lord of Parliament. He was Provost of Eton under the Commonwealth; because he wanted England to become a theocracy on Jewish lines.

OLD JUBE General Jubal Anderson Early, the *Bad Old Man*; not, as you might expect, for 'Jubal' but for *Old Jubilee*. The Mexican campaign had worn the general down so much his troops thought of him as an old man. But 'Jubilee', of course, was a pun on 'Jubal'.

OLD JUBILEE General Jubal Anderson Early (above).

OLD KNOCKBURY Archibald Campbell (1693–1790) of Knockbury, Scotland, who did much for farm-improvement.

OLD LADY, THE Frances d'Arblay (1752–1840), the diarist Fanny Burney; her family nickname even when she was young. She was hunched and short-sighted.

OLD LAIRD, THE John McNeill of Oronsay (1767–1846), Laird of Colonsay, who created prosperity in the two Hebridean islands.

OLD LION, THE William Pitt, *Aeolus*.

OLD MAC Sir Hector Macdonald, *Fighting Mac*; so called by troops in the Sudan (1885–98).

OLD MADAM Margaret Gould (died 1795), grandmother of the Reverend Sabine Baring-Gould (1834–1924), author and writer of the hymn *Onward Christian soldiers*.

OLD MAGNIFICENT James, 1st Duke of Abercorn (1811–85), Lord Lieutenant of Ireland (1866–8).

OLD MAN, THE Walter J. Travis (1862–1927), Australian who became United States Open golf champion (1902) and British Amateur champion (1904); because he started to play late in life.

OLD MAN ELOQUENT

i) Samuel Taylor Coleridge, the *Alnaschar of Modern Literature*.

ii) John Quincy Adams, the *Massachusetts Madman*. He had no equal in political debates.

iii) W.E. Gladstone, the *Dismember for Great Britain*.

- 'The Old Man Eloquent' was originally applied to the Attic orator Isocrates (436–338 BC). One of his teachers was Socrates.

OLD MAN PARR Thomas Parr (*circa* 1483–1635), an agricultural labourer reputed to have lived through ten reigns, although there is no documentary evidence. His fame was spread by John Taylor (the *Water Poet*) who like Parr lived in Gloucestershire. Also *Old Parr*.

OLD MATHEMATICS General Andrew Atkinson Humphreys (1810–83), American military engineer; so called by his troops.

OLD MOBB or MOB Thomas Sympson (hanged 1691), British highwayman who often disguised himself as a woman. He once robbed the Duchess of Portsmouth (*Bathshoba*) and Jeffreys (the *Western Hangman*) the Lord Chief Justice.

- 'Mob' was slang for a 'wench or a whore' (*The Canting Academy* 1673).

OLD MOORE Francis Moore (1657–1715), British physician and astrologer who published an annual almanac giving predictions to advertise his pills. It is still issued.

OLD MORALITY W.H. Smith, *Bookstall Smith*, Leader of the House of Commons (1886–91) and twice Secretary of State for War. He was patient, good-humoured, kind and hardworking.

OLD MORTALITY Peter Paterson (fl. end of the 18th century) who wandered about Scotland cleaning and repairing the tombs of Cameronians, extreme Covenanters named after Richard Cameron; used as the title of a novel by Scott (the *Ariosto of the North*), who saw Paterson doing this in 1793.

OLD MOTHER COUTTS Harriott Mellon, *Ma Coutts*.

OLD MOTHER HANCOCK John Hancock (1737–93), American revolutionary, statesman and first Governor of Massachusetts; so called by British troops when he was a general in the American army.

OLD NICK Field Marshal William, 1st Baron Nicholson (1845–1918), Chief of the Imperial General Staff (1908–12). Lord Fisher (*Jacky*) referred to him as 'Sir William Beelzebub'.

OLD NOLL Oliver Cromwell, the *Almighty Nose*; so called by royalists.

OLD NOLLEKENS Joseph Francis Nollekens (1702–48), father of the English sculptor Joseph Nollekens (1737–1823). 'Old Nollekens', a Dutchman from Amsterdam, was a painter, and lived in Soho, London. He was made famous by Walpole (the *Autocrat of Strawberry Hill*).

OLD NOSEY The Duke of Wellington, the *Achilles of England*.

OLD PAM Lord Palmerston, *Cupid*.

OLD PANCAKE Henry T.P. Comstock (1820–70), one of the prospectors who found the rich silver-fields called the Comstock Lode, Nevada (1859).

- See *Bonanza King*, *King of the Comstock* and *Old Virginny*.

OLD PARR Thomas Parr, *Old Man Parr*.

OLD PAUL Paul Whitehead (1709–74), British poet employed by Sir Francis Dashwood (*Hell-Fire Francis*) as secretary of the Hell-Fire Club. He was a pamphleteer and lampoonist, and older than most other members of the club.

OLD PEVERIL Sir Walter Scott, the *Ariosto of the North*; a joke on his novel *Peveril of the Peak* by Robinson (*Peter O' the Painch*). Scott had a peaked forehead.

OLD PONDER William Wordsworth, the *Bard of Rydal Mount*; so called in *Noctes Ambrosianae*.

OLD PRETENDER, THE James Stuart, the *King Over the Water*. He was given the nickname by the Hanoverians.
   • Cf the *Young Pretender*.

OLD PUBLIC FUNCTIONARY, THE James Buchanan, *Grandma*. He was a lawyer, and had a legalistic approach to administrative matters; self-applied in a message to Congress (1859).

OLD PUT General Israel Putnam (1718–90) who fought against the British at Bunker Hill (1775) and commanded at the battle of Long Island (1776).

OLD Q Lord Queensberry, *Lord Piccadilly*; part of the title of a book by J.P. Hurstone (1808).

OLD RELIABLE General George Henry Thomas (1816–70). This nickname by his troops is explained by another he won in the American Civil War, the *Rock of Chickamauga*. Also *Pa Thomas* and *Slow Trot*.

OLD ROBIN Robert Devereux, 3rd Earl of Essex (1591–1646), C-in-C of the Parliamentary army which won the battle of Edgehill (1642).

OLD ROSEY General William Starke Rosecrans (1819–98), commander of the Union Army of the Mississippi who lost his command after defeat at Chickamauga (1863), but was later reinstated.

OLD ROUGH AND READY Zachary Taylor, *Old Buena Vista*. He was prepared to accept rough-and-ready common-sense arrangements, such as his agreement to an armistice in the Mexican War.

OLD ROWLEY Charles II, the *Blackbird*.
   • 'Rowley' was a prize stud horse in the royal stables, and the allusion is obvious if you refer to the *Mutton-Eating King*. There is a Rowley Mile at Newmarket.

OLD RUBBERLIPS Mick Jagger (1943–   ), British pop star of 'The Rolling Stones'.

OLD SAM Samuel Drake (1772–1847), Briton who took his family and other actors to the American West to open a theatre in Kansas.

OLD SARAH The Duchess of Marlborough, *Mrs Freeman*, in her old age.

OLD SCROPE Henry, Lord Scrope or Scroop of Bolton (1534–92). He was the English West March Warden from 1563 until his death.

OLD SEALED LIPS Stanley Baldwin, *Honest Stanley*. He had a policy of making no comment on important matters, and was noted for his reply to inquisitive journalists: 'My lips are sealed.'

OLD SHOES Captain William Shoemaker, Chief of Detectives, Chicago (1920s).

OLD SINISTER Sir Arthur Richards, 1st Baron Milverton (1885–1978), Governor of Nigeria (1943–7).

OLD SINK OR SWIM John Adams, the *Colossus of Independence*. An American Tory (that is, pro-Britain) once mentioned to him that he should give up the idea of independence. Adams replied: 'Sink or swim, live or die, I am with my country.'

OLD SIX-MILE BOTTOM The Duchess of Montrose, *Carrie Red*; so called by racegoers. She was stout.
   • Transferred from an agricultural term. A 'bottom' is a piece of low-lying land, e.g. in a valley.

OLD SOLDIER, THE Edward (Ned) Wolfe (1728–44), younger brother of General James Wolfe (1727–59); so called in the 12th Regiment of Foot in which he was a lieutenant. He died of consumption on active service in Flanders.

OLD SOLITAIRE William Sherley Williams (1787–1849), a guide in the American West and a great loner.

OLD SQUAB John Dryden, *Asaph*, who became fat in the last years of his life.

- **See** *Poet Squab*. Squab = a short, fat person (*circa* 1700).

OLD SQUARETOES George II, *Augustus*; so called at Court.

- Old Squaretoes was a nickname for an old-fashioned pedant.

OLD STARS General Ormsby McKnight Mitchel (1810–62), American soldier and astronomer.

OLD STAYMAKER, THE Sir Alexander Thomson (1744–1817), Chief Baron of the Exchequer (1814–17); from his habit of checking witnesses and so 'staying' matters.

- Barons of the Exchequer, **see** *Green Park*.

OLD STEADFAST

i) General Steedman, *Old Chickamauga*.

ii) W.M. Woodfull, the *Great Unbowlable*.

OLD STONEFACE

i) Robert Mitchum (1917–   ), American film-star, from his impassivity.

ii) Lester Piggott, the *Long Fellow*.

OLD STONEWALL William Mortlock (1832–84), long-stop for the Surrey cricket XI. He never used pads or gloves, and stopped about 12,000 balls with only three byes against him.

OLD SUBTLETY William Fiennes, 1st Viscount Saye and Sele (1582–1662). He was, in Lord Clarendon's words, 'the oracle of the Puritans', and outwitted the King's advisers on legal points; so called by Wood (the *Ostade of Literary Criticism*).

- Cf *Young Subtlety*.

OLD SWAMP FOX, THE General Francis Marion (1732–95) who formed Marion's Brigade in the American War of Independence. He was a brave and cunning irregular fighter in the swamps of South Carolina.

OLD TATT Richard Tattersall (1724–95), a stud groom who became an auctioneer and founded (1766) the famous firm which is still the centre for horse-buyers. He was the owner of 'Highflyer', unbeaten on racecourses.

OLD TECUMSEH William Tecumseh Sherman (1820–91), Union general in the American Civil War. He is said to have created the phrase 'War is hell'. He was so called by troops serving under him.

- Tecumseh (?1768–1813) was a Shawnee chief who tried to found a united Indian nation. **See** *Old Tip* below.

OLD THAD Thaddeus Stevens, the *Grand Old Man*.

OLD THREE STARS Ulysses Simpson Grant (1822–85), 18th President of the United States of America, who was a lieutenant-general. He was Commander-in-Chief of the Union forces in the American Civil War. Also *Uncle Sam*, *Unconditional Surrender Grant*, *United States Grant* and *United We Stand*.

OLD TICK The Duke of Queensberry, *Lord Piccadilly*. He was notorious for his dissolute life.

- Farmer and Henley give 'to tick and toy', to dally and wanton.

OLD TIMBER Sir Henry Wood (1869–1944), British conductor and founder of the Promenade Concerts; a word-play on 'wood'.

OLD TIP W.H. Harrison, the *Cincinnatus of the West*; from Tippecanoe, the battle in which he temporarily defeated (1811) the Indians of Indiana, led by Tecumseh (**see** *Old Tecumseh*).

OLD TOM Thomas (Tom) Morris (1821–1908), Scottish golfer who won four Open championships, and was in fact the oldest winner of the British Open golf championships (1867), at forty-six. He was the most famous of the early professionals.

- Cf *Young Tom*.

OLD TOMMY

i) Admiral Sir John Thomas Duckworth (1748–1817) who defeated a French fleet in the relief of Santo Domingo (1806). He was hated by the men who gave him the nickname.

ii) Thomas C. Devin (died 1878), commander of Devin's Brigade in the American War of Independence. Also *Old War Horse*.

OLD TOMORROW Sir John Alexander Macdonald, the *Canadian Disraeli*.

OLD TONY The Earl of Shaftesbury, *Achitophel*. His son had the same name of Anthony.

OLD TWO TO TEN Senator Howard Baker jnr (1925–) who became Chief of Staff in the White House (1987–8). As an attorney, he usually obtained light sentences (i.e. from two to ten years) for his clients.

OLD VIRGINNY James F. Fennimore who found, with others, the Comstock Lode, Nevada (1859) and after whom Virginia City was named.

• See the *Bonanza King*, *King of the Comstock* and *Old Pancake*.

OLD VITRIOL AND VIOLETS Alexander Woollcott, the *Butcher of Broadway*; so called by James Thurber (1894–1961) because of the contradictions in his character.

OLD WAGONER Daniel Morgan (1736–1802) who began in the American War of Independence as a captain of Virginia riflemen and as a brigadier-general commanded the troops at Cowpens (1781); his army nickname.

OLD WAIT AND SEE Herbert Henry Asquith, 1st Earl of Oxford and Asquith (1852–1928), British Prime Minister (1908–16). 'Wait and see', his favourite comment, became one of the most famous catchphrases of modern times. It was first used by Asquith when replying (1910) to questions about the date for the reintroduction of the rejected Budget of Lloyd George (the *Goat*), and was picked up by the Northcliffe newspapers. Also the *Sledgehammer*.

OLD WAR HORSE Thomas Devin, *Old Tommy*.

OLD WHIG POET, THE Captain Charles Morris (1745–1838) of the Life Guards, mentioned by Timbs as 'the political and anacreontic song-writer'. Much of his material ridiculed the Tories, e.g. *Billy's too young to drive us,* a reference to *Bottomless Pit*. Morris has also been spoken of as 'The Laureate of the Steaks'.

• See *Anacreon Moore*. The Sublime Society of Beefsteaks (1735–1867) was a club of celebrities which included the Prince of Wales (*Adonis of Fifty*), Hogarth, Garrick and Wilkes. They called themselves 'Steaks'.

OLD WHITE HAT Captain John Willis (fl. 1840s–1880s), owner of a fleet of clippers, including the *Cutty Sark* which covered 363 miles in one day, a record for tea clippers. He was fond of wearing a white hat. Also *Willis o' the White Hat*.

OLD WIGS Jeffrey Dunstan (1759–97), an eccentric seller of wigs with a booth at Peckham Fair, London, at one time a muffin-man. He was elected 'mayor' of Garrat for thirteen years to protect Wandsworth Common from encroachment, and was given the mock title of 'Sir'.

• Garrat was a hamlet between Wandsworth and Tooting, Surrey.

OLD WILLIE William Dunn (1821–80), the first golf professional (1844) of the Royal Blackheath Golf Club, London, claimed to be the oldest in the world.

OLD WIZARD, THE Vladimir Horowitz (1904–89), pianist; his nickname in America.

OLD WRINKLE-BOOTS Browne Willis (1682–1760), eccentric British antiquary who wore shabby clothes and large patched, wrinkled knee-length boots.

OLD ZACH Zachary Taylor, *Old Buena Vista*.

OLIVER'S FIDDLER Sir Roger L'Estrange, the *First Tory*, one of the earliest journalists. He issued *The Intelligencer* and *The News* during 1663–6. He once played the violin or viol in the house of the composer John Hingston (died 1683) when Oliver Cromwell (the *Almighty Nose*) was a guest there.

ONE-ARMED DEVIL, THE Philip Kearney, *Fighting Phil*. He lost an arm in the Mexican War (1845–8) and was also called 'One-Armed Phil' by Confederate troops.

ONE EYE Sigtrygg or Sihtric (died 927), Norse King in York and brother-in-law (926) to Aethelstan (the *Glorious*).

ONE-EYED, THE Iain McGregor (died 1390) of Glenorchy, 2nd Chief of the Clan McGregor, son of *Gregor of the Golden Bridles*.

ONE LEG Field-Marshal William Paget, Earl of Uxbridge and 1st Marquess of Anglesey (1768–1854), Wellington's right-hand man at Waterloo (1815) where he lost a leg; so called by his family.

ONE-LEG SHADOW Walter Gould (1875–1955), American jazz pianist.

ONE-TAKE ASTOR Mary Astor (1906–87), American film actress who got it right first time.

ONE-TAKE HOWARTH Jack Howarth (1896–1984), British actor who played Albert Tatlock in the television serial *Coronation Street* from its beginning (1960) until his death. He always gave an impeccable performance.

ONE-TAKE TEMPLE Shirley Temple. *Curly Top*, for her professionalism.

ONE-TAKE WOODY W.S. (Woodbridge Strong) Van Dyne II (1889–1943), Hollywood film director; his nickname in Hollywood because of his skill and speed.

ONLY ME Mary Henrietta Kingsley (1862–1900), British West African explorer who was liable to appear in some remote place and announce to surprised traders or government officials: 'It's only me,'

OOM PAUL Stephanus Johannes Paulus Kruger (1825–1904), President of the Transvaal Republic (1883–1900), Boer leader in the South African War.

- 'Oom' = uncle in Afrikaans. It is frequently used by Afrikaner children for unrelated adult friends.

OOM PIET Petrus Jacobus Joubert (1834–1900), Commandant-General of the South African Republic (1880–1900). His cautious, artful manner gave him the nickname *Slim Piet*.

OOMPH GIRL, THE Ann Sheridan (1915–67), American film star whose sex appeal was described as 'oomph'. Her real name was Clara Lou Sheridan.

OOMPH GIRL OF INDIA, THE Padmin Kolhapur (1966–   ), film-star.

ORACLE OF COMMON LAW, THE Edmund Plowden (1518–85), British jurist and author of law books; originator of the phrase 'The case is altered'. He had given a decision but then found the property

concerned was his own; so called by Coke (below).

ORACLE OF THE LAW, THE Sir Edward Coke (1552–1634), British judge and law writer who is still regarded as the greatest common lawyer of all time. He upheld common law against the Church, the Star Chamber and the King.

ORANGE MOLL Mrs Mary Meggs (died 1691) who had a licence to hawk oranges and other food in London theatres. One of her girls was *Nell of Old Drury*. Pepys tells how Orange Moll saved the life of a man in the King's Theatre who had choked on an orange by thrusting her fingers down his throat.

ORANGE PEEL Sir Robert Peel, *Jenny*. He had strong anti-Catholic feelings – and so pro-Orange – when Chief Secretary of Ireland (1812–18).

- Cf the *Runaway Spartan*.

ORATOR BRONZE John Henley, the *Cain of Literature*.

ORATOR HENLEY John Henley (above), English clergyman noted for his oratory. He gave a series of lectures in what he called his 'oratory' in Newport Market, London, employing Sundays for theology and Wednesdays for science. *The Gentleman's Magazine* announced his death (1756) as: 'The Rev, Orator Henley, aged 64.' He was eccentric, and was also:

ORATOR HUMBUG See above.

ORATOR HUNT Henry Hunt (1773–1835), a radical politician and MP, who presided over the meeting at St Peter's Fields, Manchester when the Peterloo Massacre (1819) took place. The white hat he wore then, slashed by a sword, became a badge of reform. He was a violent speaker.

ORATOR JIM James Henry O'Rourke (1852–1919), American baseball star (Home Run champion 1880) who visited England (1874) to promote baseball.

ORATOR MUM J.P. Curran, *Longbow*. He once said that when he first appeared at a debating society 'I became dismayed and dumb.' He was, in reality, a brilliant orator and wit.

ORATOR OF EMPIRE, THE Archibald Philip Primrose, 5th Earl of Rosebery

(1847–1929), Prime Minister (1894–5), champion of Liberal imperialism.

ORCHID OF THE SCREEN, THE Corinne Griffiths (1865–1979), star of American silent films.

ORDINARY FELLOW, THE George V (1865–1936); his own description of himself which became the name of at least one public-house. The Queen (**Brenda**) called him 'Grandpa England'. Also the **Sailor King**.

ORGAN John Morgan (1929–88), BBC television presenter and radio personality; noted as an interviewer for television's *Panorama*.
* Cf 'Organ Morgan' in Dylan Thomas' *Under Milk Wood*, first a radio play (1954).

ORIANA
i) Elizabeth I, the **English Diana**, so called in a madrigal on her 68th birthday.
ii) Anne (1574–1619), wife of James I (the **British Solomon**) so called by Jonson the **Bricklayer**.
* Oriana, sweetheart of Amadeus of Gaul in the fourteenth-century prose romance *Amadis de Gaula*, is the fairest and gentlest of women.

ORINDA, THE MATCHLESS ORINDA or ORINDA THE MATCHLESS Katherine Philips (1631–64), British poetess and letter-writer who adopted the pseudonym of 'Orinda'. Dryden (**Asaph**) mentioned her in his *Elegy on Mrs Anne Killigrew*, who died of smallpox as did Orinda. Also the **Sappho of England**.

ORION HORNE Richard Horne, the **Farthing Poet**.

ORLANDO THE FAIR *Beau* Feilding; so called in *The Tatler*.
* Orlando is the Italian version of 'Roland'. the greatest of Charlemagne's knights and the hero of *The Song of Roland* as well as Ariosto's *Orlando Furioso* and *Orlando Innamorato* (by Boiardo). See **Ariosto of the North**.

OROSMADES Thomas Gray, the **British Pindar**; his nickname at Cambridge University.
* Orosmades is the Greek spelling of the

name of the Persian god Ahura-Mazda, the source of light and good, the all-knowing, the all-wise. Gray and his friends were studious and had little interest in games.

ORPHEUS BRITANNICUS Henry Purcell (1659–95), English composer. As well as producing much music for church and state occasions, he did a great deal to revive English theatre music after the Restoration.
* Orpheus, famed Thracian musician and centre of a Greek cult, whose music was said to charm trees and animals.

ORPHEUS OF HIGHWAYMEN, THE John Gay, the **Aesop of England** who wrote *The Beggar's Opera* (1728), so called, says Boswell (the **Ambitious Thane**), by a Mr Courtenay.

ORPHEUS OF SCOTLAND, THE James I, the **Law Giver**, also a poet and musician.

ORPHEUS OF THE 18TH CENTURY, THE G.F. Handel, the **Grand Old Man**.

ORPHEUS OF THE GREEN ISLE, THE Turlogh O'Carolan, the **Irish Anacreon**. He wandered from door to door, playing a harp and improvising songs.

OSSAWATOMIE BROWN John Brown, **Old Brown of Ossawatomie**; so called from his victory against the Missourians at Ossawatomie (1856).

OSTADE OF LITERARY CRITICISM, THE Anthony à Wood (1632–95), British antiquarian and historian.
* Ostade was the name of two Dutch painters, Adriaen (1610–85) and Isack (1621–49).

OTHER PRINCE OF WALES, THE William (Billy) Meredith (1874–1958) who played 669 Football League matches for Manchester City or Manchester United, and made 50 appearances for Wales between 1894 and 1924. Also the **Welsh Wizard**.

OTTO Sir Richard William Clarke (1910–75) who as a young journalist devised the *Financial Times* Index of industrial ordinary shares. He became a major influence in Government, business and academic circles.

OTTO THE TERRIBLE Otto Preminger (1906–86), Austrian-born film producer/director/actor; so called in Hollywood where he was a martinet on the set.

OUMA

i) Mrs Sibella Smuts (died 1954), wife of Jan Christiaan Smuts (**Slim Jannie**).

ii) Queen Victoria, **Drina**; her nickname in South Africa.

• *Ouma* = grandmother in Afrikaans.

OUR BILLY The Duke of Clarence, the **Flogster**, sometimes 'Billy Guelph'.

OUR CHARLEY Charles Bradlaugh (1833–91), British freethinker and politician; so called by the working classes, to whose betterment he devoted his life.

OUR 'ERB Herbert, 1st Baron Morrison (1888–1965), Labour leader and Deputy Prime Minister (1945–51); so called because he was a Cockney.

OUR GRACIE Gracie Fields (1898–1979), British music-hall singer and comedienne. Her real name was Grace Stansfield.

OUR MAN ANYWHERE Malcolm John Macdonald (1901–81), son of **Ramsay Mac**; because of the number of diplomatic posts he held around the world.

OUR MARIE Marie Lloyd (1870–1922), whose real name was Matilda Victoria Wood, a 'legendary' British music-hall star, described by the *Encyclopaedia Britannica* as 'the incarnation of the London, or Cockney, genius for low comedy'. She took her stage surname from *Lloyd's Weekly News* before it ceased publication. Also the **Queen of the Halls**.

OUR ONLY GENERAL Major-General Sir Garnet Joseph Wolseley (1833–1913), later Field-Marshal Viscount Wolseley, who outshone his contemporaries. Also **Sagrenti** and the **Tea-Pot General**.

OUR VAL Princess Michael of Kent (1942–), formerly Baroness Marie-Christine von Reibnitz; her nickname in the Royal Family and London society. The Queen is said to have likened her to a Valkyrie. She is a six-foot blonde. Also **Princess Pushy**, **Princess Tom**, **Schnitzel**.

OUTLAW, THE Edward the **Aetheling**. He lived in exile in Hungary.

OWL William Henry Russell (1802–73), pioneer of government in California.

OWEN OF THE RED HAND Owen of Wales (*circa* 1335–78), Welshman who fought with the French against the English, notably at the siege of Mortaigne where he was killed. He claimed to be the true Prince of Wales. Also **Owen the Outlaw**.

OWEN THE OUTLAW Owen of Wales, above.

OWNEY THE KILLER Owen Madden (1892–19164), British-born American bootlegger and murderer.

OXFAM Lesley Hornby, the **Matchstick**.

OYSTER EYES William (Willie) Stephen Ian, 1st Viscount Whitelaw (1918–), Chancellor of the Exchequer (1957–8), Deputy Leader of the Conservative Party (1980s) and Leader of the House of Lords. He retired from politics early in 1988. Nickname mentioned by Lord Whitelaw on television (1989). Also **William Whitehall**.

OZZY John Osborne (1948–), lead singer in the Black Sabbath pop group who formed his own band in 1980 and called it 'The Wizard of Oz'. By 1986 he was back with Black Sabbath.

P

PA Sir Francis (Frank) Robert Benson (1858–1939), 'father' of a famous British Shakespearian repertory company. He began acting with Sir Henry Irving (1838–1905).

PADDINGTON Thomas Jones (?1772– ?), well-known pugilist born in Paddington, London. He began fighting *circa* 1785 and met Jem Belcher (the *Napoleon of the Ring*) in 1799 and lost, although he stood up to him longer than any other man.

PADDY

i) Field-Marshal Hugh, 1st Viscount Gough (1779–1869). After serving in the Peninsular War, he became C-in-C, India, where he defeated the Sikhs (1849). He was an Irishman.

ii) Brendan Finucane (1920–42), British fighter pilot in the Battle of Britain (World War II).

PADDY BACKDOWN Paddy Ashdown (1941–), leader of the SLDP (1988–), because of his change of attitude early in his political career over CND.

PADDY BURKE Edmund Burke, the *Dinner-Bell*, born in Dublin; so called by Burns (*Ayrshire Poet*).

PADRONE Raymond L.S. Patriarca (1908–), Mafia boss and American gangster; nickname in New England, where he was 'in control'.

- *Padrone* is the Italian for 'master', 'lord', or 'patron'.

PAGE OF STATE TO THE MUSES, THE Edmund Spenser, the *Child of the Ausonian Muse*; so called by Wordsworth (the *Bard of Rydal Mount*).

PAGLIACCI OF THE FIRE ESCAPES, THE Ben Hecht (1894–1964), American playwright, an intellectual cynic as well as a romantic, famous for his part in writing *The Front Page* (1928).

- *I Pagliacci* (1892), an opera about a tragic clown, was written by Ruggiere Leoncavallo (1858–1919).

PAINTER PATRIOT, THE Thomas Gainsborough (1727–88), English painter who broke with tradition and painted England as he saw it.

PAINTER PUG William Hogarth, the *Juvenal of Painters*.

- Cf *Poet Pug*. 'Pug' could be used as a term of endearment, a term for a dwarf, a bargee or a monkey.

PALINURUS OF STATE, THE Frederick North, 2nd Earl of Guilford (1732–92), British Prime Minister (1770–82). Although he was Lord Guilford, he was always called Lord North from 1752 to 1790; so called by Edward Gibbon (1737–94) from his habit of dropping off to sleep in the House of Commons. North was once accused of 'slumbering over the ruin of the country'. Also *Sly Boots*.

- Palinurus, Aeneas' pilot, nodded at the helm and fell into the sea.

PALL Pauline Jackson (1640–89), sister to Pepys (the *Father of Black-Letter Lore*). She married John Jackson (died 1677).

PAM Lord Palmerston, *Cupid*.

PANCHO Richard Alonzo Gonzales (1928–), American tennis player. At forty-one, with a partner, he set a new championship record by playing 112 games (1969); also remembered for his Wimbledon match (1969), beating Pasarell, another American in a game that lasted 5 hours 20 minutes.

PANDA Mike Gatting (1957–), England captain 1986–8; so called after he had two black eyes and a broken nose from a 90-mph ball in the West Indies (1986).

PANDER OF VENUS, THE Thomas *Anacreon Moore*; so called in *Noctes Ambrosianae*.

PANTYCELYN William Williams (1717–91), Welsh hymn writer.

PAPA

i) Ernest Miller Hemingway

(1899–1961), American novelist; so called by Marlene Dietrich (**Dutchy**). Also 'Poppa'.

ii) Oscar Celestin (1880–1954), American jazz trumpeter and singer.

PAPA BEAR George S. Halas (1895–1984), American football pioneer, player, coach and manager in the Hall of Fame. He coached the Chicago Bears.

PAPER KING, THE John **Beau** Law. Many of his projects, including the disastrous Mississippi Scheme, involved the issue of a great deal of worthless paper.

PAPER-SAVING (or SPARING) POPE, THE Alexander Pope, the **Bard of Twickenham**; so called by Swift (**Doctor Presto**). Pope's translations of *The Iliad* and *The Odyssey* were written on odd scraps of paper. One page of a manuscript, for instance, was written on the back of a letter from a publisher.

PARASITE OF GENIUS, THE Horace Walpole, the **Autocrat of Strawberry Hill**.

PARKS Ronald William Parkinson Smith (1913–   ), known professionally as Norman Parkinson, British photographer of the Royal Family, among others.

PARKY Michael Parkinson, the **Mouth**.

PARLIAMENT JOAN Elizabeth Alkin (fl. 17th century), Cromwellian spy who posed as a mercury woman to trap editors of royalist newspapers during the Commonwealth.

- Mercury women were, in the words of Thomas Blount in *Glossographia* (1661–81), 'women who sell them [i.e. newspapers] by whole-sale from the Press.'

PARNELLI Rufus Jones (1933–   ), American motor-racing driver who won the Indianapolis 500 (1963).

- Cf Parnell, **Uncle Reg**.

PARSLEY PEEL Sir Robert Peel (1750–1830), father of the statesman of the same name. He set up as a calico-printer with a spinning-jenny, and became a very wealthy man. The family business won Robert the statesman the nickname of **Jenny**. His father's nickname came from the fact that he printed a quantity of calico with a parsley-leaf pattern.

PARSON BROWNLOW W.G. Brownlow, the **Fighting Parson**, more a politician than a parson.

PASSIONATE PEER, THE The Right Honourable Josslyn (Joss) Victor Hay, 22nd Earl Erroll (1901–41), Hereditary High Constable of Scotland, a well-known 'ladies' man' who was murdered in Kenya. Sir Henry Broughton (**Jock**) was acquitted of the crime, but committed suicide later.

PATCH A man named Sexton (fl. 16th century), a household jester for Cardinal Wolsey (the **Boy Baccaleur**); so called either because of the patches on his clothes or from the Italian *pazzo*, 'a fool'.

PATHFINDER, THE or THE PATHFINDER OF THE ROCKY MOUNTAINS Major-General John Charles Frémont (1813–90), American explorer and politician. He successfully crossed the Rocky Mountains in 1842.

PATHFINDER BENNETT Air-Vice-Marshal Donald Bennett (1910–86), hero of World War II who pioneered 'pathfinding' for bomber raids to ensure pinpoint accuracy. He led many such raids.

PA THOMAS General G.H. Thomas, **Old Reliable**; so called in the army of Tennessee.

PATRIARCH OF DORCHESTER, THE or PATRIARCH WHITE John White (1574–1648), an English Puritan preacher of Dorchester, Dorset.

PATRIARCH OF ENGLISH LEARNING, THE William Grocyn (1446–1519) who introduced the teaching of Greek into England, and lectured on it at Oxford University.

PATRIARCH OF NEW ENGLAND, THE John Cotton (1585–1652), a Puritan clergyman who went from England to settle in Boston (1633). He became an autocratic leader of religion there as a teacher of the First Church of Boston.

PATRICK HENRY OF NEW ENGLAND, THE Wendell Philips (1811–84) of Boston, American lawyer, orator and reformer involved in anti-slavery, women's suffrage and prohibition.

- Patrick Henry (1736–99) of Virginia,

orator of the pre-revolutionary period, famous for the phrase: 'Give me liberty or give me death.' His interpretation of 'liberty' was limited, however, since he owned sixty-five slaves at the time of his death.

PATRIOT KING, THE

i) Lord Bolingbroke, *High-Mettled Mary*, who wrote *Idea of a Patriot King* (1749).

ii) George III, the *Button Maker*, whose father, Frederick, Prince of Wales (*Prince Titi*) had been a friend and pupil of Bolingbroke (above) who influenced his son's ideas. George put himself at the head of the administration after his accession (1760), but two years later realized he had failed to achieve Bolingbroke's ideals.

PATRIOT OF HUMANITY, THE Henry Grattan (1746–1820), Irish statesman and orator, described by Irish historian P.W. Joyce as 'perhaps Ireland's most brilliant orator and one of her purest and greatest patriots'. He obtained the repeal of Poynings Law (1494), which increased the power of the king in Ireland and restricted that of the nobles and parliament; so called by Byron (*Baby*).

PATSY

i) Princess Victoria Patricia of Connaught (1886–1974) who married Admiral Sir Alexander Ramsay (1881–1972). Also *Princess Pat*.

ii) Elias Henry Hendren (1889–1962), Middlesex and England cricketer, a batsman who at his death had made more centuries than anyone else in first-class cricket, except Hobbs (the *Master*) and Frank Woolley (1887–1978). He was also a footballer for Queen's Park Rangers, Manchester City and Coventry City.

PAUL PRY

i) Frederick Gerald Byng (died 1871), younger son of the 6th Viscount Torrington (1740–1811). As a small boy he had been a page at the wedding of the Prince of Wales (*Adonis of Fifty*) to Caroline of Brunswick (1795). He was later a Gentleman Usher of the Privy Chamber and a man-about-town. Also *Poodle*.

ii) Thomas Hill (1760–1840), a journalist,

said to have been the original for a comedy *Paul Pry* (1825) by John Poole (?1786–1872).

● The first actor to play Paul Pry was John Liston (*circa* 1776–1846).

PAUSANIAS OF BRITAIN, THE William Camden, the *British Pausanias*.

PAWNEE BILL Major Gordon W. Lillie (1860–1942), friend of *Buffalo Bill*. He had been an interpreter on a Pawnee reservation in Oklahoma before he joined the Wild West Show. He later started a show of his own called 'The Great Far East Show' which later combined with Buffalo Bill's. They went out of business together in 1910.

PEABODY OF BOMBAY, THE Sir Cowasji Jehangir *Readymoney* (1812–78), financier and philanthropist of Bombay, India. 'Readymoney' was a nickname adopted by the family – Parsee merchants of the late 18th century – as a surname.

● George Peabody (1795–1869) was an American financier who among other charities endowed houses for working-class people in London.

PEACEFUL, THE or PEACEABLE

i) Edgar, King of the English (944–75). Camden (the *British Pausanias*) gives 'peaceable' (1605).

ii) Alexander II of Scotland, the *Little Red Fox*.

PEACEMAKER, THE Edward VII (1841–1910). He helped to engineer the *Entente Cordiale* which ended a twenty-year undeclared 'cold war' with France. Also the *Pragger-Wagger*, the *Sporting Prince*, the *Squire of Sandringham*, *Tum-Tum* and the *Uncle of Europe*.

PEACHES PRIOR James Prior, *Jolly Jim*. He once remarked that if British farmers could not grow apples, they should grow peaches.

PEACOCK OF THE NORTH, THE Sir Robert de Neville or Nevil (died 1387), elder brother of Ralph, 2nd Baron Neville (died 1367). He was killed by Sir James Douglas in single combat.

PEANUT POLITICIAN, THE James (Jimmy) Earl Carter (1924–   ), 39th President of the United States (1977–80). After service in the United States Navy, he built the family peanut brokerage business into a thriving concern.

PEARL OF BIOGRAPHERS, THE Christopher Hibbert (1924–) who has written books on Lord Raglan, Mussolini, Garibaldi, Dickens, Johnson, George IV and Edward VII; so called by the *New Statesman*.

PEARL OF IRELAND, THE St Brigit, the *Mary of the Gael*.

PEARLY KING, THE Derek Jameson (1929–) who has been editor of the *Daily Star*, the *Daily Express*, and the *News of the World*; so called in Fleet Street because, it was said, his smile showed a lot of teeth; now a television and radio personality. Some, because of his Cockney background, have called him 'Sid Yobbo'.

PEASANT BARD, THE Robert Burns, the *Ayrshire Poet*, son of a cottar, he worked as a farm labourer.

PEASANT-BOY PHILOSOPHER, THE James Fergusson (1710–79), Scottish astronomer and lecturer.

PEASANT COUNTESS, THE Sarah Hoggins, the *Cottage Countess*.

PEASANT POET, THE John Clare, the *Northamptonshire Peasant-Poet*.

PEASANT POETESS, THE Janet Hamilton (1795–1873), an illiterate Scottish poetess.

PEDLAR OF DREAMS, THE Lord Beaverbrook, the *Beaver*; so called by Howard Spring (1889–1965), novelist once on the staff of the *Daily Express*.

PEEK-A-BOO GIRL, THE Veronica Lake (1919–73), American film star; from her hair-style. Her real name was Constance Ockleman.

PEER, THE The Duke of Wellington, the *Achilles of England*; so called by his staff because of his aloofness.

PEERLESS, THE or PEERLESS JIM James (Jim) Driscoll (1881–1925), Welsh featherweight boxer who is regarded as one of the best stylists in the history of the sport. He held the British championship for thirteen years, and unsuccessfully claimed the world title (1909).

PEE-WEE Charles Ellsworth Russell (1906–69), white American jazz clarinettist who played with **Red** Nichols and **Duke** Ellington.

- Pee-Wee is American slang for a short person, but Russell was tall.

PEGGY A.F. Bettinson, a London businessman (1890s) and a great sportsman who helped to found the National Sporting Club (1891).

PEG-LEG Thomas L. Smith (1797–1866), American trapper, Indian fighter and horse-thief, whose right leg was amputated after he had been hit by a bullet.

PENMAN, THE James (Jem) Townshend Saward, a British barrister convicted with others (1857) of forgery of cheques and bankers' drafts. He was transported when he was fifty-eight.

PENMAN OF THE REVOLUTION, THE John Dickinson (1732–1808), wealthy American lawyer, statesman and President of Pennsylvania Executive Council (1782–85) who drafted many documents, including the Declaration of Rights and the petition to the King. Also the *Pennsylvania Farmer* (below).

PENNSYLVANIA FARMER, THE John Dickinson (above). To oppose the British claim for the right to tax Americans, he wrote *Letters from a Farmer in Pennsylvania* (1768).

PENSIONED DAUBER, THE William Hogarth, the *Juvenal of Painters*. He was Sergeant-Painter to the King (post-1757).

PEOPLE'S ATTORNEY, THE Louis Dembitz Brandeis (1856–1941), American lawyer who defended people free when they were involved in litigation over working hours and wages. He was later Chief Justice.

PEOPLE'S FRIEND, THE Dr William Gordon (1801–49) of Hull, England, philanthropist; nickname chiselled on his tombstone.

PEOPLE'S GOVERNOR, THE General Sir Reginald Alexander Dallas Brooks (1896–1966), longest-serving Governor of Victoria, Australia (1949–63). He was friendly and informal.

PEOPLE'S JOE, THE Joseph Chamberlain, *Artful Joe*.

PEOPLE'S POET, THE
  i) Sir John Betjeman (1906–84), Poet Laureate (post-1972); from his verse.
  ii) William McGonagall, the *Bard of the Silvery Tay*; so called at a banquet at Perth, Scotland (1894).

PEOPLE'S WILLIAM, THE
  i) W.E. Gladstone, the *Dismember for Great Britain*.
  ii) William Pitt, Earl of Chatham, *Aeolus*.

PEPPER James Philip Austin (1879–1965), Welsh-born American baseball star.

PERCY Patrick Ian Pocock (1946–　), Surrey cricketer. He once took 7 wickets in 11 balls.

PERFECT CURE, THE James Henry Stead (died 1886), British music-hall singer who 'made his name' with a song of that title (1861).
  • A 'cure' is an odd, eccentric or amusing person.

PERMIS The Duke of Newcastle, *Goody Newcastle*; so called for what Lord Chesterfield (the *English Rochefoucauld*) described as 'a servile compliance with the will of his sovereign' (George III). He asked *Est-il permis?* before he addressed him.

PERPETUAL MOTION Henry Armstrong, *Hammering Henry*.

PERPETUAL SECRETARY, THE Sir Dominick Daly (1798–1868), Irish-born provincial secretary of Lower Canada (post-1827); so called because of the time he held office.

PERSIAN JONES Sir William Jones, the *Admirable Crichton of His Day*. He wrote a grammar of the Persian language (1771) and translated a life of Nadir Shah.

PERSIL Norman Cowans, the *Flash*.

PERT PRIM PRATER OF THE NORTHERN RACE, THE Alexander Wedderburn, 1st Earl of Rosslyn (1773–1805), Lord Chancellor (1793–1801) who was a brilliant orator but dull in society; so called by the poet Churchill (the *British Juvenal*). Also the *Proudest of the Proud*.

PERTH TIGER, THE Dennis Lillie (1949–　), fast bowler for Perth and Australia. When he retired in 1984 he had taken 355 Test wickets. His deliveries were once timed at 100 mph. In 1988 he returned to play for Northamptonshire.

PESTLEMAN JACK John Keats (1795–1821), English poet who had been apprenticed to an apothecary and at one time wanted to become a surgeon; so called by Maginn (the *Adjutant*). In a review of *Endymion* (1818), Lockhart (the *Scorpion*) advised Keats to go back to 'plasters, pills and ointment-boxes'. Because he was a Londoner, Keats was sometimes called 'The Cockney Poet'. The disciples of Hunt were often called 'The Cockney School'.

PETE
  i) Charles Conrad (1930–　), American astronaut who walked on the Moon from Apollo 12 (1969); now an officer of the Macdonald Douglas Aircraft Co.
  ii) General Sir Harold English Pyman (1908–71), British Army expert on armoured warfare.
  iii) James Ostend Brown (1906–63), American jazz string bass player.
  iv) Major-General Sir T.W. Rees, the *Chota General*.

PETER
  i) Gladys Bertha Stern (1890–1973), British novelist.
  ii) Marshal of the RAF Charles Frederick Algernon, 1st Viscount Portal (1893–1971), British Chief of Air Staff.
  iii) Frank Laurence Lucas (1894–1967), British scholar, critic, teacher, novelist, playwright and poet.
  iv) Dr Hawley Harvey Crippen (1862–1910), murderer of his wife Cora; an American working in London as manager of a patent medicine firm. He was the first murderer to be traced by wireless when he was at sea with Ethel Le Neve, acquitted of being his accomplice.
  v) Miles Henry Easterby (1929–　), British racehorse trainer.

PETER O' THE PAINCH Patrick Robinson (1794–1855); so called by his friend Scott (the *Ariosto of the North*) in retaliation for *Old Peveril*. Robinson was Dean of the Faculty of Advocates (post-1842) and a judge (post-1843).

- *Painch* = Scottish for 'paunch'. 'Peter' was a diminutive for Patrick.

PETER PAN

i) David Steel, the *Microchap*; so called in Parliament. He was once the youngest MP.

ii) Peter Shilton (1949–   ), goal-keeper for England, claimed to be the best in the world. He hold 100 caps (1988). By May 1988 he had played a record 824 League games for Derby FC. Also *Peter the Great* and *Shilts*.

- 'Peter Pan' is the always-young central figure of the play (1904) of that name by Sir James Barrie (1860–1937).

PETER PINDAR
Dr John Wolcot (1738–1819), British satirist and poet who was editor of *The Morning Post* for some years when it was owned by Richard Tattersall (*Old Tatt*) and was better known by his pseudonym than his own name.

- Pindar (*circa* 522–442 BC) was a Greek lyric poet.

PETER SHAMBLES
William Stanhope, 2nd Earl of Harrington (1710–79), general and MP. He was eccentric, with a curious gait.

PETER THE GREAT

i) Peter Shilton, *Peter Pan*.

ii) Peter McWilliam, footballer for Newcastle United (1902–11).

- Peter the Great (1672–1725), Tsar, turned Russia from a backward country into a modern state.

PETER THE PACKER or THE PACKER
Peter, 1st Baron O'Brien (1842–1914), Lord Chief Justice of Ireland. He was alleged, when Attorney-General, to have 'packed' juries, carefully selecting those to serve and give him the result he wanted.

PETER THE PAINTER
Peter Straume, Piatkow or Schtern of Riga, a noted anarchist and painter of scenery for anarchistic dramas. The attempt to arrest him for murder developed into the 'Siege of Sidney Street', Stepney (1911). Guardsmen were used in it. Afterwards two bodies were discovered but Peter was never traced. A modern researcher claims he was really Gederts Eliass, honoured as a Russian artist.

PETER WOGGY
Sir Henry Thurston Holland, 1st Viscount Knutsford (1825–1914), Secretary of State for the Colonies (1887–92).

- 'Wog' is an offensive term for a coloured person.

PET MARJORIE
Margaret Fleming (1803–11), a young Scottish writer friend of Scott (the *Ariosto of the North*). She kept a diary and wrote some poems. Scott – who gave her the nickname – thought she would have been a great authoress.

PETRARCH OF SCOTLAND, THE
William Drummond, *Bo-Peep*.

PETTICOAT OF THE PLAINS, THE
Belle Starr, the *Bandit Queen*.

PEVERIL
Sir Walter Scott, the *Ariosto of the North*. See *Old Peveril*.

PHALARIS JUNIOR
Charles Boyle, 4th Earl of Orrery (1676–1731). His edition of *The Epistles of Phalaris* (1695) was followed by a controversy when Richard Bentley (the *Aristarchus of Cambridge*) declared them forgeries.

- Phalaris was a tyrant of Agrigentum, Sicily (reigned *circa* 570–564 BC) and was put to death himself in a brazen bull he invented in which to burn criminals alive.

PHANTOM MAJOR, THE
Colonel Sir David Stirling (1916–   ), founder of the Special Air Services (SAS: World War II); so called by the Germans because of the secrecy of SAS operations.

PHENOMENON YOUNG
Thomas Young (1773–1829), scientist, who began to decipher Egyptian hieroglyphs before Champollion (1790–1832) but treated it as a hobby and left the final work to the Frenchman. Young gave its present scientific meaning to 'energy', e.g. motive energy.

PHILADELPHIA JACK
John (Jack) O'Brien (1878–1942) American light-heavyweight boxer who knocked out Bob Fitzsimmons (the *Antipodean*) for the world title (1905).

PHILADELPHIA LADY, THE
Marian Anderson (1902–   ), American singer of the

New York Metropolitan Opera; so called after the Daughters of the Revolution had forbidden her to sing in Philadelphia's Constitution Hall because she is black. She was in fact born in Philadelphia.

PHILADELPHIA WITCH, THE Carino Favato, Italian-born American gaoled for life (1937) for her part in the murders of thirty people in insurance frauds.

PHILATELIC PRESIDENT, THE F.D. Roosevelt, the *Barrymore of the White House*. He was a renowned collector of postage stamps.

PHILOLOGUS Nathaniel Bailey (died 1742), schoolmaster-compiler of an English dictionary (1721). The nickname is carried in Greek characters after his name on the title-page of the 1757 edition. It means 'lover of words'.

PHILOSOPHER OF MALMESBURY, THE Thomas Hobbes, the *Atheist*.

PHILOSOPHER OF WIMBLEDON, THE John Horne Tooke, the *Macaroni Parson*, politician and philologist, author of *The Diversions of Purley* (1786 and 1789) which urged study of Gothic and Anglo-Saxon in order to understand English.

PHILOSOPHER SMITH James Smith (1827–97), Australian geologist and explorer who discovered rich tin deposits in the Mount Bischoff area near Waratah, Tasmania (1871) and founded the mine, which was the richest in the world.

PHOENIX OF THE WORLD, THE Sir Philip Sidney, the *British Bayard*; so called by Nicholas Breton (?1545–?1626).

PHONEY QUID, THE Admiral of the Fleet Sir Alfred Dudley Pickman Rogers Pound (1877–1943), First Sea Lord (1939–43) and C-in-C, Mediterranean Fleet (1936–9); from 'Dud Pound'.

PHUB Lady Gabriella Windsor (1981–), daughter of Prince Michael of Kent (*Maou*); so called by the Royal Family.

PHYLLIS Rod Stewart (1945–), British pop singer, famous for *I am sailing*.

PICAYUNE BUTLER General B.F. Butler, *Cock-Eye*, commander of forces which occupied New Orleans (1862). He was accused several times of corruption.

• 'Picayune' is a New Orleans term for a

nickel (or 5 cents) and can be used for something mean and contemptible. 'Picayune' is derived from a Provençal word for a Piedmontese coin, a *picaioun*.

PICCA Graham Dilley (1959–), Kent, Worcestershire and England cricketer; from 'Piccadilly'. In 1986 he took 5 wickets for 68 in one innings of a Test Match in Australia. By the end of 1987 he had taken 100 Test wickets. Also *Spotted Dog*.

PICCADILLY AMBULATOR, THE Lord Queensberry, *Lord Piccadilly*, a libertine whose Piccadilly strolls had few innocent reasons; title of a book by J.P. Hurstone (1808).

PICCADILLY PATRIOT, THE Sir Francis Burdett, *England's Pride*; so called after he had defied authority when the Speaker of the House of Commons issued a warrant for his arrest for a breach of privilege. Soldiers took him from his Piccadilly house to the Tower of London. He was released when Parliament was prorogued.

PICKLE William Hickey (?1749–1830), British author of *Memoirs* (1749–1809), first published 1913–25, whose name was adopted by Tom Driberg as columnist for the *Daily Express*. Hickey's nickname as a child was well justified.

• See *Lord of the Spies*.

PICKLE THE SPY Alastair *Ruadh* Macdonell (?1725–61), chief of Glengarry and secret agent for the *Young Pretender*. He was arrested and put into the Tower of London. He used the code name 'Pickle'. Andrew Lang (1844–1912) wrote *Pickle the Spy* (1897). Also *Red*.

PICKLOCK OF THE LAW, THE Judge Walter Rumsey (1584–1660), barrister of Gray's Inn, London who became a judge on the Welsh circuit; because he was a skilful lawyer.

• Ben Jonson (1614): 'Some crafty fellow, some picklocke o' the law'.

PIED PIPER OF PATRIOTISM, THE J.P. Sousa, the *March King*; so called in America.

PIED PIPER OF ROCK 'N' ROLL, THE Alan Freed (1922–65), American *avant-garde* black musician.

PIED PIPER OF TUCSON, THE Charles Howard Schmid jnr (1942– ?), American murderer and kidnapper; because he attracted women, three of whom he killed. His death sentence (1966) was commuted to two terms of life imprisonment. He died there.

PIET WAPEN Piet Willem Botha (1916–), Prime Minister of South Africa (1978–); so called especially when Minister of Defence. It means 'Piet Weapon'. His temper has a short fuse. He resigned from ten years leadership of the National Party (1989) after a stroke but remained President until August of that year. Also 'P.W.'. Cf. the *Big Crocodile.*

PIGEON PALEY Archdeacon William Paley (1743–1805), English philosopher who wrote *The Principles of Moral and Political Philosophy* (1785). He used the analogy of a flock of pigeons in a discussion of group actions. Also *Tommy Potts.*

PILOT THAT WEATHERED THE STORM, THE William Pitt, the *Bottomless Pitt.* George Canning (*Aeolus*) wrote a song (1802) to celebrate the fact that Pitt had steered the country safely through the Napoleonic wars.

PINCHER Admiral Sir W.F. Martin, *Fly.* A severe disciplinarian, he did not hesitate to 'pinch' ratings for minor offences.

PINEAPPLE HEAD William IV, the *Flogster.*

PINETOP Clarence Smith (1904–29), American jazz musician, inventor of 'boogie-woogie'. He would tell his band to 'boog it', his own type of rhythm.

PINETREE Colin Meads (1936–), New Zealand Rugby Union forward with fifty-five caps.

PINKEY William Penkethman, the *Idol of the Rabble.*

PINK POWDER PUFF, THE Rudolph Valentino (1895–1926), Italian-born American film star. His real name was Rodolpho Alfonzo Raffaelo Pierre Filibert Guglielmi di Valentina d'Antonguolla. He was the idol of millions of women for his film roles and the nickname was given to him by men; so called first by an American critic – based, it seems, on a story that Valentino was associated with a pink

powder dispenser installed in the men's room of a Chicago ballroom.

PIONEER GORDON Lieutenant Gordon, 98th Regiment, who went out to the Gold Coast, West Africa, before the 1873–4 Ashanti War to organize African troops. He commanded the Hausas, raised two redoubts and began to widen the road to Kumasi before the appointment of Sir Garnet Wolseley (*Our Only General*) as C-in-C.

PIOUS, THE

i) Edward VI, the *Josiah of England*, son of Henry VIII (*Bluff Hal*) and Jane Seymour. He was convinced of the divine right of kings and the truth of Protestantism.

ii) Sergeant-Major-General Philip Skippon, *Honest Skippon*. He was a deeply religious man.

* A Sergeant-Major-General was lower in rank than a Lieutenant-General. It was later cut down to Major-General.

PIPPIN Lady Anne Isabella (Annabella) Milbanke, the *Amiable Mathematician*, who married Byron (*Baby*) in 1815; his nickname for her because of her apple cheeks.

PIPPY or PIP Pierce Egan the *Elder*, his nickname among his friends.

PIRATE, THE James (Jimmy) Hill (1928–), BBC commentator on football, a former player and manager (Coventry City FC); because of his buccaneer-like beard which he later shaved off (1983).

PIRATE OF THE GULF, THE Jean Lafitte or Laffite (*circa* 1780–1826), buccaneer and smuggler, with his HQ in Barataria on a bayou near the mouth of the Mississippi. He operated in the Gulf of Mexico.

PITCHFORK BEN Benjamin Ryan Tillman (1847–1918), American spokesman for agrarian interests. He once said he would like to put a pitchfork through the ribs of President Cleveland (the *Stuffed Prophet*).

PITTER F.T. Pitman, well-known Cambridge boat-race stroke, *circa* 1882.

PITTSBURGH PHIL Henry Strauss (1908–41), killer for Murder Inc., said to have murdered 500 people.

PITTSBURGH WINDMILL, THE Harry Greb, the *Human Windmill*.

PLAIN AND PERSPICUOUS DOCTOR, THE Walter Burleigh, *Doctor Planus et Perspicuus*.

- The original Latin meant 'clear-sighted and intelligible'.

PLAIN DEALER, THE William Wycherley (1641–1716), English playwright who wrote a play of that name (1677). Once when Wycherley was in a bookshop the Countess of Drogheda, a widow, came in to ask for a copy of *The Plain Dealer*. A friend pushed Wycherley forward and said 'There is the Plain Dealer, madam, if you want him.' They were secretly married later.

PLANTAGENET Geoffrey IV, count of Anjou (*Le Bel*), father of Henry II (*Curtmantle*): nickname assumed by his father, Fulke Martel, during a pilgrimage to the Holy Land (1120–1); from the *planta genista*, the broom, worn as a symbol of humility.

- Cf *Dickon of the Broom*.

PLANTAGO The Marquess of Hastings, *Champagne Charlie* (iii); his nickname on the racecourses, from *Plantagenet*, one of his names.

PLANTER JOHN John, 2nd Duke of Montagu (?1683–1749). He had a love for planting trees, and wanted to build an avenue of elms from his home at Broughton, Northamptonshire to London (72 miles).

PLATONIC PURITAN, THE John Howe (1630–1706), domestic chaplain to Cromwell (the *Almighty Nose*).

PLATONIST, THE Thomas Taylor (1758–1835), who translated Plato and Aristotle.

PLATONISTS, THE The *Ladies of Llangollen*, ironic since they were said to have been lesbians.

PLAUSIBLE JACK John Palmer (1742–98), British actor, famous as a liar; so called by Sheridan (*Sherry*). He was no relation to *Gentleman Jack* Palmer.

PLAYBOY MAYOR, THE *Beau James* Walker of New York.

PLENIPO RUMMER Matthew Prior (1664–1721), English poet and diplomat who helped to negotiate the Treaty of Utrecht (1714), called 'Matt's Peace'. 'Plenipo' from 'plenipotentiary' and 'Rummer' from the Dutch word for a drinking-glass and the fact that Prior's uncle Sam kept the Rummer Tavern between Whitehall and Charing Cross. Also the *Solomon of Bards* and the *State Proteus*.

PLOTTER, THE Robert Ferguson (*circa* 1637–1714), political pamphleteer and conspirator involved in the Rye House Plot (1683) to kill Charles II (the *Blackbird*) and the Duke of York (the *King Over the Water*); and also in conspiracies against William III (the *Deliverer*). He was vicar of Godmersham, Kent, before the Act of Uniformity (1661) drove Puritan ministers out of the Church of England. He was never brought to trial, and died in poverty.

- See the *British Cassius* and the *Hypocrite*.

PLUM

i) Sir Pelham Francis Warner (1873–1963), cricketer who captained Middlesex and England. He founded *The Cricketer* (1921).

ii) P.G. Wodehouse, *English Literature's Performing Flea*.

iii) Richard Turner (died 1733), a British Turkey merchant who had a fortune of £300,000 but became a notable miser after he had lost £70,000 in the Charitable Corporation.

PLUMED KNIGHT, THE James Gillespie Blaine (1830–93), American Congressman and Senator who was a candidate several times for Presidential nomination. The nickname was given to him by R.G. Ingersoll (the *Great Agnostic*) when he was supporting Blaine's nomination in 1876. Blaine had been accused of taking bribes. Also the *Tattooed Man* and the *Uncrowned King*.

PLUMP Jack Goodwin (1688–1706), British thief who once stole the wheels from the Duke of Bedford's carriage.

PLUTONIUM BLONDE, THE Mrs Thatcher, *Attila the Hen*.

POCAHONTAS Matoaka or Matsoaks'ats, the *Belle Sauvage*. It means 'The Playful One'.

POCKET HERCULES, THE

i) Frank Buckle (1766–1832), champion English jockey who rode 27 Classic winners, including 5 Derbys.

- Cf the *Long Fellow*.

ii) James Grimshaw (1846–88), English jockey who won the Cesarewitch twice (1862 and 1864), The Thousand Guineas and the St Leger.

POCKET NAPOLEON, THE Major-General Sir T.W. Rees, the *Chota General*.

POCKET VENUS, THE Lady Florence Cecilia Paget (1842–1907), youngest daughter of the Marquis of Anglesey. She was engaged to Henry Chaplin (*Magnifico*), but eloped with Lord Hastings (*Champagne Charlie* (iii)) in 1864. She was small and beautiful.

POET BUNN Alfred Bunn, *Good Friday*.

POET CLOSE John Close (1816–91), British printer and poetaster; a derisive nickname. His award of a Civil List pension (1860) was withdrawn (1861).

POETICAL ROCHEFOUCAULD, THE Sir William Davenant, *Daphne*; because of the maxims in his poetry.

- See the *English Rochefoucauld*.

POETICAL SHOEMAKER, THE James Woodhouse (1735–1820). Johnson (*Blinking Sam*), however, considered he would never make a good poet.

POETICAL SPAGNOLETTO, THE James Grahame (1765–1811), Scot who wrote *The Sabbath* (1806). Also the *Sabbath Bard* and *Sepulchral Grahame*.

- José Ribera (1588–1656), painter noted for his scenes of horror, was called *Lo Spagnoletto*, 'the Little Spaniard'.

POET LAUREATE OF COLORADO, THE John Denver (1943–   ), American folk singer and composer. His real name is John Deutschendorf.

POET LAUREATE OF PUGILISTS, THE Robert (Bob) Gregson, the *Lancashire Giant*. He wrote verses, mostly about pugilists and sporting events. One of his best known was *Ya-Hip, My Hearties* (1819), sung by Jack Holmes (*Coachee*) at a masquerade in St Giles, London.

POET LAUREATE OF THE GREETINGS CARD WORLD, THE Helen Steiner-Rice (1901–81), American writer of verse.

POET LAUREATE OF THE PRIZE RING, THE Bob Gregson (above).

POET OF DESPAIR, THE James Thomson (1834–82), British poet of *The City of Dreadful Night* (1874).

POET OF GRETA HALL, THE Robert Southey, the *Ballad Monger*. He lived for the last forty years of his life at Greta Hall, Keswick, Cumbria.

POET OF HASLEMERE, THE Lord Tennyson, the *Bard of Arthurian Romance*. He had a house at Haslemere, Surrey (1868) in which he died.

POET OF NATURE, THE William Wordsworth, the *Bard of Rydal Mount*.

POET OF POETS, THE P.B. Shelley, *Ariel*.

- Cf the *Poets' Poet*.

POET OF THE AMERICAN REVOLUTION, THE Philip Morin Freneau (1752–1832) who wrote, among other works, *The British Prison Ship* (1781), which described his own experiences. His poems were said to have inspired soldiers when things were going badly.

POET OF THE CHASE, THE William Somerville (1675–1742), British writer of sporting poems, especially *The Chace* (1735).

POET OF THE COMMON PEOPLE, THE James Whitcomb Riley (1849–1916), American whose poems dealt with rural people, mostly in Indiana.

POET OF THE COMMONPLACE, THE Henry Wadsworth Longfellow (1807–82), American poet who did a great deal to make American folk themes popular abroad. There was a reaction against him after his death.

POET OF THE PEOPLE, THE Carl Sandburg (1878–1967), American immigrant with little formal education who became one of the country's great poets.

POET OF THE POOR, THE George Crabbe (1754–1832), whose poems described with stark realism the lives of poor people in British country districts. Also the *Pope in Worsted Stockings*.

POET OF THE YUKON, THE R.W. Service, the *Canadian Kipling*. He spent eight years in the Yukon.

POET PUG Alexander Pope, the *Bard of Twickenham*; so called by his enemies.
- Cf *Painter Pug*.

POETS' PARASITE, THE William Warburton, Bishop of Gloucester, the *Colossus of Literature*, who edited several editions of Shakespeare (the *Bard of All Time*) and Pope (the *Bard of Twickenham*); so called by Churchill (the *British Juvenal*).

POETS' POET, THE Edmund Spenser; the *Child of the Ausonian Muse*.
- Cf the *Poet of Poets*.

POET SCOUT OF THE BLACK HILLS, THE Jack Crawford, the *Black Hunter*.

POET SQUAB John Dryden, *Asaph*; so called by Rochester (*Virgin Modesty*).
- Cf *Old Squab* and see *Appius*.

POET WORDY Wordsworth, the *Bard of Rydal Mount*; so called by Byron (*Baby*).

POISONER, THE Thomas Griffiths Wainewright (1794–1852), British art critic, man of letters, forger and friend of Lamb (the *Mitre Courtier*). He died a convict in Tasmania where he had been transported for forgery of stock. He was believed to have poisoned a girl named Helen Abercrombie, her sister-in-law, her uncle, his mother-in-law and a friend, but it was never proved. He is said to have confessed before his death.

POISONOUS, THE Eochaid, Irish King of Argyll (*circa* 781).

POKER ALICE Alice Ivers (1851–1930), British-born saloon girl in South Dakota; from her fame as a gambler. She was the daughter of an English schoolmaster and went West with her mining-engineer husband, an expert card-sharper. Alice was a 'fast gun' and shot at least two men dead.

POKER FACE Helen Wills, *Little P.F.*.

POLE OF PADDINGTON Sir Felix John Clewell Pole (1877–1956), General Manager of the Great Western Railway. He entered GWR service at fourteen.
- Paddington station was the headquarters and London terminus of the GWR from 1852.

POLITICAL GRIMALKIN, THE Martin van Buren, *King Martin the First*; so called by De Witt Clinton (1769–1828), Governor of New York and his political enemy.
- 'Grimalkin', an old she-cat, is a term usually applied to imperious old women.

POLITICAL RATCATCHER, THE John Robinson of Appleby (1727–1802) who under the patronage of Sir James Lowther became an MP and Secretary of the Treasury in the administration of Lord North (the *Palinurus of State*), a job in which he earned his nickname by his cunning use of palace bribes to silence the 'rats', the King's enemies. He was a friend of George III (the *Button Maker*) and when he died about 300 letters from the King were found in his desk.

POLLY Pahlan Ratanji Umrigar (1926–   ), cricketer for India, the Parsees, Bombay and Gujerat. He has played in 59 Tests for India, a record number, scoring 3,631 runs and 12 centuries.

POLY R.O. Jenkins (1918–   ), Worcestershire off-spinner who scored a double hat-trick at Worcester (1949).

POLYPHEMUS OF LITERATURE, THE Dr Johnson, *Blinking Sam*.
- Polyphemus, son of Poseidon, was one of the Cyclops, one-eyed giants.

PO-FACED POM, THE Mark Thatcher (1953–   ), son of Mrs Thatcher (*Attila the Hen*); so called by Australian newspapermen after his show of indignation at having been photographed on his honeymoon (1987). One journalist described him as looking as if he had spent a month on vinegar and lemon juice.
- 'Po', from 'chamber-pot, i.e. featureless; 'pom' = an Englishman, from the rhyme of 'immigrant' with 'pomegranate' (pronounced 'pomegrant').

POMONA'S BARD John Philips (1676–1709), British author of *Cyder* (1708); so called by James Thomson (the *Poet of Despair*).
- Pomona was the Roman goddess of fruit-trees and fruit.

POMPOSO Dr Johnson, *Blinking Sam*; so called by Churchill (the *British Juvenal*) in his poem *The Ghost*, which imputed to Johnson belief in the Cock Lane ghost.

- The story of the Cock Lane 'ghost' grew from knockings heard in Smithfield, London (1762), reputed to have come from the spirit of Fanny Kent, 'murdered' by her husband. All London was intrigued by it until it was proved to have been a fraud.

POMPOSUS Dr George Butler (1774–1853), headmaster of Harrow (1805–29) and Dean of Peterborough; so called by Byron (*Baby*) in *Childish Recollections*.

PONNY

i) William Harold Ponsford (1900–   ), cricketer for Victoria and Australia. He was the only batsman to score more than 400 twice (1922–3; 1927–8).

ii) Horace Mayhew (1816–63), brother of Henry (1812–87): famous as the author of *London Labour and the London Poor*; (3 vols. 1851). Horace was a sub-editor on *Punch* and a comic writer.

PONTE VECCHIO Louisa, Duchess of Devonshire, *Double Duchess* (i); because of her passion for the game of bridge in her old age.

- *Ponte Vecchio* is Italian for 'old bridge'.

PONY BOB Robert H. Haslam (1840–1912), pioneer Pony Express rider (1860–1). Later, when he was penniless, he became a steward at the Roosevelt University, Chicago, where he is buried.

PONY MOORE

i) Mr Moore who ran the Magpie music-hall, Battersea, London, and then formed the Moore and Burgess Minstrels which starred at the Cafe Royal. He was a well-known sporting character and betted in 'ponies' (sums of £25).

ii) An Admiral Moore who also betted in 'ponies'.

POODLE The Honourable Frederick Byng, *Paul Pry*; so called because of his curly hair by George Canning (*Aeolus*).

POOH Lord Nicholas Windsor (1970–   ), younger son of the Duke of Kent (1935–   ); so called by the royal family.

POOR CON William *Consequential Jackson*; so called from 'consequential' by Wolcot (*Peter Pindar*).

POOR GULLY John Gully (1783–1863), British heavyweight boxer considered Champion of England after Pearce (the *Game Chicken*) retired. Gully was the only pugilist to become an MP and a very rich man. The nickname dated from the time he was 'discovered' in a debtors' prison. Egan the *Elder*, who spells it 'Gulley' said some amateurs 'agreed to get him released from durance vile' and paid his debts so that he could meet Pearce (1805). The fight went 64 rounds, and Pearce won. Gully lost £40,000 on his horse 'Mameluke' (1827). After a while the nickname became slightly ironic.

POOR LITTLE RICH GIRL, THE Barbara Hutton (1912–79), Woolworth heiress whose life was a series of misfortunes after she inherited $10 million at twenty-one. She was married seven times; so called by newspapers.

- Cf the *Richest Girl in the World* and see *Cash and Cary*. *Poor Little Rich Girl* is a song by Noel Coward (the *Master*).

POOR MAN'S COUNSELLOR, THE Abraham Clark (1726–94), one of the men who signed the American Declaration of Independence (1776). One of the first lawyers in America, he gave free legal advice to his neighbours.

POOR MAN'S FRIEND, THE

i) F.D. Roosevelt, the *Barrymore of the White House*. In 1932 he launched a fight against poverty in America.

ii) Senator James Couzens, the *Croesus of the Senate*.

POOR MAN'S PRIEST, THE Richard William Radclyffe Dolling (1851–1902), British clergyman working among the poor people of the East End of London. Also 'Father Dolling'.

POP

i) Sir Gerard d'Erlanger (1906–62), chairman of British European Airways and British Overseas Airways Corporation; nickname at Eton which stayed with him.

ii) Glenn Scobey Warner (1871–1954), American football coach.

iii) Lady Darlington, celebrated in London society in the 1820s; from *Poplolly*.

- William Harry Vane, 3rd Earl of Darlington (1766–1842) was a patron of the turf and a foxhunter.

iv) Bryan Robson (1967–), footballer, captain of England and Manchester United. He scored 300 League goals.

POPE DAVIS John Philip Davis (1784–1862) who painted *The Talbot Family receiving the Benediction of the Pope* (1824).

POPE IN WORSTED STOCKINGS, THE George Crabbe, the *Poet of the Poor*; so called by Horatio (Horace) Smith (1779–1849) who saw him as an Alexander Pope (the *Bard of Twickenham*) who wrote of the common people.

POPE JOAN An unidentified English girl said to have been created Pope as John VIII (855) and to have held office for two years until she was found to be pregnant. The legend is that Joan fell violently in love with a monk named Felda or Folda and wore monastic habit to be near him. She was so learned, however, she was eventually elected Pope.

POPE OF FLEET STREET, THE Hannen Swaffer, the *Bishop of Fleet Street*; so called by Frank Owen of the *Evening Standard*. It supplanted 'bishop' in the 1940s.

POPEYE John, 1st Baron Boyd-Orr (1880–1971), British scientist and first Director-General of the United Nations Food and Agriculture Organisation; so called by his family.

POPIE Walter Samuel Macqueen-Pope (1888–1960), British theatre critic and former theatre manager.

POPISH DUKE, THE The Duke of York, later James II, the *King Over the Water*.

- Cf the *Protestant Duke*.

POPISH MIDWIFE, THE Mrs Elizabeth Cellier (fl. 1679–88), London midwife involved in the 'Popish Plot' (1680).

- See *Bull-Faced Jonas*, *Duke Dangerfield* and the *Knight of the Post*.

POPLOLLY, THE Lady Darlington, *Pop*.

- A poplolly is a mistress or a light woman, (from French *poupelette*).

POPPERS or POPS Nigel Popplewell (1958–), cricketer for Cambridge University and Somerset.

POPPO John Edwards (1789–1862), professor of Greek and classical literature at Durham University (post-1840).

POPPY President George Herbert Walker Bush (1924–), his family nickname as a child. He was at eighteen the youngest pilot in the United States Navy flying missions against the Japanese. He is the 41st President of the United States of America (1989–). Also the *Wimp*.

POPS

i) Louis Armstrong, *Dippermouth*.

ii) George Foster (1892–1969), American jazz string bass player.

iii) Paul Whiteman, the *King of Jazz*; so called by his musicians.

POPSKI Lieutenant-Colonel Vladimir Peniakoff (1897–1951), leader of a long-range desert raiding group called 'Popski's Private Army' (World War II).

- Popski was a cartoon character created by Sir David Low in the *Evening Standard* before World War II, a little Russian with a fuzzy beard and a bomb in one hand. See *Shan*.

PORCHY Henry George Alfred Marius Victor Francis Herbert, 6th Earl of Carnarvon (1898–1987), London socialite. He was also Baron Porchester.

PORK BARON, THE Philip Armour (1832–1901). He founded (1867) the canned meat manufacturing and packing plant in Chicago which rapidly grew into one of the largest in the world. Pigs were the first animals processed (30,000 a year in the 1860s).

PORK CHOP Jeff Mullins (1942–), American All-State basketball player.

PORKY Edward Oliver (1916–61), American golfer, runner-up in twenty tournaments.

POSSUM, THE George Jones (1931–), American top country music singer who won a Grammy award (1981).

POSTMAN POET, THE Edward Capern (1819–94), letter-carrier poet of Bideford, Devon.

POTATO HEAD John McEnroe, the *Brat*.

POTATO JONES Captain David Jones (1870–1962), British merchant skipper who ran the Spanish Nationalist blockade (1937–38) to take potatoes into loyalist Spain. He brought back refugees.

POUGHKEEPSIE SEER, THE Andrew Jackson Davis (1826–1910), American hypnotist and spiritualist who gave a series of lectures ostensibly from trances, and wrote several books.

- Poughkeepsie is a city and port on the Hudson river 65 miles from New York.

POWERHOUSE Shirley MacLaine (1934–), American film-star, born Shirley Beaty and sister of Warren Beatty (1937–); so called as a child because of the strength of her hits in softball to score home runs.

POWHATAN Wahunsonacock, father of *Pocahontas*. He described as 'the emperor of the Virginian Indians' (died 1618).

- 'Powhatan' was the name of the Indian confederacy he founded.

PRAGGER-WAGGER, THE The Prince of Wales in University slang, especially:
i) Prince Albert Edward (Edward VII: the *Peacemaker*).
ii) Prince Edward Albert Christian George Andrew Patrick David (Edward VIII: 1894–1972), later the Duke of Windsor. Also the *Sporting Prince*, *Teddy Woodbine* and *Woodbine Teddy*.

- See note at *Tagger Ragger of St Pragger Le Bagger*.

PRAISE-GOD BAREBONES Praise-God Barbon or Barabone (*circa* 1596–1680), MP in the Barebones Parliament – one nominated in Cromwell's name (1653). He was a Baptist minister and a fairly wealthy leather-seller. His Puritan name or nickname was reinforced by his habit of praising God on every occasion. He was a Fifth Monarchy Man.

- The Barebones Parliament was given its sarcastic title after one of its most obscure and least active members. **See *Man of Sin*.**

PREMIUM MADDEN Dr Samuel Madden (1686–1765), first proposer of 'premiums' at Dublin University. They were instituted in 1734 and were prizes given to distinguished students.

PRES Lester Young (1909–59), American tenor saxophonist; so called by Billie Holiday (*Lady Day*) with whom he recorded; short for 'President'.

PRESBYTERIAN ULYSSES, THE Archibald Campbell, 8th Earl of Argyll, *Grumach Gillespie*; mentioned by Scott (the *Ariosto of the North*) in his autobiography.

- Ulysses or Odysseus, hero of the Trojan War and a shrewd counsellor. He took more than eight years of adventures to get home. 'Ulysses' is a mistake (a miswriting?) for the Latin *Vlixes* or *Ulixes*, a dialectical form of 'Odysseus', which, says Robert Graves, means 'wound in the thigh', a common form of royal death.

PRESIDENT BOB Robert Spencer, 2nd Earl of Sunderland (1640–1702), Lord President of the Council under James II (the *King Over the Water*), although he had voted for him to be excluded from the kingdom.

PRESIDENT MEESE Edwin (Ed.) Meese III (1931–), Californian lawyer and counsellor to President Ronald Reagan (*Dutch*) (post-1981); because of his power in influencing executive decisions: later Attorney-General.

PRETENDERS, THE See the *Old Pretender* and the *Young Pretender*.

PRETTY BOY FLOYD Charles Floyd, *Chock*, American gangster who was present at the Kansas City massacre (1933); nickname given to him by a brothel madam.

PRETTY DRAGOON, THE Christiana Cavanagh, *Mother Ross*.

PRETTY WITTY NELL Eleanor (Nell) Gwyn, *Nell of Old Drury*; so called by Pepys (the *Father of Black-Letter Lore*).

PRIDE OF THE FANCY, THE Jem Mace, *Gypsy*.

- The Fancy in the late eighteenth and early nineteenth centuries was the prize-ring and its followers.

PRIDE OF WESTMINSTER, THE Caleb Baldwin (1769–*circa* 1815), the coster pugilist who was champion of Westminster, where he was born. His real name was Caleb Stephen Ramsbottom.

PRIEST OF NATURE, THE

i) Sir Isaac Newton, the *Columbus of the Skies*; so called by Campbell (the *Bard of Hope*).

ii) David Williams (1738–1816), a Dissenting minister who founded the Royal Literary Fund.

PRIME MINISTER OF CRIME, THE Frank Costello (1891–1973), American gangster and syndicate boss.

PRIME MINISTER OF MIRTH, THE Sir George Robey (1869–1954), British music-hall comedian. His real name was George Edward Wade.

PRIMROSE SPHINX, THE Lord Beaconsfield, the *Asian Mystery*. He had a sphinx-like imperturbability and a liking for primroses.

PRINCE, THE Kumar Shri Ranjitsinhji, H.H. the Jam Sahib, Maharajah of Nawanagar (1872–1933), cricketer for Sussex and England who (1899) became the first batsman to score 3,000 runs in a season; sometimes 'The Prince of Cricket'. Also *Ranji*.

PRINCE ARTHUR Chester Arthur, the *Dude President*.

PRINCE CONSORT, THE Conrad Nagel (1896–1970), American silent film actor who shone in romantic roles; so called in Hollywood in the 1920s.

PRINCE ERIE James Fisk, *Big Jim*. He held control of the Erie Railway.

PRINCE JOHN

i) John van Buren, the *Jove of Jolly Fellows*, son of Martin van Buren, *King Martin the First*.

ii) General John Bankhead Magruder (1810–71), Confederate who captured Galveston, Texas (1863); so called from his bearing.

PRINCE OF BEAUX, THE *Beau* Brummell.

PRINCE OF BEGGARS, THE Sydney Holland, 2nd Viscount Knutsford (1853–1931), who showed great skill in raising money for the London Hospital, of which he was chairman.

PRINCE OF BIBLIOMANIACAL WRITERS, THE T.F. Dibdin, the *Beau Brummell of Living Authors*.

PRINCE OF CARICATURISTS, THE George Cruikshank, the *Modern Hogarth*; so called in *Noctes Ambrosianae*.

PRINCE OF CORRESPONDENTS, THE George Augustus Sala (1828–95) of the *Daily Telegraph*, perhaps the most famous of all newspaper correspondents. His large nose had its own nickname: 'Fleet Street's Most Prominent Landmark'. Dickens (the *Inimitable*) sent him to Russia (1856) and the next year he joined the *Telegraph*.

PRINCE OF DANDIES, THE

i) *Beau* Brummell.

ii) Count Alfred D'Orsay, *Le Jeune Cupidon*.

iii) M. G. *Monk* Lewis.

PRINCE OF DARKNESS, THE

i) Douglas, 1st Earl Haig (1861–1928), Commander-in-Chief, British Expeditionary Force, France (1915–18); so called by troops because of the hell he created by strategy which involved wasteful sacrifice of men's lives, e.g. the Somme.

ii) Richard Norman Perle (1941–), Assistant Secretary of Defense (1981–7) in the Reagan Administration (1981–8); because of his violent antagonism to the USSR.

- The Epistle to the Ephesians (vi.12) refers to the principalities . . . of the darkness' usually taken to mean Satan and the forces of evil. Shakespeare made it explicit in *King Lear* (III): 'The Prince of Darkness is a gentleman.' Sir John Suckling (1609–42) followed him in *The Goblins* with the same term (1638).

iii) Johnny Carson (1925–), American television chat-show personality whose enormously successful programme is put out late at night.

PRINCE OF GOSSIPS, THE Samuel Pepys, the *Father of Black-Letter Lore*; because of the entertaining nature of his diary.

PRINCE OF HALF-BACKS, THE Norman Coles Bailey (1857–1923), who played football for England and Clapham Rovers.

PRINCE OF HARLEQUINS, THE John Rich, the *Father of English Pantomime*.

PRINCE OF HIGH TOBY MEN, THE Frank Gardiner, *Darkie*.

- 'Toby' has been thieves' slang for a road since the early 19th century (from *toba*, Irish tinkers' cant). 'High toby' developed via 'tober', e.g. high tober = the main road.

PRINCE OF HUMBUGS, THE Phineas Taylor Barnum (1810–91), American circus-owner. He proclaimed his to be the 'greatest show on earth' (1871). He later joined with James A. Bailey, whose real name was Walsh. Barnum toured Charles Stratton (*General Tom Thumb*) and Jenny Lind (the *Swedish Nightingale*), but 'freaks' were always major items of his shows. Self-styled. Also the *Prince of Showmen*.

PRINCE OF JOURNALISTS, THE Jonathan Swift, *Doctor Presto*, who edited *The Examiner* (1710–11).

PRINCE OF MACARONIS, THE George Bussey Villiers, 4th Earl of Jersey (1735–1805), who earned the nickname at Court where he used the influence of his wife Frances (1753–1821), one of the lovers of the Prince of Wales (*Adonis of Fifty*), to gain position.

- See the *Macaroni Parson*.

PRINCE OF NEGRO SONGWRITERS, THE James Bland (1854–1911), American who wrote *Carry Me Back to Old Virginny* (1878). He was a familiar figure on the English music-hall stage for many years.

PRINCE OF NOVELISTS, THE Henry Fielding, the *Father of the English Novel*.

PRINCE OF PEDAGOGUES, THE William Maginn, the *Adjutant*; so called by Mackenzie (the *Man of Feeling*) in *Works of Maginn*.

PRINCE OF PETULANCE, THE John McEnroe, the *Brat*.

PRINCE OF PISTOLEERS, THE James Butler Hickok (1837–76), Illinois-born soldier, scout, spy, stage-coach driver and lawman of Abilene, Kansas. He became famous as a pistol shot when he was a boy. He married *Calamity Jane*. Also *Wild Bill*.

- See *Curly Jack*.

PRINCE OF POETS, THE
i) Edmund Spenser, the *Child of the Ausonian Muse*; so called on his monument in Westminster Abbey, London.
ii) John Milton, *Black-Mouthed Zoilus*.

PRINCE OF PRIGS, THE Arthur Chambers (died *circa* 1723), expert London thief who started to steal as a child and seems never to have been caught.

- Prig = cant for a thief since at least 1573 (Harman: 'to prigge signifieth in their [i.e. vagabonds' and criminals'] language to steale', and he quotes 'a prigger of prauncers, a horse thief'.

PRINCE OF PRINCES, THE George IV, the *Adonis of Fifty* when Prince of Wales; so called by Byron (*Baby*) in *Don Juan* (1819–24).

PRINCE OF SHOWMEN, THE Phineas T. Barnum, the *Prince of Humbugs*.

PRINCE OF WAILS, THE Johnny Ray (1927–   ), American 'crying' pop singer (fl. 1950s).

PRINCE OF WHALES, THE George IV, the *Adonis of Fifty* when Prince of Wales; so called by Lamb (the *Mitre Courtier*), from his size.

PRINCE OF WHIGS, THE The Duke of Devonshire, *Canis*; so called by Princess Augusta of Saxe-Gotha (died 1772), mother of George III (the *Button Maker*). The Duke was Whig MP for Derbyshire (1741–51).

PRINCE OF WICKET-KEEPERS, THE John McCarthy Blackham (1853–1932), cricketer for Victoria and Australia. He played in some of the first Test Matches (1882–3) and was captain of Australia for one of them. He set new standards of 'keeping'.

PRINCE OF WITS, THE Lord Chesterfield, the *English Rochefoucauld*.

PRINCE PERKIN The Duke of Monmouth, *Absalom*; so called by Nell Gwyn (*Nell of Old Drury*).

- Perkin Warbeck, the *White Rose of England*, was pretender to the throne and led an unsuccessful rising.

PRINCESS HARRY Queen Maud of Norway (1869–1938), daughter of Edward VII (the

Peacemaker). She was a tomboy when she was young.

PRINCESS KOO Kathleen Stark, *Koo*; so called in America. She was called 'Queen Koo' in one English newspaper but the nickname never stuck.

PRINCESS OF CONNEMARA, THE Mrs Bell Martin (1815–50), Irish novelist.

PRINCESS OF PARALLELOGRAMS, THE Lady Anne Milbanke, the *Amiable Mathematician*; so called by her husband, Lord Byron (*Baby*).

PRINCESS OF PUNK, THE Toyah Wilcox (1958–   ), British rock singer with clothes and hair styles designed to shock; later revealed herself to be a good actress on television.

• See the *Godfather of Punk*.

PRINCESS PAT Princess Victoria Patricia, *Patsy*.

PRINCESS PUSHY Princess Michael of Kent, *Our Val*; so called in the newspapers (post-1986) after a campaign to publicize a book she had written.

PRINCESS SUSANNA Susanna Bokoyni of Newton, New Jersey, who was 104 in 1983. She was 3 feet tall and weighed 37 pounds.

PRINCESS TOM Princess Michael of Kent, *Our Val*; so called in London society, from the name of her former husband.

PRINCESS YVONNE Princess Margaret, *Charley's Aunt*; nicknamed 'Yvonne' by *Private Eye*.

PRINCE ROBBER Prince Rupert of the Rhine, the *Mad Cavalier*. He became a privateer in the West Indies, ostensibly to help the royalist cause after the end of the English Civil War.

PRINCE TITI Frederick Louis, Prince of Wales (1707–51), son of George II (*Augustus*). He wrote *Histoire du Prince Titi* (1735), in which he caricatured his father and mother. It was an expression of his constant opposition to the King but it was never published. His son became George III (the *Button Maker*). Also *Sad Fred*.

PRINNY George IV, the *Adonis of Fifty* when he was Prince Regent.

PRINT Ison Prentice Olive (1840–86), American gunfighter, killer and cattle baron shot by an angry cowboy. He had a domineering manner.

PRISCIAN Dr Edward Craven Hawtrey, the *English Mezzofanti*; so called by Dibdin (the *Beau Brummell of Living Authors*).

• Priscianus (fl. 6th century) was a Latin grammarian.

PRISONERS' FRIEND, THE Abraham Beal (1803–72), British-born American advocate who engineered the release or pardon of 10,000 prisoners.

PROBUS Dr Joseph Drury (1750–1834), headmaster of Harrow (1785–1805). He had been a master at Eton; so called by Byron (*Baby*) who went to Harrow and had been flogged with a silken cord.

• The task of Marcus Aurelius Probus (fl. 270–80), a stern emperor, was to restore law and order to Gaul and the Rhine, but there may be a pun on 'probe us', since flogging was general in those days.

PROFESSOR, THE

i) William Ivy Baldwin (1866–1953), American tightrope walker who crossed the South Boulder Canyon on his 82nd birthday (1948).

ii) Maurice Micklewaite (Michael Caine), *Mike*; his nickname as a boy in Bermondsey, London when he had a good memory for out-of-the-way facts.

PROFESSOR OF LOGIC, THE John Black, *Doctor Black*.

PROFOUND DOCTOR, THE

i) Thomas Bradwardine, *Doctor Profundus*.

ii) Richard Middleton, *Doctor Profundus*.

PROJECTOR, THE John *Beau* Law. His many worthless projects included the Mississippi Scheme, which caused a panic in France in the 1720s.

PROPHET, THE

i) Thomas Emes (died 1707), a British quack doctor who joined up with the Camisards and published predictions.

• Camisards were French protestants who specialized in prophesy.

ii) J. Daniell, cricketer for Cambridge

University and Somerset (captain 1919–26).

PROSE BURNS OF IRELAND, THE William Carleton (1794–1869), son of a poor man. He was the author of several novels of Irish peasant life.

• For Burns, **see** the *Ayrshire Poet*.

PROSE HOMER OF HUMAN NATURE, THE Henry Fielding, the *Father of the English Novel*; so called by Byron (*Baby*).

PROSE SHAKESPEARE OF PURITAN THEOLOGIANS, THE Thomas Adams (died *circa* 1655), whose witty sermons were published in 1629. He also wrote many books demonstrating a profound knowledge of classics and theology, as well as verve and humour.

• Shakespeare, **see** the *Bard of All Time*.

PROSPERITY ROBINSON Frederick John Robinson, 1st Earl of Ripon, *Goosey Goderich*; so called by *Boney* Cobbett, after a financial crisis had followed Robinson's boast when Chancellor of the Exchequer of the prosperity of the nation. The King's speech had said 'There never was a period in the history of the country when all the great interests of society were at the same time in so thriving a condition.' It was swiftly followed by the panic of 1825.

PROTECTOR OF THE INDIANS, THE John Eliot, the *Apostle of the Indians*.

PROTESTANT DUKE, THE The Duke of Monmouth, *Absalom*; so called at the time of the rumours of the conversion to Roman Catholicism of both Charles (the *Blackbird*) and James (the *King Over the Water*) and Monmouth's aspirations to the throne.

• Cf the *Popish Duke*.

PROTESTANT MARTYR, THE Sir Edmund Berry Godfrey (1621–78), a London magistrate murdered as part of an alleged Roman Catholic plot. It was he who heard 'evidence' by Titus Oates (the *Knight of the Post*) about the 'Popish Plot'.

• **See *Bull-Faced Jonas*** and the *First Tory*.

PROTEUS Samuel Foote, *Beau Nasty*; so called by Churchill (the *British Juvenal*). Foote frequently took two or more parts in a play. Foote's riposte was to call Churchill the *Clumsy Curate of Clapham.*

• See the *Literary Proteus*.

PROTEUS CLARK Joseph Clark (died ?1696), a London posture-master, an expert in assuming various attitudes and in teaching them. A pamphlet (1691), discussing the French, commented: 'Clark, the Posture master, never knew half so many Distortions of Body as they do.'

PROTEUS OF THE STAGE, THE David Garrick, the *British Roscius*.

PROTEUS PRIESTLEY Joseph Priestley (1733–1804), British theologian and scientist who wrote about many subjects.

PROUD, THE
i) Alexander I (Scotland), the *Fierce*; nickname mentioned by Camden (the *British Pausanias*: 1605).
ii) Shane O'Neill (died 1567), dynast of Tyrone (1559–67), son of Conn the *Lame*.

PROUD BOLINGBROKE Lord Bolingbroke, *High-Mettled Mary*.

PROUD DUKE, THE Charles Seymour, 6th Duke of Somerset (1662–1748). He never spoke to his servants, communicating with them by signs, and he would never permit children to be seated in his presence.

PROUDEST OF THE PROUD, THE Lord Rosslyn, the *Pert Prim Prater of the Northern Race*.

PROUD MARY Mary Decker (1959–   ), American champion woman athlete, especially in the 1500 and 3000 metres.

PRYNNE OF HIS DAY, THE Philip Stubbs (fl. 1583–91), Puritan pamphleteer and a bitter enemy of popery. He wrote *The Anatomie of Abuses* (1583).

• For Prynne, see the *Brave Jersey Muse*.

PSYCHO Vinny Jones, *Nutcracker*; so called by Wimbledon fans.

PUBLICAN, THE The Reverend William Booth, *Holy Willie*, founder of the Salvation Army; after he had bought the Grecian Theatre and Tavern in the City Road, London (1883).

• See *Bravo Rouse*.

PUBLIC ANEMONE NO 1 Beverley Nichols (1908–83), author and women's magazines, specialist on cats and gardens.

• See below.

PUBLIC ENEMY NO 1

i) Alphonse Capone, *Big Al*; so called by the Chicago Crime Commission.

ii) John Henry Dillinger (1902–34), son of Quaker parents, bank robber and gangster. He is said to have been shot by the FBI, although there is some doubt about the identity of the dead man.

iii) George *Babyface* Nelson.

PUBLIC RAT NO 1 Alvin Karpis, *Old Creepy*, described by Edgar Hoover (1895–1972), head of the FBI, as 'the shrewdest, most cold-blooded gangster in America'. He was arrested by Hoover himself; sentenced to life imprisonment (1936).

PUCK OF SHAKESPEARIAN COMMENTATORS, THE George Steevens (1736–1800), Briton who issued four volumes of Shakespeare's plays with comments (1766); so called by Gifford (the *Bear Leader*) because of a streak of perversity.

PUD, PUDDY or THE PUD Princess Alexandra Helen Elizabeth Olga Christabel (1936–   ), cousin of the Queen; so called by the royal family.

PUD James Galvin, baseball pitcher in the Hall of Fame (1879–92).

PUDGE William Walter Heffelfinger (1867–1954), American college football player and three times a member of the All-American team.

PUFFIN The Honourable Anthony Asquith (1902–68), film director son of Lord Oxford and Asquith (*Old Wait and See*).

PUG General Hastings Lionel, 1st Baron Ismay (1887–1965), Deputy Secretary (Military) to the British War Cabinet (1940–5). He fought against the *Mad Mullah*.

PUGSY or PUGGY BOOTH J.M.W. Turner, *Admiral Booth*.

PULPIT BUFFOON, THE Hugh Peters or Peter (1598–1660), English Puritan clergyman who gained influence by his preaching in Whitehall during the Commonwealth (1649–60). He was executed after the Restoration for complicity in the King's execution; so called by Sir William Dugdale (1605–86), antiquarian and royalist. Peter was sometimes spoken of as 'a Jack Pudding' = a clown or buffoon to a mountebank.

PULPIT PHYSICIAN, THE Dr Henry Sacheverell, the *High Church Trumpet*.

PUMICE STONE Lord Palmerston, *Cupid*; nicknamed by political opponents. His abrasive qualities annoyed Prince Albert (the *Good*); a pun on 'Palmerston'.

PUNCH

i) H.B. Fairs (died 1878), British rackets champion (1876–78); he was a small man.

ii) Ernest Miller, *Kid Punch*.

iii) Charles Cavendish Fulke Greville (1794–1865), British diarist and clerk to the Council in Ordinary for almost forty years.

• The monarch is the supreme Ordinary of the kingdom, but the office of clerk to the Council in Ordinary is one without either political or secret duties. In civil law an Ordinary is one who can take notice of actions in his or her own right and not by delegation.

PUNCHINELLO See the *Great Caliban*.

PURGING COLONEL, THE Colonel Thomas Pride (died 1658), Parliamentarian renowned for having prevented MPs from entering the House of Commons ('Pride's Purge', 1648) during the Long Parliament. He was one of the judges of Charles I (the *Ahab of the Nation*) and signed the death warrant. Also *Yeasty Pride*.

PURITAN MAID, THE Mary Endicott (1864–1957) who married Joseph Chamberlain (*Artful Joe*). She was the daughter of William C. Endicott, Secretary for War in the administration of President Cleveland (the *Stuffed Prophet*: 1885–9); so called by Lord Salisbury (the *Lathe Painted to Look Like Iron*).

PURITAN PEPYS, THE Samuel Sewall (1652–1730), New England judge who kept a diary (published 1878); so called by Henry Cabot Lodge (the *Scholar in Politics*).

PURSE Franklin Pierce (1804–69), 14th

President of the USA (1853–7); so called by his friends.

PUSHFUL JOE Joseph Chamberlain, *Artful Joe*.

PUSS

i) George Leveson-Gower, 2nd Earl of Granville (1815–91), English statesman and one of the promoters of the Great Exhibition (1851). He was Foreign Secretary (1870–4 and 1880–5).

ii) Lady Isabel Burton (1831–96), wife of Sir Richard Burton (the *Modern Admirable Crichton*), who gave her the nickname. Also *Zoo* and *Zookins*.

iii) Steve Anderson (1956–80), one of the Boarded Barn killers. He suffocated himself in his cell hours after he had been sentenced to life imprisonment with a recommendation for him to serve not less than thirty years.

• See *Bouncer* and *Spiderman*.

PUSSY

i) The Princess Royal, Victoria (1840–1901). She married Frederick III, the German emperor. Also *Vicky*.

ii) Lady Emily Susan (née Caufeild: died 1917), wife of the 3rd Earl of Lonsdale.

iii) Frances Louise Stephenson (1888–1972), secretary and mistress to David Lloyd-George (the *Goat*); later the Countess Lloyd-George. He addressed her in his letters as 'My darling Pussy'.

PUSSYFOOT William Eugene Johnson (1862–1945), American advocate for prohibition, largely responsible for the Volstead Act (1919) which introduced it into America. His nickname did not derive, as is widely thought, from his methods of enforcing the Act, but because of his cat-like policies in pursuing lawbreakers in Indian territories.

PUTTOCK Aelfric (died 1051), Archbishop of York. It is an Old English word for a bird of prey, usually a kite, applied (Halliwell) to 'a greedy, ravenous fellow'.

PUTTY Lieutenant-Commander (later Rear-Admiral) Albert C. Read (1887–1967) who, with a crew, made the first transatlantic flight (May 1919) in a flying-boat of the United States Navy. The first non-stop flight was made a month later.

PYGMY, THE Lord Salisbury, the *Little Beagle*; so called by Elizabeth (the *English Diana*).

PYGMALION HAZLITT William Hazlitt, the *Dumont of Letters*. He wrote *Liber Amoris or the Modern Pygmalion* (1823).

• Pygmalion, king of Cyprus, is said to have fallen in love with an ivory statue of a girl and to have prayed to Aphrodite to bring her to life. The goddess did this, and the pair were married.

PYTHON John Dennis, *Appius*; so called because of his fiery temper.

PUTNEY Louis Dandridge (*circa* 1900–46), American jazz pianist and singer.

Q

QUAGGER, THE The Queen, especially Queen Victoria (*Drina*), university slang at Oxford and Cambridge.
- See the *Tagger Ragger of St Pagger Le Bagger*.

QUAKER HIGHWAYMAN, THE Jacob Halsey (died 1691). He was arrested when he tried to rob the Earl of Westmorland's coach in Kent, and was executed.

QUAKER POET, THE
i) Bernard Barton (1784–1849), British bank clerk and friend of Lamb (the *Mitre Courtier*).
ii) John Greenleaf Whittier (1807–92), American poet whose verse was influenced by the Quaker doctrines in which he was raised.
iii) John Scott (1730–83).

QUAKER SOLDIER, THE Clement Biddle (1740–1814), officer in the American army and a friend of George Washington (the *American Cincinnatus*).

QUAKER SOLON OF ROCHDALE, THE John Bright, the *Apostle of Free Trade*, who was one.
- Solon, Athenian law-maker (*circa* 639–*circa* 559 BC) helped the distressed.

QUAKING SOLDIER, THE Jonas Dell (died 1665), a Parliamentary soldier and a Quaker.

QUEEN Victoria Spivey (1910–   ), American singer, pianist and song-writer.

QUEEN ANNE'S GREAT CAPTAIN The Duke of Marlborough, *Anne's Great Captain*.

QUEEN BEE, THE Sue Lawley, *Lol*, appointed to the BBC's top news-reading post (1984). She won the No 1 News-Readers' Award (1987).

QUEEN BESS Elizabeth, the *English Diana*.

QUEEN DICK Richard Cromwell (1626–1712), son of Oliver (the *Almighty Nose*).

He was Lord Protector (1658–9), but was timid, weak, womanish and incompetent. Also *Tumbledown Dick*.

QUEEN ELIZABETH'S MERLIN John Dee (1527–1608), English mathematician and astrologer who gave lessons in magic to the Queen. He read her stars and named a propitious day for her coronation. Also the *Queen's Magician*.
- See the *English Merlin*.

QUEEN JACKIE THE FIRST Jacqueline Kennedy, née Bouvier (1929–   ), wife of John F. Kennedy (1917–63), 35th President of the United States (1961–3).

QUEENIE
i) Queen Elizabeth II, *Brenda*, especially in Australia. During her tour there (1980) the crowds shouted 'Good on yer, Queenie!'
ii) Michael (Mike) King (1950–   ), British professional golfer.

QUEEN MOTHER, THE Lady Melbourne, mother of the second Lord Melbourne (*Lord M*). Her daughter-in-law, formerly Lady Caroline Ponsonby (1785–1828) was so called by Byron (*Baby*). She had been Byron's mistress. See Lady Caroline Lamb (*Caro*).

QUEEN NANCY Nancy Reagan, *Dragon Lady*; for the first three years of her husband's term as President (*Dutch*).

QUEEN OF BOHEMIA, THE Ada Clare (1836–74), American, whose real name was Jane McElheney. She was notorious in Pfaff's Cellar, a New York Bohemian resort (1850s), and wrote poetry. Later she was an actress.

QUEEN OF CLEAVAGE, THE Imogen Hassell (1946–80), British actress, noted for the depth of her neckline plunge.

QUEEN OF COUNTRY AND WESTERN, THE Tammy Wynette (1942–   ), American composer and singer. Her real name is Virginia Wynette Pugh.

QUEEN OF COUNTRY MUSIC, THE

i) Muriel Deason or Kitty Wells (1919–   ), post-1952.

ii) Loretta Lynn (1962–   ).

iii) Dolly Parton (1946–   ).

QUEEN OF FLASH, THE Cher, the *Great American Navel*.

QUEEN OF HEARTS, THE Elizabeth of Bohemia (1596–1662), daughter of James I (the *British Solomon*) and wife of Frederick, Elector Palatine, later King of Bohemia; so called in the Low Countries because of her friendly manner.

QUEEN OF HORRORS, THE Ann Radcliffe (1764–1823), author of *The Mysteries of Udolpho* (1794). Also the *Salvator Rosa of British Novelists* and the *Shakespeare of Romance Writers*.

QUEEN OF ROMANCE, THE Denise Robins (1898–1985), British writer of more than 200 novels (post-1924) which sold 14 million copies in Britain alone.

QUEEN OF SHEPHERDS, THE Elizabeth I, the *English Diana*; so called by Spenser (the *Child of the Ausonian Muse*) in *The Shepheard's Calender* (1579).

QUEEN OF SOUL, THE Aretha Franklin (1942–   ), American singer.

QUEEN OF TEARS, THE Mary of Modena (1658–1718), queen to James II (the *King Over the Water*), a Catholic in a Protestant country with a tactless and pigheaded husband. Five of her children died young.

QUEEN OF THE AMERICAN STAGE, THE Mary Ann Duff, née Dyke (1794–1857), great tragic actress. Also the *Siddons of America*.

QUEEN OF THE ARABS (or the EAST or PALMYRA), THE Lady Hester Stanhope, the *Little Bulldog*.

QUEEN OF THE BLUES, THE Bessie Smith, the *Empress of the Blues*.

QUEEN OF THE BLUE STOCKINGS, THE Elizabeth Montagu, the *Madame du Deffand of the English Capital*.
  • See *Blue Stocking*.

QUEEN OF THE DIPPERS, THE Martha Gunn, one of the women at Brighton beach, Sussex, who helped sea bathers from their machines into the water. She was a favourite of the Prince Regent (*Adonis of Fifty*) who invited her to the Pavilion. The *Morning Herald* (July 1805) nicknamed her 'The venerable Princess of the Bath'.

QUEEN OF THE HALLS, THE Marie Lloyd, *Our Marie*.

QUEEN OF THE JUKES, THE Connie Francis (1938–   ), American singer who sold more than 55 million records, most of them popular on juke-boxes.
  • Cf *King of the Jukes*.

QUEEN OF THE METHODISTS, THE Selina, Countess of Huntingdon (1707–91), part of the English evangelical revival, founder of the Countess of Huntingdon's Connexion; so called by Walpole (the *Autocrat of Strawberry Hill*) for her religious beliefs.

QUEEN OF THE MOBS, THE Virginia Hill, *Flamingo*.

QUEEN OF THE MOVIES, THE Myrna Loy (1905–   ), American film star; so called pre-1939; née Williams: sometimes 'Queen of Hollywood'.

QUEEN OF THE NIGHT CLUBS, THE *Texas* Guinan, the *Female Bill Hart*, noted for her club greeting 'Hello suckers.'

QUEEN OF THE NORTHERN SEAS, THE Elizabeth I, the *English Diana*; from the size and fighting power of her navy.

QUEEN OF THE POPS, THE Madonna, whose full name is Madonna Louise Ciccone (1958–   ), American, the world's most successful pop singer.

QUEEN OF THE SILENT SCREEN, THE Pearl White (1889–1938), American film actress famous for parts in cliff-hanging serials.

QUEEN OF THE SOAPS, THE Joan Collins (1933–   ), British-born star of the American television serial *Dynasty*.
  • Soaps = television serials, a name which stemmed from the sentimental radio serials sponsored by manufacturers of soap, originally called 'soap operas' (1945–50).

QUEEN OF WIMBLEDON, THE Helen

Wills, *Little P.F.* She won the women's singles title eight times.

QUEEN SARAH

i) Sarah, Duchess of Marlborough, *Mrs Freeman*, a strong influence with Queen Anne (*Brandy Nan*).

ii) Sarah Sophie Child-Villiers, Countess of Jersey (1785–1867) who inherited her grandfather's (Robert Child, the banker) wealth. She was a patroness of Almack's and a celebrated beauty. She married George, the 5th Earl, son of the *Prince of Macaronis*.

QUEEN'S EARL, THE James Fitzgerald, 16th Earl of Desmond (died 1601), sent on an abortive mission to Ireland to establish order; in contrast to the *Rebel Earl*, his father.

QUEEN'S JESTER, THE William Frederick Wallett (1808–92), a clown who appeared before Queen Victoria (*Drina*) in 1884.

• Cf the *King's Jester*.

QUEEN'S MAGICIAN, THE John Dee, *Queen Elizabeth's Merlin*.

QUEEN SQUARE HERMIT, THE Jeremy Bentham, the *Father of Utilitarianism*. He lived in a house called The Hermitage in Queen Square, London.

QUEENY or QUEENIE Hester Maria Thrale (1764–1857). In 1808 she married George, Lord Keith (1746–1823). She assiduously attended Dr Johnson (*Blinking Sam*), and was at his death-bed.

QUEER HARDIE James Keir Hardie (1856–1915), founder of the Independent Labour Party (1893). In 1900, through the efforts of Ramsay MacDonald (*The Boneless Wonder*), Hardie himself and others, the ILP became the Labour Party.

QUIET MAN OF CRICKET, THE John Brian Statham, *George*. He does not like personal publicity, and declines to appear on television.

R

RAB Richard Austen, 1st Baron Butler (1902–82), English statesman. He made social security acceptable to Conservatives (called 'Butskellism'); so called from his initials, especially in 'Rab's Boys', the younger Conservatives (1940s–1950s).

- 'Butskellism' is compounded of the names of Butler and Hugh Gaitskell (1906–63), Labour MP who preceded him as Chancellor of the Exchequer.

RABBI SMITH Thomas Smith, *Doctor Roguery*, an expert on oriental languages. He had been a chaplain at the English Embassy in Constantinople; so called at Oxford University when he made pronouncements on the state of the Levant and the Greek Church.

RABBIT

i) John (Johnny) Hodges (1906–70), American tenor saxophonist who played with *Duke* Ellington.

ii) Wendy Turnbull (1952–), Australian tennis player, Wimbledon mixed doubles partner with John Lloyd (*Floss*); because she scampers around the court.

RABELAIS OF GOOD SOCIETY, THE Dean Swift, *Doctor Presto*.

- See the *English Rabelais*.

RACKY Lady Elizabeth Foster (1757–1824), 2nd Duchess of Devonshire; short for 'racoon' from her supposed resemblance to one. She was the daughter of the 4th Earl of Bristol (the *Earl-Bishop*).

RADICAL JACK John, Earl of Durham, *King Jog*. Although a rich man, he was the champion of the poor and of left-wing ideas.

RADICAL JOE Joseph Chamberlain, *Artful Joe*.

RAIL-SPLITTER, THE Abraham Lincoln, *Father Abraham*. For a time in his early life he earned his living splitting rails to make wooden fences.

RAILWAY KING, THE

i) George Hudson (1800–71), railway promoter who became chairman of the North Midland Railway Company, and dictator of railway speculation in the railway mania of 1844–5. He lost most of his large fortune in a railway panic (1847–8) and died in poverty; so called by Sydney Smith (the *Diner-Out of the First Water*).

ii) Jay Gould (1836–92), American financier who joined Fisk (*Big Jim*) in the Erie Railway and later bought control of the Union Pacific, Kansas Pacific and other railways.

iii) William Henry Vanderbilt (1821–85), son of Cornelius (the *Commodore*). He had interests in the New York Central and Hudson River Railway, the Lake Shore and Michigan Southern, the Canadian Southern and the Michigan Central.

RAINY-DAY SMITH John Thomas Smith (1766–1833), engraver and antiquary, writer of *A Book for a Rainy Day* (published 1845) which reviewed events of his lifetime. He was Keeper of Drawings and Prints at the British Museum.

RAJEN BABU Dr Rajendra Prasad (1884–1963), first President of India (1950–63).

RAMBLIN' RON Ronald Reagan, *Dutch*, who occasionally lost the thread of his speeches.

RAMBO

i) Ian Botham, *Both*; a nickname given to him during the England tour of the West Indies (1986).

ii) Alan McInally (1964–), British striker for Aston Villa FC. He is 6 ft 1 in tall and weighs 13 stone (189 lb).

- Rambo is the muscular central figure of films about a murderous 'hero' in Viet-Nam, a character created by American novelist David Morrell.

RAMBOYO Neil Gordon Kinnock (1932–), leader of the Labour Party and

Leader of the Opposition in the House of Commons; so called by some people in the Labour Party because of his style of leadership; mentioned by himself on television (1988); from **Rambo** and the Welsh use of 'boyo' as an affectionate epithet. Also the **Welsh Windbag**.

RAMSAY MAC James Ramsay MacDonald, the **Boneless Wonder**.

RANDY

i) Lord Randolph Churchill, the **Blenheim Pippin**.

ii) Randolph Turpin (1926–66) of British Guiana (Guyana), world middleweight boxing champion (1951).

RANDY ANDY Prince Andrew, **Bungy**, who has shown a marked interest in girls; so called in the Royal Navy (HMS *Invincible*) and the newspapers, but first at Gordonstoun after he had been seen entering the girls' school there.

RANJI Maharajah Jam Sahib Ranjitsinhji, the **Prince**.

RAPHAEL OF DOMESTIC ART, THE Sir David Wilkie (1775–1841), Scottish painter. Also the **Scottish Teniers**.

• Raffaello Sanzio (1483–1520), usually known as Raphael, the great Renaissance painter and architect.

RAPHAEL OF ENGLAND, THE Sir Joshua Reynolds, the **Bachelor Painter**; so called by D'Israeli.

RAPHAEL OF HIGHWAYMEN, THE Claude Duval or Du Vall (1643–70), Frenchman turned English highwayman; because of his 'art' and gallantry to ladies. His gravestone bore the inscription 'England's bravest thief'. He was hanged.

RARE BEN JONSON Ben Jonson, the **Bricklayer**. Sir John Young (fl. mid-17th century) caused the words 'O rare Ben Jonson' to be cut on the poet's tomb in Westminster Abbey after overhearing a casual remark by a visitor.

RAT, RATS or RATSY Robert Arthur Tourbillion (1885– ?), American confidence trickster who disappeared (1931) after having served a prison sentence; from his initials. He called himself 'Dapper Dan Colins'.

RAT, THE

i) Lady Georgina Cavendish, **Gee**.

ii) Sir Richard Ratcliffe (died 1485), a supporter and agent of Richard III (the **Boar**). Ratcliffe was killed at the battle of Bosworth.

• See the **Cat**.

RAT-CATCHER CHURCHILL Sir Winston Churchill, **Bricky**; so called by the Germans (World War I) when, as First Lord of the Admiralty, he had said of the German Fleet: 'If they do not come out to fight, they will be dug out like rats from a hole.'

RATTLER Sir Henry Morgan (*circa* 1635–88), buccaneer and Lieutenant-Governor of Jamaica; nickname in the Royal Navy where 'rattle' is slang for a prison. Morgan is reputed to have carried a large bunch of keys. Also the **Uncrowned King of Port Royal**.

RATTLESNAKE DICK Richard Barter (1834–59), British settler in California during the Gold Rush and prospector in Rattlesnake. He became a gold-train robber and was shot by a lawman.

RAZOR W.C. Smith (1877–1946), English slow bowler (*circa* 1910–20). In 1910 he took 247 wickets for 3,225 runs, an average of 13.05.

RAZZLE-DAZZLE Kenneth Wilfred Baker (1934–   ), Secretary of State for Education (1986–9), chairman of the Conservative Party (1989–   ); so called by his Cabinet colleagues because of his expertise in publicity.

READYMONEY Sir Cowasji Jehangir, the **Peabody of Bombay**. 'Readymoney' was the nickname of his family, Parsee merchants in the 18th century, which they adopted as a surname.

• There was a parallel in twelfth-century England. A London moneylender was named Lefwin Besant (1168), originally a nickname (Reaney) from the gold bezant current in England from the 9th century until the introduction of the noble by Edward III (the **Father of English Commerce**).

REAGAN'S PRIME MINISTER Donald T. Regan (1918–   ), Chief of Staff at the

White House (1980–7) under President Reagan (**Dutch**). His friendship with Reagan gave him great power.

REAL PRINCE OF WALES, THE Jonathan Davies (1962–   ), Welsh rugby hero who played for Neath, Llanelli and Wales before he turned from Rugby Union to Rugby League and professionalism (1988). He now plays for Widnes.

REBEL EARL, THE Gerald Fitzgerald, 15th Earl of Desmond (1558–83) who raised Munster in the Geraldine Rebellion (1574) and was proclaimed a traitor. He was killed by a small party of soldiers.

* Cf the **Queen's Earl**, his son.

REBEL READ Philip (Phil) Read (1940–   ), British motor-cycle racer who by the age of thirty-seven had won seven world titles; because of his dislike of authority. He was the first to lap the Isle of Man TT course at more than 100 mph (1965).

REBEL ROSE Mrs Rose Greenhow, née O'Neal (1817–64), spy in Washington for the Southern States during the American Civil War.

RECKLESS JACK John Adams, alias Alexander Smith (1767–1829), the patriarch of Pitcairn Island after the Bounty mutiny (1789); so called on HMS *Bounty*.

RED

i) Sir Felim O'Neill, the **Great O'Neill**.

ii) Henry Allen (1908–67), American jazz trumpeter and pioneer of the New Orleans marching band music.

iii) William McKenzie (1901–48), St Louis jockey who became famous as a blues blower (i.e. with paper and comb).

iv) Ernest Loring Nichols (1905–65), American band-leader celebrated for his group 'The Five Pennies'.

v) Paul Neal Adair (1916–   ), American expert at quenching oil fires.

vi) Harold Grange, the **Galloping Ghost**. He has red hair.

vii) Richard Barnard Skelton (1913–   ), with red hair. He used the nickname as a stage and film name.

viii) Harry Sinclair Lewis (1885–1951), American novelist (e.g. *Babbitt* 1922) who also had red hair.

ix) George Callender (1918–   ), American jazz double-bass player.

x) Urban Faber, baseball pitcher in the Hall of Fame (1914–33).

xi) Charles Ruffing, baseball pitcher in the Hall of Fame (1924–47).

xii) John Kelly (died 1865), father of Ned Kelly (1855–80), Australian bushranger.

RED, THE

i) Niall *Ruadh* (died 1230), King of Ulster for one month (1230).

ii) Alastair *Ruadh* Macdonnell, **Pickle the Spy**.

* *Ruadh* is Gaelic for 'red' or 'red-haired'.

REDAN WINDHAM Lieutenant-General Sir Charles Ashe Windham (1810–70), British guardsman who served in the Crimea and commanded troops at Cawnpore (1857); after his gallantry in leading the storming party on the redan at Balaclava (1855).

RED BARD, THE Hugh Hughes (1693–1776), Welsh poet.

RED BARON OF ARIZONA, THE James Addison Reavis (died 1908), American swindler. He forged deeds of ownership to vast tracts of land in Arizona, and was sentenced to six years' imprisonment (1895).

RED BILL William Thorpe, English thief sentenced to death (late 18th century) for having killed a man in a robbery, but later sent to the Hulks.

RED BUTTONS Aaron Schwatt (1919–   ), American film star who, at the age of seventeen, was a red-headed page-boy before he went to Hollywood and took the nickname with him.

RED COMYN John Comyn, Cummin or de Comines (died 1306) who led resistance to England by the Scots. He was stabbed to death after he had quarrelled with Robert the **Bruce** at Dumfries. He was a great-nephew of the Constable of Scotland, Alexander Comyn, Earl of Buchan (died 1289) and a claimant, like Bruce, to the Scottish throne. He had red hair; ancestor of the Cummings clan.

* Cf the **Black Comyn**.

RED DEAN, THE The Very Reverend Hewlett Johnson (1874–1966), Dean of Canterbury (1931–63) with Marxist sympathies, an advocate of Communism. He won the Stalin Peace Prize (1951). Also the *Spurgeon of the North*.

RED DOUGLAS, THE

i) George Douglas (?1412–62), 4th Earl of Angus, father of *Bell-the-Cat*.

ii) Archibald, 6th Earl of Angus (?1489–1557) who married Queen-Dowager Margaret of Scotland (1489–1541) after the death of James IV (the *Star of the Stuart Line*). He was brother-in-law to Henry VIII (*Bluff Hal*) and chief of Red Douglases.

RED EARL, THE Gilbert de Clare, 8th Earl of Gloucester (1243–95). He married Alice of Angoulême, niece of Henry III (1207–72) and was one of the supporters of Simon de Montfort (*circa* 1208–65).

• Cf *Rufus* (ii), the 9th Earl, his son.

RED EARL OF OSSORY, THE Sir Piers or Pierce Roe Butler, Earl of Ormonde (1522) and Earl of Ossory (1528). He was Chief Governor of Ireland (1522). Also *Red Piers*.

• Roe = Irish for 'red', from *ruadh*.

RED EARL OF ULSTER, THE Richard de Burgh or Burgo, 2nd Earl of Ulster (2nd cr.). He was twice Justiciar of Ireland (1320 and 1327). He was defeated by Edward Bruce, brother of the *Bruce* at Connor, near Ballymena (1315) and Edward became king of Ireland.

• For Justiciar, see *Roger the Great*.

RED ELLEN Ellen Cicely Wilkinson (1891–1947), British Labour MP for Jarrow (1935–47), Minister of Education (post-1945). Also *Wee Ellen*.

RED FOX OF KINDERHOOK, THE Martin van Buren, *King Martin the First*. He practised law as a young man in Kinderhook, New York.

RED GEORGE George Macdonell (1779–1870), commander of the Canadian Glengarry Light Infantry in the war of 1812 with America.

RED HERRINGS Francis Charles Seymour-Conway, 3rd Marquess of Hertford and Earl of Yarmouth (1777–1842), friend of George IV (the *Adonis of Fifty*) and a notorious rake. Gronow says he got his nickname 'from his rubicund whiskers, hair and face, and from the town of Yarmouth deriving its principal support from the importation from Holland of that fish.' Yarmouth was the original of the Marquess of Steyne in Thackeray's *Vanity Fair*.

• See *Mie-Mie*.

RED HECTOR OF THE BATTLES Hector Maclean of Duart (died 1411), Chief of the Macleans. He led the Macdonalds and the Macleans at the battle of Harlaw where he was killed.

RED HUGH Sir Hugh Roe O'Donnell, lord of Tyrconnel (1571–1602), grandson of Hugh *Duv* and known as *Aodh Ruadh*. He became The O'Donnell and a hero of Ireland. He was an ally of Hugh O'Neill, the *Great*, in the Tyrone War (1594–1603). When the rebellion was failing, he was sent to Spain for help but died at Simancas.

• *Ruadh* and *Roe* = red in Gaelic. *Aodh* = Hugh, but see the note at *Aedh of the Ague*. See the *Black* (ii).

RED INDIAN OF DEBATES, THE Lord Beaconsfield, the *Asian Mystery*; so called by Sir James Graham, MP (1792–1861). According to Graham, he had used a tomahawk to cut his way to power.

RED KEN Kenneth (Ken) Livingstone (1945–), Labour leader of the Greater London Council for five years until its abolition in 1986; so called by the newspapers. Elected MP (1987).

RED KING, THE William II (1056–1100), who had a ruddy complexion. Also *Rufus*.

RED LIGHT BANDIT, THE Caryl Chessman (1921–60), American robber and sex offender who fought the death penalty for twelve years, but lost.

RED MANE Magnus, Earl of Northumberland (killed 1449 in battle); so called by the Scots because of his long red beard.

RED NAPOLEON, THE Cochise (*circa* 1813–76), chief of the Chiricahua Apaches; because of his tactical skill.

RED PATRICK Patrick Ramsay, squire to the Earl of Douglas (1408).

RED PIERS Sir Piers Butler, the *Red Earl of Ossory*.

RED ROB Robert Macgregor (1671–1734), a Scottish farmer turned blackmailer and extortionist who demanded money from his neighbours to return stolen cattle. He was declared an outlaw, and adopted the name Campbell. He was pardoned in 1717. *Robert Ruadh* in Gaelic. Also the *Robin Hood of the Lowlands* and *Rob Roy*.

- *Ruadh* = red in Gaelic.

RED ROBERT

i) Sir Robert Birley (1903–82), headmaster of Eton (post-1948); so called at Eton. His part in the Fleming Report (1944) condemned the exclusiveness of public schools. He was educational adviser to the Military Governor of the British Zone of Germany.

ii) Robert Macgregor, above.

RED ROB MACKINTOSH Robert Mackintosh (1745–1807), Scottish violinist and composer.

REDEEMED CAPTIVE, THE The Reverend John Williams (1644–1729), a New England clergyman captured by the French and Indians (1704) and held for two years; so called from the title of the book he wrote about his experiences (1707).

REFORMED PUGILIST, THE William Thompson, *Bendigo*, after he became an evangelist.

REFRIGERATOR, THE William Perry (1963–   ), 23 stone (322 lb), 6 ft 2 in American footballer for the Chicago Bears who helped them to win the Superbowl championships at New Orleans (1986); so called after he had eaten the contents of a refrigerator at one sitting.

REGGIE NO-DICK John Reginald Halliday Christie (1895–1953), necrophile killer of six people at Rillington Place, London; hanged for the murder of his wife; the nickname comes from his sexual incompetence.

REINE BLANCHE, LA Mary, Queen of Scots, the *Mermaid*. She wore white mourning clothes for her husband, Henry

Stewart, Lord Darnley (1545–67), murdered at Kirk o' Fields.

RELIGIOUS MACHIAVEL, THE John Knox, the *Apostle of the Scots*; so called by D'Israeli.

- See the *Literary Machiavel*.

REPUBLICAN QUEEN, THE Sophia Charlotte (1668–1705), sister of George I (the *Turnip Hoer*) and second wife of Frederick I of Prussia (1657–1713). She interfered disastrously in politics.

RESOLUTE DOCTOR, THE John Baconthorpe or Bacon (died 1346), head of the Carmelites in England (1329–33). He was born in Baconthorpe, Norfolk. He advocated the superiority of the king over the clergy.

- 'Resolute' in his case meant 'resolving'.

RESPECTABLE HOTTENTOT, THE Dr Johnson, *Blinking Sam*; so called by Lord Chesterfield (the *English Rochefoucauld*): 'The utmost I can do for him is to consider him a respectable Hottentot.'

REVENUE CUTTER, THE Joseph Hume, *Adversity Hume*; so called in the Royal Navy because he challenged almost every item of public expenditure; a pun on the service vessel.

REVEREND ROWLEY POWLEY, THE The Reverend George Croly, *Catiline Croly*; so called by Byron (*Baby*) in *Don Juan* (1819–24).

- 'Rowley-Powley' or 'Roly-Poly' was a seventeenth-century term for a worthless fellow, and was so used by Johnson (*Blinking Sam*).

REX Sir Reginald Wildig Leeper (1888–1968); in charge of British Foreign Office Political Intelligence Department (World War II), once described by Goebbels as his most dangerous opponent at the Foreign Office.

REX LEGIFER James I of Scotland, the *Law Giver*.

RHODA THE RHINO Mrs Thatcher, *Attila the Hen*; so called by Denis Healey (the *Beast*).

RHODY Ambrose Burnside, *Kaiser William*, who was Governor of Rhode Island and a colonel in the 1st Rhode Island Regiment.

RHUMBA ROMEO, THE Xavier Cugat, *Coogie*.

RHYMER, THE Thomas Learmont of Ercildoune, the *Merlin of Scotland*.

RICHARD-MAKE-A-KING The Earl of Warwick, the *Kingmaker*.

RICHEST GIRL IN THE WORLD, THE Doris Duke (1912–   ), daughter of James B. Duke (*Buck*) and heiress to £20,000,000. She got little happiness from it.
- Cf the *Poor Little Rich Girl*.

RICH SPENSER Sir John Spenser (died 1609), Lord Mayor of London (1594) who died worth £800,000.

RILEY OF THE SOUTH, THE Frank Labby Stanton (1857–1927), American poet of Georgia, who wrote of the people.
- For Riley, see the *Poet of the Common People*.

RILLA Richard M. Ellison (1959–   ), Kent and England cricketer; from Ri . . . Elli. Also *Snooker*.

RINGLETS General *Autie* Custer with long hair; so called by his soldiers.

RINGO Richard Starkey (1940–   ), drummer for the Beatles; so called by his mother because of his fondness for wearing rings.

RIP Captain John S. Ford who served in Texas, working with Indians and frontiersmen for more than a decade. In 1858 he led an invasion from Brazos against the Comanches, and in May of that year fought a seven-hour battle with them near the Antelope Hills.

ROARING BOB OF THE GARDEN Robert Bensley (1738–1817), British actor who lived near Covent Garden, London, and played at the theatre there, as well as at Drury Lane and the Haymarket (1765–9); so called by Garrick (*Atlas*).

ROBBER, THE Edward IV (1442–83); nickname given to him by the Scots. The Treaty of Westminster-Ardtornish (1462) between Edward and John, Earl of Ross and Lord of the Isles, led to the break-up of the old kingdom of Argyll and divided loyalties in the Western Highlands.
- See note at *Good John of Islay*.

ROBBER BARON, THE James Fisk, *Big Jim*, financier whose attempts to corner the gold market caused a panic on Black Friday (1869). He was shot by a former business associate in a quarrel over a woman.

ROBBIE Fyfe Robertson (1903–87), BBC television personality and presenter of a number of documentary programmes.

ROBBO John Robertson (1953–   ), British footballer; winger for Nottingham Forest (1980s) and Derby FC.

ROBERTS OF KANDAHAR Lord Roberts, *Bobs*. He took Kandahar (1880) in the Afghanistan campaign.

ROBERT THE LIBERATOR Robert I of Scotland, the *Bruce*. He broke England's hold on Scotland (1314).

ROBIN BLUESTRING Sir Robert Walpole, the *Grand Corrupter*. He had a fondness for wearing the blue ribbon of the Order of the Garter.

ROBIN GOODFELLOW OF THE STAGE, THE Richard Suett, *Cherub Dicky*.
- Robin Goodfellow (Puck) was a hobgoblin or elf believed to haunt the English countryside, full of mischievous pranks and practical jokes.

ROBIN HOOD Major-General Orde Wingate (1903–44), leader of the Chindits in Burma (World War II) and nephew of *Wingate of the Sudan*; because of his methods of guerrilla fighting against the Japanese. Also *Tarzan*.
- Robin Hood, in itself probably a nickname, may have been a famous English outlaw of Sherwood Forest, whose real name by one legend was Robert Fitzooth, Earl of Huntingdon (fl. 1180–1247). One theory is that the 'ooth' became 'Hood'.
- Wingate's Chindits were members of a force containing many Burmese operating behind the lines. They were named after the Chinthey (half-dragon) statues which guard Burmese pagodas from evil spirits.

ROBIN HOOD OF COOKSON COUNTY, THE C.A. *Pretty Boy* Floyd, a 'legendary hero' of that area of Oklahoma.

ROBIN HOOD OF THE FOREST, THE Colonel Ethan Allen (1739–89) who in the American War of Independence, refused to recognize the authority of New York and commanded (1771) the Green Mountain Boys, an irregular force which captured Fort Ticonderoga (1775). He once threatened to withdraw into the desolate caverns of the mountains in defence of Vermont as a separate entity.

ROBIN HOOD OF THE LOWLANDS, THE Robert Macgregor, *Red Rob*.

ROBIN HOOD OF TEXAS, THE Sam Bass (1831–78), stagecoach and train robber in Texas. His reputation grew into folklore. It is said that while robbing trains he tipped conductors and brakemen. He once stole some grain and gave the farmer a $20 gold piece when he next saw him. He was sometimes spoken of as 'the Good Robber'.

ROBIN HOOD OF VAN DIEMAN'S LAND, THE Martin Cash, who after he was transported for housebreaking (1827), became a bushranger in Tasmania. He 'retired' and died a respectable farmer when more than sixty years old.

ROBIN MEND-ALL Probably Sir John Conyers, leader of the rising against Edward IV (the *Robber*) in Yorkshire (1469), believed to have been initiated by Warwick the *Kingmaker*, to whom Sir John was kinsman. Also *Robin of Redesdale*.

ROBIN OF HOLDERNESS Robert Hilyard of Winstead, who led a rising against Edward IV (the *Robber*) at the same time as *Robin Mend-All* (1469).

ROBIN OF REDESDALE Probably Sir John Conyers, *Robin Mend-All*.

ROBIN THE TRICKSTER The Earl of Oxford, the *Backstairs Dragon*; so called for his double-dealing.

ROB ROY

i) Robert Macgregor, *Red Rob*, who had red hair; 'Roy' from Gaelic *ruadh*.

ii) John Macgregor (1825–92), Scottish writer, traveller and canoeist. It was also the name of the canoe which he designed himself; from (i).

ROB ROY OF THE WEST, THE Jack Rattenbury (1779–1830s), Devon smuggler who 'retired' and published *Memoirs of a Smuggler* (1837).

ROBUSTIOUS EDDY Edward Eddy (1822–75), American actor who played all types of parts from Othello to circus acts.

ROCHDALE THUNDERBOLT, THE Jock McAvoy (1908–71), British middleweight and lightweight boxing champion. His real name was Joseph Bamford; because of his two-fisted attacks.

ROCHESTER Eddie Anderson (1905–77), American negro film star who played manservant to Jack Benny (1894–1947).

ROCK, THE

i) William Woodfull, the *Great Unbowlable*.

ii) *Rocky* Marciano, the *Brockton Blockbuster*.

ROCKET, THE Rodney (Rod) George Laver (1938–   ), Australian tennis player who was Wimbledon champion in the men's singles in 1961, 1962, 1967 and 1969 and the only man to win all the major singles titles both as an amateur and a professional. He became the first lawn tennis player to earn more than 200,000 dollars (1970). He was a left-hander with a powerful service.

ROCKING CHAIR LADY, THE Mildred Bailey (1907–51), American jazz singer. She made the *Hoagy* Carmichael song *Old Rocking Chair* famous.

ROCK OF CHICKAMAUGA, THE General G.H. Thomas, *Old Reliable*; after the firmness of his troops in that battle (1863).

ROCK OF NOTRE DAME, THE Knute Rockne, the *Gipper* (ii).

ROCKY

i) Rocco Francis Marchegiano, *Rocky* Marciano, the *Brockton Blockbuster*.

ii) Andrea Jaeger (1965–   ), American tennis star at the age of fifteen and showed great calmness in her play. She retired early and became a tennis expert on television.

iii) Allan Lane (1901–73), American star of Westerns in the 1930s.

ROCKY MOUNTAIN JIM James Nugent, *Mountain Jim*.

RODDERS Anthony (Tony) Adams (1966–), 6 ft 3 in defender for Arsenal and England, tipped (1987) as a future England captain.

- 'Rodders' is the nickname of a character (Rodney) in Adams' favourite television programme, the British *Only Fools and Horses*.

ROGER OF HELL Roger de Lacy, Earl of London (died 1212), ruthless Justiciar of England and Constable of Chester.

- See note below.

ROGER THE GREAT Roger of Salisbury (died 1139), Bishop of Salisbury and Justiciar of England under Henry I (*Beauclerc*). His power was second only to that of the king.

- The Justiciar was the chief political and judicial officer of the kingdom from the eleventh to the thirteenth century. He acted as Regent if necessary.

ROI DU NORD, LE Antoine Labelle, the *Apostle of Colonisation*.

ROMEO COATES Robert *Cock-a-Doodle-Doo Coates*. He believed himself to be a great actor, and insisted on playing Romeo at the Haymarket Theatre, London. He was laughed off the stage, but went on acting since he was rich enough to finance his own productions.

ROMFORD ROBOT, THE Steve Davis, the *Cool Kid*.

ROPEMAKER, THE *Ape Gabriel* Harvey; so called by Greene (the *Dying Titan*). Harvey's father made ropes at Saffron Walden, Essex.

RORY Roger Moore or O'More of Leix (fl. 1620–52), Irish rebel who plotted unsuccessfully to seize Dublin castle and raised Ulster in rebellion (1641). After capture, he escaped and became leader of the Old Irish.

- 'Rory' is a nickname derived from *ruadh*, 'red', and is often used as a first name or substituted for Roger or Roderick. The Old Irish was a group of old Irish chiefs and gentry who determined to obtain redress by insurrection after Charles I (the *Ahab of the Nation*) had decreed that the

native population should be rooted out in order to make way for new settlers.

RORY OGE Rory O'More (died 1578), Irish rebel, 2nd son of Rory O'More, captain of Leix (died 1554). Rory Oge burnt the town of Carlow and was killed after a hunt by Sir Henry Sidney (1529–86), Lord Deputy of Ireland.

- *Oge* = young or younger.

ROSCIUS BRITANNICUS

i) Richard Tarlton (died 1588), a great clown and a member of the Queen's Men. He was so comic that Elizabeth (the *English Diana*) is said to have ordered him off the stage because he made her laugh immoderately. He is reputed to have been the original of Yorick in *Hamlet*.

ii) Thomas Betterton, the *British Roscius*.

iii) David Garrick, *Atlas*.

- See the *African Roscius*.

ROSCOE Brigadier Charles Barnet Harvey (1900–), senior stewards secretary of British horseracing.

ROSE, THE Margaret (1489–1541), daughter of Henry VII (the *British Solomon*), and wife of James IV (Scotland) (the *Star of the Stuart Line*).

ROSE OF RABY, THE Cecily Nevill or Neville, daughter of Ralph Nevill, 1st Earl of Westmoreland (1364–1425). She married Richard, Duke of York (1411–60) in 1438 and was the mother of Edward IV (the *Robber*) and Richard III (the *Boar*). Also the *White Rose of Raby*.

- Ralph Nevill was also 4th Baron Raby in the Wirral, north-west of Chester.

ROSE OF YORK, THE Princess Elizabeth (1465–1503), eldest daughter of Edward IV (the *Robber*). By her marriage to Henry VII (the *British Solomon*), the rival houses of York and Lancaster were united.

ROUGH OLD TOM General Sir Thomas Picton (1758–1815) who fought through the Napoleonic Wars and several times received the thanks of Parliament. He was blunt and bad-tempered. Wellington (the *Achilles of England*) called him 'a rough, foul-mouthed devil'. General Picton was killed at Waterloo, where he wore civilian clothes with a top hat and carried an umbrella.

ROUND THE CORNER SMITH Sir Charles Aubrey Smith (1863–1948), British-born Hollywood film actor and cricketer for Cambridge and Sussex (1880s–1890s). He took the first English team to South Africa in 1888–9; from his style of delivery as a bowler. Also the *Grand Old Man of the Stage*.

ROUX, LE Alan (died 1089), brother of Alan *Le Noir* (ii). They both took part in the Norman invasion of England (1066). He was virtually the 1st Duke of Richmond, since he built a castle on land granted there. The nickname means 'red-headed'.

ROWDY

i) Richard William Bartell (1907–), American baseball star of the 1920s.

ii) Chris Tavaré (1954–), Kent and England cricketer; because he is so quiet and shy off the field.

iii) Ambrose Gaines (1959–), US swimmer who won five gold and three silver Olympic medals (1978 and 1982).

ROWDY JOE Joseph Lowe (died 1899) who established dance-halls and saloons in Kansas and Colorado (1870s). His wife, Rowdy Kate, ran a brothel.

ROYAL FAMILY OF BROADWAY, THE The Barrymores, headed by Maurice (1847–1905), an English actor (Herbert Blythe) who went to America and established the 'dynasty' after he married Georgina (1856–93). Their children were Lionel (1878–1954), Ethel (1877–1959) and John, the *Great Profile*, all of whom were outstanding performers.

ROYAL GEORGE The Duke of Cambridge, *George Ranger*; nickname in the British army of which he was C-in-C (1887–95).

ROYAL MARTYR, THE Charles I, the *Ahab of the Nation*. It was the title of a biography (1676).

ROYAL SMITH George Smith (fl. late 19th century), special Court correspondent for the Press Association for sixty years.

RUBE

i) Richard Marquard (1889–1980), baseball pitcher for the New York Giants, the Brooklyn Dodgers, the Cincinnati Reds and the Boston Braves; in the Hall of Fame (1897–1925). He won nineteen consecutive games as a left-handed pitcher – a record never equalled.

ii) George Waddell, American baseball pitcher in the Hall of Fame (1897–1910).

RUBENS OF ENGLISH POETRY, THE Spenser, the *Child of the Ausonian Muse*.

- Sir Peter Paul Rubens (1577–1640) was famous for his mythological and allegorical paintings.

RUBY NOSE Oliver Cromwell, the *Almighty Nose*.

RUBY ROBERT Robert Fitzsimmons, the *Antipodean*; because of his complexion and halo of ginger hair.

RUDE DUDE, THE John McEnroe, the *Brat*.

RUDEST MAN IN BRITAIN, THE John Fothergill (1876–1953), innkeeper of The Spread Eagle, Thame, Oxfordshire, who wrote *An Innkeeper's Diary* (1931). He refused guests if he did not like their notepaper and rebuked guests for behaviour that did not please him.

RUFFIAN DICK Sir Richard Burton, the *Modern Admirable Crichton*, from his adventurous life and his unconventional way of thought.

RUFFLE JAWS D.E. Chambers, *Frog*.

RUFUS

i) William II, the *Red King*.

ii) Gilbert de Clare (killed at Bannockburn, 1314), 9th Earl of Gloucester, son of the *Red Earl* and son-in-law of Edward (the *English Justinian)*.

RUGBY'S PRINCE OF WALES John Peter Rhys Williams (1949–) Welsh international rugby 'hero', between 1969 and 1981.

RUNAWAY SPARTAN, THE Sir Robert Peel, *Jenny*, after he had changed from an anti-Catholic policy in Ireland (cf *Orange*

Peel) and voted for the Roman Catholic Emancipation Bill (1829). One of his nicknames had been the *Leonidas of his Day*.

● See *Leonidas Glover*.

RUPERT OF DEBATES, THE

i) The Earl of Derby, the *Derby Dilly*; so called when he was Earl Stanley by Disraeli (the *Asian Mystery*) in the House of Commons (1844) and repeated by Lord Lytton (*Bulwig*) in *The New Timon*.

ii) Sir Richard Cartwright, *Blue Ruin*.

● For Rupert, see the *Mad Cavalier*.

RUSSIAN LION, THE George Hackenschmidt (1877–1968), wrestler called the *Strongest Man in the World*. Based in Britain (post-1902), he became naturalized (1950).

RUSTUM Sir Henry Lindesay Bethune (1787–1851). As a captain, he drilled the Persian army; so called in Persia. He was 6 ft 7 in tall and very strong.

● Rustum is the Persian Hercules.

RUWAN ZAFI Captain James Foley, *Empire Jim*; so called in Nigeria = 'Hot Water'.

S

SABBATH BARD, THE James Grahame, the *Poetical Spagnoletto*. He wrote *The Sabbath* (1806).

SABUT JANG Clive, the *Heaven-Born General*; so called by Indian troops = 'Daring in war'.

SACKER Dennis Amiss (1943–), Warwickshire and England cricketer. By 1986 he had made 100 centuries in first-class cricket. He played in fifty Tests.

SADDLE-BAG JOHN General John Pope (1822–92), American who, in command of the Union Army of Virginia, was heavily defeated at Bull Run (1862); so called by soldiers after he had once said his headquarters was on horseback.

SAD FRED Frederick, Prince of Wales, *Prince Titi* whose unhappy life was ended by a blow on the head from a cricket ball. He played in several matches (post-1735).

SAD SAM Samuel Jones (1892–1966), pitcher for five American League baseball teams, including Cleveland (1914–15) and San Francisco, where he pitched 271 innings with an earned run average of 2.82, a record for 1959.

SAGE, THE George Buchanan (1506–82), Scottish historian and scholar; so called in *Noctes Ambrosianae*.

SAGE OF AUBURN, THE Senator William Henry Seward (1801–72), American statesman who was Secretary of State in the Lincoln Administration (1861–5). He practised law at Auburn, New York.

SAGE OF AUCHTERMUCHTY, THE Sir John Junor (1919–), editor of the *Sunday Express* (1954–86); so called by *Private Eye*, which parodied his articles. Sir John started his career in Glasgow.
- Auchtermuchty is a small royal burgh in Fifeshire on the road between Stirling and St Andrew's, but the nickname is sardonic rather than factual.

SAGE OF BALTIMORE, THE Henry Louis Mencken(1880–1956), former editor of *The American Mercury* and author of *The American Language* (from 1918). He was born and educated in Baltimore, Maryland.

SAGE OF CHAPPAQUA, THE Horace Greeley, the *Napoleon of Essayists*. He had a farm there.

SAGE OF CHELSEA, THE Thomas Carlyle, the *Censor of the Age*, who lived at Chelsea, London.

SAGE OF CONCORD, THE R.W. Emerson, the *American Montaigne*. He lived at Concord, Massachusetts.

SAGE OF DOWN HOUSE, THE Charles Darwin, *Gas*. In 1842, after he had married (1839) his cousin, Emma Wedgwood, Darwin moved to Down House, Kent, where he lived for the rest of his life.

SAGE OF MONTICELLO, THE Thomas Jefferson, the *Apostle of Liberty*. 'Monticello' was the name of his house near Charlotteville, Virginia, designed by himself.

SAGE OF PRINCETON, THE Theodore Roosevelt, the *Cowboy President*.

SAGE OF SKINNER STREET, THE William Godwin, the *Grandfather of the Detective Story*, English author of books on politics, essays and novels, and father-in-law of the poet Shelley (*Ariel*). He kept a bookshop at 41 Skinner Street, London, and published school books.
- Skinner Street ran from Newgate Street to Holborn.

SAGEST OF USURPERS, THE Oliver Cromwell, the *Almighty Nose*; so called by Byron (*Baby*).

SAGRENTI Field-Marshal Wolseley, *Our Only General*; his nickname in the Gold Coast, West Africa; the African pronunciation of his name 'Sir Garnet'. The Ashanti War of 1873–4 is called by Africans 'The Sagrenti War'.

SAILOR Group Captain (then Squadron-Leader) A.G. Malan, *Johnny*. He was a South African who trained to enter the navy.

SAILOR JOE Vivian Simmons (1888–1965), Canadian, the world's most tattooed man with 4,831 designs on his body.

SAILOR KING, THE

i) William IV, the *Flogster*. He entered the Royal Navy as a midshipman at fourteen (1779) and by 1827 he was Lord High Admiral.

ii) George V, the *Ordinary Fellow* who became a naval cadet in 1877 and by his own initiative was promoted to Vice-Admiral before he became king.

SAILOR POET, THE William Falconer (1732–69), who wrote *The Shipwreck* (1762).

SAILOR WILLIAM William IV, **the Flogster**.

SAILORS' FRIEND, THE

i) Samuel Plimsoll (1824–98), instigator of the Plimsoll Act (1876) by which a Plimsoll line on every merchant ship prevented overloading.

ii) Agnes Weston, the *Mother of the Navy*.

SAINT, THE

i) Henry VI, *Ill-Fated Henry*; he was near canonization.

ii) Edward VI, the *Josiah of England*.

ST BARNARD CROLY The Reverend George Croly, *Catiline Croly*. He wrote *Tales of the Great St Barnard* (1829).

SAINT BOB Bob Geldof, *Modest Bob*. He raised about £100 million for the starving in Africa by the 'Live Aid' television show.

ST COLOQUINTIDA Charles I, the *Ahab of the Nation*; so called by the extreme republicans, the Levellers.

• A coloquintida is a colocynth, the bitter apple, very bitter indeed. **See** note at *Ahab of the Nation*.

ST JAMES'S PARK See *Green Park*.

SAINT LUBBOCK Sir John Lubbock, 1st Baron Avebury (1834–1913), MP who created the Bank Holiday in Britain (1871). For a time they were known as the Feasts of St Lubbock. So called especially by G.R. Sims (1847–1922) in a poem in *The Referee*.

ST MUGG Malcolm Muggeridge (1903–   ), British journalist and television personality who turned from debunking to Christianity.

SAINT OF RATIONALISM, THE John Stuart Mill (1806–73), British philosopher and author of *Utilitarianism* (1861) and *The System of Logic* (1843).

ST PADDY St Patrick, the *Apostle of Ireland*.

ST PAUL'S PHANTOM, THE Mike Gibbons (1887–1956), American welterweight boxer, born at St Paul's, Minnesota. His opponents found him difficult to hit because of his speed. Also the *Wizard*.

SAINTE-BEUVE OF CRITICISM, THE Matthew Arnold, the *Apostle of Culture*.

• Charles Augustin Sainte-Beuve (1804–69), French essayist and poet whose critical work attracted so much attention he was elected to the French Academy (1844).

SALAMANDER Lieutenant-General John, Baron Cutts (1661–1707), British soldier and MP, who showed great courage under fire. He was C-in-C, Ireland (1705).

• A salamander is a newt-like amphibian supposed to live in flames. It has been used for a fire-eating soldier, e.g. Swift (*Description of Salamander* 1705): 'Call my Lord C. a Salamander.' The C refers to Cutts.

SALVATOR ROSA OF BRITISH NOVELISTS, THE Ann Radcliffe, the *Queen of Horrors*.

• See the *English Salvator Rosa*.

SALVATOR ROSA OF THE SEA, THE Michael Scott (1789–1835), author of *Tom Cringle's Log* (1829–33); so called in *Noctes Ambrosianae*.

SAM

i) Frans Thijssen (1951–   ), Dutch midfield footballer for Ipswich and Nottingham Forest (1980s).

ii) Frederick Armstrong (1904–   ), British racehorse trainer.

SAM COLLINSON Prince Sankolinsin, Commander in Chief, Chinese Forces defending the Taku forts in the 3rd Chinese War (1859–60); so called by British troops, who said he was an Irish deserter from the Royal Marines.

SANDY Vice-Admiral Sir John Woodward (1932–), commanding the British Task Force to recapture the Falkland Islands from the Argentines (1982).

SANDY FLASH James Fitzpatrick (hanged 1787) of the Doane gang of highwaymen in New Jersey, Pennsylvania (1780s).

SANDY SHEEP Alexander (Sandy) Cruikshank (fl. mid-19th century), the Laird's Fool of the 19th Earl of Erroll, Chief of the Hays – perhaps the last 'fool' in Scotland.

SAPIENS Gildas, the *British Jeremiah*.

SAPPHO Lady Mary Wortley Montagu, the *Female Maecenas*; self-applied after Pope (the *Bard of Twickenham*), her enemy for a time, had written some lines using the name of the Greek poetess. 'Pope himself denied that she was the person meant, and indeed there seems no reason to suppose she was' (Edith Sitwell· 1887 1064: *Alexander Pope* 1930).

SAPPHO OF ENGLAND, THE Katherine Philips, *Orinda the Matchless*.

SARAH BERNHARDT OF THE MUSIC-HALL, THE Marie Loftus (1857–1940), a clever British variety star.
- Sarah Bernhardt (1844–1923), French actress, called the greatest tragedienne of all time.

SARDINE Edward, Prince of Wales, later King Edward VIII, the *Pragger-Wagger* (ii); his nickname as a cadet at the Royal Naval College, Dartmouth (1909–11). He was not tall.
- 'Sardine' is old slang (Farmer and Henley) for a sailor, as well as for someone small.

SARGE
i) Orville Moody (1933–), American Open golf champion (1969). He was in the United States Army for fourteen years.
ii) Paul Goddard (1959–), footballer for West Ham and England. He was a sergeant in the Boys' Brigade.

SARONG GIRL, THE Dorothy Lamour (1914–), American film star who wore one in many films. Her real name is Dorothy Kaumeyer.

SASSIE Sarah Vaughan, the *Divine One*.

SATAN MONTGOMERY Robert Montgomery (1807–55). At the age of twenty-three he wrote a long poem *Satan* (1830). Although the quality of this effusion is thin, it was printed by the newspapers and given a serious notice by Lord Macaulay (*Babbletongue*) in *The Edinburgh Review*.

SATCHEL Leroy Paige (1906–82), one of the first American negro baseball pitchers. He pitched three scoreless innings for the Kansas City Athletics at the age of fifty-nine (1965); so called as a youngster because he carried suitcases to the railroad station.

SATCHMO' or **SATCHELMOUTH** Louis Armstrong, *Dippermouth*.

SATRAP OF SCOTLAND YARD, THE Sir Richard Mayne, *King*.
- A satrap was a governor of a province in the old Persian empire.

SATYR, THE Charles II, the *Blackbird*.

SAUSAGE Queen Elizabeth II, *Brenda*; so called by her husband, the Duke of Edinburgh.
- Cf *Cabbage*.

SAVIOUR OF HIS COUNTRY, THE Henry Clay, the *Apostle of Liberty*.

SAVIOUR OF THE NATION, THE Oliver Cromwell, the *Almighty Nose*; so called after the battle of Marston Moor (1644) which began the decline of the royalist cause.

SAVIOUR OF THE NATIONS, THE The Duke of Wellington, *the Achilles of England*; so called by Byron.
- See *Europe's Liberator*.

SAWN-OFF LOCKIE Flight-Lieutenant Eric Lock (died 1941), British pilot who before he was twenty-one (1940) had won the

DSO and the DFC (Battle of Britain, World War II). He had short legs.

SAWNEY THE SCOT The Earl of Bute, *Jack Boot*; so called in caricatures and lampoons.
- 'Sawney' is a sneering nickname for a Scot with the secondary meaning of a fool.

SAXON NYMPH, THE Elizabeth Elstob (1683–1756), an Anglo-Saxon scholar at Oxford University who published an Anglo-Saxon grammar (1715) as well as other books on that language.

SCALIGER OF THE AGE, THE William Warburton, the *Colossus of Literature*; so called by D'Israeli.
- Joseph Scaliger (1540–1609), Italian scholar and critic, proud and abusive.

SCALY JACK Major-General John Eardley Inglis (1814–62) when a lieutenant-colonel of the 32nd Regiment (the Duke of Cornwall's Light Infantry) in India. He was hated by his men (1840s) but later became a reformed man after he married on leave (1853). He commanded troops in the siege of Lucknow (1857–8), where he made a great reputation.
- 'Scaly' means 'shabby', i.e. in the treatment of his men who gave him the nickname.

SCARFACE
i) Al Capone, *Big Al*. He was slashed by a stiletto.
ii) Joseph di Govanni (1888– ?), of the Black Hand gang, Kansas City. A still blew up in his face.

SCHEMER, THE Vincent Drucci (1895–1927), Chicago gangster and jewel thief. Also the *Shooting Fool*.

SCHNITZEL Princess Michael of Kent, *Our Val*; nickname as a schoolgirl in Sydney, Australia.

SCHNOZZLE James (Jimmy) Durante, the *Great Schnozzola*.
- 'Schnozzle' is American slang for a big nose, originally Yiddish with the same meaning.

SCHOLAR IN POLITICS, THE Senator Henry Cabot Lodge (1850–1924), American statesman and author. He wrote, among other books, a two-volume life of George Washington.

SCHOOLMASTER CAMDEN William Camden, the *British Pausanias*; so called by the York Herald, Ralph Brooke, who attacked *Britannia* (1586) for inaccuracy and plagiarism. Camden had been Second Master of Westminster School (1575) and later Headmaster (1593), but resigned on being appointed Clarenceaux King-at-Arms, an appointment which caused jealousy.

SCHOOLMASTER OF THE REPUBLIC, THE Noah Webster (1758–1843), American lexicographer who published an *American Dictionary of the English Language* (1828). He laid down standards of spelling and pronunciation which are still in force.

SCHOOLMISS ALFRED Lord Tennyson (Alfred), the *Bard of Arthurian Romance*; so called by Lord Lytton (*Bulwig*) in *The New Timon*.

SCIENTIFIC STATESMAN, THE Edmund Burke, the *Dinner-Bell*.

SCOBIE Arthur Breasley (1914–), top Australian jockey. He won the English Derby on Santa Claus (1964), and was champion English jockey four times.

SCOOP Henry Jackson (1912–83), American Democrat senator until he lost his seat in the landslide of 1980. He had been a newspaperman.

SCOOPS George Dorman Cary (1915–70), American jazz saxophonist.

SCOOTER Merlin Patrick (1932–), American racing driver.

SCORPION, THE J.G. Lockhart, the *Aristarch of British Criticism*. His vitriolic writing helped to make the reputation of *Blackwood's Magazine*, which gave him his nickname.

SCORPION STANLEY The Earl of Derby, the *Derby Dilly*, when he was Earl Stanley; so called by O'Connell (the *Big Beggarman*) who engaged with him in a vituperative debate in the House of Commons over Catholic emancipation.

SCOTIAN or SCOTTISH PETRARCH, THE William Drummond of Hawthornden, *Bo-Peep*.

• See the *English Petrarch*.

SCOTCH or SCOTTISH GIANT, THE A Scot named MacQuaill who served in Frederick of Prussia's regiment of giants in the early 18th century. He was said to have stood 8 ft 3 in tall. His skeleton in a Berlin museum is 7 ft 2 in.

SCOTCH or SCOTTISH SAPPHO, THE Catherine Cockburn, née Trotter (1679—1749), poetess and playwright. When she was twenty-two she published anonymously a defence of John Locke's *Essay Concerning Human Understanding* (1690). When her identity was known Locke (1632–1704) sent her a letter of thanks and a present of books.

• See the *English Sappho*.

SCOTCH WOP, THE John (Johnny) Dundee (1893–1965), American world featherweight boxing champion (1923–5). His real name was Joseph Carrora.

• 'Wop', American slang for an Italian, may have come from *guapi*, 'a handsome fellow'.

SCOTTISH BOANERGES, THE James Alexander and Robert Haldane (1768–1851 and 1764–1842), one brother a preacher and the other a theological writer. They formed a society for propagating the Gospel in the United Kingdom and planned one for Africa.

• The Apostles James and John were called Boanerges or Sons of Thunder by Jesus (Mark iii.17). The word is Aramaic. They once asked Jesus if he would not bring down fire from Heaven as Elijah (or Elias) did.

SCOTTISH HELIOGABALUS, THE James VI of Scotland and I of England, the *British Solomon* from his voracious appetite.

• Heliogabalus or Elagabalus (*circa* 205–22) was a Roman emperor who indulged in extravagant debauchery.

SCOTTISH HERCULES, THE Samuel MacDonald, *Big Sam*, of the Sutherland Fencibles. He was once on sentry duty over a cannon that it would have taken three ordinary men to have moved. It was a cold night, and he went into the guardroom with the cannon on his shoulder. When accused of deserting his post he replied he had not. 'I could as well watch it here,' he said. He became a porter for the Prince of Wales at Carlton House.

• See the *English Hercules*.

SCOTTISH or SCOTCH HOBBEMA, THE Patrick Nasmyth (1787–1831), landscape-painter.

• See the *English Hobbema*.

SCOTTISH HOGARTH, THE David Allan (1744–96), historical painter with a sense of humour, e.g. *The Scotch Wedding*.

• See the *Juvenal of Painters*.

SCOTTISH HOMER, THE William Wilkie (1721–72), poet, author of *Epigoniad* (1757), which has been called 'The Scottish Iliad'. It is written in the style of the fourth book of *The Iliad*.

• See the *British Homer*.

SCOTTISH MARCELLUS, THE Sir James Macdonald, 7th baronet of Sleat (1741–66), because of his grace and education. The monument inscription which extolled his virtues in Sleat church is included in Boswell's *Tour of the Hebrides*.

• Marcus Claudius Marcellus (*circa* 268–208 BC) was a Roman general who established temples to Honour and Virtue and had a keen appreciation of Greek culture.

SCOTTISH REYNOLDS, THE Sir Henry Raeburn (1756–1823), portrait painter thought by some to be the greatest Britain has produced, greater even than the man with whom he is compared.

• See the *Bachelor Painter*.

SCOTTISH ROSCIUS, THE Henry Erskine Johnston (1777–1845), actor who played Hamlet at seventeen and often appeared on the London stage.

• See the *African Roscius*.

SCOTTISH SIDNEY, THE Robert Baillie (died 1684), known as Baillie of Jerviswood, who was associated with Sir Algernon Sidney (the *British Cassius*) in the Rye House Plot. Baillie was hanged after having been questioned by the King.

• See the *Plotter*.

SCOTTISH SOLOMON, THE James I of England and VI of Scotland, who was also called the *British Solomon*.

SCOTTISH TENIERS, THE Sir David Wilkie, the *Raphael of Domestic Art* who studied the works of David Teniers (1610–90), noted Flemish artist, and genre painting in Holland.

SCOTTISH THEOCRITUS, THE Allan Ramsay (1666–1758), wig-maker and poet who wrote *The Gentle Shepherd* (1725), the first genuine pastoral since Theocritus.

- Theocritus, noted for his idylls, lived in Greece in the 3rd century BC.

SCOTTISH VAN DYKE, THE George Jamesone (?1588–1644), portrait-painter.

- See the *English Van Dyke*.

SCOTTISH WALPOLE, THE Charles Kirkpatrick Sharpe (?1781–1851), antiquary and artist.

- See the *Autocrat of Strawberry Hill*.

SCOTT OF IRELAND, THE John Banim (1798–1842), novelist, dramatist and poet, noted for his *Tales of the O'Hara Family* (1825).

- See the *Ariosto of the North*.

SCOTT OF THE SEA, THE James Fenimore Cooper (1789–1851), American who served in the merchant marine and the United States Navy and wrote sea adventure stories.

SCOTTY

i) Captain Robert Falcon Scott (1868–1912). He led two expeditions to the South Pole (1901–4 and 1910–13, in which he died); his nickname in the Royal Navy. His friends called him 'Con' (from 'Falcon').

ii) Sergeant Ronald Alan Milne (1952–   ) of the Parachute Regiment, five times British parachute jumping champion.

iii) Glynn Wolfe (1908–   ) of California, former Baptist minister, the world's most married man (26 wives and 41 children).

SCOTUS THE WISE John Scotus or Erigena, *Irish-Born John* who carried the name 'Scotus' four centuries before Duns Scotus (*Doctor Subtilis*).

- A 'Scot' (pl. Scottas) was, until the reign of Alfred the *Great* (849–99), the normal word for an Irishman.

SCOURGE OF FANATICISM, THE Robert South (1634–1716), chaplain to the Duke of York (the *King Over the Water*), who attacked various sects during his lifetime including Nonconformism, Socinianism and Arminianism, mostly by sarcasm.

- The teachings of Socinianism, forerunner of Unitarianism, and of Arminianism both rejected predestination. **See** the *Ever-Memorable*.

SCOURGE OF GRAMMAR, THE Giles Lamb (1686–1744), British lawyer and minor poet who attacked Pope's friend John Gay (the *Aesop of England*) and was given this nickname in *The Dunciad* (1728).

SCOURGE OF SCOTLAND, THE or SCOTLAND'S SCOURGE Edward I, the *English Justinian*.

SCOURGE OF THE CHESAPEAKE, THE Admiral George Cockburn, *Dandy George*. In the war of 1812–14, he sailed up the Chesapeake river and helped in the capture of Washington and the burning of the White House; so called by Americans.

SCOUT MARR Dr James William Slesser Marr (1902–65), who as an eighteen-year-old Boy Scout took part in the Shackleton expedition to the Antarctic (1921–2). He became an Antarctic expert, but never lost his nickname.

SCREAM QUEEN, THE Jaimie Lee Curtis (1958–   ), American film actress, from her many parts in horror movies; daughter of Tony Curtis (1925–   ) and Janet Leigh (1927–   ).

SCRIPTURAL KILLIGREW, THE Sir Richard Hill (1732–91). He defended Calvinist Methodism against John Wesley (1703–91). He was fond of quoting the Scriptures as his authority.

- Sir Thomas Killigrew, the *Merry Droll*, virtually an unofficial jester to the king, could jeer at anyone with impunity. He also borrowed money by quoting the King as his authority.

SCROOGIE Frank Edwin McGraw, jnr (1944–   ), baseball pitcher for the New York Mets and the Philadelphia Phillies; because of his screwball pitch. Also *Tug*.

SCULLER or SCULLOR, THE John Taylor (1580–1653), poet who was a waterman on the Thames; so called by Jonson (the *Bricklayer*). Also *Swan of the Thames* and the *Water Poet*.

- A sculler was a common name for a waterman on the Thames in those days, e.g. Pepys: 'I got a sculler for sixpence . . .'.

SCUM Cardonnel or Cardell Goodman (*circa* 1649–99), Drury Lane actor during the Restoration who attempted to murder two of the Duchess of Cleveland's children. He became a highwayman, but was pardoned by James II (the *King Over the Water*). Later he was involved in a plot to assassinate William III (the *Deliverer*).

SEA FIELDING, THE Captain Frederick Marryat, Royal Navy (1792–1848), who wrote many novels of sea life, e.g. *Mr Midshipman Easy* (1836).

- See the *Father of the English Novel*.

SEARCHER, THE Robert Fludd (1574– 1637), English philosopher and physician. He was a Rosicrucian who searched the Bible for hidden clues to 'scientific facts' and the 'real meaning' of Christianity.

SEA WOLF, THE Thomas, Lord Cochrane, the *Devil*; so called by Napoleon.

SE-BAPTIST, THE John Smyth or Smith (*circa* 1570–1612), English nonconformist minister who was a Church of England vicar turned Baptist. He baptized himself (i.e. *Se*-Baptist).

SECOND JOHN John Q. Adams, the *Massachusetts Madman*. He was the son of John Adams (the *Colossus of Independence*), who was President before him.

SECOND HOGARTH, THE Henry William Bunbury (1750–1811), English cartoonist who drew a memorable sketch of Johnson (*Blinking Sam*) and Boswell (the *Ambitious Thane*); so called by Sir Joshua Reynolds (the *Bachelor Painter*).

- For Hogarth, **see** the *Juvenal of Painters*.

SECOND SHAKESPEARE, THE Christopher Marlowe, the *Atheist Tamburlan*; so called in *Theatrum Poetarum Anglicorum* (1675) by Edward Phillips (?1630– 96).

- But see the *Father of English Dramatic Poetry*.

SECOND SOLOMON, THE James I, the *British Solomon*.

SECOND WASHINGTON, THE Henry Clay, the *Apostle of Liberty*.

SECRETARY OF NATURE, THE Francis Bacon, the *Father of Inductive Philosophy*; so called by Izaak Walton (the *Father of Angling*).

SEE-NO-MORE Admiral of the Fleet Sir Edward Hobart Seymour (1840–1929), commander of the first relief expedition to China (1900) during the Boxer Rising. He was forced to turn back.

SELIG GIRL, THE Kathlyn Williams (1888– 1960), star of the first film serial. She was employed by the Selig Polyscope Company of Chicago.

SENSE BROWNE Thomas Browne (?1708– 80), Garter King at Arms (1774) and agriculturalist; so called to differentiate him from *Capability* Browne.

SEPIA SINATRA, THE Billy Eckstine, *Mr B*.

- For Sinatra, see the *Guv'nor* (iii).

SEPOY GENERAL, THE The Duke of Wellington, the *Achilles of England*; a sneering nickname by Napoleon because of the Duke's successes as Sir Arthur Wellesley in India.

SEPULCHRAL GRAHAME James Grahame, the *Poetical Spagnoletto*; so called by Byron (*Baby*) after he had read *The Sabbath*.

SEXPOT OF THE CENTURY, THE Jane Russell, *Bones*.

SEX THIMBLE, THE Pia Zadora (1956–   ), American film actress and singer who is 5 ft 2 in tall; from 'sex symbol'.

SHADOW

i) Rossiere Wilson (1919–59), American drummer with many big bands, including that of *Count* Basie.

ii) George Martin (1942–   ), American rock singer; self-applied because he 'disappears' during business meetings, which he hates.

SHAKESPEARE IN PETTICOATS, THE Joanna Baillie (1762–1851), poetess; so called in *Noctes Ambrosianae*. Also the *Sister of Shakespeare*.

SHAKESPEARE OF DIVINES, THE Jeremy Taylor (1613–67), English bishop and author of books on theology, written in a simple but impressive style. He was chaplain to Charles I (the *Ahab of the Nation*) and Archbishop Laud (*Hocuspocus*); so called by Emerson (the *American Montaigne*). Also the *Spenser of English Prose Writers*.

SHAKESPEARE OF NOVELISTS, THE Henry Fielding, the *Father of the English Novel*.

SHAKESPEARE OF ORATORS, THE Edmund Burke, the *Dinner-Bell*.

SHAKESPEARE OF PROSE, THE Jane Austen (1775–1817) who wrote six famous novels, including *Pride and Prejudice*; so called by Macaulay (*Babbletongue*).

SHAKESPEARE OF PROSE FICTION, THE Samuel Richardson, the *English Marivaux*, whose *Clarissa Harlowe* (1747–8) is considered the first great English novel.

SHAKESPEARE OF ROMANCE WRITERS, THE Ann Radcliffe, the *Queen of Horrors*; so called by Drake in *Literary Hours*.

SHAM-BERLIN Arthur Neville Chamberlain (1869–1940), British Prime Minister (1937–40). His policy of appeasement towards Nazis with the Munich Pact (1938) earned him scorn; a pun on 'Chamberlain'.

SHAMROCK OF THE NATION, THE Richard D'Alton Williams (1822–62), Irish poet who wrote nationalistic ballads after he joined the Young Ireland movement.

SHAM SQUIRE, THE Francis Higgins (1746–1802), poor Irish adventurer imprisoned after fraudulently marrying 'a respectable lady' (1766). He was prosecuted by her relatives, obviously for false pretences. He did, however, die rich.

SHAN

i) Lieutenant-General Sir John Hackett (1910–   ), Chief of the Imperial General Staff (1980s) and a Brigadier in the war in the Middle East (World War II). *Popski* said that General Hackett 'invented him'.

ii) Elton John (1947–   ), British rock star; so called in theatrical circles. His real name is Reginald Hercules Dwight.

SHANGHAI Abel Head Pierce (fl. 1860s), American cowboy who became a 'cattle baron', owning more than a million acres and some 50,000 cattle.

SHARP KNIFE Andrew Jackson, *Hickory*; his nickname among the Indians because of his shrewdness.

SHARP OF THAT ILK James Sharp (1618–79), Archbishop of St Andrews; so called by Cromwell (the *Almighty Nose*). He was murdered by a party of Covenanters who hated him after he helped to restore episcopacy to Scotland, which they thought a betrayal.

● The inference is 'Sharp by name and sharp by nature.'

SHAVER, THE A.S. Chavasse, an Oxford University don (1880s).

SHAY Seamus Elliott (1934–71), Irish motor-cycle road racer.

SHE Queen Victoria, *Drina*; a nickname (1880s) from Rider Haggard's novel (1887) – she who must be obeyed.

SHEEPMAKER, THE Joseph Smith (died 1878), founder of the Social Institution, Manchester, who took collections to buy sheep for his community.

SHEET-IRON JACK John Allen (fl. 1876–84), American horse-thief.

SHEPHERD LORD, THE Henry de Clifford, 18th Baron Clifford (*circa* 1454–1523) who lived for some time disguised as a shepherd after his father (the *Butcher*) had been attainted at the end of the Wars of the Roses. Henry recovered the Clifford estates following the accession of Henry VII (the *British Solomon*).

SHEPHERD OF THE OCEAN, THE Sir Walter Raleigh, the *Knight of the Cloak*.

● See the *Ocean Shepherd*.

SHEPHERD SMITH James Elimalet Smith (1801–57), divine and essayist who started the periodical *The Shepherd* (1834).

SHEPHERD TOM Thomas Robinson Hazard (1797–1886), American agriculturalist of Rhode Island who specialized in sheep-raising. He also wrote on the subject.

SHERE KHAN Imran Khan (1952–), captain of the Pakistan cricket team, who had taken 300 Test wickets by 1987; so called by Pakistanis.

• Shere Khan is the tiger in *The Jungle Book* (1894–5) by Rudyard Kipling (the *Bard of Empire*).

SHERRY

i) Thomas Sheridan, *Bubble and Squeak*.

ii) Thomas Sheridan, *Manager Tom*. Johnson (*Blinking Sam*) used that nickname.

iii) Richard Brinsley Sheridan (1751–1816), British playwright and politician. James Gillray (1757–1815) published a cartoon of Pitt (the *Bottomless Pit*) uncorking a bottle of sherry. Pitt and Sheridan had been opponents in the House of Commons and Pitt spoke with great bitterness. Also the *Young Hercules*.

SHERRY-DERRY Thomas Sheridan, *Manager Tom*; so called by Johnson (*Blinking Sam*).

SHE WHO MUST BE OBEYED Mrs Thatcher, *Attila the Hen*.

• See *Ayesha*.

SHE-WOLF OF ANJOU, THE Margaret (1430–82), daughter of Rene of Anjou and queen to Henry VI of England (*Ill-Fated Henry*) whom she married in 1445. After her husband became insane, she acted with great cruelty, fighting, in fact, like a wolf for the rights of her son, Prince Edward, Prince of Wales (1453–71), killed after the battle of Tewkesbury.

SHE-WOLF OF FRANCE, THE Isabella (1292–1358), daughter of Philip IV of France and queen to Edward II of England (*Carnarvon*). By her orders, and those of her lover, Roger, Earl of Mortimer, Edward was murdered by having a red-hot iron thrust into his bowels. Mortimer (*circa* 1287–1330) was tried by Parliament and executed. Isabella withdrew from public life.

SHIFTER, THE William Goldberg (1847–94), a tipster for 'The Pink 'Un' (*The Sporting Times*) who helped to open the Star Club (1887), one of the forerunners of the National Sporting Club. He had been born in Poland.

SHIFTESBURY Lord Shaftesbury (*Achitophel*). In the English Civil War he first supported the king and raised a regiment for him, but in 1644 he went over to Parliament and became a Field-Marshal-General. He changed sides again just before the Restoration and was one of the twelve commissioners who went to see Charles II (the *Blackbird*) to invite him to return. Later he supported *King* Monmouth, was indicted for treason but fled to Holland.

SHIKARI THOMPSON Captain F.J. Thompson (died 1883) who had a passion for big game hunting in India.

• *Shikari* is an Urdu word for a hunter.

SHILTS Peter Shilton, *Peter Pan*.

SHOCK WHITE Thomas White, a Reigate cricketer who tried to use a bat wider than the wicket (1771). After that, a bat was limited (1774) to a width of $4^{1}/_{2}$ inches.

SHON SMITH DI ALABAMA Leonard Burlington Smith (died 1898), American entrepreneur and trader; so called in Curaçao in the Netherlands Antilles where he was United States Consul. He produced ice and electricity and built the country's first pontoon bridge.

SHOOTING FOOL, THE

i) Vincent Drucci, the *Schemer*.

ii) George *Bugs* Moran.

SHORTHOSE Robert II, Duke of Normandy, *Curthose*.

SHORT THIGH Robert II, Duke of Normandy, *Curthose*. Drayton (the *Golden Mouthed*) wrote (1596) a poem about him, the title of which included 'surnamed Short-thigh'.

SHOTGUN ZIEGLER Frederick (Fred) Goetz (fl. 1920s), member of the Barker gang, said to have been one of the killers of the St Valentine's Day massacre in Chicago (1929).

• See *Ma* (ii).

SHOVE Stanley Howard Shoveller (1882–1959), English international hockey player, the only Englishman to win two Olympic gold medals (1908 and 1920). *The Times* called him 'The W.G. Grace of Hockey'.

- For W.G. Grace, see the *Champion*.

SHOWBOY Kwame Nkrumah (1909–72), first Prime Minister of the Gold Coast (1952–7) and first President of Ghana (1960–6); because of his flamboyant form of electioneering. Also *Tsobo*.

SHRIMP, THE

i) Jean Shrimpton, Mrs Michael Cox (1942–   ), fashion model (1960s).

ii) Sir Henry Dudley Leveson-Gower (1873–1954), who captained Oxford (1896) and Surrey (post-1908); knighted for his services to cricket (1953). He was a small man; school nickname which persisted.

SHY MILLIONAIRE, THE Sir Max Rayne (1918–   ), British property owner who gave away at least £2,000,000 to help the distressed but does not like publicity. He founded the Max Rayne Foundation to distribute his gifts.

SIDDONS OF AMERICA, THE Mary Ann Duff, the *Queen of the American Stage*.

- Sarah Siddons (1755–1831) was a great British tragic actress, whose Lady Macbeth – it is said – never has and never will be equalled.

SIDER Herbert Sidebotham (1872–1940), British journalist, editor of the *Sunday Times* and famous as Scrutator, political commentator; his nickname at Balliol College, Oxford (1890s) which stuck.

SILENT CAL Calvin Coolidge, *Cautious Cal*.

SILENT COLONEL, THE Colonel H.C. Lowther, the *Father of the House*.

SILENT HARE, THE Francis Hare (fl. late 1700s to early 1800s); because he was so talkative. He spoke several European languages and was in Paris during the Hundred Days (1815) when he went to see Napoleon, much to the annoyance of his countrymen, who considered him a traitor.

SILKEN BEARD Sitric or Sigtrygg, Viking king in Dublin (died 1042), defeated at the battle of Clontarf (1014) by Brian *Boru*. His Norse nickname was 'Silki-Skegg'.

SILKEN THOMAS Thomas Fitzgerald of Offaly, later 10th Earl of Kildare (1513–37). He led a revolt (1534), slew the Archbishop of Dublin and besieged Dublin castle after he had heard that his father (*Garret Oge*) had been arrested for treason. *Silken Thomas* was hanged at Tyburn. He was so called because of the splendour of his dress.

SILLY BILLY

i) William IV, the *Flogster*. He was not very bright.

ii) William Frederick, Duke of Gloucester (1776–1834), nephew of George III (the *Button Maker*); for the same reason. Also *Slice*.

- A silly billy was a clown's 'stooge' – usually young – at a fair or circus.

SILLY DUKE, THE The Duke of Marlborough, *Anne's Great Captain*; from his habit of saying 'Oh! Silly! Silly!' if he did not agree with something.

SILURIST, THE Henry Vaughan (1622–95), Welsh poet and mystic, twin brother of Thomas (*Anthroposophus*); from his love of Breconshire, his birthplace, the ancient inhabitants of which were the Silures, conquered by the Romans (*circa* 78); mentioned by Aubrey. Also the *Swan of Usk*.

SILVER BILLY William Beldham (1766–1862), all-round cricketer from Hambledon, the 'prototype' English cricket club. He helped to establish batting styles still in force. He had silver-white hair.

- See *Old Everlasting*.

SILVER CAPTAIN, THE Admiral Sir Henry Digby (1770–1842). As captain of the frigate *Alcmene*, he took in October 1799 a Spanish ship laden with dollars and earned himself prize-money of £40,730. Seamen received about £180 each. Digby said he dreamed directions to the vessel. He was the father of Jane Digby (*Aurora*). Digby commanded HMS *Africa* at the battle of Trafalgar (1805).

SILVER CLOUD Lord Strathcona and Mount Royal, the *Grand Old Man of Empire*. From the post of junior clerk, he became Governor of the Hudson Bay Company. He paid Indians for animal skins with silver coins.

SILVER FOX Dennis Taylor (1948–   ), British snooker champion, winner of the 1985 Embassy World Championships.

SILVER GREEK, THE Andrea Angela (1930–   ), caddie to Jack Nicklaus (*Blobbo*) for nineteen years (pre-1982). He is wealthy. Nicklaus gave him a restaurant when they parted.

SILVER HAND Sir Humfrey Stafford (*circa* 1473) of Staffordshire, commonly called Humfrey Stafford with the Silver Hand, as the King's Bench records show (Ewen).

SILVER LADY, THE Violet (Betty) Paget-Baxter (died 1972), a friend of down-and-outs in London; because of her practical help.

SILVER-TONGUED, THE
i) Joshua Sylvester (1563–1618), poet and translator, sometimes 'Silver-Tongued Sylvester'; from the quality of his verse.
ii) William Bates (1625–99), vicar of St Dunstan's, Fleet Street, London (post-1652), an eminent preacher. Pepys (the *Father of Black-Letter Lore*) spoke highly of his eloquence but had a low opinion of the man; so called by Dissenters. Also 'Silver-Tongued Bates'.
iii) Anthony Hammond (1688–1738), poet and writer; so called by Lord Bolingbroke (*High-Mettled Mary*).
iv) Spranger Barry, the *Irish Roscius*.
v) Henry Smith (1550–1600), British Puritan cleric, called 'the prime preacher of the nation'.
vi) Heneage Finch, Earl of Nottingham, the *Dismal*.

SILVER TRUMPET OF AUSTRALIA, THE William Kelynack (1832–91), British-born missionary in New South Wales, a great orator.

SILVER TRUMPET OF THE HOUSE, THE Sir Edward Deering, Bart (died 1596), a member of the Long Parliament, with a fine speaking voice.

SILVER-WHISKERED CHAPMAN George Chapman (1559–1634), poet, dramatist and translator, praised by Jonson (the *Bricklayer*) and thought to have been 'the rival poet' of Shakespeare's sonnet; best remembered by the layman through *On First Looking into Chapman's Homer* by Keats (*Pestleman Jack*).

SIMON THE SKIPPER Thomas Hamilton, 6th Earl of Haddington (1680–1735). He was a member of 'The Flying Squadron' (*Squadrone Volante*), the party which declared for union with England. 'Skipper' was a term for a Hanoverian sympathizer.

SINBAD THE TAILOR Lord Shinwell, *Manny*; a trade unionist representing the Glasgow garment workers.
- 'Sinbad the Sailor' was nineteenth-century rhyming slang for a tailor.

SINGER OF EMPIRE, THE Rudyard Kipling, the *Bard of Empire*; so called by *Punch*.

SINGING BRAKE-MAN, THE Jimmie Rodgers, the *Father of Country Music*. He worked for the railway for 15 years. A brake-man is assistant to the conductor in America.

SINGING BUDGIE, THE Kylie Minogue (1968–   ), Australian pop singer and a former star of the Australian television serial *Neighbours*; so called in Australia. She is small.
- A budgerigar is a small parakeet, an Australian lovebird. It does not sing.

SINGING CAPON, THE Nelson Eddy (1901–67), American romantic singer in film musical comedies and operettas, often partner with the *Iron Butterfly*.

SINGING JAMIE James Macpherson (hanged 1700), son of the Laird of Invernesshire and a gipsy woman. He played the violin and composed songs. He joined the gipsies and for his crimes was declared an outlaw. He played the violin on the way to the gallows.

SINGING MOUSE, THE John Bull Binge (?1815–78). Although he sang at Covent Garden, London, he had 'a small voice'.

SINGING STRANGLER, THE Edward Joseph Leonski (1918–42), American GI who murdered three women in Melbourne, Australia, 'for their voices'. He sang before his execution.

SINGLE-SPEECH HAMILTON William Gerard Hamilton (1729–96), whose maiden speech in the House of Commons (November 1755) had an electrifying effect, but who never made another memorable one, even though he became Chancellor of the Exchequer, Ireland. His speech from 2 pm to 2 am is said to have been written for him by his friend Dr Johnson (*Blinking Sam*).

SINGULAR DOCTOR, THE William of Occam, *Doctor Invincibilis*.

SINNER-SAVED HUNTINGDON William Huntingdon, the *Coal-Heaver Preacher*.

SINNERS' FRIEND, THE The Reverend Theobald Mathews, the *Apostle of Temperance*. He went out of his way to help the worst type of social outcast.

SIR AJAX Sir John Harington (1561–1612), courtier and poet who tried to improve domestic sanitation in England. He published a tract (1596), *The Metamorphosis of Ajax*. He designed the first water-closet (1589) for his house.

• A jakes was an Elizabethan term for a privy.

SIR ALMOST RIGHT Sir Almroth Edward Wright (1861–1947), bacteriologist who introduced anti-typhoid inoculation. He was professor of experimental pathology at the University of London, where he was given the nickname.

SIR ALWAYS AND LADY SOMETIMES TIPSY Sir Beaumont Dixie and his wife (1880s).

• Lady Florence Caroline Dixie (1857–1905) was a writer and traveller who married Sir Alexander Beaumont Churchill Dixie, 11th baronet (1875). She alleged without proof that she had been the victim of a Fenian outrage near Windsor (1883) and advocated complete sex equality.

• The Fenians were members of an anti-British secret society dedicated to making it impossible for Britain to rule in Ireland. They committed many terrorist crimes in London, and the Phoenix Park murders of 1882 in Dublin.

SIR ANTHONY ABSOLUTE William Dowton (1764–1851), an English actor.

• Sir Anthony Absolute is a character in *The Rivals* by Sheridan (*Sherry*).

SIR BULLFACE DOUBLE-FEE Sir Fletcher Norton, 1st Baron Grantley (1716–89), noted lawyer and Speaker of the House of Commons. William Hickey (*Pickle*) calls him in his memoirs 'a rough violent man by nature'. Hickey, a lawyer's clerk, used to take him papers to sign. Walpole (the *Autocrat of Strawberry Hill*) said that Sir Fletcher took money from both parties in a court action and used the statements of one against the other. Norton entertained Captain James Cook (1728–79) to dinner (1776) before Cook left on his last voyage. A sound off Alaska was named in his honour.

SIR CUMFERENCE Sir Harry Secombe (1921–   ), British comedian and singer, after he had been knighted for his services to the theatre. He is stout.

SIR DAN Daniel Donnelly (fl. 18th century), Irish bare-knuckled boxing champion.

SIR GEORGE PROVENDER Sir George Warrender (fl. mid-18th century), a renowned English epicure who gave good dinner-parties, but economized on heating his house.

SIR JACK BRAG Sir John Burgoyne, *Gentleman Johnny*.

SIR LEISURELY TRUNDLE Sir Leslie Rundle (1856–1934), Adjutant-General of the Egyptian Army (1890s) and later Governor of Malta (1909–15).

SIR REVERSE General Sir Redvers Henry Buller, VC (1839–1908) who after a distinguished career found that he was no match for the Boers in the South African War (1899) and suffered many defeats.

SIR ROGER DOWLER Suraj-ud-Dowlah (?1729–57), Nawab of Bengal, whose name is associated with the Black Hole of Calcutta (1756); the pronunciation of his name by British troops.

SISTER OF SHAKESPEARE Joanna Baillie, *Shakespeare in Petticoats*.

SIXTEEN-STRING JACK John Rann (died 1744), English highwayman who wore eight strings (ribbons) at each knee of his breeches, a practice he began when he was a private coachman in London. He was always a dandy, and in court wore a large bunch of flowers at his breast and tied his irons with blue ribbons. He was hanged. Earlier he had been an associate of *Eight-String Jack*.

SIXY SMITH C.I.J. Smith (1906–79), a powerful batsman for Middlesex; so called from his habit of hitting sixes. Once he scored 66 runs in 18 minutes, including 8 sixes.

SKEE Robert Riegel (1914–), amateur golf champion (1947); later professional.

SKEETS

i) John Henry Martin (1875–1944), the first successful Australian jockey in England. He won the Derby in 1902.

ii) Richard Gallagher (1891–1955), American vaudeville and film star; from 'skeeter', a mosquito.

SKELETON DUDE, THE Edward C. Hagner (1892–1962), American, 3 stone (42 lb) and 5 ft 7 in tall.

SKID ROW SLASHER, THE Charles Sears (1949–), imprisoned after a week-long rampage in which he cut the throats of 15 down-and-outs, killing two (1981). He had been forced to live on New York's Skid Row after service in Vietnam.

SKIFF SKIPTON Sir Lumley St George Skeffington (1771–1850), British playwright and fop, one of the circle around George (*Adonis of Fifty*) when Prince of Wales. James Gillray (1757–1815) published a cartoon of Skeffington dancing, labelled 'Skiffy Skipt-on'.

SKIN AND BONE Senator William Mahone (1826–95), Confederate general and politician; so called by his men by assonance. He was small and thin, weighing just over 7 stone (about 100 lb).

SKINNER Sidney Normanton (1926–), of Barnsley FC, the only footballer to become famous after he had retired, when Michael Parkinson (the *Mouth*) confessed on television to an early hero-worship of him.

SKINNY Lesley Hornby, the *Matchstick*.

SKIP Stewart Alexander (1918–), profes-

sional golfer in the American Ryder Cup team (1949 and 1951).

SKIPPER, THE Admiral the Honourable Henry Murray (died 1865), friend of Sir Samuel Baker (1821–93), the explorer.

SKITTLES Catharine Walters (1839–1920), celebrated beautiful courtesan, mistress of the Marquis of Hartington (*Harty-Tarty*) and 'friend' of Edward VII (the *Peacemaker*). She was the daughter of a Liverpool Customs tide-waiter and won her nickname as a young girl helping in a skittle-alley. It is alleged that when she was annoyed by a group of drunken Guards officers, she threatened to knock them down like 'a row of bloody skittles'.

SLAMBINO *Babe* Ruth.

SLAPSIE MAXIE Max Rosenbloom (1906–76), American actor in boxing and gangster films; from his boxing parts and rhyme with 'Maxie'.

SLASHER, THE Kenneth (Ken) Mackay (1926–82), Queensland and Australia cricketer who played in 37 Test Matches between 1956 and 1963. He hit out without scoring many runs. He was a good medium-pace bowler.

SLASHER MARY Mary Raleigh Richardson (1889–1961), British suffragette who cut the *Rokeby Venus* in the National Gallery (1914) with a chopper.

SLEDGEHAMMER, THE H.H. Asquith, *Old Wait and See*; his nickname in the House of Commons from his forceful tactics to secure mastery in a difficult situation in Parliament.

SLICE The Duke of Gloucester, *Silly Billy*.

- Grose (1785): To take a slice: to intrigue, particularly with a married woman.

SLICK LEONARD Robert (Bob) Leonard (1932–), American baseball manager.

SLIGGER Francis Urquhart (died 1935), a don at Balliol college, Oxford University for forty years.

SLIM

i) Otis Dewet Whitman, jnr (1924–), American singer.

ii) George J. Summerville (1892–1946), sad-faced American film actor who began his career as a comedian with Mack Sennett (the **King of Comedy**).

SLIM JANNIE Field Marshal Jan Christiaan Smuts (1870–1950), twice Prime Minister of South Africa (1919–24 and 1939–48). He fought against the British in the South African War (1899–1902) but afterwards co-operated to help to found the Union of South Africa as well as having been a major factor in the creation of the British Commonwealth and the United Nations.

- *Slim* is Afrikaans for clever, crafty.

SLIM PIET P.J. Joubert, **Oom Piet**.

SLINGER Homedale Carl Nitsche (1905–82), batsman for Australia and South Australia.

SLINGIN' SAMMY Samuel Adrian Baugh (1914–   ), American quarterback for the Washington Redskins; All-America footballer in the Hall of Fame (1937–52). He was the most powerful thrower in the game.

SLIPPERY JOHN The Earl of Breadalbane, **Grey John**, said to have been as cunning as a fox and as slippery as an eel.

SLIP-UP OF THE YARD Detective-Chief Superintendent Jack Slipper (1925–   ) of Scotland Yard who failed to bring back Ronald Biggs (1929–   ), one of the Great Train Robbers (1963), from Brazil (1974).

SLOWLUGS Jock Armstrong, border reiver, captured (1606) with Tom Armstrong and Chris Irvine by Lord Howard (**Bauld Willie**). They were hanged.

- 'Lugs' are ears in Scotland or northern England dialect.

SLOW TROT General G.H. Thomas, **Old Reliable**. He was slow in his actions; so called by his soldiers, from the military command.

SLY See the **Italian Stallion**.

SLY BOOTS Lord Guilford (North), the - **Palinurus of State**.

- 'Sly Boots' is slang for a crafty person, usually one who poses as simple but is 'deep'; since about 1680.

SLY FOX, THE Henry Fox, 1st Baron Holland (1705–74), an expert in corruption. As Paymaster-General during a large part of the Seven Years' War (1756–63), he amassed a fortune, by legally retaining the interest on almost £50,000,000 that passed through his hands. The City of London called him 'the public defaulter of unaccounted millions'.

SMACK Fletcher Henderson (1898–1952), American jazz pianist and band leader.

SMALL-BEER POET, THE William Thomas Fitzgerald (*circa* 1759–1829); so called by **Boney Cobbett**.

SMALL-LIGHT THROOP Governor Enos T. Throop (1784– ?) American, who in the elections of 1830 said that the wisdom of man was a small light; so called by his political opponents.

SMELFUNGUS Tobias George Smollett (1721–71), British novelist famous for *Roderick Random* (1748) and *Humphrey Clinker* (1771); so called by Sterne (the **English Rabelais**) after the publication of *Travels in France and Italy* (1766) which was acidly critical. Also the **Vagabond Scot**.

- A smelfungus or smellfungus is a grumbler or fault-finder. Smollett is itself a nickname (Reaney), from 'small head' (*Smalheued*, 1332).

SMIFFY See **Smitty**.

SMILER Gary Lineker, **Garygoal**.

SMILEY Lyman Quick (1907–   ), American Public Links golf champion (1946); so called because of his constant grin. He took it as his first name.

SMILING DUCHESS, THE (1900–) The Duchess of York, later Queen Elizabeth, the Queen-Mother (1900–   ).

SMITH or MR SMITH Kumar Shri Duleepsinji, **Duleep**. He liked to be called by this name.

SMITHY

i) Ian Douglas Smith (1919–   ), Rhodesian Prime Minister (officially 1964–5), who brought about a unilateral declaration of independence or UDI which lasted (from 1965 to 1970, when Zimbabwe was created).

ii) Sir Charles Kingsford-Smith (1897–1935), Australian airman who flew with companions from Oakland, California to Brisbane, Australia (1928).

SMITTY or SMIFFY Michael (Mike) Smith (1955–), British disc jockey and television personality.

SMOKER John Mills (died 1749), English smuggler who tortured a Customs officer to death. He was also one of those who broke into the Customs-House at Poole, Dorset (1749). His nickname is spelt 'Smoaker' in contemporary prints.

SMOKEY

i) Walter Emmons Alston (1911–84), American baseball manager for Brooklyn (1955–6) and Los Angeles (1963) when the teams won national league pennants.

ii) Vivian Alexander Richards (1952–), batsman for Somerset and West Indies Captain; short for *Smokin' Joe*.

SMOKIN' JOE

i) Joseph (Joe) Frazier (1944–), American heavyweight boxing champion of the world (1970–3); from his non-stop 'smoking' style of furious fighting. He became a successful Philadelphia businessman.

ii) Viv Richards, *Smokey*; from his resemblance to (i).

SMOLLETT OF THE STAGE, THE George Farquhar, the *Fielding of Drama*.

• Smollett, see *Smelfungus*.

SMOOTH JOHN John or Ian Macnab (died 1653), chief of the Macnab.

SMUGGINS Nigel Lawson (1932–), Chancellor of the Exchequer (1983–9); school nickname which has lasted.

SNAKE, THE P.B. Shelley, *Ariel*; so called by Byron (*Baby*), because of his smooth, gliding manner, bright eyes and light diet.

SNAKEHIPS Kenneth (Ken) Johnson (died 1941), Trinidadian band leader killed with some of his musicians when a bomb fell on the Café de Paris, London.

SNIPE, THE Princess Dorothea Christopher-ovna Lieven, prominent in London society in the 1820s; mistress of Prince Metternich (1773–1859).

SNOBBY ROBERTS Margaret Thatcher, *Attila the Hen*; her school nickname.

SNOOKER R.M. Ellison, *Rilla*.

SNOOPY Geoffrey Dickens, M.P., (1931–), noted for raising controversial issues in Parliament; so called in the House of Commons.

• Snoopy is an American cartoon character.

SNOW QUEEN, THE Elizabeth Stuart, *Goody Palsgrave*, wife of 'The Winter or Snow King', Frederick V, Elector Palatine.

• See the *Winter Queen*.

SNOWSHOE THOMPSON John Thorensen (1827–76), Norwegian emigrant to America who carried mail across the Sierra Nevada for about twenty years. He made the 90 mile journey from California to Nevada in three days. He introduced skiing to California (1856).

SNUFF Charles Stanhope, 4th Earl of Harrington (1780–1851). As Viscount Petersham, he made a snuff mixture which was named after him. On one side of his apartment, say Gronow, were beautiful jars...'of innumerable kinds of snuff'.

SNUFFY CHARLOTTE Queen Charlotte Sophia (1744–1818), formerly Princess of Mecklenburg, who was very fond of snuff. Gronow says she was the principal cause of making it popular in England.

SOAP KING, THE William Hesketh Lever, 1st Baron Leverhulme (1851–1925), founder of Lever Brothers and Unilever, makers of soap and margarine.

SOAPY SAM Samuel Wilberforce (1805–1873), Bishop of Oxford who opposed Darwin's thesis at the famous British Association's meeting (1860); from his unctuous manner.

• See *Darwin's Bulldog*.

SOCCO THE BRACER Joseph Smith (1844–73), New York gangster.

SOCIETY CLOWN, THE George Grossmith (1847–1912), British musical comedy star. He used the nickname as the title of his autobiography (1888).

SOCK-IT-TO-ME GIRL, THE Judy Carne (1939–), English-born star of the American TV 'Laugh-In' show. It was a catch phrase she frequently used (fl. 1970s). Her real name is Joyce Botterill.

SOFTSWORD or JOHN SOFTSWORD King
John, *Lackland*, reported by the chron-
icler Gervase of Canterbury (died *circa*
1210) after John made peace with Philip
of France by the Treaty of Goulet (1200).
Gervase himself disagreed with the nickname. John lost Normandy later (1204).

SOLDIERS' BISHOP, THE The Reverend
Arthur Robins (1834–99), army chaplain,
especially to the Household Brigade
(post-1873).

SOLDIERS' FRIEND, THE
i) Sir Charles Napier, *Old Fagin*. When a
public subscription began for a statue to
him in London, the majority of those
who gave money were, or had been,
private soldiers.
ii) Frederick Augustus, Duke of York
(1763–1827), who when
Commander-in-Chief, British Army,
abolished favouritism and political
influence in gaining promotion and
introduced measures to improve the lot
of the ordinary soldier. He was called
'The Grand Old Duke of York' in a
contemporary jingle.

SOLDIERS' GENERAL, THE Lieutenant-
General Sir Brian Horrocks (1896–1985),
a brilliant tactician who out-generalled
Rommel in the Western Desert and Normandy (World War II).

SOLID DOCTOR, THE
i) Thomas Bradwardine, *Doctor Profundus*.
ii) Richard Middleton, *Doctor Profundus*.

SOLLY Lord Salisbury, *A Lathe painted to Look like Iron*.

SOLOMON OF BARDS, THE Matthew Prior,
Plenipo Rummer; so called by D'Israeli.

SOLOMON THE SECOND
i) Henry VII, the *British Solomon*.
ii) James I, the *British Solomon*.

SOLOMON OF ENGLAND, THE James I
(above).

SONGBIRD OF THE SOUTH, THE Kate
Smith (1909–), born in Greenville, Virginia.

SONNIE Robert Hale (1902–59), British light
comedian in musical comedies.

SONNY
i) Elmer Lewis Dunham (1914–),
American jazz trombonist and trumpeter.
ii) Charles Liston, the *Big Bear*.
iii) Bowen Charleston Tufts (1911–70),
burly American film actor.
iv) Sir Shridath Ramphal (1928–),
Secretary-General of the Commonwealth.

SONNY TERRY Saunders Teddell (1911–
86), blind American jazz harmonica
player and singer.

SON OF BELIAL, THE Marchmont Needham, the *Cobbett of His Day*; so called in
the *Mercurius Britannicus* (started by
Thomas Archer: 1554–1634 in 1625) before Needham took it over.
• 'Belial' the Hebrew word 'worthless',
  is used in the New Testament as a
  term for Satan (2 Corinthians v.15).
  'Sons of Belial' (1 Samuel ii 12) meant
  'wicked man'. It is not a proper name
  in its original use.

SON OF BONAPARTE, THE Jonathan
Martin (1782–1838), British eccentric
who burned down part of the south-west
tower of York Minster (1829). He was
found insane, and died in the Bethlehem
Hospital, London (Bedlam); self-styled in
notes (with the spelling 'Boneypart') he
spiked on the precincts railings.

SON OF SAM David Berkowitz (1953–),
American sex killer of six girls during attacks on courting couples. Seven others
were wounded in attacks in New York
City (1976–7); from his signature on
letters to the *Daily News* and the Police
Department; a name invented from that
of a neighbour, Sam Carr. Berkowitz was
sentenced (1977) to 365 years in prison,
and is now in an asylum.

SON OF THE LAST MAN, THE Charles II,
the *Blackbird*; so called by the royalists.
Charles I had been nicknamed by Parliament the *Last Man*.

SON OF THE PRIEST, THE Ferchar *Macin-
sagairt* or Farquhar, first chief of the clan
Ross (fl. 12th century) who in 1215 took
his clansmen to assist Alexander II of
Scotland (the *Little Red Fox*) against
rebellion. Ferchar was hereditary abbot of
Drumcliffe, Ireland and a descendant of

Niall of the Nine Hostages. Alexander created him Earl of Ross.

- *Sagairt* = priest. His nickname became the name McTaggart.

SON OF THE SAINT, THE Lord Macaulay, *Babbletongue*; so called in *Noctes Ambrosianae*. He was the son of Zachary Macaulay (1768–1838), the Governor of Sierra Leone, West Africa (1793–9) and a member of the Anti-Slavery Society (post-1823).

- The followers of William Wilberforce (the *Man of Black Renown*) were sardonically called in Parliament 'The Saints'.

SON OF THUNDER Edward Irving, *Boanerges*.

SOUPY Milton Hines (1926–), American comedian who added 'Sales' to it and used it as a stage-name. It started because 'Hines' sounds like 'Heinz'.

SOUTH AMERICAN LAFAYETTE, THE Lord Cochrane, the *Devil*: nickname given to him by the Brazilians whose country he helped to free from Portuguese rule (1822).

- The Marquis Marie-Joseph Lafayette (1757–1834) was a French general who fought in the American War of Independence.

SOUTH'S AVENGING ANGEL, THE James Wilkes Booth (1838–65), American actor who assassinated President Abraham Lincoln (*Father Abraham*) in 1865, shouting '*Sic semper tyrannis*. The South is avenged!' so called in the South after his death.

SOV, THE Queen Elizabeth, *Brenda*; so called by royal servants, from 'sovereign'.

SPAGNOLET OF THE THEATRE, THE Colley Cibber, *King Coll*; so called by Samuel Sandford.

- See the *Poetical Spagnoletto*.

SPANISH GRANDEE, THE James Duff, 4th Earl of Fife (1776–1857) who was given a Spanish title for his services in her army against Napoleon; so called in *Noctes Ambrosianae*.

SPANISH JACK John Symmonds, alias Bli Gonzales (hanged 1756) who served as a British privateer, joined a gang of smugglers and then a band of thieves in London; captured by Macdaniel, the *Blood Money Man* after the theft of a silver tankard.

SPANISH JOHN John Macdonell, *Macdonell Scotus*. He had fought in the Spanish army.

SPANISH LEWIS John Frederick Lewis (1805–1876), British painter of Spanish subjects.

SPANKY George Emmett McFarland (1928–), American child film actor ('Our Gang').

SPARROW, THE Shri Lal Bahadur Shastri (1904–1966), Prime Minister of India (1964–6), a small man. He adapted the name 'Shastri', which means something like 'Jewel of learning', and is earned by studies in Brahminism.

SPECKLED, THE Domnall, King of Dalriada (killed 642).

- See the *Fair* (iii). Domnall or Domhnull = Daniel.

SPEEDY

i) Louis Babbs, American Wall of Death rider who once made 1,000 consecutive loops (1934).

ii) Victor J. Marks (1955–), Oxford University, Somerset and England cricketer.

SPENCER BUCK Mrs Woodham (1743–1803), British singer and actress.

SPENSER OF ENGLISH PROSE WRITERS, THE Jeremy Taylor, the *Shakespeare of Divines*.

SPIDER

i) Mariel Hemingway (1961–), American film actress, grand-daughter of Ernest (*Papa*) so called in her 'teens because of her long legs.

ii) James (Jim) Kelly, American featherweight boxing champion (1938–9) and his son (below).

iii) William (Billy) Kelly, champion at the same weight (1955–6).

iv) Edgar Courance (1904–69), American jazz saxophonist and clarinettist.

SPIDERMAN Paul Hebel (1949–), one of the Boarded Barn murderers; thin as a child.

- See *Bouncer* and *Puss*.

SPIKE

i) Patrick Cairns Hughes (1908–87), British composer and critic; top British jazz musician.

ii) Edward Howard (1877–1946), American professional strong-man and the world's record blood-donor (1,056 pints).

iii) Michael Watkins (1954–), hooker in the Welsh rugby football team and its captain. He also plays for Newport.

iv) Terence Milligan (1918–), British comedian and an 'original' of the Goon Show.

v) James Kennedy (1855–?), American cattleman who disappeared after having been acquitted of the alleged murder of the Mayor of Dodge City, Kansas, James *Dog* Kelly (1878).

vi) Lindley Armstrong Jones (1911–1965), American band leader ('City Slickers').

SPIKY SULLIVAN J.L Sullivan, the *Boston Strong Boy*.

SPIN KING, THE Sonny Ramadhin (1929–), West Indian spin bowler; now landlord of the White Lion public-house at Delph in the Pennines.

SPINNING SPOON, THE Sir Robert Peel, *Jenny*; so called in *Noctes Ambrosianae*.

• A 'spoon' was eighteenth-century slang for a foolish fellow. 'Spinning' was word-play on his father's trade (*Parsley Peel*) and Peel's political gyrations.

SPIRO Jonathan P. Agnew (1960–), Leicestershire fast bowler; from Spiro Agnew (see below).

SPIRO T. EGGPLANT Spiro Theodore Agnew (1918–), Vice-President (1969–73), the first to resign under pressure. His real name is Anagnostopoulos. When I was in the USA while he was in office, people were wearing lapel badges asking 'Spiro Who?' I was never able to verify it, but I always thought 'Eggplant' was a malicious reversal of the idea of *Egghead*'. Also the *White Knight*.

SPIV Michael (Mike) Yarwood (1941–), British impersonator; school nickname.

• 'Spiv' (from 'spiff' and 'spiffing') is one who gets a living by doing as little as possible, within the law if he can (1930s).

SPLENDID SPLINTER, THE

i) James (Jim) Ray (1941–), American basketball star.

ii) Theodore (Ted) Williams (1918–), American baseball player; Hall of Fame (1939–60). He played for Boston Red Sox.

SPOFF F.A. Spofforth, the *Demon*.

SPONGE

i) Craig Chalmers (1968–), Scottish international Rugby Union player. He spends most Sunday afternoons acting as 'sponge man' for a soccer team from a public-house in his home town of Melrose.

ii) Thomas (Tommy) Baldwin (1945–), inside forward for Chelsea and Arsenal F.C's; so called at Chelsea because of the amount of hard work he could soak up in a game.

SPORTING JOE Heneage, 7th Earl of Aylesford, the *Jedge*, rake and one of the Prince of Wales' set in the 1860s-1870s. In 1876 he was the centre of a scandal when he threatened to divorce his wife, Lady Edith Aylesford, who was in love with George, Lord Blandford (1844–92), heir to the 7th Duke of Marlborough. Aylesford declared the Prince of Wales supported him, and the threat of scandal involving the Prince brought him and his wife social ostracism. The Earl went to Wyoming to ranch. George became the 8th Duke.

SPORTING PARSON, THE The Reverend John Russell (1795–1883), rector of Black Torrington, Devon, breeder of the Jack Russell terriers.

SPORTING PRINCE, THE

i) Edward, Prince of Wales, the *Peacemaker* who was interested in many sports especially horse-racing. He won the Derby twice (1896-1900) and a third time after he had become King.

ii) Edward, Prince of Wales, the *Pragger-Wagger*), with a love for steeplechasing.

SPORUS Lord Hervey, *Lord Fanny*; so called by Pope (the *Bard of Twickenham*), from his effeminate habits.

- Sporus was the favourite who 'married' the Emperor Nero (reigned 54-68).

SPOTLESS MINISTER, THE William Pitt, the *Bottomless Pit*. He had a rigid rule – for example never to accept presents.

SPOTTED DOG Graham Dilley, *Picca*.

SPOTTED JANE Margaret Rowlynson, alias dicta (= called) Spotted Jane, Cheshire, 1606. Chester Records (Ewen).

SPOT WARD Joshua Ward (1685–1761), a London quack doctor whose fame – and burial in Westminster Abbey – was assured when he treated George II (*Augustus*) for an injury to his thumb. He wrenched it, the King kicked him and cursed, but the injury was healed. Ward opened a hospital for the poor in London. He was so called from a birthmark on his face.

SPRING, TOM Thomas (Tom) Winter (1795–1851), an English pugilist who beat Jack Langan, champion of Ireland, for a purse of £1,000 (1824), a fight seen by 50,000.

SPRINGFIELD RIFLE, THE
i) David (Davey) Moore (died 1963), world featherweight boxing champion (1959–63).
ii) Tony Mayotte (1961–), American top-class tennis player with the Wimbledon singles championships in his sights. From the bullet-like serve-and-smash style of play.

SPRING-HEELED JACK The *Mad Marquis* of Waterford; from his habit of frightening people by jumping out on them from the shadows. He was noted for cruel practical jokes.

- 'Spring-heeled Jack' was a common term in the late eighteenth and early nineteenth centuries for someone who liked doing this and was used, for example, for highwaymen; also tho name of a figure in Victorian Punch-and-Judy shows.

SPURGEON OF THE NORTH, THE The Very Reverend Hewlett Johnson, the *Red Dean*, when he was a parish priest in Lancashire.

- See the *Boy Preacher*.

SQUAW KILLER, THE General *Autie* Custer; so called by the Cheyenne Indians after the massacre of Black Kettle's people at Wasjita (1868).

SQUEAKY Lynette Alice Fromme (1949–), of Charles Manson's American pseudo-religious sect. She was sentenced to life imprisonment (1975) for having tried to assassinate Gerald R. Ford (born 1913: President 1974–7) in California.

SQUINTING JACK John Wilkes (1727–97), British M.P. famous for his attack in *The North Briton* (issue No 45:1763) on the king's speech which he said was false.

- See *Immateriality Baxter*.

SQUIRE ABINGTON George Alexander Baird, Baron Auchmeddon (1861–93), a rich rake and well-known sportsman who did not like being called 'Mr Baird' (his Scottish title was not used) and preferred 'Squire Abington', which he used as an amateur jockey. His private life – which included an affair with *Lillie* Langtry – was notorious, and he was blackballed from a number of London clubs. He inherited £3,000,000 from his father. Also 'The Squire'.

SQUIRE GAWKY Lord Temple, the *Gawky Squire*.

SQUIRE MORGAN Henry Frederick, Duke of Cumberland (1745–1790), son of Frederick, Prince of Wales (*Prince Titi*) and brother of George III (the *Button Maker*); so called in *Noctes Ambrosianae*; an alias he used in an intrigue with Lady Henrietta Grosvenor.

SQUIRE OF PICCADILLY, THE William Stone (1857–1958), chairman of the trustees for the Albany Chambers, Piccadilly, London, where he lived as a man-about-town.

SQUIRE OF SANDRINGHAM, THE Edward VII, the *Peacemaker*, a country gentleman there.

STAGECOACH KING OF THE WEST, THE Ben Holladay, the *Napoleon of the West*. He took over the system of coaching and wagon-trains pioneered by John Butterfield, President of the Overland Mail Co.

STAGE BOYD William Boyd (1890–1935), American actor; to distinguish him from

William Boyd (1898–1972), 'Hopalong Cassidy' in films for many years.

STAGE LEVIATHAN, THE James Quin (1693–1766), a famous, but reputedly bad-mannered actor; so called by Churchill (the *British Juvenal*); also the *Whitefield of the Stage*.

STAINLESS David Steele (1941–   ), cricketer for Northants and England.

STALIN'S NANNY Vera Joan Maynard (1921–   ), Labour MP for Sheffield (Brightside), a fervent left-wing politician.

- Joseph Stalin, whose assumed name means 'steel' (his real name was Joseph Vissarionovich Dzhugashvili: 1879–1953) was an aggressive dictator of Russia from 1924 until his death.

STALKY Major-General Lionel Charles Dunsterville (1865–1946), in command of the Dunsterville Mission to Baku (1918); so called by Kipling (the *Bard of Empire*) in *Stalky and Co* (1899) and used by Dunsterville for the title of his autobiography, *Stalky's Reminiscences* (1928).

- 'Stalky' was schoolboy slang for someone clever or ingenious.

STALYBRIDGE INFANT, THE Samuel Hurd (1832–92), champion wrestler of Lancashire. He was 6 ft $2^1/_2$ in tall and weighed 15 stone (210 lb).

- Stalybridge is in Cheshire.

STAN The Earl of St Andrews; nickname created by himself from 'St. Andrews'.

- See *Brainbox*.

STANDARD BEARER, THE William Maginn, the *Adjutant*; so called in *Noctes Ambrosianae*. For a short time, he was a joint editor of *The National Standard*.

STAR Evelyn Edward Boscawen, 7th Viscount Falmouth (1847–1918).

STARCH JOHNNY John Crowne (?1640–1703), Restoration dramatist and favourite of Charles II (the *Blackbird*); from the stiffness of his collar.

STAR OF THE STUART LINE, THE James IV of Scotland (1473–1513), credited with the unification of the country. He was learned, wise, brave and generous.

STARVATION DUNDAS Henry Dundas, 1st Viscount Melville (1742–1811), British statesman. He introduced the word 'starvation' into the English language during a debate in Parliament on a Bill (1775) for 'restraining trade and commerce with the New England colonies'. Walpole (the *Autocrat of Strawberry Hill*) and W. Mason gave him the nickname (1781–2), sometimes using 'Starvation' alone.

STATE APOTHECARY, THE John Claudius Beresford, son of John Beresford (the *King of Ireland*); so called because of his cruelties at his riding-school in Dublin to obtain information which revealed the conspiracy for the Irish rebellion (1798). He said he had 'put a poultice on insurrection to bring it to a head'.

STATE PROTEUS, THE Matthew Prior, *Plenipo Rummer*, renowned for changes of sides in politics.

STATE'S CORRECTOR, THE Sir Samuel Romilly (1757–1818), British law reformer who obtained the repeal of the Elizabethan statute which made it a capital offence to steal from the person; so called by Byron (*Baby*).

STEEL KING, THE Andrew Carnegie (1835–1919), Scottish-born American industrialist who founded US Steel (1901). He was a notable philanthropist.

STEENIE George Villiers, 1st Duke of Buckingham (1592–1628), English statesman and favourite of James I (the *British Solomon*) who made him Lord High Admiral of England when he was twenty-seven; so called by James because he thought Buckingham looked like the statue of St Stephen in Whitehall, with the 'face of an angel'.

STELLA Esther or Hesther Johnson (1689–1728), daughter of the steward to Sir William Temple (1628–99) at Moor Park, near Farnham, Surrey; so called by Swift. (*Dr Presto*), secretary to Temple, in his letters to her, *Journal to Stella* (1766) published posthumously.

STEVE

i) Theodore Brown (1890–1965), American string bass player.

ii) Sylvester J. Wittman (1904–   ),

American airman, racing pilot and inventor of single-seater planes.

STEWARD, THE

i) Robert II of Scotland, ***Blear-Eye***. When seventeen, he was Regent for his nephew David, who became king at the age of five. Robert succeeded him (1371), and was the first Stewart (from Steward) king.

• David II, see ***Joan Makepeace***.

ii) Walter Fitz-Alan (died 1326), Hereditary High Steward of Scotland, who married Margery (died 1316), daughter of Robert the ***Bruce***. He was known as 'Walter the Steward', and was the father of (i). Walter was the first to use the name 'Stewart'.

STEWPOT Edward Stewart (1941–), British radio disc jockey with the BBC for thirteen years (post 1970).

STICKS

i) Lesley Hornby, the ***Matchstick***; her school nickname.

ii) Winston Silcott (1958–), gaoled for 30 years (1987) for murder. He led a mob which hacked P.C. Blakelock to death (1985) in the riots at Tottenham. He was on bail at the time on a charge of murder for which he was later given life, Silcott was a gangster who 'ruled' Broadwater Farm estate. Police called him the 'godfather of Broadwater Farm'.

STINKER Richard Murdoch (1907–), English comedian still acting at eighty; so called from a part he played in a radio series *Much Binding in the Marsh* in the 1940s.

STINKING BILLY The Duke of Cumberland, ***Billy***; Cumberland was so called in Scotland after Culloden.

STOAT David Gower, ***Lulu***.

STOCKWELL STRANGLER, THE Kenneth Erskine (1964–), sentenced to 40 years imprisonment (1988) for the murders of seven pensioners in 15 weeks (1987). He is believed to have murdered five others. He was said in court to have the brain of an 11-year-old child.

STOCKYARD BLUEBEARD, THE Johann Hoch (1855–1906), German-born employee of a meat-packing firm in Chicago who married 24 women (1892–1905) and

either murdered or abandoned them. He was hanged.

STONEMASON OF CROMARTY, THE Hugh Miller (1802–56), Scottish stonemason who became the most celebrated geologist of his time. His works included *The Testimony of the Rocks* (1857). He shot himself.

STONEWALL Thomas Jonathan Jackson, ***Old Jack***, Confederate General in the American Civil War, whose nickname derived from a remark by General Barnard Bee (1823–61) at the battle of Bull Run (1861): 'See, there is Jackson standing like a stone wall'. Jackson was then a major, but he became the right arm to Lee (the ***Bayard of the Confederate Army***).

STOUT, THE Aedh *Reamhar* (died 1346), King of Ulster (1344–6).

• *Reamhar* is from the Gaelic *ramh* = fat, plump or corpulent.

STOUT HARRY Henry VIII, ***Bluff Hal***.

STOUT SKIPPON Sergeant-Major-General P. Skippon, ***Honest Skippon***.

STORMY PETREL OF POLITICS, THE Lord Eldon, ***Old Bags***, Lord Chancellor (post-1799). He was a conservative who fought reform wherever he saw the need.

STRAFER GOTT Lieutenant-General William Haig Ewart Gott (1897–1942) who was shot down in the Western Desert (August 1942) after he had been given the command of the Eighth Army.

• A strafer is one who attacks fiercely; from the German *strafen* to punish, current in World War I, e.g. *Gott strafe England*, the association of which gave the General his nickname.

STRANGLER, THE Edward Lewis (1890–1966), American world champion professional wrestler who fought 6,200 bouts in 44 years and won the world title five times between 1921 and 1932. His real name was Robert Friedrich.

STRATA SMITH William Smith, the ***Father of English Geology***.

STRAWBERRY The Duchess of York, - ***Carrot Top***; a school nickname mentioned by her (1988).

STRENUOUS JEFFREY Sir Jeffrey Hudson, the *King's Dwarf*. He was a captain of horse in the English Civil War, fought two duels and was captured by the French and pirates.

STRICKEN DEER, THE William Cowper, the *Bard of Olney* He was gentle and humane but suffered from depressive mania which made him attempt suicide.

STROLLER, THE Charles Richard Gough (1962–), defender for Tottenham Hotspur and Dundee United; from the way he plays.

STRONGBOW Richard de Clare, 2nd Earl of Pembroke (died 1176), renowned for his prowess with the long bow.

STRONGEST MAN IN THE WORLD, THE
i) Eugene Sandow (1867–1925), Prussian who made his name on the British music-halls.
ii) George Hackenschmidt, the *Russian Lion*.
iii) Geoffrey (Geoff) Capes (1949–), British Olympic athlete; proved by competition on TV where he won the Transworld title (1984).

STUFFED PROPHET, THE Stephen Grover Cleveland (1837–1908), twice President of the USA (1885–9, 1893–7); so called by *The New York Sun* in the 1892 Presidential campaign.

STUFF SMITH Hezekiah Gordon Smith (1909–63), American jazz violinist.

STUFFY Air-Marshal Hugh Caswell Tremenheere, 1st Baron Dowding (1882–1970), Head of Fighter Command, RAF in the Battle of Britain (World War II). He was a lonely man and did not mix well. Also 'The Leader of the Few'.

STUMPY Floyd Maurice Brady (1910–), American jazz trombone player.

STUNT KING, THE F.E. Bussy (fl. 1920s), British business manager and developer for the Northcliffe newspapers.

STURDY JOHN John Lilburne, *Freeborn John*. He showed great courage when undergoing punishment, e.g. when he was publicly whipped from the Fleet prison to the Palace Yard, Westminster where he stood in the pillory (for having circulated publications offensive to the bishops).

SUBSCRIPTION JAIMIE Sir James Mackintosh, the *Apostate*; so called in *Noctes Ambrosianae*.

SUBTLE DOCTOR, THE John Duns Scotus, *Doctor Subtilis*.

SUBWAY VIGILANTE, THE Bernhard Goetz (1948–), American electronics engineer who shot and wounded four young men who tried to mug him in the New York underground. His action was approved by almost all Americans (1985); cleared by a court of attempted murder (1987).

SUCK-ALL-CREAM Samuel Clarke (1599–1682), author; an anagram. He was accused of stealing the best parts of other people's work.

SUDBURY DAEDALUS, THE John (Jack) Gainsborough (1711–88), brother to Thomas (the *Painter Patriot*). Jack made a set of copper wings for himself and tried unsuccesfully to fly. Both he and Thomas were born at Sudbury, Suffolk.
- Daedalus (whose name means ' a cunning craftsman') was in Greek mythology an Athenian or Cretan who obtained or made wings for himself and his son Icarus and fastened them on with wax. Icarus's melted when he flew too near the sun.

SUGAN, SUGGAN or SUGGON EARL, THE James Fitzthomas (or Fitzgerald), son of Thomas Roe, half-brother of the *Rebel Earl*. James assumed the title of Earl of Desmond (1595) and joined O'Neill's rebellion (1598). He was seized by the *White Knight* and put in the Tower of London under the name of James M' Thomas until his death.
- *Sugan* is the Gaelic word for 'a straw rope'. *Roe* = red. See the *Great* (iv).

SUGAR RAY
i) Ray Robinson (1920–89), American welterweight boxing champion of the world (1946–50) and four times middleweight champion (1951, 1951–2, 1955–7 and 1957), one of the great stylists in the boxing world. His real

name was Walker Scott, junior; so called because his good looks were sweet to the ladies.

ii) Ray Leonard (1956–), American welterweight boxer who at his peak was the highest paid sportsman in the world (1980s). He lost only one of his 33 professional fights. In 1987, after an absence from the ring of three years because of an eye injury, he defeated *Marvellous Marvin* Hagler for the WBC middleweight championship of the world. He has also held the welterweight (1981–2) and light middleweight championships. By 1988 he held five world titles at various weights.

SUICIDE SAL Bonnie Parker (1910–34), companion to Clyde Barrow (the *Texas Rattlesnake*), made famous by the film *Bonnie and Clyde* (1967); self-applied in a poem.

SULTANA, THE Isabella, Marchioness of Hertford (1760–1834), mistress of George IV (the *Adonis of Fifty*); so called in lampoons: mother of *Red Herrings*.

- 'Sultana' was a term in eighteenth to early nineteenth century London society for a whore.

SULTAN OF SWAT, THE *Babe* Ruth.

SUNBEAM Stuart Blackstock (1955–), British criminal gaoled for life at the Old Bailey, London for having shot a policeman who was permanently paralysed.

SUNDANCE KID, THE Harry Longbaugh (?1866–1908), one of the Wild Bunch, bank robber with *Butch* Cassidy. He spent some time in gaol at Sundance, Wyoming.

SUNDAY GENTLEMAN, THE Daniel Defoe, the *Father of Modern Prose Fiction*. When he was hiding from the bailiffs at Bristol (1690s), he stayed indoors on weekdays and emerged – in fine clothes – on Sundays.

SUNNY

i) Princess Alix, *Alicky*; so called first by her mother, Princess Alice of Hesse (1843–78).

ii) Charles Richard John, 9th Duke of Marlborough (1871–1934). He was quite the opposite. His nickname came from his title as Lord Sunderland.

iii) Sunil Gavaskar, the *Guru of Indian Batsmen*; from Sunil.

SUNNY JIM

i) Sir Leonard James Callaghan (1912–), British Prime Minister (1976–9); from the character in a famous cereal advertisement. He is usually smiling. He was created a peer in 1987 (Baron Callaghan of Cardiff).

ii) Sir George Clarke Simpson (19878–1965), member of the British Antarctic expedition (1910–13) and later Director of the Metereological Office, London.

SUNSET COX Samuel Sullivan Cox (1824–89), American politician; after a lavish description of a sunset printed when he was editor of *The Statesman*, Columbus, Ohio.

SUPERB, THE General Winfield Scott Hancock (1824–86), whose handling of troops at the battle of Williamsburg (1862) caused General McClellan (*Little Mac*) to report 'Hancock was superb'. The term became a nickname after a speech (1880) by Daniel Dougherty (1826–1892) nominating Hancock for President.

SUPERBRAT John McEnroe, the *Brat*; so called first by Arthur Ashe (1943–), American tennis champion and captain of the American Davis Cup team.

SUPERDAD John Knight (1936–), of Bodmin, Cornwall, who keeps 26 children (21 of them his own), a wife and a common law wife on social security pay.

SUPERGRASS Harry Kirkpatrick (1957–), a former member of the INLA given five life sentences (1983) for a plot to bomb the Royal Wedding (1981); he gave information which implicated 198 others.

- A grass (from grasshopper = copper = policeman) is underworld slang for an informer.

SUPERHOD Max Quatermann (1942–), British labourer of Slough, Buckinghamshire, who carried a giant hod to move more bricks and plaster than anyone else. He earned as much as £829 a week, and built most of a £250,000 house for himself.

SUPERMAC

i) Harold Macmillan, *Mac the Knife*; so

called by cartoonist Vicky (Victor Weisz: 1913–66)

ii) Malcolm Macdonald (1950–), British footballer who scored all five England goals in the European championships match with Cyprus (1975). He was a manager until 1984.

SUPER MEX Lee Buck Trevino (1939–), American golfer: US Open champion 1968; British Open champion 1971, 1972; Canadian Open champion 1971; US PGA Player of the Year, 1971. He was born in Mexico.

SUPERTRAMP William Henry Davies (1871–1940), British poet who was a tramp in the UK and the USA. He wrote *The Autobiography of a Super Tramp* (1908).

SUPERWAITE Terence (Terry) Waite (1939–), 6 ft 6 in special envoy for the Archbishop of Canterbury, sent on dangerous missions such as negotiations for the release of hostages held by Moslem militia in Beirut, Lebanon; so called by his friends. He is known to the Arabs as *El 'amal kebir*, 'the big man'. He himself was taken prisoner (1987) while on such a mission.

• He holds the position of Secretary for Anglican Affairs, responsible for liaison with churches overseas.

SUPPLEMENT NAPIER Macveigh Napier, the *Bacon Fly*, editor of supplements for the *Encyclopaedia Britannica*; so called in *Noctes Ambrosianae*.

SUPREMO Louis, Lord Mountbatten, *Dickie*, Supreme Allied Commander in South-East Asia (1943–6).

SURGEON, THE Steve Davis, the *Cool Kid*; from his precise and 'clinical' play.

SURLY SAM Dr Johnson, *Blinking Sam*; so called by Wolcot *(Peter Pindar)*.

SURREY PET, THE W. Caffyn (1828–1919), cricketer for Surrey and New South Wales, who coached in Melbourne and Sydney (1860s), having stayed behind after a Test Match.

SWAFF Hannen Swaffer, the *Bishop of Fleet Street*.

SWAMP FOX, THE General Francis Marion, *Old Swamp Fox*.

SWAMPY Graham Marsh (1944–), Australian champion golfer.

SWAN-NECK or SWAN-NECKED Edith the *Fair*.

SWANNY Dorothy Leigh Sayers (1893–1957), British novelist; her school nickname (because of her long neck) which persisted.

SWAN OF AVON, THE William Shakespeare, the *Bard of All Time*.

• See *Swan* and the *Sweet Swan of Avon*.

SWAN OF LICHFIELD, THE Anna Seward (1747–1809), English poetess and friend of Dr Johnson (*Blinking Sam*). Her father was Prebendary of Lichfield Cathedral, Staffordshire in the city where Johnson was born.

SWAN OF THE THAMES, THE John Taylor, the *Sculler*.

SWAN OF THE USK, THE Henry Vaughan, the *Silurist*. One volume of his poems was entitled *Olor Iscanus*, Swan of Usk, the river which flows through South Wales.

SWEATER GIRL, THE Lana Turner (1920–), American film actress, especially at the start of her Hollywood career when she wore tight, clinging sweaters. Her real first name is Julia.

SWEDISH KNIGHT, THE Admiral Sir William Sidney Smith (1764–1840), given command of the Swedish Navy and made a Knight of the Grand Cross by the Swedish king.

SWEDISH NIGHTINGALE, THE Jenny (Johanna Maria) Lind (1820–87), Swedish singer, a very popular figure in England, She made her home there (post-1859).

• See the *Prince of Humbugs*.

SWEEP John (Jacky) Barrett (1753–1821), professor of oriental languages, Trinity College, Dublin. His face and clothes were never clean.

SWEETHEART OF A NATION, THE Mary Pickford, *America's Sweetheart*.

SWEET LYRICIST OF PETERHOUSE, THE Thomas Gray, the *British Pindar*. He lived at Peterhouse College, Cambridge University (1734–56).

SWEET SINGER OF MICHIGAN, THE Julia Moore (1847–1920), American poetaster whose verses were so bad they delighted the public; so called from the title of her first book, *The Sweet Singer of Michigan Salutes the Public* (1876).

SWEET SINGER OF THE TEMPLE, THE George Herbert (1593–1633), English poet. His last poems were collected into a volume entitled *The Temple* (1633).

SWEET SINGER OF WALES, THE William Williams (1717–91), Bishop of St. David's and a Welsh hymn-writer (800 in Welsh and more than 100 in English).

SWEET SWAN OF AVON, THE William Shakespeare, the *Bard of All Time*; so called by Jonson (the *Bricklayer*) in the First Folio of the poet's work (1623).

SWEET WILLIAM

i) William Henry Draper, Q.C. (1801–77), British-born Canadian barrister who became Attorney-General (post 1841) and a judge; from his charming court manner

ii) The Duke of Cumberland, *Billy*; so called by the English after Culloden; from the flower (recorded in 1562).

SWELL-FOOT TYRANT, THE *Bloody Castlereagh*; so called by Shelley (the *Atheist*). Castlereagh had gout.

SWELL OF THE OCEAN, THE Admiral Beaumont of the Royal Yacht Squadron (1880s) with a large stomach.

● Cf *Ocean Swell*.

SWIFTNICKS

i) Captain Richard Dudley (1635–81), an English highwayman who, says *The Newgate Calender*, robbed a man at about 5 a.m. near Barnet and rode straight to Yorkshire, appearing on the bowling-green at about 6 p.m. Charged with the robbery, he was acquitted; so called by Charles II (the *Blackbird*). Dudley eventually pleaded guilty to eight indictments of robbery and was hanged. His exploits were attributed by Harrison Ainsworth (1805–82) to Dick Turpin (hanged 1739).

ii) John Nevison, *Nicks*.

SWIFTY Irving Paul Lazar (1907–), American film publicity entrepreneur. For twenty-eight years he has given lavish parties for the Oscar awards ceremonies.

SWINE-BORN Algernon Charles Swinburne (1837–1909), English poet who attacked conventional Victorian morality; so called by *Punch*, which accused him of immorality.

SWITCHBLADE KID, THE Sal (Salvatore) Mineo (1939–76), Hollywood actor; so called from the parts he played in American films. Ironically, he was stabbed to death outside his Hollywood home.

SYD David Lawrence (1964–), Gloucestershire and England fast bowler; so called from the British band leader. He has been described as 'a Frank Bruno lookalike'.

● For Bruno, see the *Black Bomber*.

SYDNEY CORNSTALK, THE Patrick (Paddy) Francis Slavin (1862–1920), Australian boxer (fl. 1890s).

● A cornstalk in Australian slang is a tall person, especially one born in New South Wales.

SYKSEY General George Sykes (1824–80), American officer; so called by his troops. Also *Tardy George*.

SYLVA EVELYN John Evelyn (1620–1706), English diarist and author; so called after the publication of his book *Sylva* (1664) which led to the planting of many millions of forest trees in England.

● Silvanus was the Roman god of fields and forests, from *silva*, a forest or woodland.

SYM or SYM THE LAIRD Simon Armstrong of Whithaugh (fl. 1520s), leader of a gang of border reivers and brother to *Davy the Lady*. Simon was a man with great power and could raise an 'army' of some 3,000 men when he needed to.

T

TAFFY Colonel David Francis Lewis (1885–1927), commanding the All-Egyptian brigade in the Sudan (1896–1900), 'Lewis Bey'; born at Welshpool, east Wales.
- From the reputed Welsh pronunciation of 'Davy'.

TAGGER RAGGER OF ST PAGGER LE BAGGER, THE The Reverend Talbot Rice, rector of St Peter le Bailey, Oxford (1890s).
- His name and title in Oxford University slang which changed final syllables into -agger, -ogger, -ugger and sometimes -ekker (see *Jekker*).

TALBOT Richard (Withycombe calls him a companion of the *Conqueror*) who is in the Domesday Book as holder of nine hides of land in Bedfordshire, probably the ancestor of the Earls Talbot.
- A talbot was a hunting dog, but Reaney suggests that 'talbot' may have come from the Old French *talebot*, someone who blacked his face to avoid recognition by his enemies (Cf *Niger*). *Talebot* means 'lamp-black' or 'potblack' in the dialect of Normandy. A hide of land is generally thought of as about 120 acres, but the amount varies.

TALBOT OUR GOOD DOG John Talbot, Earl of Shrewsbury, the *Achilles of England*.
- See above; and *Jack Napes*.

TALL SYCAMORE OF THE WABASH, THE Daniel Wolsey Vorhees (1827–97), American lawyer and politician. He was a very tall man.
- The Wabash river flows through Ohio state where Vorhees was born.

TALL TEXAN, THE Ben Kilpatrick (died 1912) of the Wild Bunch. After serving fifteen years for a robbery he committed with *Butch* Cassidy, he was killed by a baggage-car attendant in an attempted train robbery.

TALLY Natalia, Duchess of Westminster (1960-), wife of the 6th Duke (1951–).

TAM OF THE COWGATE Sir Thomas Hamilton, 1st Earl of Haddington (1573–1637), Scottish lawyer and friend of James VI (the *Scottish Heliogabalus*). He became Secretary of State (1612); so called by the King. The Earl's house was in the Cowgate, Edinburgh.

TANYMARIAN The Reverend Edward Stephen (1822–1885), Welsh hymn writer.
- 'Tanymarian' is the Welsh name of a hymn he wrote.

TAPSKY Lord Shaftesbury, *Achitophel*, after a rumour he wanted to be King of Poland.

TARDY GEORGE General George Sykes, *Syksey*.
- 'Tardy' is obsolescent in the UK, but used a great deal in the US for 'slow' or 'late'.

TARKA Sir Harcourt Gilbey Gold (1876–1952), famous oarsman knighted for his services to rowing. He stroked Leander (1896–9), winning the Grand Challenge Cup three times at Henley; President OUBC (1898).

TARZAN

i) Michael Heseltine (*Action Man*) so called in the House of Commons and in Fleet Street because of his blond good looks and after he had flourished the Speaker's mace.

ii) Major-General Orde Wingate, *Robin Hood*. He had a passion for nudity, often conducting conferences while naked.
- Tarzan, a boy raised by apes in the African forest, was created by Edgar Rice Burroughs (1875–1950).

TATTOOED MAN, THE James G. Blaine, the *Plumed Knight*. He was given the nickname after *Puck* published a cartoon of him (1884) as 'Phryne before her judges', his body tattooed with the names of the various scandals with which he was said to have been connected.

- 'Phryne' was the nickname of a Greek courtesan (4th century BC). Her real name was Mnesarete, but because of her complexion she was called 'Phryne' (toad). She was tried for profaning the Eleusinian mysteries, but she was acquitted after she (or her advocate) bared her breasts to the judges.

TAY PAY Thomas Power O'Connor (1848–1929), British journalist who founded *The Star* (1888) and *T.P's Weekly* (1902); from the Irish pronunciation of T.P.

TBW Mrs Thatcher, **Attila the Hen**; mentioned by David Frost (**Mr TV**) in a TV interview with Mrs Thatcher (1985) = That Bloody Woman.

TEACHER OF SAINTS, THE St. Finnian of Clonard (died *circa* 549), said to have begun the monastic movement in Ireland. St Columba (the **Apostle of the Highlanders**) and St Brendan (the **Navigator**) were among those who studied under him.

- Clonard is in Meath, Ireland, where Finnian is thought to have been bishop.

TEAPOT Major-General Robert Craufurd, **Black Bob**, because, says Gronow, of his 'predilection when at Eton for brewing tea in a black pot, which he kept and cherished as a soldier; although some would have it that his handsome head looked like those on old-fashioned teapots'.

TEAPOT GENERAL, THE Major-General Sir Garnet Wolseley, **Our Only General**. On the Red River expedition, Canada (1880s), he advocated tea as the only drink for his men, and took no spirits.

TEAR 'EM John Arthur Roebuck (1802–79); his nickname in Parliament. He helped to overthrow Lord Aberdeen's Ministry (1855) by a resolution for an inquiry into the mismanagement of the Crimean War (1854–56) and was chairman of the committee that did the inquiring. He was given the nickname first by *The Illustrated London News* (1858).

- See **Athenian Aberdeen**.

TEA-TABLE SCOUNDREL THE Lord Chesterfield, the **English Rochefoucauld**; so called by George II (**Augustus**) when he was told Chesterfield was working on a book about his reign.

TEDDY

i) David Thomas (1958–), left-handed bowler for Surrey and England; because of his laugh in the manner of Ted Heath (**Grocer**).

ii) Lieutenant-Colonel Henry Blythe Thornhill Wakelam (1893–1963), sporting journalist and BBC commentator. He gave the first radio running commentary on a team game (rugby) for the BBC in 1927.

TEDDY BEAR Leonard Watkins (1940–), given two life sentences (1980) for the murder of an undercover Customs official and an attempt to murder a policeman: recommended to serve at least twenty-five years.

TEDDY WOODBINE or WOODBINE TEDDY Edward, Prince of Wales, **Sardine**; so called by American, Australian, and New Zealand soldiers (World War I). He gave away packets of Woodbine cigarettes on his visits to troops in France.

- Cf **Woodbine Willie**. Woodbine cigarettes in paper packets of five were first introduced in 1909. They were priced at 1d a packet.

TEEGER, THE John Colin Dunlop (1785–1842), author of a *History of Fiction* (1814).

TEETS Samuel (Sam) Battaglia (1908–73), Chicago gangster; from his pronunciation of 'teeth', e.g. 'I'll smash you in de teets'.

TEFLON PRESIDENT, THE Ronald Reagan, **Dutch**; because nothing stuck to him – at least before the Iran arms scandal (1986). Until then , his 'reign' has been described as 'the Blue Skies Presidency'; so called first by Congresswoman Pat Schroeder.

TEL Terry Wogan, the **King of Blarney**.

TEMPESTUOUS TED Theodore Samuel Willis (1918–), American baseball player with the Boston Red Sox (1939–1960), because of his temperamental playing. He was, however, one of the best hitters of his era and made 2,654 hits, including 521 home runs.

TEMPLE LEECH, THE George Colman, the **Elder**.

TEMPORISING STATESMAN, THE
Bulstrode Whitelocke (1605–76), member
of the Long Parliament (1649–63). He
delayed drawing up charges against
Strafford (**Black Tom Tyrant**).

TENANTS' M.P., THE David, 1st Baron
Kirkwood (1872–1955), Labour MP, and
Secretary of the Scottish Labour Housing
Association, which fought rent cases for
the unemployed.

TEN CENT JIMMY James Buchanan, **Grandma**. As US President, he advocated low
tariffs and low wages.

TEN GOAL PAYNE Joseph (Joe) Payne
(1914–77) of Luton Town FC. He scored
ten goals in a 12-0 victory over Bristol
Rovers (1936).

TENNESSEE
i) Thomas Lanier Williams (1912–83),
American playwright, wrote notably *A
Streetcar Named Desire*.
ii) Ernie Jennings Ford (1919–74),
American folk singer and TV presenter;
born there.

TENTH MUSE, THE
i) Hannah More, the **Giantess of Genius**;
so called by Wolcot (**Peter Pindar**).
ii) Eliza Lucy Vestris (1797–1856),
English actress; so called by Skeffington,
Skiff Skipton.
• Sappho (late 7th century), Greek lyric
poetess, was called this.

TEN THOUSAND DOLLAR BEAUTY, THE
Michael **King** Kelly, sold by Chicago
White Stockings to Boston for $10,000
(1887), an outstanding fee at the time.

TERRIBLE CORNET OF HORSE, THE
William Pitt, **Aeolus i**, who had been a
cornet of Cobham's Horse (post-1731); so
called by Sir Robert Walpole (the **Grand
Corrupter**) who induced George III (the
Button Maker) to take away the commission because of Pitt's constant criticism in the House of Commons (1736).
• A cornet was a junior cavalry officer,
equivalent to an ensign in the infantry.
He carried the colour. Cobham's Horse
was later the 1st Dragoon Guards.

TERRIBLE TIM Tim Witherspoon (1957–),
American World Boxing Association of
America heavyweight boxing champion,
6ft 3 ins tall and weighing 15 stone (224
lb).

TERRIBLE TOMMY
i) Thomas O'Connor (1886– ?),
American thief and murderer, the last
man to be sentenced to hang in Chicago
(1921). He disappeared before execution
and the wooden gallows was preserved
to carry out the sentence 'if he should be
found'.
ii) Thomas Touhy, Chicago bootlegger,
and brother to **Terrible Touhy**.

TERRIBLE TOUHY Roger Touhy (1898–
1959), son of a Chicago policeman, a
bootlegger opposed to **Big Al** Capone in
the 1930s; shot down by an unknown
gunman.

TERROR, THE Charles Thomas Biass
Turner (1862–1944), Australian (New
South Wales) bowler who took 314 wickets in the 1888 Test matches. He and J.J.
Ferris (the **Fiend**) caused a minor panic
among English batsmen. Turner was the
only Australian bowler to have taken 100
in an Australian season.

TERROR OF FRANCE, THE The Earl of
Shrewsbury, the **Achilles of England**.
Nash (the **English Aretine**) referred to
him (1592) as 'the terror of the French'.

TERROR OF HOXTON, THE Walter Probyn,
Angel Face.
• Hoxton is a district of north-east
London.

TERROR OF TREBANOS, THE Greg
Thomas (1960–), fast bowler for Glamorgan and England; so called during the
1986 tour of the West Indies. Also
Typhoon Thomas.
• Trebanos is a town in South Wales,
north of Swansea.

TETTY Elizabeth Porter (1688–1752) who
married Samuel Johnson (**Blinking Sam**);
his nickname for her. Boswell (the **Ambitious Thane**): 'Tetty or Tetsey...is provincially used as a contraction for Elizabeth'.

TEX
i) George Lewis Rickard (1870–1929),
American sports and rodeo promoter.
ii) James Howard (hanged 1884), a
member of the John Heath gang, Arizona.

iii) Charles Bates Thornton (1913–81), American industrialist, e.g. of the Hughes Aircraft Co.

TEXAS JACK
i) Nathaniel Reed (1862–1950), bank and train robber in Oklahoma.
ii) John Omohundro (1846– ?), American army scout with **Buffalo Bill** Cody for Major-General Joseph J. Reynolds, 3rd US Cavalry, and afterwards an actor on Cody's first Wild West Show. He had worked as a cowboy in Texas.

TEXAS Mary Louise Guinan, the **Female Bill Hart**.

TEXAS RATTLESNAKE, THE Clyde Barrow (1909–34), American murderer and thief, made famous by the *Bonnie and Clyde* film; so called because of his crimes in Texas and other Southern states.
● See **Suicide Sal**.

THAT James Tate (1876–1922), husband and accompanist to Clarice Mayne (1886–1966), British variety performer. She always spoke of him as 'That', and they were billed as 'Clarice Mayne and That'.

THIN MAN, THE Maurice Blocker (1963–), American welterweight boxer defeated by the Briton Lloyd Honeyghan (1960–), for the world championship (1987).

THIRD MAN, THE Harold Philby, **Kim**. At the time of the escape to Russia (1951) of Guy Burgess (1911–63) and Donald Maclean (1913–83), there was thought to have been a third Whitehall man helping them, and there was a reminiscence of the famous Orson Welles film of that name. Philby fled to Russia in 1963.
● Cf the **Mole**.

THOMAS THE RHYMER Thomas Learmont, the **Rhymer**.

THOMAS NAPPAGH Thomas Fitzmaurice (fl. 13th century), Justiciar of Ireland. With a grant of land (1292) he created the fortunes of the Earls of Desmond, being created 1st Earl (1330).
● 'Nappagh' means 'of the ape'; cf **Apeclogge** and **Jack Napes**. For Justiciar, see **Roger the Great**.

THOMMO or **TOMMO** Jeff Thomson

(1950–), fast bowler for Australia and Middlesex.

THOROUGH The Earl of Strafford, **Black Tom Tyrant**. He had a scheme to make England an absolute monarchy under Charles I (the **Ahab of the Nation**) which he described as a policy of 'Thorough' when Lord-Lieutenant of Ireland.

THOROUGH DOCTOR, THE William Varro, **Doctor Fundatus**.

THORN, THE Elizabeth, Viscountess Melbourne (1752–1818), mother of **Lord M**; nickname given to her by the Duke of Devonshire's family because she was thought to be prickly.

THREAT, THE Lisabeth Scott (1922–), American film actress usually seen wearing a scowl.

THREE-FINGER BROWN
i) Mordecai Brown (1876–1948), Chicago baseball pitcher in the Hall of Fame (1903–16). He held the lowest average for 1906. He lost part of a finger in an accident.
ii) Thomas Lucchese (1903–67), New York Mafia chief (1930s–1960s). His real first name was Caetano. He arrived in America from Sicily in 1911 and in adult life was soon associated with bootlegging, drugs, night-clubs, property and dressmaking. His son was a graduate of West Point military academy. Thomas lost fingers in an accident as a youth.

THREE-FINGERED JACK
i) John Hamilton (1883– ?) who taught J. H. Dillinger (**Public Enemy No 1**) how to rob banks. The instruction took place while they were in prison together. Hamilton lost his finger in an accident.
ii) William White (fl. 1930s), one of **Big Al** Capone's gunmen. His hand was crushed when he was a boy.

THREE GRACES, THE The Grace brothers, Dr. W. G., the **Champion**, Edward Mills (1841–1911) and George Frederick (1850–80), all noted cricketers.
● The Three Graces, Euphrosyne, Aglaia and Thalia, were said to be friends of the Muses.

THUGEE SLEEMAN Major-General Sir William Henry Sleeman (1768–1856) who suppressed thugs in India.

THUNDER AND LIGHTNING HARRIS Sir Wythin Snow Harris (1791–1867), British scientist who invented an improved lightning conductor.

THUNDERBOLT, THE or THE ILLINOIS THUNDERBOLT Billy Papke (1886–1936), American world middleweight boxing champion (1908).

THUNDER BOLT Thomas (Tommy) Bolt (1919–   ), American golfer, US Open champion (1958); he is a temperamental player, inclined to throw his clubs about.

THUNDERBOOTS Stan Mortensen, *Electric Heels*.

THUNDERER, THE

i) Captain Edward Sterling, *Captain Whirlwind*, between 1812 and 1843.

ii) Thomas Barnes (1785–1841), editor of *The Times* (1817–41), said to have been the most powerful man in Britain at the time.

● The nickname came from a reference to a leading article by Sterling in which he wrote 'We thundered out the other day an article on social and political reform'. Carlyle (the *Censor of the Age*), in his life of Sterling's son, said the nickname was originally given to the captain who was called 'The Thunderer of the Times newspaper'. A history of *The Times* (Bowman: 1931) says that both Sterling and his editor were known by this title (which was also applied to the newspaper itself).

THUNDERTHIGHS Christina Onassis (1951–88), daughter of a Greek millionaire ship-owner; so called before she slimmed.

THURSO BAKER, THE Robert Dick (1811–66), Scottish geologist and botanist who had been apprenticed in his early life to a baker and lived in Thurso, north Scotland.

TIBBIE Talbot Baines Reed (1852–1903), British writer of stories for boys and editor of *The Boy's Own Paper* from its foundation (1879) until his death; from his initials.

TICH

i) Alfred Percy Freeman (1888–1965),

cricketer for Kent and England. He was very small. He took more than 3,770 wickets in first-class games, 304 in one season, the greatest number ever obtained (1928).

ii) George Henry West (1882–1927), Hull Kingston Rovers Rugby League player who scored 53 points in one match (1905).

● The nickname came from *Little Tich*, applied to all small men.

TICK Mark Wright (1963–   ), defender for England and Southampton FC.

TIDDY DOLL or DOL Lord Temple, the *Gawky Squire*.

● Tiddy Doll or Dol was the nickname of a celebrated fast-talking street-seller of gingerbread men in Mayfair (18th century). He dressed like a person of wealth and is pictured in Hogarth's engraving of the execution of the Idle Apprentice. His singing of 'Tiddy-diddy-doll-loll-loll-loll',the end of a ballad of that title, was well-known at the fair when Mayfair had one. His real name was reputed to have been Ford. There is now a Tiddy-Dol eating-house in Mayfair, built in 1785.

TIGER or TIGER BILL William Joseph O'Reilly (1905–   ), cricketer for New South Wales and Australia, one of the best-ever bowlers. He took 144 wickets in 27 Test matches, and a total of 744 in first-class cricket.

TIGER

i) Joseph Chamberlain, *Artful Joe*; his nickname in the mid-1890s, after Sir J. Kitson (1835–1911) had quoted in a speech in the House of Commons the limerick about the lady who went for a ride on a tiger.

ii) Edward, 1st Baron Thurlow (1731–1806), Lord Chancellor, noted for his savage speeches.

iii) E. J. Smith (1886–1979), Warwickshire wicket-keeper.

iv) Mansur Ali Khan, the Nawab of Pataudi (1940–), cricketer who played for Sussex. He was captain of India in 1964 and made more than 2,000 runs in Test Matches.

v) Helen Troke (1965–), British-born European badminton champion.

vi) Graham Greene (1904–), British author of such books as *The Power and the Glory* (1904) and *The Heart of the Matter* (1948); so called by his wife Vivien, whom he called 'Pussy'.

- See the *Perth Tiger*.

TIGER EARL, THE The Earl of Crawford, *Earl Beardie*.

TIGER TIM Timothy (Tim) Michael Healy (1855–1931), Irish M.P., lawyer and fervent Nationalist; so called after a famous comic-paper cartoon figure.

TIGER WOMAN, THE Winnie Ruth Judd (1909–), American sent to an insane asylum (1933) for the murders of two women in Los Angeles; paroled, 1971.

TIM

i) Sir Henry Birkin (1896–1933), British motor racing driver.

ii) Dr Alan Noel Latimer Munby (1913–74), British historian and bibliographer.

iii) Terence Edmund Gascoigne, Lord Nugent (1895–1973), Permanent Lord-in-Waiting to the Queen (post-1960).

TINA Margaret Thatcher, *Attila the Hen;* from the initials of her repeated assertion: 'There is no alternative' (i.e. to monetarism).

TINEMAN, THE or TYNEMAN Archibald, 4th Earl of Douglas (?1369–1424), son of the *Grim*.

- To tine or tyne in Scottish dialect is to lose, and Douglas was said to have lost every battle he fought.

TINMAN, THE

i) William (Billy) Hooper (fl. late 18th century), pugilist who was so formidable that Egan (the *Elder*) reports that Mendoza (the *Light of Israel*) forfeited a purse of fifty guineas rather than meet him; but Egan adds 'Hooper was a prominent feature in several of the mad freaks committed by the late Lord Barrymore (*Hellgate*) at Brighton and so came to be thought of as nothing less than a bully for the earl'.

ii) Frederick (Fred) Archer, the *Demon* (iii) who was very rich. It was said that

he 'rode for the tin'.

- 'Tin' is slang for money.

TINTORETTO OF ENGLAND, THE William Dobson, the *English Tintoretto*.

TINY

i) Field-Marshal William Edmund, 1st Baron Ironside (1880–1959), commander Archangel expedition (World War I) and Chief of Imperial General Staff (World War II). *The Times* spoke of his 'massive presence'.

ii) Myron Bradshaw (1905–58), American jazz drummer.

iii) Roland W. Rowland (1917–), British managing director and chief executive of Lonrho Ltd. He is far from being a small man. His real surname is Fuhrop.

iv) Hartzell Parham (1900–43), American negro jazz musician, because of his size.

TIP Thomas O'Neill (1912–), Speaker of the US House of Representatives (1977–86).

TIPPECANOE W. H. Harrison, the *Cincinnatus of the West*. 'Tippecanoe and Tyler too' was the slogan on the 1840 Presidential election. Tyler, (1790–1862), Vice-Presidential candidate, was later 10th President of the USA, after Harrison died in office.

- See *Old Tip*.

TIPTON SLASHER, THE William Perry, a pugilist who was champion of England (1850).

TISH Phyllis Preuss (1939–), American golfer; played for America five times.

TITUS Captain Lawrence E. G. Oates (1880–1912), 6th Iniskilling Dragoons and a member of Scott's (*Scotty*) expedition to the Antarctic (1910–1913). He walked out into a blizzard to die when he was convinced he was holding back the others at a time when Scott wrote 'We know the end has come'.

- From Titus Oates, the *Knight of the Post*.

TITYRUS Chaucer, the *British Homer*; so called by Spenser (the *Child of the Ausonian Muse*).

- Tityrus is the name of the shepherd in Virgil's *Eclogues* and was applied to Virgil himself.

TNT Tony Tubbs (1959–), American heavyweight boxer, 18 stone (252 lb).

TOBACCO BROWNE Isaac Hawkins Browne (1705–1760), British poet and writer whose works include *A Pipe of Tobacco*.

TOBY Gerald Balding (1936–), British racehorse trainer who won the 1969 Grand National with one of his horses.

TOEY Hugh Joseph Tayfield (1929–), off-spin bowler for South Africa, Natal and Rhodesia. He took 170 wickets in 37 Test Matches (1950s). He had a habit of tapping with his toe before starting his bowling run.

TOGO William Raphael Johnstone (1905–1964), Australian jockey successful in England. Also 'Rae', short for Raphael'.

TOGRAI SMITH Thomas Smith, *Doctor Roguery*, orientalist; so called at Oxford University.

TOKYO ROSE
i) Iva Ikuko Togori D'Aquino (1916–), American-born Japanese girl who broadcast from Japan to American servicemen (World War II). She was imprisoned (1949) for ten years, and pardoned in 1977. She lives in Chicago.
ii) Ruth Hayakawa, also born in America, who did the same thing.

TOM Professor Lloyd A. Fallers (1925–74), American anthropologist.

TOMBOY OF THE AIR, THE Blanche Stuart Scott (1891–1970), first American woman to fly solo and later a stunt pilot.

TOMBSTONE Albert Bemiller (1939–), American footballer who had wanted to become an undertaker.

TOM FOLIO Thomas Rawlinson, the *Leviathan of Book Collectors*; so called by Addison (the *English Atticus*) in *The Tatler*.
• 'Folio' has been used for a book of very large size since 1620.

TOM OF TEN THOUSAND Thomas Thynne (assassinated 1681) of Longleat, Wiltshire, ancestor of Marquis of Bath; so called because of his income of £10,000 a year and the great estate on which he lived.

TOM MIRROR Richard Estcourt (1688–1712), British Drury Lane actor and dramatist friend of Sir Richard Steele (*Little Dicky*); so called in *The Tatler* (August 1709) for which Steele wrote. Estcourt was a clever mimic.

TOM MOORE OF DIXIE, THE Abram Joseph Ryan (1838–86), Roman Catholic priest and poet who supported the Confederates in the American Civil War.
• See *Anacreon Moore*.

TOMMY
i) Commander Charles Ralfe Thompson (1894–1966), Personal Assistant to Churchill (*Bricky*) from 1940 to 1945.
ii) Arthur Alexander Thomson (1894–1968), British novelist and writer on cricket; especially for *The Times*.

TOMMY POTTS *Pigeon Paley*; so called at Cambridge University because he was uncouth and awkward.

TOM THUMB Charles Stratton, *General Tom Thumb*.

TOM TILBURY Robert Henley, 1st Earl of Northington (?1708–72), Lord Chancellor who presided at the trial in the House of Lords of Lord Byron (the *Wicked Lord*) for killing his cousin William Chaworth, a country squire, in a duel (1765). Byron was found guilty of manslaughter but, because of an old statute which favoured literates, he was discharged on paying a fine.

TOM THE TYRANT The Duke of Leeds, *King Tom*, who fought to impose harsh measures on Roman Catholics; so called in contemporary lampoons.

TOM TOUGH Thomas Blake (fl. late 1700s-early 1800s), an English pugilist who lost to Tom Cribb (the *Black Diamond*), champion of England, in February 1805.

TONKER Brian Taylor (1932–), Essex wicket-keeper (1970s).

TONY Allan Aynesworth (1864–1959), British actor whose real name was Edward Abbot-Anderson.

TONY BENDER Anthony C. Strollo (1899–1962), American gangster; his Mafia nickname.

TONY DUCKS Anthony Corallo (1913–   ), head of the Mafia family of New York, sentenced to a hundred years in gaol (1986) for murder and racketeering.

TOOM TABARD John Balliol or de Bailleul (1249–1315), a claimant to the Scottish throne, proclaimed king by Edward I (the **English Justinian**). Edward thought he would be a puppet, but Balliol rejected the English and invaded England. He was defeated, and spent three years in the Tower of London.

- 'Toom Tabard' means an empty jacket, for Balliol was considered ineffective by the Scots.

TOOK Ezekiel Chandler Gathings (1903–79), American Democrat Congressman for Arkansas (1939–69) who influenced agricultural legislation.

TOO TALL Ed. Jones, American footballer for Tennessee State (1971–3), and Dallas Cowboys. He is 6ft 9 in.

TOP and TOPSY William Morris (1834–96), British poet, artist and printer; nickname at Oxford University because of his thick mop of hair. He went up to Oxford (1853) the year after *Uncle Tom's Cabin* had first appeared in book form. 'Topsy' was later cut to **Top** and used by his friends.

TOPSY-TURVY John Massey (died 1801), a British wrestler who had a trick of throwing his opponent backwards over his head. He was hanged at Bilstone, Warwickshire for having beaten his wife to death.

TOUCHDOWN TONY Anthony Adams (1950–   ), American footballer.

TOUGH Andrew Jackson, before he was nicknamed **Hickory**.

TOUGH TONY Anthony Accardo, *Joe Batters*.

TOWN BULLY OF ELY, THE Oliver Cromwell, the **Almighty Nose**; so called by Needham (the **Cobbett of His Day**). In 1636 Cromwell inherited the farm and lands of his uncle at Ely where he was involved in controversy over draining the Fens.

TOWSER John Montague Gosden (1904–68), British amateur rider and trainer.

TOY BULLDOG, THE *Mickey* Walker. He never weighed more than 170 lb (12 stone 14 lb).

TOY WOMAN A LA MODE, THE Mrs Chevenix (died 1755), daughter of a toy-maker who married a toymaker of Charing Cross, London and, when he died in 1742, ran the business on her own. Walpole (the **Autocrat of Strawberry Hill**) bought Strawberry Hill from her.

TRADER IN FACTION, THE Milton, **Black-Mouthed Zoilus**; so called by his political opponents.

TRAITOR, THE Turchil or Thurkill, Saxon landowner in Warwickshire at the time of the Norman Conquest (1066). He did not come forward to fight. William the **Bastard** allowed him to keep his lands.

TRAITOR TWIGGS Brigadier-General D.E.Twiggs, **Old Davy the Bengal Tiger**. He surrendered federal property to Texan secessionists.

TRAMP POET, THE Harry Hibbard Kemp (1883–1960), American writer.

TRANSLATOR-GENERAL, THE Philemon Holland (1552–1637). He translated Livy (1600), Pliny (1601), Plutarch (1603) and Suetonius (1606) among other writers. He had profound knowledge of Latin and Greek; so called by Thomas Fuller (1608–61) in his *Worthies* (1662).

TREACHERER, THE Hugh de Cressingham, English Treasurer for Scotland, who died 1297 at the battle of Stirling Bridge; so called by the Scots.

TRIBUNE OF THE PEOPLE, THE John Bright, the **Apostle of Free Trade,** because of his oratory in defence of radical ideas.

TRICKY DICK Richard McGuire (1926–   ), American All-Metropolitan basketball star.

TRICKY DICKY Richard Milhous Nixon (1913–   ), 37th President of the USA, who resigned (1974) after the Watergate spy scandal – the first President ever to do so; so called because of his adroitness in politics with undertones of dubious methods.

TRIGGER Elmer Burke (1917–58), American gunman electrocuted for murder. He loved machine-guns.

TRIGGER MIKE Michael Coppola (1904–66), New York gangster for *Lucky* Luciano.

TRIMMER, THE George Saville, 1st Marquess of Halifax (1633–95), English statesman. He was neither a Whig nor a Tory, but tried to steer a middle course, 'trimming his sails to the wind'.

TRINITY JONES The Reverend William Jones (1726–1800) of Nayland, Essex; England writer on theology and defender of the Trinity.

TRI-STATE TERROR, THE Wilbur Underhill (1901–34), American bank-robber who operated in Arkansas, Oklahoma and Kansas.

TRIUMPHANT EXCISEMAN, THE Sir Robert Walpole, the *Grand Corrupter*; so called by his son Horace (the *Autocrat of Strawberry Hill*). As First Lord of the Treasury and Chancellor of the Exchequer, he was the leading financial expert and brought fiscal reform by his excise scheme (1733).

TRUE BLUE PROTESTANT POET, THE Thomas Shadwell, the *Great Prophet of Tautology*; so called by Dryden (*Asaph*) just after Dryden had joined the Court party and in the period before he became a Roman Catholic. In his feud with Shadwell he published (1682) *MacFlecknoe, or a Satyr on the True Blew Protestant Poet, T.S* which equated Shadwell with dullness.

TRUE DEACON OF HIS CRAFT, THE Alexander Pope, the *Bard of Twickenham*; so called by Scott (the *Ariosto of the North*).

TRUE LAUREATE OF ENGLAND, THE Charles Dibdin, the *Bard of the British Navy*, writer of patriotic songs; so called by Maginn (the *Adjutant*).

TRUE THOMAS Thomas Learmont, the *Merlin of Scotland*. Many of his prophecies were thought to have come true.

TRUMPET MOORE Thomas *Anacreon Moore*, who was not short of self-praise.

TRUMPETER OF PITT, THE William *Boney Cobbett*; so called in *Noctes Ambrosianae*. As a journalist, he supported the policies of Pitt (the *Bottomless Pitt*) (*circa* 1800), but later opposed them.

TRUSTY ANTHONY Anthony Aston, *Matt Medley*. *The Spectator* (1 January 1712) carried an advertisement stating that the comedian Richard Estcourt (*Tom Mirror*) would open the Bumper Tavern in Covent Garden, London, and that wines would be sold by his old servant Trusty Anthony. Everyone assumed that Aston was meant.

TRUTH TELLER, THE Charles Thomson (1729–1824), Secretary to the First Continental Congress (1774–89); so called by the Indians after his negotiations with them.

TSAR REED Thomas Brackett Reed (1839–1902), American statesman who drew up the Reed rules for the conduct of proceedings in the American House of Representatives. The nickname was given to him by his opponents.

TSOBO Kwame Nkrumah, *Showboy*.
- 'Tsobo' is the West African version of the English word, influenced by the style of spelling introduced by the Basle missionaries.

TUBAL-CAIN OF AMERICA, THE Alexander Spotwood (1676–1740), Governor of Virginia, who developed that state's iron industry and is believed to have been the first man to manufacture mineral products in America.
- Tubal-Cain, the son of Lamech (Gen iv 22) was the inventor of forging, 'the instructor of every artificer in brass and iron'.

TUBBY The Reverend Philip Thomas Bayard Clayton (1885–1972), British army chaplain (World War I) and founder of Toc. H. The first Talbot House (signallers' jargon for which is 'Toc H') was opened at Poperinghe in December 1915 in memory of Lieutenant Gilbert Talbot.

TUG

i) Admiral of the Fleet A. K. Wilson, *Old Hard-Heart*. Fraser and Gibbons say it was first given to him when he was a lieutenant in the 1860s and was a variation of 'Chug' or 'choog', although there is no general agreement on this naval tradition.

ii) **Scroogie** McGraw; so called by his parents because that is what he did as an infant.

TUMBLEDOWN DICK Richard Cromwell, **Queen Dick**, ineffective as Lord Protector.

(ii) Richard II, the **Coxcomb**. He overreached himself as an absolute monarch, and in his deed of abdication (1399) confessed himself 'useless'. He rode through London behind his successful rival, Henry (who became Henry IV, **Bolingbroke**) in humiliation.

TUM-TUM Edward VII, the **Peacemaker**.

TUNEFUL, THE Eochaid **Binnigh**, founder of the abbey at Applecross, the Scottish port for the Hebrides (673), and son of Eogan; King of Ailech (*circa* 422-5).

• *Binne* is Gaelic for melody or music.

TURNBULL THE TERRIBLE Alex Turnbull (killed in action, 1917), footballer for Manchester City and Manchester United. He scored the winning goal for Manchester United in the 1909 F.A. Cup Final.

TURNCOAT MERES George Booth, 1st Baron Delamere or De La Mer (1622–84); so called in contemporary pamphlets. He vacillated between Royalist and Parliament in the English Civil War.

TURNIP HOER, THE George I (1660–1727) who is said to have contemplated turning St James's Park, London into a turnip field. Extensive cultivation of turnips began in England in 1724 (see below).

TURNIP TOWNSHEND Charles, 2nd Viscount Townshend (1674–1738), English statesman who spent his last years at Raynham, Norfolk, in agriculture including large-scale experiments in growing turnips. He had a great influence on George I (above). Pope (the **Bard of Twickenham**) says that turnips were a favourite subject of conversation with Townshend.

TURNKEY, THE Sir Hudson Lowe (1769–1844), Governor of St Helena when Napoleon Bonaparte was a prisoner there (1815–21); so called by Byron (**Baby**).

TURTLE Admiral Sir Henry Keppel Hamilton (1890–1957), grandson of Sir Henry Keppel (the **Little Admiral**).

TUSITALA Robert Louis Stevenson (1850–94) British poet and novelist. His nickname in Samoa, where it means 'Teller of Tales'. Also the **Virgil of Prose**.

TWIGGY Lesley Hornby, the **Matchstick**; nickname given to her by Justin de Villeneuve (born Nigel Davies), photographer who helped her to become a star model.

TWITTERS Henry Howard Molyneux Herbert, 4th Earl of Carnarvon (1831–90), Secretary of State for the Colonies (1866–78).

TWN O'R NANT Thomas Edwards (1738–1810), Welsh poet. It means 'Tom of Nant'.

• *Nant* is a Welsh word for a brook, a gorge or a ravine.

TWO DINNERS Arnold, 1st Baron Goodman (1913–) because of his love of good food.

TWO GREGORIES, THE Gregory Brandon, hangman of London in the reign of James I (the **British Solomon**) and his son Richard (**Young Gregory**). The gallows became known in the 17th century as 'The Gregorian Tree' (post-1641) and 'gregory' a term for an executioner (post-1642). Grose says that Gregory, ' a famous finisher of the law', was granted a coat-of-arms by Sir William Segar, Garter King at arms (1641).

• Cf **Jack Ketch**.

TWO-GUN

i) Louis Alterie (1892–1935), American bootlegger who wore a pistol on each hip; a member of Charles Dion Bannion's (the **Arch Killer of Chicago**) gang.

ii) Francis Crowley (1911–31), American bank robber electrocuted for murder.

TWO-GUN PATTON General Patton, **Old Blood and Guts**. He always wore two pearl-handled pistols while campaigning.

TWO TON Anthony (Tony) Galento (1909–79), American heavyweight boxer who once knocked out Joe Louis (the **Brown Bomber**); famous for his catch phrase 'I'll moider de bum'.

TWO-TON TESSIE Tessie O'Shay (1918–), British music-hall star; from her size and her song 'Two-Ton Tessie from Tennessee'.

TYKE Thomas Dow Richards (1887–1971), British authority on ice figure skating . He was born in Yorkshire.

- 'Tyke' has been a nickname for a Yorkshireman since at least 1700. It is also slang for a dog.

TYPHOID MARY Mary Mallon (1868–1938) of New York City, a carrier of typhoid, the source of 1,300 cases (1903). She was detained (1915–30) after she refused to leave her employment, where she handled food.

TYPHOON, THE

i) Frank Tyson (1930–), fast bowler for Northamptonshire and England, who played a major part in winning the 1954-5 Test series against Australia.

ii) Mike Tyson, *Iron Mike*.

iii) Greg Thomas, the *Terror of Trebanos*.

TYRANT OF NEW ENGLAND, THE Sir Edmund Andros (1637–1714), British Governor of New York, New England and Virginia, of great severity. New England colonists eventually deposed and arrested him, sending him back to England, but he was released and posted to Virginia.

U

UCKERS Ludovic (Ludo) Henry Kennedy (1919–), British TV personality and author so called for seven years in the Royal Navy.

- 'Uckers' is the Royal Navy word for the game of Ludo. The word may derive from 'hucking', scraping the ship's bottom in dry dock (some of the encrustations resembling ludo counters?)

UHLAN, THE Lord Randoph Churchill, the *Blenheim Pippin* A Uhlan became known after the 1870–1 Franco-Prussian war as a daring skirmisher, and Churchill had that sort of political reputation. The *Daily News* (17 February 1883) called him 'The Uhlan of the Conservative Army'.

UKELELE IKE Cliff Edwards (1897–1971), American entertainer and film actor.

ULTIMUS ROMANORUM

i) Horace Walpole, the *Autocrat of Strawberry Hill*.

ii) Thomas Hollis, the *Dear Liberty Boy*.

iii) William Congreve (1670–1729), English playwright; so called by his friend Pope (the *Bard of Twickenham*).

iv) Dr Johnson, *Blinking Sam*; so called by Carlyle (the *Censor of the Age*).

- Cf the *Last of the Romans*. Several Romans were called *Ultimus Romanorum*, including Marcus Junius Brutus, one of the assassins of Julius Caesar.

ULYSSES George III, the *Button Maker*; so called by Wolcot (*Peter Pindar*.

- Cf the *Presbyterian Ulysses*.

ULYSSES OF THE HIGHLANDS, THE Sir Ewen Cameron, the *Black*; so called by Macaulay (*Babbletongue*).

UNBOWLABLE, THE W. M. Woodfull, the *Great Unbowlable*; because of his batting skill.

UNCLE ARTHUR Arthur Henderson (1863–1935), British politician; one of the founders of the British Labour Party in which he was an elder statesman. Winner of the Nobel Peace Prize (1934).

- Cf *Young Arthur*.

UNCLE BILL Dr Edward A. Wilson (1872–1912) who died with Scott (*Scotty*) in the Antarctic expedition (1910–1913). Scott wrote to him as 'Dear Old Bill'.

UNCLE BOB Robert Burnham, 1st Baron Renwick (1904–73), industrialist; so called by 'an immense circle of friends' (*Times*).

UNCLE DAVE David Harrison Macon (1870–1952), American folk-singer star of the Grand Ole Opry (post 1926) of Nashville, Tennessee.

UNCLE ESEK Henry Wheeler Shaw (1818–85), Massachusetts-born humorist who wrote under the pseudonym of 'Josh Billings'.

UNCLE FRED Frederick John Marquis, 1st Earl of Woolton (1883–1964), Minister of Food in the coalition government (World War II).

UNCLE GEORGE

i) George Lansbury (1859–1940), leader of the British Labour Party (1931–5), an ardent pacifist whose views forced him to resign. He was founder of the *Daily Herald*.

ii) George III, the *Button Maker*.

UNCLE JEFF Admiral of the Fleet Sir Geoffrey Thomas Phipps Hornby (1825–95). He was a Lord of the Admiralty (1851–2).

UNCLE JOE Joseph Gurney Cannon (1836–1926), American politician who served forty-six years in the House of Representatives and was Speaker between 1903 and 1911.

UNCLE MAC Derek Ivor Breashur McCulloch (1898–1967), best known of the BBC radio Children's Hour 'uncles'.

UNCLE OF EUROPE, THE Edward VII, the *Peacemaker*.

- The German Kaiser was his nephew, the Queen of Spain and that of Norway were his nieces. Queen Alexandra was aunt to the Tsar of Russia and the Kings of Denmark and Greece.
- Cf the *Grandmother of Europe*.

UNCLE REG Reginald Parnell (1911–1964), British racing driver, a 'father figure' in the sport.

UNCLE ROBERT Robert E. Lee, the *Bayard of the Confederate Army*.

UNCLE SAM General Grant, *Old Three Stars*; from his initials U.S.

UNCONDITIONAL SURRENDER GRANT General Grant, *Old Three Stars*, overall commander of the Union armies in the American Civil War; from his initials and his demands from the Confederates.

UNCONSCIOUS Kevin Curran (1959–   ), South African-born Wimbledon-class tennis player.

UNCROWNED KING, THE J. G. Blaine, the *Plumed Knight*. He held great power when Secretary of State (1889–92) under President Benjamin Harrison (1833–1908: President 1889–92).

UNCROWNED KING OF ARABIA, THE T. E. Lawrence, *Emir Dynamite*. He was a powerful adviser to the Sharif of Mecca and other Arab rulers; so called first by Sir Ronald Storrs, Military Governor of Jerusalem (1917) to American journalist Lowell Thomas.

UNCROWNED KING OF CARRICK, THE The Earl of Cassillis, the *King of Carrick*.

UNCROWNED KING OF EGYPT, THE General *Chinese Gordon*. He helped to sway the decisions of the Khedive Ismail (1830–95) and his son, Tewfik Pasha (1852–92).

UNCROWNED KING OF IRELAND, THE
i) Charles Stewart Parnell (1846–91), Irish statesman and M.P. for Cork. He was leader of the Irish National Party and a man of immense influence; so called by William Edward Forster (*Buckshot*) in the House of Commons (February, 1883).
ii) Daniel O'Connell, the *Big Beggarman*.

UNCROWNED KING OF PORT ROYAL, THE Sir Henry Morgan, *Rattler*.
- Port Royal, in Jamaica, West Indies, was once the 'capital' of buccaneers.

UNCROWNED KING OF ULSTER, THE
i) Edward Henry, 1st Baron Carson (1854–1935), Solicitor-General for Ireland and Unionist M.P. for Dublin University. He organized resistance in Ulster to Home Rule, and eventually defeated the project.
ii) John Redmond, *King John*.

UNCUMBER, ST The English nickname for St Wigefort or Wilgefortis who, although believed to be a fictitious Portuguese saint, once had an altar in St Paul's Cathedral, London; so called for the help she was said to have given to wives who wanted to rid themselves of troublesome husbands. Also 'Maid Uncumber'.
- 'Uncumber' is an old word for 'disencumber'. John Brand in his *Popular Antiquities of Great Britain* (1848 edition) quotes Michael Wodde's *Dialogue*, 1554: 'if a wife were weary of her husband, she offred otes at Poules at London to St Uncumber'.

UNFAIR PREACHER, THE Isaac Barrow (1630–77), chaplain to Charles II (the *Blackbird*) who gave him the nickname since his sermons were so detailed they were unfair to those who came after, leaving them nothing more to say.

UNION DUKE, THE James Douglas, 2nd Duke of Queensberry (1662–1711), Secretary of State for Scotland, who carried through the Union of Scotland and England (1707).

UNIQUE DOCTOR, THE William of Occam, *Doctor Invincibilis*.

UNITED STATES GRANT General U.S. Grant, *Old Three Stars*; from his initials; current at the time he was President.

UNITED WE STAND General Grant (above).

UNIVERSAL ARISTARCHUS, THE The Reverend John Hoskins (1566–1638), lawyer and wit who is said to have assisted Raleigh (the *Knight of the Cloak*) and Ben Jonson (the *Bricklayer*) in their writings.
- See the *Aristarch of British Criticism*.

UNIVERSAL CORPORAL, THE Canon Joseph Dornford of Exeter (1794–1868); so called when he was Proctor of Oxford University (1830).

UNIVERSAL GENIUS, THE Sir William Petty (1623–87), English statistician and political economist who was a professor of music and a professor of anatomy, was physician to the army in Ireland and invented a double-bottomed ship. He also carried out a land survey in Ireland.

UNIVERSAL PHILOSOPHER, THE Thomas Harriott (1560–1621), English mathematician and astronomer, geographer to the second expedition (1585) of Sir Walter Raleigh (the *Knight of the Cloak*) and a major influence on the development of algebra.

UNIVERSAL PIECE-BROKER, THE Bishop Warburton, the *Colossus of Literature*; so called by John Nicols (the *Censor-General of Literature*).

• A piece-broker in the 18th century was a shopkeeper who bought up remnants for resale – usually, says Rolt's *Dictionary of Trade* (1756), 'decayed taylors or some cunning men who have crept into the secrets of the trade'.

UNIVERSAL PROVIDER, THE William Whiteley (1831–1907) who opened the first departmental store in London (1863), and boasted there was nothing he could not provide (1860s). He was shot by his illegitimate son, Horace Rayner.

UNKNOWN PRIME MINISTER, THE Andrew Bonar Law (1858–1923), Canadian-born, Conservative British Prime Minster (1922–3); so called by Asquith (*Old Wait and See*). Bonar Law, a hard-working politician, came to power as a sick man.

UNREADY, THE King Aethelred or Ethelred II (*circa* 968-1016). He was an opportunist who sought his own ends, and was improvident and consequently *rede*-less or lacking in good advice (from the Old English *raed* = counsel).

• The Old English *unraed* meant 'wickedness' or 'folly'.

UNTAMED HEIFER, THE Elizabeth I, the *English Diana*; so called in the Martin Marprelate pamphlets for which John Ap

Henry or Penry (the *Great Make-Bate of England*) was executed for sedition. He used Martin Marprelate as a pseudonym for his violent attacks on Anglican dignitaries, especially bishops.

UPPER MACWILLIAM, THE The 1st Earl of Clanrickarde, *MacWilliam of the Heads*, known to the Irish as MacWimmian Uachtair or the Upper MacWilliam (Anglicized as 'MacWilliam Eighter') with power in southern Connaught.

• Cf the *Lower MacWilliam*. The Gaelic *uachdar* = top.

UPRIGHT TRUTH ESQ Charles Lamb, the *Mitre Courtier*; mentioned by Lamb himself with the comment 'it tickles my vanity a little'.

URCHIN, THE Archbishop Laud, *Hocus-pocus*.

• 'Urchin' in Laud's time was applied to a hedgehog, and so to someone who was prickly.

URSA MAJOR

i) Dr Johnson, *Blinking Sam*; so called by Boswell's father, Alexander Boswell, Lord Auchinleck (1707–82) because he was a bear of a man.

ii) Captain Constantine J Phipps, Royal Navy (1744–92), later 2nd Baron Mulgrave who in 1773 commanded an expedition towards the North Pole, mapped Spitzbergen and discovered Walden Island. He was a very big man, and the nickname distinguished him from his brother, the Honourable Charles Phipps, MP.

• Ursa Major is a constellation which the Greeks identified with the nymph Callisto, turned into a bear by Zeus.

URSULA UNDRESS Ursula Andress (1936–), Swiss-born American film star often seen with few or no clothes.

• Ursula = little she-bear.

U UTAH Bruce Phillips, the *Golden Voice of the Great South*. He lived in Utah.

V

VAGABOND SCOT, THE Tobias Smollett, *Smelfungus*, Scottish writer who travelled to the West Indies and lived some time in Jamaica, visited France and Italy, and lived in both England and Scotland; so called by Warburton (the *Colossus of Literature*).

VAL Eamonn de Valera, the *Chief*.

VAMP, THE Theda Bara (1890–1955), American film actress of the silent screen; from 'vampire', from the exaggerated lust for men her roles demanded. She began her career in 1915, her real name being Theodosia Goodman.

VAMPIRE KILLER, THE John George Haigh (1909–49) who admitted drinking a glass of his victim's blood after he had shot Mrs Durand-Deacon. He told the court he was addicted to drinking blood. He was also referred to as 'The Kensington mass killer', since he claimed to have murdered nine people, not for their money, 'but for their blood'. He was hanged.

VAN DIEMAN'S LAND LEVIATHAN, THE William John Turner Clarke (?1801–74), owner of vast tracts of land and great wealth in Tasmania.

VAN DYCK IN LITTLE Samuel Cooper, the *Apelles of His Age*; so called by Walpole (the *Autocrat of Strawberry Hill*).
- See the *English Van Dyck*.

VANISHING CRACKSMAN, THE Charlie Peace, the *Monkey*.

VARRO OF BRITAIN, THE William Camden, the *British Pausanias*.
- See the *British Varro*.

VAST VENETIAN, THE Primo Carnera, the *Ambling Alp*, born in Venice.

VAUDEVILLE'S GODFATHER Leonard Matchan, the *King*; because he is godfather to the children of a great many entertainers.

V.C. SAHIB Captain Rambahadur Limbu (1939–) who won the medal as a Lance-Corporal in Sarawak (1965); so called in the Gurkha Rifles in which he served until 1985. He was then the only VC on the active list.

VEE-VEE Lieutenant-Colonel Valentine Vivian (died 1969), vice-chief of the British Secret Intelligence Service, who recruited *Kim* Philby as an agent.

VEEP, THE Alben William Berkley (1877–1965), Vice-President (1949–53) to *Give 'Em Hell Harry* Truman. Berkley was very popular, and was the first Vice-President to marry in office. He was also the first to get the nickname. His wife Elizabeth Jane (1912–64) was known as 'The Veepess'.

VEILED MURDERESS, THE Henrietta Robinson (1827–1905) American sentenced to life imprisonment for having poisoned two people in New York. She appeared in court in a heavy veil. She claimed to be a descendant of George III (the *Button Maker*).

VELVET FOG, THE Mel Torme (1925–), American singer, a star at eighteen.

VENOMOUS PREACHER, THE Robert Traill (1642–1716), Presbyterian clergyman.

VERONICA LAKE Michael Heseltine, *Action Man*, in the days when his long fair hair fell over his eyes while he was speaking in the House of Commons.
- For Veronica Lake, see the *Peek-a-Boo Girl*. Cf *Goldilocks*.

VETERAN HISTORIAN OF THE RING, THE Pierce Egan, the *Elder*.

VICAR OF HELL, THE
i) John Skelton (?1460–1529), British poet, vicar of Diss, Norfolk; a pun by Henry VIII (*Bluff Hal*): Dis was a name of Pluto, god of the lower world.
ii) Sir Francis Bryan (died 1550), courtier and companion of Henry VIII (*Bluff Hal*). He is said to have induced the King to use improper language to the Princess *Bloody Mary* at a masque so that they

could test her virtue, but she did not understand. He is also said to have had to tell his cousin Anne Boleyn (the **Great Whore**) of her impending execution.

VICE-QUEEN, THE Lady Conyngham, the **English Pompadour**.

VICEROY, THE The Duchess of Marlborough, **Mrs Freeman**, who had great influence over Queen Anne, **Brandy Nan**.

VICKY Princess Victoria, the Princess Royal, **Pussy**.

VICTORIA THE GREAT Dame Anna Neagle (1904–86), British stage and screen actress who played Queen Victoria in the films *Victoria the Great* (1937) and *Sixty Glorious Years* (1938). Her real name was Marjorie Robertson.

VIENNESE TEARDROP, THE Luise Rainer (1909–), Austrian-born Hollywood film actress.

VILLAGE BLACKSMITH, THE Robert Fitzsimmons, the **Antipodean**.

VINDALOO Mrs Edwina Currie (1946–), Junior Minister for Health and Social Security (1980–8). She resigned after a furore over a statement about salmonella in eggs.

VINEGAR CRUET, THE **Alphabet Smith**; so called by O'Connell, the **Big Beggarman**.

VINEGAR JOE General Joseph Warren Stilwell (1883–1946) who commanded the U.S. forces in Burma and China (World War II); because of his temperament.

VINEGAR QUEEN, THE Sarah Lawrence, the **Holy Viper**.

VINOO Mulvantrai Himmatlal Mankad (1917–78), Indian cricketer who made a reputation in many Test Matches. In 1952, he took 100 wickets and made 1,000 runs. In another series, he made 33 catches.

VIRGIL OF DRAMATIC POETS, THE Ben Jonson, the **Bricklayer**; so called by Dryden (**Asaph**).
* See the **English Virgil**.

VIRGIL OF PROSE, THE R. L. Stevenson, **Tusitala**.

VIRGIN MODESTY John Wilmot, 2nd Earl of Rochester (1647–80), Restoration rake, neither virgin nor modest. The nickname was given to him by Charles II (the **Blackbird**) because he blushed very easily.

VIRGIN QUEEN, THE Elizabeth I, the **English Diana** who never married. The State of Virginia was named after this sobriquet.

VIRGINIA'S TUTELARY SAINT **Pocahontas** said to have saved the life of Captain John Smith (1580–1631) and who married John Rolfe (1585–1622). Their descendants include many prominent Virginian families. She became a Christian.
* A tutelar was a guardian deity in Rome.

VITAGRAPH BOY, THE Chick Kelly (1899–1956), boy film star in early Hollywood days; later Paul Kelly, the actor.

VITAGRAPH GIRL, THE Florence Turner (1885–1946), first actress to sign a film contract in Hollywood, which she did with the Vitagraph Company (1907).

VITAL SPARK, THE Jenny Hill (1851–96), British music-hall comedienne of great energy.

VOICE, THE
i) Henry Hinchcliffe Ainley (1879–1945), British actor-manager, said to have had the finest speaking voice on the London stage.
ii) Frank Sinatra, the **Guv'nor**.

VOICE, THE or JONES THE VOICE Tom Jones (1940–), British pop singer and Las Vegas sensation, born in Wales; the Welsh style of naming: real name, Thomas Woodward.

VOICE OF CORNWALL, THE David Penhaligon, **Mr Cornwall**.

VOICE OF TENNIS, THE Dan Maskell (1908–), British lawn tennis professional (1929–55) and first full-time coach to the All-English Club; radio and TV commentator.

VOLPONE Sidney, 1st Earl of Godolphin (1645–1712), First Lord of the Treasury (1690–1710). While serving William III (the *Deliverer*) he maintained links with James II (the *King Over The Water*); so called by Dr Sacheverell (the *High Church Trumpet*), whose impeachment Godolphin promoted when Sacheverell preached against the Whigs. Queen Anne (*Brandy Nan*) promptly dismissed Godolphin.

- Volpone or the Fox is the central figure in the play of that name (1606) by Ben Jonson (the *Bricklayer*).

VOLUMINOUS PRYNNE William Prynne, the *Brave Jersey Muse*. He published about 200 pamphlets and books. He was branded as a seditious libeller (1634).

VON HESELTINE Michael Heseltine, *Action Man*; so called early in his political career from his Teutonic good looks.

VOTE, THE Sir Trevor Jones (1924–   ), Liberal MP because of his election successes between 1972 and 1974; nickname in Welsh style by Liberals.

VOYAGER, THE St Brendan, the *Navigator*.

VULTURE HOPKINS John Hopkins (1663–1732), a wealthy London merchant who became a miser. He never gave to anybody and was worth £300,000, part of which he made in the South Sea Bubble (1720); mentioned in Pope's *Moral Essays* (1731–5).

W

WAGGON BOY, THE or THE WAGGONER BOY Thomas Corwin (1794–1865), American statesman, Secretary to the Treasury (1850–3). As a boy he worked on a farm, and had taken wagon-loads of supplies to General W.H. Harrison (*Log-Cabin Harrison*) when he was fighting Indians.

WAITER, THE Paul Ricca (1897–1972), of *Big Al* Capone's Chicago gang, whose name was also Paul Maglio. He was on the fringes of the Lindbergh kidnapping. He once worked as one.

- See *Buster* (xi).

WAKE, THE Hereward, the *Champion of Women*. The nickname means 'The Watchful', and was given to him in the 14th century. Reaney says of the English name 'Wake': 'Clearly a nickname, translated by the Latin *vigil*' and instances Hugo Wac, 1153.

- *Wac* (Henry Sweet's *Anglo-Saxon Dictionary*, 1897), in fact, means weak, timid, slothful. The Old English for 'watch' was *waecce*. Both words, however, derive from the same source.

WAKERS William Wavell, 1st Baron Wakefield (1898–1983), famous Rugby Union player (1920s). He held 31 England caps; his nickname at Cambridge University, which stayed with him all his life, especially in the phrase 'Champers with Wakers at Twickers'. He gave champagne parties at Twickenham for new England caps.

WALKING LIBRARY, THE
i) John Hales, the *Ever-Memorable*; so called by Sir Henry Wotton (1568–1639).
ii) John Selden, the *Champion of Human Laws*; so called by Edward Phillips (?1630–1696) in *Theatrum Poetarum Anglicorum* (1675).

WALKING PARSON, THE The Reverend A.N. Cooper (1850– ?), vicar of Filey, Yorkshire, who walked (1907) from Filey to Pompeii, 900 miles, in six weeks. He wrote *Tramps of a Walking Parson*.

WALKING STEWART John Stewart (1749–1822), a prodigious walker who after service in the East India Company walked through Hindustan, Persia, Abyssinia, across the Arabian desert and through Europe from Constantinople to England. In 1791 he crossed America on foot through Canada and the USA. He also made walking tours of France and Spain, and in 1784 walked from Calais to Vienna.

WALLOP Graham Yallop (1952–) Australian cricketer. He scored four centuries in five innings in a match against Pakistan (1983).

WALLPAPER Al Wolff (1902–), a member of Elliott Ness's team of Untouchables, 'racket busters' in Chicago in the 1920s; because when he raided an illicit distillery in Prohibition days he seized everything but the wallpaper.

WALLY
i) Paul J.W. Allott (1956–), Lancashire cricketer.
ii) Arthur Theodore Wallace Grout (1927–68), Queensland wicket-keeper.

WALTER THE STEWARD See *Steward*.

WALTZING GENERAL, THE General Thornton of the Guards who was one of 'those decrepit veterans' whom Wellington replaced (1814) by his own officers as repayment for their former services. Captain R.H. Gronow says Thornton was 'afflicted with the idea that...he was the only one who understood the art of waltzing'; so called by Theodore Hook (the *Little Pet of the Green Room*).

WALWORTH TERROR, THE James Cannon (fl. 1850s), a London sweep with seventeen convictions for assault and condemned to hang (1852) for attacks on two policemen, a sentence commuted to penal servitude.

- Walworth Road is in S E London.

WANDERING ERIC Eric Brook (1907–65), footballer for Manchester City and

England. He wandered from his position as outside-left to the centre of the field. He scored ten goals for England, including two against Italy (1934).

WAPPING ASSASSIN, THE James Flint (1953–), British boxer, because of his fighting fury.

WARLIKE BISHOP, THE Henry le Despenser, Bishop of Norwich, the *Fighting Prelate*.

WARLIKE GEORGE George Thomas (*circa* 1756–1802), Irish adventurer who deserted in Madras when he was a gunner's mate, Royal Navy, and eventually became the white rajah of Haryana, west of Delhi (1797). He tried to conquer the Punjab, but was taken prisoner and died near Murshidabad, Bengal; so called because he was a good soldier.

WARMING-PAN HERO, THE James Stuart, the *Old Pretender*. It was alleged by those who did not wish to believe his claim to the British throne that he had been conveyed to Mary of Modena (the *Queen of Tears*) in a warming-pan, her own child having been still-born.

WARRIOR or WARYER DRAKE Sir Francis Drake, the *Dragon*, English admiral and world circumnavigator who helped to defeat the Spanish Armada (1588); his nickname in the West Country where he was born.

WARRIOR LADY OF LATHOM, THE Charlotte Stanley, 7th Countess of Derby (1599–1664). She held Lathom House, Lancashire against Parliament (February–March, 1644). She was the only point of royalist resistance in the county. She was the wife of the *Great Earl of Derby*.

WARRIOR QUEEN, THE Boadicea or Boudicca, Queen of the Iceni (died 62). After the death of her husband, she raised her people to fight the Romans. She took poison after her defeat.

WARWICKSHIRE ANTELOPE, THE Richard Manks (1818– ?), British athlete who ran 18$^{1}/_{2}$ miles up and down hills in less than two hours. He also walked 1,000 miles in 1,000 hours, as did *Captain Barclay*.

WARWICK SMITH John Smith, *Italian Smith*.

WASH George Washington Loomis, jnr (1813–65), American bank-robber, killed by vigilantes.

WASHIES Ian Gregg (1955–), English cricketer.

WASHINGTON OF THE WEST, THE

i) W.H. Harrison, the *Cincinnatus of the West*.

ii) George Rogers Clark (1752–1818), American who helped to create the state of Kentucky. He was a frontier soldier, and fought in several Indian wars.

WASHY Cyril Washbrook (1914–), Lancashire and England cricketer who played memorable opening partnerships with (Sir) Leonard Hutton (1916–) in the 1946–8 Test Matches. They averaged 56 in 50 matches, in one of which (against South Africa 1948), they made 359.

WASP OF TWICKENHAM, THE Alexander Pope, the *Bard of Twickenham*; so called by Percy Fitzgerald in his *History of the English Stage* (1882).

WATCHDOG OF THE TREASURY, THE Elihu Benjamin Washburne (1816–87), American congressman; because of his opposition to extravagant spending.

WATER-GRUEL BARD, THE William Shenstone (1714–1763) who wrote *The Schoolmistress* (1742); so called by Walpole (the *Autocrat of Strawberry Hill*).
  • Water-gruel was a term (1700s–1800s) for something insipid.

WATER-GULL, THE Lord Temple, the *Gawky Squire*, because he was such a fervent supporter of Pitt (the *Grand Corrupter*), although he quarrelled with him later.
  • A water-gull or gall is an imperfectly formed or secondary rainbow.

WATERLOO HERO, THE

i) The Duke of Wellington, the *Achilles of England*.

ii) Lord Hill, *Daddy* who led the charge of Sir Frederick Adams' Light Brigade against the Imperial Guard.

WATERMAN, THE St David, the *Apostle of Wales*, possibly because that was all he and his monks drank.

WATER POET, THE John Taylor, the *Sculler*; so called in 1630 on the title page of his collected works. He was a Thames waterman and had been pressed into the Royal Navy.

WAXEY GORDON Irving Wexler (1889–1952), New York gangster and bootlegger.

WEASEL, THE
i) The Earl of Salisbury, *Little Beagle*.
ii) Martin van Buren, *King Martin the First*.
iii) Aladino Fratiannio, *Jimmy the Weasel*.

WEATHERCOCK, THE
i) Sir William Pulteney, 1st Earl of Bath (1684–1764), friend of Sir Robert Walpole (the *Grand Corrupter*). He later violently opposed him.
ii) William Windham (1750–1810), who opposed war under *Bloody Castlereagh*, but later changed sides to become Secretary at War under Pitt (the *Bottomless Pit*).
iii) Charles Townshend, *Champagne Charlie*, whose tax measures promoted the loss of the American colonies.

WEATHERGLASS OF HIS TIME, THE Samuel Pepys, the *Father of Black--Letter Lore*.

WEAVER POET OF INVERURIE, THE William Thom (1799–1850), who wrote *Rhymes and Recollections of a Handsome Weaver*.
• Inverurie is about 16 miles north-west of Aberdeen.

WEDGIE Tony Benn (1925–   ), British Labour politician who was formerly Anthony Wedgewood Benn, and before that the 2nd Viscount Stansgate.

WEDGIE BENN William Wedgewood Benn, 1st Viscount Stansgate (1877–1960), Labour MP and Secretary of State for Air.

WEE BEN Bernard Sayers, *Ben*.

WEE BLUE DEVIL, THE Alan Morton (1896–1971), QPR footballer who played thirty times for Scotland; because of his accuracy in shooting for goal.

WEE ELLEN Ellen Wilkinson, *Red Ellen*.

WEE JESSIE Jessie Anderson (1915–   ), Mrs George Valentine, British Ladies golf champion 1937, 1955 and 1958.

WEE JOHNNIE John Wilson (1750–1821), Scottish printer who published some of the poems of Robbie Burns (the *Ayrshire Poet*).

WEEPING SAINT, THE St Swithin or Swithun (died 862), Bishop of Winchester who asked to be buried outside the cathedral. The monks later wanted to move his body, but when they tried, it rained day after day for forty days, so they abandoned the idea. The superstition has grown up that if it rains on St Swithin's Day (15 July) it rains for forty days afterwards.

WEEPING WILLIE William Winter (1836–1917), British bohemian journalist and poet, because he wrote so many eulogies of dead actors during his eighty-one years.

WEEPING WILLOW, THE The Duchess of Portsmouth, *Bathsheba* who was easily given to tears; so called by Nell Gwyn (*Nell of Old Drury*).

WEG W.E. Gladstone, the *Dismember for Great Britain*; from his initials, but with undertones of Mr Wegg in *Our Mutual Friend* who was ' a great sayer of words'. *The Referee* (May 1885) mentioned a Mr James Hall who called Weg 'a great political coward'. Gladstone founded a debating society at Christ Church college, Oxford University, called 'W.E.G.'.

WELLINGTON DES JOUEURS, LE Lord Granville, *Antinous*, because of recklessness when he was Ambassador in Paris.

WELL-LANGUAGED DOCTOR, THE Samuel Daniel (1562–1619), English poet; so called by William Browne (1591–1643) in his *Britannia Pastorals* (1616).

WELL OF ENGLISH UNDEFILED, THE Chaucer, the *British Homer*, so called by Spenser (the *Child of the Ausonian Muse*) in *The Faerie Queene* (1590–6).

WELSH DRAGON, THE Colin Jones, the *Clout*.

WELSH FASTING GIRL, THE Sarah Jacob (1857–69) reputed to not have eaten or drunk after 1867. Crowds went to see her. She died and her parents were imprisoned for manslaughter.

WELSH LORD NUFFIELD, THE Sir David Jones (1887–1967), British millionaire dairy and grain merchant and philanthropist.

- William Richard Morris, 1st Viscount Nuffield (1877–1963) was the founder of Morris Motors and a well-known philanthropist.

WELSH SHAKESPEARE, THE Edward Williams, the *Cambrian Shakespeare*.

WELSH WINDBAG, THE Neil Kinnock, *Ramboyo*; so called by Conservatives.

WELSH WIZARD, THE

i) David Lloyd George, the *Goat*, a man of great political skill.

ii) Freddie Welsh (1886–1927), British holder of the world lightweight boxing championships (1911–17). His real name was Frederick Hall Thomas.

iii) William (Billy) Meredith, the *Other Prince of Wales*.

WENSLEYDALE POET, THE William Gideon M.J. Barker (1817–1855), a minor British poet who wrote *The Three Days of Wensleydale* (1854).

WENTWORTH William Charles Gore (1868–1928), British Wimbledon tennis star.

WESTERN HANGMAN, THE George, 1st Baron Jeffreys (1648–89), Lord Chancellor, infamous for his handling of the Bloody Assizes, Winchester (1685) after the Monmouth Rebellion when 329 were executed and many more sent into slavery in the West Indies. He was known as 'The Bloody Judge' in Somerset.

- See *King Monmouth*.

WESTMINSTER RIPPER, THE Mrs Thatcher, *Attila the Hen*.

W.G. GRACE OF AUSTRALIA, THE William Lloyd Murdoch (1855–1911), captain of Australia (1880–2, 1884 and 1890) He was a notable batsman and wicket-keeper.

- Cf the *Grace of Australia* and see the *Champion*.

WHACKO Harvey Proctor (1947–), former MP fined £1,450 (1987) after he had pleaded guilty to four charges of gross indecency with teenage 'rent boys'. He had been involved in 'spanking games'; so called by MPs before he resigned.

WHALE, THE Edward (Eddie) Hemmings (1949–), off-spin bowler for Nottinghamshire and England. He took five wickets in an innings seven times in one season (1987). He is a robust man.

WHEEL KING OF LONDON, THE Patrick Hearn (?1842–89). He owned 100 cabs, 20 omnibuses and 1,000 barrows.

WHIG JOHNSON, THE Dr S. Parr, the *Birmingham Doctor*. Johnson (*Blinking Sam*) was a Tory.

WHIP AND AWAY Sir Henry Lee, nephew of Sir Henry Lee (1530–1610), Master of Ordnance under Queen Elizabeth (the *English Diana*). The elder Sir Henry wanted his nephew, with a gang of 'lusty fellows' (Aubrey) to 'whip and away' someone who had offended him. The nephew refused, and Sir Henry disinherited him.

WHIPLASH WALLACE Anna Wallace, Mrs Fermor-Hesketh (1955–), friend of the Prince of Wales (*Fishface*). She married (1980) John Hesketh, brother of Lord Hesketh (*Bunter*); so called because of her love for hunting by the Prince of Wales.

WHIRLWIND, THE James (Jimmy) White (1962–), British youngest winner of the world amateur snooker championships (1981).

- Cf the *Cool Kid*.

WHISKY VAN Martin van Buren, *King Martin the First*; so called by his political opponents.

WHITE, THE

i) Aedh, King of Argyll (killed 776).

ii) Hewald, see the *Black* (i).

iii) James Butler, Earl of Ormond (fl. 15th century).

iv) Olaf, Anlaf or Amlaibh, Viking King of Lochlann (Norway) who landed in Ireland, drove out the Danes and became King of Dublin (853).

- See *James the White*.

WHITE ANGEL, THE Anna Leonowens (1834–1914), governess to the children of the King of Siam (1862–67), made famous by the musical *The King and I*; so called because of her work for the release of slaves in Siam. Slavery was abolished there in 1872. Later she lived in America.

WHITE BEAR, THE Archbishop Richard Whately (1787–1863), English theologian and logician; he 'mauled' his opponents.

WHITECHAPEL WIRLWIND, THE Jack *Kid* Berg.

WHITE DUCK, THE Aethelflaed or Ethelflaed, wife of Edgar, king of England (the *Peaceful*) and daughter of Earl Ordmaer. She was the mother of Edward the *Martyr*.

WHITE-EYED KAFFIR, THE George H. Chirgwin (1854–1922), British blackfaced music-hall comedian.

WHITE EYE JACK or THE WHITE-EYED KID Joseph Foster Anderson (fl. 1870s), friend of *Wild Bill* Hickok. After he was hit in the eye with a burning buffalo chip, he eyebrows were white.

WHITEFIELD OF THE STAGE, THE
i) James Quin, the *Stage Leviathan*; so called by Garrick (*Atlas*) to whom he was a rival in his earlier days.
ii) David Garrick, *Atlas*.
* The Reverend George Whitefield, *Dr Squintum*, was immensely popular as a preacher – in fact, many thought him the greatest orator ever.

WHITE GARDENIA MAN, THE Carl Brisson, the *Dimpled Dane* with a fondness for wearing that flower.

WHITE GHOST, THE Thomas (Tom) Finney (1922–   ), centre-forward for Preston North End and England, for whom he played 76 times. He is slight and pale.

WHITE HAIR Aedh Ui Neill, High King of Ireland (862–79). He married a daughter of Kenneth MacAlpine (died 858), King of the Scots of Dalriada.
* See the *Fair* (iii).

WHITE KING, THE Charles I, the *Ahab of the Nation*; so called by George Herbert (the *Sweet Singer of the Temple*): because he was a 'martyr'. White has long been regarded as a symbol of royalty and of goodness and purity.

WHITE KNIGHT, THE
i) Edmund Fitzgibbon (?1552–1608), Irish soldier, Sheriff of Cork.
ii) Spiro Agnew, *Spiro T. Eggplant*. Ironic: he pleaded 'no contest' to a charge of income tax evasion after having been involved in a 'backhand' scheme.

WHITE LADY, THE Lady Anne Keppel (1803–44), daughter of the 5th Earl of Albemarle (1794–1851). In 1822 she married *Coke of Norfolk*, who was fifty-one years older than herself. She had a very fair skin.

WHITE LANE C.G. Lane, the *Admirable Crichton of Oxford*; to distinguish him from another Lane.

WHITE MARQUIS, THE The Marquis of Carmarthen, later 1st Duke of Leeds, *King Tom*. His face had a deathly pallor.

WHITE MILLINER, THE The Duchess of Tyrconnel, *La Belle Jennings*, when she was a widow (see *Lying Dick Talbot*). She appeared (1690s) as a sempstress dressed in white and wearing a white mask in the London Exchange and was quite unknown. The curiosity she aroused was good for trade, and all fashionable Londoners went to patronize her. When her identity became known, her relatives provided for her.

WHITE MEDICINE PAINTER, THE George Catlin, *Medicine Paint*.

WHITE QUEEN, THE Mary, Queen of Scotland. *Mermaid*. She wore white in mourning.

WHITE RAJAH, THE Sir James Brooke (1803–68). He set up a 'kingdom' in Sarawak (1830s) and had his title confirmed by the Sultan of Borneo (1841). His descendants held it until 1946.

WHITE ROSE OF ENGLAND, THE Perkin Warbeck (1474–99), pretender to the English throne.

WHITE ROSE OF RABY, THE Cecily Neville, the *Rose of Raby*.

WHITE ROSE OF SCOTLAND, THE Lady Katherine Gordon, daughter of George, 2nd Earl of Huntly (died 1502) and wife (1495) of Perkin Warbeck (above). After his execution she married Sir Matthew Craddock.

WHITE WOMAN, THE Mary Jamieson or Jemison (1743–1833). Captured by Indians from Genesee at Marsh Creek, Pennsylvania (1758), she lived with them for the rest of her life. In 1820, the Reverend Timothy Alden, on a mission among the Senecas and Munsees, visited her and said she was known far and near by the name of 'The White Woman'.

WHIZZBANG Major-General Sir Francis de Guingand (1900–79), Chief of Staff to the Eighth Army (World War II) and one of the planners for the invasion of Europe; a 'rhyming' with 'Guingand'.

- A whizzbang was a type of field-gun shell (German, World War I). The noise of its approach and that of its explosion were almost simultaneous.

WHIZZER Byron Raymond White (1917–), American college and professional footballer who became Attorney-General in the Kennedy Administration (1961); later Justice of the Supreme Court.

WICKED COUNTESS, THE Anna Maria, Countess of Shrewbury (died 1702), mistress of the 2nd Duke of Buckingham (*Alcibiades*). She is said to have dressed as a page and held Buckingham's horse while he fought a duel with her husband, who was mortally wounded (1668).

WICKED EARL, THE Lord Wilton, *King of Melton*.

WICKEDEST MAN IN THE WORLD, THE Aleister Crowley, *Beast 666*; so called by the *Daily Express*.

WICKED JIMMY Lord Lonsdale, the *Brazen Bully*. His wild life became a legend in villages near Whitehaven, Cumberland, where people talked of his 'evil eye'.

WICKED LADY, THE Lady Katherine Ferrers (1634–60) of Markyate Cell, Hertfordshire, alleged to have committed arson and highway robbery. Her ghost is reputed still to haunt the area. In 1945 Margaret Lockwood starred in a famous film based loosely on her life.

WICKED LORD, THE

i) William Byron, 5th Baron Rochdale (1722–98), great-uncle of the poet.

Profligate and depraved, he shot his coachman dead in a fit of rage, and killed off a herd of deer in sheer wanton cruelty.

- See *Tom Tilbury*.

ii) Thomas, 2nd Baron Lyttleton (1744–79), who died of profligacy at thirty-five.

WICKED MARQUIS, THE Lord Hastings, *Champagne Charlie* (iii); nickname given to him after his death, especially by villagers of Castle Donnington, Leicestershire.

WICKEDSHIFTS Lord Brougham and Vauxhall, *Blundering Brougham*; mentioned by Creevy (1768–1838).

WICKED UNCLES, THE The four uncles of Queen Victoria (*Drina*): The Prince Regent (*Adonis of Fifty*) and the Dukes of Cambridge (1774–1850), Cumberland (*Billy*) and Sussex (1773–1843).

WICKED UNCLES OF FLEET STREET, THE Lord Beaverbrook, the *Beaver* and Lord Rothermere, *Lord Wibbly-Wob*, who formed the short-lived United Empire Party (1930s).

WICKED WASP OF TWICKENHAM, THE Pope, the *Bard of Twickenham*.

WICKED WATT Sir Walter Scott, *Bold Buccleuch*.

WIDOW OF WINDSOR, THE Queen Victoria (*Drina*), who virtually retired from public life after the death of Albert the *Good* and spent much time at Windsor castle. It was a term among soldiers picked up by Kipling (the *Bard of Empire*) in *Barrack Room Ballads* (1892). He was never honoured by the Queen because of that, although he won a Nobel Prize.

WIFFIE Margaret C. Smith (1937–), American golfer, US Women's Amateur champion (1954 and 1955) and British Ladies champion (1956). She got her nickname in Mexico, where it means something like 'Happy'.

WIGAN NIGHTINGALE, THE George Formby senior, (died 1921), British comedian with a Lancashire accent and singer of comic songs.

WILBERFORCE OF THE HOTTENTOTS, THE John Philip (1775–1851), Scottish-born missionary in South Africa, who became unofficial adviser to the Governor (Sir G. T. Napier) in Cape Town on the treatment of Africans.

• See the *Man of Black Renown*.

WILD BILL

i) J.B. Hickok, the *Prince of Pistoleers*. During the American Civil War he assumed the name of his father, William.

ii) Mortimer N. Kress (1841– ?) whose deeds, including the murder of an Indian chief, were blamed on Hickok (qv). Kress was sometimes known as 'Wild Bill of the Blue'.

iii) Major-General William J. Donovan (1883–1959) of the American Fighting 69th Regiment who headed (1942) the Office of Strategic Services which dropped agents and saboteurs into France; so called from his daring.

iv) William Cummings (1914–39), American motor-racing driver.

v) William Edward Davison (1906–89), American jazz trumpeter and cornettist, still playing at eighty; mostly because of his style.

vi) William Strathan Davis (1918–), American jazz composer, and pianist.

vii) William Lovett (died 1923), one of the leaders of the White Hand gang, New York (1920s).

viii) William P. Longley (1850–78) who is thought to have killed thirty black men in America (1866–78).

ix) William E. Mehlhorn (1896–), American golfer who won fifteen tournaments between 1921 and 1929.

x) Gordon Elliott (1904–65), American film actor, mostly in westerns, e.g. *The Longhorn* (1951).

WILD BULL, THE Vince Karaluis, Rugby League player for Australia (1958–64).

WILD BULL OF THE PAMPAS, THE Luis Angel Firpo (?1895–1960), Argentine heavyweight boxer remembered for his savage fight (1923) with Jack Dempsey (the *Manassa Mauler*). Firpo knocked Dempsey out of the ring, but eventually the latter won, although he had to knock Firpo down nine times first.

WILD COLONIAL BOY, THE Jack Donahoe, *Bold Jack*.

WILD EDRIC or EADRIC THE FORESTER Anglo-Saxon thane (fl. 11th century), son of Aelfric, *Anglo-Saxon Chronicle* for 1066: 'Eadric the Wild and the Welsh rose in rebellion and attacked the castle at Hereford and inflicted severe losses on them'. He is also mentioned by Map (the *Anacreon of the Twelfth Century*).

WILDFIRE Sir William Windham (1687–1740), Chancellor of the Exchequer (1713–14); so called in ballads. He worked for years for the overthrow of Sir Robert Walpole (the *Grand Corrupter*).

WILD SCOTCHMAN, THE Alpin Macpherson, alias John Bruce, alias John Macgregor, alias Scotchie (fl. 1860s), Australian bushranger with a gang in New South Wales. He was taken to Australia as a child.

WILLIAM THE BAD William Lowther, 2nd Earl of Lonsdale (2nd creation) (1787–1872), one of the leaders of London society with a taste for opera singers. He is said to have refused the Premiership.

WILLIAM THE CONQUEROR

i) Sir William Waller (*circa* 1597–1688), Parliamentarian soldier of the English Civil War; so called by Londoners because of his victories.

ii) William Prynne, the *Brave Jersey Muse*. The principles he fought for prevailed in the Commonwealth.

• William the Conqueror, see the *Bastard*.

WILLIAM THE GOOD Sir William Lowther, 1st Earl of Lonsdale (2nd creation) (1757–1844), father of *William the Bad*.

WILLIAM WHITEHALL Lord Whitelaw, *Oyster Eyes*; so called as he himself has said, when Secretary of State for Ireland (1970s).

WILLIAM WITHER Sir Robin Thwing, a Yorkshireman who led bands in the revolts of 1231–2 to protest against the prevalence of foreign clergy in England. He gave what he plundered to the poor.

• *Wither* = Anglo-Saxon for adversary or opponent.

WILLIS O' THE WHITE HAT John Willis, *Old White Hat*; so called in the City of London.

WILL O' THE WISP James Boswell, the *Ambitious Thane*; so called by Wolcot (*Peter Pindar*).

WILT THE STILT Wilton Norman Chamberlain (1936–), American professional basketball player who is more than 7ft tall. He holds the record for scoring 100 points in a game and 30,000 points in a season (1972).

WILTSHIRE ANTIQUARY, THE John Aubrey, the *Little Boswell of His Day*. He wrote its history.

WILTSHIRE BARD, THE The Reverend Stephen Duck (1705–56), agricultural labourer who became rector of Byfleet and a minor poet.

WIMP, THE George Bush, *Poppy*, 41st President of the USA. He was said to be sensitive and submissive. Few people see his political career as one of dynamic success.

- 'Wimp', originally Cambridge University slang for a young girl (*circa* 1900), came to mean an ineffective person behind the times. After a 1988 TV interview with Dan Rather in which Bush showed a 'macho image' over the Iran-Contra issue, Republicans boasted 'so much for the wimp factor'.

WINDMILL, THE Lauren Bacall (1924–), American film actress; so called as a model. She swung her arms immoderately as she walked. Her real name is Joan Perske.

WINDY General Sir Richard Gale (1896–1982), Deputy Supreme Commander in Europe and Commander of the 6th Airborne Division, e.g. in the Allied landings at Arnhem (World War II); so called by British troops, ex 'Gale'.

WINGATE OF THE SUDAN, THE Sir Francis Reginald Wingate (1861–1953). As Major F.R. Wingate, he was Director of Intelligence in the Sudan (1891) and later Director of Military Intelligence (1896–1898). He was a cousin of *Robin Hood* Wingate.

WINNIE Sir Winston Churchill, *Bricky*.

WINTER QUEEN, THE Elizabeth Stuart, *Goody Palsgrave*. Her husband, Frederick V, Elector of the Palatinate, was King of Bohemia for the winter of 1619–20, until his army was defeated by the imperial forces under Marshal Tilly (1559–1632).

WIRE MASTER, THE Lord Bute, *Jack Boot* who had great influence over George III (the *Button Maker*).

WISCONSIN NECROPHILE, THE Edward (Ed.) Gein (1907–84), Wisconsin farmer who dug up the bodies of women or murdered others. He was found insane (1957) and detained for life.

WISE, THE

i) Gildas, the *British Jeremiah*, called *Sapiens* and 'Badonicus' because he said the battle of Badon took place on his birthday, in *circa* 516.

ii) Duns Scotus, *Doctor Subtilis*.

iii) Ine or Ina, King of Wessex (reigned 688–726). He set up a code of laws and is reputed to have built a monastery at Glastonbury (*Anglo-Saxon Chronicle*). After his abdication he went to Rome on a pilgrimage and died there. He was credited with miracles after his death.

WISE DUCHESS, THE Sarah, Duchess of Marlborough, *Mrs Freeman*.

WISEST AMERICAN, THE Benjamin Franklin, the *American Socrates*.

WISEST FOOL IN CHRISTENDOM, THE James I, the *British Solomon*, although the Duc de Sully (1560–1641) really called him 'the most learned fool in Christendom', but the term was apparently repeated wrongly by Henri IV (1553–1610) at the time of the English alliance with the Spanish., Sully had been French envoy at the Court of James I.

WISEST OF THE BRETONS, THE Gildas, the *British Jeremiah*, a Breton saint.

WITCHFINDER, THE or THE WITCH-FINDER-GENERAL Matthew Hopkins (died 1647). He made tours of England to discover 'witches' and is said to have caused the deaths of some 3,000 to 4,000 people. He was exposed as a fraud and hanged.

WITCH OF EYE, THE Margaret Jourdain or

Jourdemain, burned at Smithfield (1441) for having conspired to kill Henry VI (*Ill-Fated Henry*). At the same time Eleanor, Cobham, Duchess of Gloucester was condemned to walk barefooted in a sheet to St. Paul's cathedral to do penance for witchcraft, and was then imprisoned for life. Jourdain and the Duchess appear in Shakespeare's *Henry VI*. They were accused of making wax images of the King.

WITCH OF WALL STREET, THE Henrietta (Hetty) Green (1853–1916), wealthy American miser who made a fortune on the Stock Exchange. She lived in squalor and left $100,000,000.

WIZARD, THE Mike Gibbons, the *St. Paul's Phantom*.

WIZARD EARL, THE Henry Percy, 9th Earl of Northumberland (1564–1682), interested in scientific experiments.

WIZARD OF BERKELEY, THE Edward Oscar Heinrich (1881–1953), criminologist at Berkeley University, California, who helped to solve many crimes, notably the train robbery and murder committed by the three D'Autrement brothers (1923). The nickname was the title of a book about him.

WIZARD OF DRIBBLE, THE Sir Stanley Matthews (1915–   ), right-winger for Blackpool, Stoke and England, with amazing ball control. He was the first English footballer to be knighted; later a coach in Canada.

WIZARD OF MANTON, THE Alec Taylor (1862–1943), top British racehorse trainer for twelve years. Horses from his stables at Manton, Leicestershire, won more than a thousand races. He was sometimes referred to as 'Grim Old Alec'.

WIZARD OF MENLO PARK, THE Thomas Alva Edison (1847–19312), American inventor who had a laboratory at Menlo Park, New Jersey.

WIZARD OF THE NORTH, THE

i) Scott, the *Ariosto of the North*.

ii) John Henry Anderson (1815–74), British conjuror and actor.

iii) John Scott (1794–1871), British racehorse trainer with great success especially with West Australia, the first horse to win the triple crown (1853): the Derby, the St Leger and the Two Thousand Guineas.

WIZARD OF OOZE, THE Senator E. Dirkson, *Irksome Dirkson*, with a honey-like voice and manner.

WIZARD OF THE CHORUS LINE, THE *Busby* Berkeley, American dance director of many film musicals with spectacular scenic effects.

WIZARD OF THE SEAS, THE Captain William Kidd (*circa* 1645–1701), British privateer and pirate who lived in New York City, *circa* 1690; because of his skill in seamanship.

WOCKA Sir Warwick Fairfax (1902–1987), chairman of *The Sydney Morning Herald* and *The Age* (Melbourne), head of an 'empire', founded in 1831, the oldest established business in Australia; from 'Warwick'.

• Cf *Young Wocka*.

WOLF OF BADENOCH, THE Sir Alexander Stewart, Earl of Buchan and Lord of Badenoch (?1343–?1405) fourth son of Robert II of Scotland (*Blear-Eye*). He burnt the town of Forres when the Bishop of Moray excommunicated him for having abandoned his wife for a mistress and he almost destroyed Elgin cathedral.

WOMAN IN WHITE, THE Mrs Perla Siedle-Gibson (1889–1971), who sang to British troopships arriving in Durban harbour, South Africa (post-1940) and to British ships after World War II. She had been a mayoress of Durban. She always wore white.

WONDERFUL DOCTOR, THE Roger Bacon, the *Admirable Doctor*.

WONDERMAC Harold Macmillan, *Mac the Knife*; so called by *Nye* Bevan.

WOODBINE TEDDY Edward Prince of Wales, see *Teddy Woodbine*.

WOODBINE WILLIE The Reverend Geoffrey Anketell Studdert Kennedy (1883–1929), army chaplain (World War I) who gave packets of Woodbine cigarettes to troops; so called by soldiers after a comic-paper character.

WOOLY Sir William Erskine, Quartermaster-General to the British Army in America, under Lord Cornwallis (1738–1805).

WORD CATCHER, THE Joseph Ritson, the *Antiquary of Poetry*. His critical work revealed many forgeries, e.g. in John Pinkerton's (1758–1826) *Select Scottish Ballads* (1784). Lockhart (the *Scorpion*) referred (1838) to him as 'this narrow-minded, sour and dogmatical little word-catcher'.

WORKER'S CHAMPION, THE Mrs Elizabeth (Bessie) Margaret Braddock, née Bamber (1899–1970), Labour MP for Liverpool (Exchange: post-1945).

WOR JACKIE John (Jackie) Milburn (1924–88), centre-forward for Newcastle United who scored 173 goals for them in 54 matches and played for England 13 times. He helped Newcastle win the FA Cup three times – in 1951 scoring the two goals to beat Blackpool.

• Wor = North Country version of 'our'.

WORLD'S FASTEST HUMAN, THE Charley W. Paddock (1900–43), American sprinter. He covered 100 yards in 9.5 sec and in 1921 was timed in 10.2 sec over 110 yards. He equalled the world record of 9.5 sec six times between 1921 and 1926, and won Olympic gold and silver medals in 1920 and 1924.

WORLD'S GREATEST ACTOR, THE John Barrymore, the *Great Profile*; so called especially for *Don Juan*.

WORLD'S GREATEST ACTRESS, THE Marie Dressler (1869–1934), especially for *Anna Christie* (1930). Her real name was Leila von Koerber.

WORLD'S SWEETHEART, THE Janet Gaynor (1906–84), American stage and screen actress; so called after she won fame before 1928; first actress to win an Oscar (1927/8).

WORLD'S WONDER, THE Elizabeth I, the *English Diana*; so called in 1591.

WOULD-BE CROMWELL, THE Samuel Adams, the *America Cato*; so called by his political opponents. He did more than any other man before 1775 to bring about the Revolution.

WRONG-WAY CORRIGAN Douglas Corrigan (1907–), mechanic to Lindbergh (*Lindy*). He decided (1938) to fly non-stop from Los Angeles to New York in an old single-engined monoplane. Then he set out to fly home, but read his compass wrongly and flew the Atlantic instead, with no radio, no maps, no water and no passport. His only food was a few fig-bars and some chocolate. He revisited Ireland on the anniversary (1988).

WRY-NECKED DICK Admiral Boscawen, *Old Dreadnought*. He had been wounded in the shoulder and held his head awkwardly.

WULLY Field-Marshal William Robert Robertson, 1st Baronet (1860–1933). He rose from being a trooper in the 16th Lancers to become Chief of the Imperial General Staff (1915–18); because of his accent. He dropped his aitches all his life.

WYN THE LEAP Wyn Davies (1942–), striker for Newcastle United and Wales. He leaps high to head the ball.

Y

YANKEE CLIPPER, THE Joe Di Maggio, *Joltin' Joe*; from the fact that he played for the New York Yankees and his batting style.

YANKEE DOODLE DOLLY Pamela Shriver (1962–), American tennis celebrity; word play on *Yankee Doodle Dandy*. She is a dolly-bird born on the 4th of July.

YANKEE HILL George Handel Hill (1809–49), American comedian specializing in Yankee roles.

YANKEE JONATHAN Jonathan Hastings, a Cambridge, Massachusetts farmer who equated 'Yankee' with 'excellent' and used it as his favourite adjective, e.g. 'A Yankee fine crop' or a 'Yankee good cider'. He was said to have been a friend of George Washington (the *American Cincinnatus*).

YANKEE SULLIVAN James Ambrose (1813–50), Irish-born pugilist who became the second official champion of the USA (1848). He was killed by vigilantes in California, where he had gone as a prospector. He usually wore the US flag as a sash on entering the ring.

YARDBIRD Charlie Parker, *Bird*.

YEA AND NAY or RICHARD YEA AND NAY Richard I, *Coeur de Lion*.

YEASTY PRIDE Colonel Thomas Pride, the *Purging Colonel*; so called in lampoons. He was alleged to have once been a drayman.

- 'Yeasty' in the 16th century meant 'swelling', e.g. 'with yeasty ambition' (1598).

YELLOW, THE

i) Aedh *Buidhe*, King of Ailech (1260–81).

ii) Aedh *Buidhe* (died 1444), royal heir to Ireland and Prince of Clannaboy (1426–44).

- Clannaboy, see *French John*. *Buidhe* = yellow in Gaelic.

YELLOW EARL, THE Lord Lonsdale, *England's Greatest Sportsman*. He always drove in yellow carriages or cars.

YELLOW HAIR Baltan O'Neill, joint King of Ireland (579–572 BC).

YELLOW KID, THE Joseph Weil (1877–1973), American swindler; so called because of his interest in his youth in the cartoons of that name by Outcault (the *Father of the Comic Strip*). It first appeared in October 1896.

YELLOWSTONE KELLY Luther Sage Kelly (1849–1928), American army scout to General Nelson A. Miles (*Bear Coat*).

YIP Edgar Y Harbury (1898–1981), Broadway lyricist, e.g. *The Wizard of Oz*, (1939).

YOGI

i) Lawrence Peter Berra (1925–), American baseball player for the New York Yankees; their regular catcher for 14 seasons. He played 148 games without error (1957–9); later manager,

- From the American cartoon character Yogi Bear.

ii) Alan Evans (1951–), British world darts champion.

YORKSHIRE LAD, THE Tom Foy (died 1917 at the age of twenty-eight), brilliant young British music-hall comedian.

YORKSHIRE RIPPER, THE Peter William Sutcliffe (1946–), a British long-distance lorry driver, imprisoned for life (May 1981) for the murders of 13 young women in five years (1975–80) and attacks on seven others; so called in the Press because his methods paralleled those of *Jack the Ripper*. He was removed to Broadmoor (1984).

YORKSHIRE WITCH, THE Mary Bateman (1768–1809), née Harker, executed for poisoning a woman. She posed as a fortune-teller and professed to know magic.

YOUNG, THE
  i) Art *Og*, King of Ulster (1514–19).
  ii) Olaf, King of Dublin, killed in Scotland (874).
  iii) Sir Niall *Og*, the *Great O'Neill*.
  • *Og* or *Oge* is Irish for 'young'. Art = Arthur.

YOUNG ADVENTURER, THE *Bonny Prince Charlie* Stuart. The 1745 rebellion was a desperate venture.

YOUNG ALFRED Alfred (1874–89), son of the Duke of Edinburgh (*Affie*); grandson of Queen Victoria, *Drina*.

YOUNG AMERICAN ROSCIUS, THE Samuel Houghton Cowell (1820–64), American star of the English music-hall. He sang *Villikins and his Dinah* at the Grecian and the Canterbury.
  • See *Bravo Rouse*, the *Great Little Robson* and the *African Roscius*.

YOUNG ARTHUR Arthur Henderson, Lord Rowley (1893–1968), son of *Uncle Arthur* Henderson.

YOUNG BEAR, THE Edward Ellice (1810–80), son of the *Bear*. He was MP for St Andrew's Burgh for 44 years.

YOUNG CATULLUS OF HIS DAY, THE Thomas *Anacreon Moore*; so called by Byron (*Baby*).
  • Gaius Valerius Catullus (*circa* 84 – 54 BC) was a Roman lyric poet, flexible and versatile, with a mastery of many metrical forms.

YOUNG CHEVALIER, THE *Bonny Prince Charlie* Stuart. His father assumed the title of Chevalier de St George. It was included in a Jacobite marching song, *Charlie is my Darling*, written by the *Flower of Strathearn*.

YOUNG CHUB Maurice William Tate (1895–1956), Sussex and England bowler who took 2,786 wickets at an average of 18.8 runs each. He made 1,000 runs and 242 catches, and played in 39 Test matches. His father's nickname was 'Chub'.

YOUNG CUB, THE C.J.Fox, *Carlo Khan*; a play on 'fox' and the fact that as a young man in politics he held unpopular opinions and was 'insubordinate' to his elders.

YOUNG DUTCH SAM Samuel Evans (fl. mid 19th century), son of *Dutch Sam*, whom he followed into the ring.

YOUNG ENGLISH GIANT, THE James Toller (1795–1819), reputed to have been 8ft 1 1/2 in at eighteen and to have been 8ft 6 in when he died. Presented to the Tsar of Russia and the King of Prussia.
  • Cf the *British Giant*.

YOUNG EUPHUES Thomas Nash, the *English Aretine*; so called by *Ape Gabriel* Harvey.
  • See the *Ape of Envy*.

YOUNGER, THE
  i) George Colman *George the Grinner*, son of George Colman the *Elder*.
  ii) Thomas Howard, Earl of Surrey and later 3rd Duke of Norfolk (?1473–1554) Earl Marshal of England (1553).
  iii) Edmund Calamy (1671–1732), grandson of Edmund Calamy the *Elder*.
  iv) Pierce Egan (1814–80), novelist and son of Pierce Egan the *Elder*.
  v) Sir Henry Vane (1613–62), English statesman executed for high treason, having been an active Parliamentarian; to distinguish him from his father, Sir Henry Vane (1589–1654), also a statesman.
  vi) *Garrett Oge*, the 9th Earl of Kildare.
  vii) William Pitt, the *Bottomless Pit*.
  viii) Major-General A. Macdonald, *Colkitto*.
  ix) Isaac Gosset. *Milk-White Gosset*.
  • See *Rory Oge*.

YOUNG GREGORY Richard Brandon (died 1649), London's principal hangman who is said to have executed Charles I (the *Ahab of the Nation:* 1649). He lived in Rosemary Lane near the Tower of London. He also beheaded the Earl of Strafford (*Black Tom Tyrant*) and Archbishop Laud (*Hocuspocus*).
  • See the *Two Gregories*.

YOUNG GRIFFO Albert Griffiths (1871–1927), Australian lightweight boxer who claimed the world featherweight title (1890). He won 54 and drew 48 out of 105 fights in America; one defeat was against Jack McAuliffe for the world featherweight title (1894).

YOUNG HERCULES R.B. Sheridan, *Sherry*; so called by Garrick (*Atlas*).

YOUNG HICKORY

i) Martin van Buren, *King Martin the First*, thought of as the spiritual successor to Andrew Jackson, *Old Hickory*.

ii) James Knox Polk, the *Napoleon of the Stump*. His friendship with Jackson (above) directed him into politics.

YOUNG JACK John William Hearne (1891–1965), Middlesex cricketer; to differentiate him from J.T. Hearne (1867–1944), also a Middlesex cricketer.

YOUNG JENKY Lord Liverpool, *Blinkinson*, son of *Jenky*.

YOUNG JOHN Iain MacGregor of Glencarnick (1668–1744).

YOUNG JUVENAL, THE

i) Thomas Lodge (*circa* 1558–1625), English novelist and poet; so called by Robert Green (the *Ape of Euphues*). Lodge's best-known work is *Phillis*, (1593), a volume of sonnets, songs and lyrics.

ii) Thomas Nash, the *English Aretine*.

• See the *English Juvenal*.

YOUNG LUTHER Thomas Edwards (1599–1647), Presbyterian preacher of violent sermons. One of them attacked Archbishop Laud (*Hocuspocus*).

• Martin Luther (1483–1546), a German reformer, violently attacked the life-style of Catholic priests and nuns.

YOUNG MARSHAL, THE The Earl of Chatham, *Aeolus*; so called when a young man by his uncle, James, 1st Earl of Stanhope (*circa* 1673–1721), soldier and statesman, who delighted in his nephew's soldier-like qualities which later earned him a cornetcy in Lord Cobham's Regiment of Horse (afterwards the 1st Dragoon Guards).

• See the *Terrible Cornet of Horse*.

YOUNG NAPOLEON, THE

i) General B. McClellan, *Little Mac*.

ii) Tommy Burns (1881–1955), French-Canadian boxer whose real name was Noah Brusso. At 5ft 7 in, he was the smallest man to win the world

heavyweight title (1906–8). In March 1908, he knocked out Jem Roche in 1 min 28 sec, the shortest heavyweight fight on record. Sometimes called 'Tammy'.

YOUNG OX, THE Domnall Ui Neill, King of Ulster (died 1260), son of Aedh the *Handy*. Domnall was killed in battle with the MacLochlainn.

• Domnall or Domhnull = Daniel.

YOUNG PRETENDER, THE Charles Stuart, *Bonny Prince Charlie*.

• Cf the *Old Pretender*.

YOUNG ROSCIUS, THE W.H. Betty, the *Infant Roscius*.

YOUNG RUFFIAN, THE Jack Fearby (fl. 1790s), a daring and courageous prizefighter, given the nickname, says Egan the *Elder*. 'from his athletic figure and determined resolution'. In later life, however, he was 'a walking skeleton', (Egan's *Book of Sports* 1825).

YOUNG SCROPE Thomas Scrope, 10th Lord Scrope of Bolton (?1567–1609), English West March Warden (1592–1603); to distinguish him from *Old Scrope*.

YOUNG SUBTLETY Nathaniel Fiennes (?1608–69), MP in the Long Parliament (1640–53), son of *Old Subtlety*.

YOUNG TARQUIN Charles II, the *Blackbird*; so called by Needham (the *Cobbett of His Day*).

• Lucius Tarquinius Superbus (*circa* 543–510 BC), King of Rome, was a tyrant.

YOUNG TOM Thomas (Tom) Morris, junior (1851–75), British Open golf champion at the age of sixteen (1868–70); died in his sleep at the age of twenty-four after the death of his wife; to distinguish him from *Old Tom*.

YOUNG VARMINT, THE Henry Havelock (1795–1857), later Major-General Sir Henry, hero of the relief of Lucknow (1858); his nickname as a subaltern in the Rifle Brigade (1815–19).

• A varmint, from 'vermin', has been used for a troublesome child since at least 1773, apparently from northern dialect.

YOUNG VICKY Princess Victoria, *Moretta*.

YOUNG WILLIE William Dunn (1870–1952), Scottish-born American golfer, unofficial American Open champion (1894) to distinguish him from his father, *Old WIllie*.

YOUNG WOCKA Warwick Fairfax (1961–), chairman of the *Sydney Morning Herald* and *The Age* (Melbourne) in succession to his father Sir Warwick Fairfax (*Wocka*).

YOUNG ZOILUS John Dennis, *Appius*.

 • See *Black-Mouthed Zoilus*.

YOUR LAVISHIP Lady Caroline Lamb, *Caro*; nickname given to her by her father-in-law, Peniston Lamb, 1st Viscount Melbourne (1770–1828) because of her extravagance.

YPSILANTI RIPPER, THE John Norman Collins (1947–), who raped and tortured seven girls to death (1967–9) in Ypsilanti, Michigan; gaoled for life (1969).

 • Cf *Jack the Ripper*.

Z

ZANY OF DEBATES, THE George Canning, *Aeolus*; so called by Lamb (the *Mitre Courtier*).

ZANY OF HIS AGE, THE John Henley, the *Cain of Literature*; so called by Pope (the *Bard of Twickenham*) in *The Dunciad* (1728).

ZAP Graham Gooch (1953–), Essex and England cricketer, captain of England (1988, 1989); because of his Zapata-like moustache.

- After Emiliano Zapata (1883–1919), Mexican revolutionary bandit.

ZEALOUS DOCTOR, THE Dr. H. Sacheverell, the *High Church Trumpet*.

ZEALOT OF REBELLION, THE John Hampden (1594–1643), leader of resistance to ship money; so called by Johnson (*Blinking Sam*).

- Ship money was old tax levied in time of war to provide money to build ships. It was revived by Charles I (the *Ahab of the Nation*) and Hampden had an obligation to provide 20 shillings. (In the early 17th century a chief architect was paid £1 a week and a labourer about 1 shilling a day.)

ZED Zaheer Abbas (1946–), batsman for Gloucestershire (for 13 years) and Pakistan (1970s–1980s).

ZERO Samuel Joel Mostel (1915–77), American comedian and film-star; because of his low marks at school.

ZIGGY Florenz Ziegfeld, the *Glorifier of the American Girl*.

ZIMRI The Duke of Buckingham, *Alcibiades*; so called by Dryden (*Asaph*) in *Absalom and Achitophel* (1681).

- Zimri was a captain of Judah who conspired against the king.

ZOO or ZOOKINS Lady Isabel Burton, *Puss*; nicknamed by her husband (the *Modern Admirable Crichton*).

ZOOT John Haley Simms (1925–85), American saxophonist who played with Woody Herman's band (post-1947).

ZUTPHEN HERO, THE Sir Philip Sidney, the *British Bayard*, who, mortally wounded at Zutphen (1586) and offered a drink of water, pointed to a soldier and said 'Give it to him; his need is greater than mine.'

ZUTTY Arthur Singleton (1898,–1975), American jazz drummer.

BIBLIOGRAPHY

(see also those listed under the Key (p.xi)

Arlott, John (ed)	*The Oxford Companion to Sports and Pastimes*	OUP	1975
Ashton, John	*The Dawn of the XIXth Century in England*	T. Fisher Unwin	1906
Bacheller, Martin (ed)	*The 1980 Hammond Almanac (Time)*	Hammond Almanac Inc	1980
Bailey, Trevor	*A History of Cricket*	Allen & Unwin	1978
Barrère, A and Leland, G.	*A Dictionary of Slang, Jargon and Cant (2 vols)*	The Ballantyne Press	1890
Barrett, N.	*Purnell's Encyclopaedia of Sport*	Purnell	1974
Barton, M and Sitwell, O	*Sober Truth*	Duckworth	1930
Bede, the Venerable	*A History of the English Church and People*	Penguin ed.	1956
Blyth, Henry	*Caro: The Fatal Passion*	History Book Club ed.	1972
Blyth, Henry	*The Pocket Venus*	Weidenfeld & Nicolson	1967
Blyth, Henry	*Old Q: the Rake of Piccadilly*	Weidenfeld & Nicolson	1967
Blyth, Henry	*Skittles, the Last Victorian Courtesan*	R. Hart-Davis	1970
Boase, Frederic	*Modern English Biography*	Frank Cass & Co	1965
Boswell, James	*London Journal*, 1762–1763	W.Heinemann Ltd	1950
Brent, Peter	*T. E. Lawrence*	Weidenfeld & Nicolson	1975
Brough, James	*Lillie*	Coronet Books	1975
Brown, Dee	*The Westerners*	M. Joseph	1974
Carey, M & others (ed)	*The Oxford Classical Dictionary*	OUP	1949/ 1966
Chambers, R. (ed)	*The Book of Days (2 vols)*	W & R Chambers	1863
Chilton, John	*Who's Who of Jazz*	Bloomsbury Book Shop	1970
Chilton, John	*Concise Dictionary of National Biography*	OUP	1969

Dekker, Thomas	*The Guls Hornbook (1609)*	J. M. Dent & Co (The Temple Classics)	1904
Dinneen, the Rev.	*A Smaller Irish-English Dictionary*	Irish Text Society	1920
Dugan, James	*The Great Mutiny*	André Deutsch	1966
Egan, Pierce	*The Book of Sports*	William Tegg	1832
Egan, Pierce	*Boxiana*	G. Smeeton (facsimile: Dennis Prestidge)	1812 1971
Egan, Pierce	*The Directory of Infamy*	Mills & Boon	1966 1980
Elwin, Malcolm	*Lord Byron's Wife*	Macdonalds	1962
Ewen, C. L'Estrange	*A Guide to the Origin of British Surnames*	John Gifford Ltd.	1931
	Encyclopaedia Americana	Americana Co.	1974
Fraser, G. M	*Steel Bonnets*	Barrie & Jenkins	1971
Fraser, J. and Gibbons, J.	*Soldier and Sailor Words and Phrases*	Routledge & Sons	1925
Frere, James and the Duchess of Bedford	*Now...the Duchesses*	Times & Anthony Gibbs & Phillips	1964
Frey, Albert R.	*Sobriquets and Nicknames*	Tickner & Co, Boston	1888
	Encyclopaedia of Jazz	Quartet Books	1978
Garmonsway, G.N. (trans.)	*The Anglo-Saxon Chronicle*	Everyman (J. M. Dent)	1962
Halliwell, J. O.	*A Dictionary of Archaic and Provincial Words*	Geo. Routledge & Sons.	1924 ed.
Hargrave, Basil	*Origins and Meanings of Popular Phrases and Names*	T. Werner Laurie	1911 1922
Hart, J. D.	*The Oxford Companion to American Literature*	OUP	1941
Hartnoll, Phyllis	*The Oxford Companion to the Theatre*	OUP	1967
Harvey, Sir Paul	*The Oxford Companion to English Literature*	OUP	1932/ 1940
Hibbert, Christopher	*The Roots of Evil*	Weidenfeld & Nicolson	1963
Hibbert, Christopher	*The Personal History of Samuel Johnson*	Longman	1971
Hibbert, Christopher	*George IV*	Longman	1964
Hibbert, Christopher	*The Court at Windsor*	Longman	1972
Howard, R. W.	*Hoofbeats of Destiny*	Signet Books	1960
Hyamson, A. M.	*A Dictionary of English Phrases*	Routledge	1922

Jamieson, John (ed. John Longmuir)	*A Dictionary of the Scottish Language*	W. P. Nimmo	1867
Johnson, Capt. C. (Daniel Defoe)	*Lives of the Most Notorious Pirates*	Folio Society (1st:1724)	1962
Johnson, Capt. C. (ed. Manuel Schonhorn)	*A General History of Pyrates*	J. M. Dent	1972
Jones, M. Wynn	*A Cartoon History of Britain*	Tom Stacey	1971
Joyce, P. W.	*A Child's History of Ireland*	Longman Green	1898
Junkin, A. K. H.	*Cornwall and its People*	J. M. Dent	1945
Kent, William	*An Encyclopaedia of London*	J. M. Dent	1937/ 1951
Kightly, Charles	*Folk Heroes of Britain*	Thames & Hudson	1982
Latham, Edward	*A Dictionary of Names, Nicknames and Surnames*	Routledge & Sons	1904
Leland, Charles G.	*The English Gipsies and Their Language*	Kegan Paul, Trench Trubner & Co., Ltd	1893
Lockhart, J. G.	*Narrative of the Life of Sir Walter Scott*	Everyman (J. M. Dent)	1922
Longford, Elizabeth	*Victoria R. I.*	Weidenfeld & Nicolson	1964
Lovette, Lr-Cdr Leland P., USN	*Naval Customs, Traditions and Usage*	US Naval Institute	1939
Macksey, J & K	*The Guinness Guide to Feminine Achievements*	Guinness Superlatives	1975
Maclean, Fitzroy	*A Concise History of Scotland*	Thames & Hudson	1970
McWhirter, Norris	*The Guinness Book of Records*	Guinness Superlatives	1971/ 1989
McWhirter, Norris	*The Guinness Book of World Records*	Guinness (Bantam Books)	1981
Marples, Morris	*University Slang*	Williams & Norgate	1950
Mencken, H. L.	*The American Language*	Alfred Knopf	1955
Moncreiffe, Sir Ian	*The Highland Clans*	Barrie & Rockliff	1967
Nares, Robert	*Glossary....to Shakespeare and His Contemporaries*	J. Russell Smith (1st: 1822)	1867
Nash, Jay R.	*Bloodletters and Bad Men (3 vols)*	Warner Books Inc	1975
Nevill, Ralph	*London Clubs; their history and treasures*	Chatto & Windus	1911/ 1969
Noble, V.	*Nicknames*	Hamish Hamilton	1976

O'Faolain, Sean	The Irish	Pelican Books	1947
Partridge, Eric	A Dictionary of Slang and Unconventional English	Routledge and Kegan Paul	1937/ 1949
Partridge, Eric	Name into Word	Secker & Warburg	1949/ 1950
Partridge, Eric	Here, There and Everywhere	Hamish Hamilton	1950
Pearsall, Ronald	The Worm in the Bud	Weidenfeld & Nicolson	1969
	A Picture History of Boxing	Hamlyn	1978
Percy, Sholto & Reuben (Thomas Byerley and Joseph Robertson)	The Percy Anecdotes	Frederick Warne & Co (n/d (1st: 1820)	
Radford, Edwin	Crowther's Encyclopaedia of Phrases and Origins	John Crowther	1945
Rayne, John (ed.)	Reminiscences of Capt. Gronow (1795–1865)	Bodley Head	1964
Rayner, J. L. & G. T. Crook (ed.)	The Newgate Calendar (5 vols)	Navarre Society	1925/ 1926
Reaney, P. H.	The Origin of English Surnames	Routledge and Kegan Paul	1967
Reid, J. C.	Bucks and Bruisers	Routledge and Kegan Paul	1971
Rienits, Rex & Jean	A Picture History of Australia	Hamlyn (Australia)	1969
Robbins, R. Hope	The Enclyclopaedia of Witchcraft and Demonology	Peter Nevill Ltd	1959
Roberts, K.	Captain of the Push	Angus & Robertson	1964
Scott, Sir Harold	Scotland Yard	André Deutsch	1954
Sell, H. B. & V Weybright	Buffalo Bill and the Wild West	New American Library	1959
Sitwell, Edith	The English Eccentrics	Dennis Dobson	1933
Smith, J. T.	The Streets of London	R. Bentley	1849
Sutherland, Donald	The Yellow Earl	Molendinar	1980
Timbs, John	Walks and Talks About London	Lockwood & Co	1865
Townend, Peter (ed)	Burke's Peerage	Burke's Peerage Ltd.	1987
Utley, R. M.	Frontiersmen in Blue	Macmillan & Co	1967
Van Thal, H. (ed.)	The Prime Ministers	Allen & Unwin	1974
Wagner, Leopold	Names and Their Meanings	T. Fisher Unwin	1892
Walford, Edwin	Old and New London	Cassell, Petter & Galpin	n/d

Wannan, Bill	*Australian Bushranging*	Rigby Ltd	1963/ 1978
Watson, Owen	*Longman Modern English Dictionary*	Longman Group Ltd	1976
Weekley, Ernest	*The Romance of Words*	John Murray	1912/ 1945
Weekley, Ernest	*The Romance of Names*	John Murray	1914
Weekley, Ernest	*Surnames*	John Murray	1917
Weekley, Ernest	*Words and Names*	John Murray	1933
Welcome, John	*Fred Archer: His Life and Times*	Faber & Faber	1967
Weseen, Maurice	*A Dictionary of American Slang*	Geo. Harrap & Co., Ltd	1934
White, T. H.	*The Age of Scandal*	Jonathan Cape	1950
	Who's Who	A & C Black	1982/ 1988
	Who was Who, a cumulative index	A & C Black	1981
Wilson, Colin	*A Casebook of Murder*	Mayflower Books	1969/ 1971
Wisden, John	*Wisden's Cricketers' Almanac*	J. Wisden & Co., Ltd.	1980/ 1988
Withycombe, E. G.	*The Oxford Dictionary of Christian Names*	OUP	1946

also radio, TV and newspapers.

INDEX

356